Indexed in

INOM

Plato's Socratic Conversations

Michael C. Stokes

Plato's Socratic Conversations

Drama and Dialectic in Three Dialogues

The Johns Hopkins University Press
Baltimore

© 1986 Michael C. Stokes

All rights reserved. No part of this publication may
be reproduced, stored in a retrieval system, or transmitted in
any form or by any means, electronic, mechanical,
photocopying or otherwise, without prior permission
in writing from the publisher.

First published 1986
by The Johns Hopkins University Press
701 West 40th Street
Baltimore, Maryland 21211

Library of Congress Cataloging-in-Publication Data

Stokes, Michael C.
  Plato's socratic conversations.

  Bibliography: p.
  Includes index.
  1. Plato.   2. Socrates.   I. Title.
  B395.S76 1986   184   85–24074
  ISBN 0–8018–2976–3

Photoset by Redwood Burn Limited,
Trowbridge, Wiltshire
Printed in Great Britain
at the University Press, Cambridge

In Memoriam
F.J.A.C.

Contents

Preface	ix
1 Introduction: Platonic questions	1
2 Socrates and a pair of generals	36
The first scene: motives	37
The first scene: values	41
Socrates changes plan	66
A transition	87
Nicias' contribution to the discussion	90
Final scene	111
3 Socrates and a tragic poet	114
Diotima	146
4 Socrates meets Protagoras	183
Plato's introduction	183
The scene with Hippocrates	184
The approach to Protagoras	193
Protagoras' explanation and Socrates' doubts	199
Socrates' attack	203
Protagoras' Great Speech	209
Socrates' initial question, 328D–330B	258
The Unity of the Good Qualities	263
Interlude 334C–338E	311
Simonides' poem 338E–347B	313
The return to the parts of goodness 347B–349B	323
Courage and wisdom: the first round 349B–351B	327
The good life and pleasure 351B–359A	349

Wisdom and courage again	420
Conclusion	437
Epilogue	440
Notes	455
Bibliography	495
Index of passages referred to	505
General index	509

Preface

This book, intended as a contribution to the study of Greek literature as well as Greek philosophy, has gestated over a long time, and on the way it has lost some of its sheen of novelty and gained in return only a number of debts. Its original purpose, to propound and exemplify a new way of reading Plato, has changed to the consolidation and furtherance of a method tried out by various scholars (most notably in French and German), but not much used for the exposition of whole dialogues or whole conversations. The Introduction shows the differences between this method and the interpretative habits of a generation of English-speaking Platonists, mostly of philosophical bent. The following chapters deploy the method in as systematic a reading of the dialogues concerned as lies within my powers. The three dialogues chosen for treatment are *Laches, Symposium* (or rather the conversation between Socrates and Agathon which forms its centrepiece) and *Protagoras*. The Epilogue is less a summary of results than an answer to some pertinent questions.

Those familiar with the scholarly literature will be aware of the scholarly debts I have incurred, not least from those whose views I have ventured to criticize. I have been unable since September 1983 substantially to alter what I have written and particularly regret my inability to take proper account of the valuable papers in the first volume of *Oxford Studies in Ancient Philosophy*, or of L. Goldberg's *Philosophical Commentary* on the *Protagoras*.

I have not, however, written with only professional Platonists in my sights. Eschewing Greek script in my text, I have reduced even my transliterations of Greek words to something like the minimum possible if the reader is to see Plato's point without the obscuring veil of English ethical terms. I have tried to explain such Greek terms as I have used in this way. The intention has been to enable readers to follow Plato (and my exposition of him) either in English or in

Greek or indeed in both simultaneously. To this end I have used a particular English translation as a basis for each dialogue; but my use of them has been unscrupulous, in that in many places I have substituted renderings more suited to my purposes. I hope I have signalized all such places in the notes, but it is human to err. The notes incorporated into the text are bare references to Plato's or other ancient works, to tell the reader where the exposition has got to or to enable him to look up a passage discussed. The end-notes not only explain my deviations from the excellent translations I have used, but also conduct, without the slightest intention of attempting bibliographical completeness, the more detailed and controversial episodes of scholarly in-fighting. There has, however, been no attempt to conceal from readers of my text the existence of other interpretations. Indeed, the persistent flow of readings of Plato different from mine forms the principal justification of this book, and it seems pointless merely to state, rather than argue out, the differences. The normal university student of Plato, be he Hellenist or philosopher in aspiration and knowledge, needs to bear constantly in mind the absence of any consensus, and the great scarcity of facts, concerning the right way to interpret Plato. The same goes for the interested layman. I hope that the student, his teacher, and his interested friend will all find this book helpful.

The responsibility for the book's conception belongs quite largely with my students, in the Universities of Edinburgh, Cornell and Durham. The interpretations given here were designed in the first instance neither for my own benefit nor for that of my fellow-interpreters, but for my pupils. Often in class their looks or questions of puzzlement and arguments in protest have clarified my ideas or the exposition of them. It is not their fault, but mine, if obscurities of mine or difficulties in Plato remain unilluminated. Without their constant stimulation, and their patient tolerance of intellectual experiment, I should certainly not have written this or any other book on Plato.

I have benefited in other ways from the Universities I have mentioned. All have paid me generously to do, for the most part, what I wanted to do, and to do it in the company of interesting, learned and critical colleagues. Durham and Cornell in particular have been unstinting in their grants of sabbatical and other leave for Platonic study. Cornell allowed me to devote a semester simply and wholly to reading Plato; Durham has given me three terms' sabbatical and one term of other leave to write this work. I am exceedingly grateful to those colleagues who stood in for me on those occasions, either as teachers or as administrators.

One of these terms of leave from Durham was made possible by the Leverhulme Trust's grant of a Research Fellowship. That term, enabling me to spend many months consecutively in thinking and writing, was crucial to the book's completion; I here acknowledge with deep gratitude the Trust's munificence. Only those who have vainly striven to develop a consecutive line of argument in the brief intervals between one set of courses and another will fully appreciate my great indebtedness to the Trust.

I am most grateful to the Trustees of the Jowett Copyright Fund and to the Publications Board of the University of Durham for subventions towards the cost of producing the book.

I am indebted to several Libraries for help; most particularly to the kind and friendly staff of Durham University Library for affording me a most pleasant atmosphere in which to write, and for innumerable inter-library loans.

Several bodies have at one time or another listened to immature versions of the views here published, and have helped me with criticism and/or encouragement. I am especially indebted in this regard to the Society for Ancient Greek Philosophy, to the Northern and Scottish Associations for Ancient Philosophy, to the Newcastle and Durham Ancient Philosophers, to the Departments of Philosophy at Cornell and Durham Universities (and especially to Mr R. J. Delahunty, formerly of the Durham Department), and to the Director and Fellows of the Center for Hellenic Studies, to the staff and students of the University of Marburg, and to the Classical Association branches of Manchester and SE Scotland; to all, my hearty thanks.

Individuals who have helped me are numerous, and I cannot possibly rehearse all their names here; but I should like to thank especially David Robinson for many stimulating and informative talks about Plato; my Durham colleagues Peter Rhodes, David Thomas and Ernest Bowcott for references I had missed; Yvonne Harper, who bore the brunt of the conversion of my messy typescript, interlarded with barely penetrable handwriting, into a typescript fit for a publisher, and Isobel Williams, Debbie Clough and Pat Croft, who performed smaller but still substantial parts of the same wearisome task; and Anne Sheppard who helped with the arduous task of reading proofs.

I owe a special debt to my wife and to our children. Not only have they put up with the moods and tensions inseparable from this kind of work, and supported me through them all; they have also tolerated, far more often than they should have had to, my absence of mind or body. They have suggested no single sentence of this book, but it would certainly not have been finished without them.

Lastly, I would record my lasting gratitude to two teachers, neither of whom, to my great regret, lived to read the book. The first is Professor W. K. C. Guthrie, whose lectures on the *Protagoras* at Cambridge roused my interest in its problems, and impelled me to lecture on it myself – though he would not have wished, I am sure, to be saddled with any responsibility for the results. The second, but not the lesser, is Mr F. J. A. Cruso, formerly Assistant Master at Eton, who died as the book was nearing completion. As my Classical Tutor for six years, he displayed a marvellous patience and warmth of kindness; his breadth of interest, his wit, his notable histrionic powers, all opened new worlds to me; his fair, open and critical mind not only sharpened my interest in literature but stimulated my distrust of received opinion; and he possessed in full measure that priceless gift of a teacher, the understanding heart. I wish this book were more worthy to be dedicated to his memory.

Durham   Michael C. Stokes

Note to the reader

References to the texts discussed are printed within brackets in the text, e.g. (359D). The reader will find it best to have to hand *either* a Greek text (preferably the *Oxford Classical Text*) of Plato's *Meno, Laches, Symposium* and *Protagoras, or* the following translations:

Meno: W. K. C. Guthrie, *Plato, Protagoras and Meno* (Penguin, 1956)
Laches: R. Kent Sprague, *Plato, Laches and Charmides* (Bobbs-Merrill Library of Liberal Arts, 1973)
Symposium: W. Hamilton, *The Symposium by Plato* (Penguin, 1951)
Protagoras: C. C. W. Taylor, *Plato's Protagoras* (Clarendon Press, 1976)

I regret that R. W. Sharples, *Plato, Meno* (Aris & Phillips) appeared too late to be used.

1 Introduction: Platonic questions

Hellenists and philosophers have vied with each other in our time for the soul of Plato, for the interpretation of Plato to our generation. At one time the philosophers seemed, in the English-speaking world at least, to be winning. Those whose training was at least as much in philosophy as in Greek, and who approached Plato from a point of view almost entirely philosophical, have, writing in English, shed a far brighter light recently on Plato's writings than scholars whose training and bias are those of Hellenists brought up in a still largely literary tradition. A host of philosophical papers and monographs – one thinks with special gratitude of Gregory Vlastos and the late G. E. L. Owen – have illuminated the premises, inferences and conclusions presented in Plato's dialogues. The Clarendon Press is in course of publishing an excellent series of philosophical commentaries on new English translations. Anyone comparing, for example, the commentary of C. C. W. Taylor[1] on the *Protagoras* with that of J. and A. M. Adam[2] published just over seventy years earlier will, even after making every allowance for differences of purpose, see at once the great progress we have made in this century towards an understanding of Plato, and how much of it is philosophical rather than philological in origin and content.

But the philosophers have not had it all their own way. There is a steadily accumulating body of writing by scholars determined to do justice to Plato's literary art no less than to the 'wiry argument' of Plato's Socrates.[3] This present work subscribes to, and attempts to further, this growing movement in the study of Plato. To be fair, not a little of the literature treating Plato's works as the dialogues they are, rather than the philosophical treatises they are not, has come from the pens of professional philosophers. One might mention Gerasimos Santas for his treatment of Socrates' discussion with Polus in the *Gorgias*, or Paul Woodruff for his recent account of the *Hippias Major*, with its close attention to the character of Hippias.[4] But very few philosophers indeed have undertaken the task of interpreting a dialogue from start to finish, through passages overtly philosophical and manifestly literary alike in exploration of the relation between the parts and the whole. A notable contribution of that sort from a Hellenist was Michael O'Brien's article on the *Laches*, written as early as 1963.[5] G. B. Kerferd's work on the Sophists has greatly improved our understanding of several personages with whom Plato's Socrates crosses swords.[6]

Continental European scholarship, largely unaffected by the analytic movement in English language philosophy, has done a good deal for Plato's dialogues.[7] A long line of works on Greek morals in general have helped to place Plato's thought in a richer context than the nineteenth century could achieve.[8] There have been explicit protests, such as R. H. Weingartner's, against the more one-sidedly philosophical interpreters.[9] If there is still a need, it is for a thorough and systematic study, throughout individual works, of the intellectual stance, personal, moral, and professional, of Socrates' principal interlocutors.

The need for such studies will continue so long as commentaries come from the presses with overwhelming emphasis on the logic of the argument at the expense of its portrayal as a dialectical exchange. This looks like being a long time. The domination of Platonic scholarship by philosophers is part of a wider process, the breaking open of the Classical discipline as it was practised in England and America (though not in Germany)[10] in the nineteenth century and its transformation into a set of more or less closely interrelated specialisms.

The process is welcome and salutary, as well as inevitable. One of its most welcome by-products has been the wider dissemination of Platonic ideas than old-fashioned Hellenists could ever have achieved. Far more people can read Vlastos or Taylor on the *Protagoras* with some notion of what is going on than could seriously tackle Dodds' edition of the *Gorgias* or similar works of Greek scholarship. But so long as philosophers continue to write as if Plato's Socrates simply puts his own views to his respondent, obtains an affirmative answer whenever necessary, and proceeds along a clear and unilinear path of argument, so long it will remain necessary to protest in the name both of interpretative caution and of fairness to Plato.[11]

Since Weingartner's protest, one of the best statements of what is needful has come from the pens of B. A. F. Hubbard and E. S. Karnofsky, in their lively and stimulating 'Socratic commentary' on the *Protagoras*. What, indeed, could be more admirable than their statements of purpose in its Preface? 'Looked at in one way, the *Protagoras* is a literary and dramatic masterpiece,' and (on the same page) 'From yet another point of view this is a serious philosophical work...,' and (again) 'Perhaps, therefore, one of the most important features of the commentary is that it brings these disparate literary, polemical, philosophical and didactic elements together, and helps the reader to relate them to each other.'[12] What is immediately striking about this is that it should need saying at all: the need is symptomatic. Next, it raises a question: ought we to regard these as 'disparate elements' at all? Would Plato have thought of them so? Or would he have wanted to say that the drama lay in the argument, and the argument in the dramatic interplay of personality, profession and belief? Perhaps even Hubbard and Karnofsky have not gone far enough in the eradication of the assumptions of much philosophical writing on Plato.

A few years ago it would have been a tediously complex process to elicit those assumptions in detail from the notes of philosophical scholars on individual passages; it is less so now, though still not easy. Recent scholarship has some rather more explicit remarks to show than some of the older writers on the subject. But it will, nevertheless, help to begin with a couple of concrete examples of such assumptions in actual use. Concreteness apart, the examples may convince the reader that the method of interpretation here questioned is alive, well, and comfortably ensconced in the English-speaking world. Indeed, it seems at times that the abler the interpreter, the more firmly he embeds the relevant assumptions in his interpretation. The following examples are from the work of outstanding interpreters; otherwise there would be little point in citing them.

The first comes from Paul Woodruff's commentary on Plato's *Hippias Major*[13] – a dialogue whose genuineness we should surely now recognize despite its chequered history in twentieth-century scholarship. Commenting on a word he renders 'law-abiding', Woodruff says, 'For Socrates the goodness of Spartan laws is not at issue: all laws are good.' (284D6–7) Now Socrates may have believed this, either within or without the pages of Plato; I have no wish to deny it. But the suggestion that this passage of the *Hippias Major* commits him to such belief carries little conviction.

According to Woodruff's rendering, Socrates says in his preceding speech: 'But look here. Don't lawmakers make law to be the greatest good to the city? Without that, law-abiding civilised life is impossible.' Here the Oxford text prints Socrates' final sentence as a question, not as an assertion; and its editor Burnet was clearly right: the Greek has 'and' before the words 'without that', and one can hardly link a question and an assertion with 'and'. Woodruff's Achilles' heel is the punctuation, and in that he is typical of many editors and translators, *because*, one would suppose, *they do not see any great importance for their purposes in the distinction between a question and an assertion in a sentence of Socrates*'. Hippias, one must admit, replies: 'True' – literally 'You speak true things.' This might appear to indicate a preceding assertion, since a question has no truth-value; but 'You speak true things' is by a not uncommon Platonic idiom a possible reply to a question: the respondent assents to the proposition put to him for choice between truth and falsehood.[14] So Socrates is not committed yet; all he has done is to ask questions.

Next, Socrates draws a conclusion from the answers he has received. 'So when people who are trying to make laws fail to make them good, they have failed to make them lawful – indeed, to make them law. What do you say?' Initially, it is possible that he puts the conclusion in the form of an assertion; but it is equally possible that he does not: Greek does not always distinguish verbally between question and assertion. Even, however, if Socrates does assert the conclusion, there is no good reason for taking such an assertion as committing *him* to its truth; rather, he explains what his respondent Hippias has committed himself to in previous responses. That the conclusion is there simply to be put to the respondent emerges clearly from Socrates' coda, which should, more literally, read 'Or how do you say?' This shows that the whole speech constitutes a question, whichever punctuation one puts after Socrates' conclusion drawn in its first part. The upshot is that Woodruff begs the rather slippery question whether Socrates is committed in this passage to any of the propositions he puts to Hippias; and in begging it he assumes, in my opinion, the wrong answer.

But we have not yet finished with our example. Terence Irwin also has things to say about the passage in his *Plato's Moral Theory*.[15] In his view, the passage, together with one from Plato's *Minos* (if that be indeed Plato's), shows that Socrates 'takes *nomos* and *nomimos* to mean (a) "what is lawful, i.e. right and legitimate," and not (b) "what is lawful, i.e. permitted by positive law."' But if we look at the whole passage again in the light of our previous remarks, we find rather that Socrates is asking Hippias whether he (Hippias) takes what is 'lawful' to be what is right, or whether he (Hippias) wishes after all to say that what is lawful is a matter of positive law; and it is Hippias who, in the sentence following the ones quoted above, says: 'In precise speech, Socrates, that is so. But men are not accustomed to use words in that manner'; Hippias thus accepts that for him 'lawful' means, strictly, 'right', or 'legitimate'. Irwin, like Woodruff, has assumed Socrates' commitment to the propositions he puts as questions to the person he is interrogating.

Indeed, Professor Irwin's book contains our second example[16] concerning a passage of Plato's *Lysis* on which a good deal hangs. According to Irwin, 'The *Lysis* commits Socrates to the rejection' of a theory which 'assumes that components "contribute to" and are "chosen for the sake of" the final good, and also, unlike instrumental means, are goods in themselves. But Socrates *maintains* that no good chosen for the sake of the final good is chosen for its own sake or is a good in itself.' (*Lysis* 219C1–D5, 220A6–B5) Further, 'Socrates *commits himself* to two principles:

LC If A chooses x for the sake of y, A does not choose x for its own sake.
LG If x and y are goods, and x contributes to y, x is not good in itself.

These two principles rule out component means; and since virtue prescribes what contributes to happiness, LG implies that it cannot prescribe goods in themselves. Socrates cannot accept NTV, or even the limited prescription of components conceded to virtue by TV. The *Lysis* recognizes only the pattern of rational choice displayed in a craft: and this pattern demands TV.' (Significant emphases here are mine. The rebarbative sets of capitals are Irwin's: TV means 'the technical conception of virtue', and NTV 'the non-technical conception of virtue.'[17]) The reason why this passage of the *Lysis* is important lies in Irwin's view[18] that in the *Republic* 'Plato insists that something can be both good in itself and good for its consequences; this is exactly what LG denies.' Irwin writes his account of Plato's development quite largely around this supposed contradiction between the *Lysis* and the *Republic*.

It would be absurdly over-ambitious even to attempt here the *disproof* of such a development in Plato's thinking. What needs noting now is that Irwin's interpretation of the *Lysis* (we will leave the *Republic* on one side) and his extraction from it of a doctrine which contradicts other doctrines depend either on taking Socrates' crucial speeches as grammatical assertions or on taking the questions put to Lysis and his friend Menexenus as, in effect, assertions to which Socrates is committed.

Irwin (as quoted above) mentions two short pieces close to each other in the *Lysis*. In the first, three sentences of Socrates' have no question mark in the Oxford text; of those the first two are possibly questions, and in the third Socrates is explaining the meaning of an earlier question. Irwin's second passage in the *Lysis* opens with a question, 'Isn't the same true of the beloved also?', and only then proceeds to explain what 'the same' refers to. This whole speech of Socrates constitutes a question, as a similar speech did in the *Hippias Major*. Irwin, like Woodruff, has begged the question whether Socrates is asserting or interrogating, presumably because he (Irwin) feels at liberty in any case to take a question as, in effect, an assertion. For both these scholars the difference between a Socratic question and a Socratic assertion would appear to have little or no significance. Perhaps the assumption that there is no significant difference is true; but it would be a pity if the case for a significant difference were to go by default. The assumption has no obvious intrinsic probability; and it tends to reduce the dialogue-form to a *merely* formal matter.

A point apparently in its favour – not a decisive one – rests on the fact that Plato, like his contemporaries, did not punctuate regularly.[19] The reader may be tempted to draw the conclusion that Plato cannot possibly have intended to make a distinction between two types of sentence we should distinguish by punctuation. The conclusion would be overhasty. The Socrates at least of the early dialogues often claims ignorance, and usually adopts an obviously questioning stance. The absence of punctuation should accordingly lead us to the conclusion that we ought to read as a question any sentence of Socrates in an interrogatory passage, unless the sentence is identified by its actual words as an assertion or other non-interrogative utterance. Once Socrates has embarked on a bout of interrogation Plato's readers will have expected questions, not statements, from him. In order to counteract his readers' expectations, Plato will have had to indicate plainly in the words of a given sentence or speech his intention to have Socrates formulate an assertion. The burden of proof rests on those wishing to take any sentence of Socrates in an interrogation as other than a question. Common sense suggests that the burden of proof rests also on those who wish to take a question as, in any case, equivalent to, or masking, an assertion by Socrates or Plato.

Around this kind of topic it is worth quoting some remarks with general implications from a recent controversy between Professor D.J. Zeyl and J.C.B. Gosling and C.C.W. Taylor. The controversy is admirably and unusually lucid. I have taken the remarks below out of context and abbreviated them, but not, I hope, misleadingly. The words cited centre on the copiously disputed hedonistic passage in the *Protagoras*. Leaving the substance of that passage for later discussion in a consecutive interpretation of that dialogue, we focus at present on the terms and framework of this controversy.

Zeyl says:[20] 'Some commentators, relying on the *fact* that Socrates *customarily* [emphases mine] expresses views as questions to which he invites the interlocutor's assent, claim that [certain questions] may be taken as expressions of his own view, whether he advocates it sincerely or ironically. But this will not work here: Socrates' questions do not simply have the form "*p*?" but the form, "do you think (say) that *p*?" Socrates want to elicit *Protagoras*' views [emphasis Zeyl's], rather than express his own [Zeyl cites three separate Greek expressions for "you say" etc.] . . . and his questions provide no evidence for his own views on the matter. They are simply diagnostic.'

Gosling and Taylor say:
1 '. . . most of the surviving ancient works in which *specific views are ascribed to [Socrates]* are by Plato [emphasis mine].'[21]
2 'A great deal of what is put into the mouth of Socrates in Plato's dialogues represents Plato's own views.'[22]
3 '. . . unless there are indications to the contrary, the views attributed to the main speaker in each dialogue (i.e. Socrates, in the dialogues with which we shall be concerned) are the views of Plato.'[23]
4 In one closely argued instance, 'The interrogative form is clearly rhetorical.' In the same instance, it is 'clear' that Socrates 'is not merely raising questions' or 'finding out what the interlocutor thinks'.[24]

Clearly Zeyl is not in agreement with Gosling and Taylor on the interpretation of the passage, towards the end of the *Protagoras*, which engages their attention. But he and they do seem to be in agreement on certain fundamental issues concerning the status of questions asked by Socrates. Zeyl suggests that it is a *fact* that a question put by Socrates, and not tagged specifically as diagnostic, customarily expresses Socrates' own view. Taylor and Gosling consider themselves free, as Zeyl does not, to take even a question apparently so tagged as expressing Socrates' view. Their argument suggests that, where it is 'clear' or otherwise interpretatively convenient, Plato's readers are at liberty to treat the interrogative form of what Socrates says as rhetorical – evidently not in the sense that the verbal form of the question is influenced by considerations of rhetoric, but in the sense that the question is equivalent to a statement of the questioner's own views. Combined with the suggestion that views ascribed to Socrates are Plato's (unless there are indications to the contrary), this would allow a question of Socrates' to offer Plato's view. What would count as an 'indication to the contrary' is clear in the present instance, to which we come later, but is hardly clear in general, and, as the history of Platonic interpretation shows, is liable to become a somewhat subjective matter.

Gosling and Taylor say nothing to indicate that they are doing anything unusual or remarkable in taking a Socratic question as 'rhetorical' in the required sense. But they do not explicitly go as far as Zeyl may be going when he says that Socrates 'customarily' puts his views in the form of questions to which he invites the interlocutor's assent. It is not wholly clear what Zeyl means: whether he means 'Most of Socrates' questions put a view of his and invite the interlocutor's assent', or 'On most of the occasions on which Socrates puts his views, he puts them in the form of questions inviting the interlocutor's assent.' But, either way, Zeyl is presumably aware that, unless a substantial proportion of Socrates' questions express his views, Zeyl's opponents will be relying on a case open to a doubt (on grounds of paucity of examples) which he does not press further. Zeyl seems to believe he needs support for taking a Socratic question as, simply, a question, since he invokes in his support here the *tagging* of the questions that concern him with phrases such as 'Do you say . . . ?' and the like.

Whatever one may think of the rights and wrongs of the controversy over the passage in the *Protagoras*, or of the *Hippias* and *Lysis* passages mentioned earlier, it is not difficult to see how beliefs and interpretative practices such as these are open to abuse – which is not to say that they are always or systematically abused. They open the way to the subordination of dialogue and drama to philosophical argument, to such an extent as to raise the question why Plato should bother with the dialogue form at all. They offer the philosophically minded interpreter a handle for turning the dialogues into the philosophical treatises to which he is, historically speaking, more accustomed. It is one of the main contentions of this work that Socrates' questions are meant as questions, both by the fictional[25] Socrates and by his creator or manipulator Plato.

The chief way of arguing for that contention is, inevitably and properly, by investigating in systematic detail some key passages and dialogues to see if they gain in coherence from treatment as genuine duologue rather than covert treatise. Generalizations about dialogue, and speculations about what Plato could or could not have brought himself to do, are unlikely to cut much ice without such investigations. The proof of the interpretative pudding is in the patient eating, even the mastication, of Plato's works, scene by scene and argument by argument. Only thus will we see whether the more extreme philosophical interpreters have or have not abused in some respects the methods which have – it must be stressed again – brought so much illumination to Plato in our generation.

Before, however, we set our hands to that plough, there is a particular furrow awaiting our attention: we may find some guidance in a passage in which Socrates offers some questions and observations about his own questions and observations. It will not offer more than guidance; the general approach does not stand or fall by the interpretation of this single passage. We should be rather careful about the presuppositions of this discussion. Some of it is dialectical in the sense that it rests on premises belonging to other people and not necessarily to me.

If a great deal of *Socrates* represents Plato's views, and *if Socrates'* questions often embody *his* views, then there is a fair chance that, in *Socrates'* questions or observations about his own questions, we shall find Plato's view of Socratic questioning. Of course, we are not dealing with absolute certainty here. It does not follow from 'A high proportion of Socrates' views are expressed as questions' that 'A high proportion of Socrates' questions express his views.' Nor would it follow from 'No Socratic questions tagged as diagnostic express his views' that 'All Socratic questions not tagged as diagnostic do express his views'. But it would be curiously arbitrary to draw a line neatly excluding from the questions giving Plato's views just those referring to Socrates' own procedures. We cannot settle thus arbitrarily the fundamental issue for Platonic interpretation, viz: when is the interrogating Socrates putting his own view and when not? But simply and solely for the purpose of argumentative experiment, we may take a passage of the *Meno* and see where it leads us *if* we start by supposing that Socrates puts his own and Plato's views to his interlocutor Meno.

The episode concerned is that of the slave (82A–86A): in it Socratic argument brings the slave, confident at the start, to acknowledge his ignorance of the matter in hand, and later to a recognition of the truth. Plato clearly intends to use the slave and what happens to him as an illustration of what has happened, and of what Socrates hopes will happen, to Meno in the dialogue at large.[26] Hence the importance of the episode for the understanding of the *Meno* as a whole, and indeed for the investigation of Plato's whole understanding of his own procedures.

With respect to that investigation the slave episode presents a highly unusual phenomenon which is both an advantage and a disadvantage. The reader of the *Meno* knows when Socrates is putting a true point to the slave and when a false one. The topic is no slippery philosophical one, and concerns no subjective values, but is a matter of elementary geometry. As there is no suggestion that Socrates is mistaken or in any doubt over any geometrical issue, Plato's readers, for once, know for certain when Socrates is offering his own beliefs to the interlocutor and when he is not. In a conversation billed as a paradigm of Socratic questioning that offers a singular benefit. But at the same time the very certainty of geometry has certain drawbacks. The transfer of what we learn from the slave episode to other Socratic conversations suffers from the difficulty in the other discussions of deciding what Socrates believes. It is not enough to say that Socrates cannot possibly believe some particular proposition he puts in the form of a question to an interlocutor on his usual topics; notoriously, opinions can and do differ as to what Socrates can or cannot possibly have believed. The slave conversation may be revealing; but immediately we try to use its revelations we run the risk of arguing in a circle. But with both advantage and disadvantage in mind let us see what we actually find in the scene with the slave.

The investigation may start with the question how far Socrates' practice bears out Zeyl's implied distinction between questions tagged and untagged as diagnostic. Zeyl implied that tagged questions are readable as putting propositions for which Socrates takes no responsibility; untagged questions put propositions Socrates is prepared to take on board.

Some types of Socratic question are clearly irrelevant here: for example, those demanding a selection from an unspecified list of alternatives within a certain class, such as 'How many times...?' (82C, 82D, 83E, 84E).[27] Of the relevant questions in our passage, several carry tags such as 'Do you say that...?' Nearly all of these fall at the beginning of Socrates' refutation of the slave (82E–83B). They put false opinions to the slave, opinions he has expressed earlier, and for which Socrates can in the nature of things take no responsibility whatever. 'You say that the side of double length produces the double-sized figure? Like this, I mean... Think for a moment whether you still think that you will get it from doubling the side.' A couple of speeches later, 'It is on this line then, according to you, that we shall make the eight-feet square, by taking four of the same length?' And again, 'Let us draw in four equal lines, using the first as a base. Does this not give us what you call the eight-feet figure?' All this reminds the slave and Meno of the false opinions the slave has already expressed. The slave must hold and express those opinions before Socrates can refute him. In this instance it is perfectly clear that Socrates does not hold the opinions in question. He has tagged with an overtly diagnostic expression exactly those questions he cannot himself accept.

But a further case of tagging complicates matters. The final sentence (85B) of the slave-boy's interrogation reads, '... so ... it is your personal opinion that the square on the diagonal of the original square is double its area.' Modern editors and translators print this as a statement, not as a question, but it is very hard (as often with conclusions) to be sure which Plato intended. But, whether question or assertion, it is tagged, and it offers the slave a true proposition certainly believed by Socrates. This would appear at first sight to obliterate Zeyl's distinction.

But there are fairly clear reasons for regarding this as a special case. Coming right at the end of the interrogation, it has the effect of nailing down the victim's responsibility for the conclusion reached. Socrates' tagged speech makes double sure that the victim cannot say afterwards, 'Socrates, that was your conclusion, not mine.' It makes a lot of sense for Socrates to tag both the false propositions at the beginning and the Socratically acceptable – and indeed true – proposition at the end, and thus pin them firmly on the respondent. Indeed the function of the tag appears to be just this, to pin the responsibility for the proposition clothed in the question firmly on the respondent.

Socrates may, however, have different reasons for doing this. One obvious possible reason is his dissent from the proposition; another is the need to make sure the respondent does not disown a conclusion. If we wish to argue that Socrates did believe a proposition tagged in this way, we shall either have to argue that it is obviously true, or we shall have to show that Socrates had a special reason for preventing wriggles by the interlocutor, or both. But the difficult thing to believe is that Socrates regards *himself* as *committed* to a tagged proposition, whether or not he *thinks it true*. If we wish to argue for such commitment, then the burden of proof weighs heavy on our shoulders. One way of discharging it would be to show that the proposition embodied in the question thus tagged is deducible by Socratically acceptable logic from other propositions to which Socrates is committed. This last proviso will, I think, allow Socrates to be committed to the conclusion of the geometrical argument, but will avoid committing him to propositions tagged earlier in the conversation.

As for untagged questions asking about propositions which Socrates certainly believed false, there is one such in the slave episode which proves that such things are possible, but suggests that caution is advisable. Socrates asks the slave 'And is four times the same as twice?' (83B) The slave of course disbelieves the proposition thus proffered which is manifestly false. The obviousness of the falsehood fits in with our previous results; Socrates does not need to disclaim responsibility for the proposition that four times is the same as twice, a proposition that nobody at all likely to be talking to Socrates would accept. But the obviousness of the falsehood here is due to the cut-and-dried nature of the subject matter. In the ethical and similar areas Socrates normally inhabits it is not so easy to be sure when a proposition is obviously false. One cannot rule out the possibility of a proposition seeming obviously false to Socrates or to Plato which does not seem so to us. There are dangers, therefore, inherent in a procedure which assumes Socrates committed, or liable to be committed, to any proposition offered in an untagged question and 'not obviously false'.

If anyone doubts that obviousness is hard to pin down, let him inspect an ethical question from the *Meno*. In the course of an interrogation on the nature of goodness (73A), Socrates asks 'Is it [then] possible to direct [anything] well – city, or household or anything else – if not temperately and justly?' and Meno replies 'Certainly not.' Now this question apparently embodies the proposition that 'It is possible to direct city, household, or anything else well but not at the same time temperately and justly.' Does the question commit Socrates to that proposition? Most of us would surely say not. Does it commit Plato to that proposition? Emphatically not.

But it is not easy to see exactly why we should return these emphatically negative answers. Is it *obvious* that a good and successful life must involve temperance and justice? The Thrasymachus of Plato's *Republic* would not suppose so,[28] and we may doubt if Thrasymachus was alone in his day any more than he would be in ours. Are we to take Meno's denial as evidence for Plato's or Socrates' beliefs? If we are, then by what right do we suppose Meno to represent Plato but Thrasymachus not? Because of other questions Socrates puts elsewhere? But then we would have a conflict of evidence. Why, indeed, should Meno represent anyone but himself? It is possible to argue that (a) Socrates assumes Meno's assent, and that (b) without Meno's assent the argument would not get under way. To (b) the reply comes that only this particular argument cannot get under way; other moral outlooks than Meno's receive different treatment in other dialogues. To (a) the simple reply is that it is false, for two reasons. First, the grammatical form of Socrates' question makes no assumption about the answer to be expected. Secondly,

Socrates is not so much assuming Meno's assent as building, in his line of questioning, on Meno's general attitude to morals, already expressed. But this second point deserves expansion.

Socrates' questioning here, and Meno's answers, arise out of the sort of person that Meno is – or perhaps, to avoid awkward historical questions in this particular case, we should say out of the sort of person Plato portrays.[29] If we look back at the speech Meno volunteers in answer to Socrates' earlier request for a statement of what goodness is, we find Meno saying that the goodness of a man is to be able to practise the affairs of his city, and in doing so to benefit his friends and harm his enemies (71E). Readers familiar with the *Republic* will instantly recognize a statement in its first Book of what 'justice' is. The statement is not entirely Socratic, but is obtainable from an ordinary, if wealthy, man.[30] Meno, in fact, is offering, as a presumably indispensable part of what he means by 'the goodness of a man', a course of action known to serve in some not outlandish quarters as a criterion of 'justice'. In that same speech Meno describes 'the virtue of a woman' as to manage the house well, being 'careful with her stores and obedient to her husband.' Meno's Victorian ideal housewife surely embodies the virtue or good quality the Greeks called *sôphrosynê*, temperance, moderation, good sense, a sense of one's limitations.[31]

Meno, then, has already deemed justice essential for a man's goodness and moderation for a woman's. Now, when Socrates (73A) asks Meno whether *he said that* the goodness of a man was to run the city 'well', and of a woman to run the household 'well', he is recalling Meno's statements. But, as elsewhere, he recalls them a trifle inexactly. Meno did say (71E) that the goodness of a woman was to run the house well, but the adverb 'well' is absent from his words on the goodness of a man. We, like Meno, may let that pass; for it will hardly count as good unless done well. Socrates' next question is the one that concerns us. It is a more complex matter, and it is not tagged as coming directly from Meno. Roughly speaking, Socrates asks whether it is possible to administer anything well without administering it justly and moderately. The following questions (73A–C) lead Meno through the reasoning that justice and moderation are both essential to any good administration, that men, women, and presumably old and young too, all need justice and moderation to act well. The main point is that justice and moderation are both together essential for good administration. But Meno had not expressly said that. He could consistently have replied that the goodness of a man was justice, and excluded moderation, and that the goodness of a woman was moderation, and excluded justice.

So far as the development of this line of questioning goes, Plato has allowed his Socrates to gamble and made the gamble come off. But is it a reasonable bet? Yes, for the most conspicuous characteristic of Meno's answers is their conventionality and lack of originality. It is pretty easy to predict that Meno will not exclude moderation from the goodness of a man – especially since he is tied to no limiting definition of the term 'moderation' – and specially easy to predict that he will not tolerate an unjust woman. This last prediction is borne out, for what the point is worth, by Meno's admission a little later (73D) that justice is either goodness or a good quality. Meno has given normal and respectable answers to Socrates' questions, being, in the pages of Plato, a normal and respectable person. But Socrates does not force the answers upon him, and Plato does not inconsistently or illogically or unreasonably manipulate him.

Socrates might want to agree with Meno. But it is difficult to see why he should be said to be committed to any of Meno's judgments. Nor is Plato committed to them. Certainly their conventional nature would have carried little weight with either, so far as we can discern. Socrates' readiness to take on board moral commitments (if he is ready) is quite irrelevant to this whole passage. It is not Socrates who is about to undergo refutation, to be reduced to acknowledged ignorance and despair. The question Socrates puts to Meno about justice and temperance draws on Meno's character and on his positive eagerness to commit himself, and not, in the first instance, on Socrates' own commitments; Socrates, it is well to observe, went out of his way at the beginning of the dialogue to avoid any commitments, pleading total ignorance of what goodness is.

What gives Socrates grounds for asking this set of questions is not his own commitment to one set of answers, but Meno's general character. The untagged question is untagged simply because the answer Socrates doubtless hopes to get is not formally equivalent to anything Meno said earlier. The lack of a tag or label does not show that Socrates is prepared to take on a responsibility either for the proposition ostensibly embodied in the question or for any one answer to the question. Is any answer to the question obvious? I hope that by now that deserves a resounding 'No'.

Indeed, obviousness is a slippery concept when it is applied to ethical propositions. What is more, the interlocutor's answer, as I think emerges from the preceding discussion, does not serve to confer obviousness on a proposition. The slave indeed rejected the suggestion that four times is the same as twice (83B). One might be tempted to suppose that the interlocutor's rejection, preferably with contumely, was meant to be a sign to us. To suppose this would be an improvement on the belief that Socratic questions contain propositions Plato is committed to; it would include the interlocutor's words in the evidence for Plato's thought.

But once we have crossed that barrier it is difficult to know where we stop. How do we distinguish interlocutors who do from those who do not represent Plato's thoughts? By informed instinct? Does the same instinct enable us to decide which propositions need an interlocutor's assent before they become certifiably Platonic?

The preceding discussion may, and indeed should, have suggested the importance of delving into the particular interlocutor's antecedents and characteristics as portrayed in the dialogue concerned, before we accord any status to his replies under Socratic questioning. A proposition may look false, or true, as the case may be, to one particular kind of interlocutor, or indeed to one particular kind of reader. Meno, in the early ethical passage, cannot complain that Socrates is treating him unfairly. Can Plato's reader complain of unfair treatment? I think not. On the face of it, if Meno is not untypical,[32] in the relevant respects, of a substantial body of readers, then that body of readers has no cause for complaint. If the reader is not like Meno, but has a different set of values, then he can claim that the refutation is not aimed at him. But then Plato has not said, suggested, or even hinted that it is. So what is unfair? But were there any people like Meno? It would be most surprising if there were not. Ambitious young aristocrats prepared to pay lip-service to justice and moderation are not, and doubtless were not, rare birds – especially if left to put their own gloss on the terms 'justice' and 'moderation'.

But we should return to Socrates' treatment of the conversation with the slave. At certain important stages Socrates asks Meno for certain observations. The form and nature of the questions and observations deserve inspection. Before he even speaks to the slave, Socrates asks Meno (82B) to pay attention to see whether the slave is recollecting or learning from Socrates. The demonstration will fall flat if Meno catches the slave learning from Socrates, and the dialogue will come to a halt. Meno as a character is formally uncommitted, but clearly as an author Plato is not.

After the first bout of questioning, Socrates asks Meno (82E) whether he sees that he is teaching the slave nothing, but just asking him questions. Meno, so far, is quite right to accept. By the next interlude (84B–C) Socrates' questions to Meno include this: 'Now notice what, starting from this state of perplexity, he will discover by seeking the truth in company with me, though I simply ask questions without teaching him. Be ready to catch me if I give him any instruction or explanation instead of simply interrogating him on his own opinions.' Meno does not challenge Socrates on this point, now or later, though quite capable elsewhere of mounting a challenge.

When the slave has discovered the correct answer to the geometrical problem (85B), Socrates asks Meno a number of questions with the same burden, namely, whether the slave did discover the knowledge or opinions he now has after questioning, or whether someone taught him. Meno accepts that nobody taught, rather than questioned, the slave, and that the questioning investigated the slave's own opinions.

How far is Socrates committed to this view of his intercourse with the slave? He later says (86B) that he would not vouch absolutely for the rest of the whole passage down to their agreement on recollection and immortality, but would favour continued inquiry, for a moral reason which Meno vehemently accepts. But nothing here cancels Meno's agreement that Socrates has not instructed the slave but questioned him on his own opinions.

Whether we find this agreement convincing is less important at the moment than two facts: first that Socrates puts and Meno accepts the relevant proposition; secondly that without this, at any rate, Socrates has no answer to Meno's query (often called a paradox)[33] about the possibility of Socrates' inquiry into a subject he claims to know nothing of. Nothing has cancelled Meno's agreement; and unless the whole has at least provisional force as far as the absence of instruction from Socrates the dialogue will simply not hang together; for Socrates cannot, on a subject of which he knows nothing, instruct Meno but can only question him. If the questioning of the slave is a form of instruction, then Socrates' programme is incoherent.

In the context of our present inquiry, we are not entitled to assume Socrates' commitment to the propositions he puts to Meno here or elsewhere. But if we do, purely for the sake of argument, accept such a commitment in this passage, then some interesting observations emerge. Socrates is then committed to the view that his questioning here, which he and his author elaborately dress up to look like the dialogue with Meno, passes no information to the slave, but only diagnoses his opinions.

If Socrates is telling Meno this, by putting questions to him in such a way as to inform him, then what he is telling Meno is that he is not telling the slave. He is telling Meno that he is doing nothing more than activate the opinions already held by the slave. But if the process of questioning the slave does not in such key points resemble the interrogation of Meno, then the dialogue is incoherent, since the slave episode provides, as we saw, the answer to Meno's doubts about the possibility of proceeding. The only significant respect in which the dialogue with the slave differs from that with Meno is that in the slave passage Socrates knows the answer before he starts, whereas in the *Meno* as a whole he claims (with good reason, up to a point) not to know the answer.

But if Socrates does not inform, but only extracts the slave's opinions, in a case where he knows the answer before he starts, then *a fortiori* he will not be informing Meno. And we have no reason to suppose that Meno is unique in this matter. If Socrates is not telling his respondents anything, then he is certainly not telling them his own opinions.

But let me recall, in case of objection, that the crucial point here is not *our* acceptance (which I suspect we should withhold, for reasons given below) of Socrates' claim. The significant thing is that Socrates makes the claim.

Why is this fact of such overriding importance? Because those same scholars who suppose that Socrates' questions are not extractive but informative also believe that one should normally take Socrates, or the principal figure of the dialogue, as conveying Plato's own views. There exist no abnormal indications to the contrary here, unless we take Socrates' later disclaimer as such; and we have argued that that can hardly extend in any radical form to Socrates' account of his own questioning without imperilling the structure of the dialogue. *Ad homines* we could argue that, if Plato's irony and aloofness from his readers extended thus deep into the structure of his dialogue, then perhaps we should abandon the attempt to extract Plato's thoughts from Socratic questioning. Of course, we could drop the claim that Plato's principal figures represent him in some fairly close way. But most of us feel instinctively that Socrates, the Athenian Stranger, and perhaps other such figures bear at least some resemblance to their literary creator. The feeling is independent of the problem whether such figures, when they are overtly mere questioners, are covert informers.

At this point one could imagine a rude objector (not unlike the objector towards the end of the *Protagoras* (355C)) uttering with a hollow laugh the single word 'Baloney'. We can see the slave learning from Socrates; some of us try ourselves on occasions to teach by what is called the 'Socratic' method, and know it can be done. That is one reason why the line of argument Socrates and Meno develop has seemed to many people quite unconvincing. But Meno is convinced? Well, Meno is easy enough to convince. But things are not so simple as that; Meno is no fool. He notices the difficulty of *ignotum per aeque ignotum* (75C), he is capable of putting together either a general statement of dissatisfaction (as 'I somehow feel that this is not on the same level as the other cases.' (73A)) or a specific argument of some dialectical weight (as in the objection to Socrates' inquiry into something he claims to know nothing of (80D)). But perhaps this is one of those occasions when some suppose Plato to paralyse the interlocutor in order to allow Socrates a hollow victory? Perhaps he does, and this is; but Plato would not, presumably, paralyse the interlocutor on behalf of a view of the discussion which Plato did not accept; and it is Plato's view, not its validity, which concerns us here.

But Plato is perhaps actively hoodwinking his readers? Perhaps he wishes to lull our suspicions to sleep while his Socrates teaches us under cover of questioning Meno and the slave? Against this suggestion the moral argument that Plato could not have so deceived his readers has little weight; if one is determined to dislike Plato, such an argument will leave one unmoved. But there is another argument to explore. The thrust of this is that neither the slave, nor Meno, nor Plato's reader, has any right to assume that any given question submits Socrates' own opinion. For Socrates does once slip the slave a question embodying a false proposition, namely that four times is the same as twice (83B). The importance of this proposition lies not in itself, but in the apparently straight face with which Socrates puts the corresponding question to the slave.[34] After it – and it happens quite early, in the first, destructive part of the conversation with the slave – neither the slave, nor Meno, nor Plato's reader is entitled to assume that any question is a mere disguise for the transfer of an opinion of Socrates' (or indeed of Plato's). The slave, and the reader, must be on his guard.

But who has put the slave and the reader thus on the *qui vive*? Socrates, in the dialogue, and Plato as its creator. This is not, one would think, the act of a deliberate deceiver. The reader, like the slave, must think for himself. Socrates has made the point explicitly very nearby (83D):

BOY   I think it will.
SOCRATES   Right. Always answer what you think.

But then is this perhaps an even more subtle piece of deceitful window-dressing by Plato? There comes a stage at which such questions are impossible to answer, when someone's determination to believe is strong enough to resist *any* argument. What one can say is that there is no point of the discussion at which we can pin Plato down and say: 'Here you have given the slave, or Meno, words which are dramatically implausible in this kind of mouth.' Plato needs no further defence against a charge of hoodwinking, since he is of necessity open with his readers about the kind of people he portrays.

But suppose there is no hoodwinking going on; we still have to take on board the point that virtually all of Socrates' questions to the slave in the constructive part of the conversation embody propositions Socrates must believe in, because he knows enough elementary geometry to know their truth. Other subjects, however, are not (we must repeat) like that: neither Socrates nor we know what is courageous or what is just, and so forth. Nevertheless, the crux of the matter is that one could still read Socrates in the slave passage as putting his own views to the slave for acceptance or rejection, and then go on to argue that other passages ought to behave in the same way. One objection to such an argument would be that if Socrates were consistently to put his views to the slave, and not warn the slave to the contrary, then he would in effect be telling the slave, and one could readily imagine Meno saying to Socrates, 'Come off it! You're telling him what to answer.' But Socrates does not consistently do this. He sometimes expects the slave to choose between possibilities within a certain range, as when he says 'How many times...?' He also expressly warns the slave to answer as he thinks, a warning which still stands. The best that one could do for the line of objection would be to say that in the constructive part of the slave dialogue Socrates puts no proposition to the slave which runs counter to Socrates' views and does put a number which embody them.

But anyone wishing to extrapolate from this to other passages is beset with the same difficulties as before: the difficulty of telling when Socrates is offering his own opinion, a difficulty we have already mentioned, is matched by another, namely, the problem when Plato's Socrates is being constructive and when destructive. The dialogue with the slave boy contains a clear warning when the change to constructiveness takes place, and so does the *Meno* as a whole. But other dialogues are more disputable and again the dispute is not always resolvable by objective criteria. How, in the last resort, do we *know* when Plato's Socrates is putting forward his own views?

In favour of a genuinely undogmatic Socrates, one who truly explores, rather than tells, stands a type of question we have yet to examine. This type has Socrates putting to the interlocutor both a proposition and its contradictory. If this type puts Socrates' own view to the respondent, then, on the face of it, Socrates' view is either an uninteresting disjunction or a contradictory conjunction. Examples may make the significance of this easier to grasp. In the destructive portion of the slave episode we find Socrates saying (and here the translation is mine (83C)): 'Will it not be based on a line longer than that, but shorter than one this length? Or is that not so?' The words 'Or is that not so?', often omitted by English translators, appear in the Budé French translation as 'Oui ou non?' They show Socrates putting two alternatives to the slave, and leaving the choice to him. The slave bears the responsibility for that choice, and indeed accepts it by saying 'I think so' – and it is precisely here that Socrates emphasizes the obligation on the slave to answer as he thinks.

Very similarly Socrates offers Meno 'Yes' or 'No' as alternatives in a passage (85C) where Guthrie's rendering is 'But these opinions were somewhere in him [the slave], were they not?' As a rendering of the Greek (which almost certainly says 'Or not?'), this 'were they not?' is surely misleading. The reader might incline to doubt the genuineness of the choice offered by this Socratic 'Or not?' But, if so, he/she should ponder the implications of a passage in the *Gorgias* (453D) where Irwin's recent version[35] correctly has Socrates ask, 'Whoever teaches about anything, does he persuade about what he teaches, or not?' and Gorgias (I desert Irwin's version) says, 'No indeed, Socrates; rather he persuades above all else.' Here, as Dodds notes in his commentary,[36] the alternative put by 'Or not?' is explicitly rejected in favour of the first, which suggests strongly that it is a live alternative requiring notice to be taken of it; the effect is indeed rather like the Budé 'Oui ou non?' cited earlier. A passage rather like the *Gorgias* one is to be seen in the *Meno* (88A):

> SOCRATES Yet we also speak of these things as sometimes doing harm. Or would you object to that statement?
>
> MENO No, it is so.[37]

There the choice is perfectly genuine. The answer to the question is not obvious, though Meno has previously agreed that, e.g., unjustly acquired wealth is bad or harmful (78D). But, as we have already suggested, if Socrates puts a genuine choice between two contradictories then his relationship to the question is more complex than that of somebody simply putting his own views to a respondent. Is his view a conjunction, a disjunction, or one of the disjoined alternatives? If it is one of the alternatives, then which? The one the respondent agrees to? But that, as we saw, brings little help.

If the objection still stands that Socrates' questions and the respondent's answers *together* tell Plato's readers in such cases what to believe, then the objectors are again playing into the hands of those holding that the respondent's responses deserve close and systematic study. For if question and answer must indeed be studied together, then the dialogues will not yield up their secrets to those who listen only to one side of the conversation. In that case we must bug the telephone, as it were, rather than eavesdrop at one end of the line.

If the objector steps back and says, in effect: 'All right, let's except disjunctive "*p* or not-*p*?" questions, obvious falsehoods (if there are any), questions tagged with a reference to the respondent's own opinions; let us say that all the rest are Socrates' opinions thrown at the respondent', then in answer let us urge the greatest possible caution. How can we be sure that Plato meant everything else to be Socrates' opinions? How could a Greek reader have known? Or how would a listener, even if, as Gilbert Ryle suggested,[38] Plato himself took the part of Socrates? A question is, after all, a question; when does the audience or the reader wake up to the supposed fact that a question is for practical purposes a statement? And have we exhausted the categories of question which cannot, or cannot easily, assert? How are we to know when we have exhausted such categories? Perhaps most difficult of all to answer: why did Plato choose this form of philosophic communication when the treatise form lay open to him? Simply because of the historical accident that Socrates was a talker and not a writer? Surely that is a *non sequitur*?

It is true that our knowledge of the treatise form as it was in Plato's early manhood is not as extensive as it could be. Treatises on rhetoric there most certainly were, and medical works too. There were also the treatises of those of the Presocratic philosophers who wrote in prose, from Anaximander in the sixth century BC through Diogenes of Apollonia in the late fifth. But, admittedly, we do not know how consecutive and thoroughly reasoned such treatises were. Recent work such as Malcolm Schofield's on Anaxagoras has tended to play down the systematic aspect of late fifth-century expository prose.[39] But continuous prose was nevertheless a vehicle in use for exposition. Whatever a treatise by Plato would have looked like, whether systematic and cogent or unsystematic and unconvincing, the question still requires an answer, why Plato did not speak straightforwardly in exposition of his views. In this context, Richard Hawtrey's recent rebuke to Taylor gains in significance.[40] He accuses the distinguished commentator on the *Protagoras* of giving no answer to the question why Plato should ever have written the dialogue; so far as I can see, the accusation is just. The treatise is, on the face of it, a better vehicle for the communication of views than the dialogue.

A possible explanation of Plato's adoption of the dialogue is his acceptance of a literary fashion of his time for Socratic dialogues; but our ignorance of such literature is profound,[41] and, whether or not Plato's treatment of the dialogue was as radically original as many Platonic scholars have believed, it is surely unlikely that Plato adopted the dialogue form *merely* because it was fashionable to do so. The late and unreliable biographer Diogenes Laertius is our main source for the titles of dialogues written by Socrates' younger friends, some of them probably older than Plato. How many of these titles are the fruits of literary forgeries of later date it is now impossible to know. The remaining fragments of dialogues by, most conspicuously, Aeschines of Sphettus, share some characters and some themes with Plato's works; they would suggest, *if* they are representative, that the principal character had things much more his own way here than in Plato, and that there was rather less by way of dramatic interplay of character and belief than is the case in Plato. Certainly this is true of the surviving Socratic works of Xenophon.

It is *possible* that in the early years of the fourth century, following the death of Socrates in 399 BC, the readers of such literature came to assimilate a convention by which a question from Socrates was regarded as both leading and representative of the author's own views. But Plato himself pretty certainly began writing, and presumably circulating, his dialogues in the 390s; that leaves very little time, in my judgment quite inadequate time, for such a convention to be a significant factor in the development of the dialogue as we know it from Plato's early period, at least down to and including the *Symposium*, probably the latest of the dialogues we shall be concerned with. We know too little to be one hundred per cent sure; but neither the dictates of literary fashion nor the example of Socratic talk seems to suffice to explain fully Plato's choice and development of the dialogue form. Perhaps these were necessary conditions; but it would be surprising if so acute a reasoner found them sufficient. More likely to have been decisive are considerations based on what can be done with the dialogue form that cannot, or can only with difficulty, be done in other forms.

Further, even if certainty in this area is unattainable, there are some questions in the dialogues which leave a very un-Socratic after-taste. Is there any serious student of Plato who will maintain that, when Socrates asks Callicles in the *Gorgias* (490C) whether the better man should have more clothes, he is putting to Callicles his own, Socrates', view of the matter? Or Plato's? Let me stick my neck out, and say I do not believe that to be a Socratic or Platonic view. But Socrates does not tag the question; and Callicles' refusal of assent is hardly evidence, one would have thought, for Socrates' or Plato's dissent. Most readers of Plato have their scepticism aroused, rightly or wrongly, in this kind of way, even if they may differ over the question where to give it free rein. But then the dialogue becomes a very inefficient method of communication, for the Socratic question by which it supposedly communicates becomes a vehicle of ambivalence.

In this situation it is possible to suppose that Plato intended his readers just to pause and think. Possibly at every question of Socrates' we were meant to step back and wonder whether the embodied proposition is being implicitly communicated or denied. But then there are, as we have noticed, some Socratic questions which hardly embody a proposition at all without the respondent's reply. It is at all times difficult, on this hypothesis, to know what Plato intends us to think, and how. The protreptic and educational value of the dialogues may be high, but their communicative value low. It is difficult to refute a view such as this; but it is equally difficult to establish it. It does little or nothing to explain the dialogue form, for a writer intending us to think about the truth or falsehood of propositions can equally well expound them in a systematic treatise.

If we could devise a model of interpretation that would both give Socrates' questions a consistent value, and avoid weakening the communicative clarity and force of the dialogues, while at the same time offering an explanation of the dialogue form that made Plato's choice more than a historical accident, we should not hesitate to abandon these embarrassments. Perhaps no such model is available. But this work is an attempt, in detail and for a small number of dialogues or conversations, to supply one and to put it to use. Its success can only be measured, as with most hypotheses, by its explanatory power, by the number of dark places on which it throws light. Its defects will be apparent from the number of obscurities it creates or at least fails to elucidate. But it deserves, I hope, not sympathetic, but rather systematic consideration.

The hypothesis runs, in bald outline, something like this. In the *Laches*, for example, Socrates talks to two typical generals, though they are of different sorts; in the *Symposium* he talks to a poet, of a particular sort, a successful tragedian who is also of long-standing homosexual inclinations focused on a single partner; in the *Protagoras* he talks to one sophist in the main, though also to a group of them. All the characters he talks to in these dialogues are successful and even distinguished in their own lines. Furthermore, Socrates talks to them, not about the technicalities of their trade as such, the dramaturgy of a tragedy, or the construction of a speech, or the tactics of a battle; but rather about what may roughly be called the philosophy either of their trade – about courage, or prowess, in the *Laches*, and about educating a citizen to Protagoras – or of their personal lives – about love to the homosexually attached Agathon in the *Symposium*. In each conversation the principal interlocutor/s is/are invited implicitly or explicitly, by Socrates or someone else, to expound what they think. They do so, naturally with varying degrees of sophistication and fluency, and at various lengths. They use premises and modes of argument more or less appropriate to their speciality or to their dominant personal characteristic. When they have finished, Socrates elicits further thoughts by questioning. The questions resolve unclarities left behind by the interlocutor's original statements, or supplement them, or otherwise arise out of them. The argument developed out of the questions and answers may use not only the premises but also the modes of reasoning of the interlocutor's original remarks. The conclusion of the argument thus developed may be a doctrine recurring in a whole group of dialogues, and hence one we may confidently label Platonic – for why else would he wish to arrive at the same kind of conclusion so often? Alternatively the conclusion may be simply one which contradicts what the respondent or interlocutor originally or in the course of the interrogation admitted or said. The two types of conclusion overlap.

Much of that, so far, would arouse hardly more than a flicker of scholarly interest. It is indeed fairly common currency in Platonic interpretation. But now suppose this process of either reducing to contradiction or bringing to a Socratic conclusion on pain of self-contradiction to be the *whole* point of at least the early dialogues. Suppose that Plato intended to show that a certain typical person from a certain significant class habitually used ways of thought and expression which laid him open to such reduction or compelled him, in consistency, to adopt Socratic views. Suppose, indeed, that all Socrates' questions are intended to elicit the respondent's answer, and no question is intended to inform us or the interlocutor. Then, after all these suppositions, try to imagine how Plato could better have done this work of reduction than by the use of dialogue. The easiest way to present us with significant but typical personages is dramatically. The easiest way to bring before us their characteristic modes of thought and speech is by putting characteristic speeches into their mouths. Of course, some dialogues may be more successful than others: their principals may be more lifelike, more typical, more significant. One wonders how many tragic poets in Athens had long-standing homosexual attachments.[42] One wonders much less how many sophists use the kind of cliché of rhetoric that, as we shall see, lands Protagoras in dialectical trouble. In that respect the *Protagoras* will be ultimately more, or at any rate more generally, significant than the *Symposium*. On the other hand love is doubtless a subject of even wider appeal than education.

You may ask where Plato's own views come into this. How did he either express or prove them? Here one has to agree with E. N. Tigerstedt[43] that Plato, like any other writer of drama, 'keeps aloof from his readers' (or listeners). His own opinions emerge only from a comparison of the conclusions to which in different dialogues Socrates seems to be anxious to drive different people, or from Socrates' rare statements, where these are not demonstrably bound to the particular context. As for the proofs, it is, it would seem, perfectly legitimate to suppose that Plato kept them *either* to himself *or* to his pupils. If one is to believe either of these suppositions, the former is perhaps preferable, though the preference may be based on nothing but prejudice; ancient reports of Plato's esoteric doctrine, for what they are worth, do not, I think, extend to additional arguments for views known from the extant works, but concentrate rather on alleged additional doctrines.[44] But it is also legitimate, and surprisingly plausible, to suppose Plato to have had no universally valid proofs, and to have believed in none. He could well have wondered from what universally agreed axioms such proofs could start. He may have written his dialogues in the belief that the best one could do was to start from such axioms as a given person or kind of person might be willing to supply, either in expansive and volunteered speech or under close interrogation. Plato perhaps intended to show that a certain type of person, with a typical viewpoint, habitually used ways of thought or expression laying him open to reduction either to self-contradiction, or to Socratic tenets, or both. In this way we can suppose that *all* Socrates' questions have the aim of eliciting the respondent's view, and that any other purpose is, if present at all, of secondary importance. If we paint such a picture as this of Plato at work we may find it difficult to see how he could have done the job better than by dialogue, by putting characteristic speeches into typical mouths. If this were a true picture, then Plato's ideas on what he should (at least provisionally) accept would have been governed, at least partly, by his ability to drive, or to imagine Socrates driving, people of various sorts towards one kind of conclusion rather than another. He may also have observed the greater difficulty of reducing some beliefs, and some people, to absurdity or to contradiction than other beliefs or people.

As for the communication of Plato's views, on this kind of reading he expresses them by contrast with the kind of thoughts and expressions he shows up as inconsistent, and by the kind of conclusion his Socrates frequently drives his interlocutors to. He also, occasionally, has his Socrates volunteer assertions without obvious contextual necessity. From these indications we can, though slowly and with much travail, build up a picture of what Plato thought. The dialogues reveal in this way the notions – in so far as he had positive notions – of their creator. They do not, on this hypothesis, offer straightforward proofs of doctrine for every step of which Plato would take responsibility.

This suggestion does nothing to rob Plato's dialogues of philosophical significance or even greatness. It is the age-long experience of philosophy that demonstrably certain or universally acceptable axioms are hard to come by. Though we might nowadays disclaim the practice of using our opponents' faulty logic or expressions against them in our own arguments, one has to use not only the axioms but also the logic which is acceptable to those one wishes to convince. We should remember, and Professor G. E. R. Lloyd has recently reminded us at length,[45] that Plato lived in an age which possessed no universally accepted system of logic or of reasoning. The best one could do to convince someone was to use not only his admitted premises but also his own implied logic. The person concerned might not always be convinced – he might perceive his own carelessness in either admission or implication – but he could not then come back at Socrates without eating words. In the absence of a systematic and widely acknowledged calculus of argument, it is (once again) difficult to see what form would have suited Plato's purposes as here painted better than the dialogue form. This coherence of purpose and form, of keen thought and dramatic vigour, may serve to recommend the interpretative hypothesis here outlined as at least worth pursuing.

In the controversy over the hedonism of the *Protagoras* from which we took statements about Socrates' questions at the outset, one weapon deployed by Gosling and Taylor was the need to take the *Protagoras* seriously.[46] 'If we take the Protagoras seriously, on the other hand, we seem to have to posit an inexplicable period of euphoria.' 'If we are not to take it seriously, we need some persuasive account of how to take it.' By 'taking the *Protagoras* seriously' these scholars seem to mean (in part) 'taking Socrates' questions to Protagoras to convey Socratic and Platonic belief.' Whether the attitude to the dialogues taken here is persuasive or not, and whether in particular the *Protagoras* is persuasively interpreted, are matters for readers to decide. But they should not decide either way on the basis of a simple decision to take Plato seriously. There is more than one way of taking Plato seriously. Indeed one way of doing so is to pay more serious attention to the dialogue form than is fashionable in some quarters. If this results in the explanation of that form less by the biographical accident – however important – of Plato's association with the great talker Socrates, and more by a deliberate and rational and literary choice on Plato's part, that may be an additional recommendation in an age which has tended to exchange biographical for literary explanations of literature.[47]

Taking the dialogue form seriously includes taking

Socrates' interlocutors seriously. This in turn includes examining the constraints placed upon them by the context in which they speak. These constraints on occasion prevent the characters concerned from giving to Socrates an answer apparently obvious then, and certainly obvious now. There are different types of such constraint. The two types separated below are not unrelated and are indeed united in the constraints on Meno analysed above.

The first type arises from the kind of person Socrates' victim is. Protagoras and Gorgias both, in the dialogues named after them, accept (not in identical ways) the primacy of the intellect; Gorgias fails to reject the intellectualism of Socrates; Protagoras actively embraces it; modern interpreters have not always failed to notice that a Sophist could do no other.[48] If the Sophists claimed by intellectual means to exert a profound influence on their pupils' lives, they could hardly rate the things of the intellect low on their scales of importance. It is precisely this which gives Socrates (or his literary creator) the opportunity to appear as the one and only consistent intellectual of his time.

The second constraint on persons subject to Socratic interrogation is what they have already said. They are under obligation, in Socrates' presence, to remain consistent, and if they do not they are defeated. Some accept defeat, others give up one or more of the offending group of propositions. Their inconsistency may be direct, in that they enunciate in the course of the discussion two propositions evidently contradictory, or it may be indirect, in that they utter two propositions of such a kind that Socrates can, by analysing the consequences of one or both, arrive at an inconsistency.

In this account, the words 'analysing the consequences' are far too logical for Plato's day in both connotation and denotation.[49] The consequences of a proposition p in Socratic dialectic include not only propositions directly deducible analytically from p, but also those deducible from a combination of p with other propositions, q, r, etc., such that q and r are inescapable for Socrates' victim either for logical or for professional or for personal reasons. The personal reasons often include words uttered by the person involved at an earlier stage of the conversation, whether or not under the particular stimulus and pressure of Socratic dialectic.

The consequences of a proposition in this 'dialectical' sense include its logical consequences, since a normal person finds it hard to resist conclusive logic when he recognizes it. But dialectical and logical consequences are not identical sets; dialectical consequences range much wider, and include far more propositions, than logical consequences. But dialectical consequences are Socrates' concern in the dialogues, or parts of dialogues, discussed in this work. This concern is important for the dialogues' interpretation, and it is specially important for the present type of interpretation to realize that people in Plato's dialogues commit themselves to propositions unfortunate for their later admissions even before Socrates starts to question them.

The often seemingly artless, or at best only dramatically artful, conversations before the Socratic chains of question and answer begin may thus be vital to the argument. No proposition advanced at any stage by any of Socrates' companions should pass without scrutiny for its possible effect on the subsequent discussion. The same goes for inferences or modes of inference, however casually drawn or exemplified in the course of conversation. One engages in talk with the Platonic Socrates at one's peril. If one does not watch one's step and bridle one's tongue one falls to his assault. Socrates does not always refer back to such remarks or inferences of his victim, but nevertheless he makes use of them, and sometimes does so explicitly. The varying openness of Socrates' dialectical behaviour constitutes a difficulty, and perhaps goes far to account for the procedures not being common knowledge. In the end we shall have to confront the question why Socrates is not more, and more consistently, explicit. But that is a question posterior to discussion of the procedures themselves.

Critics may be inclined, especially but not only if their bias is that of the philosopher rather than the Hellenist, to take a mildly cynical view of this whole programme. They may think that Plato's fallacies are about to receive a coat of whitewash, to be swept under the carpet, or whatever metaphor one cares to use for the fraudulent defence of an admittedly great but perplexing philosopher. But it is decidedly no part of the programme to insist on the removal of all fallacy from the pages of Plato. Of course he will have committed some fallacies. Naturally also, he sometimes starts from unacceptable premises; that is why I am not a Platonist in the philosophical sense. But the number of apparently fallacious arguments and apparently incredible premises to be found in Plato may become more intelligible if we allow ourselves to believe that it was not Plato's intention to convince or to convict everybody at once.

To suppose the dramatic element in the dialogues less important than it is, is today a much commoner mistake than to underestimate their argumentative content. It is easier for a philosopher to ignore a dramatic setting than for a Hellenist to ignore the argument.

More insidious is a belief, from time to time seen in print or heard at academic gatherings, that Plato's arguments do not appeal to reason. Plato appears to condemn rhetoric, but practises it.[50] Plato condemns poetry, while composing the most exquisitely refined of poetically coloured prose. Plato attacks mimetic literature in mimetic form. If Plato distinguishes false rhetoric from true, the distinction stands or falls by the truth or falsehood of the content – and why should we take Plato's word for that? The question is good. But it misses the point of Plato.

Plato's Socrates is capable of rhetoric, of gorgeous, moving and persuasive prose; but more normally he preaches and practises dialectic. He includes in that practice many techniques of persuasion, such as imagery, whether metaphor or tellingly graphic illustration. He employs even in his more sober discussions many disreputable tricks of the rhetorician's trade. But his basic practice is not to overbear the opposition with the weight of his formidable stylistic virtuosity. It is to show that other views than his own, using the word 'view' in an extended sense, are internally inconsistent; and he invites or leaves us to draw the conclusion that his own view is not. Socrates is in no danger of making the same mistakes as a Laches, an Agathon or a Protagoras. Partly this is because he lacks their pretensions – he puts forward in the early dialogues very few if any views of his own, which is of course one way to avoid putting forward inconsistent views.

To discover what Socrates and Plato think, one has to work from the kind of view they appear to reject, or to find inconsistent with other views. But that is an operation fraught with the utmost difficulty, leading through many an intellectual minefield, and not attempted here. Our subject is rather Socrates' dialectical refutations of other people.

Plato has indeed made it difficult to discover what he thought himself. The ancients put it more poetically: according to one of them,[51] Plato dreamt he had changed into a swan which flew from tree to tree, causing the greatest trouble to those who wanted to shoot him down. One thing is certain: at the end of this book, and of many more yet, he will still be flying. The best one can hope for is to cast on the shadows between the trees a little more light by which to catch and observe the manner of his flight.

2 Socrates and a pair of generals

At the heart of the whole discussion lies the concrete detail of what Plato wrote. The reader is invited accordingly to take down his text or his translation (or both)[1] and follow the argument step by step as Plato unfolds it. He or she should check against it at every turn the features to which attention is drawn in this book. At each step we shall stop and see where Plato's characters have arrived, and what further routes are open (or, it may be, closed) to them. Their personal characteristics, their previous admissions, and the logic of the sequence of questions, answers and submissions, all require appreciation. The analysis assumes the realism – or at least the plausibility – of the conversation: one cannot analyse the arbitrary. Such detailed study will show, among other things, the truth, the exactitude, and the profundity of Nicias' insight (188A) that the victim of Socrates' interrogation 'submits to answering questions about himself concerning both his present manner of life and the life he has lived hitherto. And when he does submit to this questioning ... Socrates will not let him go before he has well and truly tested every last detail.'

English-speaking writers on Plato are generally agreed that the *Laches,* in which Socrates encounters the two generals Laches and Nicias, is about courage. They usually treat the serious transaction of Plato's business with courage as beginning nearly half way through the work with Socrates' first questioning of Laches.[2] Some writers in English have in the past accused Laches of philosophical ineptitude or inexperience, leading him to give the answer Socrates wants:[3] this could obviously develop into an accusation against Plato of cheating. All three of these positions are in truth oversimplifications. European and American scholarship has in recent years shown them to be so. Dr Évelyne Méron[4] has argued convincingly that 'courage' is not an adequate rendering of the Greek *andreia* (etymologically 'manliness') as Plato uses it in the *Laches.* Dr Reinhard Dieterle,[5] in a Freiburg dissertation made public in 1966, propounded the view that the dialogue's argument develops out of the prologue, the opening conversation which precedes the Socratic interrogations of Laches and Nicias. He argued further that every step carries Socrates' interlocutor with it, that the argument is 'constantly oriented towards the partner.'

One reason for writing this chapter is to make sure that these views receive from English-speaking students more than the passing attention Guthrie (for example) gave to Dieterle in his *History of Greek Philosophy*.[6] Another is the need to develop them further. It is necessary to show, as Dr Méron does not, that Plato's usage of *andreia* in the *Laches* has firm roots in ordinary unphilosophical Greek. It is possible to find much more in the *Laches* prologue. And even Dr Dieterle is insufficiently systematic in following the reactions of the interlocutors to Socrates' questioning. It is not enough to treat Socrates as imposing his views from time to time in order to further Plato's purposes. At every step we must examine the reasons for the interlocutor's implied surrender; and we must bear in mind the question to what extent it is possible to impose one's views by questioning.

Further, the interpreter ought not to over-estimate the clarity of the implications assignable to the remarks of Socrates' partners; often their ambiguities share the responsibility for the direction taken by the argument. The course of the argument to be charted is involved, even convoluted, to a degree elucidatable only by minute study of detail. Lack of consistency in detail, and of system in the exploration of Platonic people's seemingly casual remarks, may have prevented the interchange and intertwining of ideas, essential to the dialogue, from wider acknowledgment. If so, then the reader must bear with the detail in the interest of conviction.

The first scene: motives

Our first topic must be the motives of the characters as revealed in the first scene. Lysimachus opens the dialogue on his own and Melesias' behalf, addressing Nicias and Laches.

The fame of the latter pair as generals was, we may be pretty sure, sufficient to win instant recognition at least from cultivated Athenian readers.[7]

Lysimachus and Melesias need and receive more introduction. Lysimachus, in expounding the request he has to offer, explains both the identity and the motives of himself and Melesias (178A–180E). These two are elderly men, the sons of the famous Athenian politicans Aristides the Just and Thucydides, and have now sons of their own on the threshold of manhood. Their request is for honest and frank advice. They express a desire to educate their sons, and an interest in the educative possibilities of the technique (demonstrated by one Stesilaus just before the dialogue opens (178A, 179E, the name at 183C)) of fighting in armour. The two old men invite help from Nicias and Laches in the knowledge that the generals too have sons.

The expressed motivation for the invitation is twofold (179C). Either the generals have made their sons' education their active concern, or they have neglected it. In the first case, presumably, their advice will be worth having as that of experienced fellow-parents. In the second case, the invitation will serve as a reminder of their paternal duties and a suggestion of a joint pursuit of the matter. So far as Lysimachus' words go, he and Melesias are approaching Nicias and Laches not as generals but as fathers.

But we may doubt if just any concerned, or potentially concerned, fathers would suffice in general or would be appropriate in the particular circumstances. Granted that Plato's Athenian and reasonably cultivated readers would know of Nicias and Laches as military men; granted also that military command in Classical Athens depended heavily on political skills – the 'generals' were elected; granted these propositions, it is tempting to detect a deliberate parallelism between Nicias and Laches on the one hand and the eminent fathers of Lysimachus and Melesias on the other.

When Lysimachus and Melesias tell us they were the subject of paternal neglect, the whole scene gains in clarity and sharpness. It is fitting that the eminent, such as Nicias and Laches, should not, like Aristides and Thucydides, neglect their sons' training in adolescence. Either Nicias and Laches are not doing what eminent fathers should do, in which case they need a reminder and perhaps help from victims of fatherly neglect, or they are and have been showing a proper paternal concern, in which case they can perhaps advise Lysimachus and Melesias. But if we ask why their advice should be sought rather than that of any other responsible Athenian father, the reason is obvious: it is their known political and military eminence which makes their advice worth having, as it would have the advice of Aristides and Thucydides if they had shown any interest.

True, Lysimachus makes no mention of this.[8] But it would have been obvious to Plato's contemporaries, as we can see from Laches' treatment of it as obvious in a later speech (180B). Laches, indeed, draws the parallel we have just drawn for ourselves: 'As for what Lysimachus said just now about his father and Melesias' father, I think that what he said applied very well to them and to us and everyone engaged in public affairs'. But at the same time Laches expresses astonishment (180C) at the failure to take Socrates' advice too.

The recommendation of Socrates arises directly from Socrates' demonstrated concern for education; but again there is more to be said. Laches tells Lysimachus later (181A–B) not to let the man get away because, as he says, 'I have seen him elsewhere keeping up not only his father's reputation but that of his country. He marched with me in the retreat from Delium...' Here the ground for including Socrates among the advisers is none other than his military prowess. To suppose Lysimachus and Melesias – or Plato's original readers – ignorant of the prowess of Nicias and Laches in the same sphere is to attribute undue naivety to them. To attribute to Laches a feeling for the relevance of Socrates' soldierly services, but none for the relevance of his own, would be surprising. The explicit statement of one motive and the implicit suggestion of another ought to leave, one supposes, some slight confusion in the mind of an attentive reader of this opening scene about the motives of the main participants and the reasons for their presence.

This possible confusion may seem a triviality of no significance to the philosophical reader, and of only limited interest to the connoisseur of literature; but to judge it so would be an error. The construction of the early part of the scene lends to some of Socrates' later questions a point and a relevance they would otherwise not possess, and the point is of a kind we shall frequently meet.

Socrates' questions are virtually never mere fishing expeditions, but almost always arise out of the context. Here Socrates has heard Laches introduce him both as one interested in the young and their education and as a doughty fighter; being younger and less experienced 'in these matters' (181D), whatever 'these matters' may mean,[9] he listens to Nicias and Laches before speaking himself. When the two generals differ, he draws attention (184E) to their need of an expert, and *then* (185B) points out the exactly relevant unclarity in their thinking: they have not agreed on the exact subject of their deliberation, the exact subject in which they need an expert. One respondent then (185C) replies 'Aren't we investigating the art of fighting in armour and discussing whether young men ought to learn it or not?' Socrates' subsequent line of questioning elucidates the point that they are really deliberating about the young men, not about the fighting in armour. It is an expert in education they need, not in fighting.

With this, the soldierly prowess of Nicias, Laches and Socrates loses most of its relevance. The importance of that lies in its consequence, that the generals' technical expertise is useless for the discussion, which turns largely on values; the Platonic Socrates in the *Apology* (21B–22E) illustrates his life's work with examples of experts whose technical knowledge he did not impugn, but whose authority on other topics (to him of greater significance) he denied. This is fundamental; Socrates' later questioning of the generals is in part addressed to it; and the opening pages of the *Laches* prepare the ground for it. The seemingly verbose and artless opening conversation has more than the trivial concerns it carries on its face.

But, the philosophical reader might ask, what is that to him? Does it matter that Socrates should develop his questions naturally out of the preceding remarks? Is that not a point of purely literary interest? We may be in no position to speak for the philosopher, and what is to count as philosophical or as philosophically interesting is notoriously a matter for debate. But – without entering that debate here – it surely ought to interest a philosopher to observe that some questions exercising the Platonic Socrates arise from the variety of vague and hardly formulated everyday attitudes of people ordinary in everything but their special skills. If Plato and his Socrates are in important respects 'ordinary-language' philosophers, then present-day philosophers emphasizing or opposing the emphasis on ordinary language ought at least to be cognizant of those respects. At least the sight of Plato developing Socratic or Platonic paradoxes from ordinary people's assumptions and language ought to serve, for good or ill, as an object-lesson.

The first scene: values

Motives have thus turned out more significant than one might have supposed: but Plato's early dialogues are about values. The ways in which terms of value appear on the lips of his characters in the *Laches'* opening scene illuminate the subsequent discussion. Socrates' questions, even whole lines of interrogation, will depend on the views stated or implied in the early speeches of his interlocutors.[10]

The first indication in the text of a concern with values, or with opinions about them, arrives as early as Lysimachus' very first speech, which Socrates does not necessarily overhear.[11] The topic Lysimachus and Melesias think Laches and Nicias 'if anyone' will have studied is 'the sort of training that would make the best men of them' (179B). Lysimachus and Melesias, in elaborating on their request for advice, do not suggest that values might be subject to differences of opinion. They treat the question (literally) 'how they may turn out very good' as a question about the means to an agreed end.

The sort of values they have in mind become clear as Lysimachus unfolds their intentions (179C–D). They want their boys to emulate their famous grandfathers' great services to the Athenian state, on the unspoken assumption that the kind of thing which brings great renown in peace or war is a great service. Their warning to their sons predicts a lack of *glory*[12] as the penalty for neglect of parental advice. It is in that context that they again state an interest in 'the question what form of instruction or practice would make them turn out best.' The word 'fine', constantly on Lysimachus' lips to describe (e.g.) his father's activities and the technique of fighting in armour, sometimes means '*praise*worthy'.[13] These old men's values are of the utmost banality. What counts for them as successful living is very much what the world in general esteems as success. Nicias and Laches, moreover, take no issue with their elders on this point; we suppose their values also to be either unconscious or conventional or both.

But this is not quite the whole story; another chapter opens with Lysimachus' attitude to Socrates and his father Sophroniscus. Admittedly the reader depends here on some gentlemanly courtesies of Lysimachus to Socrates as the son of an old friend. But Plato's reader must treat 'façons de parler' as ways not only of speech but of thought. Plato has no method of exposing his characters' ways of thought other than through their words; words betray mental processes none the less real for their largely habitual and subconscious nature.

Lysimachus, then, responds (181A) to the news that the Socrates before him is the one praised by his children with the remark that Socrates takes after his father, who was the best of men. Now it seems pretty unlikely that the boys praised Socrates for his worldly success, which was far from conspicuous.[14] They will have praised him for other good qualities. Indeed, Lysimachus himself, in praising Sophroniscus as the best of men, will certainly have been judging him by standards very different from those he applied to his father, himself, and his ideals for his son. Historians did not, and still do not, blazon the name of Sophroniscus across their pages in letters as large as those given to the statesmen Aristides and Thucydides. History knows him only because he became the father of Socrates. The merit Lysimachus finds in him is that of an old friend and companion, with whom he never quarrelled (180E).

But if that makes Sophroniscus the best of men, then what fault have Lysimachus and Melesias to find with each other? And why (to ask a philosophical, rather than psychological, question) are they so anxious for their sons' worldly success?

There is not only something new to this conversation about Lysimachus' use of 'best' here; there is something difficult to reconcile with his judgments of value as expressed in his desire for his son. What is more, the difficulty is a common one: how many of us want our children to grow up generous, upright and gentle, and at the same time want them to 'get on in the world'?

To ask this question raises an educational problem, if one conceives education as more than the inculcation of facts and techniques. Does one try to show how compassion and generosity and honesty lead to worldly success? Does one take a less difficult line and urge one's children to pursue worldly success only to the extent that the pursuit does not conflict with moral rules? Does one tell them, in effect, to be worldly competitors without scruple for six days a week only? Or does one, like many parents, muddle along with a mixture of all three? If worldly success consists, as it does in the eyes of Lysimachus and Melesias, of political office and military command, is a man who achieves such success a good man regardless of other qualities or actions? Or does he need other qualities to make him a completely good man? To put the matter in the terms of Socrates' later talk in the *Laches,* is a soldier's success, or are the qualities necessary and sufficient for that success, the whole of goodness or only part of it?

It would appear from the remarks made by Lysimachus to date that he would say either (a) that there existed two quite separate ways of being a good man or (b) that there existed a single unified goodness, and that the qualities necessary and sufficient for political success did not constitute the whole of it. Lysimachus and Melesias show no signs of adopting (a). Socrates (and we) would perhaps be right to suppose that (b) is more representative of their position. Right or wrong, this supposition would harmonize fully with Plato's practice (deliberate or merely mistaken) of assuming the univocality of words such as 'goodness' whose meaning Socrates questions.[15] Analysed thus, Lysimachus' apparently innocuous remarks leave the way open for pointed discussion whether soldierly prowess is the whole or part of a man's goodness.

Since the dialogue ends with an impasse on precisely this

question, with Nicias committed apparently to the beliefs that *andreia* is the whole of goodness and that it is a part of goodness, anything on this topic in the opening scene is sure to repay inspection, whether it comes from the old men, from Nicias, or from Laches. Laches is indeed the speaker in two passages bringing goodness and 'bravery' into connection. In Dieterle's opinion the second of these suffices to show that *andreia* is in Laches' view *the aretê,* goodness itself or *the* good quality. I differ, and will try below to expose the ambiguities of that passage. The first passage (184B–C) does in my view, though not everybody understands it in the same sense, commit Laches to the equation of goodness and *andreia*.

Laches here, nearing the end of his speech condemning Stesilaus' art of fighting in armour, warns of possible unfortunate consequences of laying claim to it. In view of possible disagreements I translate the relevant lines myself as literally as possible, and leave the crucial terms in transliterated Greek: 'And then it seems to me that if a *deilos* man should think he knew the art, by becoming more *thrasys* he would become more conspicuous in his true nature; but in the case of an *andreios* man, everyone would be watching him and if he made the smallest mistake, he would incur a great deal of criticism. For the claim to such knowledge is matter for grudging dislike; so that unless a man is remarkably superior in *aretê* to the rest, he cannot avoid ridicule, if he lays claim to this knowledge.'

Two points are worth making about this: the first is that it offers valuable supporting evidence for Méron's view that *andreia* has to do with strategic efficacy more than with a meritorious feeling, and as much with success as with daring. This, which is essential for a correct understanding of these lines, forms a necessary preliminary to the second point, the relationship of *andreia* and goodness.

The meaning of andreios

Méron[16] bases her view on two later passages: in one (191C) Socrates illustrates *andreia* with a stratagem which (irrelevantly to bravery) brings success; in the other, the common opinion that (190D) Stesilaus' art tends to produce courage is, she argues, better understood as referring to skill in fighting than to bravery. Somewhat confusingly she insists that the French word 'courage' covers all the nuances of the Greek *andreia*. Being otherwise in agreement but less optimistic about the English 'courage', I prefer to stick to the transliterated *andreia,* or to refer to 'courage' *in quotation marks,* when referring to the complex of ideas represented by *andreia*. Méron does not mention the sentences translated above, though they only make sense on her assumption that *andreia* means on occasion 'skill in fighting'.

This understanding of the passage deserves demonstration. If we take the contrasted pair *deilos* and *andreios* there to mean respectively 'cowardly' and 'brave' in the normal sense of those words in current English[17], a curious argument results. Laches then says that a coward *(deilos)* who thinks he has Stesilaus' art gains confidence (becomes *thrasys*) and thus reveals his true cowardly nature. A brave man *(andreios)* who thinks he has the technique will be watched for every slip and, if not markedly superior in goodness *(aretê),* he will be laughed at. This will not do in the context. The passage falls immediately after, and obviously refers to, the tale of Stesilaus; and on this interpretation the reference to Stesilaus is impossible, since whatever faults Stesilaus may possess, cowardice is not among them so far as we know. He certainly does not become conspicuous for cowardice. It is in any case hard to see how boldness could make a man's cowardice conspicuous, unless he bit off more than he could chew and then ran away; and Stesilaus does not run away. Stesilaus in the story comes to grief not through any moral defect but through incompetence.

Clearly preferable to this – and indeed the only way to make sense of Laches' words – is the interpretation of *deilos* as 'unskilled' or 'inadequate at fighting', and of *andreios* as 'skilled in fighting'. If an unskilled man thinks he knows (for example) the skill of Stesilaus, he becomes confident and bold *(thrasys),* and thus runs into situations he cannot handle, revealing his incompetence. But if a skilled fighter *(andreios)* lays claim to an art such as Stesilaus says he imparts, then, according to Laches, he is closely observed and if caught out is the victim of cruel ridicule. *This* moral exactly fits Laches' fable of Stesilaus' discomfiture.

But to this reading of the words *deilos* and *andreios* and their relatives there is an important objection, which needs to be met, but hardly figures in Méron's account.[18] Hellenists will observe that the Lexicon gives no such meaning for the *andreios/deilos* contrast as 'skilled/unskilled' or 'good/bad at fighting'.

The Lexicon gives no examples under either member of the contrasting pair. But perhaps it is the Lexicon which is at fault? That great English scholar Jebb, editing Sophocles' *Electra* (983), rendered *andreia* by 'prowess' – and reasonably so, since both daring and success are highly relevant at that point. Jebb did not think the rendering deserved any comment.

Passages in Euripides and Thucydides tell the same story. In Euripides' play *Andromache* (683), a speaker, in defence of Helen of Troy, says that till her actions formed a *casus belli* the Greeks were ignorant of war; they then turned to the *andreios*; contact, the speaker says, is what teaches mankind. The speaker's point, as her contrasts make clear, is that after Helen's stirring up of strife the Greeks improved as fighters; and the old translation of E. Coleridge[19] is correct in saying that Hellas' sons 'turned to deeds of prowess'. Electra, in Euripides' play of that name (949ff.), speaks of her need for a husband 'not like a girl, but of manly *(andreios)* quality', and she shows what she means by continuing, 'Their children depend on war.' What Electra needs, then, is a husband not merely manly and brave, but capable and competent at fighting.

Thucydides the historian, too (II 89.2), mentions *andreia* in one of his speeches (never easy to interpret) in a way simpler to understand if we suppose a possible meaning of the word to be 'good at fighting', whereas bravery, pure and simple, is *tolma* or 'daring' and the bold man is *thrasys*. The Athenian admiral Phormio, speaking to his men before the battle of Naupactus, tells them not to be frightened of the Spartans. He offers several reasons why not: especially that

> that in which they trust most as they attack, namely, the appropriateness to themselves of being *andreios,* they have confidence in just because they are for the most part suc-

cessful on account of their experience in infantry fighting, and they think they will do the same on board the fleet. But we shall have more right than they to make such claims, if indeed they can make them on land since they have no advantage in *eupsychia* at any rate, but each side is bolder as a result of its greater skill.

Phormio takes the Spartans to place trust not so much in their own courage as in their general fighting qualities; the supposed evidence supporting the Spartans is not that of courageous deeds but that of repeated success. *Andreia* here, as in some other military contexts, is not just courage, though it can include or refer to courage; it is the sum total of the qualities and skills which make a good soldier.

Thucydides' Athenian and Spartan commanders use the arguments appropriate to their respective situations: since the Spartan knows his men have little experience or skill in sea warfare, he plays down the element of skill and plays up that of sheer 'guts', which he naturally assimilates to *andreia,* as affording the hope of effectiveness and hence of victory. The Athenian Phormio grasps the nettle of Spartan renown for effectiveness in war, points out its restriction to land warfare, and (naturally) tells his men that they will be the more confident, bold or assured because of their skill and experience at sea. One should be chary of reading into this exchange a debate, or even traces of a debate, on the nature of courage, though one could hardly deny the possibility of such debate.[20] What we find here is rather differing but easily explicable uses of the word 'courage'.

Andreia with the sense 'skill in war' is thus well established in Greek usage, at least in that of the more cultivated speakers, and does not come factitiously from the mind of Plato; but to say this is emphatically not to deny that our 'courage' is in many passages the best translation of *andreia.* Indeed, in Thucydides' account (II 87.3), the Spartan commander before Naupactus uses the word in precisely that sense and (as Phormio does not)[21] as an equivalent to *eupsychia* or 'good-souledness'. We are saying rather that *andreia* or 'manliness' covers other qualities in addition to courage.

Laches (184B), in using *andreia* to include or to refer to

skill, and the other qualities going to make up a good soldier, commits himself to some fairly close relationship between at least one sort of *andreia* and sheer soldierly competence. It is therefore highly significant that Laches is the respondent to some Socratic questions in the later debate which assume that technique falls within the purview of *andreia*. The questions fit the respondent's previously expressed or implied views. But it is also significant that Laches' usage is nothing out of the ordinary for at least an educated Greek. If Socrates shows up some incoherence in Laches' thought, incoherence deriving from the variety of contexts in which he uses the word *andreia,* then his literary creator Plato is not arguing narrowly *ad hominem,* or setting up a mere Aunt Sally, but is rather attacking confusions to which his contemporaries at large were liable. That is why it is particularly important to establish the normality of Laches' vocabulary and of the use he makes of it.

But we have not yet finished with the moral Laches draws from Stesilaus: now that we are sure that *andreia* there means the sum of those qualities which make a good fighter, we may turn to the relationship between the good fighter and the good man.

Goodness and skill in war

Whatever later passages may or may not say, the one from which this discussion arose (184B–C) does put in the mouth of Laches a close connection between goodness in general and the quality or qualities of a good and successful soldier. It contains two disjoined conditions; the second arm of the disjunction is that if the claimant to Stesilaus' art is *andreios,* i.e. (as we now know) an effective soldier, he will be closely watched, and, if he makes even a tiny mistake, will be harshly spoken of. This, Laches says, is because the claim risks resentment, such that the claimant will be the butt of ridicule if he is not superior to the rest in 'goodness'. If we ask what good quality is needed in superior measure for a pupil of Stesilaus to escape ridicule, the answer is surely very simple: what such a man needs is effectiveness in war. Superiority in that will tend to eliminate even small errors such as meet with a ribald reaction if (and only if) accompanied by a claim to skill. In

Laches' cautionary tale Stesilaus failed in effectiveness and in no other quality. Goodness is, pretty clearly, the same quality here as that in virtue of which a man is *andreios,* and not *deilos:* efficiency in war.

One might want to evade that conclusion, and there are two moderately promising escape routes; but both are dead ends. The first supposes that goodness here merely *includes* soldierly effectiveness; what blocks this is the sheer irrelevance of any other good quality to the avoidance of ridicule by a failed 'expert' in fighting. From this it does not follow that Laches would not on other occasions and in other contexts use the word 'goodness' to denote other good qualities he is not thinking of here. But it is clear that in this context Laches is thinking of superiority in fighting as a necessary and sufficient condition for the attribution of 'goodness'.

The second escape route takes *andreia,* 'manliness', here as a wide term incorporating all the qualities that make up a rounded, good, human being. Considerations of relevance cut this off too: this time the irrelevance of other qualities than fighting ones to the story of Stesilaus, whom we have come to know only as a fighter and teacher of fighting. The conclusion is after all hard to evade that Laches' use of words implies an equation of 'goodness' with soldierly competence.

Much more doubt surrounds the emergence of a similar equation from other portions of the opening conversation, portions concerning the conduct of Socrates at the battle of Delium.[22] Laches drops a broad hint of his views in the first of these passages (181A–B), and follows up later. Socrates, according to him, behaved at Delium in a manner worthy not only of his father but of his country. If others had been like him on that occasion, Athens would have avoided defeat. Now Lysimachus had just described Socrates' father as 'the best of men'. Laches, therefore, treats Socrates as behaving worthily of 'the best' when he displays prowess on the battlefield. He says nothing specifically of courage, but emphasizes the avoidance of defeat, and the martial quality or qualities necessary to that end.

Without saying precisely that such qualities make a good man, Laches gives the impression that that is the most natural way to take his remarks. But it is possible to take him here either as simply equating military prowess with goodness or as saying something different. A possible reading of his remarks would say that (a) Sophroniscus is good for non-martial reasons (as indeed Lysimachus' context suggests), (b) Socrates is possessed of a different sort of goodness, namely, the martial, and (c) Socrates is martially good to a degree worthy of his father's degree of other kinds of goodness. If Laches did mean this, then he could be construed as believing in a unified goodness of which Sophroniscus' and Socrates' virtues formed each a part. Laches' views here are hard to pin down.

Not much easier is his later enlargement on the same topic (188C–189B). Laches is there expounding his attitude to 'discussions' or 'arguments' or 'words' (all the same word in Greek, almost throughout). His willingness to listen and learn depends on the proviso that the words fall from the lips of good men, or that the 'teacher' is a good man – the context makes abundantly clear that the word 'good' does not signify merely 'good at teaching'. Socrates has evidently satisfied this proviso in Laches' judgment since the day of Delium. 'This,' Laches says to Socrates (189B), 'has been my opinion of your character, since that day on which we shared a common danger and you gave me a sample of your valour – the sort a man must give if he is to render a good account of himself.'

Here the vocabulary used is significant. Sprague's 'valour' renders *aretê*, the normal abstract for 'goodness' in Greek. The word 'good' in the phrase 'a good account of himself' is apparently, in Sprague's English syntax, the equivalent of the Greek 'justly' or 'righteously'. The sample Socrates has given, or the test he has passed (to offer another approximation to Plato's Greek), is in goodness. But, as Sprague and Dieterle have clearly seen,[23] the only relevant kind of goodness is a martial quality. If Sprague's 'valour' means 'courage', that would fit Laches' reference to shared danger; but 'and', joining clauses as in the sentence translated above, may indicate an addition rather than a mere repetition, and it is highly likely that Laches means here, as in his previous reference to the retreat from Delium, to laud not only Socrates' courage in the strict sense of that word but also his general effectiveness as a fighter. Either way, 'goodness' refers to a quality elsewhere denoted by *andreia*.

But there is again, and more seriously this time, a possibility of reading 'goodness' as a wider term than *andreia* and inclusive of it. 'Goodness' earlier in Laches' speech (188C) had a more general ring. 'Whenever I hear a man discussing goodness[24] or some kind of wisdom, then, if he really is a man and worthy of the words he utters, I am completely delighted to see...'; 'And (188D) such a man seems to me to be genuinely musical... rendering his own life harmonious by fitting his deeds to his words...'; 'Let (189A) Solon grant me this point, that the teacher should himself be good...'; 'To you (189B), then, Socrates, I present myself as someone for you to teach...'

There is no sign of restriction to fighting efficiency here. But even the relationship of a narrower term to a wider one may not suffice to disentangle Laches' knotted expressions. Even if 'goodness' does start this speech as merely inclusive of *andreia,* nevertheless Socrates' demonstration of his *andreia* is in Laches' eyes sufficient proof of his goodness. Hence, it would appear, the following alternatives are open: (1) Laches ignores at the end of his speech the more general import of its beginning, or (2) he intends 'goodness' to mean *andreia* throughout, or (3) he regards the possession of *andreia* as guaranteeing the possession of the other qualities making up complete goodness, or (4) he thinks of Socrates as having demonstrated his possession of *a* goodness, or *a* good quality, namely, *andreia,* which is specially relevant to the subject of their present discourse.

Laches goes far to rule out (4) by the suggestion that Socrates is at liberty to teach and refute Laches on whatever subject he likes. Laches' previous remarks around 'goodness' incline one to suppose (1) or (2) correct, despite other possibilities arising here. Of these two, (1) is perhaps supported against (2) by the same consideration which rules out (4). A consideration apparently supporting (2) is the expression 'if he really is a man', an expression calling to mind 'manliness' or *andreia;* but such was emphatically not, earlier, the force of Lysimachus' description of Sophroniscus as 'best of *men*' (my emphasis) (181A). Either (1) or (2) would involve Laches calling *andreia* 'goodness' as he did earlier; but this passage is much less conclusive than the moral to the fable of Stesilaus.

A complication is Laches' use of 'justly' in his assertion (189B) that Socrates has given him a sample of his goodness which a man must give if he is to give a sample justly. Evidently Laches approves of giving a sample justly. But it is not evident that he would approve of a just action which was not 'courageous'. Still less is it evident that he would rank justice as a good quality on a par with 'courage' as a good quality or as a part of goodness. The relationship of justice and *andreia* simply does not become clear in this speech, or in anything else that Laches says in the opening scene, so far as I can see.

Clear as Laches was that *andreia* means being good at fighting, only once is he quite unambiguous that goodness *is andreia*. The rest of the time he is, as one might expect of an ordinary gentleman and soldier with no special reason to be careful of his words, unclear. No actual contradiction stands in his remarks; he stands less close to self-contradiction than Lysimachus. Such confusion as there is in his values is less than that in the two old men's. His principal concern is with soldierly prowess; and indeed it is not quite clear whether he could accept without implied contradiction that such prowess is only part of what makes a man good.

That anyone should value the soldierly above all other good qualities, even, on occasion, to the exclusion of any other contribution to a man's goodness, may sound extraordinary to some modern ears. But the context of these utterances repays attention, as do Greek habits of speech. Laches turns out not to be as untypical as he may sound; if he were untypical, the dialogue would then be suspect of arguing too narrowly *ad hominem* – and though, in my view, the *Symposium* affords an example of Plato doing just that, the *Laches* is very different.

First, the context: Stesilaus' is a military art, and Laches and Nicias are both generals of some standing. The universe of discourse for the story of Stesilaus and its moral is military. Other, and more recent, military commanders have been heard in such contexts to describe a good soldier as 'a good man'. In times of prolonged, even if not continuous warfare, it is easy to think like that and to treat the soldierly qualities as the ones which count most, or even as the only ones to count at all.[25] But A. W. H. Adkins, K. J. Dover[26] and others have pointed out that the world of the Classical Greeks was one in which warfare of one kind or another played a substantial role for much of the time. Civil war was for many Greek states the mere continuation of politics by other means, and wars between states were common. The ability of city or faction to defend itself was essential. Military prowess was an important contribution the individual citizen could offer to the community.[27] In certain contexts it was reasonable to use 'goodness' to mean 'military prowess', as it was to use it of political or financial success or of the qualities making for such. It is a fact that the Greeks did use the term goodness to denote soldierly excellence.[28]

Copious illustration of this last fact is unnecessary here in view of the extensive modern literature,[29] but one example may be of interest and lead to the question whether 'goodness' is ever in Classical literature equivalent to *andreia* not only in the sense 'military prowess' but also in that of 'courage' proper. Herodotus' account of the battle of Plataea (worth reading in this context for other reasons besides the reference to the battle in the *Laches* (191C)) devotes a paragraph (IX 71) to the question who acquitted themselves best in the fight. On the Greek side the Tegeans and Athenians behaved well, but the Spartans excelled all in goodness. As A. D. Godley's Loeb translation has it, 'Of this my only proof is (for all these vanquished the foes opposed to them) that the Lacedaemonians met the strongest part of the army and overcame it.' This accords clearly with the understanding of 'goodness' as 'prowess'.

This answer presupposes the question 'who had the greatest success?' The Spartans did, in that they defeated a larger force. The question who was bravest did not arise, and, if it had, would have needed more information.

The historian proceeds to the question which individual distinguished himself most. Here the question who was bravest might be thought to raise itself, though ultimately its relevance is doubtful. A previously disgraced man who wished to die appears to the Spartans inferior in goodness to a man who had presumably the normal fear of death to contend with. One might be tempted to suppose the overcoming of fear to be an essential feature of goodness in this type of situation; this would make the question at issue one of courage. That is not the only nor the most likely reading of Herodotus' account. More probably the point is simply the achievement of 'great feats' (as Godley has it) by the men in question, and the disgraced Spartan's feats did not count as fully his on account of his suicidal frenzy and consequent (as we should put it) 'diminished responsibility'.[30]

The reason for preferring this second reading is the great rarity and indeed (so far as I know) the non-existence of clear examples in Classical Greek literature of 'goodness' used as the equivalent of courage proper. Ordinary Greek writers used it to refer rather to what Dover[31] has shrewdly called 'that combination of bravery and skill which we look for in a fighter' – it being presumed that a man killed either in victory or in defeat had shown that combination.

Exhortations to 'be good men' need not, it seems to me, refer only to bravery, though their meaning is hardly susceptible of precise analysis. 'Bad' and 'badness' are, somewhat similarly, used where 'cowardly' and 'cowardice' would be quite appropriate; but then cowardice is a sufficient, though not a necessary, condition of failure or inefficiency on the battlefield, and the word 'bad' may *mean* 'inefficient' while *referring* to cowardice.

In his invaluable *Platon, Lexique,* E. des Places gives as one sense of *aretê* ('goodness') the French 'courage'; that may be right in French, but the passages des Places cites from Plato for this sense could very plausibly refer to the whole complex of qualities required for military success, and it is success which appears to be the criterion of 'goodness' in such contexts. If Plato uses the words for 'good' and for 'manliness' on occasion to refer to properties strictly moral and internal, Plato is suspect of accommodating usage to a philosophical intention to internalize the virtues;[32] it is unsafe to illustrate general usage of 'moral' terminology from Plato.

The reverse process is more illuminating; what Plato's unphilosophical characters say and mean is frequently closer to normal usage than remarks or questions put by Socrates to his familiars. In the case of 'goodness' as 'soldierly quality' it is clear that Laches' use of these as equivalents is normal, rather than sophisticated or philosophical usage. Were he to mean 'courage' proper by 'goodness', he would be uncharacteristically modifying normal usage. This suggests both that 'goodness' is for him in some contexts 'soldierly goodness' and that *andreia,* for which in one passage (184C) 'goodness' is a mere replacement, also referred to qualities likely to lead to soldierly success, and not just to courage proper.

Nicias' attitude is very different, though Plato has given us only hints of it. We do hear (180C–D) of his interest in educating his sons in music and similar subjects. He is interested (181E–182A) in keeping the young out of mischief, indeed out of their usual pursuits. The importance he attributes to warlike training is avowedly contingent on the situation in which Athens finds herself. In his eyes (182C) military arts are 'fine' and valuable. But he offers no hint of their supreme or all-embracing value.

Rather, Nicias places high value (188A–B) on something very different indeed, namely, his intercourse with Socrates. This reminds him, he implies, of things he has done which would not meet with approval; and he thinks it does him no harm to be so reminded – surely a clear case of understatement. In fact he says further that talk with Socrates gives a man the ability to 'pay more attention' or 'devote more forethought' to the rest of his life. His esteem for Socratic questioning is due not to Socrates' military prowess but to his capacity for making men think. Evidently Nicias does not embody, represent or urge the claims of a soldier's virtue in as solid a way as Laches; and it is perhaps for that reason that Plato named his dialogue about *andreia* not after Nicias but after Laches.[33] Nicias is potentially more interesting on another topic needing at least a brief notice.

This topic is the 'courageous' and the bold. In defence of Stesilaus' art, Nicias declared (182C) that 'this knowledge will make every man in war both bolder and "more courageous" by a large margin than he was before.'[34] In the scholarly literature two contrasting views about this are available: one that Nicias is equating boldness (or confidence) with 'courage', the other that he is distinguishing them.[35] The form of Nicias' sentence offers no guide here, given the ambiguity of the word 'and' in rhetorical contexts. But Méron is right in suggesting that *andreios* or 'courageous' here must refer not to what we should call courage, since no such art as Stesilaus' could rationally be expected to develop any such internal moral quality, but to something like 'soldierly skill'. Since there is no suggestion that the word for 'bold' or 'confident' refers to or denotes such skill, we may presume that Nicias is indeed distinguishing confidence from 'courage' here. This passage is in this respect consistent with the later one where Nicias explicitly makes a distinction between *andreia* and confidence or boldness (197B).

But there is no a priori reason for supposing complete consistency in all Nicias' utterances, and in at least one major respect Nicias changes his mind in the course of the discussion. At the earlier stage of the argument we have reached (182C), he cannot have envisaged with any clarity the doctrine he later propounds (194E–195A), that 'courage' is the knowledge of things to be feared and not to be feared. For he distinguishes this, roughly as a knowledge of values, from any technical knowledge; and there is nothing in Stesilaus' art remotely likely to inculcate any knowledge of values; hence, on Nicias' later definition of 'courage', there is no truth in this earlier suggestion that Stesilaus' art makes men more 'courageous'. Nicias shifts his ground in the course of the dialogue.

Does Laches also change his mind in the same area? In a series of remarks we have examined already (184B–C), Laches evidently distinguishes the bold or confident from the 'courageous' or *andreios*.[36] The claimant to Stesilaus' art who is in fact *deilos* becomes more confident, etc., a sentence revealing the compatibility of *deilos,* the standard opposite of *andreios,* with 'confident'. But this obviously results in the word 'confident' being applicable where the word 'courageous' is not. So Laches does at first have in mind some distinction between *andreios* 'courageous' and *thrasys,* confident. Yet when Nicias invokes a similar distinction Laches rejects it with misplaced contumely (197C). Nicias claims that lions differ from deer not in courage, but in the possession of confidence, daring, and fearlessness. Laches objects. Is he entitled to object after implying the relevant distinction himself?[37]

A close look at this second passage suggests that he is. His objection to Nicias is not that there is no such distinction between 'confident' and 'courageous' as Nicias employs, but rather that Nicias is misusing it. Nicias calls 'confident' and not 'courageous' a class of creatures ordinary language calls 'courageous'. Nicias distinguishes the 'courageous' from the bold by the intellectual advantages of the former; and it is this way of distinguishing which Socrates means to defend (ironically or no) by deriving it (197D) from the great Prodicus, and which Laches rejects as unworthy.

How Laches would distinguish the pair of words we do not know, and we may plausibly suppose that Laches himself is conceived as not knowing. Laches does not change his mind because he does not know his mind; Nicias does change his mind. We may think that formal consistency is not always a virtue; whether Plato thought it always was is unclear, though he makes it amply clear that he regarded it generally as such.

Before leaving the values of Socrates' interlocutors and proceeding to examine those of Socrates himself in this opening scene, we may summarise our findings. We saw that Lysimachus and Melesias treat goodness now as a matter of avoiding dispute between friends, now as a matter of worldly success, whether political or military, in either war or peace. They commend, with the description 'just', a course of action in no obvious way connected with 'courage' or with worldly success.

Laches, on the other hand, treats goodness on occasion as a matter of simple military prowess, and there is no occasion on which he certainly expresses any wider understanding of it. The word 'just' appears on his lips only in saying (rather obscurely) that Socrates gave in battle the sort of sample of goodness that a man must give if he is to give a sample justly.

Nicias is interested in, and values for educational purposes, other pursuits than the military – with what ultimate motives he does not reveal. His generally mild tone includes no specific mention of rival claimants to the title of 'goodness' such as justice. The forethought, for example, to which he finds stimulation in Socrates' refutations of him – to what end is it directed? To what end did he seek a training in 'music' for his son? We do not hear, and if we gain the impression of more broad-mindedness in Nicias than in Laches, it is a somewhat woolly, not to say empty, broad-mindedness. This could even explain the readiness of Nicias to change his mind in the ensuing discussion. At all events, we have only Socrates left of all the characters in the opening scene.

Socrates in the opening scene

Socrates does not reveal much of his own values in scenes such as this, preferring to ask questions, rather than offer expositions. Indeed, one needs to see at each step how Socrates gets his interlocutors to agree on a proposition capable of furthering his argument; one is examining still, on the whole, others' reactions rather than the views of Socrates himself. The explanation of those reactions, however, often lies in the precise nuance of a Socratic question, or the order and logical connection of his questions.

The externals of the matter are soon told. Laches introduces (180C) Socrates as a first-hand student of subjects and practices for the young;[38] Nicias backs this up. The young sons of Lysimachus and Melesias speak for the first and only time in the dialogue to confirm their frequent and laudatory mention of Socrates; we do not hear for what they praise him (181A). Laches makes his point about Socrates at Delium. Hearing this chorus of praise, Lysimachus coopts Socrates into the discussion, and puts a direct question to him (181C). Socrates gives away nothing, but turns the question into an interrogation not of himself but of Nicias and Laches. Only if he has something to add will he add it after the generals have spoken. Nicias' and Laches' lengthy answers reveal their assurance and wide experience. But they differ markedly on the merits of Stesilaus' training. Nicias thinks it beneficial, Laches not. Conscious of the difference, Laches suggests (184C), and Lysimachus agrees to ask Socrates to cast his vote.

Socrates, though his reaction is relevant to the whole situation, still says little overtly about his values, preferring to ask questions. The first to fall victims to his interrogation are the two old men. Asked if he intends to follow the majority advice, Lysimachus suggests in a rhetorical question the absence of alternative.

Dieterle[39] is right to allude to democratic political practice at this point. Plato wheels on the uncommitted Melesias to answer the question whether he agrees, and whether on the topic of gymnastic exercises for the boys he would follow a majority vote or take the advice of someone trained and practised under a good trainer. Melesias (184E) thinks probably the latter. In his next response he is unsure whether he would follow the trainer or the four men he has around him. Various reasons are available, and none certain, for this hesitancy: unwillingness to contradict Lysimachus, unwillingness to commit himself, unwillingness to admit aloud something less than complimentary to his four friends. But Melesias does emphatically agree that any question, to be decided respectably, needs to be decided by expertise, not by the counting of votes.

Does Socrates make an assertion here, with which Melesias agrees, or ask a question, to which Melesias answers 'Yes'?[40] Socrates' 'I think' does not settle the point: it is not clear whether that parenthetic word inhibits a questioning tone, or what, in any case, it applies to: alternative possible applications are to the virtues of deciding on the basis of knowledge, or to Socrates' surmised reason for Melesias' hesitant assent to the virtues of such decision. This last alternative is obscured by Sprague's choice of connecting particle in English: her 'So' in 'So I think...' renders the Greek word normally meaning 'for'.[41] In the presence of these two ways of taking Socrates' 'I think' we cannot, and the other characters also cannot, be sure that Socrates is expressing his own views in this speech rather than analysing Melesias' reasons for speaking as he does. Socrates has introduced knowledge to the discussion, but hardly in such a way as to make his own views clearly and positively known. The succeeding sentences given to Socrates, after Melesias' assent, are introduced by another Greek word, also rendered 'So' by Sprague, which has a well-deserved reputation for complexity, and may or may not introduce a question or mark an interrogative tone.[42] The possibility is strong that Socrates, though introducing the topic of knowledge and of an expertise relevant to their present problem, does so in a manner committing him to no positive view.

Melesias' reactions are puzzling. He replies with a fair degree of assurance to the question whether the trained gymnast should be listened to rather than the majority; he assents with certainly no more assurance to the suggestion that the trained gymnast would be more persuasive than his friends.[43] But to the general rule Socrates puts to him he responds with absolute confidence. It is unlikely that Melesias is proceeding logically by either induction or analogy from one relatively weak example to a strong conclusion. So is Socrates merely bullying, and Plato merely manipulating, Melesias? Possibly; but a more charitable interpretation would point out the ease with which we can imagine somebody reluctant to accept aloud the uncomplimentary implications for his friends of a particular case, but prepared to accept the general rule as plausible. An element of plausibility in the generalization, absent from the particular case, derives from the mention of knowledge, which sounds perhaps more authoritative than the mere training mentioned in the example of the gymnast.

But we still have to ask why Melesias should accept a suggestion, namely, the superiority of expert to majority judgment, which is so anti-democratic in its implications. Here, despite the absence of any formal induction, the particular case of the gymnast is highly relevant to the generalization. In the context of that example the relevance of expertise is pretty obvious, and Melesias, like (we need not doubt) many another Athenian of impeccably democratic leanings, simply does not make any connection between such obvious cases and the theory of politics.

Melesias' answer differs from Lysimachus' in this passage because the context in which he gives it is different. The need to establish such a different context without having laboriously to engineer a recantation from Lysimachus possibly accounts for Melesias' emergence in this passage from the shadows he inhabits for the rest of the dialogue. It seems clear that Plato's plans for this dialogue did not include any use of the Socratic elenchus or refutation to devastate either of the two old men; Socrates is gentle with them.

Whether in question or by assertion, Socrates (184E–185A)

backs up the application of their general rule to their particular present situation by emphasizing the importance of the subject under discussion. In the process he offers a hint as to what that subject is and in what they need an expert. The risk the two old men are running concerns their sons, and their turning out good or bad. To all appearances Melesias unreservedly accepts this statement of the problem and of its supreme importance to them. He accepts also the suggestion that they look for someone who has undergone instruction and practice in the relevant subject. His agreement acknowledges the connection between the general statement of the authority of knowledge in decision and the particular case of the well-taught and practised trainer. Melesias, however, is astonished by Socrates' next question (185B): what art is it of which we are looking for the teachers? The sophisticated reader, thinking the answer obvious, pauses to ask whether we had not settled the question, at least in clear implication, with Melesias' agreement that the problem was about the boys' education. At Nicias' ensuing intervention (185C) it is possible for a reader to feel some surprise that he, who 'claims later on ... to be an old hand at Socratic discussion', is 'unprepared for this shift from the study of a particular art to the education of the whole man.'[44] There ought, surely, to be some feature of the preceding series of questions and answers which has put Socrates' friends, both old and new, off the scent, and misled them about the subject of discussion.

The first such feature is the form of a particular question Socrates puts to Melesias the first time he addresses him (184D–E). The Greek here means literally 'If there were some deliberation for you about the gymnastic exercise of your son as to what he ought to practise, would you obey the majority of us or that one of us who happened to have been trained and to have practised under a good trainer?'[45] Significant here is the assumption that the hypothetical deliberation would be about the gymnastic exercise of the young man. This corresponds pretty closely to Nicias' query, 'aren't we investigating the art of fighting in armour and discussing whether young men ought to learn it or not?' (185C). The same query, one may readily imagine, passes through Melesias' mind as he expresses his baffled failure to see the force of Socrates' question what they need an expert in.

But there is also a deeper background to Melesias' and Nicias' bewilderment. We saw that whereas Lysimachus and Melesias approached Nicias and Laches originally for advice in their capacity as concerned parents (so far as the old men's actual words went), and Laches introduced Socrates as one concerned for education, Laches assumed, doubtless correctly, the relevance of Socrates' military prowess (and, by implication, of his own). So the soldierly qualities of the two generals and of Socrates might be thought germane to the discussion. At least the existence of such an expertise in military matters, called *andreia,* has been established as acceptable to the company. But no one has suggested in the dialogue so far that there is such a thing as expertise in, as opposed to concern for, the education of the young for success in life. In fact, since Plato was almost certainly mistaken in the belief that there is such an expertise, it is in no way surprising that Melesias has not thought of it, and that Nicias, rather than shift the discussion to it, should stick to the letter of the preceding conversation. Plato has so arranged the conversation that Socrates' interlocutors need convincing of the relevance of educational expertise, and need to have the complexities of their motivation resolved. It is against this background that we should see the interrogation Socrates now pursues. The argument's direction to these two purposes lends a unity, usually missed by interpreters, to the whole scene down to this point. This unity is embodied in the truth of Socrates' remark that they have not yet agreed what the subject of their deliberation is. Socrates, then, seeks the admission that they require an expert in the education of young men, and pursues a line of questioning of some apparent – but hardly real – complexity (185C–E).

The argument's inductive shape, its procedure from examples to generalization and then back to the original question, is, as Sprague says, typically Socratic.[46] Its apparent preoccupation with ends as opposed to means would also be characteristic of him. But it is open to doubt whether the argument either assumes or demonstrates 'the primacy of ends over means'. The assumption would exhibit no obvious plausibility and no obvious acceptability to these particular interlocutors. Greater realism results from the supposition that Socrates aims his interrogation at the identification of the original datum and problem.

In the case of the medicine and the eyes (to take Socrates' first illustration), the problem is not what to do with the medicine, but how to heal the eyes whose condition is given: a man is not given a medicine out of the blue and asked what to do with it, but has eyes in a certain condition and must decide, or get someone else to decide, what to do about them. Similarly, when a man considers whether to put a bridle on a horse, his original problem is most unlikely to be the bridle; his problem is the horse. Similarly again, the given, in the case before us in the *Laches* at large, is the young men. The opening of the dialogue after Stesilaus' exhibition should mislead nobody; the reason why this art is under consideration at all is for the young men's sake, as Lysimachus explains. The boys are the thing worrying him and Melesias; and the first question raised about them is what training will make the best possible men of them (179B). Without the horse the question what to do with a bridle would not normally arise; and without the boys the old men would probably not have been watching and would certainly not have been worried about the art of fighting in armour.

Though Socrates talks, as nearly as conversational fourth-century Greek will allow him, of ends and means, the interpreter should beware of making his talk seem more abstract and theoretical than it is. Socrates' line of questioning depends on practical considerations. This explains the immediate acceptability to the company, unused as they mostly are to abstract thought, of the admissions Socrates seeks. Unlike the modern editor,[47] Plato could not direct his reader by a footnote to another dialogue where he had discussed the relation of means to ends; the interpreter must, with only the very rarest exceptions expressly indicated in Plato's text, make each dialogue intelligible as it stands; that is the function of the above piece of interpretation, and once again it brings out the dramatic realism with which Plato constructs the conversation, and the absence, in his handling of the characters, of any wilfully deceptive manipulation of them.

Socrates does strike one note in this particular interrogation which might be thought – wrongly, I believe – to ring a little strangely in the ears of the generally practical men gathered to watch Stesilaus: the introduction of the soul (185E). True, there is some evidence that the emphasis Socrates placed on the soul was in some way odd;[48] we may suppose that not all his beliefs about the soul (whether expressed in Plato's works or elsewhere) were such as to be familiar to all his or all Plato's contemporaries. But in the context of the *Laches* there is no reason to suppose that the company would have jibbed at Socrates' importation of the soul into their talk. One of the best words for 'bravery' in Classical Attic Greek was *eupsuchia*, 'good-souledness,'[49] and the mention of the *psuchê*, or soul, is frequent in contexts of military endeavour from the fifth century BC onward.[50] Socrates has not so much shifted the discussion as opened up a new terminology for it; his terminology is acceptable not only to Nicias who knows him but also to Laches and the rest. Its acceptability is clear from the contrast between Laches' silence at the mention of soul and his quickness to object to Socrates' next step.

The next step is the conclusion that since they need expert advice, and the subject in hand is the souls of young men, they must consider whether any of them is expert in the care of souls, able to care for a soul in a way inspiring respect ('finely' rather than, as Sprague has it, 'well'), and having learnt from good teachers. This step and the previous acceptance of the link between the recipient of good teaching and the expert are both open to challenge. Laches asks challengingly whether Socrates has not seen cases of greater expertise without than with the benefit of teaching. This appeal from experience and belittling of the power of teaching come naturally from Laches who has appealed to his experience of Stesilaus and his like, and doubted the efficacy of their teaching.

Laches' intervention enables Socrates, who is far from denying the evidence of experience, to complete his point. If the self-styled expert cannot point to his teachers' expertise, he must have concrete and agreed examples of his own expertise to show. In accordance with his own treatment of Stesilaus, Laches concedes this, and Socrates urges the present company's needs to inquire which of them has teachers of agreed excellence or has agreed samples to show of his own teaching prowess – that is, pupils acknowledged to be good men. Disclaiming (186B–C) any such evidence in his own favour, Socrates presses the two old men to ask for the generals' qualifications.

The conversation proceeds at a leisurely pace towards the interrogation of Laches and Nicias. Lysimachus' assent (187B–D) to the inquiry meets with a rueful reply from Nicias (187D–E) to the effect that Lysimachus cannot be personally acquainted with Socrates, or he would know what he was letting them in for. Both Nicias and Laches submit, however, to Socratic scrutiny. Laches' implicit claim (189B) to at least some knowledge marks him out as a prime victim.

But possibly the most important point in the leisurely conversation is one neglected by recent commentators, and yet of potentially vital significance for the understanding of the dialogue as a whole in all its multi-faceted irony. Lysimachus asks, and indeed stipulates (189C), that Socrates shall, *vis-à-vis* Laches and Nicias, stand in his place and ask the relevant questions on the boys' behalf. This stipulation Socrates accepts. In the ensuing passage of arms Socrates in some sense represents, not just himself, but also the two old men who opened the dialogue. He stands in their place to ask his questions.

Plato stands aloof from us in all his dialogues but this looks as if it adds one more layer of aloofness to the *Laches*. Not only is Plato hiding in some sense behind Socrates; Socrates can in this work cloak himself in the guise of two old men and their sons. We know of the boys only their enthusiasm for Socrates. The old men's views have received in the opening scene a careful and dramatically convincing exposition. For his questioning of the generals Socrates stands in for their commonplace and somewhat confused minds. In these circumstances the reader should beware of too facile belief that Socrates' subsequent questions, or even his rare statements, convey his or Plato's views.[51] Everything in the more continuously dialectical portion of the dialogue must lie open to fresh scrutiny.

Plato's reader must scrutinize it in the awareness that

Socrates has given away nothing of his own values in the opening scene, except perhaps the importance he attaches to education, and that he is under no obligation to give away anything more in what follows.

Socrates changes plan

One could now expect Socrates to elucidate the names of the generals' teachers or their own agreed triumphs of education. Either would involve agreement on the goodness of certain people. But agreement on who was good might in this company be difficult, and would necessitate making up the two old men's minds for them on their values. Socrates cuts through a prospective inquiry into a lot of tedious personal details by raising what he rightly considers a more fundamental question.

He says (189E), and it sounds like common sense, that the imparting of something requires the knowledge of what is to be imparted. The imparting of sight, for instance, to the eyes necessitates knowledge of what sight is. Asked (190B) if the proposal is that they should advise on the imparting of goodness to the boys' souls, Laches agrees, and also accepts that that necessitates knowledge of what goodness is.

Though this may have a smell of Socrates about it, it is not unreasonable; the importance of setting one's goals in teaching will not have escaped any teacher of repute, and expert advice on the subject carries the same sort of responsibility. Assuming that they are claiming to be expert advisers, Socrates asks, as Dieterle[52] pointed out (and not 'states'), whether they claim to know what goodness is. Laches' assent totally disregards the implicit disagreements and difficulties of the preceding discussion. His own vague previous claim to knowledge (189B) in the area under discussion is still no doubt ringing in his ears.

More dangerously still, for one in the presence of Socrates, he agrees, when asked, that knowledge entails the ability to express it. Socrates is not necessarily committed here either, since again his remark is interpretable as a question.[53] But the victim's assent to this is necessary for Socratic refutation to have its full effect; without that assent the failure to produce an adequate definition does not prove the respondent's ignorance.

Socrates has successfully changed plan; but the further transition, from discussion of goodness to that of *andreia,* holds further traps for the unwary. Comparison with the preceding conversation reveals fresh ironies. 'Let us not', says Socrates (190C), 'investigate immediately the whole of goodness – that would perhaps be too great a task – but let us first see if we are adequately equipped with respect to knowledge concerning a part. Then it is likely that the investigation will be easier for us.'[54] This sounds innocent enough; and Laches agrees. Socrates asks if they should choose the part thought by most people[55] to be inculcated by fighting in armour, namely, *andreia.* Laches might be expected to demur, and rather pointedly says that is what is thought. Socrates draws the obvious procedural conclusion and asks what 'courage' is (190D).

Laches, presumably in contrast to Socrates, shows no signs here of appreciating the difficulties of their previous talk. The suggestion that *andreia* is a part of goodness slips past him regardless of his previous use of goodness to *mean 'andreia'.* He does not notice that his position on the relation between *andreia* and goodness has now shifted closer to the old men's. His usage was and is unreflecting. But Socrates lets him down, as we shall see, fairly gently. Socrates, on the other hand, may be presumed to know what he is doing. Not being committed previously to anything relevant to the relationship of goodness to *andreia,* he now appears to take on board the commitment to a part–whole relationship. The question must arise why he does this.

The question is the more pressing because, in the view of many interpreters, Plato's Socrates does not believe that, e.g. 'courage' is part of goodness.[56] The well-known Socratic paradox of the 'unity of the virtues' means, as most Platonists think, that courage, moderation, justice and so on are all the same quality of soul. Some, it is true, have given up this interpretation, holding instead that Socrates believed only the much weaker doctrine of the mutual implication of the virtues.[57] They urge the interpretation in that sense of passages such as the present, taking them to indicate Socrates' respect for distinctions inherent in ordinary moral language.[58]

Those who stick to the older view, rightly in my opinion, reject such an interpretation of these passages, finding in them the use of 'courage', 'justice', and so forth to denote the popular, not the Socratic conception of what each of these qualities should be. These scholars suppose the good qualities to be, if Platonically conceived, one and the same, but, if vulgarly conceived, distinct and separate.[59] On this view, Socrates' language in discussions such as this in the *Laches* is merely concessional, a concession to the vocabulary of his respondent.

General support for this latter kind of view need not imply the crediting of it with the whole explanation of the language Socrates adopts. In the *Laches*, if Socrates is indeed practising concessional language, he is conceding the wrong thing to the wrong person. For Laches has said nothing construable with certainty as making *andreia* a part of goodness, and at least one thing showing him to believe goodness equivalent to *andreia*. For Socrates to put to Laches now that goodness is the whole of which *andreia* is merely a part is to offer a concession not to Laches but to popular usage, and not to the person he is addressing but to other persons.[60]

Viewed simply as a question put to Laches, Socrates' suggestion about discussing a part of goodness looks like a mere fishing expedition designed to trap. The suggestion does indeed lay the foundation for the later impasse; but nothing compels us to interpret it as gratuitously devious. If we ask who, in the preceding conversation, has said things implying either the ambiguity of 'goodness', which Plato's Socrates usually fails to consider, or a part–whole relation between 'courage' and goodness, the answer comes back that Lysimachus did. In whose place did Socrates agree to question Laches and Nicias? In Lysimachus'. The most plausible answer to the question why in this particular place of this particular dialogue Socrates should use such an assumption is that it is the assumption, in Plato's view, of the person or persons Socrates has agreed in some sense to represent. Whatever Socrates had not heard at the dialogue's very beginning, he had assuredly heard the part most significant in this regard, namely, Lysimachus' opinion of Sophroniscus.

Laches, in accepting without demur the implications of Socrates' suggestion, is of course thoughtless; Plato has underlined his thoughtlessness with one of the several ironies of this section of dialogue. Socrates, at the very moment of tempting Laches to confuse his beliefs on the subject of goodness, addresses him not by name, but as 'best of men' (190C). The form of address is conventional in Greek; but the other addresses of this general type occur at significant places in the dialogue,[61] and this one is surely too appropriate to be accidental. Further, the bland suggestion that it will be easier to define 'courage', apart from tempting Laches to belittle the difficulties, has the telling irony that the proposition supposed to diminish the difficulty has the effect of increasing it. The putative ease of defining 'courage' is delicately stressed by talk of what they shall do after finding the definition. Further, when Socrates says, in effect, 'What about the part of goodness Stesilaus' art has to do with?', Plato's readers should not forget that Laches used 'goodness' for the qualities of a soldier, for 'courage', in reference to Stesilaus' art.

Fortified in the belief that not everything Socrates says must be taken at face value as his own opinion, we may now investigate the actual tenor of the dialectical episode which follows.

Socrates' questioning of Laches

Both the course and the merits of Socrates' bout with Laches have been the subject of scholarly debate in the last decade or so. Scholars used, for example, to treat Laches (wrongly) as guilty of simple logical error, in the shape of a confusion between universal and concrete instance, by way of misunderstanding Socrates' questions. The obverse of this was the representation of Socrates as patiently explaining to a somewhat unintelligent Laches what he was trying to do. Professor Alexander Nehamas has demolished this.[62] There has been dispute between Drs Detel and Graeser on what Laches' answers to Socrates actually amount to, and whether the first of Laches' answers to the question Socrates really means to put to him is separately refuted or not.[63] The whole badly needs fresh examination in the light of the context.

Laches' first answer is a case in point. Socrates asks him (190E) to say what 'courage' is, and he replies that if a man remains in the ranks and fights he is 'courageous'. Socrates applauds, but goes on to explain that Laches' answer was not what he had in mind in framing the question. Nehamas has correctly pointed out that what Laches has done is not to give a particular example where Socrates asks for a generality; it is rather to give too narrow a generality.

The point needs stressing that the fault for this misapprehension of Socrates' purpose lies not with Laches so much as with Socrates. As Richard Robinson pointed out a generation ago,[64] the question 'What is X?' may be seeking a wide range of possible answers according to the context. The context in the *Laches* does very little to make clear what kind of answer Socrates is looking for.

Laches' reply makes at least something of what information he has, and is consistent with much of what he has previously said. The context loads the dice against him. They have witnessed Stesilaus' exhibition, and discussed at some length the pros and cons of his art – if it is an art. After the discussion has turned to goodness, Socrates himself brings it back to its original theme. Asking (190D) which part of goodness they should select for investigation, he suggests the one inculcated, in the opinion of some, by Stesilaus' art, namely, 'courage'. He refers to that art as 'the technique of fighting in armour'. Receiving Laches' agreement, he immediately puts the question what 'courage' is, and goes on to suggest that once they have answered it they shall discuss how to imbue the young with 'courage'. In this context it is perfectly reasonable that Laches should think Socrates expects him to say what Stesilaus' art, by intention, enables young men to do: that is, to become good hoplite fighters. The good hoplite, in the first instance, stands firm in the ranks, at the crucial time of impact and subsequent hand-to-hand fighting. Any other soldierly skill will show itself not in the first instance, but (normally) when the battle has been lost and won by the giving way of one or other hoplite force. It is hardly Laches' fault if this answer proves too narrow for Socrates' taste. The context points him in the wrong direction; and Socrates (190E, 191C–D) (as he admits) has had a full share in the creation of that context.

This would be a sufficient defence of Laches if he had said, as in Nehamas' paraphrase, 'Courage is to fight the enemy and not retreat.'[65] But Laches does not in fact (as Nehamas well knows) say quite that. What he does say is (to use Nehamas' own rendering, more literal in some respects than Sprague's) 'Know well that if someone were willing to fight the enemy, remaining at his post, and did not retreat, he would be courageous.' Now this does not mention 'courage' at all. It mentions indeed a particular hypothetical example of it – and this may be the source of the canard saying that Laches confuses universal and instance. But of course Laches says about this particular hypothetical instance nothing that is not perfectly appropriate to such an instance; he uses the word 'courageous' as a predicate correctly, and does not use the word 'courage', either as subject or predicate; Sprague's 'a man of courage' might just possibly mislead the Greekless reader.

One of the differences between Laches' first answer and the kind of answer he gives when Socrates has explained himself is that the first neither contains a mention explicitly of 'courage' nor implies that 'courage' is grammatically subject, whereas the later ones do have a clearly implied 'courage' in the abstract as their grammatical subject. This suggests that Laches' first answer exhibits, from Socrates' point of view, not one fault but two. It not only is too narrow a statement for Socrates' purpose, it also is not in due form.

But this is perhaps a venial fault. If Laches had replied, in the same sort of form but with sufficient generality, that if a man endures in his soul in some way then he is 'courageous' Socrates could perhaps have been expected to translate that for himself into terms using the abstract 'courage'; he contrives a similar translation at a later stage (191E) of the discussion. Laches' use of the form 'If a man does X, he is "courageous"' is, however, a symptom of his failure to produce the level of generality Socrates desires. It offers a sufficient condition of being 'courageous', not a necessary condition. In so far as Socrates is interested in conditions at all, what he would like is doubtless a set of conditions both necessary and sufficient. The form 'If X, then Y' is not of itself going to produce them; and the form using the abstract as grammatical subject is perhaps more likely to produce the desired result.

If Laches' formally somewhat inappropriate answer springs perhaps from his inexperience of Socratic conversation (188E), his narrowness also, though easily excusable in context, may reflect his earlier blinkered vision. Laches began by assuming the relevance of military expertise to their educational discussion; his account of Stesilaus in action treats only military action as relevant to the inquiry. Of wider qualities he says but little: an obscure mention of justice (189B) is supported only, in effect, by his suggestion that it is difficult to say that any study is useless (182D) – a mainly rhetorical point aimed at placating others rather than at expressing his own views, as becomes apparent from a later sentence in the same speech (184B). His judgment, on the whole, is based on and limited to his own experience, whether of Socrates or of Stesilaus, in action. This trait combines with the immediate context to lend an air of realism, of suitability to his character, to his reply to Socrates' question what 'courage' is, and to the somewhat similar answers in which he persists for a while.

These things help to explain also Laches' apparent forgetfulness of Socrates' prowess in defeat,[66] let alone other less heinous lapses. In asking (191A) how a soldier in flight can display 'courage', he perhaps forgets indeed the field of Delium, but could defend himself by urging the prior duty of a good hoplite not to put himself in the position of the beaten Athenian army. His attachment to the military context accounts for his rejection of the relevance of Socrates' Scythian example by reference to the hoplites he evidently believes are the exclusive concern still of the discussion. The Scythians, it is worth observing, were probably far from Laches' experience. But every schoolboy knew of the Spartan victory at Plataea, and Laches is prepared to agree that they won by means other than standing firm in battle. The possibility for a hoplite to win in retreat convinces him of something; it is not easy to say of what, since he replies with somewhat obscure reference only 'You are right' (191C). But the simple statement that a man is brave who stands his ground makes no further appearance, and Socrates' explanation of what he is really after follows, destroying the power of the immediate context to limit Laches' horizons.

Before we examine the range of contexts Socrates presents to Laches, we must stop to look at another statement Socrates has offered in the course of his interrogation. For one so cagey in the opening scene Socrates is indeed rather prodigal of pretty direct statements or clear implications in this part of the discussion. One thing he first implies, by congratulating Laches on saying so, and then himself emphatically states, is that 'That man is "courageous" ... whoever fights the enemy while remaining at his post' (190E–191A).

Not all commentators realize quite how surprising is Socrates' agreement to this. The normal understanding of Socrates' ethics is rather different. If one's virtues are determined simply by actions such as standing firmly in the line, then it is hard to see what becomes of the Socratic paradox of the unity of the virtues. It was as a cognitive quality of the soul that the virtues were unified. The requisite action did not therefore guarantee possession of the virtue concerned. Indeed, this is perhaps the most centrally important legacy of the Platonic Socrates to Aristotle and the Stoics. Yet here, in the *Laches,* we find Socrates agreeing, to all appearances quite gratuitously, with the suggestion that every man who performs a certain type of action does so in virtue of the good quality or virtue concerned.

Again we must choose; did Socrates believe in a weaker form of unity of the virtues? Did he on occasion simply forget for concessional purposes his own deeper doctrine? Again we have in this dialogue a third choice; the old men Socrates stands in for are not for one moment to be suspected of any sophisticated or unusual ethical doctrine, and Socrates is perfectly justified, as their representative, in agreeing that a man, in whatever state of soul, who stands his ground in battle is 'courageous' in the normal use of the word.

If we may regard this admission by Socrates as in a sense concessional, it is much more than merely a use of vocabulary in a way his interlocutors can understand; it is a gratuitous agreement with a proposition the Platonic Socrates would most probably have found extremely difficult to accept. The best available explanation of this agreement is Socrates' status as someone else's representative. The timing is significant: no sooner has Socrates agreed to represent Lysimachus than he starts to offer suggestions or statements, and ones conflicting with his own usual attitudes.[67]

This rescues the plausibility of one suggestion on Socrates' lips; it is harder to save from implausibility Laches' ready acceptance of a 'courage' extending as far as Socrates expands it in the effort to widen Laches' vision (191C–E). But here one must recall the threefold usage of *andreia,* to mean 'courage' proper, 'soldierly qualities', or in general 'manliness'. The first two of these will account without difficulty for Socrates' mention and Laches' acceptance of *andreia* in war and at sea. Physical courage is often a requirement in the face of illness, poverty, or (under ancient conditions) in affairs of state. One can experience danger, fear and pain (or 'distress') in any of these contexts, and it is reasonable enough to talk of courage concerning them. Laches has already perceived that 'courage' has a wider application than he first thought of, and is naturally to be imagined as willing to go a little further in that direction. But psychological plausibility of this particular kind might, even if admitted, appear a little unfair philosophically.

Even the sense of 'manliness', available to investigators of *andreia,* will not fully account for Laches' agreement with Socrates' very wide application of the word. Agreed that some self-control is the pride and privilege of manhood, still the view was not without support in Athens, that a real man was one who took such steps as were necessary to satisfy his desires, at others' expense in preference to his own. We have Plato's Callicles in the *Gorgias* (491C–E), whether fictitious or not,[68] to bear witness to Plato's observation of such attitudes. For Callicles *andreia* is quite possible without self-restraint or moderation. But Callicles is a defiant opponent of values upheld by community and consensus; Laches is not – and presumably was not.

Socrates uses a very simple technique to draw Laches away (if he needs drawing away) from such paths; he treats the control of the passions as a battle, which the *andreios* man is good at fighting. If this were the only case of such a metaphor in Greek literature, it would look like ultra-special pleading, *ad hominem* in the worst way; but in fifth-century Greek poetry, especially in tragedy with which Laches is to some extent familiar, the closely connected metaphor of conquest or defeat is used, both actively of the passions defeating a man, and of a man being overcome by passion(s).[69] Defeat is of course constantly thought of in military contexts, in Greek as in other languages. To think of the ability to avoid defeat by the passions as the ability to fight well against them was likely to be attractive to Greeks at large, and specially so to a general. But skill in fighting is, for Laches as for many others, *andreia*.

Both physical and internal battles demand, as Laches sees clearly only a few lines later (192B–C), what in plain English people call 'guts'. Approving of decent self-restraint, Laches is quite happy, given the opportunity, to include it in the *andreia* of which he approves so strongly as to call it on occasion 'goodness'. Simply as a general, moreover, Laches would do well to remember that the Greek soldier needed the ability to make light of sundry bodily ills and privations.

The case needs considering from both literary and philosophical standpoints. From a literary point of view, it might seem inadvisable, but is nevertheless in this case justifiable, to refer to what Laches sees a few lines later. It is justifiable by consideration of the problem Plato faced as a writer in this part of the dialogue. He had to allow Socrates to present Laches with a sufficiently wide range of spheres offering the chance to show *andreia*; he had to make such a range and its acceptance intelligible to his readers; but he could not allow Socrates to explain, nor Laches to observe too obviously at the time of asking, what they had in common; Socrates cannot reveal in advance, nor Laches anticipate too early, the first proper definition Laches manages to offer of 'courage'. Given the desire to write the dialogue in something like its present shape Plato has little alternative to allowing the point of his list of 'courageous' people to seep out later.

Philosophically speaking, Laches has already been guilty of something very like self-contradiction in using 'goodness' to mean '*andreia*' and (without making any apparent distinction) in accepting for *andreia* the status of a part of goodness. This constituted first a narrow and then a wider view of 'goodness'. There is nothing out of philosophical character in Laches' using *andreia* itself similarly in senses both narrow and wide; indeed it is perhaps legitimate to see in the two sets of usages the same vagueness over the relation between goodness and manliness in the adult male.

The range thus given to *andreia* makes Socrates' vague question what is *andreia* even harder to follow. So Socrates has to illustrate the sort of answer he wants by the example of speed (192A). The purpose of the illustration is narrow. Socrates is not necessarily developing a full analogy between 'courage' and speed. Any misgivings one might have about treating 'speed' as the same sort of power, or quality, as courage need stifling in this context. Plato's Socrates needs only to find some word of an abstract nature used in a wide variety of contexts and of a wide variety of activities, and to show how the word can denote the same property (to use the vaguest word) with respect to each context or activity. For this limited illustrative purpose the example of speed will do very well. It enables Laches to see the level of abstraction at which Socrates is operating; on the way it serves to illustrate (in silence) the virtue of answering a question 'What is X' with a sentence beginning 'X is...'. Laches is now able to answer Socrates' vague question at least in the form Socrates wishes.

The external story of Socrates' treatment of that answer is easy to follow, but the inner detail has evoked much disagreement among interpreters. Laches starts by suggesting as a description of 'courage' the phrase 'a sort of endurance of the soul' (192B–C). After a brief interrogation he accepts its replacement by 'wise endurance' – presumably still of the soul (192D). Socrates asks him for the province of the wisdom concerned, and it emerges that a range of actions performed with technical competence are in Laches' opinion less brave but wiser than the corresponding actions performed without the appropriate degree of technical competence. This casts doubt on the description of 'courage' as a wise endurance. Socrates obtains Laches' admission of failure, and his agreement to seek Nicias' help.

So far, so (relatively) simple; but there are knotty points of detail covered by the bland language of such a summary including the following:

1   The meaning of 'a sort of endurance': 'something more or less like endurance,' or 'one particular type of endurance'?
2   The fate of the definition 'A sort of endurance': is it refuted or merely modified?
3   The word 'wisdom': does it mean 'technical expertise', or is it a distinct and wide intellectual quality?
4   Socrates' question 'Is it so with respect to everything both great and small?' (192E): is he offering a choice between things of moral or technical import, between greater and lesser risks, or no such specific choice?
5   The supposition that 'courage' is 'fine' (192D): where does it come from?

We may consider these in the order given.

1   'A sort of endurance'

Scholars sometimes argue that 'a sort of endurance' must mean 'a particular kind of endurance', on the basis of an exchange in the *Meno* where Socrates painstakingly draws the distinction between 'goodness' and 'a particular kind of goodness', and on the strength of a row of Platonic passages which use 'a sort of' literally rather than in mere vagueness.[70] Read in the same way, a piece of the *Charmides* offers a close parallel: Charmides defines 'moderation' as 'a sort of quietness' (159B). But the *Charmides* passage has itself proved open to a different reading, to say vaguely 'something like quietness'; and there are other places where 'a sort of' is as vague in Greek as it is in Sprague's well-chosen English rendering.[71] If the context in the *Laches* is not decisive, no parallels are likely to be so.

Fortunately the *Laches* context does, in my opinion, decide this particular question. Socrates says (192C), after accepting Laches' reply as *an* answer to his question, 'As I see it, you don't regard all endurance as "courage";[72] my judgment is based on this: I practically know, Laches, that you regard "courage" as a very fine thing.'

Andreas Graeser recently took this as merely confirmation by Socrates of what he already knows from Laches' earlier locution 'a sort of endurance'; but that seems improbable.[73] To say, if you have just been told something, that you conclude it from other evidence, without mentioning that the other evidence is 'other' or that it is additional in any sense, is so odd a proceeding as to justify our ruling it out. So at least Plato did not intend Laches *simply* to mean 'one particular kind of endurance'.

So far the context is decisive; but that leaves open two possibilities: either Laches means 'something like endurance', or Plato intended the ambiguity his words actually present. If the latter, then Socrates' following speech clarifies the situation: if Laches' words are ambiguous, at least he does not really believe that all endurance is 'courage'. Laches will either have to say what sort of endurance, or find a better word than 'endurance' to express what he thinks. What the two sets of parallel passages adduced by previous interpreters surely suggest is the correctness of this line of interpretation. They suggest that 'a sort of' is indeed ambiguous in some contexts. They fail to suggest that it bears either of its two possible meanings exclusively here in the *Laches*. For what the point is worth, and that is not much, the parallel answer of Charmides may also be an intentional ambiguity on Plato's part. The ambiguity of Laches' original answer and definition lends some spice to our second question.

2   Is Laches' original definition refuted or modified?

Wolfgang Detel[74] has forcefully suggested that Socrates actually refutes Laches' first definition, which Detel understands as saying unambiguously 'something like endurance'. A major difficulty with that view (pointed out by Graeser[75]) is that Socrates does not say at any point that he has refuted the definition. Another difficulty is the lack of clarity we have found in Laches' words. Formal refutation would mean disentangling the possible meanings and refuting them seriatim. Socrates does not do this. Instead, he persuades Laches to replace the unclear expression 'a sort of' by the epithet 'wise'. Does that constitute a refutation of some less formal kind?

In this connection, the structure of the persuasive argument repays attention. For formalizations of it the reader stands referred to Detel and Graeser; an approximation to the admissions Laches makes runs as follows (192C–D):

(i) 'Courage' is Fine.
(ii) Endurance with Wisdom is Fine (and Good).
(iii) Endurance without Wisdom is not fine.
(iv) *From (i) and (iii):* Endurance without Wisdom is not 'Courage'.
(v) *and* Endurance with Wisdom is 'Courage'.

Here step (iv) follows, as noted, from (i) and (iii).[76] But (v) does not follow from (i) and (iii). Indeed (v) would be, if Socrates were arguing on his own account, nothing more than a guess. But viewed not as an independent argument from Socrates but as an elucidation of Laches, the line of questioning, and of Laches' admissions, makes better sense; and it is surely significant that this small section of the dialogue both begins and ends with a statement or question about what Laches thinks rather than about the truth of the matter in hand (192C, 192D fin.).

Laches' suggestion was either that 'courage' is a particular type of endurance or that it is something vaguely like endurance. By the end of this section of interrogation unwise endurance, and nothing else, has been ruled out. This already narrows down Laches' view, whether he was precise or vague in his original definition. The question is still open whether there is anything else needing to be ruled out. But Laches has no notion of such further narrowing of his conception, and why should he have? It is quite natural for him to accept the first narrowing process as final and embrace the suggestion that he meant 'wise endurance' in so far as he meant endurance at all.

Laches, then, may reasonably accept Socrates' apparent conclusion; but may Socrates legitimately draw it? A prior question is whether Socrates actually does draw it; the answer depends on whether Socrates' speech 'Then, according to your view, it would be wise endurance which is courage' is a question or a statement, and, further, whether the conclusion concerns Laches' meaning or the substantive point at issue. Whether Socrates puts his conclusion as question or as statement is hard to say in a context containing both statements and questions from him; and the phrase 'according to your view' could indicate either Socrates' certainty that the conclusion follows or his strong belief that Laches (not necessarily for reasons of strict logic) will accept it.

It is not safe to denounce Socrates' logic here; it need not be his logic which is at fault. All it is safe to say is that Socrates elicits from Laches a conclusion unlikely to prove unacceptable to a Laches in this context. If strict logic were an absolute requirement, Plato would be playing an unfair game; but here as elsewhere Socrates' speeches do not represent a unilinear, autonomous piece of reasoning, but form only half of a conversation.

It would seem right to hold Socrates not to have refuted Laches, but rather to have persuaded him to accept a narrowing of his original thesis. Neither Plato nor his Socrates appears to claim more. But what does this narrower version mean?

3   The meaning of wisdom

Mrs Sprague rightly renders the Greek words *phronesis* and *epistêmê* by different English words, namely, 'wisdom' and 'knowledge', making thus clear to the attentive reader that 'knowledge' here refers to technical skill; but it is an open question whether 'wisdom' also refers to technical skill, or to a more general quality.[77] Does 'wise endurance' mean 'endurance accompanied by skill' or 'sensible endurance'? Scholars have held both views, though they have not, to my knowledge, brought the question out firmly into the open. The problem requires a brief summary of Greek usage.

Whereas words for knowledge and skill invite the question 'knowledge of what?' and 'skill at which?', it is fairly clear that, though always possible, such questions are far from compulsory in fourth-century usage with the word for 'wisdom'. 'Wisdom' can have a clearly marked sphere, such as the doctor's sagacity concerning diet in Plato's *Gorgias*; but it is the ordinary word for 'prudence', 'sagacity', or (in Aristotelians' language) 'practical wisdom'. Aristotle's discussions of the relevant words in the *Nicomachean Ethics* reveal no hint that 'prudence' ever in normal usage meant 'skill' or 'technical knowledge'. If one wished to give 'wisdom' a particular sphere one had, I think, to specify; without specification the word refers to a general capacity to deal with the problems of living.

In the *Laches* the introduction of words from the relevant stem *phron-* lacks any such specification; Socrates' question 'in what respect it is wise' (192E) is the first indication in this dialogue that such a specification is possible. It follows that when Socrates first (192C) uses the words 'wisdom' and its opposite 'folly', Laches will have heard no overtones of particular skill or technique, but only the denotation of general prudence or imprudence. Socrates will have appeared to be asking simply whether foolhardiness counts as 'courage', or whether discretion is at least a part of valour.

This situation might conceivably, but does not probably, change as the conversation develops. Socrates asks, indeed, for the province of the 'wisdom' concerned. But then we all know that a person can be wise or prudent in relations with the opposite sex, but hopelessly unwise and, e.g., extravagant in financial matters – and we do not need to talk of special skills or knowledges in either case; we talk rather of common sense. Socrates' question does not, so far as I can see, suggest to Laches that he has in mind any technical skill. One can, in many spheres, back up one's prudence and give it more of a cutting edge by technical expertise, but the expertise and the prudence remain distinct, and there is no obvious reason why Laches should suspect Socrates of confounding them. The same goes for the series of questions which follows. In the one about spending money to make money (192E), it is assumed for the purposes of the question that the man in the case has sufficient monetary expertise to be sure of his ground; but the question whether he is to be called 'courageous' could be a question about his prudence and general common sense in enduring the temporary loss for future gain rather than about his possession of monetary expertise.

In the other examples too, technical skill could be a presupposition of the exercise of prudence rather than be itself the prudence or 'wisdom' involved. The doctor exercises common prudence in not yielding to his son's desires; his medical knowledge is the necessary background to the exercise of his prudence, in that without it he would have no good reason for refusing. But, in refusing his son, of all people, he is exercising more than just medical skill. The 'wise' soldier (193A) too is, arguably, exercising prudence rather than simply deploying his tactical skill. The folly of the other camp could be either tactical stupidity or foolhardiness, or desperation; nothing in the context obliges Laches or the reader to suppose that 'folly' here is restricted to the lack of military expertise.

The subsequent examples (193B–C) do explicitly mention technical expertise, but Socrates is careful to ask at the end of them whether the inexpert are foolish to do the things they do. This step in the interrogation licenses the conclusion that the foolishly enduring are not 'courageous'. There is no need to suppose that the technical inexpertness displayed in the examples would, by and of itself, have licensed the same conclusion, without Socrates' intermediary step mentioning imprudence or folly.[78]

In short, nothing in the passage obliges us to suppose that the participants are confounding the *phronimos* man, the 'wise' or sensible man, with the technically expert; and we should not assume without such obligation any change in the meaning and overtones of 'wise' and its derivatives within this short discussion.

4   The reference of 'great and small'

It would make sense in a purely Socratic context (if such a thing existed) for 'great and small' to express the differing importance between technical knowledge (small) and moral knowledge (great). Would it still make some sense even with technical knowledge excluded from the purview of 'wisdom'? 'Wisdom' would then display itself in contexts of little significance or of greater significance for the general tenor of one's life. Which contexts would Socrates have thought of little significance? The distinction between significant and insignificant contexts would seem to boil down to that between moral and technical – at least we can be pretty sure from Plato's *Apology* that his Socrates thought the significance of technical accomplishment trifling. But no action, in the full sense of that word, is morally insignificant.

Much more plausible, now that 'wisdom' excludes technical proficiencies, is a reference by the adjectives 'great and small' to the size of the risk involved; that is to the magnitude of the endurance. Thus if the financier in Socrates' first example knows he will get his money back and more, then he is not taking any risk to speak of, and the endurance called for amounts to little, if anything, more than a reasonable steadiness of nerve. In his second example virtually no risk (the son's displeasure?) arises from the doctor's refusal of the son's request. Again only reasonable firmness of temper is needed. Both these would qualify as 'small' in terms of risk.[79] In the case of the soldier, lives are potentially at risk; but the one whose life is less at risk is the wise or sensible one. The wiser, the less the risk, and the less endurance or steadfastness is required; the more risk, the less sensible. There is a clear trade-off here; Socrates' loading of the dice makes clear that Plato recognized this. He presents Laches with choices which, in the context of courage alone or of wise endurance, Laches could hardly make otherwise than he does.

But the context, as Méron[80] has pointed out, is not one of simple courage alone. *Andreia* means not only courage but the sum of all the qualities needed for a good and successful soldier.[81] Laches, to maintain clarity and consistency, ought to think hard whether, as a qualification for *andreia,* success is more important to him than endurance, or steadfastness, or what in ordinary English we should call 'courage'. This is essentially the same question as whether he thinks the sensible soldier (the one more likely to be victorious) more *andreios* than the one who stands firm against the odds. This in turn means that Socrates' suggestion of 'wise' endurance as representing Laches' intentions was fully concordant with Laches' views as expressed not only in the immediate context but also in the Stesilaus scene. One could plausibly attribute the suggestion's acceptance not just to the dubious logic or the persuasive dialectic of the interrogation, but to its fundamental agreement with Laches' most deep-rooted beliefs. But this only makes it harder for Laches to make up his mind whether to follow his instinctive reaction and refuse the title of 'courageous' to someone justifiably confident or to follow a common Greek usage and award the likely winner that title. The instinctive reaction is surely related to the proposition that 'courage' is 'fine' – which leads us to our last question.

Méron[82] believes the non-reflective nature of 'courage' to be Laches' basic tenet, and his acceptance of the contrary view under interrogation to be mere inadvertence. But that, in view of the earlier scene, will not do.[83] The trouble Laches experiences is due not to inadvertence but to a genuine conflict between his strongly held opinions. It is extremely difficult for him to make up his mind whether to follow one instinctive reaction, in refusing to concede 'courage' to the justifiably confident, or to follow his own and other Greeks' usage and concede it to a likely winner. If one of these conflicting views were a mere slip of the tongue, there would be no profundity, nothing of any philosophic importance, in this section of the dialogue. Why should Plato bother to construct an argument on the shallow and shifting foundations of a momentary inadvertence? Méron does not face this question; if she had, she might have devoted more attention to the proposition, clearly related to both Laches' views, that 'courage' is 'fine'.[84]

5   The origins and function of '"Courage" is fine' (192C).

In its immediate context this proposition emerges in close relationship to the goodness of 'courage'. Though Plato himself probably thought of 'good' and 'fine' as coextensive terms, they were not necessarily so for all of his characters. It might depend, for instance, on whose admiration was necessary to entitle something or somebody to the epithet 'fine'. When Nicias starts from 'The "courageous" man is good' (194D) and Laches from '"Courage" is fine' they are not necessarily saying the same thing.

However, Socrates puts, and Laches accepts, the propositions that endurance with wisdom is 'fine and good,' and that 'endurance with folly' is 'harmful and bad in its effects.'[85] Socrates reserves for a separate question, tagged with a reference to Laches' own opinion, the proposition that Laches will not call 'fine' that which is 'harmful and bad in its effects'. By this second agreement Laches has blocked one way out of his subsequent troubles. He cannot now say that he admires, or calls 'fine', the firm (or enduring) but unsuccessful. The firmness which is foolish and leads to failure is not fine. He might like to say, for example, that he admires the firmness of such people, but deplores their folly. But to say this he will now have to abandon a position he has taken up. He has said that firmness accompanied by folly is not admirable. He has *not* said that firmness is admirable and becomes more so when accompanied by wisdom but less so when accompanied by folly.

It may have been because Plato (and his Socrates) perceived the temptation to say what Laches has not said that Socrates asks two separate questions. Asked directly whether endurance accompanied by folly was 'fine', Laches might have said that the endurance was fine; the temptation to say that such endurance is beneficial is rather less. But once he has admitted that endurance with folly is harmful his respect for success constrains him to deny that such endurance is 'fine'.

Socrates' shaping and ordering of his questions is artful; but its artfulness does not amount to chicanery. Laches makes no slip; he gives his answers to the questions as asked, in full accord with his views expressed earlier on the relation of goodness, military skill, and success.

But has Socrates any prior indication that Laches followed the normal Greek pattern of *admiration* for success in war and for courage? He has, though not total certainty. First (181A–B), Laches praised Socrates' own conduct at Delium as conducive, if reproduced by others, to the avoidance of defeat. Secondly (188E–189A), Laches says, apropos of that episode, that he tested Socrates' deeds and found him worthy of 'fine' remarks and of all freedom of speech – this just when he is insisting that a man's deeds harmonize with his words before he is worth listening to. Laches is inexplicit that Socrates' (or others') military prowess is 'fine', but says enough to justify Socrates' claim (192C) 'almost to know' that Laches held *andreia,* 'courage', to be fine. Further, Laches is no likely praiser of folly; his values include too high an estimation of success. Socrates is taking little, if any, risk of receiving inconvenient answers to his questions on this theme.

Neither Socrates nor Laches is in difficulties yet. But Laches (not Socrates, who is only asking questions) will be in trouble if he admits after all to admiring those who show a daring unlikely to be successful. His trouble will concern *andreia* if he uses that word, like most Greeks, for what we should call bravery as well as for the sum of the qualities required of the successful soldier. Socrates and we have no reason to suppose Laches to stand out against such usage. There is accordingly a sense in which it is natural for Laches to say that the soldier less likely to win is more *andreios*. Laches' instinct to say such things explains why he treats the inexpert well-diver as braver than the expert and more *andreios*. This treatment explains his eventual downfall; he is prepared after all to accord the title of 'courageous' to the unsuccessful but daring, despite his explicit unwillingness to suppose that the unsuccessful are admirable.

What could help to remove this confusion is a distinction between two senses of *andreia*. But Socrates put Laches off the scent of that hare by his request for what is common to all cases of *andreia*. It is, we may stress again, usual for Plato to ignore the possibility of different senses of the words Socrates seeks a definition of.[86] The course of the discussion with Laches suggests that Plato was aware that the common usage of the word was diverse, but did not analyse the ambiguity here brought out. Aristotle's account of 'courage' is peculiar, but suggests that though conscious of some difficulties with *andreia* he did not see them in terms of this ambiguity.[87] Plato therefore probably did not see them in quite those terms either; Plato had an excuse for his failure – if it be a failure – to see them thus, since he was in any case interested in a cognitive state of soul which he perhaps thought was the true 'courage' and lay behind, or constituted, real success or bravery in war or peace.

At all events, it is not only Socrates' question which has put Laches off but also his illustration of it with the example of speed. Laches has already agreed at least provisionally to look for what is common to all the examples of *andreia*, following Socrates' illustration. He offered the statement (192B) that 'Courage is a sort of endurance of the soul' with the proviso 'if it is necessary to say what its nature is in all cases.'

The univocity of *andreia* is thus a working assumption. If Laches is now going to proclaim its polysemy he is going to have to withdraw that provisional agreement, and make a song and dance about it; and Plato is going to have to make something clear which it is very doubtful whether he saw with sufficient clarity. But in all this there is no suggestion that Plato was dealing unfairly with Laches or his readers. Laches' answers suggest that he applies the single word *andreia* to two or more different things without having fully worked out either the reasons for applying his word or the question which of the qualities concerned he values the most. We have no reason to suppose him unique.

The upshot of this analysis of separate questions arising from the skirmish with Laches is that Socrates obtains from Laches a clarification and modification of his original thesis. The clarifying development of Laches' original ambiguous definition takes a form based, as it can be with some confidence, on remarks Laches has already made. It narrows 'courage' down to *sensible* endurance – or something like it – and to endurance in situations where a risk to the enduring agent makes itself felt. Endurance without the necessary technical skill to back it up then appears not to be sensible, and hence ought not to rank as 'courage'. But Laches feels that it is none the less braver, and hence more *andreios* in a different sense (a difference he does not detect). Thus he cannot maintain both his definition of *andreia,* and all of the following: his instinctive feelings about bravery, his view that *andreia* is something admirable, his disapprobation of anything that is not sensible and not likely to lead to success. He does not like this total situation – presumably because he wishes to maintain all of these. To alter his definition is one way out of his troubles, though not the only one. Socrates gives him no opportunity to select a way out, but asks instead if he would like help.

A transition

Socrates makes what has appeared to some a concession to Laches before requesting Nicias' aid. He appears to some to concede an element of truth, if only of a preliminary kind, to the suggestion that 'courage' is a kind of endurance. Dieterle, for example, one of the most cautious interpreters of the passage, suggests that we are with 'endurance of the soul' on the way to 'courage'.[88] But, though this may be true of Plato's readers, Socrates says nothing to Laches to indicate that he is on the way to anything except further inquiry. Laches himself agrees wholeheartedly that they have no share in 'courage' so far as speaking goes, and that the consequent lack of harmony in their lives has nothing 'fine' about it. Socrates speaks of obeying what they have said, to a certain extent, and, in answer to Laches' immediate question, specifies the remark that orders them to endure (193E).

Many have supposed the dialogue as a whole to contain unrefuted the suggestion that endurance is part of 'courage', relying in part on this passage. Opponents of that general view, including Irwin,[89] do not all deal with this passage in particular. The relation of this part of the dialogue to the whole is a complex topic, but needs at least brief discussion here.

The first thing to notice is that Plato's people have not hitherto said anything which could strictly carry an *order* to endure. The quality of *andreia* is a part of goodness, and therefore presumably itself good; and they have agreed that it is also 'fine'. But they have not, most emphatically not, agreed that *andreia* is any sort of endurance, or contains endurance as a part. The notion has indeed just been refuted, so far as Laches is capable of defending it.

The upshot is that in the absence of any sustainable connection between endurance and what is good or 'fine', Laches has no reason, strictly speaking, to find any recommendation of endurance in the preceding argument. If so, then Socrates has no such reason either, since the whole argument was conducted in terms of Laches' admissions and judgments. It would surely be quite out of philosophical character for Socrates to make, and to urge on his partner, an assumption not recommended by the preceding argument and forming part of the nexus of propositions which has led to contradiction.

Much the same needs saying about the rest of Socrates' speech of encouragement (194A). The second sentence is a conditional one, certainly not committing Socrates to a belief that endurance itself is in truth 'courage'. There is no reason in the previous argument for the belief that this condition is fulfilled, and some reason – namely, Laches' inability to sustain it – to support the view that the condition is not met. All Socrates is saying is that *in case* endurance is courage, they should endure; for *in that case* courage itself will laugh at them as not pursuing the search courageously.

But Socrates and Plato are not the same person, and Socrates' lack of reason for conceding anything to Laches does not entail Plato's lack of reason for dropping his readers a hint. The speech of Socrates here might function in some such way.

But we are ill-advised to take a hint of this kind from Plato unless we are satisfied that such a hint is a necessary interpretation of the passage concerned, and it is hard so to satisfy ourselves about this particular example. From the point of view of the fictional Socrates this speech is a piece of urbanity, suggesting the continuance of the discussion, and doing so in terms which the soldierly Laches can be expected to appreciate and understand. From the point of view of Plato, the piece reminds the reader of some of the heads of the preceding talk in an elegant and civilized way, without ostensibly committing Socrates to anything substantial. It also continues the motif running through the dialogue of the needed harmony between words and deeds.[90] There is no need to read anything of philosophical significance into a piece of elegant urbanity. It remains possible, but is not probable, let alone provable, that Plato is dropping a strong philosophical hint. One would surely expect an artist of Plato's stature to leave his readers in no doubt.

But in any case to suppose a concession here would disturb the basic symmetry of the argumentative portion of the dialogue, a symmetry important and too little observed. The symmetry works like this: respondents produce three definitions of 'courage' in due Socratic form. The first one is Laches' 'a sort of endurance', which mentions only endurance, or 'guts', and no intellectual quality whatever. Socrates shows to Laches' own satisfaction that he cannot really have meant that. The next stab at Laches' meaning is the suggestion that 'courage' is the combination of two qualities, one of 'guts' and the other with intellectual overtones, though not those of any specialized intellectual pursuit. This combination proves unsatisfactory to Laches. The third, which is about to appear from the lips of Nicias, is a purely intellectual one, which also proves in the end unacceptable to its principal supporter in this dialogue. Pure guts, guts with intellect, and pure intellect; that is the sequence. At the end of that sequence it is reasonable for Socrates to suggest, as he does, that they have not discovered what 'courage' is; what is left? This ostensibly exhaustive sequence, with all the shape and air of a complete elimination of possibilities, would be confounded if Socrates or Plato were to drop a hint that the second one, or even the first, contained a large measure of truth. In the context of the dialogue, all three prove unacceptable to their propounders. It is not plausible to suppose that in the middle of this lay-out Plato inserted a resuscitation of one or more of the views killed.

If it is tempting to urge that Plato must have believed one of the three possibilities he thus lays before his readers, the reply must be that, if so, it is not obvious that the one he believed is the combination view, at least when he wrote this dialogue. It is not clear to me that Plato believed this at any point of his career.[91] If asked bluntly, he might have prevaricated, suggesting that it depended whether his questioner meant 'courage' in the popular sense or in the sense in which Socrates preferred to use the word. To take a brief urbanity as settling this complex question would be to lose one's sense of proportion.

Nicias' contribution to the discussion

We have so far anticipated analysis under this head as to show the place of Nicias' substantive suggestion in the dialogue's symmetry. We have also seen, in a previous exposition, that Nicias in the early part of the dialogue does not appear to hold that 'courage' is the knowledge of things to be feared and not, which is the doctrine he eventually produces. What has happened between then and now to change Nicias' mind? Has he just suddenly recollected what he has heard Socrates saying many times before? To entertain such an explanation would be to debit Plato's account with a curious arbitrariness in the basic construction of a dialogue which has given successive generations of readers the impression of an organization both incisive and delicate. It is perhaps worth suggesting that the symmetry of the dialogue goes far to explain Nicias' change of mind.

Once Socrates and Laches have eliminated mere 'guts' and the combination of that with the intellectual quality of prudence and good sense, there remains to be broached the third possibility, that of a purely intellectual understanding. What, from Nicias' point of view as a long-standing friend and partner of Socrates, makes their omission of that third possibility more surprising is that Socrates is himself known to be an intellectualist, as Nicias goes on to explain. On the face of it, it is not necessary to credit (or debit) Nicias with a sudden conversion to the Socraticism he has listened to so often; nor is it necessary to suppose that Nicias was always a Socratic and forgot himself at the moment when he supposed that Stesilaus' art could make men more 'courageous'. Nicias could have changed his mind as a result of the preceding discussion, and of his reluctance to defend either of the two positions from which he has seen Socrates drive Laches. The alternative he prefers to defend instead is sufficiently obvious as an alternative omitted from the preceding discussion to anyone who has followed its course with attention.

Nicias' change of mind is in any case of limited scope. He believed before that Stesilaus taught a genuine subject, whose study and practice conveyed the good quality of *andreia*, soldierly skill. He still believes that one is good at what one is 'wise' or skilled at (194C). But he now supposes the skill at which one must excel to deserve the title 'courageous' is different from that of Stesilaus. This new belief, however, does not make an appearance for some time; at the start of Nicias' contribution he is not saying anything he could not have accepted earlier. He deviates from old paths only with the suggestion that the *andreios* man possesses the ability to distinguish the fearful from what is not fearful (194E–195A).

This point illuminates the introductory lines of Nicias' portion of the argument, but it does not necessarily exhaust the scope of his development. In order to believe that *andreia* consists in the knowledge of things to be feared and not to be feared, Nicias must perceive that it is more than just the ability to succeed in war. Indeed, if his present account of 'courage' is to be the whole story, the skills needed in war, such as that imparted by Stesilaus, fall completely outside its purview.

What Nicias would seem to have perceived is that Laches came to grief because he confused under one heading, 'courage', both soldierly skills and bravery. Nicias seems accordingly to adopt a policy of benign neglect towards those skills whose acquisition he had so warmly recommended at the outset: and this policy, like the introduction of the purely intellectual alternative, finds an explanation in the attention Nicias has paid to the argument between Socrates and Laches. To suppose this means that Plato has understood the implications of his characters' remarks. This again implies Plato's awareness of the diverse usage of *andreia,* but again does not imply his perception of it as a straightforward ambiguity. Whatever the truth of that, Nicias is not bound by Laches' acceptance of Socrates' demand for one definition of *andreia* in all the various contexts of its use. Nicias is much less concerned with usage than Laches.

The relation just outlined between Nicias' views and the whole previous conversation helps to explain Laches' reactions to the developing exposition of them.[92] Prodded by Socrates, Nicias explains that he has heard Socrates say that in those respects in which a man is wise he is good, and in those respects in which a man is stupid he is bad. This makes a great deal of sense, provided the words 'wise' and 'stupid' be taken as meaning 'wise *at something*' and 'stupid *at something*'. Socrates agrees with what Nicias says. He can do so – provided we remember that vital phrase 'at something' – without deserting the common sense attitude of the old men he is representing. To be good at something is indeed to be an expert at it. Nicias next draws the conclusion, proceeding from general to particular, that if the 'courageous' man is good, he must be 'wise' or expert. It is worth noting, and is seldom noted, that Socrates does not commit himself to agreement with this conclusion. All Socrates does is to turn to Laches with the questioning 'Did you hear that?' Laches' reaction is that he has heard but does not quite understand.

His lack of understanding is entirely credible. Nicias originally supported Stesilaus as a producer of 'courageous' soldiers. By this he meant good soldiers; but the preceding discussion has strongly suggested that the more prudent and skilled the soldier the less 'courageous' he is after all. Nicias is now suggesting that the 'courageous' man is an expert; but if so, in what? and if, as must seem to Laches likely, Nicias means that a 'courageous' or successful soldier is an expert in fighting somewhat on the model of Stesilaus, then what becomes of Laches' earlier objections to such experts? Nicias' suggestion, coming at this stage and in this form, is bewildering. One has to remember Laches' total ignorance of Socratic ethics to appreciate his bewilderment.

Socrates' explanation of Nicias' meaning does not help. Socrates turns the generalization of Nicias about people into a definition of *andreia* itself, though not a complete one. 'Courage' is a sort of wisdom. This clearly excites Laches' scorn (194D, 195A); Stesilaus had, we know (183D), devised a 'wise' trick;[93] and where did his 'wisdom', here meaning 'expertise', get him? To ridicule.

But Socrates, knowing (as Laches does not) the sort of thing Nicias is likely to be driving at, suggests (194D–E) asking Nicias what 'expertise' he is thinking of. He eliminates some absurd possibilities, to show, presumably, what sort of question he is asking, and then puts the original question in a slightly different form. From the word 'wisdom' he shifts to 'knowledge'; this enables him to ask not only 'What knowledge?' but (as an alternative) 'knowledge of what?'. One important consequence of this is that Nicias need not now answer with the name of a recognized art, craft or expertise, which would be difficult to find for the kind of moral expertise that Socrates expects Nicias to have in mind. At the same time the words here used for 'wisdom' and 'knowledge' overlap sufficiently in Greek usage for Laches to go on using 'wisdom' without (apparently) noticing any difference.

When Nicias specifies in accordance with this terminology the knowledge of what is or is not to be feared, both in war and in all other spheres, Laches becomes abusive. His reaction is again intelligible in context. As becomes increasingly clear, Laches interprets the knowledge of what is or is not to be feared in a certain sphere as synonymous with the normal expertise in that sphere. He has good reason: the person who knows what to look out for and avoid in war is likely to be a competent soldier; the man who does not is not. In the absence of anything specifically about values in Nicias' statement, there is no reason why the un-Socratic Laches should even think of values. Hence previous considerations about expertise apply here; and there is an additional consideration, to the effect that Nicias is apparently expecting his 'courageous' man to be expert in war and all other spheres. No wonder Laches shows his impatience. He brusquely rejects any connection between 'wisdom' and 'courage'. The rejection is fully in accord with our interpretation of his thinking. We can see that Nicias, as Laches reasonably understands him, is standing the previous discussion on its head, and then piling one absurdity on another.

By his use of 'wisdom' and by the examples he puts to Nicias, and by his own generalization apropos of the farmers, Laches makes plain his need for an explanation of Nicias' meaning: the explanation is forthcoming in terms which do much to explain the subsequent course of the argument. The doctor, Nicias says by way of example (195C), can tell what is healthy and what is unhealthy for his patient; he cannot tell whether it is better for the patient to recover or to die. He asks Laches whether he is prepared to admit that it is better for some folk not to live, and Laches, like many of us, is indeed prepared to accept that. Laches accepts also a difference between the things to be feared by those for whom death is better and the things to be feared by those for whom it is not.

All the discussion about what is better is conducted in the present tense; not because the relevant propositions about advantage are true only at the present time, but because they are timelessly true of certain types of people in certain types of situation. The present tense, in Greek as in English, is the tense most commonly used for timeless truths. We need not enter here into the vexed question whether Plato recognized the existence of such a class of true propositions, since it is immaterial for the point here being developed whether Plato thought of them as timelessly or as permanently true. The relevance of all this will become clear when we come to the final bout of questioning Socrates aims at Nicias about the nature of knowledge and its relation to tense.

The first whiff of a reference to the future in discussing

what is and is not to be feared is from the lips of Laches, not of Nicias. Asked by Socrates whether he understands Nicias' explanation, Laches interprets it as equating the 'courageous' with the prophets (195E). Who but a prophet will know whether it is best for a man to live or die? Laches indicates a necessary connection between prophecy and the requisite knowledge. We and he have no right to surprise when Nicias assumes in his reply that the reference was to the prediction of future events. At this point Nicias allows the future to creep into the expression of his view too.

Nicias' view proves still to be hard for Laches to understand. Indeed, Dieterle did well to point out that Laches is more interested in refuting than in understanding it, though Dieterle goes too far in stressing Laches' naivety:[94] Nicias' view is genuinely hard to understand for one uninitiated into Socratic thinking. Nicias holds, as he explains, that the prophet knows the signs of actual events to come in future; but no prophet can tell whether what is going to happen is good or bad for the person(s) involved. Even now, Nicias does not use the future with direct reference to the goodness or badness of events for people. He uses no tense at all, getting by in the relevant clause without a verb. But in whatever tense or in no tense, Nicias' exposition further bewilders Laches. The latter is clearly searching for a kind of person, with a recognized designation, to express Nicias' meaning. The obvious sort of name, in the context of a knowledge, would be that of a kind of craftsman or technician or expert. But of course there is no recognized name for the expertise in what is good or bad for human beings, since there is not commonly thought to be any such expertise. If there is such an expert, then he (or she, or it) sounds like a superhuman being; and that is what the baffled Laches finally supposes Nicias to have in mind – if, indeed he has anything specific in mind, and is not just wriggling (196A–B).

In thus interpreting Nicias, Laches has for some time deserted the method of questioning favoured by Socrates for the elucidation of people's views; and Socrates gently brings the conversation round to an interrogation once more, an interrogation to be conducted on behalf, now, of Laches, as well as on his own. We thus find the Socrates who has plausibly represented the two old men now representing also the vigorous general. It is of course easier to represent others, especially diverse others, in questioning than in statement. Socrates' questions do not, since they are mostly based on what Nicias has already said, betray those he claims to represent. Where they are not based on what Nicias has said, Socrates' next series of questions have a firm foundation in ordinary Greek usage, such as the two old men might easily recognize, and such as Laches was no doubt championing in associating knowledge of the fearful and non-fearful with the expertise appropriate to each sphere. It is normal Greek ways of thought and speech which here oppose Nicias' way of speaking.

Socrates begins with the merest recapitulation (196C). Nicias did say that 'courage' is the knowledge of things to be feared and not to be feared? Yes. Socrates follows this up with a reminder that since neither doctor nor prophet has in his professional capacity the requisite knowledge, it is not something that any Tom, Dick or Harry would know. Isn't that what Nicias said? Now this effectively mirrors Laches' bafflement as to what special breed of person Nicias can possibly be talking about; but as an argument in its own right it borders on the grotesque.

The implied argument is that

(a) The knowledge of experts such as doctors and prophets does not include or require the knowledge of what is fearful and what is not.

Therefore

(b) Not everybody has the knowledge of what is fearful and what is not.

In addition, it is tempting (no doubt for Socrates' hearers as well as Plato's readers) to interpret (b) as an example of litotes, a gentle way of making the more extreme pronouncement that

(c) Very few people have the knowledge of what is fearful and what is not.

It should be obvious that even (b), let alone (c), does not follow in the least from (a). But, we observe, Nicias has never said either (b) or (c); Socrates' only justification for attributing (b) or (c) to Nicias would be that (b) or (c) did follow from what Nicias said. Hence, Socrates has no justification for attributing (b) or (c) to Nicias.

Nicias' willingness to accept the limited number of people displaying 'courage' must derive from an initial conviction that 'courage' is relatively rare, or, at least, not a universal quality. The rarer it is among human beings, the better for Socrates' subsequent argument. Why does Socrates bank on Nicias accepting the attribution? The only reason I can think of is that he believes Nicias to have in mind the knowledge of values, and both himself accepts, and believes Nicias to accept, and supposes those he represents also to accept, the rarity if not the superhuman status of such knowledge. There would present all the less difficulty in that the Greeks generally recognized that almost any knowledge or skill was the special province of a relatively few people.

But one normal view now comes into conflict with what Nicias says. Socrates firmly expresses his own view of the matter. Nicias' view necessitates the refusal to call any animal more 'courageous' than another. The argument appears to be as follows:

(c) Very few people have the knowledge of what is fearful and what is not.
(d) The reason for the state of affairs described by (c) is that the subject of the relevant knowledge is difficult.
(e) What men find difficult to know an animal cannot know.

Therefore

(f) No animal is more knowledgeable in the relevant subject than any other.

Perhaps the weakest link in this chain is (e). For the argument requires (e'): What men find difficult to know an animal cannot know *at all*; and that is not obviously true. One animal might have a slightly brighter glimmering than another. The *therefore* between the first three propositions here and the fourth is dubious. The argument is more rhetorical than logical. But the company have been thinking of the knowledge concerned as either god-like (Laches) or exceptional among human beings (Nicias), and have shown no concern with degrees of knowledge or of ignorance.

At all events Laches expresses disquiet (197A) with a different proposition, namely, the argument's conclusion, (f). We all, he says, call some animals brave; are they then wiser than a lot of human beings ('than us'), or is Nicias venturing to sustain a different usage from everyone else? This appears also to evade any fine distinctions of grading: human beings could vary in the degree of courage they exhibit, and animals could also vary, but at a lower level. But nobody in the dialogue is interested in fine points of this sort. Laches is accustomed quite simply to call an animal such as a lion 'courageous', sees no way in which Nicias could share that usage without making some animals more knowledgeable than at least some human beings, and finds that ridiculous. He thinks he has found a conflict between Nicias and common sense.

Nicias' answer shares the assumption of *total* ignorance on the part of animals, but expresses a desire to use words differently from most people including Laches. The difference deserves a brief analysis. Laches was at first content to label any endurance or persistence 'courage', but agreed fairly readily to stop calling foolish endurance 'courage'. (192B–D). That was because foolish endurance is harmful to the agent, and so not 'fine'. His present attitude suggests, if he is to be consistent, his readiness to call animal courage 'fine'. One passage may persuade us of his consistency in this regard: he speaks of the animals called 'courageous' as being deprived by Nicias of the 'honour' which everybody else is ready to accord them (197B–C). Nicias may or may not insist on 'courage' being 'fine', but he does indeed refuse to accord the honour to animals. He refuses to give it to any creature which in ignorance and without forethought displays boldness or daring (197A–B). Laches thought rash and foolish daring, presumably not likely to lead to success, not worthy to be called 'fine' or 'courageous'. Nicias says nothing about success, for the excellent reason that Greek poets often liken a great warrior to a lion precisely because the lion's fighting prowess normally (in the popular view) leads it to success.[95] The ultimate success of the endeavour, or its likelihood of success, are irrelevant in Nicias' view, and have to be so. Not content with neglecting sheer instinctive daring as a factor in 'courage',

Nicias also, by implication, denies a place in it to fighting prowess. Nicias has completely abandoned the basic categories of Socrates' discussion with Laches; those categories were, as we saw, basic also to Greek usage. No wonder, then, that Laches thinks Nicias' way of drawing his distinction a mere sophism unworthy of a leading citizen, and leaves the task of elucidating Nicias' views further to Socrates (197D–E).

After making sure that Laches is still formally a partner in the investigation, Socrates starts by establishing (since Nicias disagreed so fundamentally with Laches in the argument just completed) their agreement on three fundamental matters. These are the status of 'courage' as a part of goodness coordinate with other parts, a definition of 'what is to be feared', and a point about the nature of knowledge in relation to the tense of the proposition known. All three matters deserve discussion.

At the beginning of the conversation, Socrates says, they were considering 'courage' as a part of goodness; Nicias has to agree, but it is much less clear why he agrees with Socrates on the next item. 'Did you too answer about this that it is a part, there being other parts, which taken all together are called "goodness"?'[96] Nicias has not given, or joined overtly in, any answer to that effect. It was only Laches who agreed to conduct the investigation on the assumption that 'courage' is a part of goodness. We have seen that Nicias offers in the opening scene no clear implication that he believes in several good qualities, including 'courage', making up in sum a unified 'goodness'.

Dieterle[97] suggested that Nicias and Socrates have in mind a passage at the beginning of Nicias' intervention (194D). There 'Nicias sets out from the general concept of goodness and on that basis treats "courage" as a knowledge.' Nicias sets out rather from the good, wise and brave *man*; but there is some truth in Dieterle's suggestion. Each man is good in those respects in which he is wise, Nicias says he has heard Socrates say; and if the courageous man is good, then he is wise. Further, Nicias accepted by implication that 'courage' was only one knowledge among many, and presumably also one goodness among many.

One thing only is lacking: an expression of belief in a single general concept of goodness. Nicias does not use the word 'goodness' in the dialogue at all, and his general assent (180A) to Lysimachus' opening statement of purpose is the nearest he has come so far to expressing a belief in a single goodness made up of subordinate good qualities. This is vague – like much else in Nicias' views. Plato, whether by choice or not, has given Laches much clearer and firmer views than Nicias.

All one can say with certitude is that Nicias' silence, when he could have protested about the plan to examine 'courage' as part of goodness, entitles Socrates at least to ask whether Nicias meant to join in the plan and accept its basis. For this Plato's word 'answer' is perhaps ill chosen, but is understandable. Nicias himself does not, and surely need not, quibble. It would seem that the status of 'parts of goodness' for specific virtues made sense in the Athens of Plato's day. Nicias has said nothing to indicate with any clarity what qualities other than 'courage' he regards as good; so Socrates with one swift question (198A) finds out that he accepts 'moderation', justice and similar qualities as good. He needs, if he is to make out the knowledge of good and bad to be the whole of goodness, to know which sort of quality Nicias will include in the list of virtues.

In addressing this question to Nicias Socrates once again appears to commit himself to the doctrine of parts of goodness, raising the same problems as elsewhere when he says this sort of thing. Socrates even names, in his own person, three parts. This time he is the representative not only of the two old men who might be expected to share a commonplace view of the virtues, but also of Laches, who has readily agreed (as Socrates delicately reminds us and his respondent) to treat 'courage' as a part of goodness. We are scarcely obliged to take this doctrine as an expression of Socrates' own faith.

The next point (198B) ought to be very clear, but has not always been so. Socrates, with a caution engendered naturally by Nicias' difference from Laches' usage in the matter of 'courage' words, makes sure there is no such difference in their usage of 'fear' words. The 'fearful' is what induces fear, the 'cheerful' is what does not. It now becomes clear, incidentally, that in this dialogue at least the word 'fearful' or 'what is to be feared' does not mean 'what *ought* to be feared'; the relevant issues do not rear their heads. What could be the subject of disagreement is the definition of fear. Fear is the expectation, according to Socrates, of a bad thing to come. Both the term 'expectation' and the reference to the future are potentially debatable.

Méron[98] has suggested that the future reference of fear is a mistake, that past events can arouse fear. This is perhaps simply a question of what is to count as fear. One knows, for example, what it is like to lie and sweat at night over a narrow escape from a bad accident the day before. But the feeling concerned could appropriately be described as the recollection of fear, rather than simply fear. Right or wrong as a point of usage, Socrates' reference of fear to the future is wholly reasonable, and likely to find acceptance in more sophisticated company than he has in this dialogue.

The term 'expectation' presents a more far-reaching problem. Plato has suffered rebuke in some contexts for using an intellectual word such as 'expectation' in the definition of an emotion such as fear. In the *Laches* this point is not of great importance, however significant it may be elsewhere in Plato's works. The argument in this part of the *Laches* is not directed to the merits or demerits of an intellectualist ethic, but hinges rather on the confinement of 'fear' and 'the fearful' to future reference. Nicias is already supporting an intellectualist position; he thinks of knowledge as a sufficient condition of goodness. The argument considers the internal coherence of such an outlook, or at least its consistency with other views reasonably attributed to Nicias; Nicias is in no position to object if in the course of such consideration Socrates reduces the emotional life of man to intellectual terms. The pass is already sold.

The question is not whether Socrates and Nicias are justified in putting and accepting the relevant proposition, but whether Socrates has not now ceased altogether to represent the view of Laches and the old men. Socrates is at pains to suggest that he has not: he starts the long sentence about fear with a reiterated use of the first person plural, and continues to the end retailing what 'we think'. Has Socrates (and has Plato) cheated here? The answer to this is 'Minimally, if at all.' The proposition Socrates actually *uses* is not the abstract definition of fear, but the agreement about the fearful; and the agreement about the fearful holds that it is the expected bad. So far as this goes, it is true, and it goes far enough, for Nicias did not originally speak of fear but of the knowledge of the fearful and non-fearful. That one does have additional reactions to impending bad things other than simply expecting them is true but irrelevant. For Laches and the old men to object to the abstract formulation 'Fear is...' would demand not only an alertness, but also, in context, a churlishness which they do not exhibit elsewhere.

The third premise, about the nature of knowledge (198D–E), would demand more attention than it does if others had not already paid sufficient. Gregory Vlastos some years ago propounded an interpretation of this part of the *Laches* as making knowledge of future truth simply *entail* knowledge of the same truth in the past and present.[99] To take Socrates' example, Vlastos understood the knowledge of what *was* healthy and *is* healthy to entail the separate knowledge of what *will be* healthy. In consequence, he took Socrates' point to be that the possession of one virtue implies possession of the others. But that is not the only interpretation available. If we accept on other evidence Socrates' espousal of the paradoxical view that courage not only entails, but actually is the same state of soul as the other virtues, we can very easily reconcile that with the present passage. For Socrates could be suggesting that the knowledge of what was healthy is the same *piece of knowledge* as the knowledge of what is and what will be healthy. Indeed, it looks as if that is just what he is suggesting. He speaks of there not being one knowledge of what was the case, another of what is the case, and another of what will be the case, but of them all as being the same knowledge (198D–E). This would be curious language if *all* he meant was that knowledge of the future truth entailed knowledge of the past one.

Socrates illustrates the point with a reference to generalship and prophecy, a reference seized upon by commentators[100] as a palpable hit at Nicias for his conduct (later than this dialogue's dramatic date) in the Sicilian campaign. The illustration is appropriate to a Nicias who has said about prophets what this one has in this dialogue. Earlier (195E–196A), when reproached by Laches with equating the brave and the prophets, Nicias distinguished prophets, who know only what is going to happen, from the 'courageous', who know what is better or worse. Nicias distinguishes also those who know what is better or worse from those with the knowledge of a technique such as generalship.

Socrates now (198D–199A), seeking Laches' explicit assent for doing so, puts the view that in questions of war the art of the general is the art most fitted to take thought for the past the present *and the future*. The general presumably knows what results normally follow from what actions in what war situations. The prophet presumably knows what signs normally presage what outcomes. The prophet, if that be correct, cannot do more than tell the general in advance what will happen; whether that outcome be favourable or unfavourable, it is still up to the general to do his best, according to the rules of his specialism, to secure the most favourable outcome possible.[101] The position is debatable, but tenable, and it would leave us with a consistent Nicias (though Nicias does not explicitly assent to Socrates' view here).

Nicias does agree that knowledge of past, present and future are identical pieces of knowledge. He accepts Socrates' reminder that he has called 'courage' the knowledge of what is to be feared and what is not. Things to be feared and not are respectively future bads and future goods or neutrals (199B).[102] Knowledge of future goods and bads is identical with knowledge of past and/or present bads; this branch of knowledge does not differ from others in this respect, and Nicias cannot say it does without abandoning the generality of the rule he previously accepted. Hence, Socrates suggests (199C), Nicias' definition defines only a part of 'courage'. Socrates explains his debatable formulation: Nicias' original definition makes 'courage' the knowledge of future goods and bads; his views on knowledge make 'courage' the knowledge of all goods and bads. For Nicias to deny either of these would be to eat his own words.

Debatable here is the notion of 'part'. The defining phrase in Nicias' original definition, Df. (i), is included in, is 'part' of, the defining phrase of the definition deriving from his views on knowledge, Df. (ii); does that mean that the definiend of Df. (i) was part of the definiend of Df. (ii)? I doubt it. Nicias' views on knowledge imply the *identity* of the definiend of Df. (i) with that of Df. (ii). Not one of his views implies the inclusion of the definiend of (i) in the definiend of (ii) as part in a whole. Socrates' use of the term 'part' and Nicias' acceptance of it beg a question. But the question is scarcely important to the argument. 'Courage' was a part, but turns out to be the whole, of goodness; Nicias defines not the whole of 'courage' but a part of it. There is no logical nexus here; the notion of 'part' appears in Socrates' statement of his objection to Nicias' Df. (i) apparently for literary reasons only: these might include reasons of pleasing symmetry and the enlivening effect of an apparent paradox, an effect visible also in an earlier passage, where Socrates offers his definition of fear (198B).

The proposition that knowledge of past, present and future are identical pieces of knowledge is a debatable one for other reasons, not least because it needs more philosophical unpacking. It obviously does not mean that to know that a particular apple is hanging on a particular tree is to know that it was hanging there last year and will be hanging there tomorrow. What Nicias says is untrue of the knowledge (if there is such) of contingent truths. It is true, if at all, of general truths.[103] If S is a general subject, and P is a predicate generally applicable to members of the class S, then (Nicias presumably means) the knowledge that S is P is identical with the knowledge that on all future occasions S will be P and with the knowledge that on all past occasions S was P; which is of course a much stronger proposition than 'If A knows S is P, A knows that S always will be P and A knows that S always was P.'

In this context what Nicias says earlier (195C) of the doctor's expertise is interesting. The doctor, according to Nicias, knows 'the healthy'. This is untensed, and is doubtless all one piece of knowledge in the required sense. It presumably includes something like:

> The doctor knows what will bring or maintain good health,

and
    The doctor knows what is bringing or maintaining good
    health,
and
    The doctor knows what always has brought or maintained
    good health.

It is, I suspect, nonsense to say that the doctor knows what brought or maintained good health at 2 p.m. yesterday, or that he knows what will bring or maintain health at 6 p.m. tomorrow. But the doctor does know that a sound diet did always and always will conduce to health and is conducive also for today's patients. To know that 'an apple a day keeps the doctor away' *is* to know that it always will and always did.

As his doctor knows 'the healthy', so Nicias' 'courageous' man knows 'the fearful and non-fearful'. The implications are similar. The 'courageous' man ought by parity of reasoning to know what was, is and will be fearful. It may sound as if there is a gap looming up in the argument. '*A* knows what always was, is and always will be fearful' and 'What is fearful will be harmful' imply together only that '*A* knows the kind of thing of which it is, always was and always will be the case that it will be harmful.' This is not the same proposition as '*A* knows the kind of thing of which it was, is and will be the case that it *is* harmful.' Yet it is this latter that Socrates' point and argument require.

But that hardly matters in practice: for practical purposes, the badness of things which were going to be bad is already in the past, in so far as tense is relevant to their badness. The gap in the argument hardly needs plugging. The knowledge of the 'courageous' man in Nicias' definition is of the fearful and non-fearful, that is of the bad and the good-or-neutral. The 'courageous' man knows the good and the bad. Indeed, Nicias implies as much in a question pretty clearly meant as 'rhetorical' on the subject of the doctor (195C). The question speaks of the doctor failing to know whether health is better than sickness for the patient, and also of death from disease as being (in the present tense) better for some than recovery. Pretty clearly Nicias intends his 'courageous' man to know what his doctor fails to know. Thus the 'courageous' man, in knowing what is fearful and what is not, knows not just what will be better, but what *is* better. Indeed, in context the distinction between what is better and what will be better is not easy to draw.

There is thus quite a strong sense in which the roots of Nicias' final difficulty lie in his earlier admissions. It is impossible, given the conversational vagueness of his earlier remarks, for Plato's reader (or for Socrates) to be absolutely sure; but a gamble on Nicias accepting that knowledge of future goods and bads is knowledge also of present goods and bads is a fairly safe bet. From there to the form of generalization Nicias actually accepts is a long step in logic; but Nicias has in any case given away as much as Socrates actually needs to confute him. Socrates' questions arise naturally out of Nicias' previous remarks in the dialogue, and there is nothing implausible about such a person accepting the generalization he does. The relation of previous admissions to Socratic questioning has too often escaped notice.

Whether Nicias is obliged to agree with the whole of Socrates' next speech is another arguable question. His reply is noticeably lukewarm (199E): 'I think you have a point'[104] or perhaps 'I think there is something in what you say.' The first part of it is a question whether a man with the knowledge of all good things, in all tenses and in all respects, and of bad things likewise, is in any way deficient in goodness. Scholarly interpreters urge the Socratic and paradoxical nature of this.[105] But Nicias cannot object on these grounds. He himself inserted into the discussion the notion that 'courage' is a matter not of 'guts' or endurance but one of intellect and knowledge. The point and purpose of his intervention will fall if he now submits an amendment to the effect that 'courage' is the whole knowledge of good and bad, but such knowledge is not decisive for goodness. What distinction will he draw, between goodness as a whole and 'courage' as a part, which will make knowledge an adequate account of 'courage' but not of goodness?

This last question, however, is no merely rhetorical one, but has a possible answer, which concerns the second question in Socrates' speech. One could suggest that at least part of human goodness consists of success in obtaining good things; such a view was not unknown in Greece. It is held, for example, by Plato's Meno, who supports it with the authority of the poet Pindar (*Meno* 77B). To flee from the fearful is not the same thing as escaping it, and not to flee from, but to endure, the non-fearful, is not the same thing as obtaining it – whether it be good or neutral. To know what is good is not to obtain it. Now if we denude 'courage' of its connotations of success whether in battle or elsewhere, and make of it an attitude or state of mind or soul, then its connection with the obtaining of the good things of life ceases to be clear. If we dissolve that connection, then it is not, if we adopt the 'success' view of human goodness, the case that 'courage' is goodness, or entails goodness. One might claim that 'courage' was the knowledge of what to fear and what not, and still maintain that human goodness as a whole was more than just the knowledge of what was good and what not. Human goodness as a whole might demand the attainment of the goal whereas 'courage' was a matter only of seeking it. Socrates' second question of this speech (199D) comes in at this point.

He treats the man who knows what is good and what bad as knowing how to deal rightly with gods and men; he treats the man who knows this as knowing not only how to 'deal circumspectly' with things to be feared and not to be feared concerning gods and men, but also how to provide himself with the good things. This at least seems a clear case of proceeding illegitimately from 'knowledge that' to 'knowledge how'. Socrates leaves obscure the transition from knowing that something is good to knowing how to get it. But he eases the transition by the use of the verb Sprague acutely renders 'belongs', which can also mean 'befits'. The ambiguity of this verb is useful. It is perhaps morally fitting that the man with the knowledge of good and bad should obtain the good; but it is not clear that in fact the ability to obtain the good is so fittingly distributed. However, once we are willing to grant that the person knowing good and bad is uniquely fitted to attain the good and to know how to behave to both gods and men, it is a relatively small step to the proposition that such a person possesses the virtues other than 'courage', such as temperance (or 'moderation') and justice, whose status Nicias had accepted earlier (198A), and 'holiness', reasonably to be included in the 'etcetera' Nicias had also agreed to.

The argument as a whole has a complexity belied by the rather easygoing treatment it tends to receive. But it seems to depend in outline on two presuppositions: first that 'courage' is a matter only of knowing what to fear, which Nicias has suggested himself explicitly; and secondly that the other virtues also are matters of knowledge alone, which Nicias has not suggested and has to accept only on certain conditions.

Nicias did say that a man who is wise in some respect is also in that respect good (194D); but the relevance of that is again a difficult matter. If that means that 'courage' is the knowledge of what to fear and what not,[106] then by parity of reasoning it ought to mean, say, that 'moderation' or temperance is the knowledge of what to desire and what not. Though this would leave untouched the notorious problem of defining justice, it would lend a degree of respectability to Socrates' and Plato's procedure in this passage. But only a degree: the phrase 'parity of reasoning' is not very compelling, and becomes less so simply because of the difficulty of applying the reasoning to justice.

Nor can Socrates shelter behind the phrase 'knowledge of how to associate with them correctly' with which his question ends; for the point at issue is at bottom precisely how the knowledge of what is good and what is bad can be translated into the knowledge of how to deal with one's fellows. The knowledge how to deal with gods and men forms rhetorically a neatly placed intermediate between knowledge of good and bad at one extreme and the virtues of justice and 'moderation' at the other. But rhetoric differs from both logic and dialectic, and it looks rather as though we have here a case only of rhetoric.

Perhaps the best one can do for Plato and his Socrates here is to suggest that Nicias at the outset drew no distinction between the kind of knowledge involved in being good at something and the kind involved in knowing the fearful and non-fearful. It remains most uncertain whether Plato's Socrates deliberately cashes in on this sequence of Nicias' thought or whether Plato and his Socrates remain blissfully ignorant of any problem. If Socrates is cashing in on Nicias' failure to draw the necessary distinction, then he is cashing in on something often attributed to Socrates himself: Nicias represents at least part of his original suggestions as Socratic. The part specifically so labelled is the suggestion that one is good at what one is wise at.

No such 'Socratic' label attaches in the text to the further suggestion about the definition of 'courage'. But he would be a bold man who insisted that the definition was not Socratic and rescued Socrates' procedure thus. But the suggestion deserves a moment's study. Socrates in the *Republic* (429B–C) 'posits' and obtains assent to the definition of courage as 'the power preserving through everything the right and lawful opinion about what is fearful and what is not.' This manifestly bears a close relation to the definition in the *Laches*, but equally clearly is not quite the same. Is the power which preserves right opinion about a thing the same as the knowledge of that thing? The Socrates of this part of the *Republic* does not suggest it, but in view of the well-known Platonic suggestion that one thing distinguishing knowledge from opinion is the former's permanence, it could be so.

In the *Protagoras* (358D), by arguments analysed in Chapter IV below, Socrates drives Protagoras to the admission that 'courage' is the knowledge of what is to be feared and what is not. This is the corner-stone of his refutation of Protagoras' doctrine that one can be most courageous without being at all wise. There remains a residue of uncertainty whether Socrates is committed to the particular conclusion he reaches in the overthrow of Protagoras' theory; Socrates is not, as we shall see, committed to belief in every step in that argument.

But these two pieces of Socratic conversation give us a presumption that Plato intends Nicias to be using a formulation he had heard on Socrates' lips; whether Socrates offers it for the sake of argument or of commitment remains uncertain. Nicias himself is perhaps, as Plato portrays him, not the man to care about this particular uncertainty.[107]

We have, however, said enough on a topic where such uncertainty reigns. More significant is Socrates' putative defence against a charge of neglecting, in the argument with Nicias, the feelings and emotions.[108] If Plato *deliberately* made

Nicias argue *from* knowledge that certain things are fearful and certain things not, *to* knowledge how to deal with the fearful and the non-fearful, then he could argue in his Socrates' defence (not quite conclusively, as we have seen) that the omission of the emotions from the climactic argument of the dialogue was due to the nature of the theory Nicias put forward which, alas, neglected the emotional nature of man.

If the accuser, warming to his task, said that Socrates, the originator of the theory, could not shelter behind Nicias, Plato could then produce a defence based on the dialogue's structure. He could argue that his Socrates had earlier refuted the other possibilities, that 'courage' was simply a matter of 'guts' and that it was a combination of the intellectual and the emotional.

Plato's accuser would (at least nowadays) refuse to give up. He would stress the nature of those earlier refutations, as involving the attitudes of one particular (if not in any relevant way peculiar) man. At this point, Plato might well retort that this was the only kind of refutation he knew. His Socrates refuted views as people actually held them, together with and in the context of other views forming a supposedly coherent outlook on the whole relevant field of thought. What he would certainly be able to urge, with a justice not fully appreciated by all his critics, is the necessity of taking a dialogue as a whole, and not seizing on the argument with Nicias as if it were wholly independent of the context surrounding it. Over the dialogue as a whole, the accusation of ignoring the emotional side of courage will not stand up.

There are other accusations Plato and his Socrates have to answer. One concerns the limitation of what is fearful to *future* evils. The suggestion that one can fear, or show courage concerning, the past, as in the case of bereavement, receives an answer from its originator:[109] one shows courage rather in the face of the years of loneliness to come. Does one show courage in the face of *present* conditions unpleasant or otherwise harmful? It is arguable that one is showing a rather different quality from 'courage' if one refrains from weeping or gnashing of teeth when subjected to unpleasantness. If we accept that distinction, then we shall perhaps not reject out of hand the proposition that what looks like 'courage' in the face of present unpleasantness is construable as 'courage' in the face of its continuation in the immediate future. The distinction between the present and the immediate future is not an easy one to be precise about. The point is not of great importance ultimately for the argument in the *Laches,* since if knowledge is not time-bound at all it is irrelevant whether 'courage' is bound to the future alone or to either present or future; in either case 'courage' is not knowledge.

Perhaps typical of the numerous criticisms aimed at this part of the *Laches* is Santas'[110] to the effect that Socrates does not examine the question whether one can have general and law-like knowledge of good and evil. Santas adds that Socrates assumes without question that one can. What this whole approach neglects is the fact, of more than mere literary significance, that it is not Socrates but Nicias who injects the assumption of such knowledge into the discussion. It neglects also the place of the emotions in the earlier discussion, and the structure of the whole. Having, to all appearances, forgotten at this point the previous refutation of Laches' suggestion that 'courage' is a mixture of the intellectual and the emotional, Santas makes bold to accuse Socrates of having forgotten his own list of feelings. The implied neglect of dialectic and literary structure alike is unfortunately all too common a feature of philosophical interpretations of Plato's earlier dialogues.

Final scene

Nicias' confession of failure ushers in a scene exhibiting the attitudes of the various characters to knowledge and ignorance. Laches with open sarcasm (200A) derides the wisdom of Damon, transmitted to Nicias, which has failed to ensure his success in the search for 'courage'. Nicias in reply imputes to his fellow-soldier a share in their ignorance of what 'courage' is, and an eye only for others' ignorance, rather than his own. He expresses confidence that Damon will enable him to correct anything which did happen to go amiss in his statements. He promises to teach Laches. Nicias, despite his failure, has no doubts of his eventual knowledge; Laches displays an arrogant contempt for the 'wisdom' of Damon trusted by Nicias. Neither would appear to have learnt much from Socrates. Laches has not learnt the power Socrates apparently attributes to knowledge, and Nicias has not yet realized how difficult that knowledge is of attainment. They are agreed only on one thing (200C–D): neither is any good at educating the young, and the two old men would do best to entrust their sons' education to Socrates.

Socrates' demurral (200E) is characteristic of him. His devotion to moral education appears. Yet he represents himself as having turned out every bit as ignorant as the others of the subject at issue. He urges them all to join in a common search for the best possible teacher for themselves and for the young men alike, and not to be ashamed at their age to go to school. What he suggests is not, one observes, a joint search for 'courage', let alone for 'goodness' as a whole. They have tried such a search, and failed in it. He suggests a search for someone less ignorant than themselves. *This* search is the one Socrates prosecutes throughout his life. This is the search he portrays in Plato's *Apology* (21B–23B) as enjoined upon him by the god of Delphi. Himself not claiming knowledge where he had none, he conducted a search for a truly wise man, and questioning the experts in each field found their knowledge of their own expertise impressive, but their claims to knowledge outside their field mistaken. It is no accident that he has in this dialogue sidestepped the technical question of the military relevance of Stesilaus' art, and probed the generals' knowledge of goodness, only to find it wanting.

The representative old man, Lysimachus, declares himself (201B) ready to learn with the young men, an implied confession of ignorance. But then Lysimachus and Melesias at the outset of the dialogue admitted their personal inadequacy. They are from the beginning anxious to find people competent to advise them in their search for an education for their sons. Their combination of modesty with a sense of the potential value of education makes them not wholly unsuitable people for Socrates to represent *vis-à-vis* the generals' claims. They evidently retain these qualities to the end of the dialogue. A willingness to learn and to take counsel concerning their search characterizes them no less at the end than at the beginning of the dialogue. It is no accident that in the last resort Socrates has more in common with the most ordinary Athenians in the dialogue than with the two most distinguished. He is in deeper sympathy with those who ask, than with those who with positive assurance answer, the profoundest questions.

3 Socrates and a tragic poet

Not all of the *Symposium* is dialectical; but the part which is is just that where Socrates is most active. Far more of the dialogue than is normal in Plato's prime consists of a succession of speeches long by Socrates' standards. Naturally, since the speeches are on the same topic, Love or Eros, there are intellectual interactions between the speakers; but the war of opinions, though real, takes place mostly at arm's length, in a way very different from the close in-fighting of Socratic dialectic. Only one long passage is dialectical in the Socratic sense. That is the discussion Socrates has with his host Agathon, tragic poet and the beloved (in a homosexual sense) of another of his guests, Pausanias. This chapter concerns itself with this particular part of Plato's *Symposium*. The object is to develop a dialectical analysis of Agathon's speech and of Socrates' reaction to it, and also of the continuation of Socrates' dialectical riposte in the reported (or, more probably, imagined) conversation between Socrates and the priestess Diotima.

Treatment of the conversation with Diotima as a piece of dialectic is not new;[1] to interpret it as directed against *Agathon* may raise some hackles. Despite the greatly advanced understanding of Agathon's speech in Sir Kenneth Dover's recent edition, the use of the speech in detail, as in this chapter, to explain the course of Socrates' interrogation may lift scholarly eyebrows. The whole piece, at the centre of one of Plato's greatest masterpieces of the dramatic art, has until recently been treated with a reverence it does not deserve rather than with the critical admiration it earns. In this atmosphere not only Gregory Vlastos' keen critique of Plato's doctrine,[2] but also Dover's robust edition came like a breath of fresh air. Dover, attaching a higher value to Plato's literary art than to his philosophy, maintains[3] that Plato writes 'from first to last as an advocate'. Between this interpretation of Plato as a subtly rhetorical persuader and the interpretations of philosophers mystical or analytical who (in agreement with Plato or not) regard him as a master-builder of consecutive arguments, there stretches a wide gulf. It may be possible to find a middle way along the path of dialectical interpretation, to show how Plato's gift of rhetoric and skill in argument both subserve the aims of dialectic.

This is not an academic skirmish, but it may begin by inspecting what seems a specially harsh remark of Dover's: introducing Socrates' interrogation of Agathon, Dover offers a brief but pregnant characterization of the Platonic Socrates' technique,[4] including the two following phrases: 'swift and bold in forcing fallacious inferences and assumptions on the collaborator in the dialogue...' and 'assisted both by the fallacies which the collaborator has himself committed and by the intellectual paralysis which strikes down the collaborator at any moment of Plato's choosing.' The sets of passages referred to in illustrating these two descriptions are different but overlapping. The descriptions raise, when placed side by side, a question or two. Does Socrates force fallacious inferences on his collaborator, or does the collaborator himself help the Socratic line of argument? Or are both true, but of different passages? If Socrates produces so many weak arguments in this whole passage, in how many does his collaborator Agathon actively assist, and why? How many fallacious inferences does he allow Socrates to force on him, and why? Dover's readers will, of course, easily find his answers to the questions 'how many?' But the question 'why?' is less easily answered.

A relevant question would be 'How many dubious arguments can an advocate produce without forfeiting the confidence of those he addresses?' Were Plato's contemporaries specially likely to miss or to ignore fallacious inferences in the dialogues, whether collaborator-assisted or not? Is it necessary to suppose Plato so unscrupulous an advocate? The answers to these relevant questions might turn out to be simply 'Yes.' The unpalatability of a historical statement is no indication of its falsity, and Plato's admirers may be wrong. But a fresh analysis of the text may bring out some relevant but neglected considerations – neglected by others besides Dover, but specially relevant to the questions Dover has raised with such refreshing directness. The analysis will proceed step by step through Socrates' dialectical encounter with Agathon; it draws explanations and illustrations of many steps from the speech Agathon has just made. Agathon's speech, as we shall see, is the basis of much of the dialectic. Whether the fact that Plato composed Agathon's speech too lays him open to charges of 'fixing' the discussion remains to be seen.

According to Agathon's poetic speech, Eros is both the most beautiful[5] and the best of the gods. He analyses the god's beauty and goodness into their most important constituent qualities. He defends the attribution of each to Eros with a brilliant poetic or rhetorical conceit. Rhetorical is the mention (four times) of evidence and (once) of testimony, in a technique derived from, or at least resembling, that of the orator Gorgias.[6] Gorgianic also are the cadences of the first sentence of his actual encomium (p.68, 195A). Socrates draws attention in the dialogue to the rhetorical antecedents of Agathon's style on this occasion (p.73, 198C). But we should not forget Agathon's profession as a poet.

It is extremely difficult here, as often in Greek prose literature, to distinguish poetical from rhetorical colour. Metaphors, elevated and abstract vocabulary, and personifications were as much the stock-in-trade of some orators as of some poets. Quotations from poetry such as Agathon's from Homer (p.68, 195D; see also p.71, 197C) could stem from poet or rhetorician. But one should constantly recall the occasion of the whole dialogue, a party to celebrate Agathon's first victory as a tragic poet, and the presence of Aristophanes, as comic poet obviously a foil to Agathon. Agathon's exaltation of his own poetic profession in the speech, comparable to Eryximachus' obeisance to the medical profession in his speech, draws the reader's attention to something he is in any case unlikely to forget (p.70, 196E; and (I think) p.72, 197E). The banter between Socrates and Agathon before the latter's speech would in any case remind the reader – even if it does distinguish dinner-party from theatre – of Agathon's profession (pp. 70ff., 194A-B).

As Dover points out, the rhythm of Agathon's peroration owes more to poetry than to rhetoric (197D–E).[7] Excusing some of Agathon's failures of logic, Dover adds[8] that 'The speech is appropriate to a man whose business in life is the manipulation of language.' It was as poet, rather than as rhetorician, that Agathon conducted that business, and it is reasonable to suppose that tricks (however obvious) such as the personification of Love are representation not only of Agathon's prowess as a speechmaker on this great occasion, but also of his poetic gifts.

Socrates' response is characteristic. It opens (p.73, 198B) with a mixture of admiration for Agathon's style and blunt attack on his matter. It seems, he says, that it is of no importance if one's praise of Love ascribes good and beautiful qualities to him falsely. Agathon's concluding disavowal of total seriousness (p.72, 197E) takes some of the sting out of this, but fails to inhibit Socrates' onslaught. Socrates' ensuing promise of a plain statement of the truth about love uses a rhetorical cliché with an irony presumably no less deliberate than the similar promise at the opening of Plato's *Apology*.[9] But before he speaks in that way (which ought to mean before he speaks the truth!) he has a few small questions (like the small point he wishes to clear up after Protagoras' great speech in his dialogue (329B)) to put to Agathon. Exactly where Socrates stops questioning Agathon and starts putting his own, supposedly true, opinions, will turn out to be a more difficult question than it might sound. It is doubtful whether Socrates ever does in this dialogue launch into a self-contained speech like the ones preceding his effort. Socrates' statement (p.79, 201D), on beginning his account of Diotima's discussions with him, that he 'will leave Agathon in peace' is perhaps no more than a surface truth, deserving no unreserved acceptance. The one thing we should believe with no reservations whatever is that Socrates will take characteristically full advantage of his permission from Phaedrus and the rest to 'make a speech in the way which he himself thought right' (p.75, 199B).

Socrates' first question sounds indeed trifling, but it does both arise naturally out of Agathon's speech and point forward to later developments. Since, he says (p.75, 199C–D), Agathon has given a magnificent and beautiful account of what Love is like, could he supplement it? Is Love such as to be of something, or of nothing? Dover's paraphrase is neat: 'Is he of such a kind as to stand in an "of"-relationship . . . or not?' Socrates offers an explanation more necessary in ancient Greek than in modern English, whereupon Agathon answers in the affirmative. Editors normally expound this question by showing how the proposition Agathon thus accepts furthers the development of Socrates' argument. They do not normally look back to see if the question arises naturally out of Agathon's speech; but indeed it does.

Agathon has used the word *'eros'* in two different syntactical contexts: (a) 'absolutely', that is, with no accompanying expression to limit its reference; (b) with a noun in the genitive case, the case used for 'of' in normal Greek and in Socrates' question. As a divine person, Eros may naturally be syntactically unqualified, as in (a): examples are 'No pleasure is stronger than Love' (p.70, 196C–D), or 'awkwardness is incompatible with Love' (p.69, 196A). But usage (b) does turn up twice in Agathon's speech, in the expressions 'love of Aphrodite' (p.70, 196C) and 'love of beauty' (p.71, 197B). The difference between (a) and (b), one may remark, does not coincide with a distinction between Love as a person and love as an emotion; the distinction would be harder to justify in the second of our two cases of (b). Nor is the object, or type of object, of Eros clear without specification. Dover again well says that '[Eros] can denote any very strong desire';[10] and the previous course of the whole dialogue has not confined Eros to sexual desire. It would therefore be legitimate, for example, when Agathon says 'No pleasure is stronger than Love', to ask 'Love of what? Do you have any particular object, or a general one, in view?' The 'absolute' use may, or may not, imply, or require supplement by, a general expression in the genitive case. It is simply not clear from Agathon's speech which view he wishes to take, or how he would answer these questions. Before Socrates can use the proposition which apparently underlies his question, he must make sure that Agathon accepts it. He cannot proceed without that acceptance.

Admittedly Socrates' question is a little tricky. In form it is much more likely to suggest one of the proffered alternatives than the other. In asking 'Is Love of something or nothing?'

(p.75, 199D), he invites[11] Agathon to consider whether there could be such a thing as Love of nothing, a question not altogether easy to answer at short notice in the affirmative. But the question is not wholly unfair. It is not, for instance, at all clear that either Socrates or Agathon would have accepted as an instance of a desire that is of nothing, or not of something, 'the experience of desiring or fearing, without forming any idea of what it is that one desires or fears ... in dreams.'[12] Either character might object that such a desire was Eros of something unknown, or of something undefined, rather than of nothing, and not of something at all. The only tricky element in Socrates' question is the word 'nothing', which in this context recalls the schoolboy who, receiving instructions to write nothing in the margin, wrote 'nothing' in large letters. To be in love with whatever 'nothing' denotes would be similarly eccentric.

A less biasing version of Socrates' query would be 'Can there be Love which is not of some particular thing?' But however we phrase the question, it is at least a plausible view that Agathon's is the right answer. Equally reasonable is the supposition that Agathon would have meant to presuppose no other answer by his usage: nothing in the 'absolute' usage actually implies the absence of an object rather than the need to supply a general one. Socrates' question is a reasonably fair attempt at clarification both for himself as a character in the dialogue and for Plato in communication with his readers. It arises out of Agathon's speech and is not a bolt from the blue. Socrates is right to describe his request for an answer to it as a request for a supplement to the speech on a point of detail.

Even the illustrations Socrates uses to explain his question use material from the speech of Agathon. Agathon has indeed used the expression 'father of' (p.72, 197D, cf. p.75, 199D–E), and Socrates' other examples, of 'brother' and 'sister', are of course closely related concepts. It is perhaps ironic that when Agathon used the expression 'father of', he used it metaphorically, without any apparent thought of physical offspring such as the 'son' and 'daughter' of Socrates' illustrative question.

Since the placing of Socrates' questions thus in their context as a response to Agathon's effusion gives them so pleasing a drift, we may continue in the same vein. Socrates' next question (p.76, 200A) is 'Does Love desire the thing that he is Love of, or not?'[13] Commentators again stress the importance of this question for Socrates' whole line of interrogation, but again hardly investigate its relation to Agathon's own words.

Consider Agathon's verbal fireworks on the subject of 'moderation', rendered by Hamilton 'self-control' (p.70, 196C). Everyone, the poet says, admits that 'self-control is mastery over pleasures and desires, and that no pleasure is stronger than Love. If then all pleasures are weaker than Love, Love must be the master, and they his subjects. So Love, being master over pleasures and desires, will be in a pre-eminent degree self-controlled.'

Is Love here a pleasure or a desire? It is hard and distasteful to unravel Agathon's gossamer. But in the first part of this argument Love is a pleasure, and as such second to none. But Love in the second half of the argument is also 'master over pleasures and desires', apparently on the basis of his superiority over pleasures. His superiority over desires ought then to be of the same sort as his superiority over pleasures; no other logic – if 'logic' is not a misnomer – explains the reasoning. So Love ought also to be a desire, and, as such, second to none. Are desires also pleasures? If Love masters pleasures and desires, and is for that reason 'moderate' or 'self-controlled', does it remain, itself, a superior pleasure or desire? Of course, Agathon, whether as poet or as rhetorician, does not want his listener to ask such questions; but these are nevertheless the kinds of question a relentless philosopher might reasonably be expected to put to him.

Agathon is at bottom obscure, and his obscurity leaves room for doubt of his seriousness of mind and clarity of belief in treating Love by implication as a desire. Later in his speech (p.71, 197A–B) he is not much clearer: 'It was under the guidance of desire and Love that Apollo discovered...' We remind ourselves that it is possible for 'and', in Greek as in English, either to link different things or to conjoin rhetorical synonyms (or near synonyms). In this passage the obscurity of Agathon's previous mention of desire, first assimilating and then opposing Love to it, does nothing to help. The total disappearance of desire for the rest of this particular argument, while suggesting, and indeed creating the impression, that desire is more or less the same as Love, does not actually imply their identity. The 'Desire' of which Love is the father in Hamilton's version of Agathon's peroration is a different word in Greek from the other 'desires' of the speech (p.72, 197D), but even if we treat it as synonymous we may find it difficult to work out the precise logical relationship implied by metaphorical fatherhood, and shall hardly have confidence in the results. Agathon has, in sum, left vague the relationship of Love to desire. It should accordingly surprise no one that Socrates asks a clarifying question, and obtains an answer in line with the general impression Agathon has created.

But Socrates' question (p.76, 200A) is not yet wholly clear. To explain his asking whether Love *is a desire* or not is not fully to explain what we have in the text, which is a question whether Love *desires* or not. To equate Love with Desire is decidedly not the same thing as to make 'Love' the grammatical subject of the verb 'desires'. But it is Love's function as the subject of 'desires' which, accepted by Agathon, enables Socrates to continue his line of questioning. Why should Socrates put the question as he does, and why should Agathon answer it so conveniently in the affirmative? Dover again, though not in this connection, supplies the basis of a reply to these queries.[14] On the view that Love is the beloved, not the lover, he comments: 'This was characteristic, but not consistently so, of Agathon's speech; it has been implicitly rejected ever since 200A5.' This does not suggest, and the suggestion deserves an airing, that our passage might be composed the way it is because Agathon's speech is composed the way it is. Agathon does on occasion give Love characteristics appropriate to a lover. For example (p.69, 196A), Love is supple of form, and Agathon's evidence for this is that Love could not otherwise enfold ('wrap himself round') everything. Enfolding is here hard to distinguish from the lover's embrace. A poet might urge that this is nothing but pretty allegory; but, allegory or not, it is characteristically the lover who enfolds or embraces. Allegory is a plea in mitigation, not evidence against the fact. The fact goes far to explain Socrates' question.

If allegory in this passage were the only reason for attributing to Agathon the fusion of Love and lover, one might not wish to be heavy-handed. But the poet may again have fused the two in his treatment of Love's attributes. Again his words are far from clear (pp.69ff., 196B–C): '... in his dealings with gods and men Love neither commits injustice against either nor suffers it from them.' A reckless statement, indeed. But Agathon argues for it on these grounds: 'When he is passive it is not because violence is put upon him, for violence never touches Love, and when he is active he never employs it, for everyone "wishingly" serves Love in everything, and what one "wishing" party agrees with another "wishing" party the laws, rulers of the city, declare just.'[15] Of course violence is pandemic in the history of human love; but if the vague language of Agathon's first point means that violence cannot compel someone to love, then he says what many people, falsely or truly, have believed. One does not normally become a true lover under violent compulsion, even if true love should on occasion supervene. But it is the *lover* who cannot be violently compelled to feel love; one cannot literally subject a passion to violence, and nothing, whether violent or otherwise, could literally 'touch' love.

A resolutely unpoetical and literal-minded listener, with an eye (and ear) to what precisely the poet is saying, might therefore naturally suppose Agathon to be thinking of the lover when he mentions love here. The supposition would surely gain support from the very absurdity of the suggestion that violence has no contact, in a wider sense, with Love. It is at least charitable to suppose Agathon to be thinking of the lover here. Whether in making his second point Agathon has in mind agreement by or with the lover, the beloved, or both, is moot; it is already established that, despite receiving from Agathon many attributes of a beloved, Love does figure in his speech as the representative lover. In this capacity Love not only is desire, but feels desire. If Agathon has not been consistent – and, e.g., Love as Ares' 'capturer' is no lover (p.70, 169D) – that is all the more reason for Socrates to probe his meaning. Agathon is true at least to some of what he has already said in the speech when he answers Socrates' question (p.76, 200A) in its entirety in the affirmative. He has implied that Love desires that of which it is the love.

We may take the next group of questions together (pp.76–7, 200A–E), and extract an assumption from them. Socrates asks whether Love possesses or does not possess what he desires and loves: Agathon says he probably does not, and when pushed is prepared to say that necessarily he does not. The shift from probability to necessity is, perhaps, one way in which Plato and his Socrates can mark a specially important point; at least the point is of cardinal importance for the subsequent course of the argument. If, however, one must lack what one loves and desires, then one cannot, for example, desire to be strong if one is already strong. Socrates suggests that one can, on the other hand, desire the continued future presence of things which one already has. Here it seems to be assumed that love is the desire to possess something, the desire for something to be present or to belong to the lover.[16] We have seen that there is justification in Agathon's speech for the supposition that he will accept an equation of Love and desire; and all that Socrates needs after that is the admission that all desire is for possession. He could then assume Agathon's assent to the proposition that Love is a desire for possession.

Indeed, that is the apparent sequence of thought as the text of the *Symposium* has it; but the assumption that *all* desire is for possession is not made explicit, but rather worked into the texture of Socrates' speech, disposing of the problem of the strong man's desire for strength. Without such an explicitly universal assumption, the reader might want to deny that love of a person was the same sort of desire as that for less personal objects and to suggest that to treat the two as the same is to equivocate.

We need, therefore, if we are to maintain our use of Agathon's speech, to be quite sure that Agathon would be willing actually to treat Love as a desire to possess. We saw that Agathon was less than fully explicit in equating 'Love' and 'desire' over the whole range of their applications, though affording Socrates a toehold for his dialectic. We should next examine, 1, what he says or implies about possession and its relation to Love or desire. About the relation to Love of the desire of good things, we can seek enlightenment in a passage about Apollo. We then need to know, 2, whether Agathon envisaged any desire for things not good. We may, further, look, 3, for signs of a failure by Agathon to distinguish between desire of an object and love of a person. We may, lastly, see, 4, whether and why Agathon can be committed to the notion that desire ceases at the moment of possession.

1   According to Agathon (p.71, 197A), Apollo, like other deities, discovered various arts under the leadership and teaching of love and desire. Plainly, though inexplicitly, it is Apollo and the other deities who experience the relevant love and desire. The object of that love and desire is presumably the arts he eventually discovers. Theoretically, Apollo might have been inspired by love of a third party to work on archery, medicine, and prophecy, but this was neither mentioned in the letter nor in harmony with the spirit of Greek myths. Now Apollo was manifestly not in possession of the arts he desired before he discovered them. Doubtless when Agathon speaks of the beautiful things through whose love all good things have come to gods and men (who did not possess them before) he includes these arts among them. But if all good things have come to men through desire, then desire must precede the acquisition of anything good. One desires something good before one has it and at a time when one does not have it. We are on the way to the doctrine that one desires and loves only what one does not possess. But we are still a long way from that goal. So far we have dealt only with good things. Does Agathon envisage any other object of desire?

2   For reasons which will become apparent we enter on this topic by examining the relation holding, according to Agathon, between good and beautiful, bad and ugly. We start with the pair beautiful/ugly. Agathon in his speech declares (p.71, 197B) that love is obviously of beauty, since love is not attached to ugliness. This may mean (see below) that love is only of beautiful things, since it is not of ugly things. Here the word 'since' is significant. If Agathon is prepared to argue that love is obviously of beauty (or of beautiful things) on the grounds that it is not of ugliness (or not of ugly things), then in the absence of any explicit distinction it is reasonable to assume that he sees no state between beauty and ugliness (or

nothing which is neither beautiful nor ugly). If there is any such state (or thing) he appears to ignore it as not being available, according to his logic, as an object of love. His argument is one by elimination; if available, the *tertium quid* would have needed elimination. Hence, in interpreting Agathon on love, one may ignore the possibility of a state neither beauty nor ugliness (or of a thing neither beautiful nor ugly).

Let us turn to the pair good/beautiful. On this pair it is not legitimate to use Agathon's admissions from the end of his argument with Socrates (pp 78ff., 201C). If it were, we could dive into the appendix which Socrates adds to his main line of questions and come up with Agathon's agreement that good things are beautiful.[17] But that later agreement itself demands explanation, so that we cannot make use of it to unravel a tangle earlier in the dialogue. In his main speech, Agathon offered in some sense a separation of goodness and beauty. He treated the good qualities and the beauties of Eros as distinct, setting them forth mostly in distinct parts of his speech. 'Mostly', because at the end of his encomium Agathon links the good and the beautiful in a single sentence, perhaps to provide a felicitously summatory climax before his peroration. In that final sentence (p.72, 197B) he says that (all) good things arise from the love of beautiful things.[18]

The best way to proceed from this point is by way of supposing for the sake of the argument that (contrary to Agathon's later admission mentioned above) there exists a good thing which is not beautiful. On that hypothesis there would exist, according to the climax of Agathon's speech, a good thing which arises from the love of beautiful things but which is not itself beautiful. Since Agathon has implied the identity, at least for objects of love, of non-beautiful and ugly, a *non-beautiful* good arising from the love of beautiful things would be ugly. An ugly thing would have arisen from the love of the beautiful. That may sound to us plausible, rather than absurd. But how does it happen, in Agathon's discourse? If by accident then love is not responsible, and not all good things arise through love, as Agathon says they do. If love *is* responsible, then love must produce something ugly. But, according to Agathon, one cannot hand over or impart what he does not possess. As Agathon puts it (pp70ff., 196E), 'no one can impart or teach to another what he does not possess or does not know.'¹⁹ So love must be in possession of something ugly, in order to be able to impart it – and the Greek for 'impart' here is a word meaning simply 'give', a word of the most general kind, not to be limited to the arts. This result, that love must possess something ugly, would be thoroughly out of keeping with the spirit, even though it does not formally contradict the letter, of Agathon's encomium on Love as the happiest and most beautiful of the gods.

This reduction of Agathon to near contradiction deserves supplement: we showed earlier that things which come to gods and men come, according to Agathon, because the things are themselves the objects of desire. Hence, all the good things which come are beautiful, being the objects of love. By parity of reasoning with our previous argument, if there is a beautiful thing which is not good, it will be bad, and hence not an appropriate gift for the Love of Agathon's encomium. Good things and beautiful things ought indeed to be coextensive classes according to Agathon. But, on the other hand, even the weaker 'All good things are beautiful' would match rather ill with Agathon's primary division of his praise of love between good and beautiful qualities. Agathon has had things both ways in his speech. What Plato is doing in creating a character who has things both ways, is a question still to be deferred.

3   What of the two types of desire? Did Agathon distinguish or fail to distinguish the longing for an impersonal object from the love of a person? Most of his speech was concerned with attributes more or less fancifully shown to belong to the god of human love in its sexual form(s). But the god's 'wisdom' is another matter. Partly sexual, in that Eros is expert in the creation of living animals, Eros' 'wisdom' appears in his function as the instigator of arts which he must possess before he can hand them on. Sexual love, as the modern world knows, can be the source of a poet's skill or wisdom – personal love can (as apparently in the case of the composer Elgar) inspire a creative artist. But Apollo and the other deities Agathon mentions did not, so far as we can see, acquire their arts in this way. There is no reason to suppose

Agathon to be thinking of sexual love here.[20] The sentence giving the case of Apollo is a continuation[21] of an argument making Love, as the teacher of the arts, expressly the same god as the deity responsible for procreation: Apollo's sentence makes him *also* the pupil of Love – presumably the same deity again. Apollo's Love, then, is the same Love as is involved in procreation. The person of Eros in Agathon's speech confounds the personal and sexual aspects of desire with a more general desire.

We may even suspect that Plato represents Agathon as half aware of this, since Agathon describes Apollo as acting under the guidance of Love and desire, in what looks like an effort to assimilate two distinct things. Nevertheless, half aware, wholly aware, or unaware, Agathon in his argument requires his listeners to forget the distinction which Socrates and Agathon appear to forget in the subsequent discussion.

It is not enough, in order to rebut this, to suggest that sex and the arts are different skills or wisdoms of Eros; they are indeed, but in Agathon's view they are skills of the same Eros, and it is more than one kind of *Eros* that he needs to fend off Socrates' questions. All this may serve as a reason for Agathon's and Socrates' convenient lapse in forgetting the difference between general desire and love. It does not of itself excuse Plato for so constructing his argument, nor does it yet shake the modern reader's tendency to believe that Plato is cheating. But it is easier to finish with Plato's Socrates before we turn our attention to Plato himself.

4 The ceasing of desire at the moment of possession is bound up with the argument that desire for what one possesses is in fact a desire for continued future possession which is not yet to hand. Two questions about this argument deserve an airing here. One is how this too is supported by Agathon's encomium; the other is how to defend it against Dover's powerful attack, of which more below.

The particular case at issue between Socrates and Agathon is that of Love's beauty. Agathon could say that Love desires his beauty to be continued, and it is in this sense that love desires that of which it is the love. By this means he could have hoped to evade the admission he tumbles into that Love (at present) lacks beauty. But Socrates has chosen his ground well. For Agathon has himself closed off this last escape-route. He appeared to hold in his speech that Eros is *always* beautiful. For that reason he need feel no desire to be always beautiful. To desire the continuation of his beauty would be to desire what is already, to use Socrates' terminology, 'in his power' or, as I should prefer to render it, 'available'.[22]

Three passages of Agathon's speech are relevant (p.68, 195B–C; p.69, 195E; p.69, 196A). Eros 'stays always with the young', as Plato has it; Hamilton slightly obscures my point by rendering this sentence as 'His whole life is passed in the company of the young.' Secondly, Agathon said on the subject of Love's tenderness that Eros, touching as he does 'always' the softest of the soft, is himself the tenderest.[23] Thirdly Agathon remarked that Love is *always* at war with unseemliness ('awkwardness is absolutely incompatible with Love'), and that is why Love is supple. Altogether four attributes make up Love's beauty according to Agathon. The word 'always' finds itself associated with three of them. This is already a proportion we cannot ignore. The fourth, Love's beauty of complexion, does not carry the word 'always', but Agathon does tell us that Love not only 'settles' wherever he finds a spot that is flowery and fragrant, he 'abides' there (p.69, 196B).

But does Love not still have the power to wish for his beauty to last? Does availability of fulfilment exclude the wish? For Socrates, arguing as he does from Agathon's words, I think the answer to this is that Love's beauty is *necessarily* permanent. In his excursus on health and strength, Socrates adduces the case of the strong and swift-footed by saying that 'these people must inevitably possess these qualities at the present moment, whether they want to or not, and who would desire that?' (p.77, 200C).[24] It is clearly the inevitable and necessary that people do not, as Socrates gets Agathon implicitly to admit, desire. But the probabilities are that Love is, in Agathon's speech, necessarily and inevitably beautiful. The section on sensitivity says (p.69, 195E) that, clinging as he does to the softest of the soft, he is necessarily most soft. It is not clear whether the necessity of this passage is what mediaeval logic apparently called the *necessitas conse-*

quentiae or is the *necessitas consequentis*. It could refer to the necessity of Agathon's reasoning or to the necessity of the conclusion in itself. But Agathon will certainly, and Plato probably, have been ignorant of this distinction.

And there is more to come. 'It is the nature of Love to hate old age,' says Agathon (p.68, 195B); and Love presumably cannot escape his nature. His youth, then, is also an inescapable feature of his being. There is no point in Love wishing to be young or wishing to be tender; both are inevitable whether he wishes or not. Again, it may be relevant that Love *possesses* gracefulness in a special way, for he is 'always' at war with gracelessness (p.69, 196A).[25] Whatever degree of relevance this last observation has, Love possesses half his beautiful qualities necessarily; that is, in the manner which for Socrates (with Agathon's agreement) appears to make desire pointless. Agathon has indeed gone quite a long way towards covering Socrates against a charge of ignoring a sense in which desire maintains itself over time during possession of the desired object. If Agathon were to oppose Socrates on these issues, he would have to evince a degree of dialectical subtlety not normally within the range of Greek tragic poets in the fifth or the fourth century BC.

But we should return to Dover's attack on this whole argument of Socrates', an attack which remains hard to counter. Indeed, in its own or other modern terms it is (so far as I can see) unanswerable. It runs like this:[26] 'A real interlocutor might say, "I am wise/rich/strong in many ways or to a great extent, but I wish to be wise (etc.) in more ways or to a greater extent."' Clearly, this would demolish Socrates' argument as an independent piece of reasoning. But we have already seen that to treat Socrates' reasoning as independent of its wider context is to miss at least some of its point.

The thorough exploration of Dover's criticism and Socrates' probable answer would take us too far afield at present. But the reader might like to bear in mind that the reasoning agreed between Socrates and Agathon can be rescued on certain assumptions looking as if they had at least a place in the pages of Plato. The trouble with Socrates' argument, as Dover has seen, is that it does not suffice to exclude Love's possession of *some* beauty; it suffices only to exclude his absolute and entire perfection of beauty, a perfection which Agathon has not, strictly speaking, attributed to him. But the ascription of even some beauty to Love would run into trouble if (a) Beauty were a beautiful thing, and (b) Love lacked all beautiful things. It would then follow that Love lacked all beauty. How far we are entitled to lend these assumptions to Socrates, to Agathon, or to both is a question to be deferred. But it is perhaps worth remarking that (a) and (b) cannot simply *replace* Socrates' whole argument; for at least (b) depends, in the *Symposium*, on that argument, or on something very like a part of that argument, for its plausibility.[27] Let us keep (a) and (b) in mind.

Socrates now recapitulates Agathon's replies; and we may collect our thoughts too. Every question Socrates has asked has been explanatory of Agathon's original encomium. In each question Socrates either extracts from Agathon a relatively clear inference, or he asks for the resolution of a difficulty or ambiguity. But it is not until Socrates renews his questioning after recapitulation that Socrates for the first time quotes expressly from Agathon (p.78, 201A). Why this is so is a question as much about Plato as about Socrates, and the reader is asked to suspend any disbelief until we discuss what Plato is doing here. Suspension may draw encouragement from the fact that Socrates began (p.75, 199C–D) with a reference to the speech, in the shape of a request for a supplement to it, and now begins anew with another reference to it.

This symmetry suggests, though it does not prove, that the distribution of explicit mention of the speech, as opposed to oblique reference, is due at least in part to formal literary considerations. This possibility may stave off a few obvious objections while we finish Socrates' line of questioning. That line, after a brief collection of the premises, hurries, perhaps a little too rapidly, to its conclusion (pp.77–8, 200E–201B). It needs a somewhat more formal exposition to make it readily intelligible; 'somewhat' because I am no logician. I submit both a more formal and a more discursive version of some parts of the argument, in the hope that some clarity may emerge.

Socrates and a tragic poet

A (more formal, and denoting Love by the symbol L)
1. $(L) (\exists x$ such that L is L of x)
2. $(x) [(L$ is L of $x) \rightarrow (L$ desires $x)]$
3. $(x) [(L$ desires $x) \rightarrow \sim (L$ possesses $x)]$
4. $(x) ([[(L$ possesses $x) + (L$ desires $x)]$ means $[(L$ possesses $x) + (L$ desires the continued possession of $x)]])$
   [Hence 3 cannot be refuted by an apparent example of (L possesses x and L desires x).]
5. $(x) [(x$ came to the gods) $\rightarrow (x$ came to the gods through the love of beautiful things)]
6. (a) When things came to the gods, the Love concerned was of beautiful things *because*
   (b) $(L) [\sim (L$ is of something ugly)]
7. $(L) [(L$ is love of $x) \rightarrow (x$ is beauty) $\therefore$ nec. $\sim (x$ is ugliness)]
8. $\sim (L$ possesses beauty)
9. $\sim (L$ is beautiful)

B (more discursive)
1. All cases of Love are Love of something.
2. All Love desires that of which it is the Love.
3. No Love possesses what it desires.
4. If Love claims to possess what it desires, the claim means 'Love desires the continued possession of what it already possesses.' [Hence 3 cannot be refuted by such a claim.]
5. All things came to the gods through the love of beautiful things.
6. (a) Love was on that occasion 'of' beautiful things because
   (b) there is no love of ugly things.
7. All Love of something is love of beauty, because Love cannot be attached to ugliness.
8. Love does not possess beauty.
9. Love is not beautiful.

This is still too brief, and its logic needs examination. A few preliminaries are necessary before we broach the peculiar difficulties of 7. At least 2 is either meaningless or false, and 3 and 4 are meaningless or hopelessly irrelevant without it; but, as Socrates says, Agathon has already agreed to 1, 2, 3 and 4. 5 is avowedly from Agathon's speech in praise of Love; 6(a) is lightly modified from that speech. 6(b) is specially important for Socrates' dialectic, being essential for the derivation of 7. Its importance lies in the impossibility of drawing any general conclusion about Love from 5 and 6(a) alone; so far as Love is concerned, 5 and 6(a) are 'singular' propositions, relating what happened on a single occasion. 6(b) is the first admission to afford Socrates a general expression. But it suffices. As we have seen, Agathon's argument by elimination is such that, if it is enough, in order to prove that the love experienced by the gods is of beautiful things, to exclude the ugliness of any object of love, then not only is no object of love ugly, but also no object of love is neither ugly nor beautiful. There is, then, a sense in which the general connection of Love with beauty is a consequence of 6(a), 6(b) and the linking 'because'.

But in what sense is 7 to be taken? The sentence 'Love is of beauty' is open, in Greek as in English, to two quite different interpretations.[28] This may become clearer if we consider the sentence 'I love (all) small things.' If that were true, I could say, without altering my feelings or the sense of my remark, and without doing violence to language, 'I love smallness.' There would not normally be any question of my (abstract?) love for the abstract concept of smallness; the object of my love would be every concrete example of smallness. The case of 'I desire smallness' is similar, though with a complication. 'I desire smallness' can mean 'I desire small objects' (or, in some contexts, 'I desire a small object of a certain class'); but it could also mean 'I desire to be small.' At least linguistic intuition suggests that it could; but I admit that 'I desire smallness' does not sound very natural to me in either sense. 'I love smallness' sounds to me much more natural; but so far as I know, Greek offers no such difference between 'love'-words and 'desire'-words, and desire appears with abstract objects no less often than words for 'love'. This adds a slight complication, in that 'I love smallness' would not normally be understood as saying 'I love to be small.' But the central point, in danger of obfuscation by such detail, is that as an object of verbs such as 'love' an abstract noun may *either* denote a property *or* serve as a collective noun for things possessing that property. 'I love beauty' may signify *either* 'I love the abstract "beauty"' or 'I love all beautiful things in so far as (*or* to the extent that) they are beautiful.'

The significance of this ambiguity in Plato's context is crucial. For it follows without difficulty from 5, 6(a) and 6(b) above that all Love is of beauty in the sense that all Love is of beautiful things. But if, in 'all Love/desire is of beauty', 'beauty' be read as a property, then the original 'all Love is of beauty' does *not* follow from the propositions corresponding to the circumstances delineated in 5, 6(a) and 6(b). Yet it must be the *property* 'beauty' which Love desires and hence lacks, or Socrates' and Agathon's joint conclusion that Love is not beautiful will not follow. From the reading with 'beauty' as a collective no conclusion helpful to Socrates can be drawn; yet the reading with 'beauty' as an abstract property is *not* a legitimate conclusion from Agathon's previous admissions. Plato's Socrates appears at 7 simply to have equivocated on two senses of 'Love is of beauty': a sense in which it follows from 5 and 6, and another quite different sense in which 8 follows from it.

But the expression 'Love of beauty' came in the first instance from Agathon's encomium, and ought therefore to receive scrutiny in its context there. Its source, we recall, is the last paragraph before the formal peroration (p.71, 197B). In that paragraph the sentence 'Similarly, it was the birth of Love – love of beauty, no doubt, since Love cannot attach himself to ugliness – which composed the troubles of the gods' stands rhetorically parallel to the next sentence but one: 'But as soon as this god was born, the love of beauty gave rise to all manner of blessings for gods and men.'

I have quoted the second of these sentences exactly as Hamilton's generally admirable translation has them. But the translation obscures a point of logic, even while it demonstrates that the translator was to some extent aware of it. For the Greek says there not 'love of beauty' but 'love of beautiful things'. The translator's interpretation is right, in that 'love of beautiful things' is surely to be taken as Agathon's own gloss, saying less ambiguously what he meant, on his earlier

'Love of beauty'. This gloss could only arise if 'Love of beauty' uses 'beauty' as a collective giving a proposition which, though it follows from Agathon's earlier remarks, does not help towards the conclusion. Agathon says nothing – or nothing explicit – about any sense of 'Love of beauty' which might help Socrates. Why, then, should we acquit Socrates and/or Plato of the fallacy of equivocation? What sort of defence, if any, could one put up? Or what sort of plea in mitigation?

One should not dismiss out of hand the possibility of Plato's having made an honest mistake. It is not so easy to disentangle the various uses of abstract nouns that one should necessarily expect a sure touch in the matter from a philosopher, however gifted, of the fourth century BC. But there is an alternative to the theory of an error by Plato. That is an error by the Platonic Socrates, knowingly composed by Plato. If Plato did knowingly assign such an error to his Socrates, it would be difficult, and Plato has not obviously tried, to tell the reader of this sort of narrative whether Socrates made the error knowingly or not. If he made it knowingly, his intentions might have been either deceitful or dialectical. If there were any remarks in Agathon's encomium bearing on relevant distinctions these might or might not constitute evidence that Socrates was deliberately exploiting Agathon's words here as elsewhere rather than deceiving him by mere rhetorical sleight of hand. The decision would have to rest on considerations such as the degree and the clarity of the relevance of Agathon's reasoning to Socrates'. Different people might reach different views on such questions. But the evidence, such as it is, deserves exposition, whether the conclusion be positive or negative.

First, Agathon said in his speech that Love is of beauty; only several lines later did he use the expression 'love of beautiful things'. The listening Socrates could not, as a reader could, glance forward and back from one expression to the other. Agathon's first remark was ambiguous. It is a question whether the consistency of Agathon's later sentence with only one of two possible meanings necessarily excludes the other meaning from all Socratic consideration. Agathon is not always, in Socrates' eyes at least, consistent. Perhaps

Socrates and a tragic poet

Socrates should strive to obtain full clarity about Agathon's thinking, by putting a question and seeing what answer Agathon gives. Agathon might be unclear on the precise meaning of his own words, and might inadvertently acquiesce in an equivocation on them. Socrates, one might argue, is not obliged to correct his interlocutor's reasoning. But, if one takes this view, in as bald a form as this, then one is attributing to Socrates a greater degree of cynicism than is necessary elsewhere in the dialogues we are analysing and one is confirming the most damaging suspicions of Plato's methods.

Perhaps more typical of Socrates' and Plato's procedures would be the exploitation of other, more transparent equivocations in Agathon's big speech. Thus Agathon plays twice (p.70, 196C and 196D) on the verb Hamilton renders by the English words 'mastery', or 'be (the) master'; Agathon uses it as it suits him to signify either 'control' or 'be superior to'. It is difficult to believe that we are not intended to take this as a deliberate pun on the part of Agathon. Possibly also (but not more than possibly), the use of Eros to cover both personal love and desire for an object struck Plato as a similar exploitation of ambiguity. Perhaps Plato so constructed Agathon's argument as to make it risky for him to attack Socrates for equivocation; the risk would lie in exposure to the '*tu quoque*' or 'pot and kettle' retort. The use of one's opponent's modes of inference, however faulty, is a feature of Socratic dialectic on more than one occasion. But in order to postulate an instance of such practice here, we should have to believe, e.g., that Plato thought the ambiguity of the abstract 'beauty' as easy, or nearly as easy, to detect as that of control/superiority. This is, on the whole, hard to believe.

One could look for an escape-mechanism less damaging to Plato's repute in the logical relationships between 6, 7 and 8 as Socrates himself relates them. The most relevant passage of dialogue forms part of Socrates' summary of previous admissions (p.78, 201A–B).[29] He asks Agathon to confirm that Love is of an object, and that the object must be something Love lacks. He then reminds Agathon of what he said, or rather something like what he said.[30] In Socrates' version the activities of the gods were set up as a result of the love of beautiful things; for there could be no love of ugly things. In truth this is 'something like' what Agathon said (p. 71, 197B). This is not quite the context in which Agathon mentioned 'things', and he did not actually mention ugly things at all. He did mention ugliness.

Socrates' next piece of recapitulation, after Agathon has accepted the account of his remarks so far, is 'If that is so, Love will be love of beauty, will he not, and not of ugliness?' This too is not absolutely exact as a repetition of Agathon's words, as Hamilton and other translators have clearly noticed. Agathon had not ventured 'Love of ugliness', but had used a preposition meaning here something like 'attached to'. Agathon's statement that Love does not attach himself to ugliness is perhaps composed deliberately so as to avoid the collocation 'Love of ugliness', and to suggest that what is really being denied is that Love is *of* ugly *things*. But, if so, Agathon's suggestion is at best very indirect. If not, then Socrates' variation here on Agathon is of little or no significance.

But the nagging question remains, where do the ugly things come from which Socrates introduces in the second of his two recapitulatory questions? Was he justified in extracting them from the beautiful things that Agathon does mention? So far it looks as though Socrates may have done little or nothing but tidy up Agathon's syntax in his request for confirmation. But, if we look closer, we shall find he has done rather more.

What Socrates has done is to put the two sentences he has tidied up into a close logical relationship. *If* the first is true, he asks, isn't the second true (p. 78, 201A)? And Agathon agrees, presumably not only to the second proposition, but also to the logical relationship. But this raises the same difficulty as we had before, in a sharpened form: for the allegation that the proposition offered in the second question follows from that offered in the first is false, if the second be taken in a sense which will allow the subsequent deduction of Love's lack of beauty. So why should Agathon accept that 'Love is of beauty' follows from 'Love is love of beautiful things' in a sense allowing the inference that Love lacks the property of beauty?

If Agathon's simpler ambiguities will not suffice to answer

this question, what will? Has Agathon done anything similar with abstracts and their collectives? The answer to this is 'Yes'. It does not follow, however, that this affirmative is relevant to the question what Plato is doing. The similarity of inference between Socrates' line of questioning and passages of Agathon's speech could be coincidental. But we have seen that Agathon's speech is the source of other apparent peculiarities of Socrates' questioning, and we shall see more such evidence in what follows; though coincidence cannot be excluded, a hard look is in order at the possibility that Plato has deliberately constructed a likeness between Agathon's encomium and Socrates' chain of questions.

The relevant passage concerns old age (p.68, 195A–B). Love flees from old age, says Agathon. Old age, he adds, is swift; it comes upon us more swiftly than it should; Love by nature hates it, and will not come within a mile of it. Love's hatred, in this last sentence, comes into the picture presumably 'since one does not usually fall in love with old people', as Dover has it.[31] For practical purposes 'old age' stands for 'old people' here, and presumably also in the first statement too, to the effect that 'Love flees from old age.' The two statements depend for their immediate plausibility on the fact that the old are not normally the subjects or objects of sexual passion. But the intervening image is somewhat different. 'Old age is swift' or 'Old age moves fast' cannot be taken to mean 'old people are swift': it means, as Agathon promptly explains, that old age comes too rapidly upon us. 'Old age' here does not stand for 'old people'. Yet the old age that Love flees from is the same word in one and the same occurrence as the old age which is swift.

If one wanted to stretch a point in order to save the fictional Agathon's sentence and its image from confusion, one could suppose that Love's flight from old age stands after all for the fading of sexual passion and sexual attractiveness as one grows old: Love, in that case, flees *as* old age swiftly approaches us;[32] we then have to construe the last sentence of Agathon's conceit as saying that Love does not come within a mile of old age in the sense that years before we grow old our passions are spent. But whatever the young may think of old age, it is adequately known that sexual passion does not fade away completely in middle age, long years before old age creeps up on one. Further, the most obvious and natural interpretation of Love's revulsion from old age is not this but the one Dover gives. The inference should be that Agathon has (understandably) been careless about 'old age': it represents *both* old age *and* old people at the same time in the course of the same argument.

Furthermore, he has produced a sentence which needs an abstract to function as a collective and as a genuine abstract at different points in its argument. 'Old age' is both an attribute, which belongs to people at one time but not at another, and the set of people advanced in years. Indeed this shift contributes not a little piquancy to the poetic effectiveness of Agathon's image. More significantly for our present purposes, the shift is very like the one we have noticed in Socrates' interrogation of Agathon on the topic of beauty.

What would happen if Agathon were to tax Socrates openly with foisting a logical blunder on him? The accusation could reasonably contain a statement that in the particular case at issue, that of beauty, Agathon had got it right. His remark about the love of beautiful things had shown a correct understanding of his own usage of 'beauty'. Justice would suggest that Socrates ignore the dubious logic of other arguments. Socrates could, however, have retorted that if he was making a mistake in logic, perhaps Agathon would explain the mistake? Suppose Agathon were (improbably) capable of such explanation, Socrates could follow up with a request that he eat his words about old age, which take a prominent and rather important position at the opening of his encomium. Agathon could agree to do this; he could even go on to declare that his treatment of old age belonged to the admittedly playful parts of his speech (p.72, 197E). But retraction here, as elsewhere in Plato, would lead to loss of face and is therefore put off till too late. (One answer Agathon could not give: he could not say he had used 'beauty' only in the collective and never in the abstract sense (see p.69, 196A and 196B).)

But would a reader capable of appreciating the logical difficulty of Socrates' handling of Agathon on beauty and beautiful things also appreciate the ambiguity of 'old age' in

Agathon's trope? One cannot be sure, and certainly one cannot be sure that Plato would have so judged; but the possibility remains alive.

So far we have expounded a difficulty in an inference Agathon accepts (p. 78, 201A). The inference runs *from*

A   (i) Love is of beautiful things *because*
    (ii) Love is not of ugly things
to
B   (i) Love is of beauty *and*
    (ii) Love is not of ugliness.

We have suggested a possible parallel with an inference Agathon draws in his own speech. But a flawed inference invites the suggestion of extra premisses to restore logic, and we should inspect this particular inference with that in mind.

We could try adding to the premisses here a further assumption, of a type much discussed in Platonic scholarship, to the effect that

C   (i) Beauty is a beautiful thing and
    (ii) Ugliness is an ugly thing.[33]

We should remember that B may be taken in two ways, one which is legitimately deduced but useless, and the other illegitimate but helpful to Socrates. The helpful sense of B follows by the simplest of syllogisms from A and C:

(i) Love is of beautiful things;
Beauty is a beautiful thing;
therefore Love is of Beauty.

(ii) Love is not of ugly things;
Ugliness is an ugly thing;
therefore Love is not of Ugliness.

But this simplicity of reasoning is purchasable only at a price. The price is the compulsion to answer the question why Agathon should tacitly accept assumption C. Even if we could establish Plato's perception and employment of the potential importance of C in this context, a further question would remain. One could still have to decide whether Plato thought Socrates could establish from Agathon's main speech Agathon's belief in C and hence expect Agathon to acknowledge B in the sense Socrates needs, or whether Plato thought that his Agathon had assented to both A and (by implication) the required sense of B for reasons independent of C. The second alternative we have, in effect explored already; let us look at the first. Exploration is the more urgent in that Socrates tacitly uses the assumption that Beauty is a beautiful thing in the dialogue for purposes of considerable philosophical significance.[34]

Let us search Agathon's encomium for something comparable to C. Does he anywhere treat an abstract as an instance of itself? If to treat Love as a lover is to do so, the answer is clearly 'Yes'. But the relation of Love and lover is not that between abstract and instance: Love is not the same thing as loverhood. The relation is rather that between passion and victim (or beneficiary). Eros *possesses* the attribute of gracefulness, but eros 'possesses' Ares. Plato's Agathon shows no detectable signs of confusing Love with loverhood before confounding Love and the lover. Nor does old age, in the passage analysed above, find itself confused with, or by implication designated as, an old individual; it stands rather either for an abstract or for a collective and it is not *an* individual that Love avoids but the whole class of the old. Nor does the conjunctive phrase 'characters and souls' (p.69, 195E) confound a soul which instantiates a character with the character in a relevant way: 'character' and 'characteristic' are distinct things. It is in fact very difficult to read out of Agathon's speech directly any example of a confusion between abstract quality and concrete instance. If Agathon is guilty of any confusion it is more likely to be that between abstract and collective. It results that Agathon's speech offers no *direct* support for the proposition that beauty is itself beautiful.

But, whether Plato realized it or not, there is indirect support for the beauty of Beauty in Agathon's speech. Agathon does refer to the beauty of Eros. He excludes, as we have seen, the possibility of anything being neither beautiful nor ugly. It is extremely unlikely that he would countenance for a moment the suggestion that beauty is ugly. Can one imagine him agreeing that the very beauty he attributes to Eros is ugly? If not, he must then suppose that Beauty is beautiful.

The exclusion by Agathon's argument from elimination of the third class, of things neither beautiful nor ugly, is perhaps of more far-reaching significance than he ever dreamt of or than Plato's readers have normally supposed. If one is confronted with the stark choice whether beauty is beautiful or ugly, and is forbidden to say that it is neither, there can be very little doubt which most of us would choose. The alternative likely to be most popular, that beauty is not the sort of thing to be either beautiful or ugly, is ruled out. The only further alternative would be to deny the meaningfulness of the question; but many of us, including an Agathon, might have grave difficulty in distinguishing between 'The question whether X is beautiful or ugly is meaningless' and 'X is neither beautiful nor ugly.' What is more, with this additional premiss we can account for Agathon's acceptance of the inference from A above to B. For it becomes the simplest of syllogisms:

> Love is of beautiful things;
> Beauty is beautiful;
> *Therefore*
> Love is of beauty.
> *And*
> Love is not of ugly things;
> Ugliness is an ugly thing;
> *Therefore*
> Love is not of ugliness.

But, before we accept this on Agathon's behalf, there are two precautions we must take in the matter of quantifiers. The inference we have made Agathon accept depends on 'Love is of beautiful things' being construed as 'Love is of *all* beautiful things.' Now, in the outline of Agathon's reasoning given at the outset of this discussion, proposition 6 commits him to the proposition that there is no love of anything not-beautiful or ugly; but it does not commit him to the proposition that Love is of *all* beautiful things. And proposition 7 has to be construed as being about beautiful things, rather than about beauty, in order to yield 'Love is of all beautiful things', in the sense that 'There is no beautiful thing of which there is not Love.' Indeed it is doubtful, in the absence of any quantifiers, whether it would yield the required proposition even if taken in that sense. If there is any indication at all in Agathon's speech that he would accept 'There is no beautiful thing of which there is not Love', it is to be found in the definite article in one sentence. The sentence reads (p.71, 197B): 'On account of loving (the) beautiful things all good things have come to gods and men.' Generalizations about the Greek definite article strike many scholars (including me) as risky. A determined interpreter could, I suppose, read the article in this sentence as referring back ('anaphorically') to the particular things loved by the gods specified earlier in Agathon's paragraph. But such a reading would be doubtful. The whole tone of the sentence is one of airy generalization. Socrates could with a fairly high degree of probability on his side understand Agathon to be saying that *all and only* beautiful things are the object of Love.

We must unpack a second precaution: if 'Love is of beauty' is to lead to 'All love lacks beauty' (which seems to be needed), it must be *all* love that is of beauty. But the first of our two syllogisms above shows *not* that *all* Love is of Beauty, but that *some* Love is of Beauty. A man might, obviously, urge that his love for his wife is not the same love as the love of beauty. Why, then, even granted the propositions we have granted, should his love of his wife not be beautiful? Why should it lack beauty? I do not know any valid answer to the question as put; and the feature of the *Symposium* which takes account of it is not easy to define.

This feature concerns not a narrow philosophical or dialectical point, but the dual nature of Eros. Eros is both passion and god. It is hard to be sure in the *Symposium* which the speakers are talking about at any given moment, and difficult to know whether Plato or his characters were any clearer than the modern reader. The unwary modern reader may be misled by the modern practice of using upper-and lower-case initial letters; no such graphical aid was available to the Greeks of Plato's day. But one suspects that for the guests at the *Symposium* the eros a man feels for his wife was not just a passion felt by one individual for another; it was also an instance of the god's presence. The god Eros is not present piecemeal; nor does Agathon distinguish more than one god of the same name, as Phaedrus rather unusually did in his earlier speech. The god, the whole god, one must presume, is present in every case.

In Agathon's speech, it is Eros who touches each person and makes a poet of him; it is 'this god' who teaches any craftsman of note; Eros teaches and guides Apollo and the other gods. There are not many gods Eros, even if there are many passions of an 'erotic' nature. If there is an Eros who loves, desires and lacks beauty, it is that same Eros who is present in the man who loves his wife. In the religious context of Agathon's speech, the distinction between 'some love' and 'all Love' is difficult to maintain. We may reasonably doubt if Plato, in this religious context, ever even spotted the logical problem with which our second precaution was concerned.

It could be concluded from 'Love is of beauty' in the syllogisms above that there is only one beautiful thing, namely beauty. But this conclusion is subject to at least two difficulties, one minor and one major. The minor is that in Agathon's speech we hear of Love not only of beauty but also of Aphrodite (p.70, 196D), and that Socrates makes Diotima refer to 'the beautiful and Aphrodite who is beautiful' (p.82, 203C). But it is not hard to believe that in both contexts Aphrodite symbolizes beauty; and Diotima might be using 'and' to link two equivalent expressions rather than two different things. But Diotima on beauty and the beautiful is a large topic, to be deferred for consideration of other things she says.

The major difficulty is that Agathon speaks of other beautiful things besides beauty. Beauty for him is not the only thing which is beautiful. Indeed, if it were, much of his argument would collapse. But that at least does not have to worry Socrates, who is by no means concerned at this juncture to do the best he can for Agathon. Socrates himself can continue to speak of beautiful things in the plural, and cause his Diotima to do the same. For Agathon is in no position to say him nay. Socrates and Diotima might want ultimately to say something like 'Beauty is the only thing which is truly beautiful; all the other things called beautiful are only pale imitations'; indeed it looks as if to save his own consistency Socrates would have to take refuge in something of this sort. But there is no need to attribute any such suggestion to Agathon. Socrates is, as we shall see, conducting a dialectical argument with Agathon throughout, and if Agathon cannot voice the necessary criticism without eating words, that is good enough in dialectic. But on Diotima, Socrates, and Agathon there is more to be said, and it must wait.

There are, meanwhile, a couple of points to illustrate the explanatory power of the present hypothesis, that the line of reasoning through which Socrates takes Agathon draws on Agathon's indirect implication that Beauty is a beautiful thing. The first explains the shape of the inference whose acceptance by Agathon we have been discussing. That inference went from A – Love is a beautiful thing *because* Love is not of ugly things – to B – Love is of beauty *and* Love is not of ugliness. The presence of 'because' in A as opposed to the 'and' which links the twin propositions of B is susceptible of double explanation. It mirrors the 'since' appearing in the parallel context in Agathon's speech (p.71, 197B); and, as we have just seen, the argument by elimination enshrined in that 'because' contributes an important premiss to the argument needed to get from A to B. No such 'because' is necessary in the conclusion B.

The second illustrative point concerns an objection to Socrates which we have already canvassed, but deferred.[35] The objection runs that Love need not lack all beauty simply because he lacks some beauty: that one can be wise in some respects and to some degree but desire to be wise in other respects and/or to a higher degree, and that the same is true of the desire 'to be beautiful' or 'of beauty'. One can rebut this argument on the assumptions that Love lacks all beautiful things, and that beauty is a beautiful thing. If we accept that beauty is a beautiful thing, we have, it would seem, no reason to deny that any degree of beauty is to some extent a beautiful thing.[36] If Love is of, and hence desires, and hence lacks, all beautiful things, then Love by that token lacks all and any degree of beauty. Agathon is committed to 'Love is of, and hence desires, and hence lacks Beauty' in the sense that 'Love is of, and hence desires, and hence lacks all beautiful things.' Once we have committed him also to 'Beauty is beautiful', he cannot then deny that Love lacks beauty, nor, without qualifying 'Beauty is beautiful', can he qualify 'Love lacks beauty'. But it is difficult, in view of the argument given above, to see how he could possibly qualify 'Beauty is beautiful'.

The whole train of thought behind Socrates' interrogation of Agathon is now of a piece. It remains uncertain whether the last parts of it depend on a type of logic Agathon has used, or on propositions deducible from Agathon's remarks, or both. But a connection with Agathon's words of praise for Love is discernible – admittedly with varying degrees of ease and clarity – throughout. The easier and clearer connections encourage one to persevere in discerning the others; and the whole gains from such perceptions a coherence and force contrasting sharply with the arbitrary illogic usually charged to Plato's account. Plato's Agathon sheds the foolish weakness he is often saddled with, just as Socrates sheds his overbearing rhetoric. This passage, at least, can now be read as a *dialogue*.

Agathon (p.78, 201B) admits the force of Socrates' dialectic. He (Agathon) spoke without knowledge as he now says. Indeed, he had not thought through all the consequences of his remarks. But Socrates has not yet finished with him and adds a rider (p.79, 201C). Agathon's encomium praised both the beauty and the goodness of Love. Agathon has now admitted the difficulties in his version of Love's beauty; what about Love's goodness? Socrates takes a short cut here. If we wish to discover whether Love possesses good things, what about the relationship between these and the beautiful things Agathon has admitted (p.78, 201A) that Love is of, and implied that he lacks? Hence Socrates' question whether Agathon thinks good things are beautiful.

This is an annoying question for Agathon, who has, as we saw earlier, had things both ways on this matter in his speech. But though theoretically, having had it both ways, he could now refuse to agree that good things are beautiful, he would not have been very likely to take that way out of Socrates' following chain of argument. For the word for 'beautiful' in Greek has a wide range of meanings including such as 'fine', 'respectable', 'estimable' and so forth.[37] Things which have the high value of 'good' put upon them are normally esteemed and respected. They are certainly not 'ugly', 'disreputable', etc., which is for Agathon the only alternative.

There is nothing out of the way about Agathon's admission.

This and the immediately subsequent responses of Agathon give the following argument:

> Love lacks all beautiful things;
> All good things are beautiful things;
> *Therefore*
> Love lacks all good things.

Thus quantified, the argument is simple and valid. It does not, for example, require the additional premiss 'All beautiful things are good'. Its validity is unaffected by any subsequent remarks in the dialogue on the relationship between 'beautiful' and 'good'.[38]

Diotima

Socrates ostensibly leaves his argument with Agathon now, and recounts his conversations with Diotima, a Mantinean prophetess who may or may not be a historical personage. But in the talks as recorded Socrates takes over the part of Agathon, and Diotima that of Socrates.[39]

The *Socrates* of the story (distinguished here by italics) has accepted exactly the same propositions (p.79, 201E) as the Agathon of the *Symposium*; and Diotima, although she has naturally not heard Agathon's encomium, and the ensuing discussion, bases her argument on Agathon's admissions and implications, or (occasionally) corrects them.

The first revelation of this situation is Socrates' first question to Diotima, when she says that Love is neither beautiful nor good: 'What do you mean, Diotima? ... Is Love ugly and bad?' The stupidity of this question, if stupidity it is, is not Socrates', but only *Socrates*'; that is to say it is Agathon's. To be sure, Socrates and Agathon have not expressly agreed together on the point. But the exhaustiveness of the alternatives 'beautiful or ugly' was for practical purposes assumed by Agathon, and used silently by Socrates in his dialectical attack on Agathon. Since *Socrates* represents Agathon, it is quite in order to put the mistake in the mouth of *Socrates*. It is accordingly unnecessary for the understanding of the passage either to imagine a youthfully ignorant or incompetent Socrates or to ascribe this sort of error to a Plato capable of correcting it himself. If Diotima corrects a misapprehension, or mis-expression, of *Socrates*, then the Platonic Socrates is correcting a misapprehension or mis-expression of Agathon's.[40] Dover's note on this passage[41] expounds magisterially the probable reasons for this exchange of roles.

Diotima points, then, to the middle way: the admission that Love is not beautiful does not entail that Love is ugly. She illustrates this with the example of the middle place occupied by true conviction between wisdom and ignorance (p.80, 202A). This particular triad will prove useful later, but is not wholly irrelevant to the wider context here. Agathon has no grounds for rejecting this Socratic or Platonic triad, and some for welcoming it. He has just admitted to knowing nothing of what he said in his encomium (p.78, 201B); it may console him a little to know that he need not for that reason acknowledge all his expressed opinions to be false. Ignorance has received no other mention from Agathon; but true speech accompanied by false did attract passing attention in a conditional sentence of his encomium (p.68, 195C): 'If Hesiod and Parmenides spoke the truth' about the gods, then the events they spoke of happened by the agency not of Love (as they implied) but of Necessity. Agathon can readily acquiesce in a middle way between knowledge and ignorance. He should likewise welcome, now that he cannot consistently maintain Love's beauty, the news that he need not call Love ugly. But Agathon, if he had not retired from the argument, ought to have taken a good look at the effect on his previous admissions of abandoning the mode of inference exemplified by 'not of ugliness, so obviously of beauty'.

This abandonment has in fact an unfortunate, though not completely destructive, effect on propositions 6 and 7. It removes from them all argument, and thereby reduces them to mere assertions. Love was on a particular occasion of beautiful things, and all Love is of beauty. Now that 6(b) has gone, it is no longer plausible to deduce 7 from 6, even if we retain throughout the summarizing use of 'beauty' to represent 'all beautiful things'. The 'because' of 7 is now no more convincing than the 'because' of 6. As a chain of proof, the argument along which Socrates led Agathon now has a vital link missing. But as a dialectical discussion it retains a good deal of strength. At the time of his speech Agathon asserts that Love is of beautiful things, and does not wish to deny that Love is of beauty (p.71, 197B). As for the dubious logic with which 'Love is of beauty' is handled, most, but not quite all (admittedly the most cogent part) of the dialectical justification for it has been removed with the removal of the 'not ugly, therefore beautiful' argument. But *Socrates* at the end of his first conversation with Diotima accepts that he interpreted Love as the beloved, and for that reason made him beautiful. That implies that for *Socrates* Love (as a passion) is still of the beautiful, at that stage of the argument. Neither Socrates, nor *Socrates*, nor Agathon has yet been given any reason for *denying* the proposition that Beauty is beautiful, even if one link in the chain leading to the assertion of it is now weakened. Hence they have no reason to deny that there is Love of beauty; and they have no immediate reason for abolishing the personification and the resultant universalization of Eros. Also Socrates in his own capacity has no obvious reason for forcing Agathon to deny any of the propositions concerned. If neither Socrates nor Agathon has any good reason to deny a proposition, then the proposition is acceptable in dialectic between the two.

Plato's readers may observe that *they* no longer have such support for the beauty of Love's object(s) as they had before, or for Love's lack of beauty. But readers sharp enough to notice the destruction of the supporting argument will not have shared Agathon's commitment to it in the first place. Consequently, such readers will not have accepted that Socrates has proved his case in the chain of reasoning about Love in the following passage. But this is a matter of concern only to those who construe Plato's dialogue as a step-by-step exposition of what is intended to be a universally valid proof. To those who expect Socrates' lines of questioning to have force only against the particular interlocutor or his congeners, it constitutes no problem at all.

Diotima's next step with *Socrates* (p.80, 202C) is to ask for his confirmation that all the gods are happy and beautiful. Again this opinion is largely Agathon's. Early in his address

Agathon implies (even more clearly in the Greek than in Hamilton's English)[42] that all the gods are happy (pp.67ff., 195A). Eros, as the best and most beautiful, is also the happiest. It is reasonable to suppose, though it is not a cast-iron inference, that Agathon takes the gods' happiness to consist at least partly in beauty and goodness. It is not yet relevant, though it might be relevant to the posterior question why Plato writes in this way, that not everybody in the Greek world believed that all gods were beautiful.[43]

The further point admitted by *Socrates*, that 'happy' *means* 'possessing good and beautiful things'[44] is not deducible from Agathon's more concrete remarks, but is at least consistent with his picture of Love. Love *possessed* beautiful qualities (such as gracefulness (p.69, 196A)) and these are sufficient testimony to his beauty (p.69, 196B). Love *possesses* also a share of moderation (p.70, 196C). We may infer that Love possesses the creative art, and that that also supplies a part of his goodness (pp70ff., 196E). We recall that it is as the most beautiful and *best* that he is the happiest of the gods. Diotima may here be making use of the general understanding of the term 'happy', but in doing so she is neither using vocabulary strange to Agathon or to *Socrates*, nor asking *Socrates* to say anything to which the individual Agathon could not have assented without fear of inconsistency.

Diotima next (pp.80ff., 202D) recalls admissions *Socrates* has previously made. In truth they are admissions Agathon made, but of course *Socrates* admitted just about the same things to Diotima. Love desires good and beautiful things because he lacks them. The word 'because' here is not exactly anticipated by Agathon, but Agathon was nevertheless constrained to accept both Love's lack and Love's desire of beautiful things and of good things. Agathon also accepted that desire is always accompanied by lack; and the causal connection which Agathon did not explicitly accept plays no part in what follows. That indeed was the position Agathon was in when Socrates decided to leave him ostensibly alone. The premisses are now complete; and the conclusion to this particular syllogism now follows.

As Dover's excellent summary has it,[45] '(1) All gods are happy, (2) "happy" means "possessing what is good and beautiful", but (3) Eros does not possess what is good and beautiful, therefore (4) Eros is not happy, therefore (5) Eros is not a god.' Socrates appears not to like this conclusion: his reply is 'No, it *seems* not' (p.81, 202D).[46] Agathon could not be expected to like it either, especially when Socrates appears to be suggesting that he had really believed it all along. We have left normal Greek belief a long way behind here, and Agathon with it; but *Socrates* has no escape, given his and Agathon's previous answers and admissions.

So Eros is no god. No character in the *Symposium* treats him as a mortal. As a spirit, therefore, he occupies a middle place. About this spirit Diotima tells a story (pp.81f., 203B–E), which again plays (either by adaptation or by contradiction) with themes from Agathon's speech and the ensuing conversation. Love's mother, Poverty, is poor just as Beauty is beautiful. Love is, as Agathon had been constrained to admit, in love, and in love (concerning Beauty) with Aphrodite, as in Agathon's speech. The principle of like-to-like, operative in parts of Agathon's speech, operates also in Diotima's: Diotima's Love dwells with Want,[47] as Agathon's accompanies the young. At times, as she is entitled to after Agathon's avowal of ignorance, and after the whole conversation, Diotima gives the lie direct to Agathon's encomium. Far from being tender and beautiful, as Agathon had said (Diotima says 'as most people imagine'), he is hard, which Agathon has pretty clearly denied (pp. 68–9, 195C–196A). Love in Diotima's picture has no dwelling, but in Agathon's the god had his dwelling in the minds of men (p.69, 195E). That Love is brave, Diotima will accept, but only in the same breath as she says Love is a *desirer* of wisdom (p.82, 203D). There is nothing here about Love being superior to desires, or possessing anything or anybody such as Ares. Love's skills are not here those of the creator, but rather those of the magician and alchemist. Love does not possess wisdom, but seeks and yearns for it, abiding in the middle between wisdom and ignorance – that middle ground of whose very existence Agathon seemed in his speech to be unaware. A god would be wise, like Love as Agathon depicted him (p.70, 196D–197B), but Diotima's Love is no god.

At the end of this particular speech of Diotima's, we find a strong expression of a motif common in the mouth of the Platonic Socrates. Socrates is accustomed in the pages of Plato to say harsh things, as Diotima does here (p.83, 204A), of those whose ignorance of their own ignorance obstructs their path to knowledge.[48] But this, Socratic though it sounds, is in no way inconsistent with any of Agathon's views, though it leads to a slight modification, or rather development, of them. Lack is no longer quite enough; it is conscious lack that is a necessary condition of desire. But that disrupts previous arguments not a whit; it remains established that the desiring person lacks what he or she desires.

That Socrates' Diotima should call Love 'brave' even while denying his wisdom is *not* in accordance with Socrates' own habits when he is speaking strictly; the concession to popular – doubtless including Agathon's – usage suggests that it would be a mistake to look in this particular speech of Diotima's for any precise statement of a deep Socratic conviction. The speech, despite its relative lengthiness and its mythical content, is as much *ad hominem* in its aims as anything in Plato. It serves, so far, as a summary in mythical terms of the dialectical discussion to date.

The development of Agathon's ideas on wisdom now proceeds apace. Diotima explains to *Socrates* that the philosophers are those between knowledge and ignorance (p.83, 204B). Love's connection with this is that Love is love concerning 'the beautiful', and wisdom is one of the most beautiful things. Dover comments rightly that 'This step in the exposition is made possible by the fact that [the relevant Greek word] has a much wider range of meaning than "beautiful".'[49] Another necessary pre-condition of Diotima's procedure is Agathon's previous linking of wisdom with other beautiful things of which Love is the love. Agathon treated technical accomplishments under the head of wisdom, and treated them apparently as among the beautiful things whose desire brought all blessings to gods and men (p.71, 197A–B). Further, wisdom is a virtue, a good quality or 'goodness' (pp.69ff., 196A–D); and Agathon has admitted that good things are beautiful.

The wide range of meanings of 'beautiful' in Greek makes possible Agathon's detailed expression in his encomium; it is these which lend bite to Diotima's line of argument. Backing from the interlocutor is always helpful to a dialectician even when making use of a popular view. That Diotima is indeed making use again here of elements from the preceding conversation is clear from her otherwise unaccountable and unwarranted assumption that Love is not merely the Love of wisdom but also a *lover* concerning the beautiful and of wisdom (p.83, 204B). We have already found the origin of this apparent mistake in Agathon's main speech.

Again, Love's intermittent 'wisdom' is due in the myth to his parentage. His mother, Poverty, is neither 'wise' nor 'resourceful'. The Platonic Socrates, for what the point is worth, does not normally dissociate poverty and wisdom. Love's father, Contrivance, or, as Dover well has it, 'Resource', is both 'wise' and resourceful.[50] For this to be plausible, 'wise' should be interpreted, as often in Platonic Greek, to mean 'clever' or 'skilled'.[51] It means 'skilled' in all sorts of ways in Agathon's speech; *Socrates* is not going outside Agathon's vocabulary and usage at this point. It is not immediately clear what kind of wisdom Love is the love (or the lover) of; but if Diotima is ultimately guilty of equivocation on two senses of 'wise' she can plead in mitigation that no profound wisdom is denoted here, and, if such is denoted later, then she has carried her interlocutor with her all the way to that later development.

The present analysis of Love's nature ends with an additional verbal reminiscence of Agathon, coupled with an implied admission that Diotima is judging *Socrates'* mental processes on the basis of something Agathon had originally said. The verbal reminiscence lies in the word 'delicate,' which would remind the reader of Agathon's peroration, where Love is the father of Delicacy (p.83, 204C, cf. p.72, 197D). The implied admission consists in Diotima's statement that *Socrates* has made Love the beloved, rather than the lover, and has for that reason made him 'supremely beautiful.' All *Socrates* had said was that 'Eros is a great god and one of the beautiful' (p.79, 201E). It was Agathon who made him 'most beautiful' and 'father of Delicacy' and heaped blessings upon him (esp. pp.71–2, 197C–E). Diotima's florid expressions here fit Agathon's encomium much better than they fit the terse opening gambit of *Socrates*.

After thus finishing a section of her discourse, as she had begun it, with a pretty direct allusion to things said earlier, Diotima turns (p.83, 204D) to answer a question from *Socrates* on Love's advantages for men. The real Platonic Socrates had begun by complimenting Agathon on his division of Love's praise into two sections, on the god's nature and on his effects (p.75, 199C). The corresponding boundary between Love's nature and his effects in Socrates' own discourse falls not in the conversation overtly between Socrates and Agathon but, as Socrates warns (p.79, 201D–E), in the middle of *Socrates'* conversation with Diotima. This fact illustrates the continuity of Diotima's and *Socrates'* discourse with that of Socrates and Agathon.

Accordingly, on the *Socratic* or Agathonic premiss that Love is 'of beautiful things,' Diotima asks 'In what does love of beauty consist?' (p.84, 204D) or, more literally, '*What* of beautiful things is Love?' Given that Love stands in an of-relationship with beautiful things, what, the question asks, does Love desire to do to or of those things? *Socrates* replies 'to attain possession of beautiful things.' This is good Agathonizing. Agathon had talked of gods and men attaining possession (with the same Greek verb in a different tense) of good things, because of the love of beautiful things (p.71, 197B). Here and elsewhere in the argument, there seems to be an underlying assumption that good things are beautiful. Some believe that good and beautiful are supposed to be coextensive, that not only are all good things beautiful, but all beautiful things are assumed to be good.[52] Commentators call to witness certain popular Greek views,[53] and indeed such views are relevant to Plato's argument. But the situation is not quite straightforward and Diotima assumes, as we shall shortly see, less than some have thought.

Diotima pushes her question further. What does a man obtain who attains the possession of beautiful things? Once the mere possession of beautiful things is insufficient, Agathon's original encomium supplies no helpful answer to this new question. For Agathon, if one reads that whole speech with care, beauty was a necessary, but not certainly a sufficient condition of Love's happiness. What is the possession of beauty or of beautiful things a sufficient condition of? Diotima does not answer her own question at once, but offers in some sense a substitution of 'good' for 'beautiful'. Putting now the question, 'What will have been gained by the man who is in possession of the good?' (p.84, 204E), she receives from *Socrates* the answer 'happiness'. *Socrates* finds this question easier than the preceding one, because his answer gives a common Greek view of 'happiness'. The immediately subsequent speech says, in sum, 'All men desire to possess good things.'

Do we *here* have an assumption that beautiful things are good, as well as *vice versa*, that the terms 'good' and 'beautiful' are coextensive or even, for practical purposes, mutually substitutable *salva veritate*? It is tempting to think so; but neither Diotima nor *Socrates* says so.

What Diotima does here ask Socrates to do is perhaps not immediately obvious. The translators (not Robin) tend to make her say things like 'Let us change our terms, and substitute good for beautiful.' But there is nothing in the Greek to represent 'our terms' here; and it is perfectly possible to read Diotima as offering not so much a change of terms as a change of topic.[54] A more literal translation may bring out this point. 'Just as if someone, changing, and using the good instead of the beautiful, were to ask: "Come, Socrates, the desirous person desires good things; what does he desire concerning them?"' Nothing here necessarily implies the limitation of the change to terms, as opposed to topics.

Nor is there any necessity to derive the generalization that 'the desirous person desires *good* things' from Agathon's agreement that all desire/love is of *beautiful* things. The generalization about good things is admitted quite separately, in a further question and answer a few lines below (p.84, 205A). Evidently, however, so ready an admission as *Socrates* offers there raises the further query for us whether and how that generalization is justified in this context. But the answer to our query need not depend on, or derive from, Agathon's admissions about the beautiful.

Could it be that Diotima and Socrates regard it as obvious that all men desire good things (i.e. things good for them), and indeed desire to possess them? They agree that the possession of good things constitutes the good life ('happiness'); and they agree further that it is unnecessary (or even wrong)[55] to ask why anyone desires the good life. The implication is surely clear: the desire for the good life, and hence for the possession of good things, is universal; otherwise the question would arise, as they agree it could not, why one person desires happiness (when others do not). This is not the only passage in Plato where the universal wish for good things is assumed. True, the Socrates of the *Meno* (77–8) and of the *Gorgias* (466–8) elicits an argument for it; but in the *Charmides* (167E), and even in the long-winded *Philebus* (20D), he is permitted to assume it.

The easiest way of accounting for what might otherwise pass for an unaccountable and unpardonable philosophical liberty is that of Santas:[56] people desire what they desire under the description 'good for them', and not under the description 'bad for them'. If asked what sort of life they desired to lead, Greeks commonly replied 'a happy life', or a 'good' or 'well-governed' life. They might have, as Aristotle later said (*EN* 1097b 22–4), very different sorts of life in view when offering this reply, but they would agree to a life under the descriptions 'good,' 'happy', and so forth.

On the other hand, the proposition that all men desire *beautiful* things is not nearly so well-recognized a truth in the Greek philosophers. Things beautiful, fine or honourable (to offer again several translations of this complex word) were not necessarily 'good', or 'advantageous to the agent'. It is a regrettable fact of life that people do not always aim in the sphere of conduct at what is 'beautiful', or 'lovely' or 'honourable' – even under those descriptions. From this state of affairs it follows that to derive 'All men desire good things' from 'All men desire beautiful things' would be in normal Greek usage to put the cart before the horse and to derive the easier proposition from the more difficult. Even in the context of the *Symposium*, where desire of the beautiful is so much to the fore, there is no need to derive desire of the good from desire of the beautiful.

Further study of the text shows an argument for the universal desire of the good which has not received as much attention as it might (p.85, 205E). It is unfortunate that Hamilton's translation omits, and Dover's commentary draws no attention to, the argumentative conjunction in Plato's Greek. Love, Diotima says, is not desire of half or whole 'unless that half or whole happens to be good, [*since*] men are quite willing to have their feet or their hands amputated if they believe those parts of themselves to be diseased.' Diotima's evidence is empirical. It is deployed in rebuttal of Aristophanes;[57] it is not of universal truth, nor, if it were so, would it prove the universal truth of the proposition that men desire the good. But it constitutes a reason for preferring Diotima's view to Aristophanes', and it places no reliance on the proposition that 'good' and 'beautiful' are coextensive in reference. *Socrates* chooses to accept it, perhaps the more readily since *Socrates* represents Agathon, and the argument's target is the other poet present at the banquet. However that may be, Diotima's formal invitation to *Socrates* to draw the conclusion that men desire without qualification what is good is accepted. It would be unwise to forget that this conclusion is a doctrine closely and constantly associated with the Platonic Socrates; but Plato makes others than Agathon accept it, and he may genuinely have thought it a truism.

If we wish to explore the relation between desire for the good and love of the beautiful in Diotima's exposition, it is well to look with some care at a passage we have so far omitted, falling in the middle of Diotima's discussion of the universal desire for the good. The passage begins (p.84, 205A–B) with Diotima asking *Socrates*, and herself supplying the answer to, a highly pertinent question: if the love, or desire, for good things is common to all men, 'Why is it, then, Socrates, if all men are always in love with the same thing, that we do not speak of all men as being in love, but say that some men are in love and others not?' Diotima's answer to this is to the general effect that there is a distinction to be made between two different senses of 'love', one in which it is applicable to all men and one in which it is applicable only to some.

Diotima illustrates the nature of this distinction with an example of another word which behaves, in Greek, in a somewhat similar way. Her illustration repays inspection in our present context, since the example is drawn from Agathon's own vocabulary and usage.[58] The Greek word concerned is that for 'poetry', *poiesis*, which means also, etymologically and in some non-philosophical writers, 'making'. The nearest analogue in modern English is perhaps 'creation', usable either generally or in a specifically artistic context. Agathon himself had depicted Love as a poet, a poetic creator (pp.70ff., 196E). For Agathon, again, Love is the creator of all animals by the union of the sexes. Agathon had separated, clearly enough, creation in the artistic sense and biological creation: he had talked of 'artistic' creation and of the 'creation of all kinds of living beings'. The second of these appears to be a separate illustration of Love's wisdom, and not to be confused directly with the 'poetic' or 'artistic' creation mentioned just before. Diotima's selection of this example is assuredly no accident. Not only is Agathon himself a poet, but he has also committed himself to the existence of the two types of 'creation' under that description, one much wider and more general than the other. The wider use of the word 'creation' is less common than the artistic use; by *poiesis* a normal Greek normally meant 'poetry'.

Similarly, there are, Socrates urges through Diotima, two different uses of 'Love' (p.85, 205D). One of them is wider: it denotes any sort of desire, preferably strong. The other is a form of the wider, just as poetry is a form of creation: it denotes the passionate attraction of one person to another, which we call 'being in love'. When Socrates speaks of the wider sense of 'love,' he is referring to that desire which Diotima had persuaded *Socrates* to agree was 'always' of the good (p.84, 205A). What the prophetess is going to do with the distinction, what she is about to make of the lover who loves the beautiful as opposed to the desirous who desires the good, is a question which must wait till we have dealt with the word 'always', which has rightly disturbed the *Symposium*'s most recent editor.

Agathon has agreed that everything loved is good, and that one wants to possess everything one desires; but to possess it '*always*'? Dover points out Diotima's pun on this word.[59] At first her argument requires 'always' to go with the verb 'desire', '... all perpetually desire to be in possession of the good ...?' (p.84, 205A). Here 'perpetually' means not 'eternally', but 'on each and every occasion'. Later the argument requires 'always' to go closely with the Greek verb for 'possess'. 'Love is desire for the perpetual possession of (more literally "perpetually to possess") the good' (p.86, 206A). 'Perpetual[ly]' here means 'permanent[ly]'. Verbally the two passages echo each other, even more than this account would suggest, in that the Greek order of words puts the word 'always' in each place next to the Greek verb for 'to be'. Dover says with respect to this procedure, without mincing words, that the later of the two propositions 'does not rest on reasoning at all.' If we may mince a word or two, the later proposition rests on faulty reasoning: the fault is equivocation.

This time, the Platonic Diotima would not be justified in laying the fault in its entirety at Agathon's door. It is true that Agathon had said relevant things, but their relevance is only partial; it does not afford a full exculpation of Socrates and his Diotima, let alone of Plato. On the topic of Love's youth Agathon had said (p.68, 195B), 'He is always with the young';[60] in the Greek, the adverb 'always' stands in the sentence next to the verb 'is-with', and most naturally would be taken as qualifying it. Several lines below (p.68, 195C), 'always' stands in the Greek (as in Hamilton's English) next to 'young', and this time would most naturally be taken as qualifying that epithet. If a shift in the grammatical association of 'always' were the only flaw in the reasoning Diotima asks *Socrates* to accept, she would have adequate precedent in Agathon's speech.

But this is not the only failing of Diotima's line of questioning. The possibility perhaps remains that Plato thought it was, but, if so, Plato was wrong. Diotima used 'always' in more than one sense; Agathon had not. In Agathon's argument the word means, at its first appearance, 'on each and every occasion', and throughout the argument it may retain that sense without detriment to the reasoning. Love may thus be young on each and every occasion. Of course, Love is, for Agathon, immortal; and no doubt Love is for him also eternally young: 'immortal and ageless' is a cliché of early Greek poetry.[61] If an immortal being is young on each and every occasion as it arises, it follows that he is for ever young.

If Plato thought of his Socrates construing Agathon as sliding from one sense of 'always' to another, and made his Socrates follow suit accordingly in his Diotima's argument, then Plato made a mistake: he failed to observe that his Agathon, assuming Love's immortality on the basis of popular belief, has a right to slide from one 'always' to another which Diotima does not have. Diotima apparently sets out to show that men wish to possess good things not merely on each occasion as it arises, but for ever. She cannot legitimately assume what she is trying to show. Our conclusion is irresistible: this time, unless she claims exemption on the ground of other equivocations by Agathon, Diotima must confess to disobeying the rules.

It is not clear whether Plato made his mistake here wittingly or unwittingly; but at any rate his Diotima is daringly open, in an inexplicit way, about it (p.86, 206A–B). Her conclusion that love is the desire to possess the good always is followed in her very next sentence, by 'Now that we have established that love is always this...' In this second sentence Hamilton correctly renders the Greek 'always' by 'invariably'; the word means 'on every appearance', as it did at the outset of Diotima's argument. Yet this sentence echoes its immediate predecessor, which starts in Greek with 'is' and has 'love' in the middle and 'always' at the end.

It is almost as if Plato were challenging his readers, or causing Socrates to challenge his audience. It is scarcely believable that *this* is unwitting. But that does not prove that Plato had not made a mistake in his dialectical justification for it, rather than constructed a deliberately feeble argument in the form of a verbal trick. But was this really all that Diotima, Socrates, or Plato could produce by way of argument for an important plank in the platform? Was Plato here wholly dependent on this rhetorician's trick, or dialectician's peccadillo, for support? I think not; I believe Plato, after making use, consciously or not, of a mistake, betook himself to devices less disreputable and more in accord with normal dialectical procedure. But this view requires a foundation in an understanding of the general shape of Diotima's argument in the climax of the dialogue. So to that argument we must now return.

We left it at the point where Diotima has distinguished the 'lover' properly and narrowly so called from the desirer, who universally desires the good. She has argued by a mixture of fair and foul means that the universal desire for the good is a desire to possess it for ever. She now asks 'In what way and by what type of action men must show their intense desire if it is to deserve the name of love?' (p.86, 206B). The answer she comes up with is that the function concerned is 'procreation in what is beautiful, and such procreation can be either physical or spiritual.' There is a contrast in Diotima's sentence between what love is, and what deserves, or 'would be called by [as the Greek has it]' the name of love.

It is much to the point to observe that there is a similar contrast between 'being' and 'being called' earlier in the discussion, where Socrates has his Diotima distinguish two senses of *poiesis*, creation (p.85, 205A–D). Hamilton's translation obscures the contrast in that earlier context, but it is there in the Greek, which makes poiesis *be* something large, and *be* the cause of anything's coming-to-be, and makes the craft processes *be* 'creations' and the craftsmen *be* (etymologically speaking!) 'poets'; whereas the narrower field of music and metre is *called* poetry. Similarly Eros *is*, in sum, every desire for good things, and to that desire the *name* Eros is not given; the people who are *called* lovers (*erastai*) are those with a particular passion.

Now after Diotima has developed the nature of the general type of Eros, and argued that it desires good things for ever, she turns to the question what the particular province of desire is to which the *name* Eros is normally given (p.86, 206B). She asks, in fact, 'in what type of action the passion' must be shown 'to be *called* Love'. Not only is there a clear symmetry in the uses of the verbs 'be' and 'be called' in the whole passage; the Greek root I have rendered 'passion' is the same in each occurrence, despite Hamilton's variation between 'passion' and 'intense desire'. The point is clear: the desire for procreation in the beautiful is not identical with the desire for the good; the former is a particular case of the latter. The former is also that form of the latter to which the name they have in common is most normally and most precisely applied. There is no need here to suppose any *close* relationship between 'good' and 'beautiful'; it is not on this occasion the beautiful which is itself good, but rather the procreation in the beautiful which is good (as the object of desire), though even this is not explicit.

When Diotima speaks of 'either physical or spiritual' procreation, she leaves *Socrates* behind. Agathon had both thought of Love in terms other than the purely physical, and mentioned the physically procreative activity of Love; but he had not spoken of the spiritual force of Love as procreative. He had, moreover, spoken of the desire not of procreation, but simply of 'the beautiful things' as the motive force in divine and human spiritual creativity (pp. 70ff., 196D–197B). When, therefore, *Socrates* confronts Diotima's answer to her own question about the particular activity associated with the particular desire called Love, he requires further explanation. Indeed, as the reader will recall, he had at first not even understood what the question was driving at (p. 84, 204D). When asked 'What is the aim of the love which is felt by the lover of beauty?', the only answer that came to his mind was 'to attain possession of beautiful things'; of any further aim he had no idea. Now that not only that original question but also Diotima's answer have been expounded to him, his bafflement demands still more explanation.

Diotima proceeds to give the required clarification. All human beings, on reaching a certain maturity, desire to procreate. To do so, they need the cooperation of a beautiful partner. Physical procreation, which Agathon of course understood, receives discussion first. Plato has been accused of ignoring the elementary fact that sexual desire is mostly desire for intercourse rather than for the procreation of children. Dover draws a conclusion about the argument's logic: 'The argument requires the assumption that humans, like animals (207A5–C1), are impelled by forces of which they are not aware.'[62] But Plato's Diotima has a defence ready against *this* attack, in a sentence which (my Greekless readers need a warning) Hamilton omits, in the belief (shared with several editors) that it is not Plato's (p. 86, before 'There is something divine', 206C5–6).[63] The sentence says, 'Sexual intercourse between a man and a woman is [a] procreation.' Diotima, as Dover himself adds, 'treats the ejaculation of semen by the male, rather than the complete process of creating a child, as [procreation] of that with which the male is "pregnant" ("fertile" will sometimes be found a less paradoxical translation).' But this, so far as the present passage is immediately concerned, sits a little uneasily beside Dover's remark on the passage's logic. For if the ejaculation of seed by the male in the female is procreation, then in full heterosexual relations the desire for procreation and the male desire for intercourse will be the same thing.

If, as Dover's note suggests is possible, Plato is thinking of the female secretions in orgasm as also a form of procreation, then much the same will be true of the female as of the male desire; but I confess to a suspicion that Plato has in mind, here at least, only the feelings of the male – and that despite Diotima's womanhood. To say this is not to dismiss Dover's objections to the passage's logic; it is only to postpone them to the place where they arise more pertinently. Diotima has not yet construed male desire for intercourse as a desire for immortality.

But she proceeds to introduce immortality in the next sentence: 'There is something divine about the whole matter; in pregnancy and bringing to birth the mortal creature is endowed with a touch of immortality.' The plausibility of associating the ejaculation of semen, in heterosexual contexts, with immortality rests obviously on the possibility of the conception and birth of a child. 'Pregnancy', in fact, contrary to the reader's expectations at this point, means something like 'the urgent need for relief by intercourse from sexual tension'; the 'burden of pregnancy' (as Hamilton's translation has it later in this paragraph) 'can hardly', as J. S. Morrison once wrote,[64] 'be anything else but the seed which is held back in the presence of the ugly.' If pregnancy is thus construed as an urgent need to ejaculate seed, and 'giving birth' as such ejaculation, then the most plausible way of associating 'pregnancy' and 'giving birth' with immortality is to associate them with the necessity of perpetuating the species. If we ignore masturbation, as Diotima does (her version of Eros is directed towards a partner), and recall that in some Greek thinking the female was merely the receptacle for the child, which grew from the father's seed, then the swelling accompanying male desire, and the distresses of male sexual tension, are felicitous analogues to the swelling of the pregnant female and the pangs preceding the moment of giving birth.

Indeed on these views heterosexual intercourse is, as Diotima says, a kind of giving birth. If a desire to give birth is in any way construable as a desire for immortality, then in that way and to that extent male desire for intercourse will be a desire for immortality. But it is worth noting that in this particular speech of her developing exposition Diotima has not yet so construed it; she has said so far only that the production of offspring is the kind of immortality available for a mortal animal, and that mature human beings desire the production of offspring.

Diotima talks also of the desire to produce offspring 'in what is beautiful', and this expression also makes it clear that she has male desire in mind (p.86, 206C). Women do not produce offspring 'in' a partner. Again it is not women who *particularly when pregnant* are excited by the proximity of a beautiful (or even a handsome) partner; and it is not pregnant women who are excited at the prospect of *something beautiful* ridding them of the burden they are carrying (p.87, 206D). But Diotima is presumably aware that women do fall in love and do experience sexual desires.

Diotima, Socrates, and Plato are busily using language in such a way as to gloss over this difficulty. They attach the language of pregnancy to the (male) lover without overt specification of his sex: Plato's Greek cloaks the sex of the beloved, as often of the lover, in forms grammatically either possibly or necessarily neuter in gender. Only once, near the end of this speech of Diotima, is there a masculine participle, rendered by Hamilton 'the possessor' – and even that is a generalizing participle, for which the masculine is compulsory in Greek.[65]

It looks as if Plato's use of language is due to a desire to appear to be talking about all sexual love without actually talking about the female's love of the male. This suits the parallel between physical and spiritual procreation: in spiritual as in physical it is the active partner who seeks to procreate in the beautiful, and is hence (according to Diotima) a *lover*; the passive partner, in either heterosexual or homosexual contexts, is more normally in Greek a 'beloved'.[66]

We should turn back for a moment to the insistent criticism that men and women desire intercourse for its own sake, and are so far from desiring it for the sake of offspring that they very often take action to avoid even the possibility of their intercourse producing a child. The point is well taken; but the phrase 'for its own sake' would, we may be sure, have worried Plato. Indeed, he would have had some reason for worry: there are all sorts of motives for sexual intercourse, and it is not at all clear that we have it for its own sake rather than for pleasure, for relief of tension, for the satisfaction of a tense partner whom one loves, for comfort and closeness in situations of shared anxiety, and for many other reasons which married (or indeed unmarried) couples can readily supply. These and similar motives might seem irrelevant; but for Plato they would most probably be relevant. If he had to produce a single term which would cover them all, it seems likely that he would suggest the word 'pleasure'. But the *Symposium* is not about pleasure; to bring it in would immeasurably lengthen a discussion already long enough. Plato could fairly claim to have written elsewhere on the subject. He does not, and need not, recognize the need to expound his whole philosophy in any one dialogue – not even in the lengthy *Republic* or *Laws*. So he gives Agathon, in this episode of the *Symposium*, no word about pleasure which may need picking up by Socrates or Diotima, and leaves the subject for other works. If this deserves castigation, the more's the pity.

Diotima's difficult paragraph ends (p.87, 206E) with a sudden and far from easy correction of Agathon's or *Socrates'* doctrine, a doctrine which up to now she has been holding against him. She now apparently denies that Love is of the beautiful. If she is indeed straightforwardly denying that, then much of her previous dialectic is without foundation. But the denial need not, as a matter of Greek idiom, have its full face value. In Greek 'not X but Y' can mean 'not so much X as Y',[67] and the distinction between these two is important here. Diotima is far from ignoring the beautiful in what follows, and she has just referred herself to the 'violent emotion concerning the beautiful' (a set of expressions she is far from disowning) felt by the 'pregnant'.

What Diotima does disown is the suggestion that Love is not merely *concerning* but actually *of* the beautiful.[68] For her, it is not the possession of beauty or the beautiful that the lover desires, but the production of offspring in partnership with a beautiful beloved. In Diotima's book, all love (that is, all desire, in the widest sense of 'eros') is *of* the good, to possess it. Love in the narrow sense, sexual desire, is the desire to have offspring by a beautiful mate; nothing in this part of the *Symposium* says that love is the desire to *possess* a beautiful mate, in the sense of treating 'as items at our disposal those whom we love.'[69] Obviously we do in a sense desire to have a beautiful mate by whom to produce, and with whom to rear, offspring; but that is not by any means the same thing. What we desire to possess is not even the children which are to result from our union; children are not here 'items at our disposal' either. There is absolutely no reason to suppose Diotima, or Socrates or Plato thought they were; for Diotima stresses that the (presumably good) thing whose possession is desired is the kind of *immortality* conferred by children.[70]

But even this weakened version of Diotima's denial creates problems. If Love is not *of* the beautiful, or *of* beauty, then the skein of argument against Agathon will begin to unwind. If Love is Love of immortality, then Love will, on the principles dialectically at work in the previous argument, lack immortality; that much will stand. But the dialectical line leading to Love's being neither beautiful nor ugly will be snapped off at the point where Love had to be of beauty in order to lack beauty. The refutation of Agathon's views, and of the 'youthful' views of *Socrates*, collapses.

But this need not worry Diotima or the mature Socrates of the *Symposium*; for the refutation of *Socrates* and of Agathon was based in any event on the interlocutor's own premisses, and these need not coincide with, or derive any support from, Socrates' own beliefs. Agathon's admission (p.78, 201B) that he knew nothing of what he had said in praise of Love stands. And if Love is still not immortal, and is obviously (as before) not a mortal, then his status as an intermediate form of spirit will stand too, and much of Diotima's famous myth with it.

At one point in particular Plato made his Diotima cover herself against some such emergency as the present: in that myth she spoke of Love as having 'an innate passion *concerning* the beautiful and so *for* Aphrodite herself as being beautiful' (p.82, 203C); the first half of this phrase will stand even if the second half must now fall.[71]

Furthermore, if Love needs a beautiful partner in order to produce the offspring he craves, he will still, in mythical terms, be strenuously searching for the beautiful object of which he is in such instrumental need. Additionally, since the beauty of wisdom is certainly not a point to be retracted, the mate for whom Love searches may well be wise, as in the myth (p.83, 204B). Some of the poetic power of the myth would be lost with the destruction of the picture of the spirit neither beautiful nor ugly, neither wise nor ignorant, and of his consequent parentage. But much of the substance remains, and we may be sure that Plato knew this. Poetically we may have lost, but philosophically we are largely compensated. Perhaps it is fitting that the refutation of a poet should light such a poetic fire, and that the maturer thought of a philosopher should extinguish it, only to raise a theory from the ashes.

One thing at least should be abundantly clear: as soon as Diotima drops the identification of the object of desire with the beautiful, her argument does not depend on or imply the equivalence of the good, which *is* the object of desire, and the beautiful. The beautiful might in many cases coincide with the good; indeed we have not, I think, cancelled the agreement that good things are beautiful. But it is not the beautiful which Diotima takes to be the object of desire, at any rate of sexual desire. Beauty gives rise to deep and tumultuous desire, but the desire is for something other than the beautiful. We should accordingly renew our wariness about the possibility of supposing Diotima's earlier 'substitution' of 'good' for 'beautiful' (p.84, 204D) to have been a substitution of one term for another equivalent to it; we should continue to take the substitution rather as an introduction of a new, though highly relevant, topic.

The next speech of Diotima (p.87, 206E–207A), immediately following the introduction of 'procreation in the beautiful' as the object of desire, fails also to offer any equivalence of 'good' and 'beautiful'. Procreation provides the only form of immortality available to mortals; and, once granted that we desire to possess the good for ever, what we desire is immortality in possession of, or 'accompanied by' the good. This sentence seems to me counterfactual, in that I have never met anyone who seriously desired to be immortal, but it does seem to follow from the premisses Diotima has elicited earlier in the argument: Agathon and *Socrates* have not said that they wish to possess good things only so long as they are there to possess them, but that they wish to possess them for ever. What we are supposed to desire, therefore, is 'immortality as well as the good,' or, as the Greek has it, 'immortality too'. Now in all this, whatever other objections it is open to, there is not a whisper of the equivalence or of the coextensiveness of 'good' and 'beautiful'. There is no reason to suppose that the good, whose accompaniment is evidently necessary to make immortality desirable, is the same as the beautiful, in which those desiring such immortality wish to procreate offspring. The beautiful is doubtless good in so far as it enables us to achieve immortality by procreation; but this sentence is not evidence even for that. Further, the passage says nothing about possessing the beautiful, or about the beautiful belonging to one; it speaks rather of the desire for the good to belong to one.

Whatever the sense or force of this argument, the next one Diotima produces is at least equally difficult to pin down (pp.87–9, 207A–208B). It is difficult to see what she intends as explanation or assertion, and what as proof. Dover's summary is characteristically sharp: 'We see in animals the strength of the impulse to reproduce, rear and protect offspring; this *proves* [my emphasis] that mortal nature strives after immortality.'[72] But does Plato's Socrates think of this as proof? After listening to Diotima's exposition of animal phenomena and her explanation of them by a desire for immortality, *Socrates* expresses surprise (p.89, 208B) and asks her: 'Am I really to believe this?' – or, more literally, 'Are these things truly so?' This is hardly the language of someone accepting a proof, or of a great writer portraying the acceptance of a proof. The text affords scarcely any reason for thinking that Plato intended in this passage to present a proof.

Diotima's reply to this question of *Socrates* is significant:

'Certainly you are [to believe this]'; and she adds: '*Since ...* [my emphasis].'[73] In contrast to what precedes, *this* is the language of someone presenting, if not a proof, at least an argument. After developing the argument, Diotima uses a Greek word construable as 'therefore' (p.90, 208E).[74] *After* this inference-drawing word Diotima places statements of the alleged motives not only of spiritual but also of specifically sexual and bodily love. This shape of the text makes it reasonable to suppose that the earlier explanation of the motives behind procreation is simply *an* explanation, and as such is not intended as an argument in its own favour. The actual argument comes, if this is right, somewhat later.

Opposition to this interpretation might start with Diotima's frequent request, whether rhetorical or genuine, for the explanation of the reproductive urge (pp. 87–8, 206E–207A, 207A, 207B–C), and her answers to her own request which elaborate on the desire of immortality. Surely, the opposition might say, she must be using the 'fact' of universal desire for reproduction and rearing to prove, or at least to provide evidence for, her explanatory hypothesis of a universal desire for immortality. But the argument thus constructed would be sound only if a longing for immortality were the only available explanation for sexual desire. But this is obviously untrue, and is not mentioned, let alone pressed, by Diotima or *Socrates*. All that we have is a series of assertions by Diotima that the correct explanation of reproductive desires and parental concerns lies in an urge for immortality. *Socrates'* final '... am I really to believe this?' fits this situation exactly.

Diotima's speech *following* that expression of surprise also fits; for Diotima *now* (p.89, 208B), *after* her previous assertion explaining the desire for procreation by a desire for immortality, produces an entirely distinct argument to show that we desire immortality. She markedly refrains throughout from using any argument from sole explanation to prove the universality of a desire for immortality. In this context, incidentally, Diotima's factually mistaken generalization that all animals care for their young (pp.87ff., 207A–B)[75] ceases to have any argumentative significance; it occurs in a non-argumentative passage, and if Plato wants to explain something which is not universally true it does not matter much for the dialogue and its argument as a whole.

If we are going thus to distinguish one section as an assertion from another as an argument, we must at least take account of the similarity of structure they exhibit. At the opening of her assertive paragraph, Diotima tells Socrates not to be surprised.[76] Her asserted explanation follows. Surprise opens the argumentative paragraph also (p.88, 207C). You would be surprised, says Diotima, unless you were to consider men's concern for posthumous glory.[77] The one paragraph says 'Don't be surprised at the facts; here is an explanation of them.' The other says 'You would be surprised at the facts if you did not consider the following.' The syntactical differences between prohibition and statement here do not mask a close similarity of underlying structure. But in this similarity there is a substantial difference. To say, in effect, 'Don't be surprised; here is an explanation' is not to rule out other explanations. To say, in effect, 'You would be surprised, if you did not consider the following explanation' is to assert that what follows is the only explanation; no other would remove the initial surprise. The first paragraph offers *an* explanation; the second offers a *unique* explanation. The second produces an implicit argument which the first does not.

The notion that the explanation of the second paragraph is unique depends on the assumption of man's rationality; but that assumption has deep roots in the whole context of the *Symposium*. Diotima has been prepared to assume it from as early as her remark that 'With men one would suppose such behaviour to be the result of rational calculation' (p.88, 207B).[78] I shall not be alone in rejecting that assumption; but it has more force in the *Symposium* than it would in most other contexts. For if men's devotion to Love is irrational, then what becomes of the praise of Love? If Love confers benefits, those benefits must be describable in rational terms; otherwise they will not be benefits in the required sense. A benefit is something one could rationally desire. Agathon tried, however illogical his choice of means, to persuade a company assumed to be rational that Love offered benefits to gods and men. The point is not that Socrates' or Diotima's argument is exempt from criticism; far from it. The point is rather that this assumption of the argument is not readily challengeable in its dramatic context.

Besides this assumption there is at least one other feature of the argument demanding attention to the context of its utterance. Diotima's 'rational' explanation of ambition, of the love of honour, is this (p.90, 208C–209A): human beings spend money, trouble and endurance of dangers and death for the love of immortal glory. Alcestis' willingness to die for her husband Admetus, Achilles' to die in avenging Patroclus, or the Athenian Codrus' to die in order to preserve his kingdom for his sons, all are explicable only on the basis of their desire for an immortal remembrance of their goodness. Those 'pregnant' in body turn to women and beget children; those pregnant in spirit beget the offspring appropriate to spirit. 'What is that? Wisdom and the rest of goodness.'[79] The answer warns us already, by making wisdom only a part, and not the whole, of goodness that Diotima is not enunciating Socratic views on ethics. She is using language concessional to popular usage.

The concessional mode of Diotima's speech comes out also in what she says about poets. She declares that all poets 'are' (*not*, with Hamilton, that they 'may be said to be') begetters of wisdom and the rest of goodness. Surely Socrates held no such exalted view of the function and capacities of poets? Or of imaginative craftsmen in general? That is most certainly not the impression given by Plato's Socrates in the *Apology* (22B–C) or elsewhere? It is not only in his moral language but also in his doctrine of literature that Plato's Socrates here attributes to Diotima a concession – to whom? Partly, no doubt, to the company at large, granted the poetic and theatrical occasion of the banquet in the *Symposium*; but most obviously to Agathon himself, the tragic poet honoured by, and host at, the banquet. What we have here is Socratic urbanity; no one on *this* occasion will grudge the poets their compliment. But we have here also the superb dialectical skill which hits on precisely the proposition which Socrates' opponent will not wish to deny. If Diotima is still arguing with Agathon – and we have no good reason to suppose she has stopped so arguing – then her proposition makes sense.

But what of Diotima's next sentence, to the effect that 'far the greatest and most beautiful branch of wisdom is that which is concerned with the due ordering of states and families, whose name is moderation and justice' (p. 90, 209A)?[80] It is a reasonable question whether this is a dialectically acceptable, or merely a Socratic, suggestion. Less immediately flattering to Agathon than its predecessor, it is certainly more in keeping with normal Socratic attitudes. It makes moderation and justice, themselves treated as a single quality, into a branch of practical wisdom. If this is not quite the full Socratic doctrine that all these virtues are the same quality,[81] it comes uncomfortably near the weaker version that makes each of the other good qualities a branch of wisdom.

Further, unlike Diotima here, Agathon had to all appearances distinguished moderation from justice in his encomium. For he had made justice consist in avoiding the use of force, and moderation in the restraint of desires (pp. 69ff., 196B–D). 'Practical wisdom', as opposed to the 'wisdom' which is a skill, Agathon had not even mentioned.

Diotima's words here need not, however, represent a mistaken concession to a Socratic view so much as to those elements in popular views which served to give Socrates a peg on which to hang his dialectic. Restraint and justice are not so far apart as they may appear on the surface. In Agathon's speech, for example, justice is abstinence from force. In the context of Love, that is one form of self-restraint, of the control over one's desires which is moderation. The union in a single phrase and entity of these two qualities is not beyond the bounds of normal, or of Agathon's personal, understanding. But similarly the Greeks often meant by their word *sôphrosynê*, or 'moderation', something very like the rather Victorian English 'good sense', and that is also often the meaning of the word *phronêsis* I have rendered (like many translators of Aristotle) by 'practical wisdom'. There is no reason to suppose that Diotima's words would have raised her audience's linguistic hackles.

Further, Diotima here makes poets begetters of wisdom and the rest of virtue, and also makes into parts of that same wisdom some qualities vital to the state's welfare. Agathon, of all people, is hardly the man to deny or to question that.

Nor is he likely to cavil at the flattering suggestion that as a poet he might be one of those 'spiritually pregnant with these qualities', who 'finds much to say' about them to his 'beautiful and noble and gracious' friend (p.91, 209A–C). Neither Agathon nor the rest of Socrates' audience is in the least likely to complain at these remarks, however specifically Socratic some of them may sound to us.

Finally (p.91, 209C–D), and most significantly of all, when Socrates' Diotima says that 'everyone ... would rather compose a memorable poem than procreate real children',[82] we need not take refuge in the suggestion, however tentative, that 'Perhaps the notion ... would not have seemed so grotesque to a Greek as it does to most of us.' For Socrates and his Diotima are not addressing just 'a Greek', any more than they are addressing 'most of us'. Socrates, through his Diotima, is once more addressing Agathon. Agathon is a poet, to start with; and we know, as Plato did, that Agathon and Pausanias were for a long time a homosexual couple.[83] If Plato's representations are correct they were a couple for at least twelve years, and, if an anecdote of the late writer Aelian has any basis in fact, for some time more. We should surely presume, from the silence of the *Symposium*, that Agathon was not married.[84] In addressing an unmarried poet of strong and well-known homosexual disposition, it is not 'grotesque' but at one and the same time urbane and dialectically skilful to suggest that everyone believes a great poem more worth producing than a live child.

Socrates here, as often in the early dialogues of Plato, is playing on his interlocutor's professional vanity. Neither Agathon himself nor any of his guests, as he celebrates his first artistic triumph, is likely to rise up in protest. Plato's reader may suffer a shock; but, if so, he should reflect on the difference between the fictional, context-bound Socrates and the philosophic dramatist Plato. He should not lightly speak of Plato's 'assertion' in cases of this sort. It is not necessarily Plato who is to be credited (or debited) with every proposition or argument advanced by the Socrates of the dialogues, or by one of Socrates' imaginary interlocutors. Even Socrates' apparent assertions, let alone his questions, deserve to be looked at in their context before they are attributed to Plato.

After the immortal renown of poetic masterpieces comes the great work of legislators such as Lycurgus and Solon (pp.91ff., 209D–E). In this we need see no serious interruption of the dialogue between Socrates and Agathon which is cloaked under that between Diotima and *Socrates*. As Diotima flatters Agathon by the implied comparison of his poetic triumph with those of Homer and Hesiod, so she exalts the poets in general by comparing their soul-children with those of the great political heroes. We may be meant to recall the poet's words, quoted by Agathon, 'the law, the sovereign ruler of society' (p.70, 196C); and Diotima offers a reference to the beauty attaching to the laws, a motif which will reappear in her following paragraph.

The double nature of the dialogue makes possible, we may think, a nicely ironic touch in the Socratic self-depreciation which follows (p.92, 209E–210A). When Diotima speaks to *Socrates* in depreciatory terms, her words can be understood either as a normal variety of Socratic mock modesty or as depreciating Agathon, whose part *Socrates* is playing. For this reason it is not certain whether Diotima says 'So far, Socrates, I have dealt with love-mysteries into which *even* you could probably be initiated', or says '... into which you *too* could...' (emphasis in each case mine).[85] The relevant Greek 'particle' can mean either 'even' or 'too' according to context, and the context here makes the ambiguity rather neat. One wonders whether Plato meant his readers to grasp both senses, one ('even') striking at Agathon, the other harmless to *Socrates*. Plato's scene-setting here would allow for such subtleties, but in the nature of the case it is impossible to be quite sure of them.

Be that as it may, the first portion of what Diotima thus introduces is in some respects repetitive, in others not. It goes over again the mysteries into which *Socrates* has already been initiated, but it develops and orders in logical stages the pursuit of the beautiful in this world.[86] There are thus two *versions* of the Lover's progress, the second of which, going beyond the first, falls into two *sections*. The prophetess introduces her first section (p.92, 210A) with the instruction 'Try to follow,' and the second (p.93, 210E) with the symmetrical instruction 'Try to pay the closest possible attention.'[87]

The first step in the first, repetitive, section is attraction to beautiful bodies, and the begetting of 'beautiful arguments' (Hamilton's 'sentiments') on one of them. In her previous version, Diotima had spoken, in one and the same sentence, of the parallel attractions of beautiful body and beautiful soul, and spoken of 'arguments' with which the lover abounds (Hamilton has 'has much to say') in the presence of both beauties conjoined in one person. Now she separates the beauty of body and soul more sharply: a single beautiful body, under proper guidance, can provoke the begetting of beautiful arguments. In the earlier version of a lover's history, 'He welcomes beautiful bodies more than ugly ones' (p.91, 209B);[88] and Diotima then uses the singular of the person who combines beauty of soul and of body after mentioning the general attraction of beautiful bodies in the plural. In the second version also, beautiful bodies come first in the plural (p.92, 210A),[89] followed by the singular, used with greater emphasis than before, of the person on whom one begets beautiful arguments.

It is after these beautiful arguments, though not explicitly because of them, that the next step takes place: that step is the realization that the beauty of one body is brother to the beauty of another, and that indeed the beauty of all bodies is one and the same thing. This realization should make the young man the lover of all beautiful bodies, thinking but little of the one to whom he was previously attracted. Only now, in this second version, does the lover turn to beauty of soul. On finding it, he values it more highly than beauty in body. The consequence is the willingness to be satisfied with a modicum of the bloom of youth, so far as the body is concerned, so long as the soul is fair. The lover then procreates arguments with the effect of making the young better. These correspond closely to the 'arguments' of the first version, with an abundance of which the lover 'takes the education' of his beloved 'in hand' (p.91, 209C). According to the first account the soul-children of the loving pair are comparable to poetic and legislative masterpieces, on the second (p.92, 210C) the arguments produced *touch on* the beauty of laws and practices.

From the kinship of the beauties of various practices the lover graduates to 'knowledges' and to their beauty; no longer finding satisfaction in the beauty of the individual boy, adult, or practice, he turns to and contemplates the wide sea of the beautiful, and produces numerous beautiful arguments in the ungrudging pursuit of wisdom. The first version of the lover's growth had nothing of the pursuit of knowledge(s) and in particular of the final knowledge. But it is part of the nature of Eros, as Diotima has previously expounded it, to pursue wisdom; and Agathon in his original encomium had not only spoken of love dwelling in souls (p.69, 195E), and avoiding the soul past or lacking its bloom (p.69, 196A), but also found beauty, and the object of Eros or desire, in the arts (which might just as well be called 'knowledges') attained by the various deities (p.71, 196E–197B). We are still in the circle of ideas licensed by Agathon in his speech and/or argued previously by Diotima right down to, but not including, the single knowledge which Diotima just barely mentions in the last sentence of the first section of her second version (p.93, 210D). In the second section of that second version, introduced by the above-mentioned request to try and pay attention, what is radically new, and not necessarily available to *Socrates*/Agathon, is the final visionary end of the young man's rightful pursuit.

Before we apply our dissecting knife, not without sentimental regret, to that visionary beauty, we should make one observation in Plato's defence. Since Freud, it has been tempting to argue that Plato displays ignorance of even the most rudimentary facts of human male development. It is doubtless the case that the normal human male adolescent feels a generalized sexual urge before his desires crystallize on a single beloved individual. The view is then superficially attractive that Plato ignores, and even reverses, this order of development. But for this attack to make itself good, it would be necessary to suppose (a) Plato's *first* version of the lover's growth puts the individual passion developmentally before the general urge, and (b) that Diotima's *second* version depicts, or purports to depict, the normal stages in the adolescent male development.

Neither of these suppositions will stand up to examination.

The *first* version (p.91, 209A–B) does state Diotima's view of normal development, but proceeds from plural beautiful bodies to a single person with some beauty of body and of soul; the *second* states her view not of how the young in fact develop but explicitly of how she thinks they *ought* to develop, and will, if rightly guided (p.92, 210A). We have every right both to doubt the possibility of altering the development, and to disagree with her evaluative 'ought'; but we have no right to convert what is explicitly evaluative into a mistaken statement of fact.

The single knowledge Diotima's young man eventually perceives is of a kind of beautiful thing which she is about, after this long preparation, to describe. Her description, from here on, does not mention 'beauty' at all. It speaks rather only of 'the beautiful' and 'the beautiful itself' or 'a beautiful thing...' Translators often obscure this fact in the interests of readability and plausibility of English.[90] But the precise importance of the fact thus obscured is doubtful. The present passage appears to be a star example of 'self-predication' in Plato;[91] 'self-predication' means here the phenomenon whereby, it is held, Plato attributes the property F to the property F itself.

This is not the place to discuss the full range of problems in Plato concerning self-predication. An example of self-predication would be 'Justice is just'; the analogous sentence 'Beauty is beautiful' does not actually appear in the *Symposium*. But it is not, as my readers will by now have realized, wholly irrelevant. Plato may have believed it to be true, or he may have seen how to derive it from the remarks he attributes to Agathon, or indeed both.

When Diotima puts into the rightly developing lover's mind the thought that 'if it is right to pursue the beautiful in outward form, it is great folly not to acknowledge that the beauty of all bodies is one and the same,'[92] she cannot be using the abstract 'beauty' to represent 'all beautiful things'; she must mean 'beauty' as a property.

Beauty as a property inherent in souls is probably what she is talking about a few lines below, too. In view of the habit thus established, it is probably right to read the subsequent references to 'the beautiful in activities and institutions' (pp. 92ff., 210C) as the customary way of expressing an abstract in Greek by the definite article with the neuter singular of the relevant adjective. As the beauty of one body was 'closely akin' to that 'in any other', so the whole of 'the beautiful' in activities and institutions is closely interrelated.

In fact Diotima seems to be using 'beauty' and 'the beautiful' interchangeably here. In these contexts neither is a collective; both are abstracts. This does not mean that Plato or his Diotima could necessarily have enunciated the distinction between abstract and collective, or that they were aware of any difference.[93] We are merely construing the text in the most plausible way. The upshot is that, so far at least, 'beauty' is the same thing as 'the beautiful'; and it is reasonable to suppose that 'the beautiful itself' is beautiful, since, apart from sounding (and reading) as if it must be, it receives later the alternative label '[that] itself which is [truly] beautiful' (p. 94, 211C–D).[94]

If indeed beauty is beautiful, in Diotima's climactic speech, then we cannot shirk, but cannot finally answer, the question why. Two answers suggest themselves. It is possible, as we said earlier, that Plato, and hence his Diotima, made an honest category-mistake, perhaps misled by some of the features of Greek usage just mentioned. It is equally possible that Diotima and her creator did know what they were doing, and were drawing on the indirect support for it which can be extracted from Agathon's encomium of Love.

To try to decide whether the first of these propositions was true would take us very far afield, and involve us, for example, in a detailed discussion of some of the most difficult arguments in Plato's *Parmenides*.[95] There is a limit to the number of dialogues which can be treated in detail in a work such as this, and the *Parmenides* is not our subject here.

But perhaps the most significant point lying within our present compass is this: if Plato were allowing Diotima to draw on the implications of Agathon's speech, as he has certainly allowed some other *ad hominem* remarks to escape her, it would not follow in the least *either* that Plato did not believe, himself, the proposition(s) one of his characters drew from another, *or* that he was not constructing a serious work of philosophy. The supposition that Plato believed, with more or less conscious awareness, that beauty is beautiful is not incompatible with the proposition that he knew he had not proved it in the *Symposium*; and the knowledge that he had not proved it would not make his attitude to his work any less serious. There are other serious philosophical purposes than proof. Perhaps, for example, Plato thought he had shown that if you speak as Agathon in this dialogue speaks, and are the sort of person Agathon is, then you will in the end be forced in the name of consistency to accept sundry Platonic propositions – unless, that is, you are prepared to abandon your most characteristic modes of thought and speech, modes bound up with your very profession and way of life.

To return to Diotima's account of the beautiful itself: she presents, as one might expect, some ideas new at least to this dialogue, but she also continues to move in the realms of thought that the answers of *Socrates* and Agathon inhabit. Her discourse examines the beautiful object of the ultimate knowledge and contemplation from a point of view relevant to the tenor of the previous discussion. 'First of all' (p.93, 210E) we hear that the beautiful is eternal. Under this head, it neither comes to be nor is destroyed, it neither grows nor is wasted away, but it exists for ever. In this it is distinct from the other beautiful things participating in it, things which come to be and perish without effect of any kind on the beautiful itself. They are mortal[96] by contrast with its immortality. Its contemplation confers immortality on the contemplator, if any man has immortality (p.95, 212A). This sentence demands to be read in the light of what Diotima said earlier about the only way in which mortal beings can lay hold of immortality (p.89, 208B). What they needed there was offspring; the offspring might be physical or moral and intellectual. The contemplator of the beautiful itself has most certainly moral and intellectual offspring. This offspring is true goodness (p.95, 212A).[97] It is the offspring of 'contact' – one is tempted to suppose this a sexual metaphor for spiritual intercourse[98] – with the truly beautiful rather than with its images.

Perhaps this metaphor conceals an argument. The context needs to be laid out. The lover's desire is for the procreation of offspring in the beautiful. It is by such procreation that the mortal lover can achieve such immortality as is granted to mortals. What one desires is what is good, under the description 'good'. In, or in contact with, what is truly beautiful, says Diotima, one procreates what is truly good, true goodness. It is difficult to be sure what all this means; Diotima speaks here in metaphors and in riddles. Does the steadfast contemplation of 'the beautiful itself' induce in the mind the knowledge of what is truly good? And if so, why? Agathon might supply some of the background to this kind of assertion with his doctrine that everything good which has come to gods and men has come from the love of beautiful things (p.71, 197B). But from that to the suggestion that the truly good comes from the love and contemplation of the truly beautiful is a long step, across a gap unbridgeable, so far as I can see, by logic or dialectic. Perhaps the necessary argument is concealed in the metaphor. Perhaps Diotima means, even if she does not say, that intercourse with a mere image cannot procreate real progeny, and it needs a real union with a real partner to procreate real offspring. But if that is the intended line of thought, whatever plausibility it may possess is outweighed to our way of thinking by a strange view of what is 'real'.

Where does the idea of truth, or of reality, come in? Diotima does not derive it explicitly from any source, and its appearance is rather sudden. It may – though one cannot be sure – derive from the other main line of thought in Diotima's peroration, a line to which we now turn. This starts with the word 'next' (p.93, 211A) and was, the reader will recall, preceded by what came 'first of all'. According to this second part of the exposition, the beautiful itself differs from the beautiful things participating in it in that 'it is not beautiful in part and ugly in part, nor beautiful at one time and ugly at another, nor beautiful in this relationship and ugly in that, nor beautiful here and ugly there, as being beautiful to some people and ugly to others.'[99] Nor is 'the beautiful' *in* anything else. It exists on its own account with itself for ever, being of one kind only.

The principal implication of all this is that the beautiful itself is pure beauty, with no admixture, whether spatial, temporal, or relational, of ugliness; in this it is unlike the beauty attached to mortal things, whether physical or intellectual. Even the participation of mortal things in it has no effect on the beautiful itself, and neither does their coming-to-be or passing-away. The single knowledge which constitutes the last step in love's growth has the beautiful itself for object, and that alone. To contemplate it is to contemplate the beautiful in a state of purity, unmixed and undefiled; it is to contemplate something of one kind only. It is at this point that 'truth' makes its first appearance in the argument. It is therefore reasonable to suppose that Diotima thinks truth goes with purity and derives from it.

This is all the more reasonable because Plato's characters elsewhere associate the two notions of truth and purity. The *Republic* (586BC) and the *Philebus* (53AB) supply examples. The *Philebus* also supplies an argument, though not a strong one, for the association. The argument rests, apart from a dubious analogy, on the thought that a pure X is in some sense more genuine X than an impure X is. Obviously this is true in so far as the impurities of an impure X are by definition not X and an impure X is therefore not all genuine X. But an impure X is nevertheless an X, a real X, and not a mere shadow or image of an X. One must convict Diotima of a mistake. Probably this mistake is also Plato's; its recurrence, and the total absence of any justification of it in the whole passage of the *Symposium* from Agathon's speech on, are clear enough evidence of either a mistake or a piece of deliberate rhetorical deception. We have found no evidence for the latter in Socrates or Diotima so far, and should be reluctant to accept it now.

If we give Plato the benefit of the doubt here, we still have a problem on our hands: in the matter of immortality, in what does the superiority of the lover and contemplator of 'the beautiful' consist (pp.94ff., 211D–212A)? The beauty he contemplates is immortal. But that does not transfer immortality to him. Diotima does not actually say that it does. She says rather that the contemplator will become immortal 'if ever any man can' – which is, by a common Greek idiom, equivalent to 'more immortal than any other man.'[100] By means of *this* offspring, a man will enjoy a higher degree of immortality than by any other. No ordinary child, and no ordinary intellectual masterpiece, will confer such immortality as the production of true goodness. It is left vague in what sense one leaves behind one the true goodness to which one has given birth; it is left vague by what process one gives birth to true goodness. But in all the vagueness of Diotima's surely mystical belief, one relationship with what precedes is fairly clear. Goodness is a good thing; and immortality with what is good is what *Socrates* agreed to be the object of every man's, and especially of every lover's, desire (p.86, 206A). The highest available immortality and true goodness together – what more could a follower of Agathon and *Socrates* desire?

Let us rake up an old question, and satisfy ourselves that there is in all this no scintilla of evidence that Diotima or Socrates or Plato treat the beautiful and the good as the same thing, or suppose that 'good' and 'beautiful' are synonymous terms. What men desire is the good: immortality, so far as possible, with good. What is possible is the procreation and preservation of offspring, physical, intellectual or moral. The desire for such immortality, is, as Hamilton's version says of the glory sought by past heroes, 'the incentive of all actions' (p.90, 208D); but this is not a desire directly to possess the beautiful so much as to procreate offspring in the beautiful. It is, however, the desire for what is good. The functions of the good and of the beautiful in the argument and its exposition are quite different. When she says (p.94, 211C) that the other stages of the lover's progress are 'for the sake of'[101] the final 'beautiful', Diotima means not that 'the beautiful' itself is the good, but that the highest available good is the contemplation of it and procreation by it of moral offspring.

Who keeps alive the memory of true goodness? Evidently the poets, of whom Agathon is one. Perhaps, in Athens, especially the tragic poets, in whose chief annual competition Agathon has just won first prize for the first time. It would be difficult to think of a theme more suited to a discussion with Agathon on this occasion. Of course Diotima does not directly address Agathon; but, in addition to such appropriateness of her speech to Agathon's party as we have noticed, we observe that Aristophanes, also a guest, sees in Socrates' narrative of her discourse a thrust aimed at him and is clearly right to do so (pp.95ff., 212C). Diotima's argument aims at

Agathon and his company. It is none the worse – it is indeed much the more coherent – for that.

'Coherent,' the reader may say, 'yes; but convincing?' Let us again be clear that *neither* the tailoring of the argument to fit round a particular person, his profession, his way of life, *nor* the unacceptability to Socrates, to the company at large, to us too, of several premises of the argument, imply in the least that Socrates is in any way ironic or deceitful in telling us that he believes what Diotima said (p.95, 212B). Nor do they imply that Plato failed to achieve what he set out to do. He need not have set out to convince all his readers, nor to make his Socrates convince all his audience. It is not clear that he believed it possible to produce an objectively convincing proof of his views. We may never know why he held those views himself. It may be the simple truth that the only reason he could give himself, and that Socrates could give himself, was their ability on successive and numerous occasions to show dialectically from other people's opinions, linguistic habits, and professional pride that those other people ought to hold Socratic or Platonic beliefs. Whatever the truth of this, Agathon in the *Symposium* falls another victim to the Socratic practice of turning inside out the whole way of thought, speech, and life of his interlocutors.

4 Socrates meets Protagoras

On Plato's *Protagoras* successive analyses by the philosophically expert of individual arguments or groups of arguments[1] have been matched in recent years by at least one beautiful *explication de texte* by a French Hellenist,[2] and by ever deeper accounts in English of Protagoras' relation to Athenian society.[3] Our understanding of the dialogue's unity has also deepened.[4] Some ambiguities in the expressions used in it have long been common knowledge.[5] But analysis of the dialogue as a conversation, as a succession of dialectical discussions, may still help to explain the often apparently tortuous argument.

Plato's introduction

The opening conversation between Socrates and an unnamed friend begins on a note of banter. Socrates has been in pursuit of the young Alcibiades (309A). Not perhaps so young as he was? But Socrates has been in 'more beautiful' or 'finer' company (309C).[6] In the face of his friend's doubt Socrates asks, in a form clearly expecting the answer 'yes', whether the wisest is not likely to seem more 'beautiful'. In this question at least Socrates, despite the gentle humour of this scene as a whole, can be taken seriously. Beauty of soul for the Platonic Socrates is more important than that of the body, and wisdom is at least a key virtue of the soul. Socrates now suggests that he has been with the wisest man of the day, 'if you think that that description fits Protagoras' (309D).[7] This sentence alone would not commit Socrates to the belief that Protagoras was wiser than his contemporaries; the conditional constitutes almost a disclaimer. This in turn casts ironic doubt on Socrates' previous description of Protagoras as 'more beautiful'.

The tension in this scene between the serious and the amusingly ironical adds to the fun. Socrates' words partly reflect his own high moral usage, and partly make concessions to popular language. But his nameless companion by no means dissents from the proposition that Protagoras is the wisest, and appears to endorse it without suspicion of irony, by his eagerness to hear what passed between Socrates and Protagoras. In this short scene Plato has raised some of the deepest questions of the dialogue. What is the relation of wisdom to that which is morally (or at least non-physically) handsome? Does Protagoras have wisdom? Common opinion may be that he does; but is the common opinion, represented by the unknown friend, right?[8]

One more point foreshadows subsequent conversation, though it is difficult to imagine even the most alert reader picking it up at first reading. Socrates in his first speech appeals to poetic authority. But the appeal, couched in the form of a question, does not commit Socrates to acceptance of such authority. 'Aren't you an admirer of Homer?' he asks, and his friend does not demur (309A). The acceptance of poetic authority by the sophists and their public is one topic of the discussion later of Simonides' famous poem (338Eff.). Socrates will there implicitly reject poetic authority, despite his defence of Simonides' particular poem and despite his use of a poet's weight in the introductory conversation. Again there is an agreeable tension between Socrates' use of a poet's weight in discussion and his unwillingness later to accord any weight to the expounders of poetry. One feels the tension when reading the dialogue a second time. It would be interesting to know how widely the views of the Platonic Socrates on poetry were available before the *Protagoras* itself passed into circulation.

The scene with Hippocrates

Thus even before Socrates' narrative there are philosophical questions in the air. The narrative itself begins with a mild surprise. Socrates' friend asked for the discussion between Socrates and Protagoras; but the story commences with Hippocrates (310A). He burst in, all eagerness, and said firmly that his news was nothing but good: 'Protagoras has come.' Here already there is matter for Socratic reflection; what is good or beneficial about the arrival of Protagoras? After suitable description of Hippocrates' haste the unspoken question is answered. Hippocrates, more explicitly than Socrates' unnamed friend, declares Protagoras wise (310D). This is in answer to Socrates' question whether Protagoras is behaving unjustly to Hippocrates: the latter says 'Yes,' on the amusing and quick-thinking ground that Protagoras does not pass on his wisdom to Hippocrates.

Any Socratic ought to prick up his ears at this. For Hippocrates calls Protagoras wise but unjust, and if this was not one of the very first of Plato's dialogues (and possibly even if it was), Socrates would be expected to believe it impossible for Protagoras to be in the full sense both unjust and wise. Of course many other people will at times have believed off the cuff in the compatibility of wisdom and injustice, and Hippocrates marks himself as one of them, and not a Socratic, by his remark. After this no reader of Plato's early ethical writings will have found surprising the later launch into a discussion of the question how the virtues are related. Socrates, conceding Protagoras' wisdom (again more explicitly than in the opening scene), suggests that the gentleman will pass on his wisdom for a fee. This neatly removes the suggestion (incompatible with full Socratic wisdom) of Protagoras' injustice.

It also serves to raise some suspicion of irony – a suggestion not wholly absent earlier. If Socrates is to concede wisdom to Protagoras as explicitly as this, what can Protagoras' wisdom be? All sorts of people could as professionals be described as 'wise', skilled or knowledgeable. Does Socrates really believe that Protagoras has the moral knowledge Socrates prizes? Or is he alluding to some other sphere of knowledge? Socrates suggested to the unnamed friend that Protagoras' wisdom, if he has it, makes him more 'beautiful' than Alcibiades – evidently in some non-physical sense. What precisely is Socrates' meaning and what exactly is his judgment on Protagoras?

That Hippocrates is only repeating the general consensus about Protagoras appears as he explains to Socrates why he seeks an introduction. Everybody, he says, praises the man

(310E). He adds, revealingly, that everybody says he is 'wisest' at speaking. Does this answer our previous inquiries? If we can thus limit Protagoras' 'wisdom', then it does. Protagoras can be a clever verbal trickster and still be unjust, and Socrates can surely grant him this cleverness without judging him morally wise? But Socrates is not satisfied; as they must while away the time before Protagoras is likely to be available, he tests the strength of Hippocrates (311B) by a characteristic chain of questions. These are, naturally enough, related to what Hippocrates has just said.

The young man intends to go to Protagoras and pay his fee – to become what? Before Hippocrates has time to answer, Socrates presses on him an explanation of the question. He means, as his illustrations make clear, what profession will Hippocrates learn from Protagoras? Now we know what Hippocrates (and according to him everyone else too) thinks Protagoras' skill is. It is 'wisdom' at speaking. But Socrates (and doubtless Plato) wishes to make a point. As doctors instruct in doctoring, and sculptors in sculpting, so a sophist ought analogously to instruct in sophisting: does Hippocrates want to be a sophist? Hippocrates blushes at the very idea (312A), whether from modesty or from horror. He easily accepts that he seeks the sophist's instruction for its educational value, as a continuation of his education by the teachers of literacy, gymnastics and instrumental music. So one sort of skill is ruled out for Hippocrates as the sophist's skill. The sophist does not transmit to his normal pupils the sophist's art, but a subject of more general import. In fact (though Socrates does not say so), unlike the doctor and the sculptor the sophist has no function of any direct use to a youth such as Hippocrates except to teach him something. The question what he teaches is therefore of some urgency; Hippocrates has said nothing yet to convince Socrates that he knows the answer.

Hippocrates is about to betake himself to Protagoras as to a sophist, and entrust his mental and moral self (or 'soul') to his training. But Socrates would be surprised if the youth knows what a sophist is. If he does not, he cannot know whether Protagoras will be a good or a bad thing. Hippocrates greeted Protagoras' arrival as a good thing (310B). We conclude either that he did not *know* that when he said it, or he knows after all what a sophist is. Socrates would not be surprised if he knew neither. Hippocrates thinks he does know. The sequel is predictable already to a reader acquainted with the Platonic Socrates. Socrates' wisdom in the *Apology* consisted in not thinking, as other men do, that he knew what he did not known (21C–D). So we expect Hippocrates to learn that he does not know what a sophist is, that is to say what he teaches.

Hippocrates' reply, that a sophist knows wise things, is understandably vague. The word 'sophist' was indeed widely applicable to various sorts of expertise in fifth-century Greek.[9] But Hippocrates' suggestion is not illuminating in the present context, and Socrates brushes it aside. The 'sophist', despite the etymological connection between the word and the Greek *sophos* conventionally rendered 'wise', has no monopoly of wisdom. Painters, carpenters, all have their craft-wisdom. What is the sophist's craft? The answer now comes back; he knows how to make a clever speaker. Now this is a curious answer in the face of the models Socrates has given. The painter and carpenter make paintings and furniture, or they produce (as trainers of apprentices) clever painters and carpenters. By analogy the sophist should be able to produce both sophists and some other product. A clever speaker is not like a painting or piece of furniture; he would more resemble a successful apprentice. Hippocrates is, however, sticking to the other analogy on offer, that of the teacher of reading and writing. The primary teacher's product is competence in elementary language skills, the sophist's is analogous. Hippocrates seems to be right.

There have accordingly been critics of Socrates' argument here.[10] They have urged the existence of a technique of persuasion applicable to any subject, which Protagoras offers and Hippocrates wishes to learn. There is force in this criticism. One should not answer it, even though Plato might have wanted to, by fleeing to another dialogue. True, the *Gorgias* deals with a 'craftsman of persuasion' claiming also to teach morals. Now Plato did not set out to write the *Gorgias* in setting out to write the *Protagoras*. The argument must diverge somewhere. But the use of these truths in defence of

Socrates' argument is open to two objections. First, why write the *Protagoras* at all? Secondly, what right do we have to assume this kind of inter-dependence between dialogues? We do better in the first instance to interpret the *Protagoras* as an independent whole. 'Independent' because we have no evidence of any intention to supplement other works; 'whole' because other parts of the dialogue are relevant.

The problem arises from Hippocrates' meek affirmative to Socrates' question (312D–E): 'The music teacher no doubt makes you a clever speaker about what he teaches you, namely music. Isn't that so?' To which most of us would reply: 'No. He gives musical knowledge, not articulateness – not *qua* music teacher.' Nevertheless when testing in music we frequently test not only the performance of tasks but also the capacity to express verbally some principles behind the performance. There is a certain plausibility to Socrates' questioning suggestion.

Further, Socrates later puts to Protagoras a very similar suggestion. The argument Socrates lays before the sophist (319Bff.) is that the Athenians in their wisdom summon experts before the assembly when technical matters are on the agenda. The inexpert are unacceptable advisers. Plato and (so far as I know) his commentators say nothing here about the necessity for skills of communication to accompany the expertise concerned. Protagoras fails to raise the supposedly obvious question. He does not deny the statement that the Athenians listen to technical experts. He omits to ask if the experts need any other skills such as rhetoric to secure the Athenians' attention. From beginning to end of his Great Speech he does not mention rhetoric, either to affirm or to deny its necessity. Socrates, again, makes no mention of rhetoric in his subsequent interrogation. It is not therefore just Hippocrates' apparent stupidity that we have to explain in this matter. It is also very unlikely to be Plato's stupidity which has so constructed his dialogue; if any reader decides to take that view, he is welcome to stop reading either Plato or discussion of him.

We should rather suspect that in Athens, as in other democracies of more recent date,[11] the attitudes of ordinary people to oratory and rhetoric were ambivalent. Several Athenian speeches – some of them brilliantly put together – begin with a disclaimer of skill in speaking.[12]

That kind of skill one left to one's opponents. One might point the moral, perhaps, but not adorn the tale. The very disclaimer is an example of what it disclaims, almost self-refuting. But there it stands. Inexperience of the law, the desire to acquaint the jury with the plain facts of the case, a lack of the gift of the gab: all are commonly attributed to the speaker. Litigiousness, the preparation of speeches or even of speakers, skill in presentation: these are things one's opponent evinces or needs. Plato's Socrates may or may not have been indulging a taste for parody when he began the *Apology* with a contrast between persuasion and truth and the association of clever speaking with dishonesty.[13] He may indeed have been telling the strict truth, as he or Plato saw it. But the truth of his opening gambit will have been indistinguishable by a mass audience from skilled pleading. Of course the practice of such disclaimer is advantageous to the speaker, or it would not be a practice. The Athenians in assembly and law-court were continually offered the spectacle of two sides speaking with more or less eloquence in favour of opposing viewpoints. It can hardly have escaped their notice that approximately half these eloquent men supported losing causes. If the People became aware of their mistakes, a scapegoat was ready. They had been misled by those orators with their fine phrases.

The ordinary Athenian had another reason for suspicion of rhetoric. It more often resulted from expensive training than from natural ability. But in either case it was given to few. It was not only the speakers' putative dishonesty that gave rise to suspicion; it was their very superiority to ordinary people. Ordinary citizens were articulate enough for ordinary purposes; to seek or employ a higher articulateness was invidious, élitist, suspect. Cleon the politician in Thucydides cleverly plays on suspicions of cleverness;[14] and it looks as though Thucydides thought such a man would think such tactics sound psychology. The so-called Old Oligarch[15] thinks the people of Athens prefer plain folk like themselves as leaders. How such an intelligent conservative thinks is highly relevant to Plato. At the same time inherited wealth and the education it could buy were the object of respect.¹⁶ But though the system to a large extent depended on rhetoric there was something the Athenians did not quite like about rhetoric. They listened avidly and followed frequently; but they could also laugh at themselves for doing so.¹⁷

One might suppose this to be irrelevant to Plato's young Hippocrates, who is not a man of the people. He can raise enough money to pay Protagoras, certainly no cheap sophist. What did the upper classes think about rhetoric? Of course they bought it. It was a mode of self-defence as well as of political activism. But were they happy about it? Take the Theban herald in Euripides' *Suppliant Women*; for him the upstart orator's power over the people is a plague to the 'better sort'.¹⁸ But that is not a reason for the upper classes to eschew oratory. Such reasons, however, there were. The Athenian envoys to Melos¹⁹ give one, when invited to private discussion; it is no use, they say, making long speeches to mass audiences which may deceive them; better the opportunity to raise each point of disagreement as it occurs. Continuous harangue may be too alluring, too easily capable of evading counter-argument. Moreover, the noble and wealthy are as likely as the masses to feel that one ought not to need rhetorical skill; plain speaking should do. Indeed Pindar, addressing his noble patron, scorns learning; inherited knowledge is true 'wisdom', and straight speaking will bring one to the fore under whatever constitution, monarchy, oligarchy or democracy.²⁰ Like many Athenian litigants, Pindar appeals to the perhaps naive, but persistent, feeling that the unvarnished truth ought to suffice.

If that is the view one chooses to take up, then one will the more readily accept the suggestion that to know the truth is to be a good expositor of it. Hippocrates is not going against the grain when he accepts such a suggestion. He may appear muddled, and possibly is meant to appear callow; why, after all, seek out Protagoras in the hope of being trained as a speaker, if skilled speech is not necessary? The question is good; Hippocrates is indeed muddled. But then many people (and not only young and callow people) were and are muddled. Socrates and Plato deal with real people, rather than with abstract argument. There is nothing psychologically implausible about this particular confusion; indeed we have seen that ambivalent attitudes to rhetoric were widespread. But if one wants to acquire skill in speaking, and one believes (however inexplicitly) that this means knowing the subject of speech, then it follows that the teacher of speaking must teach that subject. One looks accordingly for a general subject to cover the wide range of public speaking. The sophist teaches speaking; so what subject does he teach?

Plato's Socrates asks Hippocrates this question just where it becomes pertinent. It is at our peril that we accuse either Socrates or his manipulator of muddle in such a case. To treat the unphilosophical Hippocrates as a victim of Socratic cheating is hardly permissible without first being careful that the rules are clear, and that it is certain what kind of person Socrates (and presumably Plato) is addressing. The Platonic Socrates insists that he only asks questions without supplying answers. Perhaps his interpreters could try taking him at his word. To do this is not to take Socrates in all seriousness as a man with a genuinely open and inquiring mind;[21] far from it. It is to take Socrates as using ordinary people's confusions to further confound them. Ordinary people are often confused, and the Platonic Socrates is notoriously acute.

We are not dealing here simply with the facts of Athenian democracy. The facts are clear. The man who wished to sway the decision of an Athenian assembly, for whatever kind of reason, needed 'qualities of nerve, application and expression that eliminated all save a comparatively few.'[22] But the facts were not always openly acknowledged. It is not quite right to say that the theory differed from the facts: the scattered hints of democratic thinking in ancient Athens have rightly been refused the dignity of a 'theory'.[23] What one can speak of is the myth of democracy, or better of two myths. The first is that the best counsellors are those of intelligence and understanding. Athenagoras, the Syracusan democrat, says so, in evident expectation of his audience's belief.[24] To know one's stuff is to be a good politician. The second is that one may listen to politicians, but need not believe what they say. Thus says the defendant of Lysias' 25th Speech, a man with an axe to grind but grinding it cleverly and playing on popular suspicions of the type.[25] The one myth assumes that persuasiveness accompanies understanding, the other assumes that persuasiveness is the cloak of venality. Both are heard in the late fifth and early fourth centuries, and both thought acceptable to a mass audience.

The power of a myth should never be underestimated; if Plato's youthful Hippocrates both wants to learn the art of speaking and prefers to avoid the implication that it consists in something other than the plain statement of ascertained truth, there is nothing in our text to make us suppose him out of the ordinary. Plato goes out of his way to emphasize his youthful eagerness, his impetuous haste to obtain an introduction to Protagoras (e.g. 310E–311A): we are certainly not meant to think of him as any clearer of mind than the average young man of good family was, or indeed than the average young person of today wishing to enter university and gain a degree in the Humanities.

Indeed his hasty impetuosity is the subject of a brief harangue by Socrates (313A–314C); he points out that Hippocrates himself thinks his soul more important than his body, but that, though he would have consulted extensively before entrusting his body to a trainer, he has consulted nobody before rushing to try and see Protagoras. This though his soul is decisive in the success or failure of his life. This though he knows neither Protagoras personally nor what a sophist is in general. Nothing in this is out of keeping with what precedes. Hippocrates is abashed.

What follows again foreshadows a point to be made later by Protagoras. Continuing the comparison with the body, Socrates asks (313C–D) whether the sophist is a sort of grocer selling food for the soul. Hippocrates' question what the soul feeds on receives the reply, 'Things learnt.' Grocers do not know what is good for the customers, they just advertise their wares. Perhaps sophists behave analogously? The condition for safety of purchase is the knowledge what is good for you; and without it one is exposed to risks greater in the case of the sophist than in that of the grocer. One does not consume the grocer's wares on the spot; but one learns the sophist's teaching as he teaches, and cannot consult after purchase as to whether such consumption was wise. The comparison may seem crude, but it is in part unconsciously echoed by Protagoras (351B): courage arises from one's nature and from good nourishment of the soul.[26] The question what is good nourishment for the soul becomes vital. But for the present we may observe only that, though Socrates' language is perhaps intended pejoratively (one doubts whether Hippocrates' wealth is derived from trade), there is nothing in the comparison of grocer and sophist to which Protagoras would naturally take overt exception.

Indeed, nothing could please the sophist more than Socrates' final suggestion that they consult in the matter with the sophists themselves! They are 'wise' themselves, are they not? In the case of food one consulted a doctor who knows what to eat in what quantities when; one did not consult the grocer. Socrates only said earlier (313D–E) that *perhaps some* of the sellers of instruction do not know what is good and bad for the soul. But his bland assumption (315C), in describing Protagoras as 'wise', that the present company are not among those thus ignorant is devastatingly ironical. The irony, however, passes over the head of Hippocrates in his eagerness to meet Protagoras. The question raised in the reader's mind, whether Protagoras is or is not cognizant of the beneficial or harmful nature of his wares, is not one which Plato allows Hippocrates himself to raise.

The approach to Protagoras

The following pages of narrative and description serve to put the sophists and the deference paid to them in a humorous light. The elegant circles described by Protagoras' listeners to keep out of his way (315B), the questioners listening to Hippias (315C), the divine – but (alas!) inaudible wisdom of Prodicus (315E–316A), all receive irreverent attention. Even the tribute to Prodicus is both too exaggerated and (in any case) belied by the sequel. Yet if *these* sophists, listened to by so many distinguished people, have not the knowledge Socrates and Hippocrates seek, who (one may ask) has? The serious question lies behind the surface gaiety.

The initial approach to Protagoras is quiet and private. Hippocrates is presented (316B–C) as a scion of a great and fortunate house, the equal in natural ability of any of his contemporaries. He wishes to become 'famous in the city'[27] and believes that will happen if he spends time with Protagoras. Protagoras, offered the choice, prefers to discuss not privately but rather in the presence of others, including (doubtless for the sake of showing off) the other sophists. When all are duly assembled, Socrates puts his point again (318A). This time the statement about Hippocrates is outwardly different. He desires to spend time in Protagoras' company – it is not specified why – and he wishes to know what will be the result of doing so. Protagoras addresses his reply to Hippocrates: each day Hippocrates spends in Protagoras' company he will get better. Socrates, whether or not still on Hippocrates' own behalf, counters with the question, better at what?

This bald summary covers a complex passage. Socrates' suggestion that Hippocrates wishes to become 'famous in the city' is not repeated in public, perhaps to spare the young man's blushes. But the suggestion itself was not a clear result of the previous discussion between Socrates and Hippocrates. Hippocrates wishes to become a skilled speaker, but it is not quite clear how he thinks this will help him. He believes in the efficacy of rhetoric, but is unwilling to reject the sufficiency of plain exposition. He has not said what subject he wishes to learn, because he is unsure what the sophist teaches. With this result Socrates' second, more reticent way of putting the matter is in greater agreement than the first; the one thing Hippocrates is sure of is his desire to visit Protagoras. If Hippocrates does want to become a successful politician, that can only be a deduction by Socrates from the opening enthusiasm the youth displays for Protagoras' brand of rhetoric. Since it is only Socrates' deduction we cannot be quite sure what its content is. In the *Theages* (126A) (whether by Plato or not) the expression 'famous in the city' is applied to the likes of the great Athenian statesmen Themistocles, Pericles and Cimon, *by Theages*. Socrates merely *asks* if that is the way Theages uses the expression, as no doubt many others would naturally have done. Put into Hippocrates' mouth, the desire Socrates mentions can only be to end up a successful politician in that normal sense. On

Socrates' lips the expression might refer to a very different type.

But even if one confines oneself to Hippocrates' desire, there is – and was – more than one way of succeeding in politics. Between Aristides the Just and Hyperbolus, to speak only of fifth-century Athenian politics, a great gulf stretches. We have seen already that the content of Protagoras' teaching is a possible issue; and he himself allows it to become a live problem. For in response to Socrates' initial private introduction Protagoras tells us, directly or indirectly, several things relevant both to what precedes and to what follows. First, he claims by implication (and later openly) to practise the 'sophistic art' and to be a sophist (316CD). He suggests, and with reason, that to take people away from their normal company, whether contemporary or older, whether family or other, and claim to make them 'better' is invidious. He alleges – and there is no reason to suppose the allegation ironical or humorous in tone – that his predecessors were less open; they concealed their purpose behind the title of 'poet' (Homer, Hesiod, Simonides) or 'purveyor of Mystery-rites' or 'of oracles' (Orpheus and Musaeus), or 'gymnast' (Iccus or Herodicus), or 'musician' (Agathocles, Pythoclides and others). All these were, according to Protagoras, sophists and practitioners of the sophistic art.

This is a passage the commentators often skate over, resting content with a digest of biographical information. Yet its importance for the structure of the dialogue is great. First, the variety of sophists lends colour in retrospect to Socrates' doubts whether Hippocrates knows what a sophist is. What relevant property or qualification do all these figures have in common, which enables Protagoras to say that they are all crypto-sophists? Secondly, this is the first, but assuredly not the last, mention of Simonides. Simonides is a sophist – but according to Protagoras later in the dialogue (339Aff.) he has written a contradictory, and hence bad, poem about questions of great relevance to Protagoras' claims to teach 'goodness' or to impart the necessary for 'success'. We are losing something if we fail to observe the need to compare that passage with this one; and accidental coincidence may be ruled out, for Simonides, fine poet though he was, was not the obvious poet to rank with Homer and Hesiod and single out from the serried ranks of their successors. The question of poetic authority looms large in the *Protagoras*, very properly in a searching discussion of education; for the poets, as Protagoras makes amply clear in the dialogue itself, were central to normal Athenian education.[28]

The passage implies certain sophistic procedures, and affects Protagoras' claim to fulfil Hippocrates' needs. Poets apparently were not regarded as teachers of vivid and compelling speech; their educational value lay more in *what* they said (though not in every detail, e.g., of boat-building in the *Odyssey*). Aristophanes' comedy *Frogs*, portraying Aeschylus and Euripides as political and moral rivals for public esteem, has a serious point.[29] If Athenian rhetorical commonplaces sometimes drew on poetry,[30] that was a matter of content rather than form. Plato's awareness of the importance to education of poems' substance and his disapproval of actual poetic content reappear in his expulsion from the *Republic* of most existing poetry. If the educational value of poetry (high or low) lay in its content and substance, then if the poets are practitioners of the sophistic art the sophists too as their more overt successors must have something substantive, rather than merely formal, to transmit. In this they differ from the gymnasts, whose concern is to build a body as a tool, not to impart substantive knowledge.

If Socrates wishes, he now has a quite legitimate and reasonable excuse for inquiry into the substantive subject Protagoras teaches. What kind of sophist is he? Like the poets or like the gymnasts? Plato knew, and so presumably did his readers, that the sophists taught a good deal by expounding the meaning of poetry and discussing what it said – and that this was no new practice in Athenian education. The suggestion that like the poets they had something to say is a reasonable one; it is evident that the fifth-century sophists were not pure and disinterested scholars. Exposition of poetry will have meant teaching or preaching on the basis of the poet's text. Protagoras later in this dialogue takes an interest in Simonides' subject matter, in the truth or falsehood of his message. Such an interest can hardly have come as a surprise, or novelty, to Plato's readers. When Socrates has finished his 'exposition' of Simonides' poem,[31] Hippias has his own exposition of it ready for performance (347A–B): it is perfectly clear that the performance is one of a standard sophistic type. We have no reason to suppose Plato is falsifying Protagoras' views when his Protagoras says (338E–339A) he believes a large part of education to be skill in the field of poetry, the ability to perceive what is rightly or wrongly composed. Since Protagoras' claim is to educate people (317B), we should assume that the subject matter of the poets and its analysis form an important part of the basis for that claim. It may seem strange to us that Protagoras does not make himself out simply as an instructor in the formal aspects of rhetoric, and thus evade the Socratic questioning which follows. But if Plato had allowed him to do this, the dialogue would have been untrue to life. A sophist was expected to have something other than the purely formal to talk about, and his pretensions lived up to expectations. Socrates is arguing not with a logical abstraction but with a human being. There is no reason to believe Hippocrates' expectations (so far as they were clear) to have been any different. The sophists' mode of teaching clever speech was a short cut to the wisdom otherwise to be acquired in the school of life.

A further aspect of Protagoras' teaching becomes clear in this preliminary and private discussion. Protagoras has the makings of an intellectual snob. He claims (317A) that the denial of sophistic pretensions is immediately transparent to the keen gaze of the politically capable: the masses, however, perceive virtually nothing, merely repeating what they are told. The theme of the 'masses' and of the sophist's evaluation of them runs through the dialogue, and helps to push Protagoras into some tight corners. Here we get, presumably, Protagoras' genuine view, so far as he has a consistent view of the matter at all. This is the view he is willing to air in front of a prospective pupil from a great and wealthy house: but such were, for the most part, his normal clientèle[32] and, genuine or not, this was doubtless the view in which he encouraged them. Protagoras' view of democracy, in effect, is that it is a waste of time; the multitudes have no independent thoughts, and merely parrot their leaders' arguments. But this is not a view he thinks fit to express before an audience. Even before an audience of sophists, pupils, patrons and the like, he cannot openly deride the democracy in Athens. The commitment of such as Alcibiades and Callias to the democratic constitution was certainly not absolute; but openly to acknowledge its qualifications would not do. One reason why was that the teaching of gentlemen to speak in public presupposed a crowd to be swayed; rhetoric took its rise from the coming of democracy to the Greek world. Another reason was the actual physical danger involved. Greek democrats tended to have a short way with their radical opponents. Hippocrates himself will have been brought up in this atmosphere.

Parts of this private scene are now duplicated in public (317Eff.). Hippocrates' desires are made known, as we saw, in slightly abbreviated form. He wishes to know the consequences of indulging in Protagoras' company; the word 'pupil' is not on Socrates' lips, for reasons which will become clear when the question is broached whether goodness can be taught. Protagoras replies not to Socrates but to the young man (318A). Socrates is still very much Hippocrates' representative in putting his question. The reply declares that Hippocrates will be 'better' every day he attends. Just as Socrates asked Hippocrates before, so now he asks Protagoras to be more specific. Just as he offered Hippocrates examples of crafts whose experts could speak 'wisely' on them, so now he offers Protagoras examples of professional expertise which the experts pass on. The examples start with the famous painter Zeuxippus, and then strike nearer home, bringing out by implication the relevance of Protagoras' remarks in private. Orthagoras is a flautist; would not a pupil of his become each day a better flautist? One wonders whether Orthagoras, like Agathocles and Pythoclides the musicians, was supposed to be a 'closet' sophist, and, if so, how Protagoras distinguishes his teaching from theirs, and wherein lies his expertise. Indeed Socrates' climactic question to Protagoras (318D) is what Hippocrates would be better at, and 'concerning what' he would be the better, for Protagoras' company.

This argument can only be understood in the light of the syntax of 'good' and 'better' and their semantics in Greek, which were not at all points the same as in English. 'Good' in

Greek, the highest word of commendation, had strong political overtones. It carried part of the tone of 'successful' in English. A good man was a man whose life was as a whole a successful life. Success would then, as now, have been measured differently by different people in different moods and circumstances. A good life would be one that served its purpose; and there is notoriously more disagreement over the purposes of Man than over the purposes of, e.g., a knife. As in English, so in Greek 'good' can occur in such contexts as 'good at' some activity. The greater variety of Greek syntax in such contexts need not bother us here.

Protagoras, then, answers Hippocrates' question by saying that he will emerge from each day's education a better man. Socrates asks him in retort 'better at what?' We are inclined to protest that one can be a better man without being better *at* anything. But Plato's Socrates repeatedly ignores this point; he treats goodness as a skill.[33] But to say that this simply vitiates his argument is to oversimplify. The question remains, by what criterion Hippocrates would become the better for Protagoras' company and in what respect his life would be a more successful one than otherwise. What does Protagoras impart which has this remarkable effect? Any teaching of something one does not know will make one 'better' in some respect; even though Protagoras is so 'wise', if he learnt something new, he would be the better for it. In what respect will Hippocrates be the better? An unspoken but powerfully latent question is 'What counts as success?'

Protagoras' answer again ends by getting him into trouble, and is best taken with what follows. But it is worth remembering that, since Socrates had pointed out to Hippocrates earlier that the sophist's expertise and teaching stand in need of delimitation and definition, and Hippocrates had admitted this, Socrates could still up to this point claim to be representing Hippocrates. This will be of some interest later.

Protagoras' explanation and Socrates' doubts

Protagoras begins with a negative remark (318D): he is not like the other sophists. They corrupt the young – an astonishing piece of 'knocking copy' – by taking them as they emerge from the arts or skills and dragging them back again against their wishes. They teach 'arts' such as arithmetic and other mathematical subjects and 'music' (probably here music in our sense). What his pupils learn from him is not what they learn from the likes of Hippias. From Protagoras the young learn what, and only what, they came to learn. The subject is 'good counsel' or 'wise deliberation' concerning their family affairs and concerning the city's affairs. This is to enable them to manage their family as 'well' as possible, and to excel in capacity to act and to speak on the city's business. Socrates is not quite sure that he follows, and asks Protagoras if his promise is to teach the political art and to make men good citizens (319A).[34] Protagoras accepts this as an exact account of his programme.

Protagoras again makes admissions here which land him in eventual dialectical difficulty. His account of his profession raises problems and contains inherent ambiguities. The most obvious trouble arises from his wording of the claim to differ from the other sophists.

Fifty years ago G. M. A. Grube demonstrated the capital importance of this claim for the organization of the dialogue as a whole.[35] Protagoras rejects the mathematical studies of Hippias, only to find himself at the end of the conversation constrained to admit the necessity for an art of measurement (357B–358A). But he is in difficulty long before that. For, formally, his admission that he teaches the political art is in plain contradiction with his immediately preceding distinction of himself from his colleagues. They teach 'the arts'. He taught 'good deliberation'. Yet what he imparts is an 'art' no less than what they impart.

True, the notion of 'art' is vague at this period, and it is the Platonic Socrates who appears in our sources to take the first steps to clarify and sharpen the word's use. But even if we accept the perhaps rather extreme view[36] that 'any kind of purposive activity of which the speaker approves may be dubbed a[n art] by him and thus endowed with intellectual respectability', we shall still be unable to rid the sophist of the necessity to think again, and, if possible, explain himself. No doubt it *is* possible. Protagoras need only specify 'mathematical' arts for rejection, to save himself at any rate for the time being. But he does not apparently see the necessity, nor perceive the consequences, of allowing Socrates to foist on him the term 'political art'.[37] Socrates himself does not bring out the contradiction yet; he leaves it to cause trouble later.

But why does Socrates, and (more urgently still) why does Plato so foist a Socratic view of things on Socrates' interlocutor? Can we say of this passage in particular, to use the words of E. A. Havelock, 'In the so-called aporetic dialogues various opinions elicited from the respondent can be reduced to apparent contradiction by the device of getting each of them re-worded in terms of the questioner's own principles'?[38] Readers of the *Protagoras* have often protested at Socrates' handling of Protagoras here. But there are good reasons for it. Protagoras claims to possess an 'art' himself, presumably a body of knowledge in some sense organized, organizable or organic (if indeed it is not merely a way of earning a living).[39] He claims to impart a 'subject' or 'learnt thing' which is describable as a whole in a succinct and orderly way. This learning is concerned with exactly what his pupils seek and no more. Unless their thinking is vague (which he can hardly admit), his subject is strictly limited. In Platonic Greek, what you have learned is closely correlated with what you know, and what you know is a knowledge or an 'art'.[40]

All this is less a theory than it is a habit of thought and of linguistic usage. The epistemological status of what he teaches is represented by Plato as a problem Protagoras has not faced. Whether that is unfair to the historical Protagoras is a question not decidable without close analysis of the *Theaetetus*, a by-way we need not follow, since Plato does not follow it in the *Protagoras*. One may doubt whether it would have been unfair to the majority of sophists, and even more whether it would have been unfair to their pupils to suppose them not to have demanded clarification of the question in the way Socrates eventually does.

We may proceed to another objection made to the passage in recent years.[41] The objection makes a clear distinction between being a good politician (or indeed statesman) and being a good citizen, and urges that to be the former 'is at best *a necessary condition of being a good citizen, another necess-*

ary condition being the possession of the moral qualities,' such as 'loyalty, public-spiritedness and a sense of fairness.' This criticism depends on the supposition that the words used by Protagoras are far less slippery than in fact they are. If 'good counsel', 'good' management and the capacity to speak and act politically (presumably also 'well') are plainly and uniquely interpretable in terms of worldly success as opposed to, and to the exclusion of, unworldly values, *and* if a 'good citizen' is one who possesses unworldly virtues such as loyalty and fair-mindedness as well as the qualities more obviously conducive to political success in a worldly sense, then evidently a clash between the two passages develops. Evidently by interpreting a 'good citizen' in terms partly 'unworldly', while restricting 'good counsel' to 'worldly' contexts, we have made it impossible to call 'good counsel' a sufficient condition of 'good citizenship'. But we should be very careful not to allow ourselves to criticize Protagoras' or Socrates' logic here on the basis of what we ourselves mean by a 'good citizen'. We should be at least equally careful not to read prematurely into Protagoras' remarks here the qualities that he later appears to think essential for a participant in human society. Those later appearances will need discussion, at some length. But there is no need to stir up that hornet's nest yet. In the responses Protagoras offers Socrates here at the outset of their encounter there is no *need* to take a 'good citizen' as anything other than a successful citizen, successful in the worldly politician's sense.

We should, however, bear in mind that if the role of the successful citizen prove to require or to consist of less worldly qualities, then by the same token 'good' or successful counsel or administration may require or consist of those same qualities. The evaluative words 'good' and 'well' do not yet have any clear descriptive content.[42] It is too readily assumed that Hippocrates' needs are also unambiguously worldly or competitive. So in the first instance they doubtless were; but Socrates has undermined his apparent certainty in their preliminary conversation. True, Protagoras has not been privy to that conversation. But any notion that youths of Hippocrates' type in general were single-mindedly clear what they wanted must depend on the suggestion that their values and ideals were free from confusion. Plato would most assuredly not have accepted that suggestion; and neither should we, without further investigation which is best postponed until more specific terms of commendation enter the discussion.

Socrates' attack

Socrates begins (319A) with an expression of admiration, qualified by a conditional clause reminiscent of his earlier conditional assertion of Protagoras' wisdom (309D), but with an extra tinge of doubt. He explains his doubt whether the political art is teachable, despite his respect for Protagoras. His reasons for doubting start from the views he attributes to the Athenians, whom he also calls 'wise' (319B).[43] This is certainly ironic on one level. Socrates shows, e.g. in the *Crito*, that he does not respect the opinions of 'the many'. What he cares about in that dialogue is the convincing of Crito. Socrates' account of his mission, in the *Apology*, makes no sense if he truly thought the Athenians wise. We may be pretty sure that Socrates' statement in the *Protagoras* of the Athenians' wisdom does not fully represent his true opinion. Few have supposed that it does. The point has rightly been seen as putting Protagoras ultimately in a dilemma.[44] If the disproof of his sophistic pretensions rests on the principles of Athenian democracy, he is forced to abandon either the principles or the pretensions (or indeed both). In fact he abandons neither. The whole raises the question why Plato should face his character with this dilemma when he himself was apparently a severe critic of the democracy. If the premise of an argument can be put forward only with heavy irony, why argue thus at all? The question deserves a tentative answer.

Socrates began the discussion as the representative of Hippocrates. Hippocrates is not opposed to the democracy, and seeks the technique of public speaking presumably in order to succeed in democratic politics. Socrates' objections to Protagoras are based on Athenian democratic practice. It is plausible to suppose that Socrates is acting still as Hippocrates' representative. Hippocrates is not responsible for the characteristic lucidity and consequentiality of Socrates' discourse, but Socrates' questions to Protagoras are just the ones Hippocrates ought to ask. True, Socrates represents the questions as springing from his own intellectual biography; 'I didn't think that that was something that could be taught, but since you say that you teach it I don't see how I can doubt you.' (319A–B). But that sentence on Socrates' lips is also heavily ironical. It is not Socrates' practice to take his views from other people. His overt acceptance of Protagoras' authority could only be genuine if he thought Protagoras 'wise' in a very strong sense, without irony – which is unlikely. Hippocrates, however, has expressed no real doubt of Protagoras' wisdom, even if he cannot characterize it verbally; and he began with a firm conviction of it (310D). Hippocrates may reasonably be regarded as a democrat with élitist leanings, and as such he would receive adequate representation here. It would then be Hippocrates and his like who believe in the wisdom both of democratic principles and of the sophists, and need to have the two reconciled. Certainty is unattainable on such points; but this hypothesis at least makes dialectical sense of an argument otherwise difficult to understand.

Whatever the truth of this explanation, Socrates puts forward his criticisms on the basis of the Athenians' wisdom. They are basically two. The first is that the Athenians take advice from experts and reject inexpert advice in fields they deem learnable and teachable, and believe to be matters of 'art' (319B–C). The context makes clear Socrates' assumption that the Athenians think of things learnable and teachable as coextensive with matters of 'art'. Incidentally this confirms that Protagoras' claim to purvey a subject, a 'thing learnt', entails a claim to purvey an 'art' – an entailment Protagoras says nothing to weaken. On the subject of the city's administration the Athenians take advice from all and sundry, whatever 'art' the adviser normally practises, and whatever his wealth or poverty, without either enquiry who taught him or objection to the untaught. From this Socrates deduces (roughly speaking) that they think the 'art' of political advice to be teachable.

Secondly, the 'wisest' and 'best' of the citizens, exemplified by Pericles, cannot or do not educate those one would expect them to if they could (319E). Again it is very doubtful if

Socrates approves of these well-known and conventionally admired statesmen: such are not the feelings he appears to evince in the *Gorgias*, nor need we find such in the *Meno*.[45] It is never safe to ascribe a conventional judgement to the Platonic Socrates. But Hippocrates would most naturally be expected to share the normal Athenian veneration for Pericles. Anyhow, the second argument falls into two portions, Pericles' treatment of his son and of his ward. Pericles' son received from his father training in everything that depends on training, but in the subject of Pericles' own 'wisdom' he received no teaching from his father or from anyone else. His ward Pericles removed from Alcibiades' company and had educated in another household – but only for six months, after which he acknowledged the experiment's failure and returned the boy to Alcibiades.[46]

These arguments have been criticized, and with some reason, as tending to show only that success or goodness is not taught, not that it cannot be taught. As the critic remarks,[47] 'the fact that [the same word] spans "taught" and "teachable" renders the discrepancy more difficult to detect in Greek.' The two positions are almost equally fatal to Protagoras as a sophist. If the Athenians do believe, or if Hippocrates and the rest of his potential pupils are led to believe, that no one teaches goodness, the consequences for Protagoras' trade will be immediately disastrous. That would mean the Athenians' or his clientèle's disbelief in Protagoras' own teaching. The impossibility of teaching goodness would add to Protagoras' present failure only the impossibility of redeeming it. This would add only slightly to the disgrace of one who had been for a generation claiming to teach it. To save his face, Protagoras must eventually show that the subject is acknowledged to be not merely teachable in the abstract, but in fact taught. At least he must reconcile this thesis with the principles of democracy as Socrates (meeting with no dissent) expounds them.

But Socrates' actual arguments need more attention. Like Protagoras in his opening remarks adverse to the other sophists, Socrates distinguishes the 'arts' from the field of political deliberation. The distinction rests on the calling in of experts on the one, but not on the other. In the one case it is normal to inquire who taught the speaker the relevant 'art'. In the other such inquiry never takes place. This creates a presumption, or so Socrates would have us believe, at least that, in the Athenians' opinion, nobody teaches the non-art in question – whether or not it is possible to teach it. If they did think of goodness as taught and teachable like the 'arts' in general, then their behaviour is anomalous.

Socrates' second main argument (319Dff.) takes the 'wisest' of the 'wise', the most distinguished single politician of recent Athenian history, and uses him as an example of successful Athenian politicians in general. Pericles' withdrawal of his ward Clinias from the house of Ariphron is merely an example of failure to teach; but such a person's failure suggests (without proving) impossibility. What suggests it more strongly is Pericles' failure even to attempt to teach his sons, or to have them taught, the political goodness he himself so conspicuously possessed. This is not (as one might object) because Pericles was too busy to attend to his sons' education; he had them taught anything dependent on teaching. If the subject were teachable, who should be better at either teaching it or selecting a teacher than the pre-eminent expert? If the experts cannot teach the subject, then who can? If, in addition, they can find no teachers, there are none available. This argument works, in so far as it does work, by showing that Pericles either could not or would not pass on his expertise; evidently it is not the case that he would not; so he could not. The same goes, says Socrates, for many other prominent experts in the field: neither their own family nor any outsider received the political 'art' from them. The suspicion grows that the 'art' is not merely subject to an unusual famine of teachers, but liable (shall we say?) to peculiar difficulty of teaching. One is used to *some* experts being bad teachers: but all of them?

The Athenians in their 'wisdom' (Hippocrates, doubtless, among them) count Pericles as 'wise' and successful; Socrates does not say in support anything more than his general endorsement of Athenian 'wisdom'. The two parallel ascriptions of 'wisdom' in the one speech, to the Athenians and to Pericles, are doubtless both ironical. They are popular, not Socratic, evaluations.

The difficulties facing Protagoras are now acute. They concern more than his dubious democratic credentials. Not only does his public refusal to reject the wisdom of the Athenians contrast with his private readiness to say (317A) that the masses perceive nothing and are intellectually incapable of more than parroting. He has distinguished 'arts' from what he teaches, and yet has accepted that he teaches the 'art' of politics; and now he meets the suggestion that the Athenians do not think his subject to be an 'art' nor any teachers of it to be available. He implied it was not an 'art' that he taught, but nevertheless he admitted that he practised one, the sophistic 'art'. It is scarcely surprising that the relation between teachability and knowledge (or what one learns) returns with redoubled irony at the end of the dialogue (361A–C). Even if the vagueness of the word 'art' is at fault, Protagoras must, in order to extricate himself from this complex tangle, clarify his notion of 'art'. This, as we shall see, he signally fails to do. The failure is fundamental to the whole argument. But Protagoras does have his successes, and his reconciliation of democracy with sophistic education is at least a temporary one.

Socrates' own position is not free from difficulties. He has introduced the phrase 'political art' himself (319A), but not unambiguously as one he would himself accept. He suggests that Protagoras 'means' or 'is talking about' the 'political art', and is promising to make men good citizens. This is preceded by an inquiry whether he has correctly understood Protagoras, and is clearly put in a questioning tone. An inquiry of this sort would normally presuppose the existence of the political 'art'. But Socrates is not necessarily committed to that here. He could be offering the term 'political art' to Protagoras as an interpretation of his claim without himself endorsing the existence of the thing referred to in the claim or the interpretation. Socrates' next sentence is a statement, but he hedges his bets in it. 'Indeed, you have a fine work of art then, if indeed you do have it. For I will be frank with you; I didn't think it a teachable thing.'[48] Obviously this pair of sentences in itself would not commit the speaker to 'art' as a description of Protagoras' activity. The less Socrates is committed to that and similar descriptions the better for him. He does commit himself in the same speech to the Athenians' wisdom (319B), their authority to speak on matters such as these; and he then lends them the expressions (319C–D) 'a subject which they think can be learned and taught' and 'what they regard as a technical matter', these expressions occurring in positions making them equivalent. Here 'technical' again renders an expression containing the Greek for 'art'. Socrates represents the Athenians as equating the teachable with an 'art'. After accepting their authority, he should accept this view, or this use of language, as he accepts others. His further acceptance from the Athenians of the non-teachability of Protagoras' subject, and hence of its status as a non-art, may lead to trouble. To the degree that he has accepted the term 'art' as descriptive of the sophist's political subject, he is now near self-contradiction.

But Protagoras cannot formally convict him of the contradiction unless he can show that he was committed to the term 'art' by his earlier inquiry – which would be an elusive demonstrand. Most Platonic chronologies assume that Socrates has already in previous works been committed to thinking of goodness as an 'art', but that does not commit him here. For all that, the seeds are sown here of the remarkable turnabout at the end of the dialogue (361A–B). There Socrates points out that Protagoras has been maintaining simultaneously that goodness is teachable but not knowledge, while Socrates has been defending simultaneously the positions that goodness is knowledge and that it is not teachable. The term 'knowledge' can in many contexts replace the word 'art'.[49] Socrates is left in that passage with a commonly held view (that goodness is not teachable) in opposition to a notoriously Socratic tenet, the status of goodness as an 'art' or 'knowledge'. The situation is closely parallel to that in the *Laches*, where the commonly held view of courage as a part of goodness is left in conflict with the Socratic idea that goodness is knowledge. In each case the final clash of doctrines is anticipated at the start of the discussion and receives careful preparation. Plato's elegant shaping of these dialogues deserves attention for the light it may throw (as we shall see) on his philosophical intentions.

Protagoras' Great Speech

Protagoras' reconciliation of his teaching with democratic principles takes broadly the form of casting Socrates' premisses in his teeth and offering very different deductions from them.[50] The Athenians take advice on political questions not from selected experts but from Tom, Dick and Harry? That is because every Tom, Dick, and Harry possesses in some degree (not of course all in the same degree) the requisite expertise (322D–323C). Socrates cannot perceive the identity of the teacher (and nobody inquires about it)? That is because everybody teaches it (327E–328A). The community should reject the inexpert in politics, if there should be such an aberration, as it rejects (e.g.) the inexpert shipbuilder (325A–B). The failure of statesmen to educate their sons in statesmanship is due to the sons' comparative lack of natural ability (327B–C)[51] – a nice touch, this, in the democratic context, with its built-in distrust of inherited characteristics and power, and at the same time a nice 'come-on' for Hippocrates, whose natural endowments Socrates has described as rivalling any of his contemporaries (316C).

A similar enticement for the sons of Pericles, who are present, forms the speech's climax; there is still hope for them, they are young yet, and Protagoras is better at bringing people on towards 'goodness' than most (328B–D). But if Pericles let his sons run loose, to pick up goodness by chance, that was presumably because everyone they encounter has some share of goodness. By dint of emphasizing the universality of goodness and modestly (but not utterly) minimizing his own contribution, Protagoras successfully walks the tightrope. To fall on one side would democratize his profession out of existence, to fall on the other would rouse egalitarian hackles. He falls on neither.

Three questions seem more immediately relevant to present purposes than the many others this famous speech has stirred up. The first concerns the relation between 'justice and conscience' in the myth and Protagoras' promised training of

Hippocrates in the political 'art'. The second inquires into the status of the political 'art' relative to other 'arts'. The third, singled out by Socrates as the immediate object of his dialectical probing, demands to know the exact position of the virtues, or good qualities, in the make-up of 'goodness'. All three of these throw light on the specifically dialectical nature of the speech and of Socrates' attack on it. The reader will not find here a complete account of the speech, its provenance, its implications, its rhetoric, and its general properties. The present discussion aims merely to focus attention on certain details relevant to these three questions.

'Justice' and the political 'art'

Several scholars, from at least as far back as Paul Shorey down to Taylor's recent commentary, have found a basic defect in Protagoras' whole answer to Socrates.[52] They believe that Hippocrates seeks from Protagoras the ability to shine in competitive politics, that Protagoras talks in both the mythical and the argumentative portions of his speech about values such as 'justice' and 'conscience', and that these 'cooperative' qualities are at best a necessary, and not a sufficient, condition of the kind of political success Hippocrates and his like want.[53]

The best and most detailed exposition of this general view comes from the pen of A. W. H. Adkins.[54] It shows the pitfalls in a democratic society for a sophist offering the rich, in effect, power by means of rhetoric over those unable to afford the sophists' teaching. On this interpretation Protagoras claims to teach the cooperative virtues in a society unable to tame and willing to suspect the successful man. Protagoras in this dialogue thus becomes either the victim of a prevailing confusion, or the user of great rhetorical skill to defend his profession. The claim to teach 'political and administrative skills' is supported by and interlarded with the claim to teach cooperative virtues.[55] With respect to Pericles' sons for example, in Protagoras' conclusion, '... skill is once again in the forefront of Protagoras' mind ... for lack of justice is not the complaint against them.' The speech appears both as 'the kind of utterance which might well have been made by a newly arrived sophist with the suspicions of a mass audience in mind' and as offering 'bait' for those able to afford sophistic instructions, whether inheritors of wealth and status, or newly enriched. An extra irony is to be found in the sophist's adoption of a lengthy 'disguise' such as he had explicitly abjured in his private remarks to Socrates earlier (317B).[56]

This is a brilliant piece of interpretation, shedding light on many dark corners of the speech, and doing so with a luminous clarity to which any summary such as this can hardly be anything but unfair. Much of it is indeed simply true. As an exposition of the argument it is formidable. But one is left with a feeling of uneasiness about it as an account of Protagoras' motives, as Plato depicts him in the dialogue.

Protagoras, after all, is not speaking to a mass audience in Plato's context. The audience in the house of Callias is one of Callias and those whom his porter will admit (315D). They consist of the sophists themselves and those already initially attracted to them. A substantial number of people are present, but hardly a 'mass' audience. So why should Protagoras offer in Plato's setting an address suitable for a mass audience which is not there? So that report of it could filter out? But what filtered out was likely to rouse as much suspicion as it allayed. It could all too easily be described as bait for the rich mingled with lip-service to democratic principles. Adkins himself suggests in a footnote, immediately after mentioning a mass audience, that '(The speech) may well have been modelled on (a public display) of Protagoras known to Plato.'[57] The suggestion argues a certain uneasiness in its author's mind too. It looks (though apologies are due if it is not so) as if we are being asked to believe that Plato took over the gist of a highly skilful address by Protagoras to a 'mass audience' and used it on a fictional occasion it did not suit.[58]

If this is what Plato did, then he was seriously at fault. He portrays Protagoras as answering Socrates before a particular audience with a speech designed for a quite different one; and he shows Socrates paying no attention to this point. He makes Plato give his Protagoras a 'disguise' wholly unnecessary and highly improbable in context, and then have the impertinence to be ironical about it. Plato may have done such unscrupulous things; but the absence of any suggested motive does not make it easier to believe in them. Do we have to accept so unfair a Plato?

To suppose that we do is unduly to depreciate another piece of evidence already analysed, to wit Socrates' ascription of wisdom to the Athenians. To suppose Protagoras to adopt the tone he does with a mass audience in mind is either to suppose that Socrates makes democratic noises with the same kind of purpose or to assume an unlikely asymmetry between Protagoras' and Socrates' compliments to the Athenian people. Adkins has to dismiss Socrates' reference to the Athenians' wisdom in a footnote as an attempt 'to strengthen the argument'.[59] It is, however, much more; it is the indispensable premiss of Socrates' first argument.

The two protagonists both put forward, with whatever purpose, views based on the democratic principles of Periclean Athens. The suggestion that Socrates has in mind the young Athenian Hippocrates and his natural reactions is an obvious one; equally obvious is the matching supposition that Protagoras too has in his sights Hippocrates and his like. We have no need to assume two separate groups of people who form the target of different parts of Protagoras' speech. One individual or one class of society may hold views seeming to the dispassionate observer incompatible or at least uncomfortable together. A modern parallel might be the adoption by the British trade union movement of principles both of egalitarianism and of differential according to merit. It would be rash to suppose the ancient Athenians immune from such unclarities.

It is a relevant fact that, with the striking exception of a few years around the end of a long and disastrous war, the Athenian democracy was virtually untroubled by dissent from or subversion of its principles for over a century. As in Pericles' day, so in Plato's, extremism at both ends of the political spectrum was impotent. The slogan 'cancel all debts', beloved of lower-class Greek extremists, is virtually unheard in Classical Athens, and aristocratic and oligarchic clubs do not appear to have wielded significant power. The upper middle class supplied many leaders for the democracy. The great houses were less significant in the fourth century than in the fifth, but many of them took pride in contributing to the city's defence and religious expenditure. In particular there is a dearth of evidence that the hoplite class, able to provide their own weapons but not a horse, were disaffected at material times.

A sophist could earn a good living from such people; what they wanted from him was the means to excel in or even to dominate, but not to overthrow, the democracy. The democracy might be suspicious; but so long as there was a way to the top for talent those suspicions must often have been ill founded. The picture of an upper middle class conscious of its own superiority, exposed by that consciousness to resentful suspicion, but at the same time devoted to the pursuit of political and economic power under the democracy should not strike one as implausible. If such people held simultaneously both democratic and élitist values (to use crude terms), they were far from unique.

To prepare men for success in a democracy, Protagoras naturally proclaims the values both of success and of democracy. The words with which he does so repay attention. Of skills, such as rhetoric, the art of public speaking and of exerting influences, Protagoras says nothing. Overt discussion of them would ruin his argument. He could not claim that all men have the gift of the gab, though he could (and does) draw attention to the universality of language (327E–328A). The claim that all men share in rhetoric would lead by analogy all too easily to the suggestion that all men have a share in carpentry or any other not too esoteric 'art'. 'Justice' is different. In justice all men have at least the feeling of knowledge. The Greeks bear witness to that feeling. The *De Vectigalibus*, an economic and political pamphlet attributed to Xenophon (i,1), says that 'Some Athenian leaders used to say that they knew what was just no less than other men, but were driven...'. This dictum implies that other men did indeed know. But what did the Greeks mean by 'justice'? Did they all mean the same thing? Was it always a cooperative, as opposed to a competitive virtue? How important was it?

Much the same questions need to be asked about 'moderation', 'good sense', 'restraint', all suitable translations in certain contexts of what the Greeks call *sôphrosynê*. In the myth of Protagoras, two older words are used, *dikê* and *aidôs*, for the later *dikaiosynê* (justice) and *sôphrosynê*, to which he has recourse in his more prosaic exposition. There are questions about all these words. It is not wholly clear that an upper-middle- or upper-class Athenian would have agreed that they were necessary but not sufficient conditions of success. On questions like these whole books have brought scholars no nearer agreement.[60] This is not, and is not going to become, another book about them. All that appears here is a sketch, freely borrowed from other books, even if the unwitting lenders disapprove of the use to which the borrowings are put.

First the importance of 'justice', especially when in conflict with self-interest. Here the work of A. W. H. Adkins has been of singular importance. In a series of books and articles he has argued that the highest Greek value-words, roughly 'good', and 'goodness' or 'virtue', were attached in Homer to competitive success and the qualities required for it, including courage and warlike prowess, but not excluding loyalty to a group. This attachment was hard to break, and, as concern for one's fellows became more important for the survival of society, the shift to the coupling of 'justice' with 'virtue' was hard to achieve. As a result, where competitive advantage was in conflict with 'justice', competitive advantage, with the highest value still attached to it, tended to take priority; and this was so right down to the fourth century. The problem of a moralist such as Plato was somehow to attach the highest terms of commendation to 'justice'. This view (for which the reader is urged to consult the original works) gives Plato's procedure in the *Protagoras* an appearance of enormity. He has apparently made the sophist beg the most fundamental question for ethics in Plato's day.

But the situation is complex (and apologies are in order for grossly over-simplifying Adkins' scholarly and subtle view of it). It is too complex to allow us to suppose that either Plato or his Protagoras has made a simple error or employed a mere rhetorical sleight-of-hand. Some remarks on 'justice' are overdue.[61] In the first place, the word itself did not always denote the same kind of behaviour. Indeed, Adkins is far too good a scholar to overlook such a point, and he stresses in a revealing footnote that *dikaiosynê*, 'justice' is not always the quality of cooperating fairly.[62] But one may reasonably object to the disposal of so cardinal a point in this manner.

That justice should mean different things to people in different situations is a perfectly normal feature of human society. Underdogs, after all, tend to regard their subjection as unfair, and to claim equality. Top dogs have the mirror-image tendency to look on their higher status as fair reward for their (supposed) superiority. Both frequently invoke the name of Justice. Both attitudes appear in Classical Greece and in particular in Athens. The supposition that they were never or rarely united in the same person with respect to different aspects of Greek society would be inherently implausible.

To write in general terms such as these is to invite a demand for concrete evidence. Argument from modern parallels, from group psychology, or from one's own knowledge of the world is not enough. Examination of some ancient evidence follows. Readers willing to take for granted the Athenians' common and fallible humanity may skip the next few paragraphs with my blessing.

The evidence is not of the most direct and straightforward kind, and its shortcomings need advertisement. It consists in the main of three kinds of writing, to wit the tragedy especially of Euripides, the speeches in the history of Thucydides, and the speeches attributed (not always rightly) to at least the earlier of the extant Athenian orators. All three are of debatable relevance to common Greek or Athenian values. But it would be hard to refute the suggestion that all three reflect with varying degrees of faithfulness the attitudes, emotions and discussions of their time.

Scholars write on occasion – much less nowadays than formerly – as if Euripides endorsed what his characters say, as if Thucydides used his speakers as so many mouthpieces, as if the orators were expressing their own or their clients' points of view. Whether a speech is held to express its author's views or its audience's or its readers' depends partly on how convenient the speech is for a particular scholarly view – and my readers would be well advised to guard against my own bias. What I should like to assume is that, whether or not the speeches are moulded by their authors' personal outlook, they represent, in the case of the fifth-century figures Euripides and Thucydides, what the authors think that their audience thinks that the speaker would think that his audience would accept or approve; in the case of the doubtless fourth-century speeches in the *corpus* traditionally ascribed to Lysias, they represent what the speechwriter thinks the audience will accept or approve without utter inappropriateness to the personality of his client, the actual speaker.

One needs to add that what the audience liked to think they thought is not likely to have been always or exactly what they actually thought. Likewise with their behaviour; one does not always behave as one likes to think one behaves. Obviously great caution is necessary in the handling of such evidence.[63] Even more caution is needed in using the writings of the 'thoughtful and intellectual'[64] Thucydides and Euripides than in drawing on speeches written for supposedly ordinary litigants.

We should extract some reassurance from the large measure of agreement between the set speeches of the tragedian and historian and the law-court speeches of the next generation. If one worries over the influence of rhetorical forms and formulas one should at the same time appreciate that a rhetorical formula could not become such unless its audience – or a substantial range of audiences – was inclined to accept and approve. These considerations go far to assure us that the more overtly 'literary' speeches are reasonably true to 'life'. The onus of proof rests firmly on those who would suggest a major shift between the late fifth and early fourth centuries.

Some of the various applications of 'justice' happen to emerge most clearly from Euripides. In his *Electra* (1050–54) the justice of revenge is implicitly distinguished from a milder form of justice. Orestes, after killing his mother in revenge for his father, is greeted by the Twin gods with the words 'She has her just reward: but your deed is not just.' In one application – or 'sense', if that term be preferred – the killing is just, in another it is not. Of course, the expression is deliberately paradoxical; but if there were not available more than one application of 'justice', the paradox would be unintelligible. That is evidence that Euripides thought enough of his audience would be capable in a split second of apprehending the different applications sufficiently to follow the Twins' argument. This passage, and another in the *Orestes* (416–17), point in the same direction by counting the justice of revenge as 'shameful' or 'unseemly' and as 'lawless' – two epithets not normally coupled with justice during this period, when justice is normally 'honourable' and 'lawful'.

The objection that this is merely a conflict between two rules of justice meets the retort that if justice were a single simple thing, then conflict between its various aspects could hardly arise. Conflict there is in plenty; the pages of tragedy – and not only of Euripidean tragedy – are full of it. Take for example Sophocles' play *Oedipus at Colonus*, where the chorus of Athenians acknowledge the injustice of banishing the as-yet-unidentified suppliant Oedipus (174ff.), but barely fifty lines later (228ff.), on realizing who he is, plead that one deceit deserves another in return. A similar conflict between the justice protecting the suppliant and other rules occurs (as B. Vickers has observed)[65] near the end of the play, where Oedipus' paternal curse overcomes Polynices' supplication 'if Justice still sits by the ancient laws of Zeus' (1380–82). Consider Euripides' *Helen*, where Theoclymenus' sister Theonoe has deceived him in order to free Helen, in accordance with their dead father's wishes and in spite of Theoclymenus' desire to marry Helen. Theoclymenus pleads in anger that he is in justice entitled to kill his sister, who has betrayed him – betrayal being a common form of injustice.[66] Theonoe's loyal servant protests; her betrayal was just (1624–33). The Twin gods decide, in favour of Theonoe; she is guilty, they say, of no injustice to her brother in obeying their father's just commands (1647–9).

In politics particularly, justice is open to invocation by more than one party. Demosthenes (21. 67) links equality and justice as the privileges of democracy, and Aristotle is recording not his own but ordinary democrats' linguistic predilections when he says in his *Politics* (1317b3ff.) that 'popular justice is the possession of equality numerical and not proportionate to merit.'[67] Yet in Euripides' *Ion* (1574) a goddess may say that a person 'is just to rule', i.e. has a just right to rule, and in Thucydides various speakers either say or refer to the possibility of saying that the Athenians have a just right to their empire because of their services to Greece in the Persian Wars (I 73.2, V 89, VI 83.2). This last 'justice' stands in open conflict with Pericles' acknowledgement (II 63.2) that the Athenians hold their empire as a 'tyranny' which it is unjust to obtain but dangerous to give up. Power is just or unjust according to circumstances, or according to one's point of view.

It is one of the ironies of history that the very Athenian democrats who prided themselves at home on giving all male adult citizens an equal voice and vote were the most consistent imperialists abroad. If their rationalization of this situation included from time to time an open setting aside of 'justice' as a fine but empty word, then they were hardly in a position to complain if their own oligarchs adopted a similar view. But Athenian politics are uncommonly complex, and one can say with certainty only that some people in the fifth century were willing to listen to the suggestion that 'power according to one's services' was a just principle. Normally those capable of signal service were those who for reason of wealth or birth enjoyed power to start with: but much of the complication of Athenian politics is due to the important contribution to the safety of the state made by the poorer men who served in the fleet. In view of this, equality went hand in hand with merit in Athenian political justice. Further, the scions of the old great families were by no means universally oligarchic; some, like Pericles himself, aimed to maintain their privileges by serving the democratic regime.

Justice as fairness is not always precisely a 'cooperative' virtue, and Adkins has on occasion admitted the ultimate inadequacy of the distinction between 'cooperative' (or 'quiet') and 'competitive' values. In one of the most famous and most discussed passages of Thucydides (III 40.4) the Athenian leader Cleon claims that the massacre of the rebellious Mytileneans, ordered by a previous Assembly, is just: in his argument it unites expediency with justice. When his opponent in debate, Diodotus, suggests in his peroration (III 44) that Cleon's union of justice with expediency will not work because the massacre is not expedient, it would be tempting to conclude that this is a triumph of competitive over cooperative values. But the conclusion would not bear examination. The justice of retribution demanded by Cleon is no less competitive than cooperative, if one must use such terms at all.

Justice in Greek writers is often the distribution of rewards to one's friends and punishments to one's enemies; friends and enemies are for practical purposes those who have benefited or harmed oneself respectively, or those from whom benefit or harm respectively may reasonably be expected. One half only of this double virtue may fairly be called cooperative; and even that is not lacking in competitive possibilities.

The importance of the gods in all this has sometimes been underrated. True, the really ruthless oligarch might not believe in the gods or accept their restraint on his behaviour. True also, Protagoras himself was notoriously ready to confess his ignorance whether the gods existed or not (Frag B4); and he by no means commits himself to their existence in this dialogue. But the audience he wishes to attract here is one of prospective, not past pupils, and there is no doubt of the offence he would have caused by voicing his doubts in such a context. The fifth-century 'Enlightenment' undoubtedly left the great majority of Athenians believing in their gods no less than before. To deny them would not be respectable. It was conventional to believe in them, and to accept their connection with justice. The Melians in Thucydides (V 104) plead against the mighty Athenians that the gods are on the side of justice: not on the side specifically of those who take in suppliants or those who keep oaths, but on the side of justice. Whether Thucydides believed this or not, there is no reason to suppose that the Melian in the street disbelieved it or that the Athenian reply, putting the gods on the side of the big battalions, was meant to be found convincing by Thucydides' readers.[68]

Athenians, moreover, continually remembered Marathon, conceived by them as a victory against the odds. As A. Andrewes points out,[69] a speech attributed to Lysias (2. 10) represents certain past Athenians as fighting a numerous foe but with justice on their side winning the battle. The naturalness of rhetorical commonplaces of this kind should not lead to their neglect as mere verbiage: the orator judged his audience at least to enjoy thinking of themselves as believing them.

Euripides too has several passages where the gods are reckoned to be on the just side. In his *Electra* (583–4) and his *Andromache* (439) and his *Iphigeneia in Aulis* (1034–5) speakers declare that the whole point of having gods is that they should uphold justice. In the *Suppliant Women* (219–28) Theseus expresses the not uncommon view that it is dangerous for the innocent to consort too closely with the unjust, since the divine vengeance wreaked on the latter may destroy also the former. Less ambivalent is Aethra's remark later (328–31) that she has no fear at the departure of Theseus with justice on his side. Theseus himself expresses a like confidence (594–7). Still later in the same play (608ff.) there is a brief but interesting debate; one half of the chorus believes in just gods, the other does not, and the believers rebuke the unbelievers, suggesting that their motive is fear. In fact the outcome in this play justifies the believers. In the *Heraclidae* (415–19), another mythical King of Athens, Demophon, analyses a debate likely to take place under certain conditions: one side would urge the justice of helping strangers, the other would denounce the folly of it. But the chorus (901–9) are confident this time in the punishment of the unjust, and instruct the city not to leave the path of justice.[70] In two plays a god appearing 'from the machine' claims to reward the just: Athena in the *Iphigeneia in Tauris* (though the text is lacunose) (1469) and the Twins in the *Electra* (1349–53). Without mentioning the gods (but certainly not without the audience thinking of them) the chorus of the *Helen* (1031–2) exclaim both that good fortune does not come to the unjust and that justice gives grounds for hope of safety. In the *Phoenician Women* the Paedagogus *fears* that the gods may reward a just cause (154–5). Admittedly in the *Hecuba* (801ff., 853) rewards for justice are limited to certain types under the special protection of certain gods, and in most of the cases mentioned above the gods could have a special and personal interest. But the speakers do not put the matter thus. They do not say 'Zeus the protector of suppliants will reward the just receiver of a supplication.' They say rather that the gods reward justice. It is evident that for them the treatment of suppliants is an example, from the gods' point of view, of justice in general, and that justice in general is what the gods reward.

There were instances to the contrary, of course; the wicked

flourished then no less and no less obviously than now. But religious faith tends to survive the occurrence of counter-examples. One can scarcely doubt that a normal well-brought-up young Athenian would accept the existence of the gods and their concern with justice, and would deem it more or less disreputable to think otherwise. The plea that a funeral oration, a tragedy or a sophisticated history are merely literature will not do; literary or no, they show, first, what ideas were in circulation at the time, and secondly what emotive power the writers expected the ideas to exert.

The proceedings of the Athenian law-courts deserve special attention here. The jury received no legal guidance from an impartial judge, but was sworn to decide the case according to law and justice.[71] The juries' habit of listening to extraneous matter, and the speakers' evident expectation of profiting from its introduction, have led to the supposition that when expediency was put before them the jury sought it at the expense of justice. The suggestion is, as I understand it, that in a clash between justice and expediency the latter would win because of the power of the word 'good' attached both to 'expedient' and to the type of speaker concerned. The jury, it is supposed, found more weight in the 'good' that the speaker had done to the city, by paying for religious or defence outlays, than in the plea of justice.

But the situation is less simple than this theory makes it appear. The speakers do not, at least in the orations attributed to Lysias, argue on the sole basis of expediency; the plea of justice is always there too. On occasion the argument from the speaker's services is sandwiched between two pleas for justice with no apparent feeling of incongruity. The orators in general 'attempt to show that justice and expediency coincide.'[72]

In one Lysianic prosecution (27. 2) the speaker alludes to the past practice of the defendant and his associates of maintaining that the city would profit from the jurors' acceptance of their cases. But we have only the prosecutor's word for it that the defendants made so naked a claim on the jury's self-interest; and the prosecutor has an obvious interest in destroying the character of the defendants. If this passage suggests anything, it suggests that to plead expediency over or without justice was disreputable, the sort of thing your opponents did, not you.

There is no difficulty in all this, except in the interpretation of 'justice'. Talk of 'strict justice' will not suffice; in any clash between law and justice, the letter of the law and even its spirit might go by the board.[73] Juries might prefer their commitment to justice over their commitment to law. They might then see it as just that a man who had contributed to the city should get something back. That might be strictly illegal, and even socially undesirable, but it would still be just – as the orators normally said it was. That the jurors should prefer justice in a broad sense to strict legality is neither surprising – considering their lack of impartial and skilled legal guidance – nor evidence for the subordination of justice to other ideals.

In other speeches too the just and the expedient tend to coincide. We have seen that the speakers in Thucydides use these terms, sometimes as opposed to each other. But even Cleon's opponent in the Mytilenean Debate, distinguishing Cleon's justice from expediency and arguing for the latter, still cannot do without a word claiming justice for the policy he advocates (III 47.3).[74] Even the Athenians, in their claim to empire, give reasons for regarding their rule as more just than others (I 76.3ff.).

The disregard for considerations of justice expressed at the outset of the Melian Dialogue (V 89) is exceptional, and surely not expected to gain wide sympathy. Two points need in any case to be made about it. The first is that the Athenians claim to have made 'measured' or 'reasonable' demands on the Melians, using a word often associated with 'just' (V 111.4). The second is that Thucydides emphasizes the privacy of the negotiations; it is highly doubtful whether the unfeigned and unfettered power politics of the Athenians could have been reproduced in public; the Dialogue does nothing to weaken the view that to ignore or to denigrate the claims of justice was 'not done' and not quite respectable.

It is never easy to divine the tone of fragments, but one quoted from Euripides (iv. 758 Nauck) appears to declare that 'for the base, gain ranks above justice', which, whether Euripides or his character thought it true or not, suffices to show the way some people thought. In decisions made in the plays, too, considerations of justice are, as we might expect, sometimes decisive and sometimes not. Odysseus in Euripides' *Cyclops* (476–82) decides not to save his own skin at the expense of his crew; it would not be just, and that appears to settle the matter. Orestes, too, in the *Iphigeneia in Tauris* (601ff.) declares that self-preservation would be shameful, and he prefers to save Pylades and remain himself in the place of danger. Loyalty to the group or to friendship is the kind of justice concerned, and both Orestes and Odysseus make that clear. But the clash between justice and self-interest is there, and is resolved on the side of justice, with no suggestion that other sorts of justice would have less weight. Examples of people sacrificing justice for advantage also occur, in the *Iphigeneia at Aulis* (1368–1400), the *Heraclidae* (253ff.), and the *Phoenician Women* (1239); but in their contexts and in the face of the counter-examples it will normally be found that the audience is not expected to approve.[75]

Decision is simple, as most of us are aware, when justice and expediency coincide. The orators tended to try and make the jury's decision simple, for obvious reasons. For equally obvious reasons the serious dramatists did not so simplify their characters' decisions. But people in general hoped in deciding to combine advantage with justice. The gods were with the just. In the long run, the best policy might be honesty, as in Herodotus' improving tale (I 96–8) of Deioces who attained power by making use of his earned repute for justice. The social advantages of justice were recognized; the man with an eye on gain may be good for himself but is useless to the city, for Euripides' Iolaus (*Heraclidae* 2ff.). The political advantages of concord between classes, secured by the justice of the individual citizens, were sufficiently obvious. Even the personal advantages of justice were evident to some people in some situations.

In particular, justice could function as a necessary or as a sufficient condition of goodness or 'virtue', or its synonym 'usefulness'. In one passage it is even superior in a sense to 'goodness' (Euripides, *Suppliant Women*, 594–7). Imprecision and ambiguity admittedly abound in passages juxtaposing 'just' and 'good' or placing them in parallel, or associating the 'unjust' with 'folly' (*Hippolytus* 426–7, *Hypsipyle* fr. 60, 114–

17 (=fr. 759 Nauck); *Phoenissae* 1647ff.). But Orestes' decision in favour of justice in the *Iphigeneia in Tauris* (mentioned above) draws from Iphigeneia the comment 'O best of tempers'; Euripides' Ion (*Ion* 439–43) links advice to Apollo to pursue 'goodness' with a denunciation of his clear injustice. The Athenians even of the Melian Dialogue (V 105.4), whatever their own actions, cannot get away from the implication that the Spartans will do what they think just; they accuse the Spartans of thinking just whatever is advantageous, and they represent this as incompatible with 'goodness'.[76]

Finally, the Theseus of Euripides' *Suppliant Women*, a sympathetic character if ever there was one, speaks as follows (594–7): 'I need one thing alone, to have [on my side] the gods who respect justice: for they [justice and the gods] being in support grant victory. Goodness brings nothing to mortal men, if it have not [on its side] the wish of the gods.' We need not argue here the question whether 'the gods who...' is restrictive or comprehensive in sense: the relation between justice and goodness is plain, and justice is the more important of the two. Justice ensures success.

Two passages in other poets make out that 'goodness' *is* justice.[77] One, in Theognis (147–8), whatever its original date, became proverbial by the time of Aristotle (*EN* 1129b 27). Another, dating from the fifth century and from the pen of one Timocreon of Rhodes (fr. 1 (Page) (*PMG* No. 727)), has been wrongly discounted. Its author has a complaint against Themistocles, who failed unjustly to bring him back from exile despite the claims of guest-friendship. Themistocles is unjust, and other successful leaders of Greeks against Persians are not the most 'good'. Timocreon reserves that title for Aristides. In favour of discounting the passage Adkins' argument runs like this: first, 'Aristides' justice is not explicitly mentioned'; as if it needed mention when (a) Aristides was famous for his justice, (b) no other reason for dubbing him 'best' seems at all plausible, and (c) the contrast with Themistocles is obvious. Secondly, Themistocles has violated that part of goodness which traditionally consisted in forwarding the interests of one's guest-friends, but from this it follows that traditional values were not inconsistent with an emphasis on justice, not that this passage does not pay special attention to justice. The real motives of the historical Themistocles are irrelevant; and the last argument, that 'pique plays a sufficiently large part in Timocreon's judgement to render it difficult to regard it as a considered revaluation', is also of doubtful force: an unconsidered evaluation by an underdog is worth having in itself as a rare specimen in extant Classical Greek literature. An underdog could regard justice as sufficient evidence of 'goodness'.

Aristides is the subject of another interesting passage, in Herodotus' account of events leading up to the Greek victory at Salamis (VIII 79). Ostracized by the Athenians, he arrived back at a crucial moment to tell Themistocles (an old and bitter enemy) the good news that the Persians had blocked the Greeks' flight and so compelled them to fight. Here Herodotus says that Aristides was the best and justest of Athenians. It is no use claiming here that 'best' and 'justest' are two separate words having nothing to do with each other:[78] for again, Aristides was not an outstandingly successful politician or statesman, much less so than Pericles for instance. Men were aware of his repute for justice, and that is clearly the basis for Herodotus' judgement that he was the best. Both epithets were based, as the historian takes the trouble to tell us, on examination of his 'way', his character. The particular context is one in which Athenian patriotism gets the better of private enmity; and this kind of selfless service to the community is dignifiable both with 'just' and 'good'.

It may be true, but is not to the present point, to say that such valuations of justice were hard to establish against a different traditional set of values. The difficulty of finding any persuasive philosophical argument to convince an arrogant and power-hungry young aristocrat that he should consider 'another's good' may have been great: the reactions of the sophist Thrasymachus and the haughty Callicles in Plato's *Republic* and *Gorgias* suggest that it was. But whether a view can be philosophically and persuasively argued is a very different question from whether it can be and is held. The evidence strongly suggests for fifth- and fourth-century Athens a commonly held belief, retained in the teeth of counter-example and counter-argument alike, that justice finds its reward, leads to success, is one way of achieving human excellence. It suggests further that it was not wholly respectable to deny this belief, whatever arguments or examples one might produce on behalf of such denial.

In this situation Protagoras can assume that much of his audience will be conditioned to assume unthinkingly that 'justice' in at least some of its applications is both a necessary and a sufficient condition of a successful life. By assuming (or affecting to assume) that justice entails success he is placing an unhappy onus on any opponent. If one wishes to refute or reject this assumption one must render oneself not quite respectable. Socrates too assumes something that cannot be respectably denied, namely the 'wisdom' of the Athenians. Each has put the other in a potentially awkward position.

But what of Protagoras' habitual teaching of rhetoric? Is there not a strange contrast still between the actual imparting of persuasive skill and the claim to teach justice? Have we not seen the suspicions attaching to the power of the skilfully spoken word? Indeed, yes; but what E. R. Dodds called the 'Inherited Conglomerate' of beliefs resists any process of tidying. Rhetorically argued though much litigation was, it was hardly to be expected of jurors (or of assembled citizens) that they should regard any great proportion of their own decisions as unjust. The Theseus of Euripides' *Suppliant Women* (437) again comes to the rescue with the apparently unblushing falsehood that, in a system of written law such as the Athenian, 'The lesser man with justice [on his side] defeats the great man.' False, certainly; unappealing, no. The reputation of a system of justice can, like other reputations, survive refutation by example.

We should be unwise to underestimate the power of a political myth. We may safely assume the repute of Athenian justice in Athens to have stood as high in Athens as that of 'British justice' in England or Scotland; and we may contemplate with equanimity in both societies the simultaneous recognition of the merits of the legal system and the dangers of allowing clever lawyers to address a jury. Holding justice to be beloved of the gods, the Athenians naturally thought it to be ultimately successful.

Protagoras is again being awkward. In effect, he dares his

opponent to deny such platitudinous and respectable beliefs. He can cite Athenian authority for any of them, and Socrates has chosen to admit the wisdom of the Athenians (319B). It is no incidental point that Protagoras' account gives him the substantive subject matter which, as we saw earlier, his art had to have, once he had compared himself with the poets. The subject is justice.

This allows us to draw some threads together. The theme of many, if not most, of the public speeches extant from the late fifth and early fourth centuries was justice, in relation to the particular issue. One had to justify the action or the verdict requested of the audience. One had to show that it was both just and advantageous. The plea of advantage alone was not quite proper. What one needed to be able to talk about was justice in any relevant aspect. For this purpose it was a natural, though unnecessary and in a sense over-optimistic, assumption that one had to know what was just. Who better to know and more fitting to talk about justice than the just man? The bluff soldier Laches in his dialogue (188C–E) was surely not the only man to set a high value on harmony between deeds and words.

After discussing justice at such length, it is lop-sided to be brief on *sôphrosynê*; but nevertheless brief is what this account will be. The word here rendered 'moderation' has received many other renderings. Etymologically, the corresponding adjective, in use from Homer on, meant 'of sound mind'. It naturally came, like the English 'sound', to mean (among other things) 'sensible'. The abstract can often be translated by the phrase 'good sense'. One might expect such a general word to be usable in multifarious contexts, and it was. In view of other scholars' excellent discussions, only a few points seem to be worth making here. The use of *sôphrosynê* to replace the word *aidôs*, as in Protagoras' exposition in relation to his myth, indicates the primary function of 'moderation' in the speech's argument. Undoubtedly the sophist's concern is with questions of what we should call morality, with restraint, and also with propriety. *Aidôs* and *sôphrosynê* are generally terms of 'quiet' and 'cooperative' values. *Aidôs* is more consistently so than *sôphrosynê*, and *sôphrosynê* is therefore all the more likely to be a 'quiet' concept in a context where it replaces *aidôs*. On the other hand, *sôphrosynê* as 'good sense' is obviously not confined to 'quiet' contexts. It speaks to the advantage of self, as much as to respect for others, for rules, or for one's own calmer self. Protagoras uses the word, in one context at least, in opposition to 'madness'; there it can only mean 'good sense', and is an intellectual virtue not directly concerned with quiet values (323B).

These facts make the word *sôphrosynê* or 'moderation' most useful for Protagoras' present purposes. For like most parents the Athenians wished their children, within limits, to be obedient, restrained in temper, and moderate in appetite, and they taught them accordingly: 'Do this and do not do that' (325D). But, again like most parents, they wanted their children, within limits, competitively successful, the 'good' (e.g. 325D) and 'useful' (326B) members that society must have. Protagoras is to continue the one kind of teaching as well as the other, and both together will result in a good citizen. The 'moderate' adult produced (in intention) by early training will become still more moderate, we may be sure, at the feet of Protagoras; but it may be a different kind of 'moderation'. A restrained young man may acquire a sense of his own interests and a shrewdness in furthering them. This will not be the cooperative kind of goodness required according to the myth to hold human society together, but it will be called *sôphrosynê* or 'moderation' in the same way as that cooperative virtue. The promise to teach 'justice and moderation' will include it. The intellectual and self-centred *sôphrosynê* is there, side by side with the more moral kind.

It is not as if Protagoras were the only person to juxtapose the two contrasting, though linked, aspects of 'moderation': for example, in Euripides 'if you are moderate' means 'if you know what's good for you' in reference to normally rational self-interest,[79] while other locutions using the same or cognate words refer to respect for society's rules. It is not hard to believe that in many cases respect for others was to one's own ultimate advantage. Protagoras was no Callicles (*Gorgias* 521C), to treat *sôphrosynê* (in the moral sense) as stupid. To try to be moderate and just was to aim at a respectable success. In somewhat similar fashion, Protagoras suggests near the dialogue's end that the good life is one of respectable enjoyment (351B). A decent scion of a wealthy family, such as the young Hippocrates, could be more than content with that.

The political and other arts

If Protagoras is not guilty of proclaiming a political art of a kind inconsistent with Hippocrates' and other pupils' intentions, he is nevertheless still in difficulties over the use of the term 'art' at all in this connection. Indeed, as we saw before, both he and Socrates are, in different ways and different degrees, in danger of self-contradiction on this matter. Is political goodness an art or not? We may now turn to the treatment of the term 'art', in application to politics, in Protagoras' Great Speech. The term 'wisdom' and associated words require discussion at the same time. Protagoras has received from Socrates the title 'wise' early in the conversation (318B) and his art is that of the sophist, etymologically a professional 'wise' man. Further, in his own long argument Socrates spoke of Pericles as one of the wisest and best of the citizens in respect of the goodness he has, and questioned Pericles' capacity to teach what he is 'wise' at (319E). What Pericles is 'wise' at is clearly related to the political 'art', and such a relationship between 'wisdom' and 'art' is by no means unique. To be 'wise' can be simply to possess an 'art', to be an expert.[80] Teaching supplies another connection; what can be taught is an art, and teaching is what makes the young 'wise' in a paraphrase of Socrates offered by Protagoras in the Great Speech (324D). There is in fact a whole network of interlocking terminology to be examined: but necessarily one must start somewhere, and 'art' and 'wisdom' will serve as a beginning.

In the course of his myth Protagoras tells how Prometheus stole 'the wisdom involved in art(s) together with fire' and gave it to Man (321C–D). There follows a sentence of great interest: 'The wisdom concerned with livelihood Man thus possessed, but the political [one] (or [art]) he did not possess'. The natural symmetry of this sentence would have us supply 'wisdom' or the place-filler 'one', where the Greek has only 'the political' in the feminine in concord with the feminine noun for 'wisdom'. This would pretty clearly suggest the equivalence of political wisdom and the goodness of the best citizens (which is the subject of the whole discussion). This is indeed the way most translators have rendered the sentence. But there is an alternative and equally respectable way of taking the Greek: this puts the word 'political' in the feminine gender in concord not with the supplied 'wisdom' but with the unexpressed feminine word 'art'. The ellipse or omission of the noun 'art' with adjectives structured like 'political' is familiar enough in Greek. Protagoras' audience might accordingly take him to refer here to the 'political art' and to be opposing that to the wisdom concerned with technical skills and winning a livelihood. It is not therefore clear that G. M. A. Grube was right in saying baldly that Protagoras speaks here of political wisdom.[81]

What is true is Grube's next statement, that Protagoras nowhere 'puts "wisdom" in the foreground of his teaching'. But of that more may be said later. For the present we observe that Protagoras here distinguishes the wisdom concerned with the arts either from the political art or from political wisdom, which is presumably what he later claims to be good at teaching. If the political 'art' is meant, he is back in his old difficulty; what he does not teach is 'concerned with the arts', what he does teach he will label an art. On this reading, his replacement of the earlier phrase 'involved in the arts' with the locution 'concerned with livelihood', though it goes far to explicate his meaning, does not resolve the difficulty. He ought to have stressed or explained, as he does not, that by 'involved in the arts' he meant *only* 'involved in the arts which are concerned with a livelihood'.[82] In any case, the word rendered 'livelihood' is not the right one to make a clear distinction between Protagoras' and other arts, since it can also signify 'mode of life',[83] and what the French call with convenient reticence 'la politique' is assuredly concerned with that.

If we read 'the political...' as 'the political [wisdom]', Protagoras escapes (for the time being) the charge of renewing his old contradiction about 'art', but only in order to store up trouble for himself of a different sort. For to imply here that goodness is [a] wisdom is to contradict something he says later, namely that wisdom is a *part* of goodness. On this reading we have another similarity between the *Protagoras* and the *Laches*: in each wisdom or courage is apparently both the whole and a part of goodness. Protagoras' ambiguity here goes far already to justify Socrates' later question asking after the status of wisdom (even if we leave out of account the sophist's later remark about the possibility of being just but not wise) (329E).

'Wisdom' appears in none of the more formal lists of virtues or good qualities in the Great Speech; thus far Grube was right in saying 'The absence of wisdom is conspicuous, and must be deliberate on Plato's part.'[84] But our ambiguous sentence in the myth has raised a question about wisdom, a question deserving and receiving investigation from Socrates. Plato's reader too, like Protagoras' hearer, ought to want to know precisely how wisdom stands after this sentence.

But the inexplicit nature of the sentence has further effect. Protagoras, though permitting the hearer (or the reader) to suppose him to believe in a political 'wisdom' synonymous with 'goodness', never actually utters the words 'political wisdom' consecutively or in unmistakable grammatical concord. Hence, when Socrates asks him if he thinks wisdom a part of goodness (329E), the question does not run clean counter to the sophist's explicit beliefs. Protagoras does not have ringing in his ears a warning bell such as would be touched off (one hopes) by his own previous utterance of the phrase 'political wisdom'. One is again reminded of the *Laches*, where Laches himself, in the opening chat, implies but does not expressly say that goodness is courage.

Protagoras' remarks at the end of his paragraph (321E) contain nothing of value for our present purposes. Both Athena and Hephaestus pursue arts: Hephaestus' is involved with fire, Athena's is not. How else they differ (if they do) is not specified. There is no elucidation here of any distinction between the art Protagoras teaches and the arts of the other sophists.[85] No light is shed on the question whether goodness is or is not an art. Nor does illumination come from the reference to art in connection with language (322A): 'Man articulated by the art sound and names.' If the reference to 'art' is part of the genuine Platonic text, it anticipates indirectly the later mention of the Greek language as something universally taught (as Protagoras thinks goodness is). Some editors doubt its genuineness, for reasons seeming to me insufficient;[86] but the reader is warned. In any case, if language and goodness are arts differing from other arts by their universality, that does nothing to get Protagoras off the hook of his careless implication both that goodness is an art and that what he teaches (namely, goodness) is not an art.

Also unhelpful in this difficulty is the distinction offered below (322B) between 'practical crafts sufficient to provide food' and 'the art of running a city' which men 'did not yet possess'. The political art is here separate from the art(s) of supplying food; but though Hippias might, the other sophists certainly did not teach the latter sort of art, and the geometry and astronomy (318E) taught in the fifth and fourth centuries BC were not suitable candidates for inclusion in that sort. Nor of course were geometry and astonomy handicrafts, distinguished later by Protagoras from e.g. language skills (328A). So we find here no distinction matching up to the awkward juxtaposition of art and non-art in the initial discussion between Protagoras and Socrates (318D–319A). Further, the usefulness of the phrase 'practical crafts' – more literally 'the craftsmanlike art' – for such a distinction receives another dent when Protagoras uses the word 'craftsman' to denote expertise (of a kind) in goodness (322B, 327C).[87]

The mythical conversation between Hermes and Zeus merely exacerbates the problem (322C–D). Zeus sends Hermes with justice and moderaton to mankind. Hermes questions him on his mission: 'Shall I,' he asks, 'distribute these in the same way as the arts?'[88] This ought, like Protagoras' earlier remarks about his rivals, to mean that justice and moderation (clearly related to 'la politique') are distinct from 'the arts', and indeed are not arts. Zeus' answer tangles the web further. Zeus agrees with the proposition that justice and moderation should be generally distributed, and offers as his reason that cities would not arise if justice and moderation were distributed 'like other arts'. This in turn ought to mean, and clearly does mean, that justice and moderation are arts after all. Moderation and justice are added to Man's equipment *after* the arts and on different principles, but Zeus has put them back among the arts again.

What Protagoras thinks about this himself is a question still unresolved. But the impression (on one side of the question) that goodness belongs among the arts is deepened by what follows (322D). Protagoras uses 'the carpenter's goodness ... or any other craftsman's goodness' in reference to what makes a carpenter (or other craftsman) a *good* carpenter (or other craftsman).[89] It is highly unlikely that Protagoras here refers to anything but instances of the same thing he described previously as 'craftsmanlike art'. Indeed it is the full possession of his art which makes a good carpenter, so surprise is not in order. In these passages 'art' and 'goodness' seem interchangeable without significant change of reference. In the sophist's next sentence it is equally clear that the words 'political goodness' refer to the thing previously labelled 'political art'. Both practical and political skill are types of 'goodness' and both are alike presumably arts. The distinction between a 'goodness' and an 'art' seems in danger of vanishing. Protagoras speaks in the next sentence of 'this goodness at least'[90] in reference to moderation and justice; other 'goodnesses', as we saw, are distributed differently. This again assimilates the moral qualities to the practical skills in all but distribution; and if both are goodnesses and 'goodness' is interchangeable in this kind of context with 'art', then both look like being arts. One would not like to rely solely on this inference; but we have found sufficient support elsewhere for calling moral and practical skills 'arts', and the inference is consistent with half of Protagoras' contradictory view.

The usage of the next paragraph also tends to assimilate practical skills to morally good qualities (323A). Taylor indeed renders with the English 'skills' the Greek *aretai*, more literally 'goodnesses', which (as Taylor rightly says of 'excellences') would perhaps be 'too artificial'. 'Goodness' functions here most clearly as the abstract noun corresponding to 'good' even in such contexts as 'a good flautist' or 'good at'.[91] Where Taylor has 'good at anything else...' the Greek has something like 'good at any other art'. 'Art' and 'goodness' seem to refer virtually interchangeably to what makes a good craftsman good at his craft.[92]

But in this same paragraph Protagoras implies that political goodness is not an art at all (323A–C). For after specifying what happens to the ignorant boaster in flute-playing *or any other art at all* he goes on to state that the situation of the false boaster is quite different in the case of 'justice and the rest of political goodness'. It ought to be deducible from this that political goodness is not after all an art.

Protagoras on the teachability of 'goodness' and its relation to nature and chance is only indirectly helpful to us at best (323C–324A). It is only indirectly that he suggests that political goodness is an art. He is also hard to follow on 'wisdom' (324D). Good men, he says, teach their sons things associable with teachers, and make them 'wise' therein; but they make them no better than anyone else at the 'goodness' in respect of which they are themselves good. Here Protagoras uses 'wise' and 'good' in parallel. But he does not thus commit himself to the interchangeability of the two terms, especially as he is here paraphrasing Socrates. It is also unsafe for us, as it would have been for the listening Socrates, to rely on expressions such as 'their minds are properly formed' (326B) or 'not yet expert' (326D).[93] Although these continue to suggest a substantial intellectual ingredient in the 'goodness' discussed in Protagoras' discourse, they do not specifically connect 'wisdom' and 'goodness'.

The speech ends (328C-D) with a particularly close parallel between the 'goodness' of 'good' men and the skill of a craftsman. The argument is that there is nothing surprising in sons being 'better' or 'worse' than their fathers, presumably as men or as citizens, for the sons of the famous sculptor Polyclitus are as nothing compared to their father, and the same is true of 'other sons of other craftsmen'.[94] 'Other craftsmen' here means 'craftsmen other than Polyclitus', and not 'other than politicians'. But the argument assumes the validity of an inference from the case of skilled craftsmen to the case of good men; it thus comes close to making the 'goodness' of 'good men' another craft. This is in spite of the distinction Protagoras made earlier (322B) between the 'craftsmanlike art' and the 'political art'; the sophist's slide from one point of view to the other, and his inference at the end of the speech, are helped along by the reference to 'a craftsman in this sphere [i.e. that of justice]' earlier in his exposition (327C–D).

The upshot of this analysis needs disentangling. At the very centre of the myth stands an allusion to the 'political art' that men did not have when they first tried to found cities. The unequivocal usage is supported by others less clear. An expert in goodness is a craftsman; the word goodness is used to replace, or to stand in parallel with, the word 'art'; and Zeus in the myth (not necessarily representing Protagoras himself in this respect) implies that justice-and-moderation is an art. Possibly the ambiguous phrase 'the political...' should be completed with the word 'art'. In stark contrast to all this is Hermes' firm implication in the myth, and Protagoras' own in his exposition, that political goodness is something quite distinct from the 'arts'. It results that the Great Speech does nothing to clear and much to darken the fog in which Protagoras first landed himself when replying to Socrates' earlier remarks. It offers no firm basis on which to erect a distinction between Protagoras' political art (if he has one) and the arts of the other sophists.

Other parts of the dialogue may yield the possibility of passing from 'art' to 'knowledge' and thence to 'wisdom'; but as yet Protagoras is not in trouble over this, and references to wisdom do not formally, in the absence of explicit or clearly implicit connections of this sort, affect the question whether politics is an art or not. There are, however, various expressions linking wisdom with goodness, and one ambiguous one which could be understood to refer to 'political wisdom' as an equivalent of the 'political art'. But these will not land Protagoras in any difficulty until he declares that wisdom is only a part, and not the whole, of political goodness.

One factor making Protagoras' position uneasy is his wish to combine the democratic notion that everybody is skilled in, and qualified to teach, political goodness with the fundamentally élitist idea of an 'art' with special or specially effective teachers such as himself (328A–B). This combination, whatever its degree of logical difficulty, was likely to attract the wealthy élite of a democracy. It is not therefore surprising that the source of many of its ingredients is the questioning and argument of Socrates, which are plausibly to be regarded as offering not Socrates' own views but a representation of a gilded youth's opinions and aspirations. Naturally to say all this is not to deny, but rather to emphasize, that Protagoras distinguishes between a political art known in some degree to practically all and the other arts which are known to comparatively few. Where Protagoras seems to waver is on the question whether that difference removes from 'la politique' its claim to be an art. He nowhere explains any other basis on which to distinguish relevantly between different kinds of art.

Relations between the virtues

We have already alluded to the way in which Socrates' subsequent questions about wisdom take up a point in the Great Speech. On other topics too, Socrates shows in later lines of questioning his alertness to details of his interlocutor's exposition. His whole interrogation about 'the unity of the virtues' also arises from a careful analysis of what Protagoras has said. The connection between the Great Speech of Protagoras and the succeeding discussion is less simple, and at the same time closer than some have believed. Some scholars used to suggest that Socrates' single quarrel with Protagoras is that the sophist gives no clear account of the nature of goodness.[95] On this view, simple inability to specify what goodness is causes Protagoras' downfall.

More precise views are now available. If Socrates saw unclarity in Protagoras' speech purely on the general question what goodness is, he was sufficiently trained and fearless in dialectic to ask at once that radical question.[96] Socrates ought presumably to have more specific reasons for asking more specific questions. Several scholars have rightly supposed that Socrates is worried specifically by Protagoras' bandying of terms like 'justice', 'moderation' and 'goodness' without a clear statement of their meaning and interrelations.[97] Socrates makes the point (329C) 'You said that Zeus bestowed justice and conscience on mankind, and then many times in your discourse you spoke of justice and soundness of mind [=moderation] and holiness and all the rest as all summed up as the one thing, excellence [=goodness]. Will you then explain precisely whether excellence is one thing, and justice and soundness of mind and holiness parts of it, or whether all of these that I've just mentioned are different names of one and the same thing.' Interpreters have not failed to notice this precise question. They have gone on, very reasonably, to discuss the exact nature of Socrates' own beliefs on the relation of goodness and good qualities to one another. But for the examination of Socrates' dialectic it is helpful to look further into the detail of Protagoras' Speech for exact implications about the various good qualities. Professor Roger Duncan has recently done some useful work on this, and the present discussion owes some points to his.[98]

But the precise implications of what Protagoras actually says deserve further exploration still: the options Socrates offers him on the good qualities may prove to have even deeper roots in his Great Speech than has yet been recognized. From this relatively uncontroversial beginning there may spring a similar analysis of Socrates' whole lines of argument, which are of a more disputable (and disputed) kind.

We may start with piety or 'holiness'. Nobody in the dialogue mentions Protagoras' well-known belief (Fr.B4) that we cannot know whether there are gods or not because of the obscurity of the subject and the shortness of human life. Whether Plato meant his readers to think of it, and thus add piquancy to the remarks about piety in the dialogue, is not now determinable. It is perhaps worth keeping the question in mind as one reads, but the following analysis takes no further explicit account of it. At all events, most of Protagoras' audience on this occasion will have believed in the gods, and a normal young man like Hippocrates could be expected to.

Protagoras first mentions mankind's belief in gods without using any word for 'piety' or 'holiness' (322A). Early man, for whatever reason,[99] was the only creature to believe in and worship the gods; he set about erecting altars and statues of them. A Greek would surely have included this type of behaviour in a list of pious or holy actions; certainly the destruction of temples was an impiety characteristic of rash conquerors, and not to worship the city's gods was also impious. The gods demanded worship. They also, as we have seen in discussing justice, preferred certain other sorts of behaviour. The Greek word for 'worship' did not necessarily include these. So early man, before the arrival of political goodness, possessed part of the good quality of piety, but not necessarily the whole of it.

Next (323E–324A) Protagoras includes impiety among the opposites of the good qualities, and more positively includes holiness in a list of good qualities. This would strongly suggest the involvement (to use for the present a neutral and vague term) of piety in political goodness. No distinction appears, however, between two sorts of piety, one ritual and the other moral. Since Protagoras has not mentioned piety by name in connection with ritual, he is under no obligation, stictly speaking, to offer such a distinction. But an alert listener might wonder exactly what the relation was between the religious activity preceding the introduction of the political art and the religious virtue in some way involved in that art.

An apology is due to the reader at this point, before we proceed. Talk of 'qualities' in the English plural, as in the last paragraph, presupposes that the terms listed do indeed denote different qualities, and are not different names for the same quality. It presupposes thus an answer to Socrates' first question after the speech of Protagoras (329C). To presuppose an answer to this question has its danger; it may make the question seem either otiose or unrelated to the detail of the speech. But it is difficult to furnish terms general enough which also avoid begging Socrates' question – whether in translation, paraphrase, or description.[100] In addition, the Greek of one or two passages is, perhaps deliberately, ambiguous in a way virtually impossible to reproduce in English.

The status of piety needs further investigation; but the investigation must depend heavily on passages mentioning also justice and moderation[101] and cannot proceed without simultaneous study of the implied relationships between all these qualities, and between each (or all) of them and goodness. It might seem logical to take each quality or pair of qualities in turn: but this is impractical, and it is better to go consecutively through the Great Speech, since Protagoras' words sometimes have implications in context that they might not have, or might have less clearly, in isolation. The context and order within the speech raise expectations from time to time in Plato's reader's mind which colour the meaning of subsequent sentences. Socrates need not necessarily have paid strict attention to the context or to the expectations it engenders: but it is well to assume that he plays fair until or unless it is disproved.

First let us observe that quite near the beginning Protagoras employs an expression implying that the political art has more than one part (322B). This is particularly important for Socrates: it gives him a peg on which to hang his later questions; he does not have to establish the notion of a part of goodness. Without this Socrates might have had to phrase his questions more clumsily or perhaps start from a more basic level of discussion. No doubt the end-result would have been similar. What Protagoras says is that early men could not fight the animals effectively; they did not possess the political art, of which part was the 'warlike art'. Obviously in an attempt to remedy this situation, they sought to gather together and find safety in building cities. After what we have said on the *Laches*, the close relation of the 'warlike art' to *andreia* or 'courage' should be evident. Protagoras perhaps has in mind also the necessity of hanging together in defence. But this is not explicit in Protagoras' words, which allow us at present only to deduce his notion of a division of goodness into parts, of which one (however complex itself) is appropriate to fighting. He does not mention this part again by name, either to be identified with or to be distinguished from the other good qualities mentioned.

Armed with parts of goodness, but not knowing much about the one part named so far, we come next to early men's injustice to one another (322B). This results from their not yet possessing the political art. The passage leaves obscure the relation between the warlike art and injustice (or its opposite). If injustice is a necessary consequence of not possessing the political art, then interesting consequences appear, to be taken first in isolation from other aspects of the political art. It seems possible to extract from this passage the proposition, 1, if men do not have the political art, they are unjust. From this it would follow, 2, that, if men are not unjust, they possess the political art. Given Protagoras' rather cavalier treatment of contraries and contradictories, on which there will be much more to be said later, we should eventually be able to rewrite 2 in another form, namely, 3, if men are just, they possess the political art. Now there is more than one relation between justice and the political art compatible with the truth of 3. If justice is the whole of the political art, then obviously 3 is true. If justice is not the whole of the political art, but the possession of justice entails the possession of the other part or parts of the political art, then again 3 is true. Provided the notions of 'part' and 'whole' are applicable to the political art, as they are for Protagoras, one of these conditions must be true if 3 is to be true.

It results that the 'warlike art', being a part of the political art, is either a part of justice, or the whole of justice, or a separate part of the political art, a part whose possession is entailed by the possession of justice. That justice is coextensive with the warlike art is, though not impossible, on the face of it implausible. The choice between the two other alternatives is Hobsonian. In either case, unless 'courage' has no role in fighting for survival, the possession of justice will be seen to entail the possession of 'courage' (whether 'courage' be part of justice or not). The sophist must either accept this, or (most implausibly) give 'courage' no role in fighting for survival, or have no truck with the conversion of non-injustice to justice. If, incidentally, he takes the third of these courses, he will find himself regarding non-injustice as a sufficient condition of the political art, and his situation will be in certain respects worse. Has Protagoras been careless, or have we been too strict?

If he has (or we have), we could allow him one way out: suppose that what he really meant was that, 1', if men do not have the political art, they are either unjust or immoderate or both. From 1' it follows that, 2', if men are neither unjust nor immoderate nor both, they possess the political art. From 2' it follows (if and only if we allow for Protagoras' cavalier way with contraries and contradictories) that, 3', if men are both just and moderate they possess the political art. Men's failure to possess justice then resulted (as it happened) from their failure to possess the political art; but men may also, for anything Protagoras says, have lacked certain other qualities, such as moderation. We should be able to ask him whether injustice was the only consequence of the lack of political art. If it was not the only consequence, was the lack of other good qualities the direct consequence of that lack, or did the injustice in itself entail (e.g.) immoderation? If injustice entails immoderation, then non-immoderation entails non-injustice. If we again assume Protagoras' cavalier treatment of contrary and contradictory, then in Protagorean terms moderation entails justice. Again one good quality carries another with it.

Zeus, at any rate, responds to the situation (322B–C) by sending to men both moderation and justice. He specifies no link of entailment between them; but he says nothing to rule out such a link. Indeed it is doubtful whether he rules out their identity. The conjunctions 'both ... and ...' used to join them occur elsewhere, binding things with little or no distinction between them, and occasionally conjoin things the speaker clearly wishes to assimilate rather than distinguish.[102] But the following plurals suggest, without conclusively proving, that Protagoras has no notion that the identity of justice and moderation might be in question. No normal reader or listener would be seized of such a notion; but we have to remember that Socrates was not a wholly normal listener, and what Plato's Protagoras intends need not be the same thing that his Socrates understands.

Protagoras mentions the two functions of ordering and binding (322C); we should not necessarily divide them neatly between moderation and justice even for Protagoras' mind, let alone in Socrates'. The whole passage, however, would surely give, and be expected to give, the impression that moderation and justice are distinct parts of goodness, both necessary, and neither by itself sufficient.[103]

The position of the part of goodness concerned with war would still have presented some awkwardness. Was even the combination of justice and moderation sufficient to cope with war? Yes, if one believed wholeheartedly that the gods reward the just; perhaps yes, again, if one believed with Euripides' Theseus that a just cause was more important than one's prowess. But if one describes the warlike art as a specific part of political goodness, then one raises the question of its relation to other good qualities; the question receives no firm answer in this passage.

The next passage (322E–323A) on these qualities, with further ambiguities, occurs as Protagoras begins the exposition of his myth. 'When it comes to debate on political goodness, the whole of which must proceed through justice and moderation, they are right to accept advice from anyone, since it is incumbent on everyone to share in that virtue at any rate, or else there can be no city at all.'[104] It is here equally unclear in Greek and in English whether it is the debater's advice or political goodness which proceeds entirely through justice and moderation.[105]

The effect is somewhat similar in either case: giving advice worth hearing in debate is equivalent in the whole passage to the possession of political goodness; if we assume that to tell people what is just and moderate one needs to *be* just and moderate, it then follows that, if the advice given proceeds by urging 'justice and moderation', the good quality one needs to give such advice properly is 'justice and moderation'. But *that* assumption is unnecessary in this particular argument if the antecedent of the relative pronoun is 'political goodness'. In that case it is said directly that political goodness 'all' proceeds through 'justice and moderation'. This makes the possession of 'justice and moderation' a necessary condition of political goodness.

Whether 'justice and moderation' is a sufficient condition of political goodness is another question. Nothing visible in this passage enables us to give any more definite answer to it than before; but one consideration may be relevant. If the qualities here talked about are attributable to actions as well as to persons and their characters, then Protagoras would have it that every politically good action must be 'just and moderate'. This would have the effect that if there are any other distinct good qualities going to make up political goodness (e.g. the warlike art), then the actions corresponding to such qualities must coincide with those corresponding to justice or with those corresponding to moderation, and/or with a set whose members all fall within those two sets. In fact the possession of justice and moderation and the performance of the corresponding actions must guarantee at least the performance of the actions corresponding to the possession of the art of war.

That the epithets talked about are indeed attributable to

actions is much more strongly suggested if we take the relative's antecedent to be 'advice' rather than 'political goodness', for advice is much more likely to be concerned with specific courses of action in a given situation, and it was not generalized moral sermons that the Athenian people normally listened to. Accordingly, though the effect of the choice of antecedent is not great, it is not negligible. But it remains impossible to choose definitively on syntactical grounds; so this sentence of Protagoras has left a couple of questions open.

Considered in isolation, this passage too would be possible to read as compatible with the identity of justice and moderation. The simple particle 'and' employed here can, like 'both ... and...', be used to conjoin the identical, or to link terms identical in reference. A conjunction by this means, even of two synonymous terms, cannot be ruled out. Strict rules of inference from the text would therefore make it hard to infer that there must be two entirely separate things, namely, 'justice' and 'moderation'. It would be even harder to disprove overlapping. But again the normal reader or listener would gain the impression of two distinct good qualities. The impression already gained from the myth would not lose strength through the expression 'this goodness'. 'This goodness' would most naturally (though not with absolute necessity) be taken to mean 'political goodness' as a whole rather than to refer to justice and moderation as a single good quality.

In his following paragraph Protagoras undertakes to show that all men think everyone ought to partake in 'justice and the rest of political goodness'.[106] This expression (323A, cf. 323B) ought, at least for the time being, to remove any doubt that justice is a part, rather than the whole, of 'political goodness'. There must be something 'other' than justice included in political goodness. The expression does not, however, tend either to prove or to disprove that the possession of justice necessitates the possession of the other part or parts of goodness; the words simply supply no reason for raising the question.

Protagoras' succeeding argument (323A–C) for this version of his thesis is of limited interest here. In the case of other 'goodnesses', to declare one's possession of them without in fact possessing them is matter for scorn or anger, and even for one's treatment as a madman; due modesty is labelled 'moderation'. To say falsely or even truly that one is unjust is mad. To say falsely that one possesses justice is evidently not mad, and one ought to do so; but to do so is not formally labelled 'moderate'. If it were, then it would follow that injustice was compatible with a form of 'moderation'. But it is not, and the inference fails. It is extremely doubtful whether Socrates or anyone else would be justified in inferring from Protagoras' non-employment of the term 'moderate' of certain unjust people his deliberate avoidance of such a juxtaposition of terms, and hence his belief in the incompatibility of injustice and moderation.

Protagoras says at the end of this paragraph (323C) that every man must necessarily possess some degree of justice, or not be among mankind at all. His Zeus said earlier (322D) that everyone should be capable of sharing in justice and moderation, or be killed as a plague. Nothing is awkward here; if justice and moderation are both necessary qualifications for a social being, then irrespective of their identity or difference, justice is indispensable. But we have already gained the impression, without strict proof, that moderation and justice are not identical. If we suppose, as is then natural, that in the locution 'justice and the rest of political goodness' the phrase 'the rest...' includes moderation; if, in addition, the case of 'injustice' is only an example, then the same ought to be true of moderation as of justice here; in that case someone lacking in moderation, but refraining from admitting his lack, would be to that extent moderate. So in order to be wholly lacking in moderation it is necessary to be ready to admit one's lack. But to admit one's lack would be by common consent mad; so to be wholly immoderate is to be by common consent mad. It is not thus shown that all the mad are immoderate, or even non-moderate; but since 'moderate' and 'sensible' or 'sound' are all *sôphrôn*, not many Greeks would have wanted to deny it. This set of conclusions may be useful later.

For the moment we may return to piety, whose opposite occurs in a list of vices in the course of the argument about punishment which follows (323C–324B). Qualities inborn or acquired by chance, the sophist says, are not the occasion for punishment. Qualities acquired by care, practice, and teaching are, and 'One such quality is injustice, impiety and in a word whatever is the opposite of political goodness' (323E–324A). Clearly Socrates is right in suggesting later that the word 'one' in this sentence needs explication (329C–D); the bad qualities could, if this sentence were taken out of context, be one either as being parts of a single whole or as being identical. The sentence might offer either an actual addition of separate things or a merely rhetorical conjunction of terms.[107] Various intermediate positions are conceivable. What is, in context, the role of impiety in badness?

A similar sentence will occur later in the argument, a sentence about goodness rather than its opposite: the second one says (324E–325A) that there is one thing in which all citizens must share, namely justice and moderation and piety and (in a word) Protagoras calls it 'a man's goodness'. This positive statement is easier to analyse than the negative one preceding it. We are already aware that goodness has more than one part; we are under the impression that justice and moderation are two distinct things; we think justice can reasonably be described as a part of goodness; we have been given to understand that both justice and moderation, or at least the capacity for both, must be possessed by all men in society, and that there is another part of goodness, namely, 'the warlike art'. Where does piety fit in? The complexity of the answer to this problem might go far to explain, if explanation be needed, why Socrates waited so long (328D–E) before asking his little question.

If we take goodness as a personal quality or set of qualities, without considering actions, then piety is, according to the second statement, part of it. 'Goodness' sums up a lot of qualities including piety; and piety is one of the qualities needed for community life. Its absence is fit subject for punishment, its opposite is in some sense opposed to political goodness. The single thing in which everyone must partake is justice, moderation and piety. But in that case why did Zeus send down to mankind, so far as Protagoras says, only justice and moderation? Why was piety not mentioned long before the 'lists'? One cannot dismiss the question on the ground that the positive passage on piety appears after Protagoras has avowedly turned away from myth (324D); for it is well before that avowal that the opposite of piety appears as part of the opposite of goodness, and that negative passage is pretty difficult to interpret without saying that piety is at least part of goodness.

Where then was piety in the myth? If we save Protagoras' bacon here by suggesting that piety is involved in primitive temple-building, we land him in a further difficulty, namely that man then possesses part of political goodness before Zeus sends down political goodness, and at a time when men quite simply 'had not yet the political art' (322B). The absence of the political art was apparently sufficient ground for Man's failure in fighting, for his lack of the part of the political art which is the warlike art. Why should men have possessed another part, namely piety? Myth and exposition do not seem to fit well together here.

The more we separate piety from justice and moderation the worse the fit becomes. It might improve if we supposed piety to be a sub-part of goodness, a part of justice, or of justice-and-moderation, or of moderation. Yet in what we have called the 'list' of virtues there is no hint of its subordination. Piety might be distinct from both justice and moderation, but be a necessary condition of one or both. It might be actually identical with one of them and be conjoined in our 'list' only for rhetorical effect. Either of these interpretations would explain why it was not necessary to mention piety in the myth; but neither would quite explain the coordinating, rather than subordinating, language of the 'lists'.

Protagoras is not formally inconsistent here. But his remarks raise questions about the status and relationship of the various good qualities he mentions. The listener cannot rule out even the identity of all three good qualities in the list. It is a possible interpretation of the lists, and, though not the most natural meaning of the earlier passages, it is really difficult to reconcile only with the expression 'justice and the rest of political goodness'.

If we formulate what Protagoras is saying in the terminology of actions (a formulation surely justifiable on the basis of his reference to 'doing') (325A) we find similar difficulties. If piety is omissible from the myth, but is necessary in the ex-

Socrates meets Protagoras 247

position, then where the myth appears to be saying that all actions must be either just or moderate or both, and even the exposition says that all advice must proceed through justice and moderation, which presumably means much the same thing, the exposition says further that they must be either just or moderate or pious or some combination of two or three of these. If both myth and exposition are to be believed, the class of pious actions will be entirely contained in the class of actions that are either just or moderate or both, for, if a pious action does not fall within that class, then it cannot be termed 'good' without violating the earlier stipulation. So either pious actions coincide with just actions, or with moderate actions, or with some set contained by the set of just and/or moderate actions, or we are faced with a contradiction.

If the good qualities (to return to that mode) are faculties, capacities for or dispositions toward certain types of action,[108] this leaves piety without a function: piety then produces no actions which are not already produced by either justice or moderation or both. Piety becomes superfluous. No wonder Socrates asks questions about the identity or difference of the 'power' of each part of goodness (330A); and no wonder Protagoras has a certain difficulty, as we shall see, in answering them coherently. Naturally this particular difficulty would be instantly removed by the supposition that 'justice', 'moderation' and 'piety' were all synonyms, and their conjunction a mere trick of the rhetorical trade; but then, as we have seen, other problems would arise.

Between the two lists of qualities just analysed there falls an interesting argument about punishment (324A–D). Protagoras invites Socrates to believe that the general human practice of punishing the *unjust* demonstrates the punishers' belief in the possibility of acquiring *goodness*.[109] The aim of rational punishment is deterrence, and this aim shows a belief in the teachability of goodness. This section exhibits a rapid interchange between the word 'goodness' and words containing the root-syllable for 'just'. But, more than this, the whole argument, as it stands, depends for its validity on the assimilation or the indissoluble connection of justice to moderation, and indeed to goodness. For if justice and moderation were distinct qualities, separate parts of the overall quality of goodness, then a man having or acquiring only one of them need not have or acquire the whole of goodness – unless it is impossible (factually or conceptually) to possess one of these distinct parts without the other(s).

It follows from this that when Protagoras says that the purpose of teaching justice (or deterring from injustice) indicates belief in the teachability of *goodness* he is assuming general belief in *either* the identity of justice and goodness (and perhaps also the identity of justice with moderation) *or* the inevitable accompaniment of justice by moderation (and presumably also by piety and the warlike art). If goodness and justice are neither identical nor indissolubly connected, the teachability of justice will not necessarily involve the teachability of goodness as a whole, and Protagoras' argument will formally fail.

It would be easy to rectify the failure by stating that justice is only an example, and/or that punishment is equally a deterrent from other vices than injustice. But Protagoras does not take this easy step, and translators should not, as some have done, have taken it on his behalf. The argument remains formally dubious without the assumptions on justice sketched above.

To speak with absolute strictness, Protagoras has not yet committed himself fully to this argument. Its conclusion is about the beliefs of men in general and Athenians in particular. But the sophist describes (324C) the argument for the teachability of goodness as 'reasonable' or 'right', and it turns out to constitute a major plank in his whole platform. Besides, Protagoras may be constrained in the whole ambience of this part of the discussion to cast no doubt on the wisdom of the Athenians. If so, then he is still so constrained in the argument which follows, which is derived from educational practice (325Cff.).

Parental and other adult concern for the boy's goodness manifests itself in a set of habitual instructions and evaluative remarks listed as follows (325D). 'This is just and that unjust, this seemly and that unseemly, this pious and that impious, and do these things and do not do those things.' This does not articulate the relations between what is just, what is seemly, what is pious, and what is to be done. Presumably Protagoras would concur with at least most of the instructions; but it is unclear whether the actions enjoined as just are the same as those recommended as pious, or whether the just and the pious constitute different subsets of the set of actions adults tell the boy to do. The insertion of the much more general value-word 'seemly' between the 'just' and the 'pious' does not help. Are the actions recommended as just and/or pious the sum total of the seemly actions or not? Why do the adults not even mention any 'moderate' action? The analyst retires baffled; taken by itself the passage leaves open a whole series of alternatives.

Moderation may play no part here, but it has a major role in the next stage of education (325D–326A). Parents request the teachers to insist on well-ordered behaviour. Perhaps in their concern for this[110] the teachers place the poems of good poets in front of their pupils. The poems contain advice, and the praises of good men of old. So far, so good. If well-ordered behaviour is a fresh part of goodness, we are hardly in worse trouble than before. If it represents either a part already mentioned or the whole of goodness, then this neither raises any new awkward questions nor answers any old ones.

The teachers of music do the same sort of thing as the teachers of literacy (326A–B). They take care 'both of moderation and that the young do nothing bad'. Once again we find a conjunction shrouded in ambiguity. The words 'Both ... and ...' 'are sometimes used (rarely in prose) where the thought implies a more elaborate relationship than that of mere addition.'[111] So the most authoritative work on Greek particles, I think rightly. But Protagoras uses this combination of words elsewhere in at least one instance where the second expression is not so much added to as explanatory of the first. For example, the gods (he says in the myth) (320D) 'appointed Prometheus and Epimetheus both to equip mortal creatures and to assign to each the right powers.'[112] Here it is clear that the processes of equipping and assignment are one and the same; the second locution is simply more explicit and more elaborate than the first. So Protagoras' own usage makes it possible that, in the account of education, care that the young men do nothing bad is not additional to, but explanatory of, care for their moderation. Indeed, this possibility should cause no surprise. Moderation in Greek thought is frequently the use of self-restraint in the avoidance of shameful or wrong actions. As such, it was often felt to be particularly appropriate to the young.[113]

But this produces a problem for the Socratic interpreter. How is moderation here related to the other good qualities? If added, as something quite distinct, to 'doing nothing bad', moderation is distinguished from something it often means in Greek; if explained by 'doing nothing bad' it is evidently of enormous scope. On the second, and on the whole more probable, hypothesis it would overlap certainly the art of war, and certainly also piety. Further, it is clear from many characters in Plato who speak as normal Greeks and not as Platonists or Socratics that justice also has a negative function like that assignable to the Athenians' 'moderation' in the *Protagoras*. A conspicuous example is in the second Book of the *Republic* (360B), where 'remaining in justice' is refraining from, and avoiding contact with, other people's property. In the fourth Book of the same dialogue (442Eff.), in response to his own question what a just man in his sense of 'just' would do, Socrates lists a set of actions such a man would avoid. He then insists (very plausibly) that a man avoiding such actions is just in the normal usage of the word, and he has to insist on that, and to be able to insist on that, for his whole argument to work.[114]

What follows from this is emphatically not that Protagoras *cannot* be dividing goodness into two parts, one positive (justice) and one negative (moderation). Such a division remains possible. What follows is that Protagoras' position is open to more than one interpretation; questioning is required to elucidate its obscurities. This passage could be the work of a man prepared to equate or to implicate moderation with justice, but it need not be. The place of moderation in the list of good qualities is doubtful; it seems likely to overlap some of them. The place of moderate actions in human life is problematic; does moderation consist merely in the avoidance of certain types of action? Does such avoidance count as an action in itself? If one chooses, for example, a pious action and at the same time avoids an impious one, is the choice and performance of the pious action produced by the functioning of the quality of piety, or of moderation, or of both? Is it possible to act piously, or in accord with any other good quality, without also acting moderately? Does not the possession of the positive good qualities guarantee the possession of a negatively conceived moderation? Could such moderation be conceptually distinct but not in practice obtainable separately? How in general is the functioning of moderation related to the functioning of other good qualities? This passage even alone would be capable of provoking Socrates' later questions about the functions and 'powers' of the various good qualities. Protagoras' words here have no clear implications tending to lead to any contradiction; but they are vague on just those questions which later exercise Socrates.

A short parenthesis is necessary on the connection between moderation as the avoidance of wrongdoing and the injunctions of the Athenian parents to their children (325D). The young were told by their parents what not to do; if avoiding the bad is moderation, then presumably it was moderation in which the parents were thus instructing the children. If the evaluative remarks of the parents are summarized in the commands to do this and not that, then moderation embraces the avoidance of the unjust, the unseemly and the impious. Unless Protagoras is careful about the difference between contradictory and contrary, between avoiding wrong and doing right, justice and seemliness and piety will end up as parts of moderation. Protagoras has neither said nor implied that; but it remains a possible interpretation of his remarks, among many other possible interpretations.

Protagoras does not lighten the prevailing darkness by talk (326B) of 'every aspect of human life' requiring 'grace and proper adjustment', for the development in particular of men 'useful for speech and action'.[115] This appears to add another necessary condition of goodness or of its acquisition, without being very explicit.

Explicitness is again not a feature of the sophist's description (326B–C) of the 'trainer's' function in education. This returns us to the question of war, and of the 'warlike art', in connection with courage – though the latter virtue still receives no mention by name, as R. Duncan has pointed out.[116] The trainer's job is to see 'that once their minds are properly formed their bodies will be in a better condition to act under their direction, and they won't be forced by physical deficiency to act the "coward" in battle or in any other situation.' This does again leave the role of 'courage' obscure. But it does not minimize that role as strongly as Duncan thinks. It is true to say that the word 'courage' is 'conspicuously absent' from the Great Speech; indeed it is not only true but significant. But it is doubtful whether 'if we were to define virtue as a habit of the soul, then courage would not really be a virtue according to Protagoras,' and there is nothing at all in this or any other passage to allow the inference that 'Moreover (courage) is indistinguishable from bodily fitness.' It is even doubtful whether one can say with Duncan on the basis of Protagoras' speech that 'Courage is assimilated to bodily fitness and thus reduced in stature as a virtue, to say the least.' But Protagoras' own words require analysis.

First, bodily fitness becomes in those words a necessary condition for the avoidance of some cowardly or inefficient behaviour in war and elsewhere. If bodily fitness is a necessary condition of avoiding 'cowardice', then it would appear that *a fortiori* it is a necessary condition for the display of 'courage'. But that does not make bodily fitness logically (or otherwise) equivalent to 'courage'. Indeed the context pretty firmly implies the contrary, that bodily fitness is not a sufficient condition of courage. For 'and' in Protagoras' sentence above about trainers presumably does not denote a mere addition; it would be odd to add the body's good condition for action under the mind's direction to the absence of such bodily defect as will compel cowardice. 'And' is thus equivalent either to 'that is to say' or to 'and in consequence'. The former would be an example of what the Lexicon[117] calls the 'limiting' or 'defining' sense of 'and'; the latter is exemplified in Protagoras' speech.[118] So it is a consequence or the equivalent of the body serving a rightly formed mind that the body's unfitness should not cause cowardly behaviour. The 'rightly formed mind' looks very like the person 'useful for speech and action' who results from the previous stage of education. What the trainer seems to be doing is ensuring that it is not from bodily unfitness that the citizen of sound spirit will play his proper part in battle.

Protagoras' account of the matter is superficial, but the mention of the 'useful' or rightly formed mind strongly suggests that courage is not purely physical, but dependent also on the mind. The passage suggests that a certain temper of mind is a necessary condition of non-cowardly action, and presumably also of 'courage'. The point is that the body should not let the mind down. Protagoras' Greek word for 'mind' will later provide a question; how intellectual is it? But for the present we may investigate the fit of this passage with the earlier one about war (322B).

The warlike art, we recall, was part of the political art, and by the same token of political goodness. It now appears that to avoid 'cowardly' action in war, action which presumably contravenes the art of war, one needs not only a fit body but also a certain state of mind. That state of mind is hardly dissociable from the good qualities induced by the early stages of education, namely moderation, justice and piety and any others that may have strayed into the discussion. But Protagoras is notably cagey in even suggesting what relations subsist between these qualities and the avoidance of cowardice. But the art of war is part of the political art, and the avoidance of 'cowardly' behaviour is presumably a necessary condition of good behaviour in war. It begins to look as if Protagoras meant to include 'courage' (or at least non-cowardice) in the art of war, if not to equate 'courage' with the art of war. That would make courage a part, or a part of a part, of political goodness.

But that is not all; bodily fitness can help one to avoid cowardly behaviour not only in war but also 'in other actions' (326C). Hence the avoidance of cowardly action is not simply part of the warlike part of political goodness but is equally relevant in other spheres. This raises the usual problems concerning the overlapping (or not) of the good qualities. How *is* courage related to justice, piety and moderation? Is it included in one of them? Or is it a separate quality with a distinctive function? Does the possession of a mind loaded with justice, piety and moderation guarantee participation in courage? We cannot tell, and Socrates is fully entitled to ask. But nothing in the passage directly suggests that the possession of courage entails, either conceptually or factually, the possession of any other virtue. In volunteering later (328E) that it is possible to be brave but unjust. Protagoras is not contradicting anything he has previously said.

The city takes up the educative process, in Protagoras' account, where teachers and trainers leave off. The laws instruct, in a way analogous to teachers of writing. The assimilation of law to instruction obviously helps Protagoras' general line of argument. Anyone going outside or transgressing the law is punished (326C–E). Punishment, in Taylor's clever rendering of a Greek pun, is correction; and again, in Taylor's version, 'the law corrects'.[119] 'Law' here is the same Greek word as occurred in the sophist's myth (but not his exposition of it) to mean 'justice', and it can also mean 'penalty' or 'punishment' or (legal) 'judgement'. The word foreshadows the next paragraph's juxtaposition of 'what is just' and 'what is lawful' (327Bff.). Together with the succeeding sentence referring to goodness in general, it may also foreshadow the next paragraph's juxtaposition of 'justice' (here the related word used in the exposition) and goodness. 'We benefit, I believe, from one another's justice and goodness, which is why everyone is eager to teach the next man and tell them what is just and lawful' (327B).[120]

'Justice and goodness.' The phrase could indeed, as Duncan says,[121] practically identify justice with goodness. 'Goodness' could, here, be 'appositional' to 'justice'. But though this is quite possibly what Plato's sophist intended, it is not the only way of taking his words. The listening Socrates cannot rely necessarily on this equation, nor on that of the just and the lawful. True, there are many contexts, especially in forensic oratory, where 'just' and 'lawful' have the same reference; and that for the simple reason that the jury's oath to decide in accordance with justice and the law made no overt distinction, though it left room for a wide variety of emphasis. Protagoras could, if he had been so minded, have declared 'and' here to mean, as it sometimes does, 'and in general', adding a general point to the particular one.[122] 'Goodness' could be a more general term than 'justice' here. What the laws and what the citizens teach could be what is just and in general what is lawful and good.

Another possibility is to take 'and' here to mean 'and in

consequence'.[123] On this rendering, if an action is just, it is in consequence lawful (though the converse need not be true) and the possession of justice implies the possession of the other components, whatever they are, of 'goodness'.

The listening Socrates has no obvious grounds for excluding any of these ways of taking Protagoras. Ast in his *Lexicon Platonicum* well said 'Variae ... quas part. καί habere videtur significationes non in ipsa per se insunt, sed ex orationis proficiscuntur conformatione.' Socrates cannot be sure whether justice is another name for goodness, whether goodness is a more general term inclusive of justice, or whether, in the latter case, justice is or is not a sufficient guarantee of 'the rest of goodness'. The paths thus left open bear indeed a suspicious resemblance to the ways from which Socrates will ask Protagoras to choose. If, however, justice really is to be equated with goodness, then Protagoras is in trouble; for in that case his previous phrase 'justice and the rest of political goodness' (323B) makes no sense.

The situation remains very much the same in the subsequent (second) analogy from flute-playing and its aftermath (327Aff.). An adequate flautist is to an ignorant one as any man brought up in society is to one not so brought up. That is, any societal man, however unjust, is 'just, and an expert in this matter' (327C-D), compared to those lacking society's educational advantages, and hence not compelled to care about goodness. Here 'this matter' picks up the same expression earlier,[124] and most probably refers to 'goodness' rather than to 'justice', and this probability gains strength from the mention of goodness later in the sentence just paraphrased. On this reading the sentence gives us 'just' and (by implication) 'good' again linked by 'and'; again the possible consequences are either equation of goodness and justice, or inclusion of justice in goodness, or the distinction of goodness from justice but with a guarantee of one by the other.

One further comment concerns the relation between the possession of the good qualities and the ability to talk effectively about what it is right to do. In several parts of Protagoras' speech the possession of goodness or of one or more good qualities is enough to make a good adviser or instructor in them. The gods assign 'moderation and justice' to all

(322C-D); and hence all are qualified to advise on questions of political goodness (322D–E). Good men do not uniformly make their sons better; but this is apparently because their sons' heredity chances to be inferior (324D, 326E–327C). The suggestion that they might 'have their sons taught' is not directly motivated by parental inadequacy in teaching (325C). Somehow, it seems, we all function as teachers of goodness, as we function as teachers of our native language. But we do not so function only by example, since we are all presumed capable of offering precepts to a political audience. The young serve, as it were, an apprenticeship; the apprentice learns by practice and example, but also by verbal instruction.

This attitude toward the capacity to verbalize knowledge is not conditioned only by the terms of Socrates' original inquiry about the reasons for the Athenians' readiness to listen to anybody on moral topics. It reflects also the overwhelming frequency of moral debate in Athenian law-courts and assemblies, combined with the democratic myth that anyone could obtain a hearing.[125]

But for Protagoras the poets do not just offer good examples; they are 'good poets'. The lawgivers who discover and lay down the lines of society's educational policy are 'good lawgivers'. It is not clear whether they are so because they know their stuff, or whether they are also good at persuading and teaching. Protagoras lays claim to a somewhat greater ability than other men to guide the young towards goodness (328A–B). Either he is in some way 'better' as a man than the poets, lawgivers and statesmen Socrates has mentioned, or he is better at communication. If communication is his forte, then he is open to the suspicions we have found attaching to rhetorical skills; if he is 'better' than other men, then why is he not doing, rather than teaching? Protagoras is perhaps wise to remain vague; he nowhere says or denies explicitly that goodness is a sufficient condition for the capacity to instruct; and he nowhere says or denies explicitly that a higher ability to instruct implies a higher degree of goodness.

It is time to add up the results of this analysis, first as it concerns the virtues of piety, justice and moderation. Justice, we found, was certainly in some passages a part of goodness, notably in the reference to 'justice and the rest of goodness'. In at least one passage justice was a sufficient condition for the possession of the whole of goodness. There were some passages which, were it not for the sentences implying justice's status as a part, it would be tempting to take as equating, or at least assimilating, justice to the whole of goodness, though we found none where such a reading was mandatory. The place of moderation was obscure. Normally listed as if distinct from justice and coordinate with it as a part of goodness, it appeared at times to be a necessary condition of justice. The possibility that it was also a sufficient condition of justice was hard to square with one passage, and *a fortiori* the actual identity of justice and moderation appeared to be ruled out. Passages tempting the hearer to identify justice with the whole of goodness could not be taken that way without some danger of identifying moderation also with goodness. This possibility was left open anyway (though not necessitated) by the passage associating moderation with the negative aspect of goodness; that passage did not clearly distinguish goodness from its negative aspect, but parental injunctions proved to be both positive and negative. Piety was pretty clearly a part of goodness, though its relation to the other good qualities presents an obscurity; is it identical with them, or with one of them, or is it coordinate or subordinate? Protagoras has not made himself clear.

That these good qualities must, if Protagoras is to be consistent, be parts of goodness is tolerably clear. That he may have incautiously identified two or more of them occasionally, or identified one of them with goodness as a whole, remains an open possibility. Whether, how, and in what circumstances these three qualities overlap is a thoroughly tangled question, and one which becomes even more involved if we translate it into action-terminology.

Wisdom and 'courage' both figure much less prominently. 'Wise' occurs, and 'wisdom' is ambiguously hinted at. The relation of art, wisdom and goodness is left obscure, with the gods in the myth actually contradicting themselves on the question whether political goodness is an art. The possibility of equating the political art or goodness with wisdom or *a* wisdom is left open. 'Courage' is presumably, and eventually almost explicitly a substantial part of the art of war, which is in turn a part of the political art or goodness; but 'courage' appears in other avocations than war, and in these its relation to the other and generally quieter virtues is left unexplained. It does not appear to be certainly either a necessary or a sufficient condition of the other good qualities; Protagoras nowhere suggests that it is the whole of goodness.

It remains to be seen what effect these various implications, or such of them as Socrates may reasonably be thought to have noticed, have on the rest of the discussion.

Socrates' initial question; 328D–330B

Socrates assumes Protagoras' willingness and ability to exchange brief question and answer. Protagoras does not demur: self-deprecation is not an item of the sophistic stock-in-trade as it is of the Socratic. Socrates quotes (329C) the sentences from Protagoras' speech about the moral terms he used in myth and exposition, to the effect that Zeus sent justice and moderation to men, and that justice, moderation and piety 'and all these things' were in sum one thing, goodness. Socrates' quotation, here as in the *Symposium*,[126] is inexact. Protagoras nowhere adds an 'etcetera' of this type to a list already containing justice, moderation and piety – though he does say 'justice and the rest of political goodness'. Socrates has, however, here as in the *Symposium*, reasonable grounds for his alteration to the actual words of the preceding oration. We have seen that at least 'courage', though not explicitly mentioned, might on a common-sense interpretation of Protagoras claim a possible place among the parts of goodness; wisdom as a part is less likely, unless (or except in so far as) the warlike art ranks as a wisdom, and Protagoras has not been specific about that. But at least there is some justification for Socrates' 'etcetera', and it may be in part already exploratory.

About the good qualities thus enumerated Socrates first lays two alternatives before Protagoras. One is that each is the same thing under another name; the other is that they are parts of the single whole, goodness. The first view, as we have seen, is one which might have been the sense of some sentences of Protagoras in isolation, but ought not to be their meaning if Protagoras is carefully consistent. It seems fair for Socrates to ask the sophist, in effect, whether he meant the inconsistent sense or not; and he very readily indicates, consciously or unconsciously, that he intended no such inconsistency. He opts for the parts of a single whole, as he ought if he is to be consistent.

We saw that there were problems in Protagoras' speech over the extent to which the parts of goodness overlap, and the extent to which possession of one of them implies possession of one or more of the others. We have no cause for surprise that Socrates should ask how the parts are related (329D). He presents Protagoras with two alternatives, each an analogy. Are the parts like the parts of a face or like those of a piece of gold? Exactly how the parts of a face are in his opinion related Socrates does not yet specify, but the parts of a piece of gold, he says, differ only in size from each other and from the whole. There is some obscurity in the implied question whether the parts of goodness are different only in size. It seems likely that Socrates is stressing more the similarities between parts of gold here (and hence of parts of goodness) rather than the one point of difference, despite the possibility that parts of goodness, like the parts of gold, may overlap or include one another. Some further elucidation is necessary, and after Protagoras' answer, it is forthcoming. Protagoras chooses to say that the parts of goodness resemble those of a face. This must mean that they have at least one property not in common other than size. This too is consistent with what Protagoras has already said: he is merely clarifying, at Socrates' instigation, his rather vague implications concerning the good qualities. But it remains to be seen *what* properties or kinds of property the parts of goodness do not share.

But there is another question to be answered first. We saw that one possible line of interpretation for Protagoras' critics was to suppose that the possession of one virtue guaranteed the possession of one or more (perhaps all) of the others. So we recognize the way Socrates' thoughts are tending when he asks precisely whether the possessor of one good quality must have them all, or whether different men have differing selections (329E). The sophist opts here for the second alternative, and rashly adds a reason (by way of a couple of examples) to his answer. His examples, though not implausible in themselves, land him in some hot water. Bravery, he suggests, is compatible with injustice and justice with lack of wisdom. Why should the 'fictional' Protagoras offer these examples? Why should Plato want him to? Is there some Socratic and/or Platonic 'foisting' going on? These are not easy questions.

Let us take first bravery and injustice. If one can indeed be brave and unjust then Protagoras' myth comes to mind. Men in the beginning were unjust inasmuch as they did not yet possess the political art (322B). Then, if 'courage' is at least, as we supposed above, part of the warlike art, and hence a sub-part of the political art, the earliest men could have been simultaneously unjust and cowardly. If they possessed 'courage' but not other hypothetical parts of the art of war they would have been courageous but unjust, and they must, when they acquired justice, have been just in virtue of something other than courage. In neither case is Protagoras in any immediate difficulty over his example of the brave and unjust man. Later Protagoras raises the possibility, under certain bodily conditions, of a man behaving like a coward even if his mind be properly formed (326B–C). If realized, this possibility would result in a just coward, a phenomenon certainly doing nothing to discredit the possibility of a brave man's being unjust. Protagoras has in fact said nothing to contradict the compatibility which illustrates his answer to Socrates' inquiry about the good qualities.

The case of wisdom and justice is more complex. One wants to know more than Protagoras has explicitly told us. The properly formed minds of the passage on cowardice – are they wise? And if so, why? As the inevitable result of the inculcation of justice and other good qualities? How important is moderation here? Protagoras leaves various possibilities open in the Great Speech. If justice is not quite equated with goodness, the equation of wisdom with goodness, whether explicit or implicit or not fully either, will not help the equation of wisdom with justice. If wisdom is a part of goodness, then it can happily be a part distinguishable from justice; if wisdom is the whole of goodness, it will be possible to possess justice, now that Protagoras has firmly made that a part, without possessing full wisdom. Protagoras appears thus to be safe. Where he is on dangerous ground is in his reply to Socrates' next question (329E–330A). When Socrates has heard the pair just/unwise brought together in the same breath with the pair brave/unjust, in a context where the behaviour of the parts of goodness is in question, he naturally asks whether 'courage' and wisdom, not listed previously as parts of goodness, are actually parts. It is more plausible for Protagoras to regard 'courage' than wisdom as a part of goodness; 'courage', as we have seen, is almost inescapably such; but wisdom? Protagoras is constrained perhaps by his own inclusion of the pair just/unwise in his illustrations to accept wisdom as a distinct part, despite his previous close association of it with the whole of goodness.

This might seem like a piece of cheating on Plato's part, even if Socrates in the fictional context is not to blame. Why has Plato made his Protagoras put wisdom among the parts, when he has also made it arguable that his Protagoras intends to make it the whole, of goodness? A possible and by no means frivolous reply derives from an earlier passage in the dialogue. Protagoras here says that justice is compatible with non-wisdom; Hippocrates in his first remarks about Protagoras had made non-justice compatible with wisdom (310D). The general unthinking use of words tended at some times, in some moods, and in some senses, to encourage the view that 'wisdom' was a good quality, coordinate with the others, and neither implying the others nor being implied by them. In other moods and at other times people might think of it as wise to be just. Plato's Protagoras sometimes leans one way and sometimes the other. In so doing, however, he adds no contradiction to his views over and above the fluctuation we have already noticed between goodness as an art (and hence a wisdom?) and as a non-art.

Apart from that still unlaid ghost, Protagoras raises no spectres by telling Socrates that courage and wisdom are additional items in his list of good qualities. In doing so he is merely using the vocabulary of praiseworthy qualities in ways Plato recognized as normal and puts into the mouth of an ordinary person. If Plato's Protagoras lands himself in dialectical trouble by using language in ordinary unthinking ways, that perhaps makes his troubles more, rather than less, interesting; and it is not clear that the question of fairness to a historical figure was important to Plato or need at this juncture be important to his readers. Protagoras does indeed pay the penalty for adopting a merely popular understanding of the questions involved; but the time for his punishment is not yet.

Protagoras, and perhaps Plato, sail nearer the wind when the sophist volunteers additionally that the greatest of the parts of goodness is wisdom (330A). For if that were the case, one is hard put to it to explain why he should accord justice so much, and wisdom so little prominence in the Great Speech. Duncan declared roundly that 'the most important virtue for Protagoras is justice', in summarizing the Great Speech. It is not easy to see on close analysis wherein the greater importance of justice lies, but it is indeed more prominent than any other good quality.[127]

There are, however, reasons why, even if he believes justice to be the wisest policy, Protagoras should give the palm to wisdom. One is that teaching is most closely associated with 'making someone wise', and he had himself sanctioned that association in his Speech (324D). As a teacher himself, he can hardly ignore the association. It is accordingly in his professional interest to lay stress on wisdom. The very name of 'sophist' is etymologically connected with the Greek for 'wisdom'. If in fact (though he has not said so) he was considered 'wise in speaking' (310E), above all other skills, and this was a common description of him, he would presumably know, and thus have an added interest in advancing the claims of 'wisdom'. Protagoras' remark about wisdom is on these lines fully explicable from his profession, its claims, and his own mode of life. It needs no further explanation.

Anyone still inclined to doubt the relevance of these points should inspect what Protagoras agrees to about wisdom and knowledge at a much later stage (352C–D). Protagoras agrees there that 'intelligence is a sufficient safeguard for a man' and that 'it would be an especial disgrace to me above all men not to maintain that wisdom and knowledge is the mightiest of human things.' When Socrates' early question receives an answer in harmony with this, nothing is being foisted on anybody.

The Unity of the Good Qualities

The analogy with the parts of the face

Now that the list of parts of goodness is sufficiently complete for Plato's purposes, his Socrates makes sure that the sophist still believes no member of the expanded list to be identical with any other (330A). He then attempts to elucidate the nature and extent of the intended distinctions. His first step in this direction is to ask if each part has a distinctive power. The question is explained by means of an analogy Protagoras has already accepted, that of the parts of the face. One expects this analogy, brought out again at this early and crucial stage of the argument, to have a substantial role in the argument as a whole. But more interpreters, noting that explicit reference to it disappears almost at once, take little notice of it. D. Savan is one notable exception; but Taylor's criticisms of his account were convincing.[128] Nevertheless Savan's fundamental question, what the role is of the parts of the face in the ensuing discussion, will not go away. Why should Plato introduce the analogy only to drop it?

The full answer to that question requires analysis of the argument in detail. But a brief sketch of the eventual answer may helpfully precede the analysis. A problem about similarity may receive an answer simultaneously. The discussion of justice and holiness contains references to varying degrees of similarity on the lips of both participants. These have appeared loose and slipshod to many scholars, and opinions differ as to who is most at fault and who finally has the better of this particular aspect of the debate.

Vlastos, remarking that 'The fumbling in the phraseology is extraordinary', believes Socrates' claim to be that 'Courage and Justice and Temperance are as alike as are two bits of a gold bar'.[129] But Socrates makes no such claim; his questions about the gold bar need be no claim, but could be (and in my opinion are) merely an attempt to elucidate Protagoras' rather than to clarify his own doctrine.[130] Vlastos' only explanation of the 'fumbling' phraseology is that the *Protagoras* is 'an early work in which Plato has yet to achieve the mastery of logical vocabulary and technique which he exhibits ... even in dialogues of the middle period and, still earlier, in transitional dialogues like the *Meno*.' But Vlastos says of the fumbling phraseology that he 'cannot recall its like in any of Plato's Socratic dialogues': so is his claim really that the *Protagoras* is the earliest and least logically expert of them all? And how would one set about convincing Platonists that this large-scale and highly successful drama was Plato's first essay in the genre? This *ad hoc* explanation is surely to be rejected.

But Vlastos was right to express dissatisfaction with Gallop's earlier account, which had Protagoras correct in refusing to admit the homogeneity of Justice and Holiness, while admitting that 'To make his objection conclusive Protagoras would have to specify the criteria for regarding things as homogeneous... The argument simply leaves the issues open.'[131] This leaves a question: in the absence from Socrates' questions and Protagoras' answers of adequate criteria for homogeneity, how can we call Protagoras correct? Taylor[132] is able to hold that Socrates' argument depends on his failure to distinguish two senses or applications of 'alike', namely 'alike in every respect' and 'alike in some respect(s)'. This too is a somewhat desperate expedient; if Socrates could not distinguish these, then he was not much of a philosopher, even after all charitable allowance is made for his early date in the history of the subject. And if he could not distinguish them, then how would he distinguish as he does between 'identical' and 'very like' (331B)? Taylor suggests no reason why Plato should have made his Socrates argue so blindly.

Two questions then lie before us: why Plato appears to drop his analogy with parts of a face, and why he apparently leaves Socrates and Protagoras floundering without clear criteria for similarity. It is worth suggesting that the analogy, as Socrates expounds it, fills the need for a clear criterion for similarity. The passage needing examination here is the one that illustrates 'power' by means of the analogy, 'And does each of them have its own separate power? Just as the parts of the face are not alike, and the eye is not like the ear, nor is its power the same, nor is any other part like another in power or in other ways, is it the same with the parts of excellence, that none is like any other, either in itself or in its power? Surely it must be if it corresponds to our example.' (330A–B):[133]

My suggestion is that in this passage, one of the only two in this whole section which explicitly mention the face analogy, that analogy forms the basis of Socrates' questions about similarity. The criterion for 'homogeneity' is the possession of the same 'power'. This suggestion would evidently solve both the problems we have unearthed. It accounts for the shortage of explicit references to the face analogy, in that it makes 'similarity' and its congeners a shorthand for the kind of resemblance denied to the parts of a face; and it supplies the missing criterion for 'likeness' with reasonable intelligibility and precision. But does it accord with the meaning of Plato's Greek?

The Greekless reader need not give up at this point of the argument. The necessary argument can be conducted in any language known to me. All that is needful is a hard look at the structure of the passage (330A), 'the eye is not like the ear, *nor* is its power the same' (my italics). 'Nor' is normal in English or Greek for 'and not'. We have already illustrated the use of 'and' to mark not only the addition of two distinct things, but also the conjunction of two ways of saying the same thing. The latter is particularly common where one expression stands in need of explanation or refinement; and if there is anything agreed between students of this part of the *Protagoras* it is that the 'similarity'-expressions need explaining and refining. It does not seem too bold to suggest that they receive explanation and refinement in this sentence.

The next clause, it is true, makes some difficulty; but then it makes difficulty on any available interpretation. No part, it says, resembles any other in respect of its power; so far, so good; that is what we should expect it to say. But it adds that there is no resemblance 'in the other respects', which if taken to mean 'in all other respects' would be, as Taylor points out,[134] a quite illegitimate generalization from the preceding sentence, and would foist on Protagoras a view he does not hold. It might appear (though Taylor does not suggest it), that here, if anywhere, Protagoras is led by Socrates from particular to total resemblance.

But a look forward to the next sentence suffices to rebut such an interpretation (330B); there what corresponds to 'in the other respects' is the phrase 'in itself', and there is no reason to take that phrase as denying *all* resemblance. Indeed such a universal denial would risk a contradiction, for the parts of a face (or of goodness) must have at least one property in common, namely that of being parts of a face (or of goodness). We must restrict the generality of 'in the other respects' somehow.

Taylor's restriction is plausible, viz. 'in its other aspects (i.e. in its permanent character which gives it its power)'. This forms a good parallel to the phrase 'in itself' in Plato's next sentence; 'in itself' is also explained or refined by the words 'in its power'. 'In itself' in fact *means* here 'in respect of those attributes relevant to its power', but this is not spelled out since to spell it out would convert rhetoric into manifest tautology. In the earlier sentence 'in the other respects' means presumably 'in respect not only of its power but also in respect of all other points of resemblance relevant to the determination of that power'. To spell this out would again have been to reduce rhetoric to tautology.

Socrates' rhetoric here has a clear enough basis: the most important property of a part of the face such as eye or ear, as of a part of goodness, is its 'power'. Other less significant properties may be ignored except in so far as they contribute to or help to determine that power. The use of the terms 'like', 'such as', and their congeners, in the whole succeeding argument also ignores the same less significant properties, and refers only to the individual 'powers' of the virtues. Being thus structurally possible, the interpretation of Socrates' speech in this sense should be adopted on the grounds of philosophical neatness, as removing two major difficulties at a single stroke.

Scholars have found varying numbers of theses Protagoras assents to in this passage, but so far as the good qualities are concerned we may now reduce them to the following:

1 No named part of goodness (GQ for 'good quality') is identical with any other (330A).
2 No GQ has the same 'power' as any other (330A–B).

3 At least some of the named GQs are such that the possession of one of them does not entail possession of the rest (329E).

3 may also be formulated, 'The possession of one GQ does not entail possession of all of them'; an alternative formulation of 2 which in effect appears in the text is 2': 'No GQ is like [*or* is such as] any other'.

This list omits one of the four assertions summarized by Gallop and Taylor.[135] A reader comparing their versions with this one will see that it treats their propositions 2 and 4 as two merely verbal variants on the same proposition 2. This is in accordance with the conclusions reached above on expressions for 'like', and also with another point about 2 and 2': Socrates asks (330A–fin) if 'No part of goodness is like any other, either itself or its power', and asks whether that should not obviously be asserted *if* the parts of goodness resemble their agreed analogue, the parts of a face. Protagoras assents, presumably, to this whole hypothetical proposition, and not only to the consequent. Only then is he asked, and agrees, to deduce that indeed, since he has admitted the analogy, no part of goodness is like any other; and here Socrates names each of the five good qualities separately. Socrates pursues his chain of argument with the greatest care, and makes clear its dependence on the analogy of parts of the face.

In enumerating the parts of goodness Socrates substitutes 'knowledge' for 'wisdom'. Duncan has legitimately raised, without answering, the question why.[136] The answer, or part of it, must lie in the way much of the earlier portion of the dialogue prepares the way for the final round of argument. For in that final round Socrates will take Protagoras through an argument to the effect that courage is a species of wisdom; he will then (361A–B) turn round and say that he has been arguing that the good qualities are each knowledge (and hence teachable). 'Knowledge' sounds more evidently teachable than 'wisdom'; in the *Meno* (87C) the principal interlocutor agrees with alacrity that goodness is teachable if and only if it is knowledge. I know of no equivalent passage for the teachability of wisdom. 'Wisdom' and 'knowledge' are closely related terms in at least Platonic Greek,[137] but it is hard to believe this relationship to be the sole reason for Socrates' substitution here, and the connection with the end of the dialogue should be clear.

Socrates next suggests the investigation of what each good quality is like (that is to say what power it has). First justice; is there such a thing? Protagoras and Socrates both believe there is. Protagoras had implied as much in his Speech, and Socrates, if not being purely formal, may be reminding him simply with an eye to the point that in order to have a power (or, indeed, any other attribute) it is necessary to be something.[138] Socrates' next question is 'is . . . justice, itself just or unjust?' (330C). This question has been very variously interpreted; it and Protagoras' in effect affirmative answer have been made a star example of 'self-predication' in Plato, and they have been called an example of 'Pauline' predication.[139] The first of these alternatives would make justice predicable of itself, the second would predicate the property 'justice' tautologously but not illogically of just people.

Each has its perils, and its advantages; but neither is deeply embedded in the context as we have understood it so far. Socrates suggested, and Protagoras accepted, an enquiry into what sort of thing each of the good qualities is (330B-C). This means, if our analysis is right, what 'power' each of them has. Asked whether justice is just or unjust in this context, Protagoras could and no doubt does take this to be a question about the power of justice: is it the 'power' of justice to be just or to be unjust? Socrates and Protagoras agree that it is the power of justice to be just. Socrates then treats as the same question, asked at the same time by the same imaginary questioner, whether 'justice is such as to be just'. He and Protagoras agree that justice is such as to be just.

Now this is another example of the sortal terminology Plato's Socrates has been using as shorthand for the possession of a 'power'. Recent scholarship has tended to treat the question 'Is justice just or unjust?' as primary, and the question 'Is justice the sort of thing to be just or to be unjust?' as derivable, however easily, from that primary question. In the context this is clearly wrong; it is the question 'Is justice just?' which needs interpreting in the light of the sortal question, and not the other way round. True, the word

Taylor rightly renders 'So' represents the discussion as moving from the direct to the sortal predication of the property 'justice'. But that leaves open the question whether it moves thus because sortal teminology can be interpreted as direct, or because the direct predication in this instance was an expressive further shorthand for the sortal type. In the context the latter is far more likely.

A possible retort to this argument would be that it is not the 'power' of justice to *be* just. The power to be just rests with just people, not with justice. Are we here back in the 'Pauline' interpretation? Perhaps; but if we are, it is to be observed that the analogy with the parts of a face is highly relevant. The possession of an eye *confers* (normally) the power to see; the eye *has* the power to see. Both of these are normal ways of thinking and speaking. In the context of the analogy between good qualities and parts of the face it makes very good sense to speak of, say, justice as both conferring and possessing the power of being just.

But that would still not compel Plato or his Socrates to write or speak in this way. Why does Socrates not proceed immediately to the sortal question, without stopping to ask the one involving direct predication? Motivational problems of this sort are in principle intractable; but a possible solution to this particular one may lie in Plato's reluctance ever to admit that a property may be predicable of its opposite. In the *Symposium* (211A) the beautiful itself, and doubtless 'beauty' too, are not allowed to be ugly in any respect, at any time, in any relation, at any place, or in the eye of any beholders.[140] In the *Republic* too the Forms implicitly exclude their opposites (479A–B). So they do also in the *Phaedo* (103B). To use these examples is not to import the theory of Forms in any metaphysical guise into the *Protagoras*; it is to suggest no more than that to Plato's ears the proposition '*F* is the opposite of *F*', where 'is' is the 'is' of predication, was always immediately unacceptable. If that is so, it would be natural for him to cause his Socrates to use that immediate unacceptability to elicit the required alternative from Protagoras. Such a method would be tactically unfair, but not strategically, since Socrates could argue that the 'power' of justice cannot be to issue in unjust (or non-just) actions rather than in just ones. The reasons why Plato does not want to have Socrates argue in 'power' terms come out later. (To anticipate, the disagreement between Socrates and Protagoras about similarity (331D–E) could not take place if similarity had not displaced 'power' in the argument's terminology.)

Even after all these caveats there remains a suspicion that Socrates has been allowed to trick Protagoras somehow. The question, 'Is justice just or unjust?', has always been the most suspect link in the chain of argument. The question may be intelligible in context as, in effect, a question about the 'power' of justice; but it still seems illegitimately to assume the absence of any third alternative. A natural reaction from readers of Plato here is to wonder why Protagoras does not either ask Socrates to clarify his question or simply reject both alternatives. If the question is supposed to bestow extra plausibility on the argument, over and above what is plausible about the sortal or 'power'-question, it fails conspicuously to bestow any such thing for modern readers. Nor does it seem necessary to suppose that the sophist would reasonably be expected to share Plato's metaphysical or logical predilections. Did Plato at this point construct the fictional conversation unconvincingly?

Taylor has some interesting points to make here: '341d1–3 shows Plato aware of the distinction between contrary and contradictory'; which disposes, as Taylor says, of the notion that Plato is confusing contrary and contradictory as such in the argument we are discussing. It does not wholly disprove the notion that *Socrates* was making this confusion, but it makes it improbable. It does not, however, show Plato guiltless of all confusion; there is more than one kind of contradictory involved, and Plato need not have realized this fact. The passage Taylor cites deals with a contradictory in the middle between two contraries; and this is not the same kind of thing at all as a contradictory applied to a subject to which for logical reasons neither of a pair of contraries could in principle be applicable. Yet it is a case of the latter which Socrates' would-be plausible question about justice presents. As Taylor[141] points out, 'justice as an attribute of persons cannot be said to be just whether we take "just" as "disposed to behave fairly" or as "having the correct relation between the parts of one's soul'''. Indeed, it is impossible, for the same logical reasons, for justice to be either just or unjust or halfway between.

There is nothing in the *Protagoras*, and nothing I know of in the early dialogues in general, to show Plato's grasp of these logical reasons. In particular there is nothing in the Great Speech of Protagoras having a direct bearing on them. The Speech has, as we shall see, a great deal of bearing on other confusions between contrary and contradictory, but not on this vital type. It looks as if in assuming that Socrates' question here offers Protagoras one alternative more plausible than his sortal propositions Plato makes a mistake, and foists one unawares on Socrates and Protagoras. But the mistake lies, as we saw earlier, in tactics, and not in strategy; Plato is guilty at most of having Socrates use a verbally plausible but misleading point to lend colour to a thesis not – or not yet – in need of such support. The basic thesis concerns the 'power' of justice, not the justice of justice in any other sense.

Mutatis mutandis, the same sorts of consideration apply to Socrates' next points about holiness (330D–E). It is especially noteworthy that for this quality Socrates makes no use of the 'plain predication' *question* at all; the imaginary questioner this time puts the 'sortal' question immediately and is answered in plain-predication terms. But the plain-predication format is juxtaposed with Socrates' plea to Protagoras, 'What about you? Wouldn't you give the same answer?' All we can say is that again 'plain' and 'sortal' predications of holiness are clearly equivalent, and the context alone tells us which is of primary importance. The sequel, returning to argument after the establishment of the necessary premisses, makes use, for several steps, of the 'sortal' type of expression. That, and the context as a whole, may encourage the supposition that primacy belongs to the 'sortal' here. But the full exposition of this sequel must wait on the elucidation of the plain-predication sentence we have mentioned: 'Scarcely anything else would be holy, if holiness itself is not to be holy.' This sentence, a statement offered by Socrates himself, and not in the Greek interrogative, offers some resemblance to remarks in, e.g. the *Phaedo*, which look as if they were self-predicatory (100C with 102D and 106D). Nothing is holy except by partaking in the holy itself.

But there is no need to take the sentence in the *Protagoras* to say any such thing. It could no less easily, in the context we have outlined, state that if holiness does not constitute the 'power' to issue in or to perform holy actions, then no other quality will constitute or confer that 'power'. Granted, that would not be its natural meaning out of context. But that is not the point; Plato did not write it, nor his Socrates speak it, out of context. Whether Plato thought here also to lend plausibility to a sortal or 'power'-statement by substituting a self-predicatory one, is a question hardly decidable. To a modern reader, though not necessarily to Plato or his contemporary readers, the sortal or 'power'-statement sounds actually the more plausible of the two.

At this point Socrates distinguishes himself cleanly from Protagoras. Protagoras, but not Socrates, has said that no part of goodness is like any other (330E–331A). That is to say that Protagoras has denied that any part of goodness has the same 'power' as any other; that is the sense of 'like' here, though it is not mentioned explicitly. Protagoras then accepts as a consequence that holiness is not the sort of thing to be just, and that justice is not the sort of thing to be holy. In 'power' terminology, this says that holiness does not constitute or confer the power to be just, nor justice constitute or confer the power to be holy. Holiness does not issue in just actions, nor justice in holy actions. Hence the actions in which justice issues are other than holy actions, and hence not holy actions. From here Plato's Socrates treats it as a short step in this context to the proposition that justice issues in unholy and holiness in unjust actions. If we allow, as suggested, the equivalence of 'such as to be F' and 'F' and 'having/conferring the "power" appropriate to F', this line of reasoning is at least obtainable from the text.

But it has a fishy smell. It is rotten in two places, more readily probed if the argument be restated with slightly greater formality.

1   No GQ is identical with any other.
2   Each GQ has its own power.
3   No GQ has the same power as any other.
3' No GQ is like or such as any other.

4   [3' is equivalent to 3.]
5   There is such a thing as justice.
6   [Justice is a GQ.]
7   [The own power of] Justice is [to be] just [i.e. to issue in just actions].
8   There is such a thing as Holiness.
9   [Holiness is a GQ.]
10 [The own power of] Holiness is [to be] holy [i.e. to issue in holy actions].
    Then, from 2, 3, (=3'), 5, [6], 7, 8, [9] and 10, Socrates obtains:
11 Holiness does not have the power to issue in just actions and
12 Justice does not have the power to issue in holy actions.
    Then, from 12, Socrates obtains:
13 Justice's power is to issue in actions other than holy actions.
    From 13 Socrates obtains:
14 Justice's power is to issue in unholy actions.
    Socrates also, from 11, obtains:
15 Holiness' power is to issue in actions other than just actions.
    From 15 Socrates obtains:
16 Holiness' power is to issue in unjust actions.

Some comments on this scheme are in order. The insertion of propositions 6 and 9 is both easy and necessary. Protagoras is in no position to deny either, and Socrates rightly takes his assent to them for granted. Quite why Socrates should mention the equally obvious and agreeable 5 and 8 but not 6 and 9 is not immediately evident; but 5 and 8 are questions of a type frequently put at the beginning of a Socratic chain. The re-interpretation of 7 and 10 in terms of 'power' is in accordance with the proposals already argued concerning the general drift of the passage. The phrase 'issue in' is designed to be neutral between two notions of 'power', that of capacity and that of disposition; it is not clear to me that Plato's Socrates here is able or willing to distinguish capacity from disposition. The translation of good-quality terminology into action terminology is convenient and not without warrant.

We may proceed to identify the two troublesome inferences and discuss them at some length. The first is that from 12 to 13 and from 11 to 15. The flaw in these is the same. It is not that justice and holiness do not issue in actions at all; evidently they do. The trouble is rather that 12 and 11 are both consistent, whether separately or in conjunction, with the proposition that just and holy actions at least largely coincide; furthermore this last proposition is one for acceptance of which a conventional classical Greek might readily find good reason. As Taylor argued,[143] justice could have the power to issue in actions which by virtue of issuing from it would be just, but which would be the same actions as those which are holy by virtue of issuing from holiness. Justice and holiness would then be different factors in the performance of, in great part at least, a single set of actions, and would not issue in wholly distinct sets of actions as 13 and 15 say.

Interpretation requires the examination of Socrates' next remarks (331B). Socrates himself would say that justice is holy and holiness just. In context he means that justice has the power to issue, and does issue, in holy actions, and that holiness has the power to issue, and does issue, in just actions. Socrates adds, apparently by way of an equivalent statement, that either justice is the same thing as holiness, or it is most like it, and above all justice is the same sort of thing as holiness, and vice versa. Beginning, therefore, with the denial of 11 and 12, Socrates has reached the identity, or extreme similarity, or the likeness of power, between justice and holiness. A bewildering variety of conclusions spring thus from a pair of propositions not cogently justifying any of them. If justice issues consistently in holy actions, and holiness consistently issues in just actions, then *either* justice and holiness are indeed the same thing and there is only one factor at work, *or* the two qualities are most alike, in that they have the same practical effects, issuing as they do in the same or almost the same sets of actions. Above all, Socrates thinks they have the same power, namely to issue in a certain set of actions.[144]

Now coincidence between the relevant sets of actions does not, as we have seen, suffice to prove the identity of power; but it does suffice to undermine Protagoras' original acceptance of the analogy of parts of the face. For the sense organs arguably do not perceive the same things; the ear perceives sounds, the eyes perceive shapes and colours. These look very like distinct sets of perceptibles. If Protagoras were prepared to accept that, he could not then maintain simultaneously the parts-of-a-face analogy and the coincidence of the sets of actions appropriate to the just and to the holy man. Either there is no distinction between these two good qualities, or they are very alike, but at least the distinction between their powers, if any, is a quite different distinction from that between the powers of parts of the face with which the discussion of powers began. Which means that there is no *relevant* distinction between their powers. Taken in this way Socrates' remarks present at any rate a wall of argument that Protagoras will have to work hard to breach. Protagoras has a case to answer.

Does Socrates say more than that the sophist has a case to answer? Critics treat the Socrates of this passage as a dogmatist.[145] But he does not say that his own conclusions here follow without the possibility of disagreement, and his series of questions is gently phrased. He explains what his reply to an imaginary questioner would be, and invites Protagoras to consider whether his reply would be the same. Plato too is not dogmatic here; he gives Protagoras a position in certain respects different from Socrates' and deserving of analysis – to come later.

Behind the disagreement between Protagoras and Socrates here there could lie a differing conception of the nature of a good quality. If Socrates holds, for instance, that the possession of a good quality is a certain interrelation of a limited number of parts of the soul, then he could not easily suppose that there are two different interrelationships which issue in the same actions at the same time. Different parts of the soul or different types of interrelationship would have to be brought in to explain different good qualities if that were the case, and Socrates might not want to do that. At least a close or complete overlap between the appropriate sets of actions will on this view make one of the two good qualities largely, if not wholly, superfluous. If on the other hand a good quality may be any kind of property of the personality or soul, then it is much easier to suppose the just and the holy aspects of actions which are both just and holy to be due to different properties of the soul. But, regrettably, Socrates and Protagoras do not discuss the nature of a good quality or its effect on the soul in this context.

They also fail to discuss, though Socrates may assume, a definition of 'power'. Protagoras cannot afford, if the present interpretation is on the right lines, to define the power of a virtue in terms of a set of actions issuing from it. Not having defined power at all, he need not find that alarming. But alarm should perhaps be his reaction to the problem, admittedly not brought up in the dialogue, which arises if the sets of actions counting as just and as holy coincide. If they do, then one cannot tell which of the two supposedly distinct virtues a person performing the actions possesses, by inspecting his actions. If one cannot tell which of the two good qualities a person possesses then naturally one cannot say that the person possesses one and not the other. But Protagoras has offered no outward criterion for distinguishing the good qualities other than the actions in which they issue, and nevertheless wishes to say that one can possess one good quality without possessing another (329E). True, he has mentioned in this connection only the pairs courage/justice and justice/wisdom, but in so doing he gave no sign that these were meant as the only pairs of this sort rather than as examples illustrative of a generalization. Even if it is true that in general one can have one of the good qualities and lack another, it is hardly clear how Protagoras can know it to be true.

This is an additional, if unspoken, reason why Protagoras should *want* to embrace at least some form of 13 and 15. He needs, unless he is very careful, something separating the set of just actions from the set of holy ones. He needs that not only in view of our latest speculations but also in view of the earlier analogy with the parts of the face. But the question then arises whether such a separation, and in particular propositions 13 and 15, are wholly benign. We have no definition of 'holy' from Protagoras to help us answer this question. If we venture to use one, it must accordingly be merely by way of illustration, and the utmost caution will consequently be necessary in interpreting the results. The most that can be said is that they exemplify the *kind* of difficulty Protagoras might fall into, and which he might be expected to anticipate.

Suppose, for the sake of argument, and keeping the most obvious alternative for later treatment, we call 'holy' that which is encouraged by the gods, and 'neither holy nor unholy' actions which are neither encouraged nor discouraged by the gods. This has one distinct advantage: it allows for a difference between non-holy and unholy, in accord with many critics of Plato's discussion here. Considering in the light of this proposition 13, and neglecting 15 on grounds of symmetry, we develop the following: if justice issues in actions non-holy, but not unholy, then the gods neither encourage nor discourage just actions. What then becomes of Protagoras' myth to the effect that the gods for good reason gave men justice (322B–D)? And what of the widespread Greek feeling that the gods are on the side of justice? Already we can see plenty of trouble in store for Protagoras, both in his personal capacity and as the defender of widespread views.

Protagoras need not accept Socrates' inferences to be embarrassed by his propositions. He is likely to run into some problems whether he accepts or denies 13 and 15. We should therefore feel no surprise when he temporizes (331C). He would not, he says, like to admit without qualification that justice is holy and holiness just. Things are not so simple as that. He thinks there is some relevant difference between justice and holiness. In modern and anachronistic language, more than one factor is at work, and the distinct factors correspond to the distinct descriptions of the same actions as 'holy' and 'just'. The second part of that is not in the text, but remains a solidly intelligible justification of what Protagoras does say. Nevertheless Protagoras is prepared to accept, if Socrates wishes, the form of words 'Justice is holy and Holiness is just'. What this presumably means is that Protagoras prefers to keep an overlap between just and holy actions; but he does not think he must therefore accept the identity of holiness and justice. It is now, he could say, up to Socrates to show him where he has been inconsistent if he takes this view. Socrates, as we have seen, has indeed a case of this sort to make against Protagoras; but he has not yet made it.

But Socrates finds this 'if you wish' unacceptable. Protagoras' agreement to a form of words for the sake of politeness or to allow the discussion to continue is not good enough. Socrates, one may add, has good reason for wanting Protagoras to commit himself to the assertion or the denial of 13 and 15. Protagoras, however, in reply to the implied request that he should either accept outright or reject outright Socrates' suggestions about holiness and justice, and not take refuge in a '*distinguo*' or in prevarication, launches into a harangue on whose relevance there has been scholarly disagreement (331D).

Oh yes, says Protagoras, 'Justice resembles holiness in a way; since in fact anything resembles anything else in some way or other. There is a respect in which light resembles dark,[146] and hard soft, and all the other things that seem completely opposite to one another'. Each of the two pairs of opposites actually given in illustration of this rule is a gradable one, with each term resembling the other in that they are applicable to the same set of subjects. Each thing hard by comparison with X may also be soft by comparison with Y. There is a sense in which the set of hard objects and the set of soft objects overlap extensively or indeed coincide, as Plato well knew. But he also knew that it is not the case that thereby 'hard' and 'soft' come to mean the same thing. On the present reading of the argument Protagoras' examples are highly relevant, as they are not on some others. Justice and holiness are, Protagoras appears here to accept, qualities corresponding to extensively overlapping or to coincident sets of actions. But that does not make the terms 'justice' and 'holiness' as applied to actions or to human beings mean the same thing.

Protagoras goes on to point out that the organs of perception, which they originally agreed had differing powers, and were not the same sorts of thing, resemble one another in a certain respect and are in that respect the same sort of thing after all. It is not clear what Protagoras means precisely by this; but if he means to imply that the organs of perception perceive the same things – namely, the objects of the external world – but correspond to different aspects of them according to the 'power' of the organ concerned, then the parallel with the other items in this speech is complete. The sophist continues, with pardonable exaggeration, by claiming that by using his present method Socrates could show that any two things are alike. It is not the possession of some property in common, however trivial, that is relevant; Socrates has to show that the two things in question (here, the good qualities justice and holiness) are alike in the required and relevant respect (here, in having the same power).

If Protagoras' argument is, in essence, as plausible as this, it is a matter for inquiry why Socrates is, as he recounts, amazed at it (331E). His amazement springs, to judge from the question it prompts, from Protagoras' claim that the possession of a trivial property in common is not relevant to the sort of similarity Socrates had in mind. The clear imputation is that the property Socrates is claiming to be common to justice and holiness is trivial; and Socrates has some right to claim that it is not. As we have seen, it is, by implication, the whole field of applicability of the two terms in so far as they apply to actions. Protagoras, even though by apparent implication denying the relevance of this to the 'power' of the good qualities, has still to make good the claim that it is not relevant on the assumption of the analogy with the parts of the face. 'Trivial' is not yet a word to which Protagoras is entitled in this context; and Socrates has a right to be amazed.

Protagoras has perhaps allowed his rhetoric to run away with him. At all events he can only reply, with a degree of lameness but a certain exactitude, that the resemblance in question is not exactly small, but does not have the significance Socrates attaches to it. At this Socrates sees that Protagoras will not grant him the conclusion he desires here in the form in which he desires it. He rests accordingly content with what he has been able to secure: there is a substantial similarity between justice and holiness, in that justice issues in holy actions and holiness in just actions. Such substantial similarity is no more and no less than Plato has his Protagoras admit at a later stage in the discussion (349D). It is perhaps worth adding that the version of the Greek which makes Socrates say in his next speech (332A) that Protagoras seems 'to find discussion of this point uncongenial' is tendentious, and need not represent the force of the Greek words.[147] The words do not have a neat single English equivalent, but the general force of Socrates' remark could be, not that Protagoras finds the discussion uncongenial, but that Socrates finds Protagoras to be captious or to be making difficulties. The reader may like to judge for himself whether such an accusation is a possible one for Socrates to make, and how far it would be justifiable – on the understanding that that is two questions and not just one.

This whole way of reading the argument may seem to fall a victim to the charge of reading too much into an outwardly simple piece of Greek exposition. Taylor brings this charge, successfully in my opinion, against Vlastos' reading in terms of 'Pauline' predication.[148] But the present reading gives the argument a coherence which it lacks at several places in Taylor's more literal-minded version: it makes use of equivalences implicit in the text, and merely explains in terms suggested by the opening parts of the argument passages couched in terms of similarity or of plain predication. The presence of the latter group of terms is explained by their convenience in leading to a deadlock between Socrates and Protagoras; and translation out of them is justified by the sheer necessity of avoiding the reduction of a man of Protagoras' intellectual status and calibre to saying that 'it isn't right to call things "similar" just because they have some point of similarity, however small'. Obviously such things are somewhat or slightly similar; the implausibility of the distinguished sophist's failure to notice such a point is doubly great in a dialogue in which he is elsewhere portrayed as quick and sharp on the uptake.

We have seen that Protagoras appears to find propositions 13 and 15 dangerous. It is possible that this is partly due to the deduction of propositions 14 and 16 respectively from them. In view of this possibility we should investigate whether 14 and 16 are themselves unpalatable, and whether Protagoras can escape the inference leading to them.

We need at this point to return to our experimental definition of 'holy'. If we apply it and its fellows to the stronger proposition 14 as we did to the weaker 13, interesting consequences again follow; and not unnaturally the consequences are stronger too. Justice's power will be to issue in actions discouraged by the gods. Protagoras' myth of the gods' despatch of justice, and the widespread Greek association of justice with divine power, will be under even greater pressure than they were from the proposition that the gods were neutral. The pressure is of the same kind, and the argument of the same fundamental nature; but the results are a trifle more spectacular. They remain spectacular if even some, rather than all, just actions are unholy; there will then still be some just actions actively discouraged by the gods.

If the reader at this point decides that, for all the éclat of the propositions 14 and 16, they do not really make a great deal of difference, he is logically correct. If we have already, in Socrates' eyes, a *reductio ad absurdum*, it does not greatly matter one way or the other if we now add a *reductio ad absurdius*. It matters logically all the less in that the difference in absurdity cannot be called great. Really the most that can be said for Socrates' addition of 14 and 16 is that it is rhetorically effective, that it may help to dispose Protagoras to abandon 11 and 12 as Socrates would like him to. The inference from 13 to 14 is therefore of limited importance in the total structure of the argument. I can see no reference to it in the subsequent development of the discussion. But nevertheless this twin inference has been the subject of much scholarly writing and of much indignation from readers of Plato who think Plato is cheating them. The feelings of such readers, whose indignation I used to share, may serve as an excuse for the following addition to the literature of the subject.

Scholars are mostly satisfied, whatever degree of significance they attach to the question, that Protagoras could escape these inferences.[149] They are convinced, for various reasons, that holy/unholy and just/unjust are pairs not of contradictories, as the Socratic argument (331A) appears to make them, but of contraries. Taylor[150] in particular argues that, in application to settled dispositions, to make the pairs contradictories would make children unjust in that they have no settled moral dispositions, and render unjust also acts not indicative of moral dispositions, such as blowing one's nose. These points are well taken. One might reply to the second with the argument that if one defines as 'just' or 'holy' those acts which are permitted, rather than enjoined, by the rules of justice or holiness, then blowing one's nose will be just or holy. But it is decidedly unclear whether either Socrates or

Protagoras would wish to define justice or holiness in terms of rules of this sort. If they did, the problems Protagoras faces would be slightly different, but no less hard; it would then be permitted, rather than enjoined by the gods, to perform unjust actions, if proposition 16 be accepted. This remains a small price for Socrates to pay for the respectability of his inference. A higher price might be the consequent labelling as 'holy' of the act of blowing one's nose, on the grounds that it is permitted by the rules of holiness. But there remain two subjects for discussion apropos of this question. The first is the relevance here again of Protagoras' Great Speech. The second is Greek linguistic usage in the matter of negatives and contraries. The first will show that Protagoras has not made things easy for himself. The second will show that in certain respects Greek habits of speech did not make things easy for him. Passages relevant to the first of these topics are due for discussion below.

1 According to Protagoras in his myth there was a time when Man did not have the political art (321D). The mere absence of the political art, the mere non-possession of justice and temperance, was sufficient reason for the commission of injustice. Here is an inference from negative to contradictory. It collides with Taylor's argument, mentioned above, about children, in that the non-possession of a disposition, or of a quasi-permanent quality issuing in a particular type of action, is for Protagoras sufficient condition for injustice. But the injustice concerned need not be a settled and quasi-permanent quality; it is not the sophist's express view that early Man was necessarily and without qualification 'unjust'. All Protagoras said was that 'they treated each other with injustice' (322B), and children can treat each other with injustice, settled in their dispositions or not. Therefore it is not clear that this part of Protagoras' myth will excuse Socrates entirely, though it might complicate Protagoras' escape route from Socrates' reasoning. How far Plato saw this kind of objection and counter-objection is not clear; he may have treated alike all inferences from negative to contrary regardless of the particular difficulties involved in particular inferences.

2   Protagoras would have those killed who are unable to partake of justice and moderation (322D). Simply because they lack, and are unable to acquire, these good qualities, he describes them as a 'disease of the city'. It is hard to think of these exceptional people as other than actively unjust. If they were merely to go through life doing such things as blowing their noses, they would scarcely rank as diseases of the city, or as deserving death.

3   Protagoras' two analogies between virtue and flute-playing raise more complex difficulties. In drawing a distinction (323A) between other good qualities and political goodness Protagoras directly contrasts (a) boasting that one is good at flute-playing when one is not, with (b) saying one is unjust when one is. The rhetorical parallel here, between the man not good at flute-playing and the unjust, looks like a parallel between contradictory and contrary. The same paragraph of Protagoras' speech (323C) offers a further parallelism of the same sort. It picks up the man known to be unjust (whose madness consists in confessing the truth, viz. his injustice) by the non-just man (who is mad not to claim to be just). Protagoras here encourages, though he does not formally compel, his audience to equate the unjust with the non-just.

David Savan,[151] however, saw a rather different view in Protagoras' second use of the flute-playing analogy (327C). In that passage the analogy stands between good man and expert flautist and between the ignoramus of flute-playing and the creature so extreme that the most unjust man might seem just in comparison. Savan's point is that 'between the expert flautist and the man who does not know how to play the flute at all there is the poor flautist. In the same way, Protagoras goes on, between the good citizen and the savage there are those who are neither good nor savages.' But this interpretation fails to note that those who are 'neither good nor savages' are not thereby 'neither just nor unjust'. They could equally well be unjust, and be just only by contrast with the abnormal savages. If so, they need not be 'neither just nor unjust', but could be described as 'both just and unjust' – a description which need certainly not surprise a Platonist. Similarly, between the ignoramus and the good flautist there need not lie a player neither good nor bad. They might all be describable as bad, in comparison with the expert, and good, in comparison with the ignoramus. Protagoras actually says that the unjust would seem just by comparison with the savage. There are more ways than one of describing the middle ground between extremes. Savan's point does not show that Protagoras or his creator adopted the 'neither ... nor' type of description rather than the 'both ... and ...' type.[152]

4   Another suggestive sentence appears in Protagoras' argument about punishment (324B). According to him, rational punishment is motivated by the desire to ensure that the man punished does not again commit injustice. This intention, Protagoras thinks, shows the punishers' belief in the teachability of goodness. Not to commit injustice is by implication a sufficient condition for goodness. It is naturally difficult to connect non-justice thus with Protagorean goodness, unless the non-commission of injustice is a sufficient condition of justice. But that places an obvious and major difficulty in the way of the supposition that there is a third state which is neither justice nor injustice. Furthermore, this is the only proof Protagoras offers for the vital proposition that the Athenians believe goodness to be teachable. The equivalence of non-injustice and justice is thus extremely important to his argument.

5   In the protasis of a condition clearly not counterfactual, Protagoras includes the suggestion that every man ought to act with goodness and ought not to act without it (325A). One not partaking in it ought to be taught and punished, until he becomes better. Here punishment is appropriate for ethically wrong, not for ethically neutral action, as Protagoras well knew even if he insists that punishment is not rational if 'for the sake of' the past injustice. His suggestion therefore assumes that simple lack of goodness produces wrong action, as in his account of primitive Man.

On the other hand, the remark about becoming better suggests that the man without a share of goodness is up to a point good, since under teaching he becomes not 'good' but 'better'. If this is not merely careless writing of no significance, it indicates again that the most evil man in society is good compared to the savage outsider. This passage also offers no evidence of a *tertium quid* neither good nor bad, but rather that a person can be both good and bad, or, in a sense, both good and not-good. It suggests that in one sense the non-good is punishable, and hence bad.[153]

The upshot is that Protagoras' brilliant rhetoric makes no clear distinction between contrary and contradictory in the case of some moral predicates. Indeed one of his key inferences depends on the conflation of the two. He could be excused, and Plato could have arranged for him to be so excused, if (say) justice were a matter of obedience to purely negative rules. But we have seen that such rules are not clearly attributable either to the Protagoras or to the Socrates of Plato's *Protagoras*, at any rate in the case of justice.

What of the other virtues? Moderation is a different kettle of fish. Its rules may be negative, as one possible interpretation of the music-teachers' function makes them (326A). Courage, however, behaves in the speech in this respect somewhat like justice. Prevention of cowardice is there used as evidence of a concern for goodness (326B-C). But we cannot use either moderation or courage as evidence for Protagoras' views about justice in this connection, since, long before Socrates develops the argument conflating contrary and contradictory, Protagoras has distinguished justice firmly from courage and from moderation.

Nor is there much to be gained from Protagoras' portrayal of Athenian parents as instructing their children in terms both positive and negative (325D). 'This is just, that unjust, this is honourable and that is dishonourable, this is holy and that is unholy, and "do this" and "don't do that"'.[154] The parents are perfectly entitled to say these things, whether or not they believe in a *tertium quid* between their pairs of opposites. It is unclear whether the instructions 'do this' and 'don't do that' are an addition to or a summary of the preceding moral assertions; and parents, not needing to mention every type of action to their children, may omit the morally neutral, if they believe in such, without being guilty of bad logic.

Whether Protagoras' logic is bad or not is perhaps still open to discussion; but, bad or no, it is a logic very similar to that which Socrates asks him to follow in the final step of Socrates' argument about holiness and justice. This similarity is surely at least part of the explanation for Socrates' line of questioning. The alternative to explaining Socrates' line of questioning in this way is to regard the resemblance between the implications of it and of Protagoras' Speech as coincidental. We shall have to examine other fits between Socratic interrogation and Protagorean rhetoric before deciding to rule out coincidence. But the reader may care to note the unusual frequency of Protagoras' inferences from contradictory to contrary. With his own black-and-white rhetoric dancing before his mind's eye, it would be less shocking for the sophist to fail to observe the subtler shades of grey, and for Socrates to take advantage of his failure. That Plato should portray such a sequence certainly need not shock us; he would only be doing for sophistic rhetoric what he did for poetic fancy in the *Symposium*.

As in the case of Agathon the poet, so in that of Protagoras the sophist, we have to ask whether the victim of Socratic dialectic is an isolated figure or representative of more widely held views and widely inculcated habits of thought. Was there anything in Greek linguistic usage which could have helped to dull Protagoras' perceptions at a relevant point? Was the *Protagoras* directed *ad hominem* or *ad homines*? If the former, why write it down? But we shall see that general Greek habits of thought and speech are in fact relevant.

In brief, the Greeks often used negative locutions such as 'not just' in contexts where they are readily replaceable by terms such as 'unjust' denoting apparently a contrary. In many of these contexts strong disapproval is evident. The Greek language as used by great writers of the fifth and fourth centuries BC often assumes that the action, manner or person negatively qualified is up for moral appraisal, and it omits any thought or word of the non-moral or of the morally neutral. So Demosthenes can write 'Don't do it; it isn't just' (21.183 (cf. 39.35)), and another speech, preserved in the Demosthenic corpus but likely to be by another hand, has the same expression ([42].21(cf.[25].84)). In the corpus of speeches attributed to Lysias we find 'it is not those who governed well who betrayed the city, but those who governed not justly' (20.5). The tragic poets Sophocles and Euripides do the same sort of thing; in contexts where a rebuke is obviously intended, the negative is perfectly at home. 'Not just and bad', says a character in Euripides' *Hippolytus* (942), and in his *Iphigeneia in Aulis* (399) we find the stern 'things unlawful and not just'. 'Not just(ly)' appears twice in one passage of remonstrance from Sophocles' *Ajax* (1342, 1344). The comic poet Aristophanes uses the same idiom; witness a speech from his *Plutus* (751-5). In Thucydides' 'Melian Dialogue' the Melians describe themselves as 'holy, opposed to not-just men' (V. 104). There is scarcely any need further to multiply examples. 'Holy' can be treated in the same way; a Euripidean character says 'Not holy, not just' (*Hecuba*, 1235), and Demosthenic invective (18.217) gives us 'Of course he does frightful things, or rather an act not even holy'.

The use of negatived words of approval to express active disapproval occurs also in Plato. The *Crito* supplies some neat examples. In his attempt to persuade Socrates to escape from prison Crito urges both practical and moral considerations. He introduces the moral ones by saying 'What's more, Socrates, I think you are taking in hand something not just' (45C). Evidently Crito means 'something unjust', and he conceives of his remarks as strongly dissuasive. So Socrates, I think, takes him; for in his reply he proposes to consider whether to escape would be just or not, and suggests that if just it should be done, and if not, not – and in the same speech he declares that the only question before them is whether they will be acting justly or unjustly (48B–D). Similarly, in a more rapid exchange whose logic is not easy to follow (49C), it looks as though 'not just' is picked up in the same sense by 'unjust'. Crito accepts both the suggestions concerned. When the laws of Athens hold their imaginary conversation with Socrates, 'things not just' are referred to with the verb 'act unjustly' (51C, 51E). More doubtful examples occur towards the end of the *Crito*, perhaps under the influence of the general structure and tone of the sentences involved (52E, 54B). Possibly Plato represents Socrates as deliberately picking up Crito's phraseology.

In the *Protagoras*, then, if Socrates and Protagoras are using 'not-holy' and 'not-just' to mean 'issuing in actions not-holy' and 'issuing in actions not-just', it would be in complete accord with Greek idiom, and presumably in accord with normally unphilosophical Greek thinking, to assume that the not-holy and not-just actions are respectively unholy and unjust. This transfer of the epithet from the virtue to the actions in which it issues seems to be legitimated by the foregoing interpretation of the argument as a whole. The upshot is that Socrates and Protagoras are not guilty of (respectively) pushing and accepting a blatant fallacy in the matter of the not-just and the unjust.

There might appear to be an element of overkill in my argument here. If normal Greek usage accounts for the turn taken by Plato's discussion, then why invoke dialectic at all? Why should Socrates be construed as *both* taking advantage of Protagoras' indiscretions *and* using linguistic habits to make a point? There are two answers to this pertinent question. The first, observing the number of associations of contradictory and contrary in Protagoras' Great Speech, asks in return whether this number is likely to be there by pure coincidence. The second, perhaps in the last analysis less subjective, urges that Socrates is not entitled to assume Protagoras' unthinking acceptance of every common viewpoint. He is not entitled to assume it for two reasons; first, because common views often contradict each other, and Socrates has to tease out, rather than assume his victim's contradictions; secondly, because Protagoras' relationship with the man in the Athenian street is an uneasy one, forming a substantial theme of the dialogue and needing at this stage delicate handling. Protagoras must be, in the context of the dialogue, convicted out of his own mouth. On this interpretation, Plato's own creative procedure would be unfair only if the sophists in general and Protagoras in particular were clear and forthright on the relation between their thinking and that of ordinary Greeks. It is at least open to question whether this was the case.

We observe, in the course of this piece of philosophical conversation, some places where reference back to Protagoras' Great Speech sheds light. In other places we find that the admissions made by Protagoras at the outset of the discussion are highly relevant to its later course. The commitments entered into by the sophist, as in his myth or in his acceptance of the image of parts of a face, return to plague him. As a treatise, or part of one, developing a continuous and wholly explicit argument of Socrates' own, the whole passage would present many dubieties. But interpreted as a dialogue, as a conversation with cut and thrust, with give and take, it wears an altogether different look. It is worth considering whether the dubieties are due less to Plato himself than to a mistaken method of reading his work.

Wisdom and moderation (332A–333B)
The second argument of this group concerns wisdom and moderation. Its clarity of structure belies its complexity of detail. The structure is indeed amply familiar to scholars, and may be set out as follows:
1   Wisdom is opposite to folly.
2   Moderation is opposite to folly.
3   Each thing that has an opposite has only one opposite.
Therefore 4 Wisdom and moderation are one and the same thing.

Obviously the conclusion 4 is inescapable only if two conditions are fulfilled; if the premisses 1 and 3 are true, and if no equivocation occurs on any term of the argument. But there can at this date be scarcely anyone who is satisfied of these conditions' fulfilment. Scholars have protested at Protagoras' acceptance without argument of 1 and at flaws in the reasoning used to support 2 and 3. The fallacies most commonly appearing in the indictment are the 'contradictory–contrary fallacy' (to use now G. Klosko's helpful shorthand),[155] and equivocation. Some accounts do not wholly separate the two fallacies thus distinguished, taking 'opposite' to mean either 'contradictory' or 'contrary' and taking Socrates to equivocate on this double meaning. How far these charges are justifiable in the argument's context is a reasonable question to ask. The answer requires examination of all the premisses 1, 2 and 3, the unargued 1 no less than the others.

1   'Folly' is a common and philosophically innocent word in

English and a standard antonym for 'wisdom'; hence, e.g., the delightful air of paradox surrounding the description of James I of England as 'the wisest fool in Christendom'. But Plato's word for it, transliterated *aphrosynê*, is neither common nor innocent. In Plato's genuine works it appears 22 times, of which 7 are in this section of the *Protagoras*. The remaining 15 would hardly entitle it to the epithet 'common' even with respect to Plato. In poetry it is, like most words ending in *-synê*, uncommon before the fifth century BC; Homer has it only 3 times and the lyric poets seldom. The fifth-century tragic poets have it rather more often, Aristophanes, significantly a comedian, not at all. In prose literature it is again unusual; Herodotus uses it only twice, Thucydides once (and that in a passage couched in direct speech and exhibiting 'a meaningless play on words').[156] The Attic orators hardly appear to know this word for 'folly': so far as I have found, only Isocrates, in his pamphlet *On the Peace*, uses it. There were other words available. Plato's choice of word is unusual, and demands attention; Socrates may not be wholly innocent in the opening question of this section (332A). But of what then can he be guilty?

There are two advantages of the word *aphrosynê* for an argument with the purposes of Socrates' here. To assimilate moderation with wisdom, as Socrates intends to do, is to intellectualize moderation and/or to ethicize intellectual excellence. The latter is supported by the choice of *aphrosynê* in that, while having an intellectual ring about it, it resembles closely in sound and form the standard word for moderation, *sôphrosynê*. Only the initial syllables of the two words are different, and the initial alpha of *aphrosynê* is the same common prefix as marks *adikos*, unjust, as the opposite of *dikaios*, just. This prefix is indeed both the etymological relative and the semantic equivalent of the English prefix 'un-'. 'Foolish' and 'foolishly' sound, in the words Plato chooses here, like the opposites of 'moderate' and 'moderately'. At least, in the absence of any such word as *phrosynê, there is nothing in Greek usage which sounds or looks more like the opposite of *aphrosynê* than *sôphrosynê* does.[157]

It is not only the form of his chosen word, but also its usage, which is convenient for Socrates' argument. Like several other Greek words, *aphrosynê* occurs in contexts spanning the gulf we should want to set between intellectual and moral. Moral and prudential considerations are not easy to tease into separate strands in early Greek thought, and lack of attention to reasonable considerations of the virtue of prudence is easily attributed to intellectual inadequacy. When Homer speaks of the 'folly' of Penelope's suitors in the *Odyssey* (24, 457), he refers not only to their morally dubious stance with respect to the laws of hospitality, but also to their foolish failure to take into account the possibility of Odysseus' return. The analysis of some later passages is a highly subjective business; it is simply not clear how moral the word sounded to a Greek ear. But at least it is at home in 'moral' contexts. Bacchylides speaks of *'illicit aphrosynê'* in a passage contrasting justice with *hybris*, violence (15, 67). The chorus of Euripides' *Bacchae* use *'lawless aphrosynê'* to describe King Pentheus' resistance to the power of Dionysus in lines hard to interpret as purely prudential (387). Yet Euripides' Achilles in his *Iphigeneia in Aulis* describes as 'folly' a stance he clearly admires morally (1430). Hence, while remaining a suitable antonym for 'wisdom', *aphrosynê* is in usage no less than in form a good opposite for *sôphrosynê*, moderation.

It is all the better an opposite, in that *sôphrosynê* itself has a chequered history. Helen North's admirable exposition in her book *Sophrosyne* makes it unnecessary to trace that history here. Briefly, the word began as a mainly prudential one, and gathered moral force during the centuries after Homer. In the Classical period of Athens it was available for both prudential and moral contexts, meaning either 'good sense' or 'restraint', 'moderation'. The latter is not just a Platonic or technically philosophical usage; it is, for example, clearly implied in Agathon's encomium of Love in the *Symposium* (196C), just about the last place in which to look for the technically Platonic. A word so versatile finds a suitable antonym in the infrequently but rather vaguely used *aphrosynê*. Vagueness is indeed a feature of Socrates' language in this section of the *Protagoras*. Socrates has multiplied words with both moral and intellectual force; his further locutions 'rightly' and 'not rightly' can, in Greek as in English, occur in contexts either of intellectual correctness or of prudential soundness or of moral choice. Plato's Socrates, here as elsewhere, makes use of popular confusions and imprecisions; if a word has a foot in two camps, he uses it to assimilate one to the other. The charge of equivocation he could probably answer with the retort that not only the characters of the Platonic dialogues but also Greeks at large failed to spot the equivocation, maintaining a unified understanding of words such as *sôphrosynê*. So long as *they* thought thus, Socrates could convince *them*. It would be time to find other arguments only when *they* ceased to think on such lines.

Proposition 1, however, says nothing yet of *sôphrosynê*, but rather of 'wisdom'. Here Taylor[158] accuses Socrates of 'ignoring ... the wider [viz: the non-prudential] aspects of *sophia* ["wisdom"].' Protagoras, Taylor says, 'intends the terms, not in the narrow sense of "prudence", but in the wider sense of "intellectual distinction".' In support of this attack Taylor cites a later passage (349D) where a different word with the connotations of 'stupid, ignorant' is opposed to 'wise'. It is not quite clear that this criticism is fair to Socrates. In the first place, Protagoras has not yet delivered himself of his later remarks, and *Socrates* cannot be taken to task for ignoring them, whatever one may think of Plato. In the second place, the universe of discourse in which proposition 1 finds a place is, if our interpretation of the previous argument is correct, that of actions, so generalized intellectual excellence is not relevant. In the third place, it is unclear that *aphrosynê* has no overtones other than the prudential. In the fourth place, Protagoras' own use of words in his previous remarks and verbal commitments is in this case, as in others, very difficult to interpret.

In one use of 'wise' (321B) Protagoras laid himself open to precisely the attack Socrates develops. If we look at Epimetheus in the myth, we find him described as 'not being altogether wise'; now here generalized intellectual excellence is not likely to be in point, since Epimetheus' distribution of the powers to the creatures is thoroughly ingenious, and what is relevant is the failing for which Epimetheus was named, namely, his lack of prudent foresight. He finds himself at the end of his exercise with no suitable powers left for Man. To the kind of 'wisdom' envisaged here, 'folly' or *aphrosynê* is an entirely appropriate antonym. True, Protagoras also uses the word 'wisdom', with appropriate qualification, for technical skills. But, even though Protagoras himself was inconsistent on the relation between goodness and technical skill, the universe of discourse for the argument between Socrates and Protagoras about actions does not appear to include technical skill. So the usage of 'wisdom' to denote 'technical skill' is irrelevant to proposition 1.

The sophist's other uses of 'wise' and 'wisdom', whether within the sphere of actions or not, have up to now been vague and hard to pin down. What Protagoras means by 'wisdom' as a part of goodness (330A) he has never explained. As an attribute of distinguished statesmen 'wisdom' (if Protagoras meant to apply it to them (324D)) is equally vague, but at least could refer to that practical foresight so conspicuously lacking in Epimetheus. (It should not by now need special emphasis that Socrates' own uses and understanding of 'wise' (e.g. 319B) and its relatives, in this or other dialogues, are wholly irrelevant to the answers extracted from or statements volunteered by Protagoras. In general, the victim of Socratic dialectic is convicted out of his own mouth as far as possible, and not out of Socrates'.) In so far as the word 'wise' does have uses in contexts more moral than the one concerned with Epimetheus, it matches not too badly with 'folly', which we have found also in such contexts in Greek. Protagoras cannot complain that proposition 1 requires him to fly in the face of popular usage or is inconsistent with his own.

We have ruled out some of Protagoras' uses of 'wisdom' from consideration in the present context on the grounds that they are not within the universe of discourse delimited by the context of the statement of proposition 1. Did Plato know enough to do the same? If the question be phrased in terms of Plato's knowledge of logical rules and terminology the answer might need long discussion and would probably be negative. But that Plato had in practice the necessary abilities is immediately clear. Plato's Socrates carefully specifies in this very argument the relevant area, namely that of sound, in which two words are opposites (332C). The words Taylor quite appropriately renders 'high-pitched' and 'low-pitched' are words of many different English equivalents, and many differing sets of contexts in Greek. Characteristic, but by no means universally appropriate, would be 'sharp' and 'heavy' respectively. To make these words opposites, the relevant universe of discourse needs specification as much as it would for the English 'sharp' and 'flat'. That is of course why Socrates supplies such a specification with the limiting phrase 'in sound'.

The upshot is that in Protagoras' vocabulary 'wisdom' can mean 'good sense', and that *aphrosynê* or 'folly' is a sound, if rare, antonym for it; and that *in context* it is this sense of 'wisdom' which, alone of those he clearly knew, Protagoras ought to have in mind. It has come out that, if 'wisdom' has a wider meaning than the prudential, so does *aphrosynê* or 'folly', though admittedly 'wisdom' extends more in the direction of 'cleverness' than *aphrosynê* does in the direction of 'stupidity'. The force of this last concession is weakened by the sheer irrelevance to the context of 'cleverness' or technical skills.

The argument accepted by Protagoras for proposition 2 runs as follows (332A–C, 332D–E):

2.01 When men act rightly and beneficially, they are-moderate (and not the opposite).

2.02 They are-moderate by moderation.

2.03 Those who act not-rightly act foolishly and, in so acting, not are-moderate.
Therefore

2.04 Acting foolishly is the opposite of acting moderately:

2.05 (a) Actions performed foolishly are performed by folly.
and
(b) Actions performed moderately are performed by moderation.

2.06 An action performed by strength is performed strongly, an action performed by weakness weakly.

2.07 An action performed with speed is performed speedily, an action performed with slowness slowly.

2.08 (a) An action performed in the same way is performed by the same property
and
(b) An action performed in the opposite way is performed through the opposite property.
Therefore (from 2.08b, a version of 2.04, 2.05a and 2.05b)
2   Folly is the opposite of moderation.

The briefest glance at this suffices to show that the key proposition is 2.04. The rest is spun out, presumably to close every loophole, at tedious, repetitious and (in the MSS) inaccurate length.[159] The heart of the proof lies in the deduction of 2.04 from 2.01, 2.02 and 2.03, and it is this kernel of argument which has raised philosophical hackles.

2.04 itself would not have appeared strange to a Greek. *Aphrosynê* and its relatives, as we have seen, look like the opposites of *sôphrosynê* and *its* relatives, and function thus in several Greek authors.[160] But that merely makes the conclusion (2.04) itself acceptable; it may, in a curious sort of way, excuse, but does not lessen, the dubiety of the argument leading up to it. One trouble with the argument is that it *either* treats 'contradictory' as equivalent to 'contrary' *or* uses the word 'opposite' throughout to *mean* 'contradictory'. The second alternative seems to me, as to Taylor,[161] much the less plausible. The first, however, requires exploration, proposition by proposition.

2.01 is plausible in itself, as Taylor again sees, if 'moderation' be taken to mean here 'good sense'. But the difficulty is to fit 2.01 into Protagoras' beliefs or admissions. In the light of the position he has taken up in response to Socrates' questioning after the Great Speech, one would expect Protagoras to deny that all right actions are moderate actions. They could be right, in the sense of being (e.g.) thoroughly courageous, without being moderate, since it is more than possible that for Protagoras courage does not entail moderation. Protagoras seems, with this admission that all right actions are moderate, to give away far too much. But if that is the whole truth of the matter, we should have hard words to say of Plato, if not of his Socrates. Has Protagoras let slip anything which could after all make it difficult to deny 2.01?

This is the place to look back to an important sentence of Protagoras' Great Speech (322E–323A). He there said that either all political advice or all political goodness must 'proceed through justice and moderation'. If that meant anything solid at all, it ought to have meant either (a) that justice and moderation were the same thing, and this one thing was a necessary condition of any action's being in accordance with political goodness, or (b) that justice and moderation were distinct but both necessary features of actions in accordance with political goodness.[162] There were reasons for him to deny (a), so that he is now left with (b).

A third way, if he were capable of thinking it out, would be the assertion that justice and moderation are both essential to the good man but not to his every action; that just actions need not coincide with moderate actions, even though the good man will do both. Even if he did get this far the sophist would have to admit, after the argument about holiness and justice, that some moderate actions are unjust.

Apart from any personal moral repugnance in face of that position, he would then be open to some awkward questions. If moderation is restraint, what is the point of an action in the service neither (being restrained) of the agent's own desires nor (being unjust) of his fellow men? If moderation is prudence, is it not, on the whole, prudent to be just?

Protagoras is left with (b), including the assertion that moderation is a necessary feature of action in accordance with political goodness. It thus results from things he has already said that he ought to agree to the plausible-sounding proposition 2.01 laid before him (332A–B). Its vocabulary offers him no chance to escape. 'Rightly' and 'beneficially' are clearly terms of approval associable closely with 'goodness'. Neither term in isolation indicates the interests or aims served or the identity of the beneficiary; the question of self- or other-serving goodness is not raised by Socrates' question. There is every reason why Protagoras should be prepared to give it an affirmative answer.

Socrates is taking advantage of a slightly muddled Protagoras. He is not explicit about it; but then we have found other examples of inexplicit argument of this kind. This is not the clearest example of the type. But it would appear that Plato is not only relying on the blurring in contemporary vocabulary and thought of the line between the moral and the intellectual. He is making his Socrates depend also on what Protagoras has specifically said. For Protagoras' remarks Plato, of course, bears the creator's responsibility. He makes his Protagoras throw around, with rhetorical effect but intellectual casualness, words like 'justice'. He deals with the resulting problems together with those arising from the moral–intellectual complex, enmeshing his Protagoras in both at once. Though this particular case of the technique is not of the most certain, such a reading is worth consideration; there is a close fit between other series of questions and Protagoras' speech, and Socrates treats other interlocutors similarly. The acceptance of this case would have the not unwelcome effect of making Socrates' reasoning in this passage less, rather than more, opportunist.

On 2.02 it is possible to be brief. It is clearly intended as analytically true. But in case of temptation to dissociate the good qualities from the corresponding types of action more sharply than Socrates does on my interpretation, there is another relevant sentence in Protagoras' speech (323B). In his first musical analogy Protagoras attributes to normal people (without distancing himself from it) the view that modestly telling the truth about one's abilities *is* moderation.[163] The doctrine that being-moderate, acting moderately and possessing moderation are necessarily linked is not one that Protagoras can easily or even consistently resist.

2.03 presents harder problems. In part it is the converse of 2.01. Whether directly or indirectly[164] it says that when men act not-rightly they act not-moderately, whereas 2.01 said that when men act rightly they act moderately. 2.03 cannot be deduced from 2.01. So where does it come from? How does foolishness come in? At least two things are stated clearly in 2.03:

2.03a All not-right actions are foolish.
2.03b All not-right actions are not-moderate.

It is not immediately plain, as Taylor points out, that a third proposition is asserted, namely:

2.03c   All foolish actions are not-moderate.

But if Socrates does not state or secure Protagoras' statement of it here, then he must be supposed to assume throughout, without expressing the assumption, the incompatibility of folly and moderation. The assumption could indeed be deduced from or 'on the basis of' the ordinary meaning of the terms. But in that case why all the fuss? Why purport to argue the incompatibility of folly and moderation while in fact assuming it? By the time Socrates has arrived at 2.04 he evidently thinks he has connected the concepts of folly and moderation in such a way as to show that they are at least incompatible, if not more sharply opposed. The only place for him to have connected them is in 2.03, which must therefore be read as indeed connecting them. No merely external connection, no simple addition of one to the other, will succeed. So we should take 2.03 as including 2.03c; the participle translated above 'in so acting' will then be more than merely temporal ('when so acting') and be more causal ('in so far as they so act'). The sentence then implies, in Taylor's words: 'If anyone acts wrongly he acts foolishly and therefore (in so far as or because he acts foolishly) not sensibly [in Stokes terminology, "not-moderately"].' At least Protagoras must take the sentence in this way, for otherwise he would be able to make an objection subsequently which he does not in fact make.

But this is not the end of the difficulties. For 2.03a would appear to lack credibility. Why should Protagoras accept that all not-right actions are foolish? There are reasons why he should not. If 'right' means 'morally right' (or perhaps 'cooperatively right') then 2.03a begs large questions, and if 'rightly' (as Taylor says) 'should be taken in the widest sense of "doing the right thing"', then there are many other reasons than folly for failure to do the right thing, reasons such as weakness of will or even bad luck. But it may be replied that Protagoras does not have the nerve to deny the long-term folly of uncooperative actions here or elsewhere, and he has professional reasons, to be discussed later, for discounting the effects of weakness of will or of luck.[165] If 'rightly' means 'in a well-thought-out way', again Protagoras could accept 2.03a without demur, and this may be his line of thought. But in that case he has other problems on his hands. In that case either 2.03b is extremely dubious or moderation too is a matter of intellect; he should either reject 2.03b or agree that moderation is an intellectual virtue, and thus abandon the distinction (such as it is) between moderation and wisdom.

Can Protagoras reject 2.03b? Only if he is prepared to admit that a moderate action may be wrong; and this he no doubt finds difficult: Zeus himself sent Hermes with moderation. But nevertheless Protagoras could, if pressed, since he has stressed the difference between the good qualities, instance a moderate move which is not right because there is a move (recommended by another good quality) which is in some sense better. But an action not in accordance with a virtue is liable, after Socrates' and Protagoras' first argument, to end up contrary to that virtue; and Protagoras finds conflict between the virtues hard to deal with. Indeed 2.03b is all too easy for Protagoras to accept.

2.03b has also some warrant, allowing for the vagueness of the sophist's language, in the Great Speech. In the account of Athenian education there (326A) the musicians take care of moderation and that the children do nothing bad. If, as is perhaps the most plausible view, 'moderation' and 'doing nothing bad' are rhetorical doublets, then moderation is roughly equivalent to 'doing nothing bad'. 'Bad' and 'not-right' are pretty clearly close relatives. On this interpretation Protagoras implies that moderation excludes not-right action; not-right action will then be, as 2.03 says it is, not-moderate.

But ultimately both this interpretation of Protagoras' earlier words and the plausibility of 2.03b itself rest on the traditional view of moderation or *sôphrosynê* as the quality in virtue of which one refrains from bad or wrong actions.[166] If Protagoras wants to reject 2.03b he will have a bad time not only from Socrates but from those who shared in this tradition.

It does not follow that Protagoras must accept 2.03c, the most important component of 2.03. Why should he be prepared so closely to relate the opposite of wisdom with the negation of moderation? The trouble lies deeper than the usage of 'folly' or 'moderation'. It concerns, I think, the vagueness of 'wisdom' in the mouth of Protagoras and of his typical admirers. When Protagoras speaks of the great statesmen, he implies that they fail to make their sons wise in the wisdom of their fathers. The art of the statesman is at issue. Statesmen were more noted for their practical intelligence than for their moral qualities, but Protagoras will not or dare not preach the dissociation of the statesman's art from justice and moderation. Protagoras treats justice and moderation as the crucial components of political skill, and skill or art (*technê*) is almost indistinguishable in many Greek contexts from wisdom.[167] Protagoras is none too consistent in his belief that he teaches an art, but he will not, if asked, deny it. Yet he takes wisdom to be only a component of political goodness, of what it takes to be good at politics — although it is the 'greatest', in some undefined sense, of such components (330A). That is inconsistent. It is not surprising if he answers Socrates' questions in ways that turn out to be inconsistent.

In this particular case, when asked if all foolish actions are not-moderate, he thinks, no doubt, of actions not in accord with the statesman's wisdom, with that skill which he himself claims to impart. Either such actions are not-moderate, or they are not-just, or they are in some way not-good. But he cannot afford to escape by saying this, rather than agreeing that all foolish actions are not-moderate; for the escape will lead to the admission that the relevant sort of wisdom is the whole, not a part, of political skill or goodness. Protagoras gives away one bastion rather than give up the defence altogether. Socrates' procedure is to put questions forcing his opponent into the open whatever answer he gives.

But we have still not arrived at 2.04 (332B). On the way to it lies the crevasse set between 'not moderate' and 'the opposite of moderate', between contradictory and contrary. Plato could not claim that 'un-moderate' is a common idiom for 'excessive' or 'self-indulgent', as 'not just' was for 'unjust'. Protagoras himself has committed no transition or deduction from the contradictory of 'moderate' to its contrary. All he has done is to label 'mad' one action (namely, not laying claim to justice) which consists of failure to do something moderate. One cannot build any relevant generalization on this. But if Plato knew what was going on in the case of justice, he presumably knew what was going on in the case of moderation. Our argument that he probably did know in the case of justice therefore creates a presumption that he knew in the case of moderation. If he did know, then he could have relied on Protagoras' usage in the case of justice to excuse Socrates' line of questioning and account for the apparently simple-minded answer. Having accepted the transition between contradictory and contrary in one context Protagoras is in no position to reject it in another – unless he is ready with a clear discrimination between the two cases, which is implausible.

3   Socrates asks (332C–D) whether each thing that has an opposite has only one opposite. If the opposites are gradable, then there is indeed only one notion that fits each end of the relevant scale, each end towards which the scale tends. It seems reasonable to allow Plato and his characters the analytical truth of this point. Having failed to distinguish two different scales, the intellectual or mental and the moral, Protagoras falls victim to the argument. He himself has used madness, mental derangement, as an apparent opposite to moderation; it needs no unjustified generalization to bolster the claim that Protagoras cannot now complain if moderation takes a place on both the mental and the moral scale. But these considerations do not exhaust the subject.

Protagoras' Great Speech includes in use a few pairs of opposites. In particular he labels the pair good/bad as opposites (323D–E). The pair of which 'fine' is a member crops up in the same passage in the MSS; but I believe the MSS to be wrong.[168] Nevertheless 'fine' or 'honourable' and 'shameful' do occur in the parents' instructions to their children (325D).[169] It need not be coincidence that these two pairs of opposites are two out of the three put to Protagoras by way of Socratically inductive argument for 3 (332C). It is unlikely also that Socrates' choice of third example, from the field of music, is unrelated to Protagoras' choice of flute-playing for an analogue of goodness (323A, 327A). Socrates is moving here within the circle of ideas trodden out by his opponent.

This much could be true without compelling Protagoras to admit only a single opposite to each opposite. We need to go deeper. We need in particular to examine the remarks in the Great Speech about political goodness and its opposite. These are obviously relevant to Socrates' line of questioning about opposites.

Qualities, Protagoras said, which are won by care, practice and the absorption of teaching are, if the relevant bad quality is attributable to someone, the subject of anger or of punishment (323D–E). The expression used for 'bad qualities' here is 'the opposite bad things'. This in itself commits the speaker to no answer to the question whether each opposite has more than one opposite. But Protagoras goes on to say 'of these [bad things] *one* (my emphasis) is both injustice and impiety and in sum the whole opposite of political goodness'. Disregarding now the question of the identity of its constituent qualities, we find that the whole opposite of political goodness is single; it is one single thing. Turning forward a little, we renew the discovery that, in the very passage Socrates cited as he began his interrogation, political goodness itself, the goodness of a man, is *one thing* (324E–325A, cf. 330C). The two passages together constitute a conspicuous and memorable instance in Protagoras' own Speech of one opposed thing having a single opposite only. This too is an inadequate basis for generalization. It is only an instance. But it is doubtful whether Protagoras can escape by merely pointing out that it is an isolated instance.

If he is to do that, he will have to show that it is isolated and peculiar. Is political goodness unique in respect of having only one opposite? Protagoras gives, in Speech and under interrogation, no reason for thinking so. Do other opposites behave differently? Again Protagoras is and remains silent. He has, of course, the right of silence. But if he wished to return a negative to Socrates' generalized question, he would be obliged to tell us (and Socrates) in what relevant respect this particular pair of opposites is different from others. No doubt a competent modern logician would know how to set about this. But we may be confident that his eventual explanation would be beyond a Protagoras to achieve. Protagoras has left himself open to an attack he has not the skills to evade: he will not be able to deny the proposition Socrates put to him without either logic-chopping or simply abandoning a position he took up in his Speech. In a case such as this the admission of a single instance can be dialectically as fatal as the admission of a generalization.

Returning to the text at Socrates' inductive line of questioning about opposites (332C), we see that he includes the pair good/bad, and asks about two other pairs. Protagoras fails to differentiate good and bad from the others in respect of the number of opposites available. If the sophist has imprisoned himself by his remarks in the Speech, this set of answers bolts the door. Protagoras is unwilling or unable to distinguish relevantly between good/bad and the other pairs of opposites he uses or envisages, and Socrates can successfully put to him the general question whether each opposed thing has a single opposite. Socrates' success may look like Plato's empty contrivance. But if it does, we may suggest that, just as the sophist ensnares himself with his own rhetoric, so he will have ensnared the readers who found that rhetoric acceptable, and such readers will have been in a large majority.

It is curious, and need not be coincidental, that despite Protagoras' assertion that there is just one opposite to political goodness he uses in the Speech two different opposites to the adjective 'good'. In one passage he uses *kakos* and in the other the word *phaulos* (323E–324A, 326E (cf.327B)).[170] This makes clearly two opposites for a single term. But no one (least of all Protagoras) has suggested that the two opposites so used differ in meaning in their Protagorean context. Protagoras is no Prodicus to distinguish synonyms or near synonyms. This supplies an elegant precedent for Socrates' enforcement of the equation of the wise with the moderate. One would like to suppose that this precedent was not due to Plato's inadvertence. But there is no such verbal evidence in favour of deliberate intent here as there is in the matter of a single opposite for each single opposite, and one should be cautious. Even without this additional point there is a growing body of evidence that Socrates is working on Protagoras not with mere sophistry but with a clever use of Protagoras' own confusions of thought, carelessnesses of expression, and widely shared inadequacies of logic.

Several commentators accuse Socrates of cheating by omission in his concluding summary of the argument. The accusation is not hard to justify, and is made succinctly by Taylor.[171] 'Having reached a conclusion which is incompatible with Protagoras' original thesis of the non-identity of sophia [wisdom] and sophrosyne [moderation], Socrates offers him the choice of abandoning that thesis or giving up premiss 3; "each thing which has an opposite has only one opposite." He assumes without justification that premisses 1 and 2 are not open to question.' To justify the accusation, however, is not to explain Socrates' reasons for incurring it. To judge from their silence, the accusers probably put down the cheating either to deliberate policy on Socrates' part (and hence on Plato's) or to inadvertence or ignorance. Such explanations may be right.

But if the above analysis of the argument is correct, a situation emerges which is favourable to other types of explanation. Premiss 3 will then derive pretty directly from Protagoras' words uttered as long ago as the Great Speech. The thesis of the good qualities' non-identity will derive explicitly from Protagoras' initial exposition under questioning of the Great Speech's implications. Premisses 1 and 2, on the other hand, though not extracted entirely without regard to that Speech, are the result of inexplicit and/or general implications of Protagoras' words, implications not crystallized until the start of the present argument identifying wisdom with moderation. Hence the premisses Socrates omits from the list of possible retractions are the most recently developed. It could be the case that Socrates is, in effect, challenging his victim to deny something he has only just admitted; the challenge would take the form of silently assuming the impossibility of his doing such a thing. But where that would leave Plato's purposes in so constructing the dialogue is very unclear.

Alternatively, Plato may have judged that the two premisses 1 and 2 would have proved most easily acceptable to his expected readers, and accordingly have deliberately left these two unchallenged. We should then perhaps envisage Socrates as endorsing that judgment, though it is not perhaps necessary to treat the dialogue as a document so historical as that might be held to imply. It is true that our premisses 1 and 2, though not necessarily the most evidently acceptable to

Protagoras, are probably the two most likely to be accepted without question by the average Classical Greek. Both look like glimpses of the verbally obvious, whereas the average man might well distrust a logical generalization such as 3, or a proposition such as the conclusion 4 which announced the identity of two things denoted by two different words not normally used as synonyms. This interpretation would imply less obscure motives for the creative artist Plato; but we should perhaps trim our speculative sails here.

Justice and moderation (333B–334C)

Socrates plunges at once into the next argument. Protagoras, in his eventual reply, is quite open about the trickiness of Socrates' first question: does the sophist think that a man who acts unjustly performs moderately in so acting (or because he so acts)? The subsequent by-play helps to clarify the meaning of this, at least as Protagoras interprets it. It is clear that he does not take moderation here as 'self-restraint' but rather as 'being sensible in one's own interests'. Injustice is pretty clearly, as self-aggrandisement at the expense of others' rights, not an example of self-restraint, and Protagoras could not envisage 'many people' as saying it was. Hence his reply (333C), that he would be ashamed to answer in the affirmative though many people would not be, rules out the 'self-restraint' sense of moderation. The question therefore is whether injustice is sensible behaviour in one's own interests.

Protagoras could in theory, and if this were an isolated question, reply that injustice was indeed in the interests of the agent; but he has already accepted that justice is a good quality, a part of goodness (329C–D), and presumably one he helps to inculcate (328A–B (with reference to the whole of goodness)). He is neither in general any sort of immoralist, nor able in particular to go back on his former high evaluation of justice. Of course, the selfish pursuit of one's own advantage was in the opinion of many Greeks of his time the sensible policy. Admitting the spread of this opinion, Protagoras nevertheless stands out against such a popular (not necessarily majority)[172] view. Plato is not concerned with nakedly and openly immoralist views in the *Protagoras*; he is concerned rather to lay bare by implication the discrepancy, e.g., between the sophistic training in the pursuit of advantage and the claim to teach men to be good citizens considerate of others. Protagoras would be ashamed to support injustice as the right path to follow, because to do so would be to incur odium from ordinary people.

But he is also in trouble if he says that injustice is not moderate. The admission that all unjust behaviour is not-moderate would bring the two virtues of justice and moderation too close for his comfort. If all unjust behaviour is not-moderate, it is not possible to be moderate but unjust. True, Protagoras has not explicitly said that it is possible to be moderate but unjust. But he has accepted a list of parts of virtue that includes justice and moderation; he has said that the parts of virtue are related to one another like the parts of the face (329C–E). The parts of the face include, e.g., the eyes and the ears; and he can hardly deny the possibility of being deaf but not blind. Thus a negative answer to Socrates' question will endanger his consistency.

The choice before Protagoras is thus a tricky one: odium or inconsistency? He takes refuge in evasion. He would be ashamed to give one answer, though many people would give it; but he does not explicitly give the other. Socrates tries to pin him down. Is the questioning to be directed to the sophist's implied view or to that of the many people who would reject it? Protagoras seizes his chance for evasive action and suggests inquiry into that of the many. But Socrates is not going to let Protagoras stop answering questions, and insists that the sophist continues to answer, whether the opinions he is thus defending are his own or not. The Socratic claim is that only the set of views is being examined, and that if any person is being subjected to examination it is the questioner no less than the questioned. Whatever the truth of this claim, Protagoras agrees to continue (333D); he can hardly break off at this point without irreparable loss of face. On agreement, he is asked the same question again. The answer he plumps for is the affirmative, that some people in acting unjustly are moderate (*or* sensible). At the same time his choice of words is such as to leave him with no necessary personal responsibility for the views expressed. This raises a problem later when the argument is broken off; for Protagoras thereabouts shows signs of being worried (334C) and there is no obvious reason why he should be worried about the outcome of support for opinions he does not share. The point is surely that to deny those opinions would land him so quickly and manifestly in difficulties of the kind we have outlined as to be impossible; hence the necessity of a successful defence for the affirmative choice, however unpleasing.

The ensuing argument is unfinished, and, as Taylor says, 'any reconstruction of the unfinished argument must be conjectural.'[173] The usual strategy of reconstruction is to produce analogous arguments from other dialogues and show how one or other Socratic line of argument would fit the context in the *Protagoras*. Certain principles of reconstruction ought to be observed; the less the argument requires by way of completion, (a) the more intelligible Protagoras' evasive action becomes in the dramatic context, and (b) the more intelligible it seems that Plato should leave the argument where he does. The interpretation which follows tries accordingly to produce an immediate embarrassment for Protagoras at the very place of break-off. That is a consideration in its favour independent of the main thrust of Platonic interpretation being developed here.[174] However, the interpretation's appeal to Protagoras' earlier remarks will not now surprise the reader. But it should be clear that this particular interpretation is not advanced as *proof* that Plato's unfinished argument must refer, like others, to the sophist's words before the interrogation. It seeks rather to show the *consistency* of such reference with the broken torso of this Socratic argument.

Now that Protagoras has admitted the possibility of an unjust action being sensible or moderate, Socrates proceeds to introduce to the argument further terms which will embarrass his victim further (334D). Translated as literally as possible, the next question says: 'By "being moderate" you mean "thinking well"?'[175] The next continues, 'and by "thinking well" you mean "deliberating well" – in respect of their unjust behaviour?' The sophist returns an unqualified assent to the first and a responsibility-declining affirmative to the second. We have already seen that indeed he took Socrates, rightly, to be talking about good sense in one's own interest, and the gloss 'thinking well' is consonant with that understanding. But 'deliberating well' offers fresh problems.

These arise from comparison with Protagoras' claims at the very outset of the dialogue (318E). The root of the verb here rendered 'deliberate' (Taylor has 'plan') is the same as that of the noun rendered 'management' by Taylor in that earlier passage. Taylor's epithet 'proper' there renders the syllable (in this case part of a compound noun) which means 'well'. Protagoras' claim was to teach good-deliberation.[176] Socrates now asks him to agree that one can practise good deliberation in the commission of injustice. Protagoras promised to confer on his pupils, in whatever sense of 'good', good counsel, good planning, good management. Justice, he said later, is at least a necessary condition of goodness (e.g. 322E–323A); all counsel had to pass through justice and moderation. He now has to face his admissions, however unwillingly made; they compel him either (a) to divorce sound thinking from sound deliberation and planning, or (b) to accept that good deliberation can result in unjust action, or (c) to agree that the good deliberation he inculcates need not result in appropriate action at all. To choose (c) will land him in a professionally impossible position.[177] The choice of (a) is unwelcome, in that the thinking concerned is clearly marked by the context as having to do with one's choices of action. Alternative (b) appears to make justice no longer a necessary condition of goodness. Protagoras is as reluctant verbally to take responsibility for this as for the moderation of some unjust actions, and for rather similar reasons. The necessary admission accordingly takes a form disclaiming responsibility; but, as before, Protagoras cannot really evade responsibility without falling from frying pan into fire.

But Socrates has not even now finished milking this line of talk. 'And do they deliberate well if they do well in acting unjustly or if they do badly?'[178] 'Do well' here covers either or both of 'act well' and 'fare well', but it makes relatively little difference which Protagoras takes Socrates to have in mind. If faring well is in point, the question lands him in much the same set of alternatives as the previous one. That is perhaps a reason for slightly preferring the rendering 'Act well', which leads to further difficulties. The question then seeks to extract an admission that good deliberation results in acting well even in cases of unjust action. Can Protagoras resist this admission? Hardly; for his own statement of his teaching objectives included the suggestion that his pupils learnt good deliberation concerning the city's affairs, namely how to make the most effective contribution to the affairs of the city 'both by word and action' (318E–319A). Whether just or unjust, 'word and action' follow on good deliberation, and if the deliberation is good it is assumed (at least for the present) that the action is good. To balk at the admission Socrates seeks here would tend to destroy Protagoras' earlier claims. But, again, to make the admission promises to be no less disastrous. It would admit the possibility of unjust action being good, contrary to his assertion that justice is a necessary condition of goodness. Without separating goodness and good action with far more rigour than he seems capable of, Protagoras cannot escape.

With his next pair of questions Socrates looks as though he is about to rub salt in these already unpleasant wounds. The first of them is 'Do you call some things good?' Protagoras does indeed, and we might guess what things; they might well include (though they do not explicitly) the virtues, whose opposites are bad (323D–324A). What Protagoras has explicitly said is that we benefit from each other's justice and goodness (327B). If, as Socrates' next question invites him to do (334D), he admits now that what is good is what is beneficial to men, then he will have to admit that justice is good.

To articulate this will bring his difficulties into the open. What would become of his present series of admissions? It is possible, he has admitted, in unjust action to be moderate, and to be moderate is to think and deliberate and hence to do well, to benefit. So what benefits does justice confer on the agent? In so far as moderation is prudence, injustice which is moderate will be prudent, and, presumably, beneficial to the agent. We shall arrive at a situation where some injustice benefits the agent, and some justice benefits others than the agent. In so far as Protagoras claims to teach good management or the goodness of the citizen, and in so far as an important element in that goodness is justice, his teaching will not necessarily be in his pupils' own interests. Why then should they pay him large sums, and why in particular should Hippocrates entrust himself to Protagoras or any other sophist? Protagoras simply cannot afford to bring such questions into the open. He is now in danger of confrontation with one of the basic confusions of contemporary attitudes and values, a confusion underlying the whole of his original defence.

Protagoras is in comprehensive trouble. He must put a stop to the inexorable interrogation. At the point we have reached he must avoid any questioning on *which* men good things (such as justice) benefit. He evades that possible line of questioning with the quite valid but not wholly relevant rejoinder that things may be good without being beneficial to men. Desperation is the mother of quick-wittedness. The good planning and doing that the moderate but unjust achieve can be squared with 'justice is good for men' without problems by the supposition that the good achieved by the unjust is not good for men.

If this is his line of thought, Protagoras' nervousness at this point would be understandable; what sort of good are the unjust's good plans, etc., if they are not good for men? Here Socrates' next thrust fits in; in speaking of things not beneficial to men, did Protagoras mean things beneficial merely to no man, or things not beneficial to all? In context, that could be interpreted as asking about the good things done in unjust but moderate behaviour. If it is not good for men, then for what or whom is such behaviour good? If for men, then for which men? This dreaded line of questioning looms up again. Of course Protagoras could abandon the equation between good and beneficial; but that is not easy in Greek, and Protagoras' succeeding harangue shows his unwillingness to do so, in that he uses 'good' and 'beneficial' interchangeably.

The remarks Protagoras offers on the relativity of 'good' and 'beneficial' are thus true but largely irrelevant to his basic difficulty. Their irrelevance is due to his need to evade looming issues. The argument is as good as over before he starts on them. No long Socratic deduction would have been necessary to break him down once more. His claims as a teacher make the separation of the virtues difficult to maintain in the rather pure form he has accepted. His defence is hindered by his lack of a clear distinction between doing something just and possessing the virtue 'justice'. If he could make this clear, he could contend that a prudent man could do an unjust action in certain circumstances without being an unjust man on the whole or by temperament. Unjust action could then be on occasion prudent, even though to be an unjust man was not prudent. But Protagoras blurs in his own remarks the distinction between possession of a virtue and the acting upon it; and whether by accident or design Socrates uses a number of verbs in the argument which are ambiguous, meaning either 'to be such-and-such a kind of person' or 'to perform such-and-such a kind of action'.

It must be admitted that it is not wholly clear that Plato himself was as aware as he should have been of this distinction. In any case even to make the distinction would leave Protagoras with some awkward questions to answer: what unjust actions, and what proportion of unjust actions, are prudent? Where are the relevant lines to be drawn?

Whatever the precise difficulties Socrates' line of interrogation is meant by Plato to lead to, it is obvious that he did intend it to lead into difficulties. It is equally clear that he did not mean the difficulties to be immediately transparent; for he makes the crowd in the house of Callias applaud Protagoras' evasive speech, with cries of 'Well spoken!' (334C). They are presumably, however, perceptible by Protagoras, a by no means stupid or thoughtless man who is as much the victim of his own rhetoric as of Socrates' acumen. Indeed Socrates tells his listener that he was aware of Protagoras' dissatisfaction with his answers to date, and there is no reason to suppose this diagnosis false (335A–B). These considerations do nothing to discourage a certain amount of reading between the lines of Socrates' report, to gain insight into the thrust and parry of a battle not all discernable on the surface of the text. The account ventured above is probably not the only one consistent with the indications mentioned; but it aims at consistency both with them and with the general thesis that Socrates' interlocutors in Plato are required in their replies to respect all their previous pronouncements.

Interlude 334C–338E

In dramatic context Protagoras' smokescreen is successful. Much of what Protagoras says is also true, even if its truth does not blind us to the dialectical power of Socrates' counter-argument. Dramatically it also supplies a transition to the next part of the dialogue. The dialogue continues with a plea from Socrates for Protagoras to speak at less length. This plea has met with derision, on the grounds of the greater length of some of Socrates' own speeches;[179] but (a) it is up to Protagoras to plead forgetfulness if he wishes (as he does not) and (b) Socrates disclaims the intention of cutting speeches more than is appropriate. His objections to Protagoras (his plea of forgetfulness is obviously ironic)[180] are doubtless that his speech is longer than needed, and, as Alcibiades later suggests (336C–D), calculated to cause *the audience* to forget the original question. In fact the irrelevance, rather than the mere length of Protagoras' harangue, must form the gravamen of Socrates' dissatisfaction. The ironic excuse is half sham and half politeness; it is less urbane to say 'Your remarks are irrelevant' than to say 'You're going too far and fast for me'.

Socrates indeed makes to abandon the discussion. His response to the remonstrances of the company is the artful insertion into the conversation of the notion of a competition. With his usual self-deprecation, he suggests that he cannot win the race as at present constituted. Alcibiades and Hippias develop the competitive theme, over the objections of Critias and Prodicus. Even Prodicus, despite his diplomatic tone, has the rather competitive suggestion that they should assign more weight to the 'wiser' of the two principals.

In the account of Hippias' intervention (337Cff.) 'wisdom' receives further attention. The narrator Socrates describes him as 'Hippias the wise', and Hippias calls the company the 'wisest of the Greeks' and refers to Athens as 'the very shrine of wisdom in all Greece' before offering his services (by obvious innuendo) as umpire. This gives Socrates his cue. His grounds for rejecting any umpire include the assertion that none could be wiser than Protagoras, an assertion he treats by implication as simply equivalent to the assertion that none could be better (338C).

In the context, this is not merely Socratic philosophy: it is artful. Protagoras claims to be a professional wise man, a sophist. He has not demurred at being called 'wise' by

Socrates. He claims to be a better teacher of goodness than other men. Socrates is here reinforcing his vanity and his pretensions. Vanity and professional repute alike make it more difficult for Protagoras to abandon the contest. It is especially difficult when he is not clearly victorious. Socrates' offer (338C–E) to submit to questioning by Protagoras, an offer bypassing the original dispute about length of answers, is hard to refuse. The slightest suggestion of a competition, in the remark that no single judge is necessary, but the whole assembled company will sit in judgment – and Protagoras is (as Socrates narrates) virtually forced to accept a role in the discussion once more. He promises to submit to questioning at some later time, in return for the right to question Socrates now.

Simonides' poem 338E–347B

Protagoras accordingly takes his turn. He chooses to interrogate Socrates on a famous poem. His reasons for the choice come out in a brief preamble. He thinks it is a very important part[181] of a man's education to be knowledgeable about poetry. By that he means being able to grasp 'what is rightly composed and what is not', being able to distinguish the two, and to respond to interrogation. As often in Platonic discussions of literature it is pretty clear that 'what is rightly composed' means 'what is true' much more than it means 'what is aesthetically pleasing'. There is no reason to suppose Platonic discussions unique in their time in that respect. Hence, one might presume, to be able to tell what is rightly composed is to know the subject. The sophist indeed insists on the concern of his questions with goodness (339B). The transfer to poetry gives the *only* explicit difference from the preceding Socratic interrogation.

Protagoras' introductory questions are brief but pregnant. The poem for analysis is one Simonides wrote for the 'tyrant' Scopas of Thessaly. Is Socrates satisfied that the poem is well and rightly composed? Socrates has received warning that an incorrect answer to this will brand him as mistaken in an area

Protagoras rates highly among the accomplishments of an educated man. The brand will strike deeper in that he has claimed to know the poem and to have devoted special study to it. He plumps for the affirmative; the poem is well and rightly composed. Is a poem, Protagoras asks, well composed if the poet contradicts himself? Socrates can hardly give any but a negative reply to this; not for him Walt Whitman's 'I contradict myself? Very well then, I contradict myself.' But then Protagoras points out an apparent contradiction, and Socrates is in trouble.

This section clearly recalls, is indeed probably modelled on, the early stages of Socrates' questioning of Protagoras. Socrates pronounced the Athenians 'wise', presenting the sophist with a dilemma; either he agrees or he makes an unpopular assertion. Protagoras does something very similar to Socrates. The poem was evidently a famous one; not only do Protagoras and Socrates both know it by heart, but Hippias too has an interpretation ready (347A–B). The judgement of it as bad would in all probability be unpopular. Socrates, like Protagoras earlier, does not take the unpopular line. Like Protagoras, after failing to deny the Athenians' wisdom, he confronts unpalatable consequences. Plato's Protagoras is clever enough to produce a species of unpalatability specially calculated to needle Socrates. The apostle of consistency, trying all along to get Protagoras to contradict himself openly, now approves of a self-contradictory poem! No wonder Socrates is momentarily confused.

The methods by which he first extracts himself from Protagoras' dilemma and then offers his own positive interpretation of the poem have received from scholars various labels such as 'comic', 'whimsical', 'humorous', 'mocking satire', 'parody', and the like.[182] Some have supposed Plato to be showing us Socrates beating the sophists at one of their own games.[183] Grote supposed, on the contrary, that Socrates, having renounced competition with Protagoras in long speeches, is displayed here as losing the game, as 'on the lower ground as a rhetorician'.[184] Some believe that for all its inadequacies Socrates' interpretation of the poem is superior to Protagoras' in that it is more systematic, and treats the poem as a whole[185]– as if the results were anything but appalling to any serious student of poetry. Amid this variety of interpretation one thing at least should be clear: Plato did not, could not, seriously believe in every detail of Socrates' exposition of the poem as a whole. Once that is agreed, we have to ask whether 'outsophisticating the sophists' is a plausible account of the passage *in its context*. Here Grote deserves attention; his notion of Socrates' inferiority has something to be said for it. For if, as is generally agreed, Socrates' exposition of Simonides is in great part ridiculous, and if, as is pretty obvious, Plato knew it to be ridiculous, then Socrates is not beating the sophists at their own game. He is rather producing a ridiculous specimen of interpretation-play.

A way out of Socratic inferiority here would be to assume Socratic (and Platonic) burlesque. But if burlesque is the only point, then the passage is largely irrelevant to the rest of the dialogue – if we want to treat the rest of the dialogue with some degree of seriousness. It then becomes plausible to suppose the episode, with A. E. Taylor, 'intended mainly to be humorous "relief".'[186] No doubt such a view is possible. But A. E. Taylor could not point to any Platonic habit of inserting whole large chunks of broad comedy without philosophical purpose into passages of dense philosophic argument. It is well to assume, until proved mistaken, Plato's consistency of purpose throughout the dialogue.

In this sense one should take seriously G. Klosko's recent request that scholars explain 'just why Socrates is justified in using fallacies in some parts of the dialogue but not in others'.[187] Klosko was certainly right to add that 'It will not do at all to ignore the interlude (of Simonides' poem) completely and to treat the dialogue as an uninterrupted series of serious arguments.' Klosko seeks for a consistent view of the dialogue as a whole, and reasonably so; if one can find such an interpretation, one will gladly take the bull by the horns and *either* work the view of our passage as comic relief into that interpretation *or* abandon such a view entirely. Klosko himself believes that Socrates is 'outsophisticating the sophists' throughout the dialogue; but to believe this cheapens the dialogue. Nevertheless it is incumbent on one who interprets the dialogue's first half in a rather different sense to show how that sense can be extended to the Simonides passage.

In the present context that obliges one to show how the basic idea of the episode is 'dialectical' in the way that term is being used here. That is to say that the sophists in general, and Protagoras in particular, are deprived of all obvious retort to Socrates' arguments by their own professional pretensions and their acceptance of certain doctrines and methods – both the doctrines and the methods being as a rule not too far distant from the unthinking beliefs and slipshod reasoning of the ordinary man. In so interpreting the interlude on poetry we should not altogether forget the warning of Shorey that 'it is perhaps a matter of opinion whether Plato himself fully appreciated the fallacious character of the fanciful interpretations proposed in jest or in earnest by Socrates'.[188]

But we should allow Plato a little common sense, and a modicum of subtlety in understanding his own language. It behoves us to see whether and, if so, in what sense Plato could possibly regard this extraordinary passage as (in the words of a nineteenth-century editor) 'a confirmation of his own convictions on the subject of virtue as essentially dependent upon knowledge'.[189] To be sure, the old commentators were naively straightforward in their portrayal of Plato's thinking; but the dialectical interpretation may point to elements of truth in that kind of account. It may show that, if we accept sophistic modes of interpretation and sophistic educational values, then the poets do confirm Socrates' views on virtue. It may show that in this situation the sophists are only too glad to turn away from this line of inquiry, and have no great desire to answer Socrates' strictures on their method. It may indeed show Socrates tying the sophists in the same sort of knots here as in the rest of the dialogue.

How does Protagoras treat the poem? The inconsistency he finds in it lies in Simonides' combination of (a) an announcement that it is difficult to be a truly good man and (b) a rebuke to Pittacus for saying that it is difficult to be a good man (339D). Scholars have sought to set aside this apparent contradiction in many ways. Some have followed Socrates in fastening on the ambiguity of one of the verbs 'to be', a verb which can also mean 'to become'; but this view is surely mistaken.[190] By far the most plausible understanding is that which holds Simonides to have agreed with Pittacus, but to have rebuked him for not going far enough.[191] One might, but need not, follow the late Professor Sir Denys Page, who suggested in a memorable Cambridge lecture that the poet is helped by the ambiguity of the relevant Greek word between 'difficult' and 'impossible': one could take Simonides' own pronouncement, but not Pittacus', in the sense 'impossible'. That this is the poet's general drift is made quite adequately clear, even if Plato's citation of the text here is incomplete, by Simonides' later emphatic statement that only a god could achieve true goodness; its achievement is impossible, by implication, for a mortal man.

The exact proper interpretation of Simonides' lyric is not here our primary concern. But we should observe the sort of twist that Protagoras gives it. The contradiction he finds is a purely formal one; Simonides' correction of Pittacus is obviously not meant as a simple denial of what he said. But nevertheless, at first sight or hearing it sounds or looks like such a denial. To rebuke someone for saying what one has just said oneself is odd. On a purely verbal level Protagoras has a genuine point. His interpretation does not stretch the Greek language beyond what it will bear. His method is to distort the general drift of the particular poem, but not the language itself.

Much the same is true of Socrates' understanding of the first line (343E). Grammatically the word 'difficult' could be modified by the adverb 'truly', as he suggests: to do so is to commit a critical, not a grammatical blunder. Certainly the order of words in Simonides' Greek makes it quite clear that Socrates is wrong; but the wrongness is that of an extremely implausible sense, not that of the syntactically impossible. Rather different, and indeed unhistorical, is Socrates' distinction between 'being' and 'becoming' (340B). It is unlikely that in poetry of Simonides' day the two words could have been so sharply distinguished as in the philosophy of Parmenides or of Plato himself. The word rendered 'become' could in poetry mean 'be'. Socrates has ignored the true import of Simonides' words in their historical context. The unhistorical distinction saves the poet from self-contradiction by the importation of a verbal distinction alien to him but in accord with an element in Platonic philosophy. But did Plato realize he had made a linguistic mistake of a historical sort? Perhaps he conceived this too as a critical rather than a linguistic error.

Socrates supports the result thus attained with a citation of lines from another poet, Hesiod (340C–D). It was common to cite poetry as lending dignity and authority to one's views. One recalls the very opening scene of the dialogue, where Socrates (not without irony) does that very thing. The assumption is that one ought to attach weight to poetic pronouncements. In a way this assumption underlies Protagoras' concern for poetry and use of it in education. But this does not prevent him from treating the poets critically or from occasionally disbelieving them. To the question what criterion Protagoras uses to separate the true from the false statements of the poets, an answer appears in the immediate sequel to the citation of Hesiod. If Socrates is right about Simonides' meaning, then the poet is stupidly wrong, 'as everyone agrees'. The general agreement of mankind is apparently the touchstone (340E). Protagoras' intellectual relation to the general consensus of mankind remains uneasy.

Socrates does not retort directly. Instead, he appeals to Prodicus. Led on by Socrates' flattering references to his linguistic pursuits Prodicus agrees that 'difficult' could mean 'bad'. This suggestion is grotesquely arbitrary, and, as H. Gundert has pointed out, it does not help with the consistency problem.[192] But Prodicus nevertheless agrees. The result is to make him ridiculous; but that is not the only significance of his intervention. It serves the additional purpose of associating this further distinguished sophist with the critical game. Socrates can, and does, drop Prodicus the moment this particular interpretation comes under fire. Again Protagoras appeals to popular usage to refute it (341D). Socrates does not match Protagoras either in certainty or in his reliance on the popular use of words, but prefers to believe Prodicus wrong on the basis of the text.[193] This dissociates Socrates as opposed to Prodicus from distortion of simple Greek; and, as opposed to Protagoras, from reliance on a common consensus. This latter point, cropping up as it does elsewhere in the dialogue, is likely to have been more significant to Plato and his Socrates than the display of their greater skill in literary criticism, an activity the Platonic Socrates held in this dialogue (347C–348A) and elsewhere to be of little importance.

The sophists, as we have seen, do not hold that view. Hippias and Prodicus press Socrates (342A) to offer a general exposition of the poem. Socrates' preface is of much interest as well as humour. A long speech extols the Spartans for their characteristic Laconic brevity; it praises the wisdom of the Spartans as a counter-weight to the 'wisdom' of the Athenians; it transmutes the Spartan reputation for both courage and military prowess[194] into a scarcely deserved acclaim for their intellectual prowess. In particular (342E) Socrates affects to regard their brevity as the mark of an educated man, and that is a mark Protagoras himself has been unable to display consistently. Is Protagoras a truly educated man? Is he a true intellectual descendant of the Spartan 'sophists'?

When Socrates resumes his interpretation of Simonides, it is to displace perversely a Greek word (Taylor's 'rather') marking a contrast with what follows. The contrast lies not between a good man and a truly good man, Socrates says, but between being and becoming; 'truly' modifies not 'good' but 'hard' or 'difficult'. The perversity of this is not (as we have seen) that of a grammatical solecism but of a gross implausibility of sense. Socrates does not have in mind plausibilities as the common man sees them; he is concerned to stop Simonides from the 'simplicity' or 'naivety' of supposing that there are good people who are not truly good.

Why, in Socratic terms, should it be 'simple' (or 'simple-minded') to distinguish 'good' from 'truly good'? One cannot be sure,[195] but whether or not there is a Socratic point here, there are certainly Socratic points in the rest of the speech of interpretation. With an apparatus of detailed linguistic and philosophical analysis worthy of a better cause, Socrates educes from the rest of the poem's text some characteristic suggestions. It is the inexpert man who is bad; it is the 'expert and good man who, if disaster strikes, may become bad.' (344D–E). 'Doing well' in the arts becomes a matter of having learnt, and hence knowledge. The good man is directly comparable with the good writer or doctor. The only form of 'doing badly' is the deprivation of knowledge; deprivation implies prior possession, just as becoming a bad doctor implies being a good doctor (345A–B). The implications of all this are clear, though Socrates takes care *not* to spell them out in this context. The good man is the 'wise' one; 'wisdom' is equivalent, without addition and by itself, to 'goodness'. Goodness, like any other 'wisdom', is learnt – and therefore presumably learnt (as medicine and letters are learnt) from someone who teaches it. The first of these implications is a 'Socratic' view, entertained favourably by Socrates in Plato's dialogues. The second foreshadows the impasse at the end of the dialogue.

Socrates is twisting Simonides' words by reading into them his own views without concern for the original meaning. Again no grammatical solecism appears; but again none of Socrates' audience could have taken the exposition seriously as a historical account of Simonides' doctrine. The same two things are true of Socrates' further displacement of the word 'freely'. Simonides plainly implies a contradiction of the Socratic thesis that no one does wrong while wishing to do wrong. So, since Simonides is a 'wise' poet, who writes 'well', he must be robbed of his plain meaning by sheer verbal ingenuity. The displacement of 'freely' accompanies an interpretation of 'compulsion' as self-compulsion (345D–E), an outrageous distortion in conflict, though not in explicit contradiction, with Socrates' own reference to the poet being compelled to praise tyrants and their like (346B).

That Socrates next (346D) drives Simonides to the distinction between 'noble', 'dishonourable' *and neutral* makes a fitting climax. We recall the importance of the excluded middle in the series of arguments between Protagoras and Socrates which preceded this episode. Simonides must mean this distinction, says Socrates, or be ridiculous; it is difficult to resist the conclusion that Protagoras is here the victim of Socratic ridicule. Protagoras need not have recognized the full force of the last sentence (347A), with its suggestion that the most blameworthy thing is false conceit of knowledge about the important things; but it too finds a target in Protagoras no less than in Pittacus.

We have now reached the end of Socrates' version of the poem. From it we may reasonably deduce the rules of the game he is playing: if a poet 'writes well' that means, above all, that his words are susceptible without actual solecism to an interpretation agreeing with and supporting the views of the interpreter. That is doubtless what Socrates means when he says (344A–B) that 'there are many things which one could say about each of the expressions in the poem to show that it is well written'. The primary reference of 'well written' here is to the poem's consistency, which Protagoras had impugned; the poem is consistent throughout in its criticism of Pittacus' saying. But a persistent thread running through the subsequent analysis of Simonides' words is that of their pretended Socraticism.

Do the sophists approve of these rules? Of course they do. Protagoras may remain silent; but Hippias (347A) thinks highly of Socrates' performance, and Prodicus has played his part, has indeed supported an interpretation too outrageous even for Socrates (341B). Hippias even has a version of his own ready; this does not stop him from admiring Socrates' – and why should it? Hippias doubtless approves of ingenuity in reading one's own thought into a poet's words, and doubtless did the same himself. In these circles the question of Simonides' real meaning need hardly ever arise, and is clearly unimportant at least to Prodicus. Even Protagoras fastens on a purely verbal point, one imagines, only to discredit Socrates. If we do not understand the sophists thus, we have to believe their public incapable of following the most rudimentary drift of Simonides' poem, so as to be willing to go along with Protagoras' attack, or with a bold travesty such as Socrates', without demur.

From this reading of the Simonides episode it results that Socrates bases himself on a text known to Protagoras and to himself among many others. He uses a mode of interpretation perhaps lightly and occasionally caricatured, but no more – a mode likely at bottom to be acceptable to the sophists. If Protagoras were to object, he could point in reply to Protagoras' own purely verbal ingenuity in misunderstanding Simonides as being no different in principle from his own. He could certainly show out of Protagoras' mouth that poetry and the interpretation of it were important to the sophist and thought relevant to the issues raised earlier. From an acceptable type of text, by a process of reasoning not, *qua* mode of inference, unacceptable in present company, he has deduced conclusions endangering two propositions Protagoras has appeared previously to accept. For the distinctness of the good qualities appears in grave doubt if the only evil (or harm) is the loss of knowledge, and the equivalence of unjust and not-just is endangered by the elucidation of the middle term between honourable and dishonourable.

In form this passage is basically no different from many others in which Socrates more or less explicitly deduces from his opponent's premises, by his opponent's characteristic methods of inference, theses threatening his opponent's opinions and confirming views whose frequency of recurrence entitles us to label them as in some sense Socratic. To do this implies for Socrates neither approval of the premises or methods, nor disbelief of the conclusions. As we have seen, Socrates does not regard a conclusion as tainted with the argument leading to it. Rather he sees as peculiarly binding upon his victim an argument of which *the victim* can reject neither premises nor modes of inference.

Further, on this occasion Plato's purposes are not obviously suspect of differing radically from Socrates'. A highly esteemed poem, interpreted in a way intellectuals at least found exciting, is made to yield doctrines which appear to have had some appeal to Plato. We have no reason to suppose that Plato, any more than his Socrates, thought the poets authoritative on matters of moral philosophy or admired the type of interpretation that Socrates produces with the sophists' approval. One advantage for this kind of dialectical talk (for the Platonic Socrates) or writing (for Plato) is that it commits neither speaker nor writer to any doctrine absolutely. It is possible to disown a doctrine thus developed from someone else's premises by someone else's type of reasoning. The author thus retains both a distance from his readers and a provisional nature for the doctrines concerned; he shows, however, that certain people are in no position to reject them.

To range the Simonides episode under this head is to explain why Socrates can offer arguments and interpretations that seem to us wildly fallacious or wickedly wrong. It is to explain the passage without resort to mere light relief, humour, satire, and so forth. It is also to give the episode a place in the dialogue without reducing the whole work to satire. It is to make the dialogue indeed, at least this far, a consistent whole. What is more, it offers reinforcement to, and receives it from, the account given earlier of Socrates' argument with Agathon, in the *Symposium*.

The return to the parts of goodness 347B–349B

Some additional details of the Simonides episode are relevant to the main theme of Socrates' discussion with Protagoras, the relation between the good qualities. The first concerns justice and knowledge. In Simonides' poem, we read 'not bad nor altogether wicked, a sound man who knows justice that benefits the city.' (346C). M. J. O'Brien[196] has warned us that the word 'knows' here is not a sign of intellectualism in early Greek ethics. But if we look at the passage through Socratic spectacles, we see very clearly the association of justice with wisdom or knowledge. The association could take the form of the inclusion of justice in knowledge, rather than the equation of the two; but at least it looks as if the two overlap. Socrates, it is true, does not draw attention to this. Nor does he draw attention to Protagoras' earlier problems surrounding the beneficiary of justice on citing Simonides' words 'city-benefiting justice'. Simonides' word for 'benefit' here has not appeared on the lips of either Socrates or Protagoras, but the resemblance between this and, e.g., Protagoras' 'We profit, I think, from each other's justice and goodness' (327B) is there to see. It seems possible that the lack of overt recognition of it is part of the irony of the whole episode.

The second detail worth mentioning here is embedded in Socrates' remarks about Spartan wisdom (342B). The Spartans are reputed, says Socrates, to achieve pre-eminence among the Greeks not 'by fighting and by courage'[197] but by wisdom. At first glance this looks as though Socrates is dissociating wisdom from courage. But reflection brings doubt. Socrates is concerned apparently to clear the Spartans from their common repute of being courageous but stupid, and says that they are wise. This has the effect of removing at any rate one example of courage combined with stupidity, one example counter to the mutual implication of the virtues. It is, moreover, open to question whether Socrates really means to *substitute* Spartan wisdom for courage as the source of their reputation, to *add* Spartan wisdom, or to *reinterpret* Spartan courage as wisdom. Another doubtful point is how far Socrates is making concessions to popular usage in his account of the Spartan reputation.

'What Socrates really means' is not so much difficult to discover as a meaningless locution in a passage so rich in irony as this whole account of the Spartans. Nevertheless, if one were Protagoras listening with care to these remarks one would observe that Socrates is at least committed to the proposition that in ordinary usage 'courage' and 'wisdom' refer to two distinct qualities. There would be a temptation to try to make use of this in any return to the original discussion.

After some urbane but not un-barbed compliments, serving to remind the reader of Protagoras' pretensions, Socrates does indeed return to the original line of questioning (349B). Are the five names of good qualities, 'wisdom', 'moderation', 'courage', 'justice', and 'holiness', five names for one and the same thing, or is each the name for a distinct entity with its own 'power', not resembling any of the others? As before (330Aff.), it is perfectly possible to read this question as using the 'power' and 'resemblance' locutions to express the same point in different ways; the next question may be read as explaining and delimiting 'dissimilarity' by reference to the possession of different 'powers'. Socrates courteously invites Protagoras to make a fresh start; he will not hold it against Protagoras if he voices different opinions now from his earlier ones. That means that he will not use a contradiction on this topic between present and past views in his usual way. The sophist's feelings are also spared by the offer of an excuse for abandoning his old expressions; perhaps Protagoras was only putting Socrates to the test (349C–D). Accepting the implication that he had not been wholly serious, Protagoras takes advantage of the offer.

The ground on which the sophist then regroups his battered forces repays the closest inspection. He says, as he did before, that the five named good qualities are all parts of goodness. But he is now prepared to admit that four of them are reasonably close to one another. Only courage is very different from all the other four. Evidence advanced in support of the position consists in the observation (hardly new!) that many are exceedingly unjust, immoderate and stupid, but are none the less exceedingly courageous. Taylor rightly notes the subordination of the mutual implication of the good qualities to the question of their identity, in that the denial of the former is adduced as evidence in favour of denying the latter. But the principal problem here is why courage is singled out in this way, and why Protagoras abandons so much ground to his assailant.[198]

Why yield so much? We have seen the three previous rounds of argument all tending to drive a person of Protagoras' views or the like to assimilate the good qualities justice, moderation, wisdom and holiness. The basic form of the drive was the elicitation of premisses and inferences showing that actions issuing from each of these good qualities were the same as the actions issuing from each of the others. This tended to show that in so far as a good quality is, or consists in the possession of, a capacity to perform certain actions, one good quality is very like another. At least this similarity extends to holiness, justice, wisdom and moderation. If the actions in which they issue turn out to be the same, it will then be the case that the conceptual distinctions between them (if such there are) will not easily be able to find support in the argument that a person may have one of them without the others. If a person performs the relevant actions, and the good quality consists of a capacity to do those actions, it will be impossible to tell the difference from the outside between a person doing actions a, b, c, out of (say) holiness and a person doing the same actions out of (say) moderation. This we agreed was not the way the analogue of the parts of the face worked; it *is* possible to tell from the outside whether a person is blind and/or deaf.

Confronted with this line of argument, Protagoras took refuge in the irrelevant, or at best faintly relevant, long speech on the varieties of goodness. The ultimate cause of his downfall in that earlier round was not just the acceptance of the analogy but also the kind of thing he had said about the gentler good qualities in the Great Speech. The loose rhetorical talk, the ambiguous lists of good and bad qualities, the perpetual failure to be exact, all come home to the sophist as similar failings do to other victims of Socratic dialectic.

But most of the ambiguities and dubieties of the Great Speech passed courage by. None of the lists contain it; it is mentioned only indirectly, as part or whole of the art of war (322B), or as the (implied) opposite of cowardice (326C). The references (325E) to a *man's* goodness could possibly be hints at it, for courage and manliness are represented by the same Greek word (but women and children are mentioned in the same context). It is partly in response to Socratic prodding that Protagoras lists courage eventually among the good qualities (329E–330A).

But it does not seem quite right to infer from all this with Duncan[199] that 'courage, at least as normally understood, is not really virtue at all, contrary to vulgar opinion'. For Duncan's explanation of this depends heavily on his interpretation of the 'hedonistic' passage which follows; and Protagoras could not possibly foresee that turn of the argument, nor Plato legitimately foresee it on his behalf. Plato's readers would hardly thank him for leaving them in the dark about the place of courage in the earlier argument till they had worked through the 'hedonistic' argument.

On the other hand, simply to say that the Great Speech had fewer contradictions or ambiguities about courage than about the other good qualities, and that Protagoras can therefore fall back on courage after his defeat on the rest of the battlefield, is not really to explain anything. Such an explanation would lack finality unless one could assume that the Great Speech was substantially the work of the real Protagoras – an assumption many have refused to make. For if Plato composed the Speech, then the question arises why he wrote it in this way; why he made the position of courage easier to defend than that of the other good qualities.

We come back to the view that it must have seemed to Plato, as it still does to some people, easier to defend the separateness of courage than that of other virtues. The separation of courage from wisdom we have already seen (apropos of the *Laches*). Indeed the view persists today that an action can be brave or courageous even if performed in an unjust cause, or misguidedly, or impiously. Plato's own later theory of temperaments in his *Republic* (410E) and *Politicus* (306B ff.), with its opposition between the courageous and the moderate, is an example of this way of thinking. Even if it does not represent his own theory of the philosophic virtues (and I do not think it does), it shows that Plato saw the separateness of courage as an element either in a satisfactory account of the 'popular' virtues, or in the popular view of goodness and its varieties – or indeed both. One should not argue directly from Plato's later to his earlier works, and that is not what is happening here. The point is rather the inherent plausibility of the view of courage Plato appears to assume both for Protagoras and for his readers. It is likely to have been this plausibility which caused Plato to give his Protagoras no obvious confusion on courage in the Great Speech. The absence of courage from the lists of good qualities is explicable by (a) the dissimilarity between courage and the others and (b) the lack of any need for courage in internal affairs in a society where justice is supposed to rule.

Another feature of courage may also be relevant. In underplaying the role of courage in the goodness he claims to teach, Protagoras could be activated by political motives (in a broad sense of 'political'). It would be both impolitic and implausible for a sophist to claim overtly that he inculcated courage or 'manliness'. It would be impolitic because it would imply an insult to the manhood of his potential pupils and of those he never taught. It would be implausible because the kind of studies the sophists pursued had no obvious relevance to their pupils' behaviour in the test of courage on the field of battle. In the *Laches* the elderly gentlemen conspicuously do *not* think of sending their sons to a sophist to make good soldiers of them. It was other good qualities, such as justice and its congeners, which were, as we have seen, deeply involved in the art of speaking taught by virtually all the sophists. This need imply no conscious devaluation of courage.

Courage and wisdom: the first round 349B–351B

Whatever his motives, Protagoras does admit a resemblance

between the other four parts of goodness, a resemblance in which courage does not share. This special difference between bravery and the rest he founds, rationally, on an appeal to ordinary experience: 'You will find many men who are extremely[200] unjust and irreligious and wanton and ignorant, but most outstandingly courageous' (349D). Socrates stops Protagoras here to investigate his views so far. In the sequel Socrates does not impugn Protagoras' reasoning; so the object of his attack must be the truth of the premises. In particular he concerns himself with the relation between ignorance, knowledge and courage. The ensuing discussion has been reduced in recent years to a variety of brief and/or symbolic forms. But to do so can be risky, if it leads to the conclusion that some steps in the argument are irrelevant, or are even designed to confuse the issues. On the other hand simply to set out a translation in full is not necessary and would here be unhelpful. The following paraphrase attempts a middle way, retaining the essential question-and-answer format.

1   Are the brave confident, or something different? (349E) – They are confident and indeed bold to face what the many are afraid to face.
2   Is goodness fine? Is your claim to teach it a claim to teach a fine thing? – It is extremely fine.
3   Is only part of goodness fine, or every bit of it? – Every bit, as fine as possible.
4   (a) The knowledgeable are confident in the activity in which they are knowledgeable? (b) They are confident on account of their knowledge? – Yes; and (c i) The knowledgeable are in all things more confident than the ignorant and (c ii) the individual is more confident after acquiring knowledge than before (350A).
5   Have you ever seen any ignorant people in all the mentioned activities being confident (350B)? – Yes, indeed too confident.
6   Are the ignorant but confident brave? – Bravery would be shameful.
7   Bravery would be shameful because (a) the ignorant but

confident are mad and (b) bravery would then be madness and (c) madness is shameful.
8   How do you characterize the brave? Are they not the confident? – Yes, as I said before.
9   The ignorant but confident are not brave but mad (350C)?
10   And in that case too the extremely wise are extremely confident, and being extremely confident are extremely brave?
11   Therefore wisdom is bravery? – Socrates, your memory is inexact.

Confronted with the conclusion that wisdom is bravery, Protagoras diagnoses a mistake in Socrates' line of questioning and argument. This mistake he elaborates at some length by example, in default of any technical vocabulary for logic. What he illustrates is in fact an unwarranted conversion. Protagoras claims not to have said all the confident are brave, but only that all the brave are confident; he claims that Socrates' argument hinges on the premiss that all the confident are brave.

The sophist's diagnosis, like much of his argument in this dialogue, deserves our close attention; but it is not necessarily correct, and the absence of any rebuttal from Socrates does not prove it so. If Protagoras' diagnosis appears, as it does, to render otiose some of the steps and quirks in the Socratic dialectic, it does not follow that those steps or quirks are indeed superfluous. Nor does it follow, as Klosko suggests, that the steps in question are designed to make it less obvious (in a manner recommended by Aristotle) where the fallacy lies.[201] It could rather be the case that these steps are highly inconvenient to Protagoras, and that he would like to gloss over them. *A priori* discussion will not help us. It is worth investigating each step's significance. It is the more worth the trouble since some of the steps Protagoras apparently ignores are concerned specifically with his own claims as a sophist.

The question arises what Socrates' strategy is. Two recent commentators have found a change of strategy in the middle of the argument. The more hesitant and less exact of the two supposes that Socrates 'starts attempting to prove that courage is wisdom... But suddenly, for no apparent reason, he shifts to proving the converse of his original conclusion, wisdom is courage.'[202] A plausible idea, we find, is that 'Socrates has implicitly proved that courage is wisdom ... before he moves on to complete the biconditional by (fallaciously) proving that wisdom is courage'. But the interpreter adds 'There is ... however, no textual evidence to support this interpretation of the argument.' This formulation of the change in strategy will not do unless the statements 'courage is wisdom' and 'wisdom is courage' are taken as Pauline predications, rather than as the identifications they look like.

More immediately usable is Taylor's version, to the general effect that some early steps in Socrates' argument lead toward the proposition that all courageous people are wise ('$(x)(Cx \rightarrow Wx)$'); that Socrates implicitly, but not explicitly, proves this proposition, and then turns to the proposition that all wise people are courageous, and proves that too. On this type of interpretation the early placing of 4 above obscures the order of events; 4 is clearly directed to proving that all wise people are courageous, but appears in the middle of propositions aimed at proving that all courageous people are wise. The order of questions in early Platonic dialogues is as elastic as Aristotle's *Topics* would lead us to expect; but the postulate of a change of strategy would be more coherent if there were a definite single place at which the strategy changes. The intertwining of the two stages, and the absence of explicitness about them, remain puzzling.

The puzzles of the whole passage are approachable by way of comment on successive steps in Plato's discussion. It is important for the commentator to discuss each and every admission Protagoras makes. No solution is satisfactory which omits to consider the implications of all of them. So let us begin with 1, and observe that at least the first half of Protagoras' admission here is unproblematic. Protagoras openly agrees in so many words that the brave are confident. That is what he says in his later diagnosis that he has said, and nobody has ever disputed that he has said at least that. But what else does he say?

With this question the problems start. Protagoras volunteers the suggestion that the brave are bold to face what 'the many' are afraid to face (349E). The implications of this need to be drawn out.[203] There is a strong antithesis in Protagoras' sentence between 'the brave' and 'the many'. Clearly the many are not brave. On the face of it there seems to be no reason why we should not take the many to include *all* who are not brave.

One could imagine a third class, those who are not brave, but nevertheless make bold to face the same dangers as the brave and one could, further, imagine the exclusion of that class from 'the many'. The first of these imaginations will not be beyond any who distinguish between 'confident' and 'brave'. But the second is more difficult. It would require us to read Protagoras' assertion as saying that (a) the brave are confident, (b) the brave, and the confident but not brave, are bold to face what the many who are neither brave nor confident are afraid to face. This seems an unnatural way to read the sentence. More natural is to read it as saying that the many who are not brave are not bold in action, and do not have the confidence to face danger.

Strictly, Protagoras has not said that all confident people are brave; but what he has said gives rise to strong suspicion that he means the logical equivalent of this, namely, that all non-brave people are non-confident. One condition of this interpretation is a closeness in meaning of the expressions 'bold to face X' and 'confident in the face of X'; Protagoras' sentence would appear to associate them closely; we suspect, indeed, synonymy, though we cannot be one hundred per cent certain. Protagoras' remarks are vague, his terms undefined, but our suspicions of his meaning remain. When trouble arises later, it is well to remember the awkward and paradoxical fact that Protagoras both has and has not said that all the non-brave are non-confident. He has not said it in so many words; he has not, on the strictest possible interpretation of his words, implied it; but he has said it, in the sense that such is the impression his words convey.

After this we should not be surprised if Protagoras later first agrees and then denies that he has said that the confident are brave. It would not be the first time that Protagoras has fallen victim to his own loose and rhetorical speech. Unsurprising also should be Socrates' mixture in the sequel of two lines of argument, one resting on 'the brave are confident', and the other on 'the confident are brave'.

Steps 2 and 3 are less obviously relevant to the subsequent argument. They invite denunciation for superfluity or for leading to fallacy. But that goodness is fine, and that bravery, as part of goodness, is fine, are useful admissions for Socrates to extract in view of the function of 'shameful', the normal antonym of 'fine', in steps 6 and 7. The claim to teach, which puts in an appearance in 2, is more isolated; its only manifest link with what follows is through the notion of 'learning' or 'acquiring knowledge' in 4 (c ii), and in general with the idea of knowledge. This link may seem to a superficial glance tenuous, but clearly Protagoras' claims are important to the dialogue as a whole, and we shall see as the discussion proceeds how they affect this particular argument.

Step 4 is even more complicated in its conversational development (350A–B) than in the summary given above. The text has at first a single example, that of diving into wells. That exemplifies the suggestion that the experts' confidence is due to their expertise. The knowledgeable are confident, the ignorant apparently not. Taylor[204] is clearly right to call this premiss in question. 'There may be cases where the expert, on the strength of his expertise, decides that something is too risky, and is not prepared to do it, while the non-expert is willing to have a go, either because he is ignorant of the risks, or because he regards them as outweighed by some other factors.' Taylor points out that, in any form which takes account of these points, the proposition will not bear the weight the argument requires of it. But this criticism is not necessarily the whole story. Unless we are prepared to believe either that Protagoras would have given the game away without reason, or that Plato would arbitrarily have made him do so, it cannot be the whole story – and Taylor justifies neither side of this dilemma. We should surely look next for reasons why this premiss should be either generally plausible, or acceptable to Protagoras, or both. In any case we should bear in mind that Socrates is at least aware of the possibility of exceptions to the rule to which his questions seem to tend, since his next question is 5, whether the sophist has seen any ignorant people being confident. What is going on?

It is possible, but not specially likely, that what is going on is an equivocation by somebody on the word 'confident'. If we look to the inner feelings of the persons involved in the activities mentioned by Socrates, the general proposition Protagoras volunteers in response has an air of plausibility. The parent will, it is true, rescue the child where the fireman (or well-diver?) will not. But in doing or not doing something relevant to his profession the fireman will act with an inner confidence born of experience and training and unavailable to the inexpert parent. Neverthless, it is pretty clear that (whatever 'confident' meant at the outset of the discussion) by the end it means confident in behaviour rather than merely in feeling.[205] For the text suggests that one can see (350B) the confidence exhibited, and one cannot see a feeling but only the behaviour resulting from it. On the whole this is confirmed by the Protagorean sentence about 'the many' (349E): the implication of that is that those who are afraid to face a situation do not face it; the possibility of overcoming fear is there left out of account, so far as one can see. It is hard to resist the impression that the notion of equivocation on 'confidence' is special pleading, unlikely to give the solution to the real question why Protagoras should give so much away without apparent necessity.

More likely is another way of modifying the absoluteness of the propositions boiled down into 4. The modification this time is to insert in them the word 'normally'. It is true, or at least seems plausible to me, that under normal circumstances the person who goes down a well or joins in a cavalry fight with most confidence is the trained expert. Confidence here is not incompatible with a professional wariness of dangers, or with cautious procedures designed to minimize them. *Normally* experts are confident in the exercise of their expertise, and will do things the inexpert would not dream of doing. *Normally* on being trained a man will similarly be more confident than before, and will do things he would not have dreamt of before. Of course there are also things he will not do, in his professional capacity, and among these are some which an untrained person might do either from mere ignorance of risk or from countervailing motives; but such things will not come up very often, and partake of the exceptional. They would certainly be exceptions in the cases of the two arts actually mentioned by Socrates in his inductive questioning of Protagoras. We should bear in mind the version of 4 weakened by the insertion of 'normally' in assessing the rest of the argument; and we should also bear in mind the inductive procedure Socrates has used.

The induction makes it necessary to introduce at this stage the problem Protagoras sets to Socrates, the reader, and perhaps to himself, when he volunteers the generalization that knowledge increases confidence 'in all other things' (350A). How much is included? How do we fill in the blank cheque offered by 'things' (or the Greek neuter plural it represents)?

It is not easy to suggest any other interpretation of Protagoras' generalizing expression than 'in all other arts'. But then the old question crops up again; is political goodness, the subject of Protagoras' instruction, an art? Or is it not? He implies at times that it is not, but he cannot consistently maintain this, and does not in fact maintain it throughout. The mention of his claim to teach (349E) may serve to remind us that what one teaches or learns is, analytically, a 'subject', an 'art'. In the long run Protagoras must teach a subject, however he tries to dissociate himself from teachers of other subjects. That carries the implication (after Protagoras' recent admissions) that the person who knows his subject will be (normally) more confident than he was before, and (other things being equal) more confident than someone who has not learnt it. This is of course no bad thing for Protagoras. He has conveyed the impression that the confident are brave, and courage is a part, acknowledged by him, of political goodness. But it is awkward for him that teaching, learning, art and other intellectual terms should be so closely associated with courage, when he has said one can be brave without being wise. But this awkwardness does not yet appear openly.

It waits, in fact, till Socrates has a change of tack. With the question 5, Socrates shifts Protagoras' attention to the exceptions, those rash ignorant people who rush in where the experts in their knowledge will not tread. People with this sort of confidence are at least in some cases *too* confident; are they brave? Protagoras replies in 6 that they are not; they are mad, and, 7, bravery would be shameful. Clearly steps 7(b) and 7(c) are required by the argument and omitted by the sophist in normal conversational brevity and looseness. This disturbs neither Socrates nor us. But there is a deeper problem, raised by Taylor, which we must solve.

Taylor says:[206] 'Even if the state of being daring but lacking in knowledge is not itself any part of excellence, and *a fortiori* not courage, it does not follow that those in that state do not possess some *other* state which is courage.' From 'All the ignorant and confident are brave' and 'All the ignorant and confident are mad', it does not follow, as Protagoras appears to think it follows, that 'Bravery is madness' as 7(b) has it. Taylor explains that Socrates 'probably' makes in silence a causal assumption about courage and madness and their effect on action. But he stresses that his suggested line of argument is different from that in the text.

The following is also not explicit in the text. It cannot be said to claim more than probability. But apart from its immediate explanatory function, it accounts for some otherwise superfluous features of the text, and its wider explanatory power may recommend it.

Protagoras, as Plato has just (with apparent casualness) reminded us, *teaches* political goodness. Political goodness (as we have also been reminded) has parts, of which one is courage. For good measure, we may recollect that Protagoras claimed to be specially good at teaching political goodness (328A–B). Teaching confers knowledge or 'wisdom' on those who learn. The ignorant are those who have not learnt, i.e. (normally) those who have not been taught. (Those incapable of learning are sub-human (323B–C, 322D).) Presumably those, and only those, who have learnt the relevant part of goodness possess courage. In that case people in 'the state of being daring but lacking in knowledge' cannot 'possess some other state which is courage'. Lack of the relevant teaching and knowledge excludes the possession of courage. Protagoras cannot suggest that whether somebody is knowledgeable or ignorant has nothing to do with whether they are courageous or not – unless he is willing to suggest that what he teaches is not knowledge, or to confess openly that it omits courage.

Here the reader may reasonably want to put an objection. If

this is the point, and Plato saw it, why not cut the cackle by simple and succinct statement of it? What is Plato on about all this time? The answer can only lie in Plato's inscrutable purposes. But he has provided good evidence that he did see, if not the particular point, at least the general point; and he did nevertheless construct the dialogue at the length it now has.

At the end (361A–C) Socrates reminds Protagoras of the paradoxical fact that Socrates has been trying to show first that goodness is not teachable and, secondly, that it is knowledge, whereas Protagoras has been trying to show that it is not knowledge but is teachable. Now Socrates could, if Plato had been so minded, have pointed this out at a much earlier stage. It could have been the starting point. It could have been the *coup de grâce* at the end of the first set of arguments. But Plato, for whatever reason, chose not to make it so, but rather to draw out the elaborate argument that the dialogue does present. One cannot therefore object to the interpretation of individual arguments by means of thoughts about teaching and knowledge on the grounds that Plato, if he had such thoughts, would have abbreviated the argument by expressing them; for he had indeed similar thoughts, and did not in fact shorten the argument. One is left not only with a coherent explanation (expounded above) of the particular train of thought about courage, but also with an explanation of Socrates' mention, otherwise superfluous, of Protagoras' claims to teach.

Before turning to the characterization of the brave which follows, we may spend a moment considering the comparatives of adjectives which have made appearance in the argument so far. Some take virtually no account of them;[207] but they have some interest. First, the sophist has admitted that goodness (and presumably its parts) are very fine, and even 'as fine as possible'. This does not play a great part in the argument; but it does prevent Protagoras from suggesting that confidence without knowledge is a form of courage which is merely less fine or more shameful than other forms. Whether Plato saw this, or cared if he did, it is not possible to say. The inductive conclusion drawn in 4(c) is put in the comparative form, though the two examples leading up to it are both in the positive form (350A). Socrates has chosen at least one example, namely, that of cavalry fighting, where the folly of taking on the job when untrained is so obvious that no sensible person would feel *any* confidence in doing it. The example of well-diving, plausibly or no, is put by Socrates, and agreed by Protagoras, in the positive. Why does Protagoras shift, in his volunteered conclusion, to the comparative? The answer to this can again only be conjectural; but the effect of his shift is to make Socrates' next question much easier to ask. If Protagoras had admitted in the positive degree that the knowledgeable are confident and the ignorant not, it would then be difficult to get him to agree that some are both ignorant and confident. Conversely, if Protagoras had in mind exceptions such as he admits in answer to the next question, then it would be difficult for him in the first place to volunteer positively that the knowledgeable are confident and the ignorant not. The course of the interrogation flows more freely as the passage stands, with the comparatives. The importance of this will emerge below.

The adverb 'too' in the next sentence (350B) is difficult. It can mean in Greek either 'very much' or 'too much'; it is not certain which Protagoras means. The two meanings shade into each other. If he meant that some ignorant people are very confident, that would sit uneasily beside his previous agreement that the knowledgeable are more confident; it is just this sort of difficulty that Plato's Protagoras has avoided by his use of comparatives. The probability is therefore that 'too' means here not 'very' but 'more than is good for the agents'. Hence, whatever may be true of the comparatives, 'too' has probably no connection with the superlatives (possibly meaning 'very . . .') occurring later in the argument.

Smoothed thus by some not wholly incautious remarks of Protagoras, the discussion arrives at the end of 7. Socrates now has a question to put which has given rise to a lively controversy over text and meaning (350B). 'Well now, what do you say about the courageous? Isn't it that they are the confident?'[208] Socrates' question receives an affirmative answer, containing the clear implication that Protagoras has said this before. The textual controversy concerns the definite article, in front of 'courageous'. It is there in the Greek manuscripts, but some scholars have wished to emend it away.[209] Others have claimed that the meaning is the same as if it were away.[210] If it is removed or if the passage is interpreted as if it were removed, then Protagoras *includes* the class of brave people in the class of confident people. But if it is left and given full face value, he says that the class of brave people is *coextensive with* the class of confident people.

The evidence here is not of the clearest. Passages adduced to show that Plato's Socrates could use the definite article thus without making classes coextensive turn out to be inconclusive, not to say doubtful; but other people used this type of expression more loosely, as one might expect.[211] This raises the possibility that Protagoras is supposed to misunderstand a loaded question; but this possibility would make Plato's procedure so tortuous that it can pretty safely be ruled out.[212] Though medieval scribes frequently insert the definite article, especially where there is already one in a parallel position, it is perhaps best to keep the MSS reading where possible. It is also best to give Socrates exactitude of expression where possible. So let us at any rate explore the consequences of allowing both Plato's scribes and Socrates the benefit of the doubt in this sentence.

The consequences are, roughly, as follows. In the light of our analysis of 1 above, we see that Protagoras conveyed, wittingly or unwittingly, the impression that confidence was not merely a necessary but also a sufficient condition of bravery. Later, on empirical evidence, he admits some exceptions. But in an unwary moment he agrees to the proposition he implied earlier, that the confident are brave, included in the seductive form 'the brave are *the* confident'. Socrates then (350C) asks the question 9, which is a combination of elements from 6 and 7, and proceeds to 10. 10 draws on 4(c i) to show that the wisest are extremely confident, and on 'the confident are brave' to show that the wisest, because they are extremely confident, are extremely brave. This line of interpretation would have it that Protagoras' unwary answer is conditioned by his previous implications; that his mistake in agreeing to the *equation* of confident people and brave people is the result of his earlier imprecision still reverberating in his mind. In that case, when he pulls Socrates up at the conclusion of 11, and says (350C) that he was not asked whether the confident are brave, he is prevaricating; he was asked something which included that, but he was not asked that in exactly those terms.

Prolonged reflection on the whole passage leaves the impression that this interpretation is a possible one; but there are objections to it. The principal difficulty is the resulting close proximity of two propositions on Protagoras' lips which contradict each other. Protagoras has to state in one speech some exceptions to the proposition that the confident are brave and then agree in his very next words, after a short sentence from Socrates, that 'confident' and 'brave' are two coextensive classes, which implies that there are no exceptions. Scholarly refusal to accept this juxtaposition would be understandable, even if Protagoras has made a rash remark earlier. The refusal would be the more readily intelligible in that it absolves Protagoras, not from the whole but from the worst of the charge of prevarication in his 'pulling-up' speech. So let us now explore the consequences of *refusing* to accept such a mistake from Protagoras.

If we assume that either the Greek is loosely expressed or the manuscripts have added a definite article, the sophist's implication in 1 that the confident and the brave are the same people remains dormant for a little longer.

Socrates has received admission that knowledge improves confidence, and that the brave are confident, and that confident people who are ignorant are not brave. His next step is 9, still a simple reminder of previous admissions. With 10 he turns to the topic of wisdom, or knowledge. Apart from his change of terminology, to be discussed briefly below, his sentence here is ambiguous. In Taylor's clear and helpful formulation,[213] using 'daring' where I have used 'confident', one can read question 10 'either as "Since they are most daring they are therefore most courageous", i.e. $(x)\ (Dx \rightarrow Cx)$, or as "Since they are most daring (and also wisest) they are therefore most courageous", i.e. $(x)\ (Dx + Wx \rightarrow Cx)$'. Taylor can find no conclusive argument to enable us to choose; no more can I. Protagoras' diagnosis (350Cff.) assumes the first of Taylor's versions, '$(x)\ (Dx \rightarrow Cx)$', and pulls Socrates up for relying on this. But Protagoras is biased and selective; naturally biased in his own favour, he either omits or fails to notice the impression he conveyed in 1 earlier that he believed the proposition '(x) (Dx→Cx)'.

Even if Protagoras were wholly honest, his understanding of the situation need not be Plato's. If we are meant to appreciate, and imagine Socrates as appreciating, the impression conveyed in 1, then the use of '(x) (Dx→Cx)' by Socrates acquires a point; the sophist's earlier words are turned against him in a way we recognize, even though he can still deny any formal implication of the kind his opponent needs.

Suppose, however, that this point is not Plato's intention. Suppose Plato had in mind for Socrates the alternative proposition '(x) (Dx+Wx→Cx)'. This supposition puts the argument in a rather different light. We now have 1, 'All the brave are confident'; and 9, 'All the ignorant but confident are not brave.'

If the alternatives 'wise' and 'ignorant' are regarded as mutually exclusive and exhaustive, then these two propositions imply that, 12, 'All the wise-and-confident are brave'; which is '(x) (Dx+Wx→Cx)'. We have now only to make sense of the superlatives in the Greek statement of the proposition 12. But that is not simple, for to suppose degrees of wisdom implies degrees also of ignorance; and 'wise' and 'ignorant' are no longer mutually exclusive and exhaustive, but rather gradable. Indeed we have suggested that one reason for Protagoras' introduction of degrees of comparison in 4(c) was to avoid a clear-cut division between the wise who are confident and the ignorant who are not. Socrates appears to be relying on that very admission of Protagoras'. If knowledge gives greater confidence, then by the same token greater knowledge gives greater confidence still; whatever implausibilities attach to one proposition attach to the other; whatever caveats were entered for the one may be entered for the other. The greater the well-diver's expertise the more wells he will (normally) be confident in his ability to dive into. If that is at all plausible, then it is also plausible that the extremely expert will (normally) be extremely confident. But does it follow that they will be extremely brave? Clearly not. Ordinary usage is against the very idea; we do not call 'brave' those who can do, by reason of their skills, things the unskilled will not normally attempt.

It seems that the argument salvages the plausibility of the first half of 10, only to remove all plausibility from the other half. But there are some conditions under which the half thus robbed of plausibility can regain some of it. It is plausible on the premiss that the confident are brave, a premiss which Protagoras has given the impression of believing at an early stage in the conversation.

Another such condition is more complex. Plato may have had in mind a sort of informal equation which, formally expressed, would read 'Wisdom + Confidence = Bravery', and he may have thought informally that if one added to both the elements on the left hand side of this equation one was also adding to the right-hand side. This possibility strikes me with less force than it used to. It seems too difficult to think of in informal terms, and too unlikely to have been excogitated by Plato in mathematical formality. It is better to suppose that, believing Protagoras to have suggested earlier that the confident are brave, Socrates wishes to suggest that the more confident the braver – a suggestion not actually implied by 'the confident are brave' but not too far from it for a sophist (or reader) unused to close logic.

On no interpretation of Socrates on wisdom, confidence and bravery does this argument compel Protagoras to accept that wisdom is courage, that wisdom is a species of courage, or that courage is a species of wisdom; but this argument is not the whole dialogue, and we should not be too ready to convict *Plato* of logical error. Certainly the *equation* of wisdom and courage does not follow from 1 and 9 above, nor from 'the extremely wise are extremely brave'. It would not even follow from the conjunction of either of these with the proposition 'the brave are wise', which Socrates shows no interest in extracting from Protagoras. For Taylor has rightly pointed out that the coextensiveness of the classes 'the wise' and 'the brave' would not prove that wisdom and bravery were the same property. But the final stages of this argument are rapid, and Socrates uncharacteristically gives Protagoras no time to digest and answer the individual questions which are thus hurriedly sewn together. Perhaps the conclusion also is, as it were, in shorthand? It is worth going back to the place of origin of this particular argument to see how the conclusion may be understood.

There is indeed an interesting parallel between the origin of the argument and its end. The conclusion mentions in one and the same breath and speech a couple of superlatives and the identity of two virtues. The identity is derived to all appearances from the remark including the superlatives. It is unlikely to be coincidental that the argument took its rise from a remark of Protagoras which coupled the non-identity of the virtues with a point concerning a number of superlatives (349D). The relationship between the two in Protagoras' original words may elucidate the relationship between them in Socrates' conclusion. Protagoras had deployed, as his *sole* reason for asserting a difference between courage and the other good qualities, the known existence of people who were extremely gifted with courage but not with the others. If Socrates can demolish this sole reason for asserting a difference, he is entitled to claim that there is no difference, until or unless his opponent can provide another reason. On this reading, Socrates' strategy is not to prove his point of view but to demolish Protagoras' reason for holding *his*. This would not necessarily finish the argument; but it would put the ball firmly in Protagoras' court. Nothing in the text says that the argument is finished, and in fact the ball is left in Protagoras' court.

If one could press home this line of thinking, one problem, how Socrates can think he has proved the identity of courage and wisdom, would cease to be troublesome. But there are a number of obstacles. The first is that Protagoras has contended that courage is not merely distinct from the other virtues, and not identical with any of them, but actually *very* different (349D). To demolish the assertion that two things differ very greatly would not prove their identity. Secondly Protagoras' premiss was that some people are not wise but extremely brave. That means 'Not (All extremely brave people are wise).' To deny this would be to assert that 'All extremely brave people are wise'. But Socrates does not assert that anywhere. What he asserts, at best, is that 'All extremely wise people are extremely brave'; and that looks perfectly compatible with the denial that 'All extremely brave people are wise'.

Let us take the difference problem first. In admitting a resemblance between four of the good qualities Protagoras is presumably bowing to Socrates' previous dialectic. That dialectic aimed to extract an admission that the good qualities concerned were similar. In that discussion (329E–332A) similarity meant having the same 'power'; and it was the 'power' of a good quality which distinguished it from other good qualities. If Protagoras now admits that the four good qualities are similar, he is presumably responding to that earlier argument. He is therefore agreeing that the four good qualities have the same 'power', and hence are not differentiable by any distinction he has thought of yet. By contrast he says that courage is different, very different. By that he need mean no more than that, in contrast to the other good qualities which turn out to have the same 'power', courage has a distinct 'power', and is therefore a distinct good quality.

Furthermore, the argument Protagoras uses to support this distinction proves no more than that courage is a distinct quality. That a person can possess courage (to however high a degree) and not possess the other good qualities at all proves only that courage is sufficiently different not to be the same good quality; it does not prove any other difference.

Both Protagoras' assertion and his supporting argument are such that it is after all sufficient, in order to leave *any* distinction between courage and the rest unsupported, to show that Protagoras' argument for a great difference will not work. In essence, Socrates' point is that the difference of 'power' is illusory.

The second difficulty, over the denial that 'All extremely brave people are wise', is harder to deal with. Indeed it is hard to think of any way of dealing with it that does not end in convicting either Plato or at least Plato's Socrates of a mistake of omission or commission. On any interpretation this seems to be true; it is not just a vice of one particular set of interpretative assumptions. But it is worth seeing how far the present set of assumptions can reduce the element of commission and account for the element of omission in this area. Plato (or his Socrates) is perhaps guilty; but he may not be *presumed* guilty.

Let us return to degrees of comparison. In his inductive line of questioning (350A-B), Socrates requested admissions in the positive degree which would have implied, in generalized form, that the ignorant are not confident; hence the positive form of 4 (a) and (b) above. From this it would have followed without trouble that the ignorant (or 'stupid') are not at the same time extremely brave. Surprise is not in order if, as we have seen, Protagoras offers instead his own generalization, to the effect that the knowledgeable are *more* confident – a generalization which does not have the same *immediately* devastating result. Socrates must try again. Further, he must try more indirectly. If he can extract an admission that the degree of confidence is directly proportional to the degree of knowledge, then he is near his goal. For then *no* knowledge ought to imply *no* confidence; and the most ignorant (or 'stupid') will not be brave after all. Protagoras has admitted only that the knowledgeable are more confident; if he can be persuaded to agree that *the more* knowledgeable one is, *the more* confident one is, then Socrates will be able to argue that the less knowledgeable one is, the less confident one is. But that will give him the direct proportion he requires; no knowledge, no confidence, and hence *no* bravery.

At the point (350C) where the argument starts to rush to its conclusion, Socrates is in fact attempting to persuade Protagoras, under rapid fire, that the wisest (or 'more knowledgeable') are the most confident and the bravest. If Protagoras admits either of these attributes of the wisest, let alone both, he will then be in danger of admitting the direct proportion between wisdom (or knowledge) and confidence which Socrates requires. He will, for good measure, if he admits that the wisest are the bravest, be in danger of admitting that wisdom is in direct proportion to courage; and thus that no wisdom implies no courage. He will thus be in danger of abandoning his supporting statement for his assertion that courage is distinct from wisdom, and hence having to abandon the distinction itself unless he can think of some other support fast.

But Plato's Socrates skates over this with extreme rapidity; indeed it would be more exact to say that he does not mention it, and that it has to be excogitated from his text by dint of taking seriously the otherwise pointless shifts in degrees of comparison. What excuses these sins of omission? Socrates, at least, has a motive for them; if he is too direct, Protagoras will take flight. Does Plato have a motive? That, as usual, is matter for conjecture. But it is a plausible conjecture that Plato (a) thought that his argument could bother a Protagoras, but (b) did not set much store by it as an argument.

If that seems too sweeping, consider the general situation of the argument once more. Protagoras has defended himself by taking up the position that it is possible for the most stupid to be brave. In broad outline this can be demolished if confidence turns out to be a necessary condition of courage, and learning a necessary condition of confidence. Plato sees (and gives his Socrates) a possible approach to doing this by taking 'wisdom' or 'learning' or 'knowledge' to refer to the arts, skills and crafts of ordinary life. But Plato does not have in mind, in his own philosophy, any such reference for 'wisdom'. He intends some form of knowledge which, however *analogous* to such arts and crafts, is distinguished from them by its subject matter. There is no need for Plato to set much store by the argument, and hence no need for him to do more than set out its main theme in as dramatically plausible a way as possible, with give and take between two clever disputants.

But Plato's Protagoras has other problems. It is hard for him to answer Socrates by saying 'I didn't refer to arts of the kind you mention'; for if he does, he will be asked 'What kind of "stupidity" *did* you mean?' To this question it is hard to think of any answer that will not lead to his embarrassment. He has failed to formulate a distinction between the arts in general and the wisdom or 'art' of politics which he claims to teach. If he places too much emphasis on his teaching as the transmission of an 'art' or 'wisdom' he will end up unable to distinguish between 'wisdom' and goodness at all. A sophist is subject to this kind of embarrassment. If Plato does not yet bring this embarrassment out into the open that does not imply its absence.

What Plato does is once again to postpone the revelation of such embarrassments, by giving Protagoras a way out. The exit is a little ignominious, if (and only if) one looks below the surface of the text. For Protagoras extracts himself by taking one possible meaning of Socrates' words, which does not go to the heart of the matter, and denying that he had uttered words bearing that meaning – even though he had earlier conveyed the impression that the resulting proposition ('All the confident are brave') was acceptable. It is only on a superficial level that Protagoras triumphs here.

The above version of the argument uses the mutual substitutability of terms such as 'wisdom' and 'knowledge' (both occurring in this passage) and 'art' (occurring earlier). Indeed no account of the argument can do without the transition from one of these nouns to another and back without apparent difference of sense – and the same goes for their adjectival and even verbal counterparts. But Socrates is not necessarily portrayed as wholly guileless in his choice of words in context. Taylor[214] is right that 'the appearance of equivocation is illusory'; but there is more to be said.

First, the interchangeability of 'knowledge' and 'wisdom' has become dialectically acceptable since early in the dialogue. Protagoras offered no objection when Socrates introduced 'knowledge' as a substitute for 'wisdom', in elaborating on Protagoras' behalf the notion of distinct good qualities (330B). If there were to be any illicit shift in our later passage, it would be up to Protagoras to point to it, not Socrates.

Secondly, Socrates probably uses 'wisdom' and its adjective 'wise' at the end of the argument in order to make his final conclusion in the terms in which Protagoras first and most prominently mentioned the relevant part of goodness, and in which Socrates had broached the question of its identity with moderation. The reason why the whole argument is not conducted in these same terms can hardly be other than to extract answers from Protagoras as favourable as possible by lulling him with terms which will remind him no more than is strictly necessary of the points at issue concerning 'wisdom' as a part of goodness.

Somewhat similarly Socrates in the next major argument talks near the beginning about knowledge (352B), and only returns to the topic of wisdom, by that name, near the end (360D). It is naturally doubtful whether Plato was thinking of the effect on his fictional Protagoras, or on his readers. Either way, this parallel in structure between these two arguments is of interest.

Protagoras also uses the same shift in terminology when

summarizing the argument and supplying a similar one by way of illustration (350E–351B). Protagoras also introduces the comparative, in repetition of what Socrates has said. But he does not go into the detail of the consequences, leaping straight into his parallel argument from the equivalent of 4(c) to the conclusion equivalent to 11. About the intervening interrogation he is swiftly and vaguely dismissive. He assumes that Socrates meant to *prove*, directly, the equation of wisdom and courage.

It has been a temptation to commentators to follow the same path. But Protagoras may legitimately be represented as an interested party; he omits some steps of the argument altogether; there is no good reason for supposing him to be giving us a fair account. He does a good job of its kind; the steps he gives do either occur or look as if they occur in Socrates' line of questioning, and some which he omits he alludes to later, as in the distinction he draws between power which comes from knowledge or from *madness*, and strength which does not; this alludes to the distinction he wanted earlier to draw between courage and confidence. But his successful and good job is incomplete (it lacks any allusion to the superlatives) and superficial. What is more, it brings one very important question to a head.

That question has been long postponed; it is introduced now, as we shall see, only when Protagoras lays himself directly open to it. But we may postpone it ourselves for just a moment more, in order to answer in brief some queries which have arisen in the course of our inquiry into Plato's meaning in the argument about courage, confidence and wisdom.

One such query concerned the change of Socratic strategy which has struck at least a couple of recent analysts.[215] In so far as Socrates does change his strategy we are now in a position to explain the change as due to Protagoras' responses. Socrates started out, we saw, to get his interlocutor to admit something leading directly to the proposition he wanted. But Protagoras gave him, not the assertion of positive degree that he needed, but a comparative one (350B), leaving open the negative of the proposition Socrates wanted. So Socrates had to shift to other means of extraction, to methods less direct, as befitted an opponent not unable to see what was coming. The goal of the interrogation remains the same; it is the abilities of his opponent which cause Socrates to resort to indirectness. Socrates changes tactics rather than strategy. The explanation lies in the exact nature of Protagoras' replies, and in particular in the logical implications of his use of those degrees of comparison which have recently suffered some scholarly neglect. A major part of Socrates' dialectical genius as portrayed in this dialogue is his capacity to react immediately to his opponent's responses, whether casual or canny.

A probable, but less than certain, illustration of this capacity is Socrates' treatment in this argument of Protagoras' casual elaboration of the confidence of the brave (349E). If the manuscripts are right in offering the disputed definite article (350C), then that elaboration forms the basis for the resultant directly damaging admission. If the manuscripts are wrong, then Socrates still apparently makes use of it, rhetorically: he seeks to persuade Protagoras to agree to his 'superlative' sentence (350C) by juxtaposing 'most confident' and 'most brave' in such a way as to leave open the possibility that he is arguing from confidence to bravery, and to tempt into agreement a man who has conveyed the impression of belief that the confident are brave. The sophist answers as if sensitive to this juxtaposition of confidence and bravery. In doing so, he chooses a counter-attack which, deliberately or not, ignores the impression he had conveyed earlier that he found the coextensiveness of confident people and brave people acceptable.

The counter-attack makes a verbal point. The claim not to have said that the confident are brave is verbally true; the sophist has not said it in so many words. Though his criticism of Socrates is (if one ignores his conveyed impression) logically correct, the criticism rests ultimately not so much on the opinions Protagoras has (with more or less exactitude) expressed, but rather on the words he has used to express them. In this respect there is a resemblance between this criticism and some of his earlier efforts. Most of all it recalls his original attack on Simonides. That attack too depended on a purely verbal contradiction, regardless of the real import of what was being said. Protagoras' critique of a genuine poet is all of a piece with his critique of a genuine dialectician. His shallowness does not plumb the depths of either. For all his grasp of surface considerations of logic, his criticism matches the profundity not even of Simonides, let alone of Socrates. Plato has drawn his portrait with a scathing consistency, even if not wholly without respect for his quick intelligence. If this view lays Socrates open to a charge of captiousness for taking such advantage of a casual and volunteered remark, he expiates the crime by abandoning the advantage as soon as Protagoras clarifies his position, and by turning at once to the real question.

The good life and pleasure 351B–359A

If the real question of the dialogue turns out after all to be the nature of the good life (360E), then how does that question arise at this juncture? In the large literature on the 'hedonistic' passage which comes next, scholars have mostly treated it as an abrupt departure.[216] Taylor even suggests that the argument about pleasure is an afterthought. The full refutation of such a view must remain implicit in the account below, designed to set the argument firmly in its place in the dialogue as a whole.

But there are things to be said about the transitional remarks leading into the discussion of pleasure; and it seems right to start with another look at the gravamen of Protagoras' foregoing counter-attack. Protagoras develops, in illustration of his logical point, an analogy between the relationship of bravery, confidence and wisdom, on the one hand, and capability, strength and wisdom on the other. He would, he says, have agreed that the strong are capable, but not that the capable are strong – which (we may note) is in full accord with the variety of 'powers' or capabilities in the myth of his Great Speech (320Dff.). He adds (351A) quite consistently that capability comes from knowledge, but not only from knowledge. 'Spirit' (Taylor has 'animal boldness')[217] and madness are sources of capability no less than knowledge is. Analogously, not all the confident are brave, though all the brave are confident. Confidence, like capability, has more than one source. Confidence comes from 'art', from 'spirit', or from madness, the same three alternatives as capability. (Protagoras points up the resemblance, and 'art' and 'knowledge' are interchangeable terms here as elsewhere.) As capability and confidence are parallel, so are strength and bravery. As strength is due both to nature and to good nurture of the body so courage is due to both nature and good nurture of the soul. From all this two links with what follows emerge. One concerns knowledge, the other good nurture. Let us take good nurture of the soul first.

We are all familiar with the situation that there is general consensus as to what constitutes bodily strength or fitness, but a notorious level of dissent as to what constitutes a good soul. If courage derives from good nurture of the soul, then what is the good soul which good nurture is designed to produce? If courage derives from natural endowment, then from what sort of natural endowment? Protagoras here has closed one chapter only to open another. Where does he stand in the inevitable controversy on the ideals of man, on the question what is a good human soul? If he cannot say, then his answer to Socrates is hollow, and the distinctions he makes in it are vain. Confidence proceeds from 'art' or from 'spirit' or from 'madness'. Courage derives from a well-nurtured soul. If a well-nurtured soul is not one which has acquired an 'art', nor one which has 'spirit', then what is it? Evidently not a 'mad' one. Then what? No Platonist should have to search long for the answer to that one; the early Platonic Socrates can be credited with a sense of the importance of pleasure in human life without loading him with all the psychological baggage of the *Republic*. What is more natural in our context than that Socrates should enquire about the place of pleasure in the good nurture of the soul?

Of course, he talks not directly about the soul, but about the good life. But the verbal connection is evident enough. The soul is what confers life; it was always (among other things) that whose possession marked the difference between the living and the dead body. But perhaps it seems far fetched to associate this 'sense' of 'soul' with a man's *way* of life? To speak of 'the good life' here might seem indeed to be a mere pun of no Platonic significance. But Plato's Socrates does elsewhere associate the soul with both being alive and a way of life in one and the same context and indeed in the same argument.

He does so, as is very well known, in the First Book of the *Republic* (353D–E). There, in a discussion of the question whether the just live better lives than the unjust, we learn, with the full agreement of Socrates' interlocutor Thrasymachus, that a function of the soul is to live. Many have felt (more than I do) the inadequacy of Socrates' argument in this part of the *Republic*; the plausibility of the soul's function as 'living' depends perhaps on the soul giving life to the body, whereas Socrates wants, there too, to talk about ways of life. Again we need not read the *Republic* back into the *Protagoras*. What we should do is to note that, whatever the argument's philosophical vices, Plato could attribute it to the Socrates of the *Republic* without objection from a sophist.

That makes plausible the attribution to Socrates in the *Protagoras*, without the sophist's disagreement, of a somewhat similar train of thought connecting paragraphs. It is after all germane, in the context of Protagoras' chapter-opening remarks, for Socrates first to ask (351B) if some men lead a good life, and secondly to explore what makes that life good. The relevance of the exploration is both logical and verbal. The interrogation which follows is a development of the preceding one, in view of Protagoras' chosen escape-route, rather than a wholly new departure constituting an admission by Socrates of defeat.

The other question left alive by Protagoras' self-exculpatory speech is that of knowledge's place in the good life. This question lies at the heart of the matter. For, though the necessity alike of natural gifts and of good teaching is clearly fundamental to Protagoras' theory of education, it remains persistently unclear what the position in it is of 'knowledge' or 'art'. On one side lies the equivalence of 'art' and 'knowledge', and the dissociation of courage from 'art'. On the other is the equivalence of the good quality 'wisdom' and 'knowledge', wisdom being among the good qualities of which goodness consists. So far, so good; the sophist can say that he has maintained the dichotomy between courage and knowledge, wisdom or art. But he has done nothing whatever to clarify the difference between the art which is dissociable from courage and the kind of art he himself teaches. Courage is a part of political goodness which is the same thing as the political 'art', even though it does not arise from 'art'. Protagoras is a teacher, as Socrates recalls; courage is a part of what he teaches; courage is not, and does not arise from, any 'art'. What is it that Protagoras teaches? Is it not an art? Does he not convey knowledge to his pupils? If not, how does he fulfil his function as a teacher?

These by now familiar questions surely come back to the attentive reader's mind at the juxtaposition of an argument turning in part on Protagoras' claim to teach goodness with a speech making out a part of his teaching to be neither art nor knowledge. After this, no reader should find anything startling in the early rise to the surface of the argument of the Socratic question 'How do you stand as regards knowledge?' (352B) or in its subsequent role. Indeed, the whole dialogue could, with only a certain degree of oversimplification, be read as leading up to the question how Protagoras stands as regards knowledge. Protagoras' reply affords, as we shall see, an important premiss for the remainder of the argument. It forms the second such premiss, the first being the one concerning the good life which we just examined. It is unlikely to be coincidental that the language of Protagoras' preceding counter-attack strongly suggests the need for questioning him on these two subjects. The whole passage containing the counter-attack and the questioning appears to present a reasonable degree of unity. Whether that degree of unity is sufficiently high to disprove the notion of an afterthought is (I suppose) a subjective matter; the reader will easily perceive the direction in which my own argument tends.

The detail of what follows in the *Protagoras* has been the subject of many chapters, papers and notes over the last generation; but the chief interest of the whole passage, in the context of this work, lies in its general strategy rather than in its particular and shifting tactics. Though Plato's very skill in attaching the battle verbally to the preceding skirmish has concealed the point, the postponed issue of the role of knowledge in the good life is at least as important as the opening issue about pleasure. Indeed it is common for Socrates to discuss the two together, as in the *Philebus* and the *Gorgias*, to say nothing of the *Republic*. In the *Philebus* (11A, 21A–B, and *passim*) Socrates, on beginning an investigation into opinions about pleasure, moves swiftly to ask his victim for assessment of the intellectual side of his humanity. So in the *Protagoras* the question he raises about the evaluation of knowledge finds an explanation in further questions on its relation to what may (very loosely) be called the emotional elements of human life, including, conspicuously, pleasure and pain (352C–D).

These closely integrated questions here draw others in their wake: what of Protagoras' attitude to the opinions of the man in the street? How does he reconcile that attitude with the presuppositions of his life as a professional educator? Such problems are already visible on or only just below the surface of the dialogue so far. Their presence here is indicated by Protagoras' answers, at the outset of Socrates' questioning, first about pleasure and then about knowledge. Pressed to say if he agrees with the popular view that some pleasures are bad and some pains good (351C–D), Protagoras rather solemnly invokes not only dialectical safety but also the whole tenor of his life as reasons for his answer. Asked if he accepts the popular view that knowledge is the slave of the passions, he replies with no less solemnity that 'it would be shameful, for him especially, to deny that "wisdom and knowledge" is the mightiest power in human life' (352C–D). This reply elicits from Socrates a rare expression of unqualified approval and assent. This serves to underline its strategic importance.

The immediate sequel is a difficulty characteristically raised by Socrates. His and Protagoras' agreement is in discord with another popular view, that one can know the better and do the worse. People reply, when Socrates asks them to explain this phenomenon, that those who act in this way do so because they are overpowered by pleasure or pain or one of the passions. This is what conflicts with Socrates' and Protagoras' intellectualism. It is a plain fact of everyday human experience. Further pursuit of the matter promises to jeopardize the position Protagoras has so solemnly taken up. The promise of jeopardy is contained in two considerations which may look merely verbal but are absolutely fundamental.

First, the contradiction by 'the many' of Protagoras' view is sharpened by choice of words; knowledge, he says, is the 'most *power*ful' element of humanity; yet the man in the street says that the passions over*power* the person. (The italicized verbal similarity reproduces a like similarity in the Greek.) Protagoras would like to scoff at the point, as a mistake such as the masses normally make; but Socrates insists that they discuss it, and makes it hard for Protagoras to refuse. Socrates' line is that he and the sophist ought to teach people what the phenomenon really is, which they call being overpowered by pleasure. Having conceded the leadership of the discussion, Protagoras gives in (353B). But there is nothing unfair about Plato's treatment of him in this respect. There is an obvious obligation on an intellectualist of the stamp of Protagoras and Socrates here to defend himself against the imputation of disregarding manifest facts of experience. Socrates has good grounds for pressing Protagoras to allow the investigation, and the reader has no reason for doubt that Plato supposed the sophists to see those grounds. To account for the relevant facts of experience will actually help the sophists. It will do so by showing that knowledge (which they inculcate) and wisdom (to which their professional title lays implicit claim) are of greater significance than 'the many' supposed. The important point to observe here is that the sophists, no less than Socrates, are committed to some form of intellectualism; they offer an intellectual training for the good life.[218]

Secondly, Protagoras skates on thin ice in dealing with any major conflict between his own opinions and those of 'the many'. 'The many' are not readily distinguishable from the Athenians. At the outset he conspicuously failed to correct Socrates' statement (however ironic) that the Athenians are wise (319B). He has agreed with 'the many' that some pleasures are bad and some pains good (351C–D). He has publicly expressed conviction that the Athenians are (though somewhat inferior to himself) capable educators of their children in the political art (327E–328B). Yet if the Athenians are wrong about a matter so fundamental as the status of knowledge *vis-à-vis* the emotions, where is the art or wisdom they transmit to their children? Protagoras claimed at the end of the Great Speech to be a little better at teaching, not to know more. Indeed, if he knew vastly more, then what the Athenians taught their children would not have been the full political art. Yet here (352E) he is being asked to join Socrates in persuading and *teaching* 'the many' what it is to do wrong against one's better judgement. He is in danger of being convicted at least of arbitrariness in his relation to the opinions of 'the many'. Where and how to draw the line between their acceptable and their unacceptable views promises to be a knotty problem. For a man who has taken up his kind of position it is dangerous to have to say dismissively 'People have many other wrong ideas too'. It is scarcely surprising that he is shy of discussing the opinions of the many; but his manner of attempted dismissal is more dangerous still: 'But why, Socrates, must we examine the opinion of the mass of people who say whatever comes into their heads?' (353A–B). Is the education the Athenians give their children 'whatever comes into their heads'?

We may be fairly sure that Plato would not place his Protagoras in this sort of position without reason. As he apparently sees it, the sophistic claim to teach goodness implies the intellectual nature of goodness – and the sophists do not deny this; they could hardly deny the intellectual nature of the education they offer. The masses rejected then as now the notion that goodness or successful living is an intellectual matter. The sophists had to shrug off the masses' rejection. But they can hardly shrug off the opinion of the masses about the fundamental nature of goodness without removing the basis for popular morality. Some perhaps did simply abandon popular morality. But the position of those who did not was uncomfortable. Protagoras, and apparently the rest of the sophists present in this dialogue, did not; he at least is portrayed here as a moralist of no very original stamp. In any case, had they (or he) openly, in the dialogue's context, rejected the claims of popular morality, they (or he) would have met with a frosty reception from a conventional young man such as Hippocrates.

These general considerations may be particularized. The

particular case of fear reveals a special difficulty for Protagoras. When Socrates, in elaborating his question about the status of knowledge, mentions the passions, feelings and emotions supposed by 'the many' to dominate a man at the expense of intellect, the last emotion he names (though certainly not by afterthought) is fear. Presumably the knowledge concerned must be relevant to the fear. If it is, then its capacity to overcome fear is fully consonant with Protagoras' previous admission that knowledge improves confidence (350A), and that the brave and confident face things the many are afraid to face. Protagoras did not there admit the converse, or, if he did, it was by inadvertence, that all the brave are wise. But if it is not wisdom that makes people brave, which gives them the part of goodness called 'courage', then what is it? If it is no sort of knowledge or cognitive excellence, then how can a sophist teach it? If it is not knowledge, then how is it part of the citizen's *art*?

These difficulties confront any sophist wishing to claim the political art as his subject and to separate wisdom from other good qualities of the citizen. Protagoras is in extra trouble. The knowledge which improved confidence was that of the relevant art or skill. What is the knowledge which now overcomes fear? If it is still the relevant art or skill of a technical sort, then Protagoras is in danger of inconsistency. For then he must teach the relevant art or skill of a technical sort, or his pupils will not be able to overcome fear. But this he cannot do; he has precluded that possibility by his claim to teach not the technical arts like other sophists but goodness. If the requisite knowledge to overcome fear is not the relevant technique, then what is it? What Protagoras needs is a coherent distinction between the technical skills and the skill of being a good citizen; this he has so far signally failed to produce. He cannot even seize the lifeline Socrates throws him by mentioning another form of cognitive excellence called *phronesis*, rendered by Taylor 'intelligence' (352C). He cannot say he teaches *phronesis* but not other intellectual good qualities, because he has no clear idea how *phronesis* might differ from those others. His claim not to teach an art like the other sophists, but to teach the political art, remains a stumbling-block.

These considerations lead into the strategy of the whole

argument. It is possible now only to outline that strategy baldly and dogmatically; detail must be left till later, lest it swamp the outline. It depends quite largely on the thesis argued above, that the sophists are intellectualists. Socrates' point is that they are inconsistent intellectualists. They believe, because professionally they must, in the power of the intellect to govern and to decide human action. But they also believe things inconsistent with that belief, such as that no intellectual gift is required for courage. In order to defend their intellectualism they have to deal with the objection of ordinary people, that the knowledge of the 'right thing' does not constrain the agent to do it. The defence requires an account, consistent with intellectualism, of what is commonly called akratic action. To know the better and do the worse must be shown to be contradictory, and an account given which explains what really happens when ordinary people think they are subject to akrasia.

To this end Socrates conducts in his own name and that of the sophists an imaginary interrogation of ordinary people. The interrogation has them ('the many') admitting what Protagoras at the outset refuses to admit, namely that (in a sense to be expounded later) all pleasures are good and all pains are bad. On the basis of that admission 'the many' are compelled dialectically to accept that akrasia is a self-contradictory illusion. The sophists need not be too finicky about the logic of Socrates' discussion with 'the many', since Socrates is defending the sophists no less than himself.

On attaining his goal in the argument with the fictional 'many', Socrates asks whether the sophists accept then the hedonistic doctrine that formed the basis of the refutation of the many and hence of the defence of intellectualism. Unable to think on the spot of any other defence, the sophists have little option but to accept the hedonistic doctrine or something like it. Socrates then turns the searchlight of his dialectic directly on the sophists, and dazzles them into acceptance of a line of argument to show that courage is a form of knowledge. That line of argument purports to depend on a hedonistic doctrine. What the doctrine is, whether it differs from that accepted by 'the many', and whether the argument depends genuinely on it, are all points to be taken up when occasion arises.

One thing should be clear from the above summary; this account of the argument as a whole assumes no commitment by Socrates to a strictly hedonistic doctrine.[219] Even if in this dialogue Socrates offers no argument to defend his intellectualist stance save one based on a form of hedonism, it does not follow that he accepted that or any other form of hedonism. Even if the positive argument in favour of his intellectualism is based on a hedonism it does not follow that the steps in the argument are acceptable to the questioning Socrates as well as to his respondents and interlocutors. The only evidence enabling us to say for sure that Socrates was committed in this dialogue to hedonism would be an unequivocal statement or firm implication from Socrates' own lips that he accepted the commitment. We may start the detailed study of the whole passage with the resounding question forming the title of the next section.

Is Socrates committed?

Scholarly argument rages still over the questions how far Socrates commits himself in the *Protagoras* to any form of hedonism, and to what form, if any.[220] The intrinsic interest of these questions to students of Plato in general matches their particular importance for any study of Socrates' dialectical procedures in action. Can Socrates be merely asking questions without committing himself? Can he be said to phrase his questions in such a way as to imply that he holds (and is advancing) a particular view? To what extent is he supplying premises of his own? No answer to this series of problems is likely to be final; one plank of the present platform will be the offer of an explanation why no final solution is likely. The suggestion is, in development of a notable article (of 1961) by J. P. Sullivan, that Plato intended a certain degree of ambiguity in the crucial passage, and that Plato resolved the ambiguity only (if at all) by hints not themselves entirely perspicuous. This leads on naturally to a further conundrum, scarcely susceptible of universally acceptable answer: *why* did Plato make his text so difficult?

We must examine the form of the questions Socrates asks in the opening lines. Socrates' first questions (351B) take absolutely neutral form, and clearly commit him to no beliefs whatever: 'Do you maintain...?' and 'Do you think...?' Protagoras is committed by his clear and decisive answers; Socrates is in no way bound. This situation is not in the least altered by the fact that at least one of these questions would certainly, if put to Socrates, have received the same affirmative answer it receives from Protagoras. Protagoras, but not Socrates, commits himself (not for the first time)[221] to a distinction, as yet unspecified, between people who live a good life and people who live a bad life. Protagoras, but not Socrates, says that a man in pain does not live a good life; the implication is that pain excludes the possibility of a good life.

In the next question, the presentation is no longer neutral; the question includes the phrase 'Don't you think...?' which in Greek as in English 'expects' (as grammarians used to say) the answer 'Yes'. But in reply to such a question the respondent is in no way obliged to affirm. The form 'Don't you think that *p*?' is inherently ambiguous concerning even the questioner's 'expectations': it implies that *either* the questioner 'expects' the particular respondent to think that *p*, *or* the questioner 'expects' *p* to be generally acceptable. In the former case the questioner commits himself not at all to *p*: in the latter he commits himself only in so far as the commitment to the general acceptability of a proposition commits one to personal belief in it.

The reader will complain that this is just quibbling; and the reader will be right. Normally speaking, if one asks a question in this kind of way one does so because one believes that *p*, and, hence, if one asks a question thus, one creates the impression that one believes that *p*.

But the Platonic Socrates is not – and few will dissent from this – wholly normal. He pays a most unusually close attention not only to the impressions people convey, but to the exact implications of what they say. Whether he pays more attention to impressions or to implications, in his own words as much as in others', may depend on which happens to suit him at the time. It is not therefore surprising if he is difficult both for his fictional interlocutors and for Plato's readers to pin down. In the passage under discussion Socrates seems to think the proposition that the life of pleasure is a good life likely to appeal to Protagoras as to a wider public. But though

Socrates' questions might convey the impression that he too finds this proposition acceptable, they do not firmly imply that he does.

Socrates submits the conclusion of this first argument for Protagoras' acceptance (351B). 'So to have a pleasant life is good, and to have an unpleasant life is bad?' His submission can hardly commit him to agreement. Whether the relevant sentence be punctuated at the end with a question mark or a full stop (a point on which editors disagree),[222] to submit, or draw, a conclusion from premises to which one is not committed is not to endorse the conclusion; Socrates has not unambiguously endorsed the premises. Whether or not Protagoras believes Socrates to have endorsed the conclusion, he is not bound by Socrates' opinion. In response to Socrates' submission he offers no more than a conditional endorsement of the conclusion. What that does to his position we shall see later.

Socrates' next question reveals deeper complexities. This time his question 'expects', if anything, the answer 'No',[223] but such expectation, *mutatis mutandis*, may receive the same treatment as that we have given to the expected answer 'Yes'. The extra complexity results from the addition of 'go along with the majority in calling...'; this leaves the reader wondering whether Socrates' apparent hesitancy is directed at (a) Protagoras' implied agreement to a certain *proposition* or (b) Protagoras' agreement with *the majority* on a cardinal point such as the proposition represents. If the reader adopts hypothesis (a), he may wonder additionally whether Socrates' hesitancy actually implies (as opposed to creating the impression of) his own disagreement with the proposition itself.

Socrates' next sentence looks at first as if it is going to resolve the reader's query (351C). It starts with (in Taylor's version) 'What I say is ...' or (possibly) 'What I am saying is...' and on reading either of these we anticipate a statement of Socrates' own opinion; such a statement would neatly balance his remark about an opinion attributable in some sense and in some degree to Protagoras. But – and this is the crucial point here – the anticipated statement does not materialize. What we have instead is a question 'expecting' a particular answer, a form of question which (as we have seen)

Socrates meets Protagoras 361

commits the questioner to nothing firm. The general shape of the sentence is (in this kind of translation) 'What I say is ... are they not ... ?', and this shape is peculiar since the sentence offers no assertion, but a question. But the peculiarity vanishes immediately if we replace 'say' with 'mean', which is an equally legitimate translation of the Greek verb Plato's Socrates uses.

Curiously, when at a few lines' interval (351E) the pattern is repeated of the same verb being followed by a question, Taylor actually puts in his translation 'Well, that's what I *mean* ...' (my italics). Clearly the verbal form 'mean' should stand in an English rendering in both places.[224] But if we thus understand the Greek, we find in it no unfulfilled promise of a statement; we find in it no promise of a statement at all, but only an explanation by Socrates of a previous question's meaning.

To explicate a question no more makes an assertion than to ask one. Socrates commits himself to nothing more in the sentence following the one about going along with the majority than in any sentence embodying a query with an 'expected' answer. That Plato's Protagoras takes this sentence (351C) and the one following as questions is strongly suggested by his use of the word 'reply' referring to a response to them both together, a response detailing his attitude to each sentence separately. The second question containing 'I mean ... ' (351E) describes itself on Socrates' own lips as a question.

For completeness' sake we may observe that only a single interrogative speech by Socrates intervenes between Protagoras' reply to the first explicated question and Socrates' second explicated question. That intervening interrogative, 'And don't you call ... ?' is subject to the normal reservations about the assertoric value of a question 'expecting' a certain answer.

As one could readily imagine, this ambiguous and even tortuous passage has called forth a number of widely differing interpretations. Some place more weight on the questioning aspect of Socrates' remarks, others emphasize rather the 'expected' answers and the verbs taken to be verbs of assertion. Socrates is held either to be merely asking questions or to be committed to a thesis. What was radically original (so far as I know) in Professor Sullivan's article mentioned above was his readiness to admit at one and the same time both (a) that Socrates 'is trying to give the many (not to mention Protagoras and the Sophists)' 'the impression ... that he is logically convinced of the validity of his view' and (b) that 'He does incidentally give the reader several indications that this is not his true view'.[225] Plato thus expects his reader to see that Socrates is being 'ironic', but in the fictional conversation the other characters are taken in. This interpretation was a great advance on those which ignore the ambiguities of the passage; especially welcome was its implication that the ambiguities were deliberate.

The deliberateness of the ambiguities deserves separate and emphatic treatment. Examination of the rest of this dialogue shows no parallels. Socrates is normally quite clear; normally *either* he is eliciting his interlocutor's views without voicing or (strictly) implying his own, *or* he is prepared to distinguish views he accepts from those he merely elicits, *or* his irony is overwhelmingly obvious (as, presumably, in his apparent attribution of wisdom to the Athenians) (319B). The passage introducing the relation between the pleasant and the good, in so far as *Socrates* conveys a strong impression of commitment without actually implying it, a strong impression of something he does not really *mean*, is of a type of difficulty unique in this dialogue, and certainly of the rarest kind in the whole range of Plato's early and middle dialogues.

We know that Plato could be relatively clear when he wanted to be, and it is a plausible, though not a certain, inference that in this passage he did not want to be. What he may have wanted instead is to have his Socrates drive the sophists towards a certain view, and use to that end the carefully created impression that he (Socrates) believes it himself; such a policy would not be easy for Socrates or his manipulator Plato to reconcile with an equally careful abstention from active or implied espousal of the view in question. The only way to reconcile the two would be the most carefully studied ambiguity. Such care would explain what would otherwise be a sad lapse of Plato's in his capacity as a writer.

In that capacity Plato is already sailing rather close to the wind. He would be sailing even closer if he were to allow his Protagoras to take Socrates' remarks as constituting an assertion about the pleasant and the good, when, as author of the dialogue, he does not intend them to constitute an assertion. True, Protagoras is not, in this dialogue, a wholly reliable interpreter of other people. But to allow Protagoras to come down heavily on one side of Plato's ambiguity would inevitably incline the reader, in his puzzlement, to follow him.

Now at two places (both at 351E) Taylor's rendering of the Greek would cause a careful reader to deduce that Protagoras does indeed take Socrates as having asserted something. The passage concerned deserves detailed analysis. In Taylor's English version Socrates asks a question '... in so far as they are pleasant, are they not good? I'm asking whether pleasure itself is not good,' and Protagoras replies: 'As you always say, Socrates, let's investigate it. And if your thesis seems reasonable and it appears that pleasant and good are the same, then we shall be in agreement. But if not, we shall argue about it then.' Several things in this version are worth discussing in this context, some of them already treated by Donald Zeyl in a notable paper, and again by Gosling and Taylor in their book *The Greeks on Pleasure*.[226]

One question of obvious importance is whether Protagoras actually speaks of 'your thesis' to Socrates; and in fact he does not: he speaks of 'the thing under examination'. It is Taylor's view (repeated in *The Greeks on Pleasure*) that 'the thing under examination is Socrates' thesis'. But this view certainly has no place in a translation,[227] and is in any case open to serious doubt. Socrates has just asked a question; Protagoras replies 'let's investigate it'. The obvious antecedent of 'it' is surely the quesion, and when a noun meaning 'the thing under investigation' turns up in the next clause it too should refer to the question.

What seems to move Taylor and Gosling to depart from this clear train of thought (in opposition to Zeyl) is the notion that the condition which Protagoras advances is 'if the thing under examination appears reasonable' – and, 'reasonable' being apparently interpreted to mean 'with a considerable likelihood of being true', what is 'reasonable' must be a proposition, or 'thesis', rather than a question. But the phrase (*pros logon*) rendered 'reasonable' need not and most probably should not be taken in this way. I have found (by using Leonard Brandwood's indispensable *Word-Index to Plato*) nine other relevant Platonic examples of the phrase;[228] in none of them is there a clear case of evaluation of a proposition to determine its truth, falsehood, likeliness or unlikeliness. In some of them such evaluation of a proposition would seem to be excluded; in each and all the idiom can mean 'relevant', 'to the point', 'to the purpose' or 'to a purpose'. Indeed, in all the four other passages translated by Taylor and Gosling, in their respective translations of the *Protagoras* and the *Philebus*, such renderings duly appear. There is accordingly no need to regard 'reasonable' as more than an *ad hoc* expedient.

But nevertheless the expedient (as one would expect from scholars of this calibre) is not without its attractions. Protagoras' conditional sentence (351E) has a double protasis. The second half is '[if] it appears that pleasant and good are the same'. It is most natural to see a close connection between the second half and the first. Attractive, therefore, is a rendering which makes the second half, 'if your problem is relevant', straightforwardly repeat the first; since the second embodies a proposition taken from Protagoras' understanding of Socrates' question, the first will then (à la Taylor) refer to that same proposition.

But, attractive or not, this interpretation is far from necessary. The second half of the sophist's protasis might equally well mention an easily perceived consequence of the first. Now, if the question Socrates is pressing is to be relevant to the main discussion, what must the answer be? Evidently if the answer is negative, and 'pleasant' and 'good' are not related in the way Socrates is asking Protagoras if he will allow, then the discussion of the question will have advanced the main discussion not a single step. The discussion will only be to the purposes of Socrates or of Protagoras if the answer turns out to be affirmative, i.e. if Protagoras can accept the relationship between 'pleasant' and 'good' which forms the subject of Socrates' line of questioning. Hence there is a close enough connection between the two halves of Protagoras' protasis even without the second repeating the first. Hence, again, the structure of the protasis fails, after all, to add to the attractiveness of an otherwise dubious rendering of its first half.

But we cannot finish with this passage yet. For the agreement or disagreement envisaged by Protagoras demands attention. According to Taylor and Gosling, 'If [Socrates'] thesis appears reasonable, [it] will be agreed on by both parties', and 'if that thesis does not seem reasonable, the parties will dispute: it takes two to make an argument'. Against this view there is an *ad homines* argument worth an airing. Suppose the two parties decide that the thesis is not reasonable, then what is there left for them to dispute about so far as the thesis is concerned? They will already have investigated the thesis, and come to a decision. The only way I can see of allowing further dispute about the thesis would be to suppose Protagoras, when he says 'if the thesis does not appear reasonable' to mean 'if it does not appear reasonable *to me.*' But after the plural 'let's investigate it' this is implausible.

But does our other interpretation of Protagoras' speech fare any better? Yes, it does. If Protagoras and Socrates conclude that the questionable relationship of pleasant and good does in fact hold, they will agree to continue the discussion on that basis; if they conclude that it does not hold, the basis of further discussion will be open to dispute. Indeed – which is why the argument is only *ad homines* – this kind of reading seems on any interpretation of the protases to be the best way out of the difficulties concerning the prospective agreement or dispute.[229]

So far we have dealt with the outward form of this difficult passage; we should now turn to the inner substance of it. Here Taylor's commentary has proved especially valuable in sorting out the various possibilities, though it is not to be expected of any single work (including this present book) that it should exhaust them. The first thing Socrates asks the sophist (351B) is whether living well is compatible with a life of pain and misery. Protagoras understandably says not. Socrates then adds a harmless-looking rider: if a man lived his life pleasantly to the end, would he have lived well?

Our attention should be directed at two things: first, as the distinguished Finnish philosopher G.H. von Wright, writing in English, rightly pointed out, the epithet 'good' in common parlance often means 'pleasant'; any resistance to this can be met with the confident assertion that 'good' often at least *refers* to the pleasure-content of the noun it qualifies.[230]

Further, in Greek 'to live well' and similar expressions constitute a sound and established way of saying 'to lead a comfortable life', i.e. one with one's bodily needs satisfied. 'Neither good nor pleasant' looks like rhetorical emphasis, not a distinction, where it occurs in fifth-century literature,[231] and it is not only those demoralized by the great Athenian plague who will have thought everything fine and advantageous that was pleasant (or contributed to pleasure).[232] In Thucydides such thoughts are not wholly respectable; but normal (if philosophically incautious) people would say, in effect, that pleasure is the most valuable thing in life.[233] To live well is not (as it happens) a common phrase in extant Classical Greek literature, but in Homer it means 'to be comfortably off' – and a 'good life' is one with comfortable satisfaction of bodily needs.[234] Words for good and bad fortune are often closely associated with those for pleasure and pain respectively.[235] So it is understandable that, receiving with no more clue than his own expression 'good nurture of the soul', the question whether a life lived pleasantly to the end is a good life, Protagoras should say 'Yes'.

What appears to bring Protagoras up sharp is the conclusion Socrates draws, on his behalf and quite inescapably, from his two answers so far. The conclusion? 'To have a pleasant life is good and to have an unpleasant life is bad' (351C). This puts a different complexion on things. Either it gets away from '*live* well' and brings us back to a dialogue in which 'goodness' bears a different meaning from 'pleasantness' (though what meaning it does bear is still undecided), or it rings a less specific but still loud warning bell in Protagoras' mind.

Protagoras wakes up and qualifies his previous response. He now expresses the opinion that a pleasant life is a good and successful life if (and only if) it consists of the enjoyment of *fine* things.[236] Protagoras would find a life spent in scratching an itch no more acceptable, however exquisitely pleasant, than would (ultimately) the Callicles of the Gorgias (494C–495A, with 499B). We know Protagoras would find it unacceptable, for he has agreed that goodness is something 'fine' (349E). In so far as he has admitted that pleasure, experienced right through to the end, is a sufficient condition of good living, he goes back now on that admission. It is not enough just to describe Protagoras' conditional remark as a 'caveat' or 'rejoinder';[237] one must be clear that it is a rejoinder not to a thesis of Socrates' but to Protagoras' own previous admissions, which were freely, if unwarily, made.[238] Given a moment to think, and faced with the consequences, Protagoras does not after all believe a life good just because it is pleasant. Dialectically, he gets off to a very bad start in this part of the discussion.

Socrates' surprise at this implicit admission of a bad start is very natural. His plausible conclusion is that Protagoras does not after all believe all pleasures to contribute to a good life, but only fine pleasures. What enhances his surprise – or so he would apparently have Protagoras accept – is the fact that *most people* deny some pleasures a place in the good life, thinking them actively harmful; one might mention, though nobody does in this passage, the pleasures of intoxication pursued to excess. Surely Protagoras does not agree in this important distinction with the vulgar herd? Socrates is trying to clamp on Protagoras the view that all pleasures are good. That, at least, is how Protagoras understands him; but Protagoras has already rejected that view and has no desire to be shifted from his rejection.

The explicatory question Socrates asks next presents a complicated problem to the interpreter, a problem on which Taylor has most percipient things to say.[239] On the whole the course of the conversation fits best with the meaning (in a rough paraphrase) 'Aren't pleasures good to the extent to which they are pleasant?', to which an affirmative answer would imply that 'if x is pleasant, it must be overall good, no matter what other considerations . . . may be brought against it.' After his previous 'caveat' Protagoras cannot consistently affirm that, and he does not.[240]

Parenthetically, we see that the sophist does not explicitly agree that some pleasures are bad, only that some pleasures are not good; pains on the other hand, he admits are bad or not bad, or neither good nor bad. He must use 'not bad' here (at its first occurrence) for 'good'. The reason for all this inexplicitness is obscure. But possibly Protagoras has at the back of his mind some vagueness about the distinction between (a), 'All pleasure is good', a proposition readily acceptable to many, if not most, people, and, (b), 'All pleasures are good', which is, one imagines, much less widely acceptable, since it appears to assume that a pleasure's pleasantness outweighs any other disadvantages it may have.[241] 'Some pleasures are bad' would in fact deny (b) even more forcibly than 'Some pleasures are not good' does; Protagoras may have shrunk from 'Some pleasures are bad' because he confused it with 'Some pleasure is bad', which would be a forcible denial of the widely acceptable (a).

Socrates now inserts a question evidently designed either to clarify the point he wishes to make, or to render it more acceptable to Protagoras, or to do both. By 'pleasures' or 'pleasant things' does Protagoras refer to 'things participating in' or (Taylor) 'characterized by pleasure', or to things which 'produce pleasure' (351D)? Plato's distinction is hard to understand. If it is intended to distinguish between pleasure as the feeling effected by an activity and pleasure as a feature of the activity itself, it does not seem relevant to the conversation; it supplies no readily visible reason why Socrates should think his present line of questioning clearer, or his submitted propositions more acceptable, after it than before it.

Much more probable, therefore, is Taylor's other suggestion, that Socrates is extending the sense of 'pleasant' to include both 'pleasant in itself' and 'having pleasant consequences'.[242] After this, Socrates' immediate repetition (351E) of the question whether pleasant things are not good to the extent that they are pleasant is now different from the question's first occurrence. It differs in that it now includes the pleasant (or unpleasant) consequences in the factors relevant to the estimation of whether a pleasant thing is good or not. To judge from the later discussion, and especially from the element in it of a 'hedonistic calculus', Plato and/or his Socrates think(s) that with this clarifying stipulation and on this basis the doctrine that all pleasure or 'all pleasant things' are good is more widely acceptable than without it; and this is probably the case. (It runs, however, counter to ordinary usage; we do not call the dentist's drilling 'pleasant' just because it saves us from toothache.)

Socrates' reasonably lucid line of questioning receives next an attempted further clarification which has actually clouded several issues in modern times. He paraphrases his last question whether pleasant things are not good to the extent that they are pleasant, by saying that he is 'asking whether pleasure itself is not good'.

Some have imported here quite unnecessarily the notion that 'pleasure is *the* good (emphasis mine).'[243] Nothing in what has gone before has prepared Plato's reader for that, or requires it. Interpreters have devoted insufficient attention to the expression 'pleasure itself'. In Greek the emphatic pronoun (the English '-self') frequently means 'in -self' in the sense '*by* -self', or 'alone', and this usage is thoroughly intelligible here.

If that is Socrates' meaning, he then adds to his previous query, whether pleasant things are not good, the query whether pleasure by itself is not good. The second of these two queries, unpacked a little, asks whether pleasure without any non-pleasant consequences is good. This helps to explain the first query by making clear that it is now modified in the way suggested by the inclusion (not long before this) of 'what has pleasant consequences' in 'pleasant things'. 'Whether pleasant things are not good' now means 'Whether things pleasant and having only pleasant consequences are not good'. A thing which is itself pleasant and which has only pleasant consequences is a pleasure unalloyed, pleasure by itself. True, one might have expected, more straightforwardly, 'pleasant *things* themselves', but 'pleasure' in this sentence of Plato's is doubtless a mere stylistic variant for 'pleasant things'; after all, a pleasant thing is a pleasure.

But one chief reason for making pleasure 'the good' in this passage has always been what Protagoras says next. The second half of the sophist's if-clause is almost universally rendered '"pleasant" and "good" are the same thing'.[244] That, assuming Protagoras' reasonable reliability as a reporter, necessitates the discovery of something equivalent (or virtually equivalent) to this in the preceding sentence. Hence talk of 'pleasure is the good'. But closer inspection reveals cracks in this foundation. Protagoras' recapitulation, as Taylor's note admits, would, if rendered according to normal Greek usage, be taken to mean 'the same thing is pleasant and good'. This gives satisfactory sense as a way of saying that 'good' and 'pleasant' are coextensive terms, that they refer to the same set of things.[245]

That rendering would, of course, raise the problem whether that coextensiveness is implicit in anything that Socrates and Protagoras has said. Here is a suggested solution. Protagoras and his creator Plato may have been thinking of the consequences of the proposition 'To the extent that x is pleasant it is good', and may have deduced from it that if x is not pleasant at all, then it is not good at all. If what is not pleasant is not good, and there is something good, then what is good is pleasant. Protagoras has learnt wariness; Plato perhaps represents him as putting the most extreme construction he legitimately can on the propositions Socrates asks him about, and avoiding any chance of being saddled with the proposition corresponding to that construction. Protagoras, ever since his caveat that pleasures must be fine to be good, has concentrated throughout on escaping Socrates' pressure on him to accept that all pleasures are good; he now makes plain his rejection equally of 'all good things are pleasant'. To conjoin these rejections is to stand (more warily than is strictly necessary) by his assertion that pleasures are good if and only if they are fine. He agrees to *investigate* the question whether pleasant and good are *coextensive* – no more.

Socrates, having failed to secure immediately the commitment he wants from Protagoras, pursues the investigation of Protagoras' position on pleasant and good by other means. He turns (352A) to what looks like another field of inquiry altogether, and extracts Protagoras' views on the power of knowledge. Eventually he will secure a commitment he can use on 'pleasant' and 'good' from the common man, and then cleverly transfer it to the sophists.

Knowledge and opinion

It is not, of course, coincidental that knowledge is the chosen field of inquiry when the question has arisen of Protagoras' values, of his notion of the good life. Knowledge is much more important than pleasure in the dialogue as a whole. If either were an interloper here it would be pleasure. Taylor has well pointed out that Plato's Socrates regards the issue of pleasure as in a sense subordinate to that of the status of knowledge. There is sufficient indication of this in Socrates' medical simile here (352A–B). Knowledge and wisdom are the subject of this section of the argument as of the previous section. But the evaluation of pleasure and of the intellect are very closely related in Platonic talk of psychology; in discussing the good life in the *Protagoras* Plato is as concerned with the apparent choice between a life of pleasure and a life in accordance with the intellect as he was in the *Gorgias*. This is true even if his conclusion is that the pursuit of pleasure requires for its success the exercise of intellect. To conclude thus could be a reason for deciding in favour of the intellect rather than an annulment of the choice; and even if the intellectual life were the most pleasant one could not reach that position without discussion.[246]

Protagoras' answer to Socrates' question about knowledge is, as we have seen, pleasing to the questioner. As a teacher, he says, he is in no position to decry the strength and controlling power of knowledge. If knowledge is the slave of the passions, his teaching is of little value in practice. So much is evident, and Protagoras' reference (352C–D) to his professional life in this context confirms it.

But Plato's readers have long felt that Protagoras goes too far and surrenders too much. Protagoras' admission is that knowledge *always* rules, that a man knowing good from bad will be ruled by nothing in any circumstances which bids him do other than his knowledge and his ultimate self-interest bid him. On the face of it, Protagoras need not admit all this, contrary as it is to normal experience and to common sense. If knowledge regularly, but not invariably, rules the passions, then knowledge is useful, fine, controlling and worth purveying to a sophist's customers. Why should Protagoras accept a view so all-embracing?

One answer to this would look at the alternatives Socrates lays before his adversary: on the one hand knowledge as a slave, being dragged around as pictured by the common herd; on the other hand something fine, strong, leading. Given such a choice, this answer runs, Protagoras chooses the more flattering alternative. On this interpretation the choice is cleverly but falsely put, and Protagoras fails to spot the falsity, and succumbs to the temptation. On this view he ought to reject both alternatives, but actually flatters himself that he purveys an article describable as Socrates here describes knowledge. Thus Socrates cheats, and Protagoras foolishly (if understandably) allows him to cheat. This interpretation may be right; but if it is, not only the fictional Socrates but also the real Plato cheats, and the dialogue is deeply flawed. If Plato had any defence to this accusation, he has not given it to us directly. But he would perhaps have wished to turn defence into attack.

The attack could be aimed at Protagoras, rather than directly at Plato's readers. If knowledge does not invariably rule, but is from time to time overwhelmed by passions and feelings, then clearly men will differ in their constitution in this matter. Some will more often experience such defeat of knowledge than others. Whether one makes the right choices for a successful life or not will depend on one's knowledge, yes, but also on one's capacity to resist the onslaughts of passion. Does Protagoras convey to his pupils any such capacity? It is hard to see any way in which he could substantiate any such claim. Could he blame his pupils' natural endowment? Hardly, even though he refers twice to natural endowment (351A and B). For 'natural endowment' refers to a capacity to learn, not a capacity to suppress the passions. In any case, Protagoras cannot afford to allow too large a place for natural endowment in the growth of goodness, since that would correspondingly reduce the importance of his and others' teaching.

True, the Athenians pay lyre-masters to see to the moderation of the young, and their avoidance of bad actions (326A). This looks more like the training of what it used to be fashionable to call 'the will' than the inculcation of the knowledge of good and evil. But Protagoras has already agreed that moderation and wisdom are much the same, in a passage (349D) where saying that meant that their 'powers' were the same, and they were, as good qualities, indistinguishable. It is too late now for Protagoras to make the necessary distinctions, dialectically too late. Protagoras is not to blame for his surrender at this juncture.

But Socrates does not rest content with knowledge as the ruling power in Man. If he *is* cheating over knowledge, he compounds the offence by slipping in 'belief' or 'opinion' as well.[247] It is hard to separate one such outrage to common sense from another. So let us anticipate a great deal of Plato's discussion, and attend to a relevant passage where Socrates has finished with the man in the street and returned to plague the sophist. Having secured agreement to a premiss about pleasure, he continues (358B): 'So if what is pleasant is good ... no one who either knows or believes that something else is better than what he is doing, and is in his power to do, subsequently does the other, when he can do what is better...' The critics' outrage has been loud and persistent:[248] 'Knows *or believes*?' There is nothing in the preceding few pages to justify, or even to pretend to justify, the addition of the two italicized words.

Vlastos put the criticism well:[249] 'No one would seriously suggest that Socrates would have wished to say the same thing about belief ungrounded in knowledge.' Faced with this difficulty, and thinking too exclusively in terms of a 'Socratic thesis', Vlastos went on to interpret the passage as meaning that 'we cannot act contrary to what we believe *when we do have knowledge* (Vlastos' emphasis)'. This is a highly artificial interpretation of a plain sentence. Apart from its artificiality, this expedient is open to the further criticism that it ignores the status of opinion later in the argument (358C–E), where there is no mention of knowledge to obscure the issue.

Norman Gulley[250] faces the problem with the idea that 'to believe' in this passage covers only false opinion, there being no room in the *Protagoras* for a goodness consisting in true belief. Manuwald[251] has expounded the difficulties of seeing how this coverage of 'belief' could fit into the argument as a developing whole.

But Manuwald's own explanation is equally unsatisfactory. Noticing a number of differences between the phraseology of the discussion in this passage and earlier phraseology, he finds (not wholly without justification) a certain disunity in the long argument from the introduction of pleasure to the conclusion about courage. But this explanation does not really come to grips with the difficulty about the status of belief. In effect it explains this piece of cheating by pointing to other supposedly unjustified discontinuities in the argument; and it is not clear why one should allow Plato or his Socrates to get away with cheating on the grounds that he has cheated more than once.

Taylor's explanation is that '(a) Plato has true belief exclusively in mind and (b) when writing the *Protagoras* he had not yet arrived at a clear distinction between true belief and knowledge'. It is unnecessary to argue here over (b), since (a) is undefended by Taylor and is highly implausible. In essence it is subject to the same criticism as Manuwald brought against Vlastos' understanding of the passage. Plato certainly had false opinion in mind in the composition of this passage, as witness the fact that the phrase under discussion, 'neither knowing nor believing', is *only one Socratic question* away from a mention (358C) of false opinion. At the later crux of the argument (358E) we find that neither the coward nor the brave man faces what he thinks is fearful. The coward is wrong in his thinking. If Plato has only true belief in mind at the gateway to this argument, then his mind changed decisively by the time he arrives near its conclusion. Taylor's defence of Socrates' cheating only (at best) postpones the accusation; it does not answer it.

It begins to look as if Plato's Socrates has indeed introduced an assumption here, unwarranted either by common sense or by argument or by anything the sophists have admitted in the course of this long final argument. It is time we referred back once again to Protagoras' pronouncements much earlier. His Great Speech contains utterances which make resistance to Socrates' assumption about opinion so difficult as to explain exactly why Protagoras lets him get away with it. Protagoras has to let him off; and at this crucial moment no representative of 'the many' is allowed to speak, let alone protest. The argument is again *ad hominem*. But when we have examined its *ad hominem* nature more precisely we shall be able to see also to what extent it is difficult for the many to press their natural-sounding objections.

In the Great Speech the first connection between belief and action (322A) proves nothing relevant. Men believed in the gods and built temples; though this does bring together opinion and action, it does so without any inferential connection between the two. Holding the gods to be worshipful is a necessary but hardly a sufficient condition of temple-building. But the Great Speech contains three arguments which do overtly and interestingly connect by inference men's opinions and their actions. It is, however, by no means simple to tease out the precise nature of each connection in each case. Protagoras is every bit as elusive a reasoner as Plato's Socrates has proved for generations to be. It may indeed be necessary to offer a mildly and amateurishly symbolic presentation of one or more of the arguments involved, in addition to a more discursive account. The symbols may simplify the exhibition of the argument. It so happens that the most convenient order of exposition is also the order in which the arguments appear in Protagoras' speech and a descending order of direct helpfulness for present purposes. On this occasion it will also be necessary, when we have analysed Protagoras, to refer back still further to what Socrates said in his main speech of attack on the teachability of goodness (319A–320C), the speech to which the sophist's Great Speech is a reply.

The sophist had a battery of arguments for the Athenians' belief in all men having a share of goodness; its first salvo (322D) is rewarding. It speaks firmly of what certain men, namely the Athenians, do on every relevant occasion. The Athenian reaction to the relevant circumstances bears repetition. On every occasion, Protagoras says, on which they need expert advice in arts or crafts the Athenians think it right to send for the appropriate experts and refuse to listen to the non-expert. On every occasion when they need advice on political goodness they listen to every Tom, Dick or Harry. They act thus, and reasonably so, having in mind everybody's having a share in this goodness – or there being no cities. No word for belief occurs in the second sentence here, and this paraphrase avoids importing any. But clearly the

Athenians' selective practice is reasonable (as Protagoras says it is), because it is done in the belief or the knowledge[252] that it is a necessary condition of the existence of cities that each man should have a share of political goodness.

Two preliminary things need saying about this. First, the Athenians may, in fact, have often dismissed or refused to hear expert advisers irrationally and in a bad collective mood or irrelevant surge of emotion; but that is not the point. Nor is it to the point that they may not in fact have allowed any Tom, Dick or Harry to address them. Being human they doubtless did make irrational choices of speaker to listen to. But the facts of the cases are not in point. It is what Protagoras says which is in point, and what he says is straightforwardly unequivocal; whenever the assembled Athenians need advice they make the rational choice of advisers according to the subject under discussion. False though this pretty obviously was, Protagoras is committed to it.

Secondly, in isolation it would be possible to read the final sentence (323A), 'That is the reason for it', as saying that the alleged Athenian selective practices are reasonable because of the *fact* that all men share in political goodness, and *not* as saying that (a) the practices are practised because of the *Athenians' view* that all men share in political goodness, and (b) practices so motivated are reasonable. But in the context the second interpretation is the only possible one; for the next sentence probably says 'in order that you may not think you are being deceived, receive this further evidence that in truth all men think that every man has a share in justice and the rest of political goodness'.[253] This clearly implies that the previous paragraph was evidence not for the proposition that all men have a share in justice, but for the notion that the Athenians and others *believe* in men's possession of such a share.

Having said this, we can inspect the relevant implications of the passage. Protagoras is saying not only that the Athenians have a notion, and invariably act in accordance with it, but that the reason for their invariable behaviour is that notion. In this particular sphere of action, performance follows invariably on a cognitive state, and the explanation of the performance is the cognitive state. The question of erratic behaviour due to emotional disturbance simply does not arise. If it did, then one thing Protagoras could not formally say in reply would be that the Athenians are uniquely unemotional or strong-willed; for he says that 'Everyone including the Athenians' (more literally 'the others and the Athenians') thinks and behaves in the requisite way (322D). Nor is it easy to imagine Protagoras pleading that men in general are unemotional or strong-willed specially in this highly charged political matter. To all appearances his words indicate a belief that men invariably act, at least in this sphere, in accordance with, and as accounted for by, their cognitive state.

'Accounted for' here papers over an ambiguity; Protagoras could be saying either that the 'reason' he mentions is the actual *cause* or that it is the *motive* of the Athenians' invariable behaviour. It is not clear that the choice would make much difference to us now; for even if (the less favourable hypothesis) the 'reason' gives only the motive, then the sophist implies that the Athenians and the rest invariably act in this sphere on a motive supplied by their cognitive state. Nor is there any good reason why Protagoras should suppose this sphere of action to be peculiar in this respect. There should, admittedly, be no doubt that Protagoras would not have fully intended at the time to take such commitments on board; but it looks very much as though Plato's dialogue so commits him. How fair that is of Plato, how far Plato has foisted anything on anyone, and, if at all, on whom, are questions better raised after inspection of further passages in Protagoras' harangue.

Best mentioned here, however, is a specially interesting feature of the present passage. The speaker says nothing in it about the Athenians' knowledge. Of course, as we saw much earlier in this essay, the carpenter's goodness and so on are certainly related to knowledge. But do the Athenians and the rest *know* that on technical matters only expert evidence is relevant? If so, Protagoras does not mention the fact; he mentions only what all men (including the Athenians) *think*. When it comes to the Athenians' recognition that everyone ought to have a share in political goodness, the sophist does not use a verb of cognition at all; his remarks simply do not reveal whether he has in mind the Athenians' opinion or their knowledge. So far as this paragraph of his argument is concerned, Protagoras shows no sign of doubt that opinion is sufficient to sway men's actions, and no interest whatsoever in their knowledge, or in distinguishing knowledge from opinion.

If one had to choose someone past whom to try and slip the suggestion that *either* knowledge *or* opinion rules in a human being, then one would be hard put to it to find a readier victim than the Protagoras of this long speech. If that still seems a trifle exaggerated, then it is worth waiting for the implications of subsequent arguments.

We proceed to Protagoras' first argument against the acquisition of goodness by nature as opposed to teaching (323C ff.). The demonstrand, to be more precise, is that everybody thinks goodness to be acquired not by nature but by teaching. The first premiss laid down is that

1 Everybody pities, and is not angry with, and does not teach, punish, or rebuke, those who suffer a fault which he believes to be due to natural (or chance) endowment. The establishment of this premiss proceeds by induction; the examples given are ugliness, smallness, and weakness (presumably all three bodily and congenital). In Protagoras' stated opinion, men know that beauty and ugliness are the gift of nature (or chance). The second premiss comes next:

2 Men are angry with, and do punish and rebuke those who have faults remediable by attention, practice and teaching. The opposite of political goodness is a case in point, which gives us Protagoras' third premiss:

3 Everybody is angry with and rebukes everyone whose fault is the opposite of political goodness.

Obviously, says Protagoras – and this is the conclusion of this part of his argument – everybody in behaving thus has in view the proposition that political goodness can be won by attention and by learning (the latter once again the correlative of teaching). The argument is well constructed: if the premisses are true the conclusion follows, whatever one may think of the premisses themselves. Indeed it is the premisses at least as much as the conclusion which interest us at this moment.

The first premiss certainly repays attention. In a very slightly modified Taylorian translation it says: 'In the case of undesirable characteristics which people think are due to nature or chance, nobody gets annoyed at people who have them or corrects or teaches or punishes them, to make them any different, but they pity them; for instance, who is silly enough to try treating the ugly or the small or the weak in any of those ways?'[254] The mere translation brings out the connection Protagoras makes here between what people think and what they do. On the face of it, the point of the first premiss at least is that what people think of the undesirable characteristics in question governs what they feel and how they react.

There is, it is true, a small unclarity. The qualifying clause 'to make them any different' might foster suspicion that the speaker envisages people getting annoyed with other purposes in mind, or even with no purpose in mind at all but simply because they are feeling jealous, irritable, or something else irrational. But this can be cleared up; for Protagoras says that if you think the faulty person's fault is due to nature or chance, then you don't punish him in order to improve him, but you pity him, i.e. you act mercifully towards him. This clearly envisages no third way; either you punish for the sake of improvement or you show mercy; it is difficult to see where irrational punishment would fit in here at all.

The second premiss draws the same connection between cognition and action. In the case of faults remediable by teaching, etc., what men think about the origin of them is mirrored in each instance not only by their emotions but by their actions. Not just an angry feeling, but an actual rebuke is directed at anyone with this kind of fault. But whereas in the previous premiss the form of words 'not ... but ...' (323C–D) made unnecessary any reference to 'every occasion', in this second premiss we miss such a reference. But the sophist does use very general terms in his remarks, literally, '*as many* good things *as* they think come-to-be from teaching', and '*if anyone* doesn't have them but has their opposite faults ...', on them fall '*the* angers and *the* punishments and *the* rebukes'. These expressions need not imply that this is what happens on every occasion such a fault arises. But in the light of the preceding premiss, and of Protagoras' omission of any hint at the possibility of occasions on which the appropriate behaviour does not follow on the relevant belief, one would be fairly safe in supposing Protagoras to envisage no such occasion. At the very least this premiss is fully consistent with the supposition that men's thoughts determine their actions.

Similar considerations apply to the third, more particular premiss, about the example of political goodness. Protagoras says that *every*body rebukes *every*body who has its opposite(s). If he does not specify 'on every occasion', he fails here also to hint at the existence of any exceptional occasions, and to discourage the belief that there are none. Again what he says at least harmonizes with the belief that men behave on every occasion consistently with opinion or knowledge.

Does it here, more than in the argument previously analysed, matter which, opinion or knowledge? It is a striking fact that Protagoras in this exposition of the effects of human cognition on action, passes easily and with apparent nonchalance from opinion to knowledge and back again. Men do not get annoyed at what they *think* due to nature; men *know* that ugliness, etc., are due to nature, and act accordingly. In the sentence which in this particular passage is clearest on the universal effect of cognitive states on action, the cognitive state is thus one of opinion. Men *think*, Protagoras proceeds, that some good things spring from attention, etc., and as we have seen, no word of any exception to the effect of that opinion on action crosses his lips. It would be difficult, if not impossible, to claim, on the basis of this argument, that the difference between opinion and knowledge matters at all to Protagoras so far as actions are concerned. Socrates, if accused later by *this* Protagoras of ignoring that distinction, could have replied with a resounding 'Tu quoque'.

The following briefer presentation of the argument may help to clarify some of the points at issue:

1 (x) (x sees a fault he thinks or knows to be natural $\rightarrow x$ pities), and
2 (x) (x sees a fault he thinks to be non-natural $\rightarrow x$ is angry), and

3   (x)   (x sees a political fault → x is angry).
   Therefore, from 1, 2 and 3,
4   (x)   (x thinks or knows the political fault to be non-natural).

Here all values of x fall within the set of persons. In the premiss 1 'thinks or knows' is based on the alternation noticed above in Plato's use of the terms; in 4 the same disjunction is based on his use (324A) of the same construction, without a verb of cognition at all, as was found at the end of the first of this set of arguments to receive our analysis (323A).[255] The extent to which the implications marked by arrows in this transcription are not absolutely cast-iron has been detailed above. To the extent to which Protagoras adheres to those implications, he is saying that action follows on cognition. But surely, the reader may suggest, he cannot have meant to rule out irrational action? Surely he even mentions irrationality in the course of his next argument, which is clearly part of the same paragraph? That next argument also repays inspection.

Protagoras' argument[256] starts (324A) from the premiss that nobody punishes the unjust for the sake of their past injustice who does not punish like a beast irrationally. This indeed at least raises the possibility of irrational punishment. But it is not absolutely clear what Protagoras means by 'like a beast' in context. Is he saying, in effect, that some *men* on some occasions allow their passions to get the better of them and in anger worthy of a beast punish with no thought but vengeance in their heads? Or is he saying that anyone who punishes with no thought but vengeance rules himself out of the human community, and is *not really a man* but a beast? So far the former alternative is the one more likely to occur to Protagoras' audience; 'like a beast' is not the same as 'not human'.

We are justified in putting two propositions into Protagoras' mouth here: (1) Nobody punishes for the past rationally, and (2) Punishment for the past, if there is any such punishment, is irrational. It is clear also that Protagoras can distinguish between rational and irrational action, at least in the sphere of punishment, and for all that he has said so far in this particular argument, a determined interpreter could attribute to him a belief in the occurrence of any proportion, however high, of beastly and irrational punishment. Irrational punishment is a likely instance of emotion overcoming reason. In this section of this argument Protagoras has apparently covered himself against the suspicion of being the kind of intellectualist Socrates can later take advantage of.

But nagging suspicions of excessive intellectualism remain. Protagoras expresses his conclusion interestingly: 'all those who punish privately or publicly' (324B–C) hold that goodness is inculcable. This conclusion convinces only on one of two conditions: either all who punish, punish rationally, or those who punish irrationally do not count as men rather than beasts. This would make all human beings who punish (including all parents) rational beings in respect of punishment. Nothing in Protagoras' words actually excludes the possibility of a generally rational human being doing something irrational in (say) a fit of temper; but nothing here clearly envisages such an event. It is simply not clear whether the irrational counts as human or not. But whether or not Protagoras continues in this punishment-passage his neglect of human irrational action in his account of democracy, his questioner in dialectic may still legitimately probe; if Protagoras did fall into self-contradiction, Socrates would be entitled to ask after one arm of the contradiction and to leave him to bring up the other if he dared. Protagoras believes for at least part of the time in the primacy of the intellect.

If Protagoras is nearer to common sense when he shows signs of envisaging cases of emotion winning the battle against reason, then whence comes his earlier attitude? Why should he treat the Athenians as always acting rationally in their choice of speakers? The first line of answer to this question is quite simple: Socrates in his challenge treats the Athenians thus. This is where we have to subject Socrates' speech of challenge to the same kind of dissection to which we have subjected Protagoras' reply. The sophist, indeed, expressly refers us back to Socrates' speech at just the place in his reply that deals with the Athenians' selection policy (322C–E cf. 319B–C). Comparison shows that the term 'whenever', which led Protagoras into such trouble by specifying that the action concerned took place on every relevant occasion, is indeed taken over from Socrates. Protagoras' facts about the policy he says the Athenians invariably pursue are straight out of Socrates' speech – and that includes both the selection of experts where relevant and the freedom given to every Tom, Dick or Harry to speak on the general administration of the city. Both are every bit as much universal policies according to Socrates' speech as they are in Protagoras', and both are connected with what the Athenians think. Evidently Socrates' speech needs analysis.

On subjects where the Athenians *think* teaching and learning are possible, Socrates says, they always send for experts, and they remove anyone they *think* is not an expert; that is their policy, seemingly invariable, on subjects they *think* are by way of 'arts'. On state administration they allow anyone to speak without reproaching him for his lack of a teacher. 'So it's clear that they don't regard that as something that can be taught.' (319D).[257] Socrates makes no mention here of knowledge; he does mention, earlier in his attack, the *wisdom* of the Athenians. What does all this amount to? Socrates suggests that in technical matters the Athenians always do what, given their opinions on the nature of the topic and the qualifications of potential speakers, it would be rational for them to do.

On goodness, again, Socrates deduces (319D) Athenian opinion from their invariable behaviour. This deduction is difficult:

A The Athenians on this topic act unselectively.

For, obviously,

B They do not believe goodness teachable.

This is not actually a deduction of A from B; it is rather a statement that A is true, and a deduction that B is true. B is true as the only possible explanation, indeed a necessary condition of A. But if we ask why B is a necessary condition of A, we must go back to the first half of Socrates' statement about the Athenians. There we find:

C (x) (the Athenians believe x teachable → the Athenians act on *x* selectively); now if C is true, then B does indeed follow from A. That is why B is 'obvious', given A. We conclude that Socrates' deduction about the Athenians' belief of B depends on, and is deduced from, the truth of C. Hence his deduction renews his commitment to the Athenians' invariably acting in a certain way on their beliefs that certain subjects are matters of technical expertise. Socrates' connection of opinion and action in this speech is all of a piece. And, as we have seen, he does not even mention knowledge, but speaks throughout of the apparently inevitable consequences of holding an opinion.

'Curiouser and curiouser.' This might indeed seem an adventure in a philosophical wonderland; we are asking the reader to excuse Socrates for asking (358B), and Plato for making him ask, whether men follow their knowledge or opinion of what is good, on the grounds that his interlocutor is indifferent to the distinction between knowledge and opinion, and implies (at least part of the time) that action follows inevitably on the relevant opinion; next, we find that the victim of this leading question owes to none other than Socrates the supposition that cognition rules in the sphere of action. Bewildered by the apparent unfairness of a Plato who can so foist a view on Protagoras, for 'foisting' is a natural expression in this context, we notice to our further irritation that the power *of knowledge*, usually thought to be a Socratic tenet, does not appear in that opening speech of Socrates. The proposition Socrates does foist on Protagoras is precisely the proposition about *opinion* which even in the form of a question, has aroused some scholarly suspicion because of its un-Socratic nature. Clearly we have not yet got to the bottom of this problem.

The only way to touch bottom is to delve deeper into the Socratic challenge to Protagoras. Does Socrates believe anything of what he asserts in that speech and, if there is a high proportion in it of assertions he does not believe, is that *merely* irony? If it is, then Plato's 'foisting' is, we may think, inexcusable. Is there any alternative? First, how much of what Socrates says there looks like Socratic argument from Socratic premisses? Let us turn a cold and wary eye on it.

Socrates began with a statement of his previous disbelief in the teachability of goodness (319B). This might be genuinely Socratic (though it does not seem likely) and might be possible, despite the *Meno* (87B–C), to make consistent with Socrates' doctrine – if he believed it fully – that goodness is knowledge. Acknowledging our ignorance, we should proceed to the next assertion. Whether the reasons Socrates gives for believing goodness teachable are his own or not is still *sub judice*. But it would be difficult to take seriously as his own belief Socrates' suggestion that the Athenians are wise. We have no reason to suppose that it was his genuine and sincere opinion that the Athenians lived up invariably to their opinion and allowed only experts to address them on topics requiring expertise, and never rejected the requisite expert unheard.

It is no less difficult to imagine at least the Platonic Socrates, with whom we have to deal, ever in all honesty and sincerity holding that the wisest and best of his fellow-Athenians were the leading statesmen of the democracy, and that they (if they had only tried) would have been the best educators for their sons (319E–320B).

Nor, without some degree of irony, not to say falsehood, could Socrates assert at his opening (319A–B) that he finds it impossible to disbelieve Protagoras, and at the end that he bows to his wide experience, manifold learning, and originality. In fact there are very few lines of this speech which sound like the genuine and sincere expression of Socrates' own views; and none which are specifically, exactly and necessarily Socratic; his implications in the matter of the Athenians always following their opinions are presumably no more and no less tongue-in-cheek than the rest. What then is going on in our philosophical Wonderland?

To this insistent question there is a surprisingly simple and coherent answer. It is this: Socrates, in his challenge to Protagoras, is still speaking on behalf of the young Hippocrates. Hippocrates is a conventional youth, eager to shine in the democracy (316C). He wants to that end to be taught rhetoric, and the arts of government and politics. He certainly can be thought of as finding it difficult to disagree with Protagoras, for whom he has an ignorant and naive enthusiasm (310Aff.). He certainly would think highly of the Athenian political system, in which he seeks to distinguish himself. He can hardly be expected to bother himself with niceties of expression, and is just the sort of person who might make a sweeping statement implying that the theory, the myth, of democracy actually described its workings. He will certainly have had a high respect for both the ability and the citizenship of figures such as Pericles, and will have known (as who did not?) that their sons were less distinguished than they. There are notably few assertions in Socrates' challenge that could not be put into the mouth of Hippocrates with an ease which matches the extreme difficulty of taking them seriously as Socratic premises or beliefs. So has Plato given to his Socrates the job of representing Hippocrates? And is there anything in the dialogue to indicate that Socrates has this job and is not at this juncture to be thought of as speaking in his own person? Well, yes, there is, and it is worth rehearsing it.

Hippocrates' explanation of his precipitate arrival at early dawn contained a statement of his purpose; to get Socrates to talk to Protagoras *on his (Hippocrates') behalf* (310E). At their meeting with Protagoras, the first words of any substance Socrates speaks are an introduction of Hippocrates and a statement of the young man's purpose (316B). When the company are assembled to hear the discussion, Protagoras asks Socrates to explain what he mentioned before *on Hippocrates' behalf*. Socrates asks Protagoras the same question whose answer he had previously convicted Hippocrates of not knowing; what does Protagoras have to offer (317E–318A, cf. 312Bff.)? The question is represented pretty fairly as 'ours', i.e. Hippocrates' and Socrates'. Protagoras' vague reply, in effect 'improvement', earns him further questioning conducted in terms of what would happen to Hippocrates if he went to other teachers. Having thus illustrated his point, Socrates asks Protagoras to say to the young man and to Socrates asking *on his behalf* in what respect will the 'improvement' be (318D). Protagoras in answer distinguishes himself from other sophists: he teaches not the arts, but good counsel in private and public life. Socrates requests him to amplify, asking him if he means that he teaches the political art. The question Socrates puts here, whether Protagoras promises to make men good citizens, is strongly reminiscent of Hippocrates' desire to become well known in the city. Right up to the moment of Socrates' great challenge to Protagoras he is, and Plato makes quite clear that he is, speaking on Hippocrates' behalf.

The case is already strong for Socrates' approach to Protagoras being a joint affair with Hippocrates, the young man's likely views being put together in the form of argumentative questions by Socrates. Further traces of such a scheme are visible. Socrates' dialectical efforts in the dialogue's opening conversation are pretty clearly aimed at getting the young man to agree that he does not know what Protagoras teaches. Hippocrates does not want to learn from him how to be a sophist (311E–312B). He opines that Protagoras' subject is like that of an elementary teacher of letters, music or gymnastics, for general education (312A–B), but he is argued out of the supposition that the skill of speaking is Protagoras' subject (312D–E). The question in what the sophist is wise, and in what he makes his pupil wise, is the final question, whose answer Hippocrates admits he does not know, before Socrates harangues him on the enormity of his rashness in entrusting his soul to a sophist in such ignorance (313A–C). The harangue is spiced with a warning not to accept the intellectual huckster's word for the high value of his wares (313C–314B). The pair then go off to listen to Protagoras and the other sophists; presumably on the merit and nature of their teaching, since their teaching itself has possible dangers which Socrates has just pointed out (314A–B). The whole trend of Socrates' early questions to Protagoras is thus prepared for by the conversation with Hippocrates.

It is now up to Protagoras to produce a convincing account of his teaching and its value. Evidently his claim to teach goodness, a claim as arrogant as any huckster's, needs close inspection. The question (foreshadowed in Socrates' talk with Hippocrates) 'goodness at what?' has in this context a thoroughly natural sequel in the inquiry whether the particular goodness Protagoras claims to teach is in fact susceptible of being taught. Socrates has succeeded in replacing the naive enthusiasm of Hippocrates' dawn arrival with a certain scepticism, and it is this cooler Hippocrates that he now represents to Protagoras.

So it is not, after all, just Plato's Socrates who has made suggestions to Plato's Protagoras which the latter finds it convenient to take up and apparently endorse, to his later discomfiture. Protagoras faces a series of questions and arguments on behalf of a prospective pupil. They are questions and arguments such as any cool-headed and articulate prospective pupil might put to Protagoras in an Athenian milieu where the purpose of going to Protagoras in the first instance was, as Socrates well expresses it, to distinguish oneself in the city (316C), to make a name for oneself in democratic politics. Protagoras has to be able to convince someone like Hippocrates, rendered articulate by Socrates, that he has a subject to teach and of course that he knows what it is. If Plato has him, in trying to be thus convincing, using suggestions that come from such a source, that seems both natural – the question receives an answer in its own terms – and fair: Protagoras was, doubtless, no less given to taking on board sweeping statements than most rhetoricians.

One thing that the dialogue itself shows is that such easy generalizations tend to lead one into trouble, and that in particular some of them, notably some of the myths attaching to democracy in Athens, necessitate, if they are to be held consistently with themselves and with other cherished beliefs, the taking up of positions not far removed from those of that Socrates whom the democracy put to death.

A particular case of this is the supposed openness, and openness of mind, of the Athenian democracy. In the sweeping form in which Socrates, on behalf of Hippocrates, puts this forward, it is based on the unspoken and (by Hippocrates and Protagoras) unrecognized assumption that men's opinions issue in appropriate action. The sophist, perhaps not altogether consistently, but nevertheless for a spell in his self-justifying speech, uses this assumption fed him by the representative of a prospective pupil. That representative is Socrates, who then uses the sophist's commitment to the view that men do what their opinions bid them, and his apparent indifference to the distinction between knowledge and opinion, coupled with the sophist's own implied commitment as a teacher to the power of knowledge, to lead him to the doctrine that what men know or think is better or less bad will be their choice of action. The detail of the line of questioning by which Socrates achieves this still awaits our examination; but the nature and source of the assumptions from which he starts has, it is to be hoped, received clarification.

Before we return from this excursus to pick up the thread of the dialogue's argument, there are a few points of a transitional nature to be made. We must, eventually, go back to Socrates' argument at the place where 'the many' are introduced to the discussion. The 'many' differ from Protagoras on the subject of the power of knowledge, let alone that of opinion. The 'many' are not committed to what Protagoras says, nor to what Socrates said in his challenge, nor yet to what Hippocrates may legitimately be supposed to have had in mind. Hippocrates is an ordinary young man about town, with ambitions, not an entirely ordinary citizen. It is not therefore surprising that, when in his Great Speech Protagoras turns to what the ordinary Athenian citizen-parent does, it is not something implying the same intellectualism as Protagoras' own argument implied.

The sophist's account of Athenian education (325C–326E) shows indeed something much less rationalist in character. As parents, according to him (325D), the Athenians instruct the very young by telling and displaying to them what is just, holy, fine, and/or to be done, and what is none of these things. But they do not assume that their offspring will directly do only the right things, and they provide coercive threats and punishments for those who do not. The process presumably needs the reinforcement it receives from teachers of music, poetry and physical training. The poetry contains warnings, and contains (like the music) also examples of praised actions for the young to emulate. The music teachers take care also of their charges' moderation, compelling them to adapt their 'soul' to suitably gentling rhythms and (in some sense) 'harmonies'.[258] The trainer of the body (326B–C) supplies further help. The system's crown (326C–E) is the city's compulsion on its citizens not only to learn the laws but also to live in accordance with them, with no implication whatever that living in accordance follows inevitably from learning the laws; even if Plato did write that the city 'makes them learn the laws and live according to their example' (which has been doubted),[259] there is no suggestion that legal prohibitions and example are sufficient conditions of good behaviour; rather the city itself compels its citizens, by punishment of various sorts, to do what is right. In the whole account of Athenian education there is no suggestion that the young or the adult citizen will do what he thinks or what he knows to be right. External compulsion is exercised at every stage.

The Athenians as here portrayed are not rationalists of the stamp of earlier passages in Protagoras' speech. But if we ask, reasonably, how this portrayal of education squares with the earlier rationalism, the answer must be that it does not have to square with what precedes it; what precedes is something Protagoras was committed to, but to the Athenian system of education nobody is committed except the Athenians. Protagoras' views do not have to coincide with those of the 'many', and their motives need not be his.

The foregoing account of Protagoras' paragraph dealing with Athenian education glossed over a point which needs attention. The trainer of the body (326B–C) supplies what appears to be a necessary condition of avoiding cowardice, namely, a physique fit and able to serve a good mind. We should dwell on this for a moment, since the later passage from which this whole discussion arose concerned itself particularly with courage. If Protagoras were committed to the suggestion that a necessary condition of 'courage' is the physique to stand up for oneself, he could not agree that a knowledge, namely, of what is to be feared and what is not, is a sufficient condition of 'courage'. But, as already said, the sophist is not committed to the justification of all or any of the motives he ascribes to the Athenians.

Furthermore, even if Protagoras were committed to this particular point, he would still not be committed to the insufficiency of knowledge in the required sense. Several times in the course of the dialogue's final discussion Socrates stresses the question whether a man will willingly or voluntarily do the worse or more unpleasant thing *when it is possible for him not to do it*. If, as the Athenians' motive for physical education (in Protagoras' version) suggests, poor physique *forces* a man to behave in cowardly fashion, then his choice of behaviour is compulsory and not voluntary.

In parts of the Great Speech to which one may fairly say that Protagoras is committed the dominant picture is that of Man as a rational creature, acting at the behest of his cognitive faculties. Socrates relies on this picture in requiring Protagoras to accept that opinion rules, no less than knowledge. He can be fairly sure of an affirmative answer, and if he gets a negative one, he can deal with it.

But a further query must detain us: why should Socrates make such a song and dance about knowledge in the final discussion of the dialogue, and why (by contrast) should he so casually slip in the point about opinion? Two possible answers to this query come to mind, answers by no means mutually exclusive. The first is that knowledge both is in general immeasurably more important to Socrates and is in this dialogue a major theme, as opinion is not. The second is that in the Great Speech Protagoras laid great stress on opinion and belief, but curiously little on knowledge. Despite references to teaching and learning, notions generally associable with knowledge, and also to 'wisdom' and 'art', the Great Speech refers explicitly to knowing only twice, and both times in reference to things placed in contrast with goodness, not to goodness itself (323B and 323D).

The fictional Socrates can afford to take for granted Protagoras' commitment on opinion much more easily than his commitment to the power of knowledge. There is a possible reason for this way of constructing the dialogue, too. Protagoras cannot be too firmly and overtly committed in the Great Speech to the necessity and/or sufficiency of knowledge; for that would commit him too firmly and overtly and unambivalently to the doctrine that goodness is a knowledge or an art, and Protagoras' ambivalence on that matter is a vital theme of the developing discussion.

The introduction of the 'many'

The immediate context of the multitude's entrance on the dialectical scene is Socrates' suggestion that they do not agree with Protagoras and him on the status of cognition. We have now seen that that suggestion is justifiable with reference to what Protagoras said in the Great Speech. It is also justifiable in fact. The common man believes that many people know, or think they know, what is best for them, but, even when it is possible, still fail to do it. (Ovid will serve, in this context, as a common man, '... video meliora proboque, deteriora sequor'.)

The ordinary man says, on inquiry, that people are overcome on certain occasions by pleasure, pain, or some other factor, such as anger, sexual desire or fear.[260] Socrates and Protagoras have just agreed against the common man in denial of any such thing. Socrates suggests that the common man, faced with that denial, will repeat that he nevertheless has such experiences, and if his description of them is incorrect, perhaps Socrates and Protagoras would be good enough to explain how to describe them and what the experience is?

Protagoras' protest, to the effect that 'the many' are often in error and speak at random, leads to the question why bother with their opinions? Yet Protagoras had earlier (328A-B) claimed to be only somewhat better at teaching goodness than the Athenians. The contrast between these two attitudes shows him a worried man, wanting to brush the common view on weakness of will hastily under the nearest carpet. Evidently the sophist knows personally that 'the many' have a good point, since he has often, like the rest of us, shared their experience. The facts threaten to demolish the intellectualism alike of his profession and of his earlier commitments in the dialogue. He cannot know what escape route Socrates will find, but for himself he can presumably see none, in view of his recent admissions. Protagoras especially, but also the other sophists, will eventually be only too glad to accept certain premises, and certain compressed arguments, which otherwise they would be under no obligation to accept; they will be glad *because* acceptance makes possible the rebuttal of the common man's interpretation of weakness of will. That interpretation endangers certain pretensions which Plato, rightly or wrongly, thought common to them all.

The sophists have accordingly no need to examine too closely the line Socrates takes with 'the many'. If he foists dubious premises or inferences on the 'many', that does not commit the sophists to anything, but helps them against the common man. The only people with an interest in the detail of the common man's refutation are offstage, reading or listening to Plato's dialogue. Paradoxically, it is doubtful how far Plato was interested in them; if the dialogue's point was to show the sophists as compelled to adopt not merely an intellectualist outlook but one consistently intellectualist à la Socrates, then Plato had no need to worry about the soundness of their joint refutation of the 'many'.

These general points should now give way to consideration of the detail of Socrates' discussion with Protagoras. Our general suggestions already account for Socrates' contention that the opinion of the 'many' is relevant to the question immediately at issue between him and Protagoras. The question was, in Taylor's terminology, 'how courage is related to the other parts of excellence'. Naturally the particular other part of goodness that Socrates has in mind is that of wisdom; but Protagoras had admitted already the resemblance between wisdom and the three other parts of goodness (349D). It is in this context that Socrates, with, as he says, Protagoras, is to try to explain men's experience of weak will.

Men's experience is of being overcome by things pleasant but acknowledged to be bad. What makes these pleasures bad? In pursuing this further question. Socrates puts two alternatives before the 'many' (353C–D).[261] Are these pleasures bad because they give immediate pleasure? Or because they have unfortunate consequences? If they had no unfortunate, but only pleasant consequences, would they still be bad, however they produced those pleasant consequences? Protagoras and Socrates agree that it is not, in the eyes of the 'many', the production of pleasure by itself which makes these bad pleasures bad. It is rather their unfortunate, that is unpleasant, or even painful, consequences. Similar alternatives are then put concerning painful but good things: are they good because painful or because they have consequences which are agreed to lead to pleasures and liberation from pains? The pair of alternatives in each case is not necessarily exhaustive; but in each case the sophist and Socrates ask the 'many' if they wish to give any other reason for the goodness of unpleasant but good or for the badness of pleasant but bad things – and in each case it is agreed that the 'many' would choose no other alternative than those mentioned, and would chose only one of these.

The basic question thus put to the 'many' is this: if things are good but unpleasant, is their goodness due to anything other than the pleasure accruing from their consequences? and, if a thing is bad but pleasant, is its badness due to anything but its unpleasant consequences? Are there any other criteria by which the 'many' evaluate the alternatives that life throws in their way? It is essential to the present interpretation to observe that these questions are, in elaborate and lengthy form, the same question that Socrates put to Protagoras earlier (351C–E). Stripped of its rhetorical trappings and detailed precision, the question now put to the 'many' is whether a thing which is pleasant is good so long as it does not have unpleasant consequences (353C–D). We should take into account Protagoras' earlier agreement that 'pleasant' was to mean 'pleasant without any non-pleasant consequences'; we then notice that Socrates asked Protagoras in that earlier interrogation, in effect, whether, if x is pleasant and x has no *non-pleasant* consequences, x is good. The question for the 'many' to answer is whether, if x is pleasant and x has no *unpleasant* consequences, x is good. Neither Protagoras nor Socrates lays any stress on the difference between non-pleasant and unpleasant, and neutral consequences are largely irrelevant here.

But if the questions asked of Protagoras and the 'many' are very similar, the replies Socrates receives are of course significantly and even radically different. After correction of his initial blunder, Protagoras refused to be drawn in his own behalf; as a moralist he cannot bring himself to disregard moral considerations in the evaluation of choices. But on behalf of the 'many' he has no such scruples. He does not suggest that they too might pay some attention to what is 'fine' in judging what is good. He does not permit them, despite repeated opportunities, even so much as to hint that the morally fine action might rank as better than the merely pleasant one – however pleasant the latter.

On the face of it this is strange: the Athenians of the Great Speech insist on telling their children what is just or unjust, what is fine or disreputable, what is holy or unholy, and as parents they say nothing about what is pleasant or unpleasant (352D). For what the point is worth, *Socrates* had associated the many with the belief that some pleasant things are bad, and some painful things good (351C). Although this belief is about to be swallowed up in the hedonism of the 'many', it remains unclear why this should be at the expense of all considerations of morality such as justice. It is indeed, so far, just as unclear in the case of the 'many' as in that of Protagoras. So far, though Socrates' interpretation of the 'many' is at least consistent, Protagoras' is not. Three solutions to the problem of Protagoras' inconsistency present themselves, one much less flattering to the participants in the discussion than the others.

The first and least flattering solution is that Plato and his Protagoras are still under the shadow of the apparent opposition between the values of pleasure and those of the intellect. Being unable, after previous admissions, to associate the man in the street with those of the intellect, Protagoras turns to those of pleasure as more plausibly attributable to the 'many'. To do this is to lose what we should call moral values in those of the intellect. This would suit Plato and his Socrates, but would certainly not, normally speaking, suit the 'many'. It ought to suit Protagoras only in so far as he is agreed that goodness is an 'art', teachable, and a 'knowledge'. But this solution would have Socrates making use of Protagoras' difficulties to confute the 'many'. The sophist can hardly attribute a confusion of intellectual and moral spheres to the 'many' just because his own professional pretensions threaten to land him in that confusion. The lack of verisimilitude would be a glaring fault. It would be the more glaring in that the 'many' are already acknowledged to have differences with Protagoras and Socrates over the status of the intellect in the moral life, differences which it is the whole purpose of the attempted refutation to reduce. The sophists are not, and do not need to be, specially alert in the debate with the 'many', which they need to win, but limits must be set to their hebetude.

The second solution takes account of a further feature of the Athenian system of education as outlined in the Great Speech.

When Athenian parents have finished instructing their children in what is fine and what disreputable, and have added 'Do these!' and 'Don't do those!', they then presumably observe the consequences of their instruction before taking further steps. If the child obeys without compulsion – Plato's sentence is left unfinished, for there is nothing left to say or do (352D).[262] If the child is disobedient, however, they 'straighten' him with threats and blows. Now this procedure is of considerable interest to the analyst of pleasure's and pain's position in moral matters. Evidently those administering penal pain[263] believe that it is likely to be efficacious where moral instruction of a verbal kind is not. In administering the punishment they are training the children who show signs of disobedience to recognize as giving less pain in the long run those things which are 'just' and 'fine', and as giving in the long run more pain those things which are unjust and disreputable. Since the object is to get them to do the just and fine, and not do the unjust and disreputable, the training assumes that the children will do what is less and avoid what is more painful or unpleasant. That makes the Athenians, as parents, into a species of psychological hedonists. Their psychological hedonism, moreover, does not stop with their children; the city of Athens through its legal system exercises on adults coercion of the same sort, and presumably on the same basis. Protagoras verbally links the two sets of punishments by the use of the same verb 'straighten' (325D7 and 326E1),[264] and by comparing the educative function of the city to the behaviour of schoolmasters. The system of punishments too is based in Protagoras' view on a species of psychological hedonism.

Now it does not follow immediately from the proposition that the Athenians think of themselves as psychological hedonists that they are in fact, behavioural fact, hedonists. They might in fact be moralists who, without realizing it, base their choices of action on the relative justice or injustice of the courses open to them. They might be soft-hearted while believing they were hard-headed; it is possible to be incorrect about one's motives. But if one thinks of oneself as a psychological hedonist, one cannot say 'I did it just because it was morally right'; if one said this, one would acknowledge that psychological hedonism was false; and one cannot rationally believe that one holds a proposition which one believes at the same time to be false. Hence, if Protagoras does indeed treat the Athenians as believing themselves psychological hedonists, then he cannot consistently suppose that they would give any other reply to Socrates' question than the one they do give. When asked, that is, whether certain pleasures are avoided for any other reason than that they lead to countervailing pain or distress, they cannot reply that they are avoided because they are unjust or dishonourable without adding that the unjust and dishonourable are avoided because they lead to unpleasantness. Ultimately they have no other reason for avoiding pleasures and calling them bad. If Protagoras thinks the Athenians are psychological hedonists he will suppose them to answer the question 'What is your ultimate motive?' with the single word 'pleasure'.

So far as Socrates is concerned, all that matters for the moment is that Protagoras should be constrained to agree that the 'many' could offer no other answer. The sophist does not have to be any sort of hedonist himself to think that 'the many' or 'the Athenians' are. Whether his Great Speech committed *him* to a belief in psychological hedonism is more than doubtful; a belief in the moral efficacy of punishment may imply a species of psychological hedonism, but Protagoras does not commit himself to the moral efficacy of punishment – it is not his mode of teaching. What he does, indirectly, commit himself to is Athenian belief in a species of psychological hedonism: what is more, there is nothing absurd in the commitment.

But this does nothing to answer the question why the 'many' turn out to be not merely psychological but actually evaluative hedonists. They clearly believe not just that they pursue pleasure, but that pleasure is good for them to pursue. Between such an evaluative hedonism and psychological hedonism a gulf is set, which Plato's and Socrates' 'many' appear effortlessly but dangerously to leap. Plato could have bridged that gap by arguments of a kind he uses elsewhere, e.g. in the *Gorgias* (467–8), with a view to eliciting the opinion that the object of pursuit is in fact the good, what people ought to pursue. But though Plato could have constructed such a bridge he does not, in the *Protagoras*. The difficulty need not be fatal to our analysis, but remains to nag us, and there is a third solution to the original problem of Protagoras' inconsistent reports of the 'many' which may enable us to avoid it. Its exposition demands, at the risk of some repetition, a return to the text.

We recall Socrates' question to the 'many': in what respect are they (sc. the bad pleasures) bad (353C–D)? Socrates offers alternative answers: the first is that the reason for the badness is the immediate pleasure, and this has never struck readers as a very plausible answer. But at least this does offer a property possessed *in common* by all the pleasures concerned. If we wish to explain in what respect all As are B it is advisable to look thus in the first instance for a property possessed in common by all As. So Socrates offers the many a property common to all bad pleasures, namely, their enjoyability at the time. He then offers them another property which they may think common to all bad pleasures, namely that such pleasures result eventually in disease, poverty, and the like. These in turn (it is agreed) result in pain or unpleasantness (353E).

Here the bad pleasures are unfortunately not enumerated, so that we cannot inspect them to judge the plausibility of the suggestion that the only relevant common property they possess is their resulting eventually in unpleasantness. But moral disgracefulness, at least, need not be such a common property; it is no doubt possible to think of pleasures not disgraceful, not unfair to others, which result in some material damage or unpleasantness to the person pursuing them. To take an anachronistic example, the eating of sweets may lead to toothache.

The case is, however, clearer when Socrates turns to good pains (354A). There he asks the 'many' to agree to an enumeration of such pains: gymnastics, military expeditions and medical treatments. The common property of painfulness does not explain the goodness of these to the many, who are neither masochistic nor excessively puritanical. But it is hard to think of any other relevant common property except that their consequences are more pleasant than the consequences of avoiding them. In particular there is nothing *morally* fine about submitting to painful medical treatment. Such submission is, however, sensible in the patient's interests, in that he avoids greater pains or death to follow. It is this kind of common sense to which Socrates makes appeal. What other common property would ordinary people find in this hotchpotch? What else do health, good physical condition, offices and wealth have in common than the enhancement of life's pleasantness? Do they all result in any other single thing which is good?

Results are in question; Taylor's translation well brings out this point by using the English verb and noun 'result', where the Greek had also an etymologically related noun and verb (354B). Socrates is asking the 'many' (i) whether the experience itself or its consequences are the reason why they call good pains good and bad pleasures bad, and (ii) whether the multifarious consequences of bad pleasure have anything in common explanatory of their badness other than consequent unpleasantness, and whether the multifarious consequences of good pains have anything in common explanatory of their goodness other than consequent pleasure. It is not at all clear that the 'many' have any serious option but to answer as they do.[265]

But the 'many' could object to the whole procedure. They could claim that there is no single property common to (for example) good pains, except their goodness and their painfulness. Such an objection would recall a familiar criticism of Socratic dialectic, accusing Socrates of assuming that a word (often a word to be defined) covers a single class, with one universal defining property.[266] The criticism is effective in the present instance; one could perhaps divide 'good pains' into several classes, each serving a different end or having a different kind of good result. An end such as health could be good in itself, rather than because of the concomitant pleasure of well-being; fighting for one's country could be, in Horatian terms, *decorum* rather than *dulce*, and good for the former reason.

But if Plato himself were confronted with this criticism of his Socrates he might conceivably have replied with a plea of genuine and pardonable ignorance, urging that for him at the date of the *Protagoras* one word inevitably covered a single definite class, except for obvious homonyms – and he did not think 'good' a homonymous term. Thus the tacit acceptance by the 'many' of the univocity of 'good' matches similar univocity assumptions elsewhere. Even if Plato knew the dubiety of the assumption, he could be fairly sure (a) that the 'many', if summoned before him, would not spot his mistake, and (b) that the sophists, as keen as Socrates to win the dispute with the 'many', would not naturally be the people to point it out. Since the assumption helps to rule out a *moral* account of good pleasures, the 'many' can quite naturally be driven to accept a form of evaluative hedonism in which not only is pleasure good and pain bad, but also the defining property of good things, the reason why they are called 'good', is their pleasantness, and the defining property of bad things, the reason why they are called 'bad', is their painfulness or unpleasantness.

We have, then, arrived at a form of evaluative hedonism. But we have not yet, curiously enough, found anything, in the text of the discussion with the 'many', about psychological hedonism, and clearly we are going to need such, in order to smooth the way for later steps in the argument. Perhaps significantly, the doctrine of psychological hedonism appears without formal introduction, let alone proof, in the tail of the argument designed to obtain the acceptance by the 'many' of evaluative hedonism.[267]

The development of the argument with the 'many'; psychological hedonism?

So far Socrates and Protagoras have driven the 'many' to admit that in deciding whether an action is good or bad it is only the pleasantness or unpleasantness of the action itself and of its consequences which need to be taken into account. After this there is a sense in which it would be legitimate for the interrogators to assume the respondents' belief that pleasure was *the* good and unpleasantness *the* bad. But there is no need for them to make this assumption, or invite the 'many' to make this assumption, or invite the 'many' to make it, in every question asked. There is accordingly no need to take the next question (354C), 'So you pursue pleasure as good, and avoid pain as evil?', as saying anything about *the* good or *the* bad.[268]

It simply asks if men pursue pleasure as being a good thing, and avoid pain as being a bad thing.

This question may well have a double point: the first prong is the extraction of a formal admission that pleasure is good and pain bad. This – or something like it – had been refused by Protagoras in his own behalf at the very outset of the talk about pleasure. The sophist had there first admitted and later qualified the notion that it was a sufficient condition for a life to be good that it be pleasant; he had subsequently refused to agree that all things pleasant are good or that all things painful are bad. But the 'many' in Socrates' imaginary conversation accept without qualification that pleasure is good and pain bad. Protagoras had wanted earlier to insist that 'pleasant things are good and painful ones are bad' needed qualification: pleasant things are sufficient for the good life if and only if they are not only pleasant but also fine. One point of Socrates' question may be to establish that the 'many' have now gone beyond what Protagoras could accept in his own behalf.

The second prong is the establishment of the *pursuit* of pleasure by the 'many'. If the 'many' believe that they pursue things pleasant then they are adopting at least a mild and possibly a strong form of psychological hedonism; in the belief of the 'many' men do, as a matter of fact, pursue pleasure.

But these considerations do not determine the place of the question about pursuit in the chain of reasoning the 'many' are being invited to follow. The many have accepted, in effect, that, A(i), Bad pleasant things are bad because and only because they result in pains, and that, A(ii), Good painful things are good because and only because they result in pleasures. Formally speaking, this does not show that pleasures are good nor that pains are bad. To *compel* the 'many' to admit that would need another pair of questions, affirmatively answered, namely, whether that because of which (and only because of which) something is bad is itself bad, and whether that because of which (and only because of which) something is good is itself good. For whatever reason, Socrates skips this stage of the argument. Whether Plato let him do so in deliberate informality or in carelessness is not clear. At all events the 'many' have not previously admitted in their imaginary conversation that pleasure is good and pain bad, and Socrates duly extracts the admission, plausibly if not in accordance with strict logic,[269] with the question at 354C mentioned above.

The next speech of Socrates is tricky (354C). 'This, then, you think is bad, namely pain, and [this you think is] good, [namely] pleasure, since even enjoyment itself you say is bad then, when it deprives [the enjoyer] of pleasures greater than it contains itself, or produces pains greater than the pleasures in it; since, if you call enjoyment bad in any other respect and with any other result in view, you would be able to tell us [what it is]; but you will not be able'. The Greek here is very compressed, as its lack of the bracketed words indicates.[270] The original is in fact even more compressed; for the demonstrative adverb 'then' in the fourth line of my version must be short for 'only then' in order to give point to the reference to 'no other result' which follows. Hence the preceding demonstrative pronoun 'this' must stand likewise for 'this alone'. It results that Socrates, having just previously asked (in effect) whether all pleasure is good and all pain bad, asks here (conversely) whether all good is pleasure, and in his next speech symmetrically whether all bad is pain. It is this not altogether open procedure which entitles him to claim below that 'the good' has been admitted to be pleasure.

Is Socrates entitled to commit the many to the exclusion of all other goods than pleasure and all other bads than pain? Surely, after their previous admissions, A(i) and A(ii) above, yes. Suppose, for instance, that there is something else which ranks as good, namely, moral fineness. In that case an action up for assessment will be judged for value by two criteria, its production of pleasure (or distress) and its moral fineness (or otherwise). But nevertheless the only criterion for the goodness of a painful action will be, according to the 'many', its resulting in pleasures greater than the pains it contains. Its moral fineness will be relevant, and good, only in so far as moral fineness results in the agent's pleasure. Moral fineness will then be only an instrumental good, whereas pleasure will be good in itself. In this context it seems pointless for the many to reject the conclusion that pleasure is indeed, in the sense Socrates intends, 'the good'.[271]

Socrates next explains to the 'many' what his questioning is all about (354E). He is concerned with *what it is* to be overcome by pleasures. For if the nature of such events is understood, then the case against 'weakness of will' is made: 'the whole argument', Socrates says, 'depends on this'. In context, of course, this last remark addresses the 'many', and not Protagoras directly, let alone the other sophists. Not Socrates' debate with Protagoras, but their joint quarrel with the man in the street depends on the nature of weakness of will. Naturally, however, the listening sophist and his rivals will be glad to hear (as we are to read) what Socrates has been driving at.

The general subsequent course of the discussion will be to illuminate the absurdity of believing simultaneously in the two following sets of propositions (355Bff.). The first or C set consists of (i) Pleasure is the only good thing and (ii) Pain is the only bad thing. The second or D set consists of propositions embodying the belief in the possibility of being overcome by pleasures so as to do bad things or refrain from good things. To expose this absurdity the general strategy is to substitute in the D group of propositions first 'good' for 'pleasant' and secondly 'painful' for 'bad'. To be 'overcome' is in each case to yield where it is inappropriate, that is, where the 'goods' or the 'pleasures' do not in true value outweigh the 'bads' or 'pains'. Socrates extracts the agreement of the 'many' that the only question relevant to the problem whether goods or pleasures outweigh the bads or pains respectively is whether the goods or pleasures are greater or smaller than the bads or pains respectively. To be overcome is to make a mistake, to choose greater bad in exchange for lesser good, greater pain in exchange for lesser pleasure.[272]

At this stage (356A) Socrates puts for the 'many', and rebuts for himself and Protagoras, a fairly obvious objection to this whole developing line of thought. The general force of the objection is that the attractions of immediate pleasure outweigh by their very immediacy those of more distant pleasures. Taylor[273] suggests two ways of taking the thrust of this objection: (i) is that 'Socrates should add propinquity and distance in time to his list of conditions determining the value of pleasures and pains.' (ii) is as 'an explanation, overlooked by Socrates, of why it is that we often choose things which we know or believe to be less valuable than available alternatives'; the explanation then says 'that we are frequently more concerned about ... what is near ... than ... what is more distant', and adds, 'looked at in the context of ... various manifestations of this psychological principle, actions against one's better judgement appear a less isolated and consequently less paradoxical phenomenon.'

To one or other of these two (or conceivably, to a conflation of them), Socrates replies that immediate and more distant pleasures may differ, but 'Surely not in any other respect than simply pleasure and pain: there isn't any other way they could differ.' Taylor finds this 'disappointing', as either simply rejecting 'without any reasons given' objection (i) or asserting 'without argument' in answer to (ii) that 'the psychological principle of attachment to the present is itself to be explained as an effect of mistaken assessment of the amount, etc., of future pleasures according to the dimensions he had already mentioned.' Either way of taking the passage thus results in an unargued assertion by Socrates. But we ought by this stage to be distrustful of the imputation to Plato's Socrates of unargued assertion, and ready to see first what his opponents have admitted.

In the welter of second and third persons plural in this section of Plato's text it is important to keep clear which are the two sides to the debate, and to bear in mind their positions. On the one side stands the common man: on the other the imagined ill-mannered objector, no doubt a thin disguise for Socrates (and able to be ruder than Socrates in person), whereas Socrates in turn is still acting for Protagoras in addition to himself. So inspection of the force of the rude man's (or Socrates') argument demands inspection of the common man's admissions.

First, the 'many' have agreed that the only good thing is pleasure, and the only bad thing pain (354C). Secondly they have agreed that the *only* way in which a pleasure can be bad (or a pain good) is if the pleasure produces *greater* pain (or the pain *greater* pleasure) than itself. The emphases are mine, but the agreement is that of the 'many'. They cannot now go back on it as if it had never been. But if they did wish to correct their former answer, what could they substitute? They could specify that a bad pleasure is one which *either* results in greater pains than it contains itself *or* results in pains *appearing* (because of the relevant propinquity or distance) to be greater than itself. But they would then have to answer a line of interrogation on how the appearances can be relevant to true value, which was the subject of the original questions. It is far from clear how they could answer it. After their previous admissions, the 'many' cannot turn round and say that there is any *relevant* difference between immediate pleasure or pain and distant pleasure or pain. There may be an *apparent* difference in respect of size – which may cause the increased concern of which Taylor speaks: but a difference merely apparent and not anchored in reality makes (truistically) no difference in reality.

Further, since Protagoras has allowed Socrates to get away with the extraction of the two above admissions from the 'many' he cannot now, without eating words, give the 'many' any support. The recurrent 'no other' motif reveals the structure of the passage: according to the 'many' there is *no other* way (354B) in which pain is good and pleasure bad than the ones given above, and there can be *no other* relevant difference (356B) between immediate and distant pleasure or pain than the corresponding one also given above.

How does this leave Taylor's two versions of the objector's point and Socrates' 'disappointing' reply? First, (i) is ruled out of court: Protagoras cannot put the argument in that shape without retracting admissions he had passed; the 'many' also cannot put it thus without retraction. Secondly, objection (ii) could be countered with the retort that Protagoras, and not only Socrates, has overlooked the objection in conceding that the 'many' view things as he says. Again, the 'many' cannot press the objection, for they said nothing about the *apparent* relative size of pleasures and pains, nothing about the effect of pleasures and pains on our feelings of concern; everything Socrates put to them, and they accepted, spoke of size or quantity without qualification. They uttered no proviso about apparent size, or the effect of such appearance on our feelings. In order at a later stage to enter such a proviso, they will most seriously have to modify what they have agreed to.

But this, it will be argued, merely pushes the problem back

one small step. What right has Plato to make his Socrates do such things with language, either to the hypothetical 'many' or to the distinguished sophist? How can he seriously expect to persuade or influence anybody carefully reading his work if he plays dialectical tricks as dubious as this? The common *reader*, after all, is not bound by Protagoras' reluctance to modify admissions about the commitments of the 'many'. The common reader (if endowed with sufficient lucidity) will still say the sorts of thing Taylor says about cigarette-smoking in his illuminating note: 'Even at the time of pursuing the short-term pleasure they may accept that it is not worth it (i.e. not rationally justified) but yet for the time being want the pleasure more than they want their long-term happiness.' Socrates and Plato appear to have brushed the problem aside. But not, as we shall see, in ignorance; they will broach it later. Even the later answer does not satisfy; one hardly agrees with Socrates. But one can reasonably wait till Socrates actually tackles a problem before criticizing his answer.

At least our analysis should enable us to approach with confidence the next piece of this astonishingly consecutive discussion (356B). Socrates issues an instruction to the objector about immediate pleasures: to weigh pains and pleasures, nearness and distance, and say which is (not 'appears') greatest. 'If you weigh pleasant things against pleasant, you always have to take the larger and the more numerous.' Taylor's linguistic arguments[274] show that this 'have to' is not an expression of psychological necessity, but what ought to happen. We have *here* not psychological but evaluative hedonism. What is in keeping with the drift of the preceding paragraphs is that it is in a man's interest to choose the bigger (overall) of two pleasures, that in so choosing he will be choosing what will contribute to a good life for him. It is not until the next section of the dialogue that Socrates subtly insinuates a psychological doctrine.

Meanwhile we should be as careful as ever to avoid imputing any kind of hedonism to Socrates. Socrates might conceivably agree, under certain definitions of pleasure, to some circumscribed versions of hedonism. But, though he represents himself as issuing instructions for a procedure to the imaginary objector, it is pretty clear from what follows that he sets out the procedure just in order to put it to 'men', in the question, 'Perhaps it is in some way otherwise, men?' 'I know,' he continues, 'that they would not be able to say otherwise.'[275] The point, once more, is that this is the kind of procedure the common man must accept, in his apparent disregard of moral considerations. Protagoras, also, accepts only that the 'many' would be constrained to agree with what Socrates has laid before them. This is scarcely the moment for the casual commitment of either Socrates or Protagoras to hedonistic doctrines to which they have for so long avoided commitment.

The 'salvation' of our life

The next section begins (356C) with the enumeration, to secure the consent of the 'many', of kinds of thing which look bigger nearby than from a distance: magnitudes, thicknesses, and numbered sets – and Socrates adds that sounds seem louder nearby and softer at a distance, the Greek for 'louder and softer' being the same as for 'bigger and smaller'. Socrates asks, in a key question (356C–D). 'If our doing well depends on this, on doing and choosing big lengths, and avoiding and not doing smaller lengths, what would have seemed clearly to be the salvation of our life?'[276] In response to this and further questioning, the 'many' affirm that the salvation of our life would have been the art of measurement.

In this continuing exchange with the 'many', the term 'salvation' is particularly significant. It clearly concerns not only the necessary, but also the sufficient condition of a good life for man. Saving life here means producing a good life, one in which we do well. When Socrates later asks 'What would have preserved our life?', it is hard to see how this could in context be construed as demanding only a necessary condition, rather than a sufficient one. If the life involved was indeed saved, then not only necessary but also sufficient conditions for that life were fulfilled. That the life concerned is the good life is manifest from the use of the expression 'the preservation of life' in a position precisely parallel to the expression 'well-being' (356D and C). The relevant phrases here are 'So if our well-being had depended on taking steps...?' and 'And what if the preservation of our life had depended on correct choice...?' There is no apparent reason to doubt that Socrates is speaking throughout of the sufficient conditions of the good life. If he later refers to knowledge as the sufficient condition of the good life, that is not based, so far as one can see, on any blurring or neglect of the distinction between what is sufficient and what is necessary for the good life. There may be dubieties in Socrates' line of interrogation, but this is not one of them.[277]

We left Socrates giving examples, and he had not finished. He proceeds with one in which the salvation of life depends on the choice of odd and even (356E). What would save life in that situation? A knowledge. Socrates quite legitimately substitutes 'knowledge' for 'art' here. 'Knowledge' is a wider term in Greek than 'art', but Socrates does not make any illegitimate use of its greater extension. With a little nudging of terminology the necessary 'art' can be described in this case too as one of measurement. Protagoras agrees that men would admit all this. The examples lead up to a question (357A) whether, since life's salvation actually depends on correct choice in the matter of pleasure and pain, a quantitative choice as in the examples, the salvation does not lie in measurement, and, hence, in an art and knowledge. Which knowledge, says Socrates, is subject to inquiry; he is still not committed to the notion that the correct measurement of pleasures is the key to the good life. The important proposition here is that the salvation of our life consists in a branch of knowledge.

With this crowbar Socrates can demolish the position of the 'many' (357C–E). They began by saying that pleasure often overcomes even the man who knows, and rejecting Socrates' and Protagoras' proposition that knowledge always overcomes pleasure. They invited Socrates and Protagoras to explain the experience the common man knows as being overcome by pleasure. The 'many' have now in effect admitted, though Socrates does not quite spell this out, that knowledge is a necessary and sufficient condition of correct choice in the sphere of pleasures and pains. As Socrates implies, it follows that they must admit that lack of the appropriate knowledge is a necessary and sufficient condition of mistaken choice in that sphere. But (according to the 'many') pleasures and pains are goods and bads. So the relevant ignorance is the greatest and most important ignorance, that of goods and bads. And the sophists claim to cure it; Socrates ends on a suitably flattering note, drawing attention once more to the teachers' professional pretensions.

How has Socrates persuaded the 'many'? By what sleight of hand has he conjured away the power of the emotions? The 'nerve' of the Socratic Paradox is not 'laid bare' in any ambiguity of 'have to take', as has been supposed by some and rebutted by others.[278] The trick is not done by confusing directly the necessary and the sufficient conditions of correct choice. David Gallop has, however, put forward what is in essentials the solution.[279] It lies in the 'adroit handling of the term "salvation".' Extensive quotation is here in order. 'At the start (356D3–4) it is equated with the measuring art, as that which would save our life... Next (356E5–6) it is said to reside in the actual *choice* of odd and even, for which numerical arts would be needed and, we may add, sufficient.' 'Finally (357A5–B3), these two uses of "salvation" come together in a single sentence... In the "since"-clause "our salvation" is said to reside in the correct choice of pleasure and pain, whereas in the main clause it appears as the art of measurement. This conveys the impression that the correct choice of pleasures and pains actually *is* the art of measurement. "Salvation" acts as a bridge by which the concepts of knowledge and correct choice can be equated.' With this analysis of the function of 'salvation' I am fully in agreement; but there are two additional things worth saying about it.

First, there is one sentence of Plato's which, in a context of quantities such as length, awards remarkable psychological functions to the art of measurement (356D). 'The [power of appearances], as we saw, confuses us and makes us often change our minds about the same things and vacillate back and forth in our actions and choices of large and small things; but measurement would have made these appearances powerless, and given us peace of mind by showing us the truth and letting us get a firm grasp of it, and so would have saved our lives.' Here the art of measurement stills any doubt or vacillation. Knowledge calms our confusion, and in that calm enables us to grasp truth firmly.

Knowledge, Socrates leads us to suppose, makes appearances 'powerless', and the Greek word for 'powerless' can also mean 'invalid' (as opposed to 'valid'). Certainly knowledge can check, as it were, on the appearances and show their lack of validity, and this is especially easy to see in the case of magnitudes. But, side by side with this (in the present context) philosophically harmless way of speaking, there stands the philosophically tricky literal sense of 'powerless'. The word in this context gives the impression that any emotional involvement with appearances (producing, for instance, our different attitudes to the near and the distant) will be rendered powerless by the relevant knowledge. The rest of Socrates' phraseology, and especially the words 'peace of mind', deepen the impression. Once knowledge supervenes, we gather, all passion is spent. Of course things are not quite like that. That is not how human nature works. But Socrates seeks to persuade the 'many' that that is how their nature works.

What enables him to insinuate his views is the second point. In the case of lengths and numbers, when we measure or count and satisfy ourselves that we have done so correctly, our doubts, disputes and difficulties are settled. Appearances, e.g. optical illusions, cease to trouble us. We are not upset. However fierce or hectic the dispute may have been, it is a dispute no longer. But in matters of choice, as Taylor says,[280] even if we recognize, or 'know' to the full, the consequences of two courses of action open to us, even if we could measure the effects (pleasant or painful, good or bad) of each, our emotions may still be roused, our minds still clouded, by the proximity of one effect and the longinquity of another. In this case, our knowledge might conceivably render the appearances invalid, but would not help to render them powerless. In these matters there is no guarantee that knowledge will bring peace of mind, or give an emotional being a firm enough grasp of the truth. The basic difference here is that in questions of length our emotions (unless prestige is accidentally involved) are normally silent; hence the possibility of using language such as Socrates' in discussing our reactions to them. In moral questions the emotions have much to say, and knowledge cannot silence them. Socrates has no business assimilating the two situations by referring both to the single category of correct choice in which knowledge saves our life. Socrates is thus as guilty in the *Protagoras* as anywhere of assimilating moral knowledge to other, not entirely parallel, forms of expertise. He is no less guilty of ignoring (even while implicitly acknowledging) the power of the emotions. But Plato, whether deliberately or not, has lent him language such as to obscure this error. He thus enables the 'many' to respond affirmatively to questions to which they should have returned an indignant negative. What appears to them to be straightforward induction is in truth a false analogy pressed upon them with either carelessness or cunning. If it be cunning, then to discuss whether it is the cunning of dialectic or of rhetoric would be fruitless; we might call it either or both. But we should recall that rhetoric was the habitual tool of the sophists themselves. They, at least, cannot object to its use against the 'many'.

Back to the sophists

Socrates has cozened the 'many' and ended by flattering the sophists. That in itself offers no reason why the sophists should accept the views coaxed from the 'many'. But we have already found good dialectical reasons why the sophists should willingly agree with Socrates' refutation of the 'many', and with such propositions as seem to them necessary to support it. Socrates' flattery is not merely polite; nor is it merely ironical. In reminding the sophists of their claim to cure ignorance (357E), Socrates also reminds them of the vested interest they have in the rebuttal of the common interpretation of weak will. He recalls their high opinion of knowledge; the ignorance that is weakness is a lack of knowledge; claim to remedy that lack. Their claim cannot be maintained simultaneously with, and is rejected by the 'many' who hold on to, the belief that weakness of will is something other than ignorance.

At the same time as he thus looks back and draws threads together, Socrates also foreshadows the future course of the dialogue, at least in one significant respect. Still addressing a last word to the common man, he says, 'You don't believe it can be taught,' and this rejection is linked with the belief that weakness of will is not lack of knowledge. It is fairly clear, though (doubtless deliberately) not stated in full openness, that if the 'many' did accept that weakness of will was, or was due to, lack of knowledge, they would be in no position to reject the claim that it was curable by teaching. In so far as Socrates is concerned to convince Protagoras that knowledge and wisdom are goodness or the key to it, he will similarly be sustaining the very claim, the teachability of goodness, at least in essentials, which he originally doubted. From being inexplicit and below the dialogue's surface at this time, this reversal will become open and explicit at the dialogue's end. At the very least, the reader or hearer should notice, if only subliminally, that Socrates, through his address to the common man, has connected teachability with knowledge.

It is remarkable, but perhaps in the last analysis not altogether surprising, that Plato's literary art, shaping his dialogue as a whole, should express itself in tiny but detectable details of this sort. But, as usual, the detail has not only a formal function; it serves to sharpen the opposition between the sophists and the 'many', and thus more strongly to predispose the former to accept anything calculated to confute the latter.

Formally abandoning the conversation with the imagined 'many', Socrates asks all the sophists if they think he speaks truly or falsely (358A). In agreeing with zealous alacrity to the truth of his remarks the sophists are accepting only the willingness of the 'many' to answer the questions in this sequence in accordance with Socrates' suggested dialogue. The overwhelming majority of Protagoras' replies to Socrates in this passage are in such terms as to make this limitation perfectly clear. Occasional apparent exceptions or ambiguities, presumably designed to avoid monotony of expression, make no substantial difference to the reader's clear impression of the drift of the whole. So far, that is; and it is doubtful whether anything much later than the point we have reached in the dialogue could rectify that impression if Plato wanted it rectified.

But in this connection there is a genuine difficulty in the transitional conversation. According to the normal punctuation, Socrates flatly *states*, immediately after the sophists' expression of agreement, that they *therefore* agree that the pleasant is good and the painful bad (358A). This appears to draw a conclusion about the *content* of the refutation of the 'many' from what we have just labelled an assent only to the suggestion that the 'many' would say these things. Further, it appears to draw that conclusion in Socrates' own person, and in a rare flat statement from him. What higher authority can be imagined? It is scarcely surprising if scholars deduce that the sophists' expression of agreement expresses acceptance of the content of the proof used against the 'many', and hence also that the sophists' agreement to the truth of what Socrates has been saying implies that the content of the proof was said by Socrates in his own person.

But though scarcely surprising, this deduction would be erected on the sandiest of foundations. It should suffice, in order to bring it down, to argue two propositions; first, that what is commonly thought to be a flat statement is in fact a question, to which the sophists (as fictional characters) are at liberty to reply as they choose; secondly, that there is an alternative explanation of the sophists' willingness to answer it in the affirmative, an explanation fully consistent with an uncommitted Socrates.

First, then, statement or question? Should we render Socrates' utterance as 'You agree, then...' or as 'Do you agree, then...?' Taylor is merely the latest but one in a long line of editors and translators who take it as a statement.[281] But there is no good textual or linguistic objection to taking it as a question; and Taylor's own rendering of Socrates' next sentence causes one to wonder why he did not so take it. '...give your answer,' he makes Socrates say, 'according to the sense of my question.' Of course, if the word 'question' appeared in the Greek, that would settle the matter. But it does not appear. Taylor's translation, scrupulously faithful to the spirit of the original, here departs slightly from its letter. A more literal (but unreadable) translation would be: '...answer me this in respect of what I mean.' However, the Greek word for 'answer' here is Plato's standard word for response to a question, and one does not normally have the right to press for an answer to a statement. It really could not be clearer that Plato meant his Socrates to ask here 'Do you agree...?' Ambiguous though it would be in isolation, the sentence is wholy unambiguous in context. Nothing preceding it leads the reader to expect a statement, and solid evidence in the same speech clarifies and confirms its status as a question. So Socrates is, after all, not flatly stating that the sophists must agree, following the discussion with the 'many', that pleasant is good and pain bad. He is asking them whether, in the light of that discussion, they are prepared to agree.

But how can he expect or invite them to draw the conclusion about pleasure and pain from the preceding conversation if he has not drawn it himself? What does he think may have changed Protagoras' mind since he last refused an affirmative answer to the same question? Why should he expect Protagoras' mind to be changed when his own is not? We have already in effect answered these pertinent queries, but the answer will bear some repetition.

The sophists are eager to see refuted the common belief that knowledge is in practice subservient to passion, a belief supported rather firmly by the phenomenon known as weakness of will. They are, then, willing to accept anything they see as necessary to refute that belief. The query will then arise, 'Why should they believe the premiss about pleasure and pain to be indispensable?' Is it? On the face of it, yes. The refutation will not work in anything like its present form without the mutual substitutability of the pairs pleasant/good and painful/bad. Without that, indeed, the refutation will not get under way at all. Socrates (and Plato) may or may not have seen the flaws in the refutation's logic. The sophists, confronted for the first time in their lives (we must suppose) with the apparent consequences of the intellectualism implicit in their profession, are in no state to produce anything better, or even anything different, by way of confounding the common man. Socrates has thrown them a lifeline, and they catch hold of it. But Plato himself can let go at any moment he chooses; his Socrates has other lines of argument, given in other dialogues, to cling to.

In view of all this, why does Socrates not ask, or the sophists not accept, the full doctrine with which they have landed the 'many'? Why not, instead of merely 'What is pleasant is good and what is painful bad' (358A), the stronger doctrine that 'the pleasant is the only good, the painful the only bad', a proposition the 'many' have also, in some sense of it, accepted? Perhaps it is because Socrates does not at the moment need the stronger version, and there is no point in raising sophistic hackles beyond necessity. Even in their desperate plight in face of the problem of weak will, Socrates cannot be sure that the sophists will stick at nothing. If necessary he can push the sophists along by stages, proceeding from weaker to stronger version of hedonism.

It remains to be seen whether in the long run it makes any difference which version Socrates starts with. In the meantime the reader will observe that some explanation has to be forthcoming for the sophists' change of stance, for Protagoras' willingness to agree now without qualification to a proposition he felt unable earlier to accept unqualifiedly. The present explanation, that the change of mind is due to Socrates' cunning in making it worth while for the sophists to agree in order to defeat the common man, is better than any which supposes Plato to be making the sophists give in for no good reason, in order to afford Plato's Socrates a factitious victory and Plato himself a cheap one.

Socrates, anyway, has a further question to ask, arising from the combination of other propositions with the weak hedonism now admitted by Protagoras and his colleagues (358B). 'Aren't all actions fine [and beneficial] which lead to a painless and pleasant life? And isn't fine activity good and beneficial?'[282] To these the sophists agree. To understand their agreement it is necessary to go back to the opening of the whole pleasure passage, to Protagoras' first answers to Socrates on this general topic.[283] The pleasant life is good, Protagoras there said on second thoughts, if and only if the pleasures enjoyed are fine (351B–C). The attempt to get him to be consistent, and maintain that all pleasant things are good, was a failure. Now, however, Socrates has elicited agreement that all things pleasant, in total with their consequences, are good.[284] Socrates has accordingly sound reason to believe that Protagoras will now agree that all things which are pleasant in total are fine. Otherwise it will be possible to have pleasures which are not fine and still lead a life of good things – a possibility Protagoras has rejected, and with reason, since before that he committed himself to the view that all goodness is fine (and it is axiomatic that goodness is what gives one a good life). 'Beneficial' here means, and is a synonym for, 'good for the agent'. It is not *necessary* to add here that things in total pleasant are in that sense beneficial, since the sophists have admitted that they are good, which in context means the same thing. But it does no harm, and the manuscripts may be right in presenting it, though many editors bracket the words 'and beneficial' as I have above. The next question, 'isn't fine activity good and beneficial?' is the one that is odd, since the sophists have not admitted that all fine activity benefits the agent, nor that *only* pleasant things are fine. It is worth observing that no inferential particle links this question with its predecessor; it may be logically independent, and receive an affirmative answer on the basis simply of the common Greek associations of the two terms 'fine' and 'good'. This admission, unnecessary here, plays a more substantial role in the argument at a later stage (359E). In the later appearance, which takes the form of a reference back to the earlier, Socrates conflates at least the vocabulary of the two questions forming the topic of the present paragraph. It is possible therefore that they are meant to be taken closely together, and the second to ask whether *the fine activity* talked about in the first question (namely, that devoted to pleasant and painless living) is good and beneficial. But that would not fit the logic of the second appearance. It is better to suppose common usage uppermost in Plato's and his characters' intentions at both places. The association of the two words can be exemplified in Protagoras' own words in the Great Speech (328B), though not, I think, in any context unambiguously implying any one relationship between the two words.

So far, this new series of questions for the sophist(s) to answer has few real difficulties for the reader who bears in mind the dialectical situation. But the next question is troublesome (358B). We have already dealt with the matter of knowledge and opinion; but that is the apodosis of Socrates' conditional sentence, and the protasis now claims our attention. 'If what is pleasant is good,' it reads; and 'the pleasant is good' is to all appearances the premiss for the conclusion drawn in the sentence's apodosis. That conclusion is the position to which Socrates drove the 'many' (to the delighted agreement of the sophists), not on the basis of the relatively weak hedonistic doctrine that pleasure is good, but from the much stronger equation of pleasant with good and painful with bad. The stronger position had indeed appeared necessary to get the argument with the 'many' under way at all. There come to mind three explanations of the trouble, given below in what is intended as an ascending order of probability.

The first is that Plato's Socrates has for once ignored correct usage, and means here to equate the pleasant and *the* good, despite his omission of the italicized definite article. We should be wise to take this way out only in emergency.[285] The second is to suppose that Plato is here using a kind of shorthand by way of summarizing the entire discussion with the 'many'. The third is a less bald and less unconvincing version of the second. Once committed to the doctrine that all things in total pleasant are good, and all things in total painful are bad, the 'many', unless they could supply another criterion of goodness, were unable to resist the conclusion that only things pleasant in total were good. Under these circumstances, if the sophists now answer Socrates by producing another criterion of goodness, thus stopping his argument in its track, they will have to explain why they did not allow it to the 'many'. If they want in particular to urge the criterion of moral fineness, they will be in trouble for their recent acceptance that 'fine' actions are coextensive with actions pleasant in total. They might, therefore, want to resist Socrates' apparently rather simple-minded conditional sentence, but have, as usual, no obvious defensive position. Without very fast thinking, they must accept the doctrine forced on the 'many', that weakness of will is ignorance, and strength of will merely knowledge or 'wisdom'. Throughout this trial of strength the sophists are hamstrung by the inability to find an account of weakness of will both differing from that forced on the 'many' and able to sustain the primacy of intellect. Of course abandonment of the primacy of intellect would put them immediately in the clear, but professional reasons forbid its abandonment; and Protagoras in particular has been committed to its sustainment since the Great Speech.

Socrates now puts a question, or possibly makes a statement (358C–D),[286] containing a form of the Socratic Paradox that no one 'wishingly'[287] goes for bad things, and it is not in human nature to wish to go for bad rather than good. This passage makes clear that somewhere in the argument a psychological statement about men's desires has its place. It is much less clear that this psychological statement is a strong form of hedonism; indeed, no hedonism is immediately implied. The doctrine appears to be that men by nature do not desire their own disadvantage (*or* do not desire it under that description). If we combine with that a hedonism taking the form of the equation of good (or advantage) with pleasure, then certainly from the combination there results a strong form of psychological hedonism. The combination has not surfaced until this point in the discussion. If our previous interpretations were right, there has been no previous explicit admission of a strong psychological hedonism.

Indeed Socrates' only warrant for offering the general psychological statement in the paradox is, to all appearances, the bland 'it seems'.[288] If there is any more support to be found, it can only be in the earlier passage about the 'salvation' of our life (356C–357B). Socrates used the concept of 'salvation' to bridge the gap between knowledge and performance. By cunning insinuation he passed from the correct choice saving our life to the relevant knowledge saving our life. Whether deliberately or not, this tacitly assumed that knowing the correct choice entails making it. This use of 'salvation' as a bridge was not there confined to pleasures or to hedonistic conceptions; Socrates introduced it by imagining different worlds, in which things very different from pleasure constitute the good life. If our good life depended on the choice of right magnitude, right class of number, or the right number of decibels, then the relevant knowledge and ability to measure would be our salvation. The tacit assumption, buried under some of Socrates' cleverest dialectical rhetoric, is that we needs must do the best when we see it, that knowing what is good for you suffices to ensure the pursuit of it.

Once Socrates has slipped this one past the common man's guard under the very noses of the sophists, and manoeuvred the latter dialectically into accepting the conclusion of his argument with the former, he is able, for reasons already given, to count on sophistic acquiescence. But to reveal this support for this part of the Socratic paradox would be to cast a spotlight on the fatal flaw in his reasoning. So both Socrates and the sophists are content perforce with that bald 'it seems'.

Before leaving this paradox, it is worth a moment to inspect Socrates' brief account of its reception. 'All of us', he says, 'agreed to all of that.'[289] Here, for the first time, Socrates lends his own personal assent to a proposition in no temporary, provisional or equivocal fashion. The difference between the tone and content of this reception and those of previous ones strikes the reader forcibly. This time it is not just the sophists or Protagoras who agree; Socrates clearly includes himself, and emphatically at that. This need occasion no special surprise, since the doctrine agreed to is a well-known part of the famous Socratic Paradox. But it is worth notice that the sentence Socrates himself clearly agrees with, the sentence contrasting so strongly in that respect to its predecessors, is one which omits all reference to pleasure or pain. The reader is invited to consider whether this contrast with preceding sentences coincides with the other by accident or design. For my part, I think design by far the most likely explanation. Further support is thus forthcoming for the conclusion that Socrates is not committed to any form of hedonism in this discussion, and *a fortiori* that Plato is not committed either.

One more short piece of reasoning is necessary before the overt premises for the final argument are established (358D–E). On the first part of it, little remains to be said. It is a satisfactory definition of fear to say it is an expectation of bad if and only if one loses sight of the element of 'painful excitement or disturbance' which is 'essential to the emotion of fear.'[290] Protagoras apparently fails to spot this. But it is a question whether his failure is any way relevant to the argument between him and Socrates. He believes, as he has said, that a man who has knowledge of good or bad will not do other than what his knowledge bids. He has even agreed (because he cannot afford to disagree) that wisdom always overcomes, among other things, fear. Hence for him the element of emotion ought to be as unimportant as it is for Socrates. If X expects bad things to happen, X will *act* no differently, according to Protagoras and Socrates, whether or not his expectation is accompanied by emotional disturbance. But Protagoras' and Socrates' interest lies in actions and in what people will face. The following considerations should bring this out. Suppose fear to consist not only of an expectation of bad but also of an accompanying emotional disturbance. Consider two questions: (i) If X thinks A bad and is emotionally disturbed about it, will X face A? (ii) If X knows or thinks B is good but nevertheless is emotionally disturbed about it (if he has a counter-rational fear of it), will X face B?

On the view agreed at the outset between Socrates and Protagoras, the answer to question (ii) is a resounding 'yes'. X's reason will overcome the emotional disturbance. Hence we have only to consider (i); and in the situation hypothesized in (i), the emotional disturbance is on the same side as reason and tends towards the same action. The action, indeed, in both cases, is the same irrespective of the emotional disturbance. Plato does not make clear that Protagoras has seen this far into the definition set before him; he does not even make clear that his Socrates has seen it. But the odds are that Plato, with ample time to reflect on the relations between emotion and intellect, knew what he was writing; and indeed how else can one interpret him?

Socrates again commits himself openly and firmly here. Socrates does *not* say that nobody will go for what he fears; he says only that nobody will wish to do so if he can avoid it. The occasional passage quotable to the contrary is 'on a charitable interpretation',[291] merely a convenient abbreviation.

Wisdom and courage again

The stage is set for the dénouement; to change the metaphor, the weapons lie ready to hand for the final thrust towards the equation of courage with wisdom. Abandoning his talk with Prodicus and Hippias, Socrates turns explicitly to face Protagoras alone (359A). This is not a mere literary device; Socrates will on occasion use admissions only Protagoras has made. He asks him to defend, in the light of their recent agreement and of earlier admissions, his statement about the relation between the good qualities, the parts of goodness. Not, Socrates says, the very first answer on this, immediately after the Great Speech, but the second, less stringent one, after the interlude with Simonides (349D). Courage, Protagoras said then, differed markedly from the other four good qualities, whereas those four were fairly close to each other. Evidence for courage's difference was the alleged fact that a man could be most impious, unjust, immoderate, and (climactically, as we now see) stupid-cum-ignorant, and yet be brave. One of Socrates' subsequent questions was whether the courageous are confident. Part of Protagoras' reply was that 'Yes, they are confident, and ready ("goers") to face things.' What Protagoras had actually said was that the courageous are ready to face things which the 'many' fear to face. The clear implication of this was, as we saw, that the 'many' are not brave and, as a result of their fear, are not ready to face things which the courageous are ready to face.

At the beginning of the dialogue's final argument Socrates reminds Protagoras of this, and asks, for clarification's sake, to face *what* things the brave are ready; are these things the same as or different from the things that the cowardly are ready to face? Protagoras answers that they are different. To clarify the difference, Socrates asks, 'Do cowards go for non-fearful things and courageous men for fearful things?' The first half of this could mean, 'Do cowards go for things *they* do not fear?' or 'Do cowards go for things which are in some objective way non-fearful?' If the latter, then, since Protagoras says that the mass of mankind agree, he is saddling them with an unlikely view: imagine a safe but narrow bridge over a deep gorge, and an acrophobic coward: evidently the coward will *not* cross the objectively non-fearful bridge (and even a reasonably brave acrophobic will take a way round if available). More probably Taylor's version is correct, and the first half of Socrates' question means, 'Do cowards go for things they are confident about?' Taylor argues soundly also that the second half of the question asks if the brave 'go for things which frighten most people *including them* (Taylor's emphasis)'. Socrates wants to know if the sophist thinks the courageous overcome their fears.

Protagoras' answer and Socrates' encouragement of it are both of interest, and relevant to the preceding argument. Protagoras' reception of the question is twofold: first that the mass of mankind will accept Socrates' proposition, and secondly that he himself cannot accept it, being bound by his previous admissions. The previous section of the conversation ended with the conclusion that no man will *wish* to face what he fears, if he can avoid it (358E). What anyone else fears is irrelevant to this. The conclusion said nothing about what a man ought or would be best advised to fear, and that too is irrelevant. On the face of it, this shows conclusively that to be a 'goer' is to *wish* to face something. But in what way is Protagoras bound by, and compelled (as he says) to accept the logic of, the previous discussion with the many? The question is of some importance for a dialectical interpretation, and Socrates supplies the answer. Socrates' encouragement of Protagoras offers a summary of the conversation which is compressed in at least two ways. As Taylor notes,[292] it omits the proviso 'if he can avoid it' or 'except as the lesser of two evils' from the concluding paradox of the argument with the 'many' that no one goes to what he thinks bad. It omits also the word 'wishingly'. From these two omissions it is clear that Socrates' desire (and Plato's) is for brevity at the expense of accuracy. Socrates' summarizing words help to clarify what has happened.

Socrates actually says (359D): 'So if that was rightly shown, no one goes for things he thinks fearful, since giving in to oneself turned out to be ignorance-cum-stupidity.'[293] Taken by itself, this is a somewhat obscure sentence; but in context it is illuminating. Clearly the intellect, in its opinion as to what is fearful and what is not, is always and everywhere victorious; that is why no one goes (wishingly, at least) to what he thinks fearful. As a reason for this, which is the same proposition asserting the mastery of the intellect from which Socrates and Protagoras began, we are offered the proposition that weakness of will is an intellectual failure. But the logical nexus between these two propositions is not the simple 'since ... then ...' which Socrates gives in this summary. The point is rather that the chief objection to the mastery of the intellect is removed with the removal of the obvious objection about weakness of will. This Socratic summary thus encapsulates the course of the whole conversation, as we have analysed it.

Be that as it may, we find Protagoras and Socrates in this passage using the verb 'go' and its relatives to indicate a state of mind, as well as an action: a state in which one goes 'wishingly' to face something. An earlier passage, previously left ambiguous, can now be read in this same sense. Protagoras said there (349E) that the brave are confident and 'goers' to face what the many fear to face. This means that they are ready and wishing to face what the 'many' are afraid to face. The word for 'confident' reinforces this interpretation: the same word, in a passive sense, is used later for 'what people are confident about'; 'things people are confident about' are later (359C–D) interchangeable with 'things that are not fearful'. What Protagoras meant to say was that the brave are not afraid of things the 'many' are afraid of: hence that the 'many' and the brave are afraid of two different sets of things. It is because the brave are not afraid of the same things as the 'many' and (a fortiori) the cowards are afraid of that the brave wish to face them whereas the rest do not.

Protagoras' earlier utterance, helpful to Socrates at the time, left a good deal vague. In our later passage (359C ff.) Socrates tries to elucidate that vagueness. He and the sophist have agreed that what one is willing to face is not what one fears. The brave then do not wish to go, and are not ready 'goers', to face what they fear. The brave, accordingly, do not suppress fear, but rather have no fear, of the things they wishingly face. This is Protagoras' answer to the questions with which Socrates followed up his recall of the earlier passage: 'What are courageous men ready for? The same things as cowards? "No."' Protagoras here distinguishes the sets of things the brave fear and things the 'many' fear, consistently with our interpretation of the earlier passage (349E).

But in the meantime Socrates, as he reminds Protagoras (359D), has obtained the latter's admission that neither cowards nor brave men are ready to face what they fear; they both face what they do not fear, or 'are confident about'. In a limited sense, this contradicts Protagoras' statement distinguishing the sets of things feared by brave and by 'many'. But Socrates knows that it does so only in a sense; that is why he inserts (359D) the phrase Taylor unfortunately renders 'therefore', which might with at least equally good grammar and much better logic be rendered by the limiting expression 'in this respect at least'.[294] Protagoras, without attempting to deny Socrates' point (for what it is worth), replies in effect that the set of things the brave man wishingly faces is diametrically opposed to the set the coward wishingly faces. This is of course consistent with these two sets having some properties in common, or being the same sort of thing in respect of such a property. Protagoras here successfully defends an earlier admission against an inconclusive attack from Socrates. Socrates wanted merely to elucidate, and Protagoras confirms the elucidation: neither the brave nor the cowardly fear what they wishingly face, but they wishingly face very different things.

Giving examples of the sort of thing the brave face and cowards do not, Protagoras points out (359E) that one class wish to go to war, the other does not. Socrates asks, is going to war fine or shameful? Protagoras says: 'Fine.' Most people, under certain provisos, would agree with this off-the-cuff response. Certainly to go bravely to war is finer than skulking from fear. If it is fine, then by previous admission it is good; and if it is finer than an alternative, it is presumably better. Socrates and Protagoras are at one on this. The whole argument, in the form presented in this dialogue here, is as dependent on the acceptance of moral imperatives as it is on the primacy of the intellect. Socrates and Protagoras can agree on a species of moralism as well as on intellectualism; and Socrates does indeed unambiguously agree. But Socrates has more to say, and begins by pinning Protagoras down, with finicky precision. *Which* [sc. brave men or cowards?] do not wish to go to war and thus do a fine and good thing (360A)? Protagoras answers this easy question, and then Socrates slips him a harder one. If going to war is fine and good, is it also pleasant? And Protagoras replies, 'Well, that's what was agreed.'

Scholars have been severe on this exchange. B. Manuwald,[295] for example, tells us that the implied 'Everything that is good is pleasant' is a mere conversion of the earlier admission, in the transition from the 'many' back to the sophists, that all actions which tend to a pleasant and painless are good. The conversion, he suggests, defies logic. He rejects the older view of H. von Arnim, that one can refer back to the discussion of hedonism with the 'many'. Indeed, simply to use that discussion here as a place where Socrates and Protagoras have been committed to the doctrine that everything is good is pleasant would appear to be somewhat simple-minded. The answer to Manuwald's objection to Plato's or Socrates' procedure does not lie in quite that direction.

Nevertheless, the discussion with the 'many' is relevant in the sort of way we have already seen. The sophists, to defend the primacy of intellect, must adopt against the 'many' on weakness of will the line of defence Socrates shows them, since they can think of no other. That defence starts from, and reasonably seems to the sophists based on, the interchangeability of the terms 'good' and 'pleasant'. Protagoras has accordingly agreed that weakness of will is to be interpreted as intellectual error. He cannot do other than accept the argument in favour of that view and against common sense. He is therefore stuck with the doctrine that everything good is pleasant, just as much, and for the same reasons, as he is stuck with the converse. He is stuck with *everything* in the dialogue with the 'many'. In the circumstances, he does well to cut short a possibly embarrassing topic by saying that he has agreed to 'Everything good is pleasant.' He has agreed in effect. We may readily accept a Protagoras less strict than Socrates sometimes is in these matters.

But why, apart from reminding the sophist of his previous dialectical position, does Socrates reintroduce the concept 'pleasant' at all? D. Zeyl has recently found a good answer to this question;[296] but a further point requires attention. Socrates (360A) wants Protagoras to refuse to accept his proposition. But the proposition that cowards do not wish to face what is finer and better, though they know it is finer and better, is all too easily acceptable. It would chime with common sense, and in particular with the common view that fear can overcome the intellectual perception of what is right.

True, Protagoras ought not to give in after resisting so long; he ought to maintain his intellectualism. But if he were to succumb at any stage to the temptation to abandon it for the common view, Socrates would find his purpose, to force Protagoras to be a consistent intellectualist, frustrated. In particular, Protagoras might start to argue, as the moderns have, that *universal* domination of the emotions by the intellect is not a necessary concomitant of an intellect *in general* more valuable and more powerful than the emotions. Socrates is skating on thin ice.

With the addition of 'pleasant' to the proposition we are discussing, Socrates' way becomes much safer. That a coward should reject the more pleasant option is far more implausible than that he should reject the finer and better one. Socrates can offer the proposition to Protagoras now with a far higher degree of certainty that he will answer in the negative.

My suggestion here is not that the addition of 'pleasant' makes the proposition any more inconsistent with Protagoras' previous admissions, but that it makes it harder for Protagoras to adopt one particular inconsistency which is not the one Socrates wants. That is a sort of dialectical justification for the reintroduction of 'pleasant'. But we are interpreting not only a piece of dialectic but also a work of literary art. Plato has built up in his reader's minds the importance of 'pleasure' and the 'pleasant'. It is in keeping with this build-up that pleasure should reappear in the final and climactic argument, rather than vanish from the argumentative scene as if it had seen a Boojum. This suggestion is not meant to imply that purely literary motives, here or elsewhere, suffice by themselves to determine the course of a Platonic argument. It is rather a warning not to leave them altogether out of account, when they may have reinforced considerations of dialectic.

Having, for whatever reason, made his admission about cowards, Protagoras finds himself confronted at once with a similar question about brave men. Since he has agreed that cowards do not fail to pursue what (they think) is finer, better and more pleasant, what about the brave? Do they pursue what is better, finer and more pleasant? Of course they pursue what is finer and better; that is easy; but do they also pursue what is more pleasant? The very addition of 'pleasant', which made it easier for Socrates to steer Protagoras along a safe path in answer to the previous question, ought, in common-sense terms, to make it harder for Protagoras to give the answer Socrates wants to this one. But here we see Plato's Socrates' cunning in the ordering of his questions.[297] Now that Protagoras has accepted the inference from 'good' to 'pleasant', he can scarcely go back on it in his very next answer. As he says, 'I have to agree.'

But this last question suggests another kind of dialectical reason behind the reintroduction of the 'pleasant', a reason very like Zeyl's. Socrates (358E) has persuaded the sophists to accept that no one goes wishingly to do what he thinks bad (*or worse than the alternatives*). He has not asked them to agree, or formulated any line of questioning compelling them to agree, that everyone wishes to do what he thinks good (or better than the alternatives). The propositions accepted do not appear to entail those not yet agreed. Protagoras might not agree immediately, and might need more than a gentle push in the right direction. It is in Socrates' (and presumably Plato's) interest to cut the argument short at this point (360A), and offer a plausible suggestion, that people pursue what is better, finer, or more pleasant. One might cavil at the suggestion that the good the brave man pursues is pleasant; how pleasant, even in total, is war?[298] But once its pleasantness has been added to its goodness and fineness, it becomes an irresistible temptation; hence, partly, Socrates' reintroduction of the pleasant *before* the question crops up what the brave man wishes to go for. Socrates thus not only forces Protagoras' hand; he evades what might otherwise become a lengthy additional argument (with some difficulties in it, perceived by Zeyl). As for the problem why Socrates has not *previously* in this dialogue explored the connection between wishing and good, it seems likely that concentration on courage, and hence on fear, as one particular potential victor over the intellect, has led, through the definition of fear in terms of the bad, to concentration on the bad rather than the good.

Actually, the question about the brave once more omits

any reference to 'wishing' to go; but once more Plato's readers confidently supply that reference. Symmetry with the previous question strongly suggests it; and if what is finer is also better and more pleasant, it is hard to think of a sound reason for a normal person not to wish to go for it. What is more, the following line of questioning flows more naturally if the reference to wish is supplied. That following sequence has, however, caused some heart- and head-searching. For an admirably clear example, one may cite a piece from G.X. Santas. Having analysed the argument into a set of propositions, Santas writes, among many interesting things,[299] 'This argument is puzzling for several reasons... The first is that Socrates elicits from Protagoras a number of admissions ... all of which are unclear as to their source, their meaning, and their function in the argument. These statements do not seem to be derived from anything preceding them; and it is not very clear what they mean ... Further, it is not clear what function these statements have in the argument, since they do not seem to be used subsequently.' The use of these extracts is not intended as a complete reproduction of even the gist of Santas' argument, which deserves the fullest and most careful consideration, and which will in part receive criticism below. My citation shows only the general drift of Santas' conclusions, and the kind of question he most helpfully raises.

The argument (360A–E) may be encapsulated thus:

1 The brave (wish to) go for the finer and better and pleasanter? Yes.
2 The brave, when afraid, entertain no shameful fears, nor do they entertain shameful confidences? No.
3 If their fears and confidences are not shameful, they are fine? Yes.
4 The cowards, the bold and the mad, on the contrary entertain shameful fears and confidences? Yes.
5 Their confidence(s) is (are) shameful and bad for any other reason than ignorance-cum-stupidity? No.
6 That, on account of which cowards are cowardly, do you call cowardice or courage? Cowardice.
7 Cowards turned out to be cowards because of ignorance

of what is fearful? Yes.
8   Cowards are cowards because of precisely that ignorance? Yes.
9   You have agreed that cowardice is that on account of which cowards are cowards? Yes.
10 That would make cowardice the ignorance of what is fearful and what is not? Protagoras nods.
11 Courage is the opposite to cowardice? Yes.
12 The wisdom (*or* knowledge) of what is fearful and what is not is opposite to the stupidity-cum-ignorance of them? Protagoras nods.
13 The stupidity-cum-ignorance of them is cowardice? Protagoras nods.
14 Being opposite to the ignorance of these things, the knowledge (wisdom) of what is feared and what is not is courage? Proceed.
15 Do you still think some men are most ignorant but most brave? It would be impossible, given our admissions.

The first puzzle arising out of this is the source or derivation of the earlier members of this list of questions and admissions. The chief clue is the mention, in Socrates' question 4 above, of madness and boldness. These two notions are indeed conspicuously strange to the immediate context. But it is not the first time they, or something very like them, have appeared in the whole dialogue. The passage concerned has, I think, escaped notice in this connection, perhaps because the vital words are not there in Socrates' mouth but in Protagoras', and interpreters have paid too little attention to Protagoras' words. We should cast our minds back to the abortive attempt, immediately after the Simonides episode, to link courage with wisdom. In that discussion Protagoras mentions madness twice (350B–C, 351A), and he has never withdrawn – or indeed been asked to withdraw – what he said in the two passages. In both he was dealing with a kind of confidence which is not courage, and could be (though it is not quite, as one must admit) called 'bold'.

The connection between that earlier discussion and the final one of the dialogue becomes clearer still when we perceive Protagoras' suggestion in the earlier (350B) that the kind of confidence concerned would not be courage just because it is shameful. One should compare 2 above. The earlier passage also contains Protagoras' admission that courage, like all goodness, is fine. One should compare 3 above. This set of clues may not in itself be decisive; but it deserves following up. We ought to see how the relevant piece of the final argument looks in the light of that earlier piece of conversation.

First, let us notice that despite the 'So' which (unnecessarily) begins question 2 in Taylor's translation,[300] the proposition embedded in 2 does not follow in the least from what immediately precedes. From 'The brave go (wishingly) for things fine and good and pleasant', it does not evidently follow that 'The brave entertain no shameful fears and no shameful confidences.' Taylor speaks in his comment, not uncharacteristically, of Plato's doctrines and Socrates' treatment; but the question is not of these at all, but rather of what Protagoras has to agree. In question 2 Taylor felicitously uses the English 'in general'; the Greek, like the English, might give the impression that question 2 is a generalization of what precedes it. But inspection shows that it is nothing of the sort. The generalization is not *from* anything, but is just a generalization. Nothing is there in the immediate context about the brave being afraid, or the brave not doing or feeling a shameful thing, or a fear being shameful. No basis for the generalization appears in the immediate context. So whatever the provenience of question 2 may be, it is not from the immediately preceding questions.

But considered in the light of the earlier discussion of courage 2 becomes much clearer. Protagoras earlier treated the statement on his own lips, 'Courage would be something shameful', as the conclusion of a *reductio ad absurdum*. So he should, for only a few lines before this he agreed that each part of goodness was something fine (349E). In the later context (359D–E) Protagoras has agreed that what distinguishes a brave man from a coward is not that one goes for fearful and the other non-fearful things, but that, nevertheless, they go for opposite things. Neither goes wishingly for what he thinks fearful. In this whole passage, 'to think fearful' is, for intellectualist reasons, the same as 'to fear'. What the brave man fears ought then to differ in some respect from what the coward fears. Further, courage cannot be shameful; so the choice of things to fear, the choice which distinguishes the courageous from the cowardly, cannot be shameful. Against this background, against all of it, including the earlier passage on courage not being shameful, the first part of the question under 2 above makes excellent sense, and embodies a proposition acceptable to Protagoras. The second part is even more closely derived from the same earlier agreements. Protagoras rejected the claims of certain confident people to be courageous on the grounds that courage would become shameful if he granted the claim. The grounds would be inconclusive if a shameful confidence could be an essential part of courage. Protagoras treated the grounds as conclusive. Therefore Protagoras must refuse to permit shameful confidence to be an essential part of courage. If he were to reject that refusal, he would have to eat words.

Again in the light of the earlier passage, Socrates' question 3, though no less illogical, appears on the whole to be merely mischievous. The reason why Protagoras excluded shameful confidence from courage was presumably (though he never actually said so) that courage is, as he agreed, something fine. 'If something is fine, it is not shameful,' would not appear to imply the present (360B) 'If something is not shameful, it is fine,' but merely 'If something is shameful, it is not fine.' But Protagoras, though not bound as a result of past admissions to accept the peculiar logic of Socrates' question, has treated the distinction of contrary and contradictory with too little respect in the past. Also, he cannot deride Socrates' *conclusion* in this instance, since he has accepted that all of goodness and each of its parts is fine. The particular fears that distinguish the courageous from the cowardly are therefore, presumably, fine.

Question 4 is a complex one, both in itself and in relation to what follows. We may begin unravelling by setting out the propositions entwined in it, on the assumptions that the bold (but not courageous) and the mad are (as would appear from Protagoras' earlier remarks) (350B) the same people, and that both are (as common sense would suggest) distinct from the cowardly. We then obtain four propositions which Protagoras is being asked to accept or reject, as follows:

A   The cowardly entertain shameful fears.
B   The bold/mad entertain shameful confidences.
C   The bold/mad entertain shameful fears.
D   The cowardly entertain shameful confidences.

Of these, A at least looks like common sense, especially once we have accepted that cowards and courageous people fear different things; B is directly available from Protagoras' earlier remarks; C on the other hand looks on the face of it extremely implausible; and D could be made plausible, I think, but only after a substantial argument. That argument would have to run something like this:

> The coward who runs away from battle is ready to endure ('go for') disgrace.
> To 'go for' disgrace is shameful.
> To 'go for' something implies that one is confident in the face of it.
> Hence, to run away from battle is to display a shameful confidence (since confidence in the face of something shameful is itself shameful).

But Socrates and Protagoras have spelt out nothing like this anywhere. The question needs raising, whether Socrates means to ask about C and D, and whether Protagoras means to accept them. One might be tempted to explain the sentence's structure in such a way as to rule out any request for – or explicit giving up of – C. This could easily be done, by taking the cowards as the subject only of the one Greek verb 'fear' and 'mad men and foolhardy' as the subject only of the one Greek verb 'are confident'. In Taylor's English syntax this could easily be clarified by the addition of the one word 'respectively' and consequent slight alterations: 'Now the fear and the confidence respectively of cowards and of mad men and foolhardy are disgraceful.' But though this would be a possible analysis grammatically, especially of conversational Greek, it is logically impossible in this passage. For this would expunge not only the unhappy C but the vital D – vital since the logical nexus between 4, 5 and 6 absolutely requires that somebody should have shameful confidences, and that

that somebody should be the coward. So D is required. But if we keep the required D we seem grammatically condemned to keeping the more than dubious C. And there is, for good measure, a further point, suggested by Santas' questions: why are the mad-and-bold here in this sentence at all, when they play no part in the subsequent argument?

A tentative solution to all these difficulties suggests itself, one recommended only by its explanatory power. Plato's Socrates wishes to extract D from the sophist, to use in the succeeding chain of questions. But both Socrates' audience and Plato's readers (or audience) are pretty weary if they have followed the whole discussion this far. So, rather than use a longish argument, which might additionally need the support of a Socratic induction, Plato has his Socrates ask a portmanteau question, to which the natural answer, on a snap judgment, appears to be 'yes', but which conceals requests for one implausible and one unproved admission. This shortens the argument, and does so without producing for actual use anything Plato did not think he could argue convincingly to a Protagorean if he had to. If this is right, this is the second instance of Plato deliberately shortening this final discussion. As for the introduction of the mad-and-bold, Socrates was already relying in the preceding questions on the passage which mentioned them, and he inserts them in order to complete his portmanteau question. Not to put too fine a point on it, they are there to create a useful muddle.

This explanation, whatever its faults, makes it understandable why the bold-and-mad have no further role. Whether the explanation be true or false, we have seen enough to dispose us to believe that (a) the earlier passage is indeed relevant to the later, as the similarities of vocabulary would lead us to expect, and (b) that the bold-and-mad are there to further some limited *ad hoc* purpose. That purpose might be to awaken the reader to the reference back from later to earlier, thus helping to hold the dialogue together, and performing a literary no less than a philosophical function.[301]

Socrates' fifth question raises some hackles. Granted (since needs must) that cowards entertain bad and shameful confidences,[302] can we really accept, or believe in a Protagoras who accepts, that the only explanation or reason for their entertaining them is ignorance-cum-stupidity? Why should Protagoras accept this? Having seen the importance of verbal reminiscences just now, we should here (360B) be alert to Plato's recall of the motif 'nothing else' from the imaginary conversation with the 'many'. It is hard indeed to believe that this repetition of that passage's constant refrain is accidental.[303] It pays to look back at two particular occurrences of it.

The first (357E) is Socrates' polite rebuke to the common man for thinking that giving way to pleasure is something 'other than' ignorance. This thought is the reason why the man in the street does not send his son to the sophists. The common man behaves therefore as if resistance to temptation were not teachable, saves his money, and does badly. If the rejection of stupid ignorance as a necessary and sufficient condition of badness leads to such consequences for the sophistic profession, Protagoras is not likely to wish to endorse the rejection, especially in the presence (let us remember) of at least one prospective pupil. In the present context, if he does not agree that ignorance is sufficient condition of wrong confidence, he will be damaging his trade; if ignorance is not a necessary condition of wrong confidence, then whoever remedies other conditions will be a competitor, and the sophist's teaching, the handing on of knowledge, will often be irrelevant. It is not without dialectical reason that Socrates anticipated, in the above rebuke to the 'many', the conclusion of the whole dialogue. The tension in that conclusion is felt already, though not set forth with such bluntness, in this preceding argument; behind it lie Socrates' apparently silken flatteries of the sophists in his rebuke to the 'many'.

The second relevant occurrence of our formula (358B–C) heightens this tension in ways we have seen. There, for reasons already analysed, the sophists apparently accept the argument refuting the 'many' on yielding to pleasure. If one never knowingly chooses other than the better course of action, then (except under compulsion) knowing which is the better is a sufficient condition of pursuing it. This extends the scope of the refutation. No feeling, impulse or emotion will prevent the pursuit of the better any more than immediate pleasure will. Overcoming any emotion, that is doing the better action despite any impulse to the contrary, will be sufficiently explained by the possession of knowledge. Short of compulsion, no *other* explanation *than* ignorance is available for failure to take the better course. The normal explanations for pursuing a disadvantageous, or less advantageous, course are either mistaking one's advantage or being overcome by emotion. Once the latter is reduced also to mistaken opinion, or ignorance (358C), then nothing *other than* ignorance is left. The suggestion that no one deliberately pursues the worse or less advantageous course leads in this context to the supposition that one does bad things because of nothing *other than* ignorance. What about moral considerations? These cannot be a separate matter for Protagoras, who has already accepted that the fine *is* advantageous. Indeed, a reminder of this admission appears (358B) just before the passage on ignorance that we are discussing.

What else is left to Protagoras? The common man might or might not have escape-routes from Socrates' net. But Socrates is no longer trapping the common man; rather he is arguing with one who accepts both the advantages of morality and the supremacy of intellect. He is trying to force Protagoras to accept the consequences.

Ignorance-cum-stupidity is, then, the only explanation for cowardly action left open for Protagoras at this stage, and with (I fancy) a resigned air he accepts it. But the step from 'the only necessary and sufficient condition of cowardly action' to 'cowardice' is not a short one. Why does Protagoras take it at one bound, and offer affirmative answers to questions 9 and 10 on our list? Protagoras has not found it easy to separate a good quality from actions in accordance with it, but in general a good quality for him has been an inner state corresponding to, and in a sense producing, or issuing in, certain actions.[304] The distinctive feature of each single virtue was its power, expressed in the kind of action produced. If ignorance issues in the same actions, corresponds as an inner state to the same actions, as cowardice, then Protagoras will have to find another way of individuating the good qualities. Protagoras could argue that the ignorance which is cowardice is different from the ignorance which is (for example) immoderation. That would leave him with (say) four bad qualities distinguished by the object of the corresponding ignorance in each case. But he could then certainly not believe in five bad qualities, all (including ignorance) coordinate, as he had at first tended to believe; and he could not accept any longer that a man can be at the same time superlatively ignorant and superlatively brave.

We have arrived at a place in our argument where we badly need to turn to the opposite of cowardice. That is what Socrates does next (360D). Once arrived at 'Cowardice is ignorance of what is or is not to be feared,' he obtains Protagoras' agreement to 'Wisdom in that field is the opposite of ignorance in it,' and to 'Courage is the opposite of cowardice.' Assuming tacitly, perhaps on the basis of Protagoras' admission of long ago, that nothing has more than one opposite (332C–D), Socrates arrives at the equation of courage with wisdom in what is and is not to be feared. It follows that one cannot be superlatively ignorant and at the same time be courageous. Protagoras' doctrine that courage is distinct from the other virtues is demolished by the collapse of the observation to which he appealed for support (349D).

The demolition is based on premises Protagoras has been driven successively to accept. He obliges Socrates by saying that his old supporting proposition is indeed impossible *on the basis of what he has agreed to* (360E). That, the reader should observe, is not the same thing as saying simply that it is impossible. The underlined phrase reserves the right to go back over his admissions; but Protagoras does not exercise that right. Conceived as a contest, the discussion has been a defeat for Protagoras. It will be no less a defeat if he goes back now to a proposition and withdraws it than it is already when he is forced to withdraw his statement of, and evidence for, the wide difference between courage and wisdom. As a contestant he has nothing to gain by going back. It must gall him that in his effort to trap Socrates (339A) he rebuked Simonides for inconsistency; audience and reader alike should appreciate the irony of this.

Protagoras has nothing clearly to gain as a man, either. That 'fine' behaviour in accord with morality was advantageous to the agent was, if not Protagoras' belief, something he could not without embarrassment withdraw, whatever other less scrupulous sophists might think. The primacy of intellect was bound up, as he himself says, with his whole life (352C–D). From his tenacity in maintaining the separate 'powers' of the good qualities spring ultimately most of his dialectical troubles. Those that do not, spring mainly from his beliefs both that knowledge (or wisdom) is a separate and co-ordinate good quality and that he teaches an art (or knowledge) which forms the goodness of a man and a citizen. But these propositions and beliefs are ones he cannot retract without denying either his profession, or his own personal character, or what seems on the face of it to be plain common sense.

As a contestant, Socrates is the victor. But, whether ironically or not, he disclaims any competitive intent (360E). He asks all his questions with no other end in view than a search for the truth about goodness and its nature. In one of his rare assertions of personal knowledge,[305] he declares that he knows this: that whether goodness is teachable or not is most likely to become clear when the nature of goodness becomes clear. Later in his paragraph comes the assertion that goodness would appear most to be teachable, or that it would be astonishing for it not to be teachable, if all the good qualities were knowledge. If goodness were not knowledge, it would clearly not be teachable, or, as he says a little later, 'would least of all be teachable'. This, he says, makes the respective positions of Socrates and Protagoras ridiculous. Socrates has been trying to show that all the good qualities are knowledge, but that goodness is not teachable; Protagoras, after positing the teachability of goodness, has been striving to make goodness appear almost anything rather than knowledge. Socrates would like to consider next what goodness is, before going on to consider anew its teachability. But Protagoras, faced thus with renewed inquiry into the nature of the thing he claims to teach, declines the implied invitation with exquisite, if a trifle patronizing, urbanity.

Conclusion

This final exchange brings in a number of allusions to motifs significant earlier in the dialogue. The technique is familiar, as a way of rounding off a work of literature. 'Nothing other than' (for example) is recurrent in the *Protagoras*: Socrates' motive is 'nothing other than' inquiry (360E); and if goodness is anything 'other than' knowledge, it will not be teachable (361B). The inquiry, one supposes, is aimed itself ultimately at knowledge. Previously we hear that weak actions were the fruit of 'nothing other than' ignorance (355A, 358C). The 'many' could think of 'nothing other than' pleasure when constrained to think of what is good (354B–E). The price of good things depends on no 'other' feature than their size (355D–E). It was because they thought surrender to pleasure something 'other than' ignorance that the 'many' treated resistance to pleasure's temptations as something not teachable (357E). The rounding off is natural and effective. Conversationally realistic is Socrates' reference back to the figures Epimetheus and Prometheus in Protagoras' myth (361C–D, 320Dff.). More brilliant is the compelling picture (361A) of the argument's conclusion like a man mocking Socrates and Protagoras with accusing laughter – a picture surely designed both to bring to mind the 'ill-mannered' fellow (355C) who laughed at the development, under Socrates' and Protagoras' questioning, of the common man's view of weak will, and to recall the laughter imagined as the common man's reaction to the explanation of weak will to which he is ultimately driven (357D). Just as the common man was found to be laughing at himself, so at the end (361A) Socrates invites Protagoras to imagine their own conclusions mocking them for their inconsistency.

One perhaps expects, in a Platonic dialogue, that Socrates' principal interlocutors will end up unable to maintain a consistent position. But for Socrates, the apostle of consistency, the situation is far more serious. If he has been inconsistent, it is in maintaining that goodness is not teachable, maintaining the dominance of knowledge over the emotions in choice of behaviour, trying to persuade Protagoras that goodness consists in knowledge, and in completing the circle by suggesting that goodness *is* teachable if and only if it is knowledge. If indeed Socrates does have to abandon any of this group of attitudes and propositions, then to which is he least committed? It is rash even to suggest an answer to this question, when Socrates is so wary of committing himself at all. But what about the non-teachability of goodness?[306] Socrates originally advanced that, we have suggested, as Hippocrates' representative; he used arguments in its support which were based on the wisdom of the Athenians and the goodness of their statesmen, two bases he will hardly have thought of as unshakable. If the Socrates of the *Protagoras* has to drop something, it is not unlikely to be this. But we can only hope that these, and indeed all our other suggestions, do not provoke mocking, even ill-mannered, laughter from the shade of Plato.

Epilogue

I

Persistently this book has treated Plato as creating a Socrates who makes use of his respondent's positions, admissions, social function and status, and indeed anything that might give the respondent reason for finding a proposition difficult to deny. We have seen that Socrates often proceeds thus in silence that is, without drawing attention to the fact of his respondent's previous admission, need to save face, and so on. Why should Plato thus have set his readers a series of conundrums whose nature has gone largely unrecognized? Why not set out explicitly the assumptions of the argument, in such a way as to leave his readers in no doubt of where they and he stood? Despite the known difficulties of exploring a writer's intentions, these questions need at least a tentative answer if an interpretation such as the present is to carry conviction.

One may reasonably point to Socrates' partial explicitness in the passage of Plato's *Symposium* we have analysed,[1] and suggest that the lack of continual explicitness may be due, in two ways, to literary taste. First, the continual repetition of indications that the respondent is in an awkward spot could all too easily become monotonous, and monotony is decidedly uncharacteristic of Plato's early and middle writings. Secondly, and perhaps more significantly, for Socrates to point out on each separate occasion with merciless precision the exact nature of the respondent's quandary would be in stark contrast with the atmosphere of ironic urbanity suffusing the Socratic dialogues, an atmosphere essential, surely, to Plato's vision of the genre. Plato's wishes as a writer did not necessarily accommodate the philosophical clarity demanded of him by the modern reader.

But that kind of answer leaves open another question: how could Plato expect his readers, in the absence of clear signposting, to follow the route he had mapped out for them? He should have been able to count on their recollecting, e.g., that Agathon was a homosexual poet; but could he possibly count on their still recalling the details of Protagoras' Great Speech by the time they had arrived, whether in reading or performance, near the end of a dialogue of such length and complexity?

The answer to this question has many ramifications, but must receive a straightforward and brief exposition here. It notes the gradual spread of literacy and of books, and the consequent decline in powers of memory, in the Greek world of the fifth and fourth centuries BC.[2] Plato, himself a man of wide literary culture, portrays in his *Protagoras* Athenian schoolchildren as learning to read and write. But we do not know how long the schools had been teaching these skills,[3] nor to how many children, and it is not until the last third or so of the fifth century that there is fully convincing evidence for *widespread* functional literacy even in Athens.[4] One may reasonably doubt whether even then, while Plato was growing up, the reading of books was a commonplace activity for anything approaching a majority of Athenian men (let alone their less educated womenfolk). The spoken, rather than the written word may have maintained its dominance down to Plato's thirties and forties.[5] Were Plato's readers necessarily readers? We simply do not know whether he wrote the early and middle dialogues in the first instance for oral performance or written dissemination.[6] Though we hear of memoranda, people will have exercised their verbal memories far more than now. For example, Havelock has noted that Socrates and Protagoras assume that each can recall with instant exactitude the poem Simonides wrote for Scopas.[7] Writing may often have been for purposes of check or reminder for oral recitation, rather than for wholly independent use. Plato's dialogues could very possibly rely on a substantial proportion of Athenians retaining powers of memory superior to our modern norm. Such a public would not need the explicitness of reference back desirable for a constantly and fluently reading, and hence less freely memorizing, one. The evidence is not hard and fast, and we cannot *know* that Plato composed with such a public in mind; but if he did, his assumption that audience or readers recall details of speeches after a sizable interval would make sense.

The undoubtedly continuing spread in Plato's lifetime not only of functional literacy but of the *habit* of reading may also account for the failure of Plato's immediate successors to appreciate fully what his Socrates was up to. Aristotle's generation was far more book-oriented than Plato's, and would not necessarily have realized the full extent of Plato's demands that his public recall, and expect Socrates and other characters to recall, earlier passages. Not only is it doubtful whether he said much about his dialogues to his pupils, who differed on some major points of interpretation; Plato might well have *taken for granted* a less bookish society than the next generation. If Plato thus retained that distance from his public which inheres in the dialogue form (so long as the author is not a character), his successors need never have thought to look for the kind of intellectual exchange over long stretches of dialogue that we have detected.

We have suggested tentative answers to two different questions: why Plato should be so inexplicit in the first place, and why he thought he could get away with it over works of such length and complexity. The second question has received an answer closely tied to one time and place; one would not perhaps expect to find a precise parallel. But the answer to the first applies also to other arguments in antiquity, arguments of a dialectical nature we are only now beginning to understand. The dialectical interpretation of Plato may draw support from the parallel; indeed, if the interpretations concerned are disputed, it seems reasonable to treat each as supporting the other. This is all the more true, in that the Stoics, the authors of the arguments about to be mentioned, were heavily influenced by Plato, especially in ethical matters.

The type of argument concerned is a set of syllogisms by Zeno of Citium. Malcolm Schofield, in a most valuable paper,[8] has recently drawn attention to the similarities of Zeno's procedures to those of Socratic dialectic. But it is worth giving one example here of the kind of difficulty into which Zeno could have led his opponents, who are best considered as respondents. Zeno produced the following argument:⁹ 'It is reasonable to worship the gods: it is not reasonable to worship the non-existent: therefore the gods exist.' Now this argument will not have persuaded any determined atheist from Zeno's day to this. No self-respecting atheist would admit to himself the truth of the first premiss. But let us consider the predicament of such a person if asked in public to accept or deny the two premisses of the above argument. Suppose our atheist wished to deny the first premiss; he would then find himself saying in public that most of his audience were irrational. He would also be publicly refusing to concede rationality to that insurance premium of worship which the ancient communities paid to the governing powers of the universe for their safety. His denial would tend to stigmatize him as both contemptuous of his fellows and downright unpatriotic. Were he to escape the charge of unpatriotism by going to public worship, he would brand himself as irrational. In certain respects his situation would resemble that of an early Victorian free-thinker publicly asked 'Is it rational to go to church?' But if the wretched atheist turns to the other alternative, and declares it rational to worship the non-existent, he is in immediate difficulties; how can one worship what one does not believe to exist? Faced with this sort of dilemma, the atheist cannot even expound his quandary without giving too much away. Hence it is easy to see why Zeno's opponents resorted, as Schofield points out, to the production of arguments parallel in structure to Zeno's, but with true premisses and false conclusion. This was in order to show that acceptance of Zeno's premisses did not entail acceptance of his conclusion. Zeno's subtle dialectic left them with no choice but to accept the premisses.

But what still needs saying about Zeno is best deferred. The crucial point is that Zeno apparently relies on the awkwardness of public denial of his suggested propositions. According to the present interpretation, that is just what Socrates relied on. This constitutes indeed support for our method of reading Plato, in that it shows the possibility in the ancient world of arguing dialectically without dotting every 'i' and crossing every 't'.

II[10]

One consequence of this approach to Plato's works has remained implicit in the preceding interpretative chapters, but now needs to be drawn explicitly: it concerns the relationship between one dialogue and another. So long as scholars take the argument of each dialogue as a progression from one objectively established point to another, they will naturally feel entitled to use any such point in one dialogue to elucidate the argument of another dialogue. Not just the final conclusion (positive or negative), but the intermediate steps of a given work will aid directly in the interpretation of another. Not only apparently convincing logic but also apparently obvious premisses will prove transferable. Such transfer becomes a far riskier business for an interpreter treating each piece of dialectic as a wrestling match between Socrates and a particular, carefully characterized opponent or interlocutor. Any premiss, argument or principle of reasoning found acceptable by the interlocutor of one dialogue is open in theory – and often in practice – to question by a different interlocutor in another dialogue. In view of differences of opinion within one and the same dialogue (notably the *Gorgias* and *Republic* I and II) there is no reason to find this surprising. But a consequence is that it is dangerous to interpret one work of Plato's out of intermediate details of another, and this may surprise.

Surprised or not, readers of this book must accept disappointment if they expect here or elsewhere a neat tying of loose ends with reference to dialogues not specifically under discussion. They will also have to bear with the absence of a list of Socrates' (let alone of Plato's) beliefs. Such conclusions as Socrates reaches depend on the premisses and arguments acceptable to an interlocutor in each case. It does not follow that Socrates believes in them. It does follow that, unless Socrates explicitly commits himself, we cannot be sure in any given instance whether Socrates found them acceptable or not, even provisionally. An account of those passages in which Socrates does commit himself would take us into another book. It would necessitate detailed discussion of the degrees of commitment emerging from Socrates' forms of words in a whole series of passages from different dialogues, each needing discussion in its context. Some, such as the assertion in the *Apology* (41C–D) that no harm can befall a good man, are in context not merely of intellectual interest but intensely moving; but, since this book is about a style of argument, and not about a collection of conclusions, we leave them (however regretfully) aside. Apart from these, there are some conclusions towards which Socrates appears to drive so many different interlocutors as to offer grounds for the belief that the fictional philosopher and his author both hold some version of them. The unity of the virtues, in the early and in later dialogues,[11] and a metaphysical version of the Theory of Forms in the *Symposium* and other middle dialogues are moderately clear examples. But even positions Socrates frequently arrives at from premisses offered and arguments accepted by widely differing interlocutors need be no more than provisional beliefs of Plato's; it remains unclear how far Plato's commitment extends. And what premisses Socrates would himself have offered to a questioner, and what steps of reasoning would have secured his assent, are problems to which we have only (at best) tantalizing glimpses of an answer. Of course, his ability to arrive at certain conclusions habitually from the admissions of people with a range of viewpoints may have suggested to him or to Plato that these conclusions deserved at least provisional acceptance.

In any case, it seems premature to take on the synoptic task of looking at the Platonic corpus as a whole before we arrive at something approaching agreement on the meaning of individual works. The view taken of the whole ought to emerge from the interpretation of the parts. Of course, without some view, however ill focused, of the background it is impossible to inspect properly the dialogues chosen for the foreground. This is what makes interpretation an art rather than a science. But no rapid overview will do justice to Plato at this stage, and none is attempted here.

One remark, however, is necessary: one of the conversations chosen for inspection here (to wit, the *Symposium*) finds a place, according to many scholars, among the middle, rather than the early dialogues. The early dialogues, with their frequent ostensible failure to arrive at any positive conclusion at all, are much more obvious targets for an approach like the present one than the middle dialogues, which do appear to have positive and often far-reaching conclusions. To approach in this way a dialogue from Plato's middle period, often regarded as a time of confident exposition of Plato's views, through the mouth of a Socrates behaving more like a guide than a searcher, may seem heretical. But the experiment will have been worth trying if it opens eyes to possibilities often left unexplored in the treatment of such dialogues as the *Phaedo* and the *Republic*. We have no need to believe Plato so wedded to the dialogue form as to continue using it regardless of appropriateness; and study of the middle dialogues in the light of their literary form, the development of characters within them, and the relation of character to philosophical position, ought to occupy Platonic scholars more than it does. Some work of this kind has already appeared;[12] but there is room for more. The appropriateness of Socrates' arguments to his carefully characterized interlocutors needs systematic investigation in all the dialogues where he appears, and not only in the apparently negative and critical works of the early period. Only the completion, to a tolerable extent, of that investigation will make possible a truly synoptic view of the dialogues.

One must, of course, reckon with the possibility that Plato excogitated an initial plan for a series of dialogues and composed each for its place in the series. If he did, then he will, on the interpretation suggested here, have excogitated a whole series of interlocutors, or groups of interlocutors, to portray in the grip of Socratic dialectic and under compulsion to find a new consistency. This is not impossible, though I see no way to prove it. What seems most improbable is that Plato would have expected contemporary or other readers to read the dialogues as a connected series of mutually dependent works. If that was his intention, then, first, his projected series was unique in Classical Greek literature, with the sole exception, so far as I know, of the Attic tragic trilogy or tetralogy, produced under very different conditions from the dialogue, and, secondly, the occasional references from one dialogue to another, almost if not quite all in later dialogues, would have formed an utterly inadequate signpost of his intentions. Nothing in the text of the dialogues suggests at all strongly such a way of reading them; and a strong suggestion would have been needed. Plato does not invite us to read the dialogues as a series; in default of such invitation we have to read them, in the early and middle periods, as each an independent book, able to stand, and to bear its full meaning, by itself. If to proceed dialogue by dialogue forces the postponement of interesting questions, that is a pity, no doubt. But philosophers are used to postponing such questions in favour of the small but answerable ones, and interpreters are subject to a like discipline.

A corollary concerns the dating of Plato's dialogues. Scholars sometimes date dialogues relatively by comparison of two or more arguments on the same or related topics. It is hard to emphasize strongly enough the risks of such a procedure. Abbreviation of an argument may be appropriate for one interlocutor, a more expansive and gradual exposition for another. An assumption immediately acceptable to one character may need tough argument to convince another. The characters of the dialogues differ in intellectual sophistication as well as in their specific positions. Only in case of high probability that the respective interlocutors display no relevant difference could one justify dating by these means. Demonstration of such a probability would be hard to come by. The search for it, compelling the minute dissection of the characters concerned, could be of the greatest value.

III

I have eschewed any attempt to indicate or to investigate the boundary, in so far as there was one, between Socrates and *Socrates*, between the historical and the Platonic Socrates. My use of the name has normally been to refer to Plato's character regardless of historicity. Nevertheless, the reader may reasonably desiderate a brief statement of the contribution offered by this book to the solution of the historical difficulty. It is easy to be brief. This book offers no easement whatever of the difficulty.

One reason for making this clear here lies in the remarks of the previous section on the middle dialogues. So long as scholars believe, as many do, that the historical Socrates ends with the early dialogues and Plato begins with the opening of the middle set of dialogues, there will be a standing temptation to interpret any suggestion of a resemblance in the presentation of Socrates' arguments between early and middle dialogues as a hint that the Socrates of the middle dialogues is as close to the historical Socrates as the figure dominating the early ones. I should not wish publicly to take on any commitment to that particular solution to the Socratic Question; and regardless of its truth or untruth I intend no such hint. Even if one were to claim that Plato's basic method of presenting and developing an argument is the same in the middle dialogues as in the earlier – and I have purposely avoided any such sweeping claim – that would not entail the proposition that the philosophy so presented and developed is still that of Socrates rather than of Plato. The bare possibility, mentioned in the previous section, of exploring in the middle dialogues the relation between personal individuality and philosophical position carries, *a fortiori*, no such entailment. The reader will have to look for other guides than me to the difficult terrain of the Platonic borderland between biography and philosophy.

IV

There is never an end to the analysis of a Platonic dialogue; age cannot wither Plato, nor custom stale his infinite variety. But we have reached the end of our particular journey through three of his Socratic conversations, and it is time to look back and see what features stand out, to take a synoptic view of the dialogues we have been able to analyse.

Each dialogue, we saw, brought Socrates face to face with a conspicuous example of something, be that something an emotion such as Love, or a quality which underwrites success in a certain sphere, such as *andreia* or 'courage' in war, or 'wisdom' in human life at large: Laches and Nicias, examples of success, at least when the conversation takes place, in war; Agathon, in the eyes of his contemporaries, and certainly to his celebrating guests, an object of Love in the first degree; and Protagoras, the most successful in his day of the professional purveyors of 'wisdom'. Each dialogue saw the apparent expertise of this shining example brought to confusion by Socrates' questioning. The two generals admit to not knowing what 'courage' is; Agathon confesses to not knowing what he was talking about when he spoke of love; Protagoras reluctantly admits the contradictory of his initial assured pronouncement on the differences between the virtues and scarcely appears to know where wisdom stands. Each argument contains reasoning which, taken (as it often is) as a straightforward unilinear development, is rich in fallacious argument. Each in turn, when considered as a conversation, has proved rich in confusions, not so much on Socrates' lips (though Socrates is fallible) as on the respondents'. Socrates has played on those confusions and used them to elicit discordant replies to his questions.

So is the point and tenor of these dialogues purely negative? Has Plato written to show only that certain combinations of views are impossible, or at least difficult, to sustain? He has surely shown, or tried to show, the difficulties of holding that *andreia* is both bravery and soldierly skill; he has shown the difficulties of simultaneously believing that 'courage' is 'goodness' and that 'courage' is only one of the many qualities contributing to goodness, or to successful living. He has argued that if you accept that all wise men are good in respect of their wisdom, it becomes difficult to distinguish one virtue from another. He has shown that if you claim to teach goodness you are relating the good qualities again in a way that brings them all together in 'wisdom'. But what has he shown in the conversation between Socrates and Agathon in his *Symposium*? Merely that a poetically gifted homosexual adult cannot be trusted to maintain consistent views of love? What point is there in that which compares with the confutation of doubtless widespread views in the first half of the dialectical part of the *Laches*, or of the misunderstandings surrounding the place of knowledge in education which a great sophist is plausibly exhibited as holding? It looks as if the *Symposium* is almost a reduction to absurdity of the approach adopted in this book. Plato might sensibly write *ad hominem* if the victim was either exceptionally distinguished or typical. But Agathon? Why use a dialectical sledgehammer to crush a butterfly?

If one says in this context that a great artist composes for himself, and not only for his public, one runs the risk of alienating an academic audience completely. But that is in all seriousness the essence of the following answer to the question just raised. The answer is not demonstrable, or even likely to commend itself as obvious. But we may specify in advance that it does not take refuge simply in saying that Plato wrote to please himself and that no further inquiry into his purposes is necessary.

If one takes another look at those characteristics of Agathon, the poet's gift of words and the homosexual inclinations lasting into adult life, and if one asks the question which of Plato's contemporaries possessed those same qualities, then at least one probable example springs immediately to mind: Plato himself. For sheer verbal virtuosity Plato has had few equals in the history either of philosophy or of literature, and surely no superiors; and, from ancient times on, few have been able to resist the strong impression that the author of the dialogues knew about homosexuality from the inside. Like Agathon, Plato never married. The evidence is not, we may repeat, conclusive, and to argue the case in detail here would be tedious. But if Agathon found the Socratic conclusions hard to resist, would Plato have found them much easier?

But of course, the reader will urge, it is Socrates, and not the respondent, who represents Plato. What have Nicias or Protagoras in common with Plato? Does this not leave the *Symposium* just as much of an oddity as it seemed at the outset? To these questions there may be no acceptable answer, but again it seems worthwhile to explore. Exploration reveals that Nicias and Protagoras do have a good deal in common, if not with Plato, at least with his Socrates. Nicias, for one, is prepared to take on board in a dialectical discussion the Socratic doctrine that goodness is indissolubly connected with knowledge. Protagoras is prepared to accede to the suggestion that knowledge is the most important power in human life. Nicias for his part moves in a Platonic or Socratic direction only by a change of mind brought about by the preceding discussion; Protagoras on the other hand feels himself obliged by his whole life and profession to acknowledge the power of the intellect. These two are as near to Plato's Socrates on the subject of knowledge as Agathon is near to Plato in the matter of Love. If Plato is cheating in his use of any one of them, if he has with artificial arbitrariness selected in any one case a victim for Socrates who will give half the game away, then he has done so all three times. If Plato had meant to say to his readers in any of these dialogues 'I have now started from scratch and proved my case,' then he would indeed have been cheating, and would have had to plead guilty as charged. The defence, instead of rescuing the *Symposium*, would have implicated the other two dialogues in the offence.

But the whole thrust of this book is to cast doubt on the notion that Plato ever meant to say any such thing. In the final argument of the *Laches*, for example, one can read him equally well, and far more charitably, as saying something more like this: 'If you abandon the connection of "courage" with mere "guts", and are prepared to agree that it is an intellectual matter, then you must abandon the attempt to distinguish one good quality from another.'

The *Protagoras*, too, says something very like that. It says to the great sophist and his congeners, 'You too must acknowledge the power of knowledge; and if you do so, then you must admit the inadequacy of the conventional distinctions between the virtues, distinctions by which you and your pupils guide your lives and your education.' In each case Plato says, in effect, 'if you are ready to come with me this far – and you are, aren't you? – then you must come the whole way.' Whether he says these things convincingly is another matter; his Socrates is not always right, even on the assumptions of this interpretation. But he is a lot less wrong on this type of interpretation than he is on some.

The *Symposium* is a little different; it says, rather, 'If you are like me, an artist of passionate homosexual nature, holding the values I hold, acting on the belief that a great work is more important than any child, how will you conceive the nature of Love, of Desire, and of their objects?' It is perhaps a paradox that the most private and personal of the three works, the one which shows signs of concern with Plato's own inmost nature, is the greatest dramatic masterpiece to come from his pen.

But we should not neglect the possibility that Plato wrestles with himself in the others too: that he takes up the cardinal point of the Socratic faith as he saw it, the central importance in human life of the intellect and its knowledge, and argued that that faith necessitates, against common sense, against linguistic intuition, the abandonment of certain distinctions between one kind of human goodness and another. If we hold that Plato thought both Nicias and Protagoras were wrong to suppose that intellectualism harmonizes with such distinctions, we do not therefore have to hold that he came to that conclusion without intellectual struggle. That intellectual struggle has often given rise to the belief that Plato criticizes Socrates; but it is not necessary to interpret as criticism those dialogues which oppose Socraticism to the views of the 'many', for whom Plato's Socrates evinces contempt on more than one occasion, even if the 'many' include some distinguished philosophers.

It is in a special way fitting that Plato should conduct his public thinking in the form of a dialogue between the views he appears to favour and the views he appears not to. In the *Theaetetus* and the *Sophist*, both admittedly compositions of a much later date than our three dialogues, Plato's Socrates and the Eleatic Stranger both alike put forward, without opposition, a view of thinking as a conversation within the soul. If, as seems probable, Plato saw the process of thinking as an internal dialogue, conducted by question and answer, it was natural for his published thoughts to take the form of a dialogue between his favoured views and those whose popularity he recognized even in disagreement. It would not, for a man holding his views, and anxious to avoid thinking himself wise when he was not, be right to leave unquestioned the attitudes and the conclusions of dialectic he had inherited, we may suppose, from Socrates. He would, if his public thoughts were to mirror his own conception of his private ones, find himself naturally drawn to the exposition of them in the form of a dialogue of the kind we have envisaged. If, he might say to himself, I am going to hold to what Socrates seemed to be saying about goodness and knowledge, I need to posit it, and see what objections can be brought against it. I do not have to accept those objections, but they need stating. Who better to imagine questioning these views than the arch-interrogator Socrates himself? I need to draw out and face the consequences of Socratic notions, to see just how unpalatable such consequences are. What better method than to imagine those who accept a measure of Socraticism being shown up, in Socrates' way, as not facing those consequences? I need to be sure that my own attitudes and values are consistent with my beliefs; what better road to certainty than the construction of a dialogue in which a poet holding some of them is driven by Socrates along the road to others of them?

Scholars may object to this use of the interpretative imagination. It is indeed no substitute for close study of the texts. But, if after that study we make no attempt to stand back from the detail and understand the whole, we shall have betrayed the ideals of scholarship no less than if we skip the study of detail. Further, it is difficult, if not impossible, to work on the detail without having some view, implicit or explicit, of the purpose and direction of the whole. One purpose of this book is to question, and cause others to question, the assumptions underlying much recent interpretation of Plato in English. I hope and expect that others will do the like to me.

The discussion will continue; Plato's appeal is perennial. It will remain so even if the theses of this book are correct and Plato's thinking is anchored firmly in the habits of thought and speech of his own day, and in his own difficulties. Plato's is not merely the appeal of great literature, or the antiquarian interest of any ancient monument, nor is it simply the fascination exercised by a perpetual enigma. Plato's writings raise so many questions about human life in the course of their discussions that he must be a dull dog who does not find in some of them an echo of his own questionings. Perhaps professional educators, particularly but not only in the humanities, need most of all to consider, as Plato does especially in the *Laches* and the *Protagoras*, what qualities they are trying to instil, and what relation their teaching has to the successful living of their pupils' lives.

Notes
For details of works cited see Bibliography, pp. 495ff.

1 Introduction: Platonic Questions

1 Taylor, 1976.
2 Adam and Adam, 1905.
3 The quoted expression is borrowed from Vlastos (Jowett, 1956, xxxi).
4 Santas (1979, 221–55, esp. 238) and Woodruff, 1982. Woodruff relies perhaps too much on ancient biographies of Hippias. On the *Gorgias* see now Kahn, 1983.
5 O'Brien, 1963, followed up in his 1967. There is much of value also in Klein, 1965, despite its discursiveness; and see his bibliographical note, 4 n. 10. I use 'dialectic' differently from Klein (see his 27), to include *ad hominem* argument, and distinguish, as he seems not to do, between *ad hominem* argument and rhetoric.
6 See Kerferd, 1981, with list including his own most important articles.
7 See e.g. Goldschmidt, 1947; Laborderie, 1978, with a wealth of references to the classic French and German expositions of Plato; Méron, 1979, a helpful sketch paying, however, too little attention to Kerferd's papers or to Plato's motives.
8 See especially Dodds, 1951; Adkins, 1960; Lloyd-Jones, 1971; Dover, 1974.
9 Weingartner, 1973.
10 See Lloyd-Jones, in Wilamowitz, 1982, x–xviii.
11 A notable exception, sharply separating Socrates from Plato, is Klosko, 1983; this paper emphasizes the importance of Socrates' interlocutors, but came into my hands too late for detailed consideration.
12 Hubbard and Karnofsky, 1982.
13 Woodruff, 1982, 30, n. 27. I have borrowed Woodruff's translations.
14 Cp. *Meno* 84A, where Socrates' speech is grammatically one long question: 'Do you observe that...?', and Meno replies 'You speak true things.' At *Meno* 76C–D, Meno says, 'That is so' (Εστι ταῦτα), in response to one of a series of questions.

φαίνεται 'it seems so' is common in such contexts. The idiom is natural enough.
15 Irwin, 1977, esp. 296, n. 23 (and see the Index Locorum).
16 Irwin, 1977, 85.
17 Irwin, 1977, xvi.
18 Irwin, 1977, 93.
19 Some of the following references I owe to Dr J. D. Thomas, Reader in Papyrology, University of Durham: Gardthausen, 1879 I, 270ff., and on the question mark II², 1913 405ff., dating it to the ninth century AD; Thompson, 1912, 60, says, 'about the eighth or ninth century'; Turner, 1971, 10–13, esp. 11, 'No special stop was devised [in the classical period] to act as a question mark.' See further Pfeiffer, 1968, 179–181, and Reynolds and Wilson, 1974, 214–16.
20 Zeyl, 1980, 250–269, esp. 253.
21 Gosling and Taylor, 1982, 37.
22 Gosling and Taylor, 1982, 37.
23 Gosling and Taylor, 1982, 46–7.
24 Gosling and Taylor, 1982, 47.
25 By 'fictional' I do not mean fictitious; I refer simply to the obvious point that Plato's dialogues are not verbatim records of actual conversations, but authentically literary creations. See Ch. IV n. 58, below.
26 See Bluck, 1961, ad loc. for verbal parallels proving this intention; and Klein, 1965, 99–107, 175–184.
27 See Santas, 1979, 59–96 on Socrates' questions.
28 Thrasymachus at *Republic* 348C denies (1) that justice is a good quality, and (2) that justice is more profitable than injustice.
29 See Bluck, 1961, 120–126 and Klein, 1965, 36–37 with nn.
30 The crispest formulations are Socrates' at 331E–332C, but Polemarchus shows no reluctance to accept them.
31 The reader stands referred to North, 1966.
32 Cf. Hare, 1982, 3: 'that not untypical young man'.
33 See Moline, 1969, 153–161.
34 See Dover, 1982, 122, on Socrates' elaboration of this relatively simple point.
35 Irwin, 1979.
36 Dodds, 1959.
37 I have lightly retouched Guthrie's rendering here.
38 E.g. Ryle, 1966, 28.
39 Schofield, 1980, reviewed by me, *Philosophical Review*, 93 (1984) 435–9.

40 Hawtrey, 1981, 17 n. 13.
41 Laborderie, 1978, perhaps exaggerates our knowledge, but has a solidly helpful account; he relies more on Diogenes Laertius than I would, and (despite his words of caution) may overestimate the typicality of our meagre remains of Plato's fellow Socratics. I have, for the chronological reason given below, much sympathy with his conclusion (49), 'Les autres Socratiques auxquels la tradition attribue des dialogues n'ont pu exercer d'influence déterminante sur la forme dialoguée adoptée par Platon.'
42 See Dover, 1978, esp. 84 and 144 on Agathon.
43 Tigerstedt, 1977, 92ff., esp. 96.
44 I will not repeat the extensive modern bibliography but refer the reader to Vlastos, 1981, 379–403, as the most sensible writing on the subject known to me.
45 In Lloyd, 1979. Consecutive argument of anything like a formalized nature is difficult to find before Plato's old age, apart (in my view) from the isolated genius such as Anaximander.
46 Gosling and Taylor, 1982, 46, 53, 58–60. Manuwald, 1975, e.g. 45, n. 50, has a similar dichotomy between 'ernst nehmen' and 'Ironie'.
47 See e.g. Lefkowitz, 1981, and, for Plato's life, Riginos, 1976.
48 Weingartner, 1973, 109ff., Kerferd, 1981, 138.
49 See Plass, 1960, 103–115 esp. 110; *contra* (on this particular issue), Gallop, 1975, 188–9. The translation 'results', Bluck, 1955, 14 and 169, I find hard to differentiate from 'consequences'.
50 The most notable example of this tendency is Dover, 1980.
51 Olympiodorus *In Alcib.* 2, 156–62 (p. 6 [Westerink]), cf. Anon., *Prolegomena* 1, 29–35 (p. 5 [Westerink]); the references collected by Riginos, 1976, 24.

2 Socrates and a pair of generals

1 The text most conveniently available is Burnet, 1949; useful commentaries are by Tatham, 1888–1938, Vicaire, 1963, and Cron (in several editions). The translation I have used as a basis for discussion of *Laches* is that of Kent Sprague, 1973.
2 Guthrie's 'Comment', *HGP* IV, 130ff., devotes only a few lines to the first half of the dialogue and Sprague, 1973, treats the first half of the *Laches* as perhaps an introduction to the

whole group of definition dialogues.
3 E.g. Santas, 1969, 190–92 (also in Vlastos, 1971).
4 Méron, 1979, esp. 195–203.
5 Dieterle, 1966; cf. O'Brien, 1963 (also at Anton & Kustas, 1971, 203–35) and 1967, 114–17.
6 Guthrie, *HGP* IV, 132, n.1.
7 On the characters see Guthrie, *HGP* IV, 125ff., Sprague, 1973, 9ff.
8 As Sprague (1973, 4) points out, too emphatically denying the relevance of the generals' experience to Lysimachus' request.
9 Perhaps education and/or warfare?
10 Much of this will not be news to readers of Dieterle and Méron; but neither devotes much attention, in this connection, to Lysimachus and Melesias.
11 I have found no indication in the text whether Socrates is within earshot from the start or comes up to the little group on cue at 180B; did Plato not want his readers to raise the question?
12 Sprague's rendering of ἀκλεεῖς γενήσονται, 'will become unglorious', as 'will turn out to be nobodies' is elegant but fails to bring out this particular point.
13 So C. C. W. Taylor in his translation of the *Protagoras,* and Woodruff, 1982. See Woodruff 109–11; the word refers in general to the judgment of a beholder.
14 The best evidence for this is not the dirty Socrates of Aristophanes' *Clouds* (on which see Dover, 1968, xxxiii ff., esp. xlii), but the sheer unanimity of the major ancient sources.
15 For a hostile account of this see R. Robinson, 1953, but one might point out that it is up to Socrates' respondent to say if he regards a word as having more than one distinct sense, and that several respondents are not the type to discern any but the most obvious puns.
16 Méron, 1979, 197.
17 See the translations of Sprague, Jowett, Lamb (in the *Loeb*) and others.
18 Méron, 1979, 204–6, cites several passages mentioning what we would call 'courage', but the question is not what the Greeks made of courage but what they meant by *andreia*.
19 Coleridge, 1905.
20 De Romilly, 1980, 314, postulates such a debate.
21 De Romilly, 1980, misses this point. She appears, further, to ignore the clause in Thucydides, II 89.2 mentioning *andreia*.

The history of the word *andreia* still remains to be written.
22 Dieterle, 1966, 34, is too positive about the implications of these.
23 See Sprague's translation and Dieterle, 1966, 53.
24 Sprague's version has 'virtue' – a word better known to philosophers than to ordinary folk; the Greek ἀρετή functions as the ordinary abstract of ἀγαθός, 'good', and may be rendered simply 'goodness' or (in some contexts) 'a good quality', as almost always in this book.
25 For the effect of war on Greek morals see esp. Thucydides, III 82–3.
26 Dover, 1974, 161; Adkins, 1960, 225.
27 On the importance of 'contribution', see Rist, 1982, 14.
28 See Dover, 1974, 165ff., though I doubt if his passages from Lycurgus show his distinction there between *andreia* and *arete*.
29 See in general Dover, 1974, 161–70, and Adkins, 1960, though *andreia* is not in his index. Pearson (1962, 207–08) is one-sided on Athens and Sparta, but (231–3) good on Tyrtaeus.
30 Dover, 1974, 148, points out the Greeks' lack of the concept, in legal theory or practice, of ' "diminished responsibility" by virtue of insanity'; but failure to distinguish 'mad' and 'bad' need not imply failure to distinguish 'mad' and 'good'; cf. Aristotle, *EN* 1115b24–8.
31 Dover, 1974, 164.
32 As probably, for example, at *Rep.* 399E–400A.
33 Sprague has another reason: 1973, pp. 6 and 8.
34 I have here kept closer than Sprague to the order of the Greek.
35 Equating: de Romilly, 1980, 314; distinguishing: Méron, 1979, 197.
36 As Dieterle saw, 1966, 93 n.1.
37 Dieterle, 1966, 116 n. 3, says that Laches has 'die Unterscheidung in gewissem Sinne bereits selbst vorweggenommen'; he refers to Pohlenz, 1913, 27, an over subtle and at the same time inexact interpretation.
38 Dieterle, 1966, 38, notices the connection between this and 184D–E.
39 Dieterle, 1966, 37.
40 I have noticed no editor who prints a question here.
41 γάρ in conversation *can* suggest a necessary condition of what precedes, and hence come close to 'so', but hardly here.
42 Οὐκοῦν, on which consult des Places, 1929, 146–209.
43 Sprague renders both εἰκός and ἴσως by 'probably'. The

Notes to pages 61–68

second of these could be weaker; LSJ offers as an alternative 'perhaps' but gives for εἰκός in this usage (s.v. ἔοικα) only 'likely' or 'probable'.

44 Sprague, 1973, 23 n. 16.
45 Sprague's 'council' here and at the end of 184C is unnecessarily concrete; and σοί explains who would be doing the deliberation (βουλή). My 'literal' version differs accordingly.
46 Sprague, 1973, 23 n. 17.
47 See Sprague and Vicaire, 1963, ad loc.
48 See, e.g. Guthrie (who is cautious) *HGP* III, 469, and Dover (who is sceptical) on Aristophanes, *Clouds* 94.
49 See with caution Huart, 1968, 420–22.
50 See Claus, 1981, 75–8 and 87 for ψυχή as the seat of courage.
51 Vlastos, 1981, 266ff., treats it as wrong to allow Socrates to concede the falsehood of his proposition (7), 'Courage is only one of the parts of virtue', and refers to its previous admission at 190C. But if my point here is right, there is nothing at 190C itself to prevent Socrates from conceding the falsehood of a proposition there implied (nor, to do him justice, does Vlastos make any argument out of 190C).
52 Dieterle, 1966, 53.
53 Sprague, indeed, prints it as a question with Jowett[4], though Vicaire, Tatham and the Loeb do not.
54 I have lightly retouched Sprague's version here so that the first part of the sentence does not imply already Socrates' intention of proceeding to a second task, and the second half does not make Socrates talk baldly of 'having' a knowledge.
55 The Greek does not say 'everyone', as Sprague's translation has it, and Laches is himself a clear exception.
56 See esp. Penner, 1973, 35–68 and Ferejohn, 1982, 1–21. Gregory Vlastos has consistently opposed this view, nowhere more forthrightly than in *Platonic Studies*, 2nd edn, 266–9, and 418–23.
57 Vlastos' 'Biconditionality thesis', for which see *Platonic Studies*, 2nd edn, 232ff.
58 Vlastos, 1981, 225 n.8, cites in this connection *Meno* 78D–79E as unequivocally offering and strongly emphasizing the doctrine that 'Virtue is a "whole" and that Justice, Temperance, etc. are its "parts".' But the whole of that passage explores Meno's ethics, and not Socrates': thus the ἔφαμεν ('we said...?') at 79A on Socrates' lips commits him not at all. The habit dies hard of attributing affirmations to Socrates in his interrogatory passages.

At *Platonic Studies*², 418–21 Vlastos gives as a reason for doing so at *Meno* 78D–79C the assumption of different bees, figures and colours, in the examples Socrates uses to illustrate the kind of answer he wants to his 'What-is-*X*' question. But are not these examples also couched in interrogative form? Certainly the example of the bees is interrogative (72A–C); and the application of it to the virtues probably is too, since (a) Οὕτω δή at 72C6 points the parallelism between this speech and the preceding, and (b) nothing in the Greek indicates that Plato has inserted a statement by Socrates in the middle of a series of questions. It was Meno who suggested a varied plurality of virtues, and Socrates asks Meno whether the members of *this* plurality have a quality in common. Similarly, Socrates' question at 73E1 'Πότερον ἀρετή, ὦ Μένων, ἢ ἀρετή τις' arises only out of Meno's views.

Socrates' example of figure needs to be read in this context. Socrates does commit himself to its truth at 73E; but does not commit himself anywhere to the view that virtue is precisely parallel. Certainly he does not at 74A1–3. Socrates' *second* speech at 74A *is* statement, not question; it commits Socrates apparently to one single virtue which is in all these [virtues mentioned by Meno]; but it is hard to see how that commits Socrates to any *difference* between the virtues Meno names. Again, Socrates at 75A remains uncommitted to any doctrine of the virtues; he merely requires Meno to answer about colour as practice for a subsequent answer, to be based still on *Meno's* view of the virtues. The instructions at 77A are again, so far as one can see, predicated on Meno's assumptions. The statement about parts of virtue at 77D–E is qualified by ὡς ἔοικε, giving accordingly the apparent result of Meno's admissions. *Nowhere* in all this can one confidently assert Socrates' commitment to distinct and varied virtues.

59 See esp. C. H. Kahn, 1976.
60 Dieterle, 1966, 50ff., sees the passage as a concession to 'seiner Gesprächspartner und deren gedankliche Umwelt', and interprets the (surely ironic) excuse that the discussion will be easier if they take a part of virtue as meaning that the Socratic assumption of the unity of the virtues would make the discussion too hard to grasp. But one could treat the whole of goodness without any specifically Socratic assumptions, easy or difficult; and the partner and his 'Umwelt' need to be distinguished. There is no unified 'Alltagsdenken' from which Socrates can (Dieterle, 51) lead Laches to philosophy.

61 Note in this dialogue: 194B ('My friend', says Socrates in encouraging Laches to go on searching after his defeat in argument); 197E ('O blessed one', says Socrates in urging Laches at least to consider an intellectualist proposition from Nicias, and 'O best one' in stressing the need for great intellectual qualities in order to lead great affairs: 199D ('O divine one', says Socrates to Nicias in the cardinal question whether on Nicias' view 'courage' turns out to be the whole of goodness). All these are highly significant places in the drama; the present one matches them.
62 Nehamas, 1975–6, 288–306 refutes the notion that Laches and his congeners in the early dialogues confuse universal with particular.
63 See Detel, 1973, and Graeser, 1975.
64 Robinson, 1953, 55–61.
65 Nehamas, 1975–6, 295.
66 See on this D. B. R(obinson) at Jowett, 1970, vol. 2, 99, and Santas, 1969, 185.
67 I agree with Vlastos, 1982, 223 n. 5: 'It is widely assumed that, for good purposes (pedagogical or polemical) of his own, the Platonic Socrates does not scruple to profess to believe propositions he thinks false and to defend them by sophistical arguments. I reject this assumption, holding it to be inconsistent with what we learn in the Platonic corpus about Socrates' conception of the philosophic life and about his general character.' *But* I do not find it implausible or reprehensible or inconsistent for Socrates to speak as a representative of one other person *vis-à-vis* another, even if unable to fulfil the requirements for representative status of Aristotle, *Topics*, 159b27–35.
68 See e.g. Irwin, 1979, 110, and Dodds, 1959, 12–15.
69 See LSJ s.v. νικάω, II, 2 and 3.
70 See Graeser, 1975, 174 and nn.
71 Cf. Detel, 1973, 8, Dieterle, 1966, 69 and n. 2, who adopts this way of reading the *Charmides* passage, and Goodwin, 1894, 217ff.
72 I have avoided Sprague's 'every kind of endurance' in favour of the more literal 'all endurance' in order to avoid importing potentially controversial 'kinds' or 'sorts' of endurance.
73 Graeser, 1975, 175.
74 Detel, 1973, esp. 8–9.
75 Graeser, 1975, 178, pointing out the important omission of τήν γε τοιαύτην in Detel's paraphrase of the Greek.

76 Telle, 1975, 18, speaks of (iii) (her 2b) as won from (ii) (her 2a). But the argument she gives is not in the text; nor is any other inferential connection between the two steps. She over-schematizes.
77 Santas, 1969, in his account (esp. 94) clearly separates 'foolishness' from lack of skill: Telle, 1975, clearly associates φρόνησις with technical skill. Irwin appears to hold that φρόνησις is ambiguous: he speaks (1977, 47) of cases where one person 'because he is an expert or for some other reason happens to know the right answer' – though it is not easy to see *to what* Irwin's person knows the right answer. φρόνησις, 'practical shrewdness', is rare before Socrates (Irwin, 288 n. 18). We are dealing here largely with fourth-century BC usage, though poetry (including comedy) knows the related adjective φρόνιμος in a corresponding sense. On the usage of these words see O'Brien, 1967, 41 n. 46. See further O'Brien, 1967, 30–9, and Adkins, 1960, 244–6.
78 Méron wrongly assumes (1979, 5) that the context necessitates the understanding of ἀφροσύνη ('folly') as 'manque de connaissances'; she fails to take into account the background of Greek usage.
79 See Santas, 1969, 188–190; Santas adds that where there is little risk there is no 'nobility', nothing 'fine'. But the 'fine' makes no appearance, and the reader's first thoughts should perhaps be of the slightness of the endurance required. Santas, 191, has Socrates' examples compare 'two men who endure dangers *equally*' (my italics): but the risk is less for the knowledgeable.
80 Méron, 1979, 197ff.
81 So Dover, 1974, 164.
82 Méron, 1979, 200.
83 Laches does imply in the opening scene that technical knowledge is not, and does not lead to, goodness. But that does not mean that goodness or 'courage' is non-reflective. 'Wisdom' is, as we have seen, not necessarily technical knowledge, and the latter is not the only form of 'reflection'.
84 Cf. Burnyeat in Vlastos, 1971, 214: the 'only worthwhile form of attack is through premises which have and keep the respondent's assent'.
85 Sprague's translation 'of the ... harmful sort' does not bring out the etymological relation between κακ- and κακουργ-; hence my dragging in of the word 'bad'.
86 See Robinson, as cited in n.15 above.

87 Aristotle at *EN*, III, 1115a4ff., says nothing of any ambiguity; but his interesting view that 'courage' is displayed *par excellence* in battle may owe something to the fact that *andreia* refers, in the way we have seen, to a soldier's skills.
88 Dieterle, 1966, 95–100, esp. 99ff.
89 1977, 128: 'The *Laches* excludes endurance from the account of courage.'
90 See O'Brien, 1963, *passim*.
91 See Kahn, 1976.
92 Irwin, 1977, 72, criticizes the way in which Socrates moves abruptly from the proposal that courage is wise endurance to Nicias' Socratic view of it as some sort of knowledge. The abruptness is more apparent than real.
93 Sprague has 'invention' which is neat, but obscures the etymological and semantic relation between σόφισμα and σοφός.
94 Cf. Dieterle, 1966, 104ff.
95 On lion similes in Homer see Scott, 1974, 58–62, and Moulton, 1977, 139–141.
96 Sprague's rendering of this sentence (198A) is 'And didn't you give your answer supposing that it was a part, and, as such, one among a number of other parts, all of which taken together were called virtue?' The first words of this (down to 'a part') leave the question 'Which answer?' open; the Greek, in my opinion, does not. In τοῦτο ἀπεκρίνω ὡς μόριον I take τοῦτο to have for antecedent ἡ ἀνδρεία and to be, as commonly, the subject of a clause in reported speech placed outside the clause as though it were the object of the verb of speaking. My opinion implies that ὡς here is the conjunction 'that' and the word ἐστι is (to use convenient if outmoded grammatical terminology) 'understood' in the implied clause ὡς τοῦτο μόριον. It looks as if Sprague takes the ὡς here to be similar to the ὡς in Socrates' previous speech; I find this, with Jowett, hard to believe.
97 Dieterle, 1966, 119 n. 2.
98 Méron, 1979, 198.
99 Recently at *Platonic Studies*, 2nd edn, 443–4. Vlastos appeared to accept that equation rather than entailment was meant here. He promises there a fuller exposition; but he still holds that Socrates is criticizing himself on the basis of accepting that courage is a part of virtue.
100 So Sprague, and Irwin, 1977, 303 n. 65.
101 This is no doubt the force of Socrates' προμηθεῖται (198D).

102 Nicias has accepted the addition of neutrals at 198C; its omission later is presumably for brevity's sake.
103 See the general expression καὶ πάντως ἐχόντων twice at 199C.
104 The first of these is Sprague's rendering; the other is mine.
105 Socrates does not assume, as Irwin says (1977, 99) 'that the final good will require most of the recognized virtues'.
106 At 194E–195A and elsewhere Nicias suggests that courage is the knowledge of 'things to be feared and things to be dared.' Only at 195D does Nicias use the formulation 'things to be feared and not to be feared'; but that this is his meaning throughout is clear from his acceptance at 198B of the definition Socrates offers of 'things-to-be-dared' as 'things which arouse no fear'. The etymologically associated Greek verb θαρρεῖν often means 'not to be afraid'. See *Iliad*, 4, 184; 8,39; and many other passages.
107 *Laws* 646E is not a definition: the Athenian Stranger says, 'We fear, I suppose, bad things, expecting them (προσδοκῶντες) to happen.' That is not, in context, a statement that the whole of fear consists in the expectation. *Laws* 644C calls fear 'The expectation (ἐλπίς) before distress', which looks more commonplace than Socratic.
108 Santas in Vlastos, 1971, 208, is one who brings this charge.
109 Méron, 1979, 198.
110 Santas in Vlastos, 1971, 207.

3 Socrates and a tragic poet

1 E.g. Thompson, 1979, argues instructively that Socrates' speech, as a 'dialectic search for truth', is Plato's ideal speech.
2 Vlastos, 1981, 3–42: see also Levy, 1979, and Price, 1981.
3 Dover, 1980, viii.
4 Dover, 1980, 133.
5 Translators of the *Symposium* persistently render κάλλιστος by 'fairest'. This seems dangerous in modern English in a context where justice is mentioned. I use 'beautiful' for καλός in expounding the *Symposium*, though I have 'fine' elsewhere. 'Beautiful' sounds to me more like a term for the beloved than 'fine', but 'fine' is less misleading in other moral contexts.
6 Dover, 1980, 123ff. Hamilton's translation (70) has 'evidence' all five times.
7 Dover, 1980, 124.

8   Dover, 1980, 123.
9   See Burnet, 1924, and Allen, 1980, e.g. 5ff.
10 Dover, 1980, 1.
11 Hamilton's 'or can he exist absolutely without an object?' does not bring out my point.
12 Dover, 1980, 134.
13 Jowett, 1953, has a somewhat different version: '... whether Love desires that of which love is.'
14 Dover, 1980, 143, on 204C2.
15 I have modified Hamilton's version here in two main ways: the substitution of 'just' and its relatives for 'right' and its relatives, to avoid commitment to the supposition that justice is the whole of goodness (see further below on the *Protagoras*): and the substitution of the un-English 'wishingly' for 'willingly', on which see Saunders, 1968 and 1973.
16 Dover, 1980, on 204C7–206A13, understandably finds such an assumption objectionable.
17 See on the later passage pp. 145ff. below.
18 Hamilton here has '... the love of beauty gave rise to all manner of blessings for gods and men alike.' But the Greek here speaks of 'beautiful things', not beauty in the abstract, and the word rendered 'blessings' is the ordinary word for 'good things'.
19 I have omitted Hamilton's 'art', not in the original.
20 Nor is there reason for supposing the last sentence before Agathon's peroration (197B) to deal only with the love of beautiful *people*.
21 γε μήν is here 'progressive'. See Denniston, 1954, 349.
22 The word is ἕτοιμον, p. 77, 200D.
23 Here Hamilton simply omits the word 'always' in his version.
24 I have retouched Hamilton (a) to bring out the notion of 'wishing' in the Greek, and (b) to avoid (though I share it) Hamilton's assumption that the antecedent of 'that' is 'what is inevitable'.
25 The word for 'possesses' here (ἔχει) has no direct representative in Hamilton's or in Jowett's translation.
26 Dover, 1980, 135.
27 See below pp. 176ff. on the climax of Diotima's scene.
28 I owe this cardinal point to my friend and former Durham colleague, Mr. R. J. Delahunty, but he should not be held responsible for my expression or development of it.
29 Hamilton's translation, near the foot of his 77, implies, with the words 'we have reached agreement', that Socrates as well

as Agathon is committed to agreement. But the summary itself takes the form of *questioning*. At 201B1 'we have agreed' is a mistranslation of ὡμολόγηται which, as a passive, 'it has been agreed', does not specify by whom. Similarly, at p. 78, 201A8, 'Quite right' (Hamilton) is not correct for ἐπιεικῶς, which means 'Reasonably'.

30 Twice in this speech Hamilton simply omits οὑτωσί πως: he also changes 'beautiful things' and 'ugly things' to 'beauty' and 'ugliness'. Also, as Dover points out, 'troubles were composed' will not do: Plato's meaning is 'The powers of the gods were arranged'.

31 Dover, 1980, 125, which has also the paraphrase 'within a mile of old age' employed above.

32 This appears to be the drift of Hamilton's version, '... by fleeing *before* old age' (italics mine).

33 'Thing' here does not mean 'object' but is the merest space filler.

34 See below, pp. 176ff.

35 Dover, 1980, 135, on 200E2.

36 Proclus, *In Tim.*, 128, quoted by Bury, *ad loc.*, is thus mistaken.

37 See most recently Woodruff, 1982, 109–11.

38 Bury, *ad loc.*, says 'For coincidence of these two concepts. cp. *Prot.* 360B, *Hipp. Maj.* 297B,C, *Phileb.* 64Eff.' – but the two concepts do not necessarily 'coincide' here. What Bury goes on to say implies that τὸ καλόν is a species of τὸ ἀγαθόν – which is certainly *not* implied here, *pace* Galli, 1935, 148, ad loc. Galli speaks vaguely of 'L'intima affinità dei concetti *buono e bello*' and lists more passages; but no such list would prove Socrates to assume here what the argument does not require. Dover correctly states *ad loc.* that this present passage makes τά ἀγαθά a sub-class of the class καλά; but his contrast with other passages is not, I think, in the text. See further below.

39 See on this Robin, 1951, Notice, xxv–xxvii.

40 Vlastos' discussions of *Protagoras* 331A and similar passages, including this one, 1981, 249ff with nn. and 438 n.**UVP249, ignore this point, which makes it unnecessary to suppose with Vlastos, 439, that Socrates and Diotima are talking about a '*P* attribute' or special Platonic notion in this passage at least, or that this 'is Plato's way of saying that at this point he is breaking with his old teacher'.

41 1980, 137–8; see also Cornford, 1950, 71.

42 Hamilton, 'Of all the happy company of the gods Love ... is the most happy'; in the Greek there is no word for 'company' and the first 'happy' is a predicate of the subject ('all the gods') of a participal phrase.
43 Dover, 1980, on 202C6.
44 See Dover, 1980, on 202C10 for a lucid analysis.
45 Dover, 1980, 139ff.
46 Hamilton's 'Obviously not' is, I think, mistaken for Οὐδαμῶς, ὥς γ' ἔοικεν. The restrictive γ' is significant; hence my emphasis.
47 Hamilton's 'lives in want' (p. 82) is not literal.
48 See e.g. *Apology*, 29A–B, *Meno*, 84A–B.
49 1980, 143, on 204B2. Cf. n. 38 above.
50 Diotima's εὐπόρου (204B) is rendered by Hamilton (p. 83) 'fertile in expedients'; the word can also mean 'well-provided'.
51 See below pp. 185ff. on the *Protagoras*. Clay, 1975, draws out a contrast between Socrates' 'wisdom' and Agathon's (243ff., and 248ff.), notably at 175E, at 203E in Diotima's myth, and in Alcibiades' later speech. I do not think this affects Socrates' dialectic here, despite the different sphere in which Socrates is 'wise'.
52 Cornford, 1950, 72; Friedländer, 1969, 24; Dover, 1980, on 204E; Guthrie, *HGP* IV, 375, follows the same line, but more cautiously. A. E. Taylor, 1937, and Robin, 1951, lxxiii–xcv, to say nothing of Grote, 1888, III, 10, all give summaries of the whole argument which make nothing of the equation between good and beautiful, but all refer to that equation afterwards. The suggestion that the equation is presented in the *Symposium* seems to have become a *communis opinio*; and it can lead to confusion between the wider and narrow senses of '*eros*', as I think it does in J. Moravcsik's 'Reason and Eros', Anton and Kustas, 1971, at 290ff.
53 See on these e.g. Guthrie, *HGP* IV, 247, n. 1.
54 For μεταβαλών of a change of philosophical topic or tack see *Philebus* 51A; χρῶμαι here is a vague word meaning 'make use of' with no implication that 'the good' here means 'the term "good"' rather than 'the example of "good"'. (At *Protag.*, 355B, the linguistic *noun* ὀνόματι makes the sphere of application obvious.)
55 οὐ δεῖ is ambiguous; see Stokes, 1971, 146 and n.137 (on p. 315).
56 See Santas, 1964, esp. 154ff., and elsewhere, and Irwin on

Plato, *Gorgias* 467C–D. Eros in its wider sense of the *Symposium* is closer to 'wish' than to 'desire' in the distinction offered by the *Gorgias*.

57 I see no reason to suppose with Brentlinger, 1970, 15, that Socrates is here striking through Aristophanes at the physical philosophers, whatever the point of Aristophanes' original encomium.

58 Galli, 1935, on 205B makes this point.

59 1980, 144.

60 Hamilton's rendering here, 'His whole life is passed in the company of the young...', is too elaborate for my purposes.

61 See LSJ s.v. ἀγήραος.

62 Dover, 1980, 146f.

63 Cf. Vlastos, 1981, 21 n. 60, and Rettig or Bury *ad loc.*; but the sentence is clearly necessary to the argument, as Dover points out; without it the phrase 'in the beautiful' remains obscure for too long, and the fact of desire for intercourse, rather than directly for procreation, goes unnoticed. The sentence does not contradict the preceding mention of τόκος.

64 Morrison, 1964, 52. Morrison suggested further that passages of the *Timaeus* are relevant; *contra* Plass, 1978, with an unconvincing explanation of the linguistic phenomena of this part of the *Symposium*.

65 Hamilton's 'he' at p. 87, lines 5 and 8, and 'himself' at line 9 are translator's expedients: 'It' would be impossible English, and even 'he or she' would be more explicit than Plato's neuters.

66 See below, pp. 174ff.

67 On the use of this idiom to modify traditional sayings, see Easterling, 1974. But the idiom is applicable to *any* previous saying; see Sophocles, *Philoctetes*, 1358ff.

68 Hamilton here has (p. 87) 'is violently attracted to beauty', in so far as this suggests that beauty is the actual object of love here, this is, in my opinion, not in the original Greek, πολλὴ ἡ πτοίησις γέγονε περὶ τὸ καλόν. Galli, 1935, on 203C says that throughout this whole passage περὶ τὸ καλόν is 'Perifrasi espressiva, invece del Genit. Τοῦ καλοῦ, per varietà...' But the periphrasis is far too convenient logically to be a mere stylistic variant.

69 *Pace* Dover, 1980, 144.

70 On immortality in the *Symposium*, see Dover, 1965.

71 See n. 68 above. Hamilton's translation indicates agreement with Galli there cited.

72 Dover, 1980, 149.
73 I do not know why Hamilton omitted the word 'since' here.
74 Hamilton's 'Those whose creative instinct is physical...' omits again the logical connective 'therefore', clearly here included in μὲν οὖν.
75 Dover duly castigates the mistake (1980, 149) and overestimates its importance.
76 Hamilton does not reproduce the imperatival mood of the Greek, in his '... the answer won't surprise you'.
77 I take τῆς ἀλογίας, with Hamilton and Robin, to refer to 'its', i.e. human ambition's, irrationality. Dover ad loc. says 'τῆς ἀλογίας sc. τῆς σῆς'. But 'You would be surprised at your irrationality if you don't consider...' is odd and irrelevant; odd, because if Socrates does not consider what Diotima wants him to he will not realize the irrationality of not considering it; irrelevant, because the sentence is about human ambition, and its explanation, and not about Socrates.
78 This is very nearly Hamilton's version.
79 This is, in intention, more literal than Hamilton's 'if you ask what that progeny is, it is wisdom and virtue in general.'
80 Here I have, as usual, substituted 'most beautiful' for 'fairest'.
81 See on this esp. Penner, 1973, and Ferejohn, 1982.
82 This is Dover's summary, 1980, 152, from which also comes my next citation.
83 See Dover, 1978, 84 and (for Pausanias and Agathon in Macedonia) Dover, 1965, 13ff.
84 See Dover's more cautious remarks, 1978, 144.
85 The first version here is Hamilton's; Dover favours 'too'.
86 Hamilton (p.91, top) has the lover 'go in search of a beautiful environment for his children'; this is correct only if it refers to a beautiful partner in procreation.
87 Hamilton has 'Do you try to follow if you can' and 'I must ask you to pay the closest possible attention...' The translations I have printed attempted to render the repetitions of πειρῶ and the idiomatic οἷος/οἷόν τε – repetitions serving as punctuation and marking the beginning of two sections. Notice also the repeated ὀρθῶς (210A2 and A4, and again 210E3), τέλεα (210A1) – τέλος (210E3), ἰόντα and ἰέναι (210A5) – ἰών (210E4). Plato has given the whole a verbal structure to match and reveal its logical shape.
88 Here Hamilton's 'physical beauty is more pleasing to him than ugliness' is rather too free.
89 Hamilton's 'physical beauty' again conceals a concrete plural.

90 So Hamilton, and Suzy Groden in Brentlinger, 1970, and even, occasionally, Dover in his notes.
91 It is, however, seldom, if ever, cited as such in the bulky modern literature on self-predication; as assumed in the *Symposium*, it resists reinterpretation as a 'Pauline predication' (on which see n. 139 below on the *Protagoras*).
92 Most of this is Hamilton's, but the opening, down to 'form', is unscrupulously rewritten.
93 See Forrester, 1975, esp. 12.
94 My addition of 'that' is merely for convenience; that of 'truly' does not, I think, exaggerate the force of ἐστί here.
95 Discussion and bibliography most conveniently in Vlastos, 1981, 342–65.
96 Hamilton has (p. 95) 'perishable'.
97 Hamilton rightly says (p. 95) 'bring forth not mere reflected images of goodness but true goodness'. This rendering Dover implicitly rejects by saying 1980, 159, 'a5 ἀληθῆ sc. offspring'; cf. Groden's (Brentlinger, 1970) '... but to truth'. The contrast with οὐκ εἴδωλα ἀρετῆς above and the parallel with ἀρετὴν ἀληθῆ below both show that the noun 'understood' with the first ἀληθῆ must be the feminine singular ἀρετήν, not a neuter plural word for 'offspring'.
98 Diotima's ἐφάπτεσθαι is not, so far as I can discover, used elsewhere for the sexual act; but (1) the simple verb ἅπτεσθαι is so used, and (2) so are other words for 'touch' such as θιγγάνω, and (3) the closely related compound ἐπαφάω is connected by Aeschylus (?), *Prometheus*, 849–51, with Zeus' begetting of Ἔπαφος on Io – and there is a good reason for the poet's not having used the commoner verb ἐφάπτεσθαι, viz.: that no part of it begins in Attic with ἐπαφ–. A. E. Taylor, 1937, 230, with n.1, clearly associates ἐφάπτεσθαι with sexual union, but without cogent argument.
99 Here I desert Hamilton only in the final phrase, to preserve the continuing symmetry of the Greek.
100 See for examples Kühner–Gerth, 1955, II, 573.
101 Here Hamilton's 'with that absolute beauty as one's aim' is too elaborate.

4 Socrates meets Protagoras

1 See especially C. C. W. Taylor, *Plato, Protagoras* (referred to below as 'Taylor'), and Taylor, 1980, 499–518, and papers by

Vlastos from Vlastos, 1981, and also Santas, 1979, and Irwin, 1977. All the books mentioned have serviceable bibliographies. I regret, again, that I have not seen L. Goldberg's *Philosophical Commentary* on the *Protagoras*.
2 Bodin, 1975.
3 Especially Morrison, 1941, and Adkins, 1973.
4 See especially Grube, 1933, Sullivan, 1961, Gagarin, 1969, Weingartner, 1973, 45–134, Klosko, 1979, Cronquist, 1980.
5 See eg. Shorey, 1933, 121.
6 The Greek word is καλός, rendered usually by 'beautiful' in passages of this book dealing with the *Symposium*, but by 'fine' elsewhere.
7 I have substituted 'think' here for Taylor's slightly tendentious 'agree'. Gagarin, 1969, 135 and n. 8, ignores the conditional altogether.
8 Gagarin, 1969, 135ff., makes too much of Protagoras' reputation for a Socratic context.
9 See Havelock, 1957, 158–9.
10 See especially Taylor, *ad loc.*
11 See e.g. Baldwin, 1926, 96.
12 Riddell, 1877, XXI, quotes Lysias 19. 1–2 and Isaeus 10. 1. See also e.g. Isaeus 1. 1; Demosthenes 27. 2; 34. 1; 55. 2.
13 Burnet, 1924, on *Apology* 17A1–18A6 thought there was parody here: but possibly Socrates here is simply creating an opening for the Socratic-sounding point that the only rhetoric for him is telling the truth (*Apology*, 17B). Baldwin, 1926, 94, insists that 'To tell the truth needs no art at all.'
14 See Thuc. III 37 with Solmsen's comments, 1975, especially 39.
15 [Xenophon] *Ath. Pol.*, i 13, and vi.
16 Dover, 1974, 40.
17 Dover, 1974, 25ff., and Dodds, 1959, 355.
18 See ll. 409–25 (with literature cited by Collard on 412–13).
19 Thuc. V 85.
20 *Pythian*, II, 81–9, with Rodewald, 1974, 77–8.
21 This, at least, is rightly castigated by Dover, 1980, viii.
22 G. T. Griffith, 1966, 124.
23 See Finley, 1962, 9 and n. 19.
24 Thuc. VI 39. 1.
25 Lysias 25. 2.
26 Taylor's translation has 'nourishment' at 313C and 'nurture' at 351B for the single Greek word τροφή.
27 Taylor has 'eminent in public life'; for this meaning of the

Greek, cf. Plato, *Theages*, 126A, discussed immediately below.
28 On this see (with due caution) Havelock, 1963.
29 See Harriott, 1969, 149–61.
30 For instance, the 'opening formula' documented by Fraenkel, 1960, has an early poetic exemplar in the *Odyssey*, I 1–10. πολλά ... ἀμόθεν.
31 The relevance of that exposition to Protagoras' earlier history of 'sophistry' is noted by Croiset–Bodin, 1923, 61 n. 1
32 See Adkins, 1973, 10 with n. 21.
33 See e.g. *Euthydemus* 292C, where I over-simplified in Jowett, 1970, II 129–34.
34 In isolation the Greek might mean 'to make citizens into good men', suggested as a possible alternative by Taylor ad loc.; but in the context of πολιτικὴ τέχνη it must mean 'to make men into good citizens'. For the relevant relationships between words see Lyons, 1963, 155–7, 174–5.
35 Grube, 1933.
36 Adkins, 1973.
37 Gagarin, 1969, 136, sees Protagoras here distinguishing specialized from general arts. But Plato does not allow Protagoras any such distinction overtly.
38 Havelock, 1957, 209.
39 This may be the force of τέχνη at Aristophanes, *Plutus*, 905.
40 Lyons, 1963, 151–5, 159ff.
41 See Taylor, *ad loc.* 72, italicizing as cited below.
42 Observe that Callicles, *Gorgias*, 515C–D, in all seriousness accords the title ἀγαθοὶ πολῖται to leading political figures such as Pericles, and the like.
43 Weingartner, 1973, 55, says 'Socrates merely wonders about its teachability, and, using Protagoras' own techniques, supports his skepticism with three reasons that rest upon Athenian beliefs and practices.' It may be so; but readers of the *Protagoras* have as yet no evidence that this is Protagoras' own technique, and the relation of his views to popular ones has yet to be clarified, and cannot be taken for granted.
44 See e.g. Morrison, 1941, 7.
45 See Dodds, 1959, notes on *Gorgias*, 502Dff.
46 On the meaning of this passage I follow Bodin, 1975, 19–21.
47 Adkins, 1973, 4 n. 4. Guthrie, *HGP* IV, 217 n. 2, replies that in Socrates' view 'not taught' implied 'not teachable'. Guthrie describes the view thus attributed as 'not unreasonable'. But Socrates' apparent similar shift in senses of οὐ διδακτός from

'not taught' to 'not teachable' in Guthrie's passages from the *Meno* does not compel the belief that Socrates had any such explicit 'view'. Nor did Guthrie explain why Protagoras should meekly accept Socrates' implication.
48 I have adapted Taylor's rendering here, to bring out the relation between τέχνη and τέχνημα.
49 Or, come to that, 'wisdom'; on ἐπιστήμη and σοφία see Gagarin, 1969, 135 n.10. σοφία in turn is closely connected with τέχνη and its hyponyms; see Lyons, 1963, 227ff., and on σοφός 155ff., 174ff.
50 On the reasoning of this Speech see especially Kerferd, 1953, 42–5, Adkins, 1973, Bodin, 1975, *passim* and the unfailingly interesting Havelock, 1957, 167ff.
51 Protagoras' comparison with flute-playing (327C) is perhaps triggered by Socrates' example of Orthagoras the flautist (318C).
52 Shorey, 1933, 121, Morrison, 1941, 8–9, Adkins, 1973, 6ff.
53 Apart from his 1960, especially 6ff., Adkins also elucidated his use of 'cooperative', 1971, 3–5.
54 Adkins, 1973.
55 Adkins, 1973, especially 9.
56 Adkins, 1973, 10–12.
57 Adkins, 1973, 10 n. 23.
58 The word 'fictional' here as elsewhere is not intended to imply that no such meeting ever took place; see J. P. Sullivan, 1961, 22.
59 Adkins, 1973, 4 n. 4.
60 Most notably Adkins, 1960, and H. Lloyd-Jones, 1971.
61 A useful summary is Irwin, 1979, 15ff. Lloyd-Jones, 1971, and Arnheim, 1977, present views differing from Adkins', and Kahn, 1979, 12–16, makes some useful points.
62 Adkins, 1972, 132 n.
63 See Dover, 1974, 1–45, with Adkins' review article, 1978.
64 Adkins, 1960, 179, of Thucydides; cf. Solmsen, 1975, 113, on Euripides.
65 Vickers, 1973, 474.
66 Cf. e.g. Plato, *Crito*, 45C–D.
67 On equality in political theory see e.g. Kagan, 1965, 77ff., Arnheim, 1977, 168. 'The underlying principle of Greek justice is not equality but fairness', is perhaps too sweeping; extant theoretical literature is mostly aristocratic.
68 On Thucydides' attitudes see Lloyd-Jones, 1971, 140–44.
69 Gomme, Andrewes, Dover, on Thucydides, V 102.

70 On Euripides see again Lloyd-Jones, 1971, especially 151ff.
71 See on Athenian legal justice most conveniently MacDowell, 1978, and Harrison, 1971, vol. II.
72 Adkins, 1960, 214.
73 Adkins, 1960, 202. 'There is then a plea which in normal circumstances may be used to overset what we should consider to be strict justice' – which may be true, but is scarcely relevant to the question whether that plea overrode what *the Greeks* considered to be justice, strict or otherwise. In Greek thought 'strict justice' and 'legal merits' are not synonymous in all contexts; see Dover, 1974, 187.
74 See Gomme, 1962, 157ff. and n.
75 Counter-examples include the often mentioned inability of fate or gods to distinguish good from bad in a shipwreck: see Collard, 1975, on E. *Suppl.* 226–8.
76 Cf. Andrewes ad loc.
77 Adkins discusses both: 1960, 78; 1972, 94; see also Arnheim, 1977, 164–70, and especially Lloyd-Jones, 1971, 147. Dover, 1974, 68, and n. 3 suggests that the author of the Theognis couplet was 'someone whose sense of proportion had been affected by a great injury done to him by a dishonest rogue' – a temporary underdog?
78 Despite such passages as Aeschylus, *Septem* 610, σώφρων, δίκαιος, ἀγαθὸς, εὐσεβὴς ἀνήρ; see Adkins, 1972, 94, and Dover, 1974, 66–9.
79 North, 1966, 77, and see passages in her Index s.v. *Mania*.
80 Lyons, 1963, 175, 227ff.
81 Grube, 1933, 204 n.5.
82 Sprague, 1976, 18, thinks Protagoras is denying that his art is a first-order art, such as other sophists teach. But Protagoras is not nearly explicit enough about this.
83 See LSJ s.v. βίος I 1. Protagoras himself uses the word in a very general sense at 326B5.
84 Grube, 1933, 204.
85 No distinction in the Greek corresponds to Taylor's different English words 'art' and 'craft' at 321E.
86 See Deuschle; and Taylor does not seem to render the phrase. Adam and Burnet print it as genuine. See Weingartner, 1973, 58 n.9.
87 At 327C Taylor has 'an expert in this sphere'; more literally the Greek says 'a craftsman of this thing'.
88 Taylor here renders 'arts' as 'practical crafts'. But 'practical' is not in the Greek. Taylor has seen the difficulty but smoothed

it over: a good example of the immense difficulty of Englishing Plato.
89 Taylor here renders ἀρετή, 'goodness', as 'expertise', while drawing attention to the Greek word in a note.
90 'That sort of excellence' in Taylor.
91 Cf. Sprague, 1976, 19.
92 One might distinguish 'goodness' from 'art' on the basis that 'goodness' is the quality in virtue of which a man is 'good', whereas 'art' is the techniques of the good craftsmen. But Protagoras shows no sign of such sophistication.
93 Taylor here has 'when a child is still learning'.
94 Taylor here has 'in the case of the experts'.
95 Kerferd, 1953, 42–5; Guthrie, 1956, 33. Guthrie was more precise later (see below).
96 See Gagarin, 1969, n. 145.
97 See Gagarin, 1969, n. 105; Guthrie, *HGP* IV, 217–18 and 222; Versenyi, 1963, 26 n. 22; Hubbard and Karnofsky, 1982, 102ff.
98 See Duncan, 1978. My own discussion is based on my paper circulated to members of the Society for Ancient Greek Philosophy in 1971.
99 The text is doubtful: Deuschle deleted διὰ τὴν τοῦ θεοῦ συγγένειαν at 322A, with Adam's approval, but Burnet restored it. It is not impossibly redundant in the rather full style of the myth, and Taylor translates it, apparently with Kroschel's τῶν θεῶν for τοῦ θεοῦ.
100 So e.g. Taylor at 324D has the plural 'those qualities of character' where the Greek has literally 'that goodness' in the singular; I am not alone in having to face the problem.
101 Taylor normally renders this word (*sôphrosynê*) as 'soundness of mind' or (323B6) as 'sound sense'. This time he renders αἰδώς as 'conscience', and *sôphrosynê* has the function (among others) of replacing the older, more 'poetic' αἰδώς. I have chosen 'moderation' for both, partly as a conventional rendering but partly as a neutral word between intellectual and moral spheres. At 326B5 Taylor has 'are well-balanced' for the related verb – but this is at once too moral and, within the moral sphere, too general for Plato's purposes. We shall not arrive at a successful English compromise here either; I merely explain my own practice; in my context uniformity is more important than readability. See on *sôphrosynê* especially Annas, 1981, 115.
102 Taylor (very understandably) does not differentiate in English

between Greek ways of copulating expressions; at 320D καὶ
... καὶ ... ('both ... and ...') links things which are
hardly distinguished, and at 323C it links things the speaker
clearly wishes to assimilate rather than to distinguish.
103 For one commentator's distinction see Bodin, 1975, 24.
104 My translation borrows from Taylor's but attempts greater
literalness: Taylor's 'that *sort of* virtue' (my emphasis) is not
literal enough for my purposes.
105 I assume throughout that αἰδώς and δίκη are equivalents to
σωφροσύνη and δικαιοσύνη. The Speech as a whole,
especially at the join between myth and exposition, makes no
sense to me otherwise.
106 The Greek word ἄλλος 'other' has some peculiar usages (see
LSJ s.v. II 8), but these do not, in my view, affect the meaning
of this passage. The use 'in enumeration, *as well, besides*' is not
in point; and the word is not obviously pleonastic as at e.g.
Charmides 166E.
 I have substituted 'political goodness' for Taylor's 'the
excellence of a citizen' at 323A and 322B, to make ἀρετή look
in English, as it functions in Greek, like the abstract of
ἀγαθός, 'good'. Cf. Dover, 1982, 115.
107 It would be surprising if συλλήβδην ('in a word') in the
summing-up phrase ruled out either interpretation; such
words take on the meaning required by their context.
108 On the question of capacity and quality see Kerferd, 1953,
Weingartner, 1973, 61 n. 14 and Taylor's notes on relevant
passages.
109 The point at issue in my text (and, I think, in Plato's) is often
obscured by translators. Hubbard and Karnofsky are a notable
exception. Guthrie and the Loeb have 'wrongdoers', the
Jowett–Ostwald version 'evildoers', and Taylor 'wrongdoer',
or 'guilty of wrongdoing' for ἀδικοῦντας or grammatically
related forms in the Greek, forms which refer to 'the unjust',
'being unjust', 'to be unjust', etc. 'Wrongdoers' and 'evildoers' are such general terms as to give readers of these translations no hint that any particular type of wrongdoing could
be meant, nor of any problem in the relationship between
wrongdoing in general and injustice in particular. The Budé's
'un coupable' appears to suffer the same defect. Translators
have smoothed over the rough places in Protagoras' argument. Similarly, to render δίκαιος at 328C with Guthrie as
'good' is to obliterate the distinction Protagoras himself
draws between 'justice' and 'the rest of political goodness'.

δίκαιος can indeed mean 'righteous', but if the reader is presented with translations such as 'good' or 'righteous', then in this dialogue he needs telling which word Plato is using. E.g. Taylor does not tell his readers at 325D (cited below in his translation except for the restoration of 'just' and 'unjust' for Taylor's 'right' and 'wrong').

110 For associations of well-ordered behaviour with *Sôphrosynê* see North, 1966, index s.v. *kosmiotes* and s.v. *kosmios*.
111 Denniston, 514.
112 Taylor's translation here, '... to equip each kind with the powers it required' is too free to bring out my point; but the constraints upon him to translate thus support the idea that the equipment and the assignment are the same process.
113 See North, 1966, index s.v. *Enkrateia* and s.v. Youth, *sophrosyne* of.
114 See Sachs, 1963, and a selection of papers in Vlastos, 1970, vol. II. I try to take no sides here in that controversy.
115 Since we are discussing 'goodness', I have preferred 'useful' to Taylor's 'better', in order to make Protagoras no more explicit on the point at issue in English than in Greek.
116 1978, 217ff.
117 LSJ s.v. καί, and Denniston, 1954, 291 para. 5: 'Appositionally related ideas are occasionally linked by καί.'
118 Cf. 322B: 'They sought to come together *and* [emphasis mine] save themselves by founding cities.'
119 See Taylor's note on 326D8–E1.
120 This is Taylor's rendering with 'just' for 'right'.
121 Cf. e.g. Sophocles, *OT* 425 σκῆπτρα καὶ θρόνους.
122 Denniston, 1954, 291, supplies the examples of Plato, *Laws* 903C, and *Iliad* V 398, without setting up a separate category. LSJ s.v. καί, quoting *Il.* V 398, says 'sometimes'. Cf. Sophocles' *Electra*, 1121, Plato, *Apology*, 17D5, *Theaet.*, 154A3, *Crito*, 52B8–C1.
123 Cf. e.g. Plato, *Theaet.*, 161E2, 180D5, 191D8, E1; Ast, 1908, s.v. καὶ, quotes *Phaedo*, 58B, for this sense.
124 The repetition of τούτου τοῦ πράγματος from 326E to 327C–D is obscured by Taylor at 327A and 327C–D. To bring out my point, his 'excellence in something of which one is ignorant' should be 'no one must be ignorant of this matter', and his 'an expert in this sphere' rather 'an expert in this matter'.
125 On allied democratic myths see pp. 191ff. and esp. 225ff. above. Lesser men stood as good a chance as greater men.
126 See pp. 135ff. above.

Notes to pages 262–274   479

127 Here and elsewhere Duncan, 1978, 218ff., rather overstates his case.
128 Savan, 1964, 130–35, Taylor 117–18.
129 1981, 230ff., with n. 22, cited partially below.
130 *Contra*, apparently, Vlastos, e.g. 1981, 246ff.
131 Gallop, 1961, 90, and n. 2.
132 Taylor, 109, and further 110–11.
133 I have modified the beginning of Taylor's version here in order to make somewhat clearer how much of it is an expansion of a compressed Greek phrase. See the Adams' commentary for the syntax.
134 See his 111 *ad loc.*
135 Gallop, 1961, 86ff., Taylor, 109.
136 Duncan, 1978, 218. 'It is perhaps significant, but at least odd, that he substitutes ἐπιστήμη for σοφία (330B)'.
137 See Lyons, 1963, 155ff. and 174ff., on contexts in which either σοφός or ἐπιστήμων occurs; and esp. 228, on σοφός.
138 Cf. Taylor, 111 *ad loc.*
139 See Vlastos, 1981, 259–65, and for rebuttal of this 'Pauline' interpretation Taylor, 118–20.
140 See Vlastos, 1981, 58ff., esp. 66–7.
141 Taylor, 113, on 330C2–7.
142 I have recast Taylor's 'how could anything else be holy...?' as an assertion, which the Greek clearly is, to make sense of my next comment.
143 In effect, on Taylor's 107.
144 My interpretation makes sense of the 'strained and unnatural' emphasis of μάλιστα πάντων, which troubles some commentators, e.g. Kroschel. Taylor, 115–16 rightly rejects the Adams' view that ὅτι means 'because' and urges: 'Since ... the conclusion that justice and holiness are like one another *follows directly from* the admission that justice is holy and holiness just, that step which leads directly to the conclusion is treated (*loosely*) as just the same answer as the conclusion itself [emphases mine].' On my interpretation, that 'Justice is holy and Holiness is just' is the same as, and means that, Justice and Holiness are identical or very similar, or above all resemble one another (as implied in the οἷον-terminology throughout) in having the same power. The reason why Socrates here gives most emphatic expression to the weakest formulation 'Justice is like Holiness and Holiness is like Justice' is that the 'likeness' formulation is the one nearest in Socrates' treatment to the 'power' version which is really what 'Justice is holy

etc.' is all about. Naturally, since 'powers' are what distinguish different virtues, Socrates feels in consequence entitled to the 'stronger formulation' in terms of identity at 333B.
145 'Socrates *is claiming to show* that the two virtues are... identical', Taylor, 120, resting this (his 116) on 333B5–6; but 333B is preceded by 331D, where Protagoras admitted no small resemblance, and took refuge in waffle. Socrates need not let him get away with waffle. What counts is not what Socrates has shown, but what Protagoras has (reasonably or otherwise) been compelled to admit is 'obvious to us' (333B).
146 E. Irwin, 1974, cites examples of μέλας and λευκός (often rendered 'black' and 'white' respectively) which persuade me that 'dark' and 'light' are at least equally appropriate.
147 δυσχερῶς ἔχειν πρὸς τοῦτο, Socrates' phrase, has a bare demonstrative which Taylor renders 'discussion of this point'; it could be the point itself to which Protagoras objects, rather than discussion. Socrates' complaint would then be that Protagoras was refusing to concede a point already sufficiently made. The adjective δυσχερής, used of 'argument' or 'discussion' at 323D (τὸν γὰρ λόγον ᾐτιᾶτο δυσχερῆ εἶναι), could there mean 'disagreeable', 'difficult' or (as LSJ s.v. I, 3) 'captious'; it need not mean 'inconvenient' as Taylor has it. The adverb at 332A is also hard to pin down to a precise force, but δυσχερῶς ἔχειν is reasonably translated 'be annoyed' by LSJ s.v. δυσχερής III; that Protagoras is annoyed at the point is a reasonable deduction for Socrates from Protagoras' refusal to concede it and his flight to a weak sanctuary.
148 Taylor, 119, citing Vlastos and Peterson.
149 Weingartner, 1977, 70ff., saves these inferences by supposing Plato already to have in mind paradigmatic Forms; he then supposes Protagoras 'in no way' to 'do justice to the argument Socrates has made' (79). But Weingartner's Plato manipulates Protagaoras too crudely to be convincing; and in default of clear evidence from the text few will accept paradigmatic Forms in the argument of the *Protagoras*.
150 Taylor, 114.
151 Savan, 1964, 134.
152 Savan deploys two later passages, 334A and 331D; but Socrates' or Protagoras' later reasonings are hardly relevant to the dialectic of 330–31.
153 I have not discussed the question whether the laws of the city at 326ff. give positive guidance (cf. teachers of writing) or

Notes to pages 285–305   481

negative (as witness the punishment of those who 'go outside' or 'transgress' the lines traced out by the city). Protagoras associates the lawful with the just, but is not clear on this question.

154   Here my 'just' and 'unjust' replace Taylor's 'right' and 'wrong', and 'honourable' and 'dishonourable' replace 'good' and 'bad' since I keep 'good' and 'bad' for ἀγαθός and κακός rather than for καλός and αἰσχρός.
155   Klosko, 1979, 133–6 with nn.
156   Forbes, 1895, p. 94.
157   The etymological antonym εὐφροσύνη is semantically inappropriate.
158   Taylor, 122, on 332A4.
159   'In the MSS' because the tedium in particular of the passage Οὐκοῦν εἴ τι ἰσχύι ... βραδέως should cause one to suspect the work of a scribe with more conscience as philosopher than as copyist. The passage supplies examples of movement from dative to adverb when what is needed is movement from adverb to dative, as in the preceding sentence. Compare Dodds on *Gorgias*, 460B8–C4.
160   See North, 1966, index, s.v. *aphrosyne*.
161   Taylor, 127–8.
162   See pp. 241ff. above.
163   Taylor there has 'sound sense' to render *sôphrosynê*.
164   See Taylor's excellent discussion, pp.124ff.
165   One wonders accordingly why Vlastos' sharp eye did not light on the dubiety of his proposition 5, 1981, 244ff. with nn.
166   Vlastos has a nice counter-example, 1981, 245 n. 68.
167   See Lyons, 1963, as in n. 137 above.
168   The Adams defend, and Burnet printed the MSS reading, but I fail to see how the Adams could have justified their notion that goods due to nature are fine but not goods due to attention, etc. Protagoras later agrees that goodness is fine but never that it is simply due to nature. Taylor has either rendered καλά by 'good' or rendered freely Ficino's reading κακά.
169   On Taylor's rendering with the antonyms 'good' and 'bad' see n. 154 above.
170   Taylor usefully has 'bad' and 'worthless' at 323E and 326E but renders the repeated φαῦλος at 327B as 'poor'.
171   His 131, on 333A1–B6.
172   'Many people' does not say 'the majority of people'; πολλοί is different from οἱ πολλοί.

173 See e.g. Sprague, 1967, and especially Weingartner, 1973, 91, largely anticipating my interpretation. See further n. 178 below.
174 Guthrie's brief paragraph on this argument (*HGP* IV, 226–7) lacks this advantage, referring instead to an exasperation of which Protagoras shows no sign.
175 A more literal version than Taylor's 'By being sensible you mean showing good sense'.
176 This explains in clumsy English the association, obvious in Greek, between εὖ βουλεύεσθαι and εὐβουλία.
177 See below pp. 371ff., on 352C.
178 I have heavily adapted Taylor here, to bring out the participial force of πράττοντες and the symmetrical antithesis εὖ πράττουσιν ... κακῶς (sc. πράττουσιν). Weingartner, 1973, 90ff., sees at least some of these points; but his talk of 'an angry outburst of frustration' and of 'Protagoras' temper' flaring is based on nothing in the text, which has a rational place in the argument.

Weingartner says, 1973, on p. 91 'one can surely not maintain that it is possible to achieve the good in doing wrong'; if 'wrong' here means 'unjust', this is frequently maintained; the point is rather that *Protagoras* cannot maintain it. But Weingartner perceives that Protagoras' inability to escape the popular opinion here is partly due to his differentiation of the virtues. I have tried only to expound more clearly the specific difficulty caused by the differentiation of the virtues, and to treat it in isolation from the relation between Protagoras and popular thought.
179 E.g. Weingartner, 1973, 94.
180 Richard Robinson's word is 'insincere', 1953, 9.
181 Taylor and others have '*the* most important part' (emphasis mine). This could, but need not, be right. The superlative in Greek without the definite article may be merely intensive; thus the Budé 'une partie importante'. I see no reason why Protagoras should wish here to make the interpretation of poetry more important than any other facet of the educational system outlined in his Great Speech.
182 'Comic', A.E. Taylor, 1937, 253; 'whimsical', C.C.W. Taylor, 1976, 146; 'humorous', A.E. Taylor, 251; 'mocking satire', Lamb in the Loeb, 88; 'parody', C.C.W. Taylor, 145, Sullivan, 1961, 10, Weingartner, 1973, 95.
183 See Sullivan, 1961, and Wilamowitz, 1920, I, 112, on the Spartan 'philosophers'.
184 Grote, 1888, II, 285.

185 Friedländer, 1965–9, II, 24, Gundert, 1977, 25.
186 A.E. Taylor, 1937, 251; Weingartner's view is very similar.
187 Klosko, 1979, 130.
188 Shorey, 1933, 12ff.
189 Turner, 49ff., cf. Raeder, 1905, 111.
190 For a convincing argument against it see Dickie, 1978, 21ff.
191 See Dickie, 1978, Easterling, 1974, 41–3, and Gundert, 1977, 26 n. 3, citing Fränkel.
192 Gundert, 1977, 28.
193 Gundert, 1977, 29.
194 The two need not be distinguished here; see above pp.44ff. on Plato's *Laches*.
195 Protagoras implies often in the Great Speech that there are degrees of goodness, but it is not certain that Socrates is here condemning his implication through Simonides.
196 O'Brien, 1967, esp. 39ff.
197 Taylor here has 'courage and fighting qualities'; the plural is not in the Greek and raises problems. Duncan, 1978, omits the passage.
198 Duncan, 1978, 220, thinks there is something new about the appearance of courage here; but see 329E.
199 Duncan, esp. 222.
200 Taylor has 'totally'; but is anyone *totally* unjust for Protagoras?
201 Klosko, 1979, 140ff., Aristotle, *Topics*, 157A 1–3.
202 Klosko, 1979, 140; Taylor, 158.
203 Cf. Guthrie, *HGP* IV, 229. The etymology of ἴτης 'bold to face', related (presumably) to ἰέναι 'go', will become important later; a possible but sometimes awkward rendering is 'ready (or even "rarin'") to go'.
204 Taylor, 153.
205 This distinction resembles Hubbard–Karnofsky's between 'unafraid' and 'daring', 1982, 134. They ask (136) whether Socrates is equivocating.
206 Taylor, 155.
207 Taylor (155) says explicitly: 'As far as the logical structure of the argument goes, the comparatives and superlatives are irrelevant', but see his 152ff. Weingartner, 105, cites some superlatives but proceeds with the positive. Hubbard and Karnofsky pay no attention to degrees of comparison.
208 Taylor's version with 'confident' for 'daring'.
209 'Sauppe and others', according to the Adams, 1905, 175, on 350B.

210 See O'Brien, 1961, 411 and 414 n. 10.
211 See Gosling, 1975, on *Philebus*, 11B4–C2, arguing that Socrates means 'what is good' by ἀγαθόν; Gosling makes insufficient allowance for the possibility of development in the opening discussion of the *Philebus*. Passages cited by Taylor, 159 (*Gorgias* 491E, *Laches* 195E, *Protagoras* 342B), are not from the mouth of Socrates and are not uniformly convincing.
212 Taylor's idea (157) that 'Protagoras is unclear about the difference between the conditional and the bi-conditional, and consequently unclear as to what thesis it is that Socrates is maintaining' would presuppose a Plato whose dependence on his readers' subtlety is heavier than one normally expects.
213 Taylor, 155.
214 Taylor, 152.
215 See n. 202 above.
216 Hubbard–Karnofsky, 1982, 140 (with 136ff.), speak, to their credit, of 'the *apparently* [emphasis mine] unrelated question' of living well; but they seem to regard the two arguments as showing ἀνδρεία to be σοφία not in one sense, but in another. But neither Socrates nor Protagoras makes any such distinction, and it is not necessary for dialectical understanding of the conversation. In any case it would hardly mitigate, for the uninitiated reader, the effect of the 'quite remarkable abruptness' of which Taylor (261ff.) speaks. On this topic Cronquist, 1980, is good; though I disagree with some of his remarks, I accept that *one* point of introducing pleasure is to probe the distinction between good and bad cases of confidence or daring.
217 θάρσος here means 'spirit' in more senses than one; see LSJ s.v., and Taylor, 153 n.1.
218 See Kerferd, 1981, 137ff., and Weingartner, 1973, 109–11.
219 I am not clear how far Hubbard and Karnofsky agree with the outline presented here. The difficulties of discovering their views are strongly reminiscent of the difficulties of discovering Socrates' views from *his* questions. On the one hand they appear (149) to think relevant in the discussion of the 'many' the question whether *Protagoras* could deny the rationality of the assumption that 'For any two possible courses of action, x and y, no man will choose x for his own ends if he considers x more painful than y, for someone else.' Nothing like this assumption is put, or needs to be put, to Protagoras in this part at least of the dialogue. On the other hand, they put the

following hypothetical sentence before their readers (152): 'If the trio of sophists look to the audience, now, like hedonistic opportunists, it must be admitted that Socrates is tarred with the same brush.' With its context, this suggests that Hubbard and Karnofsky believe the sophists to be united in professional support of the intellect's primacy at the cost of agreeing opportunistically to a brand of hedonism they would not otherwise accept – which is substantially the view of the main line of the discussion adopted here. There is however the significant difference that, not believing Socrates committed by his question, I am not obliged to ask if Socrates is tarred by the same brush. He is not tarred at all: he may have other defences for his views. To suppose Socrates not committed to hedonism here gives his strategy more coherence and punch.

220 See especially Taylor, 162ff., Gosling and Taylor, 1982, chap. 3, and Zeyl, 1980.

221 See 323D–324A in the Great Speech. In explicating these questions Taylor's notes use the word 'preponderantly', but Socrates does not. He is asking Protagoras to accept everyday, not philosophically sophisticated, beliefs.

222 Burnet and the Adams have a full stop; Taylor translates as a question. Compare 330B, where the conclusion marked by ἄρα is surely unacceptable to Socrates as he is normally understood. Neither Taylor nor Burnet has a question mark there. At 358A, as we saw, a conclusion with ἄρα must be a question. Hubbard and Karnofsky print a question at 330B and 351C but not at 358A. Editors and translators need to think out a policy on these matters, and probably to insert more question marks than they are doing at present. It would be helpful if commentators justified their punctuation. See above, Introduction, pp. 4–7.

223 See Denniston, 1954, 47ff. Expectation is less definite with ἆρα μή ... than with ἆρ' οὐ ... The former means something like 'can it be that ... ?'

224 So Hubbard and Karnofsky.

225 Sullivan, 1961, 22.

226 Zeyl, 1980, esp. 251–5; Gosling and Taylor, 1982, 49ff., esp. 50 n. 1.

227 Regrettably, Hubbard and Karnofsky follow Taylor here.

228 The examples are *Protag.*, 343D, 344A, *Philebus*, 33C, 42E, *Gorgias* 459C (Hermann's emendation), *Theaetetus* 183B, 188A, *Laws* 643A, *Alcib. 1*, 105C.

229 Was it the unavailability of this solution which caused Turner

to write of Protagoras here 'what he actually says is nonsense'?
230 Von Wright, 1963, 10ff.
231 Herodotus, III 80, Aristophanes, *Birds*, 785.
232 See Thucydides, II 53.3; the Athenians attribute the same view to the Spartans in the Melian Dialogue.
233 E.g. the Messenger, in Sophocles, *Antigone* (1166–71); and at Aristophanes, *Plutus*, 803ff., Carion says it is pleasant to fare happily (πράττειν... εὐδαιμόνως), and his illustrations of happiness and of good things are simple sensual pleasures.
234 *Odyssey*, 17, 423 and 19, 79, and for the good life 15, 491.
235 εὐτυχία and εὐδαιμονία are associated with pleasure words and contrasted with pain and distress words, and vice versa for their antonyms: see Aristophanes, *Birds*, 127ff., where the most pleasant city of Euelpides' imagining is a set of κακά for the Hoopoe; Sophocles, *Oed. at Col.*, 798ff., οὐ γὰρ ἂν κακῶς οὐδ' ὧδ' ἔχοντες ζῶμεν, εἰ τερποίμεθα; the assumption that λυπή is κακ- at Sophocles, *Ajax*, 271–7; etc.
On this whole subject McDonald, 1978, is a mine of information. At *Medea*, 1090ff., the question of εὐτυχία is, in effect, the question εἴθ'ἡδὺ βροτοῖς εἴτ'ἀνιαρόν; at *Ion*, 658 (McDonald, 198, and cf. *Phoenissae*, 214) εὐτυχ- contrasts with λυπ-; at *Andromache*, 420, 'according to the perspective of the speaker one can be either εὐτυχής or δυστυχής without children, and ... the happiness or good fortune involved is based on an absence of pain' (McDonald, 53, cf. 79ff.) At fr. 196 (Nauck) (from *Antiope*) εὐτυχία and living ὡς ἥδιστα, not quite synonyms, are closely related (McDonald usefully refers to Snell, 1964, 88). εὐδαιμον-words appear with pleasure words at *Alcestis*, 164–9, and *Ion*, 1456–61; McDonald, 201, says on the latter that here a pleasure is a 'good event' exemplifying the εὐδαιμονοῖμεν of 1457. At *Electra*, 1357–9, the man who χαίρειν δύναται without misfortune is the man who εὐδαίμονα πράσσει, though χαίρειν may be distinguished from εὐδαιμονεῖν at *Iphigeneia in Aulis*, 1160ff. (McDonald, 281). 'Pain', on the other hand, is inconsistent with εὐδαίμων at *Iph. Aul.*, 161–3 (McDonald, 276ff.), and *Med.*, 276ff.; κακ- goes closely together with λυπ- at *Med.*, 1046ff., and contrasts with pleasure at *Hippolytus*, 382ff. (Snell 81). Good things are *opposed* to pleasant at fr. 187 (from *Antiope*; possibly they were associated by the opposing speaker in the famous debate drawn upon in Plato's *Gorgias*).
236 'If and only if' seems to be the logic here; note the limiting γε and the strong emphasis of -περ. It appears from Sophocles fr.

Notes to pages 367–381   487

inc. 665, χαίρειν ἐπ' αἰσχραῖς ἡδοναῖς οὐ χρή ποτε, that Protagoras is not more original, though more guarded, here than in his previous response.

237 Taylor, 165.
238 Zeyl's arguments to this effect, 1980, 254, do not include the point that this is a question, not a statement by Socrates. But Zeyl is surely right in interpreting an affirmative answer to it as contradicting Protagoras' previous remarks, and as contradicting an affirmative answer to the previous question.
239 Taylor, 166ff.
240 See Zeyl, 1980, 253, and n. 9.
241 Vlastos, 1969, 77–9 with n. 24, slid, without comment, from 'All pleasure is good' to τὰ ἡδέα ἀγαθά ἐστιν ἅπαντα ('All pleasant things are good').
242 This interpretation is duly adopted by Taylor and Gosling, 1982, 56.
243 Taylor, *ad loc.*
244 'Pleasure and good are really the same', Jowett–Ostwald; 'pleasant and good are the same', Taylor; 'the pleasant turns out to be the same as the good', Hubbard and Karnofsky; 'pleasant and good appear identical', Guthrie. Taylor and Guthrie come nearest to reproducing the potential ambiguity of the Greek.
245 Coextensiveness is all the argument requires at *Gorgias*, 495A.
246 Manuwald, 1975, shows how natural it is for pleasure and intellect to be considered together.
247 Zeyl, 1980, 266 n. 24, calls this 'puzzling' and promises a discussion which I have not seen.
248 Taylor and Gosling seem undisturbed, 1982, 57.
249 Vlastos, 1969, 72.
250 Gulley, 1971, 118–23.
251 Manuwald, 1975, 34 n. 33 and 38.
252 ὡς with the accusative absolute gives the *grounds* for Athenian practice.
253 Taylor, 'Just in case you have any doubts . . .' does not refer so clearly to what precedes as the Greek does.
254 I have the more literal 'who is silly . . . ?' for 'is anyone silly . . . ?'
255 See n. 252 above.
256 This discussion of Protagoras on punishment is not intended as a philosophical analysis in depth of a very complex matter. See Taylor, 90–6, and Mackenzie, 1981, 5–64 and 181–91. I agree with Mackenzie that Taylor's account is 'somewhat

overschematised' (188 n. 30); but disagree with her interpretation of the sophist's argument as tending to show that since injustice etc. are subject to punishment, 'it is clear that the corresponding virtue may be acquired by practice and learning' (188, cf. 190). Protagoras' point is that those who punish, particularly the Athenians, *believe* in the acquisition of goodness by learning (cf. 324C); and his proof assumes Athenian rationality. His argument does not even suggest that he believed in the reforming and deterrent *effect* of Athenian punishments; his concern is only with the *intention* behind them. Further, if the section on punishment does represent the views of the historical Protagoras, and Plato did hold similar views, that would still not entitle us (despite Mackenzie 190) to use the passage as 'evidence for what Plato himself believed'. Views assigned to Protagoras offer no evidence, nor even confirmation, for Plato's views.

257 Thus Taylor: the Greek has 'for' rather than 'so' (as below under B).

258 Taylor here speaks of 'rhythm and melodies'; Mr E. Bowcott refers me to R. P. Winnington-Ingram, s.v. Greek Music in the latest edn. of Grove's *Dictionary of Music and Musicians*. The related εὐαρμοστία is metaphorical here, and Taylor's 'proper adjustment' carries the right overtones.

259 The MSS are repetitive at 326C8, giving 'according to them according to example'; some editors omit 'according to example', Heindorf conjectured 'as an example' and others accept the MSS.

260 On the philosophical problems the facts raise see Taylor, 1980.

261 Taylor's version of these sentences has 'wrong' where I have 'bad'. The Greek is πονηρός, not the κακός which is usual in this dialogue for 'bad', and it has a wider range of meaning, as Taylor says, than κακός. But indeed the relevant sense of πονηρός is the one closest to κακός.

262 Taylor and others complete the sentence in English.

263 On pain and suffering in punishment see Mackenzie, 1981, 10–12.

264 Taylor, for good reasons of English idiom, has 'corrects' at 326E.

265 Taylor argues on 353C1–354E2 that the words he renders 'as Protagoras and I maintain', at 353E–354E, commit Socrates to the hedonistic statement there put into the mouth of the 'many'. Taylor's argument against the meaning 'as Protagoras

and I maintain (that you think)' is that Socrates has hitherto elicited the many's views by questions and not anticipated them directly. This will not stand against the counter that, whatever Socrates is committed to, Protagoras is emphatically not committed to any such propositions as Taylor's version puts into Socrates' mouth on his behalf. Therefore, neither Socrates nor Protagoras is committed here, and Socrates' technique with the 'many' varies – and why not? See further on this and similar passages Zeyl, 1980, 250–57.

266 See Richard Robinson, *Plato's Earlier Dialectic*[1] (Ithaca, N.Y., 1941), 58ff. Taylor, 177–8, seems not to realize that this common Platonic assumption is relevant.

267 For a succinct distinction between psychological and evaluative hedonism see Taylor, 175ff.

268 *Contra*, Taylor, 177, on 354C3–6.

269 Taylor on 354C–E2 need not be right in rendering οὐκοῦν as inferential 'so'. See Denniston, 1954, 433–5, for other possibilities.

270 This version is my own, to illustrate the compression Plato perpetrates here.

271 This paragraph takes no account of actions neither pleasant nor painful; Socrates and the many appear to assume that there are none – and it is not clear that they are mistaken.

272 On the nature of the actual absurdity I gratefully follow Taylor, 181–6 (in agreement with Gallop, 1964, 117–29, against Vlastos and Santas) except for such phrases as 'establishing his thesis'.

273 187–9, on 356A5–7.

274 189ff., on 356A8–C3.

275 These translations are mine; Taylor's omits the address to 'men' and obscures the persistent 'nothing-else' motif.

276 Taylor's translation here, 'depended on taking steps to get large quantities ...', is less literal than mine; Taylor's reason for paraphrase (194) is that 'doing large quantities' is impossible English. Yes; but it is also impossible Greek, and impossible logic. Socrates' hypothesis is deliberately paradoxical, and perhaps humorous, and I have translated accordingly.

277 Taylor, 192, on 356C4–357E8, restricts too much the force of what is agreed at 357B1–4. It is there agreed that the relevant knowledge or technique is both a necessary and a sufficient condition for leading a good life. Taylor also suggests that Socrates' and Protagoras' treatment of the 'many' ignores the difference between being regularly right and being right on

each occasion. True; but Protagoras is in no state to point it out to Socrates, since (for reasons suggested above, pp. 371–91) he allowed Socrates to get away with neglecting this distinction at 352B–D.

278 Gallop, 1964, 128; Taylor, 189ff.
279 1964, 127ff.
280 See Taylor on cigarette smoking, his 188.
281 So Turner, the Adams, Burnet, Lamb and Croiset, and the translations of Guthrie, Jowett–Ostwald, Taylor and Hubbard and Karnofsky, with Manuwald, 1975, 27.
282 I substitute 'fine' for Taylor's 'praiseworthy' and add in brackets a phrase in the MSS usually omitted by editors and translators. See below.
283 Manuwald, 1975, 28, rightly rejects Voigtländer's view that Protagoras' answer here is derivable directly from his views at 351B–C, but too hastily rejects all connection. Socrates pauses here to clarify Protagoras' new position in relation to the old. Somewhat similarly, Manuwald, 40, takes 360A καὶ ἡδύ, *and pleasant*, as *either* bitter irony *or* exalted (presumably Socratic) ethic. Neither makes any sense of what Socrates is doing here.
284 Manuwald, 1975, 40 and n. 42, denies that ἡδύ means 'pleasant in total with its consequences' in the *Protagoras*. To support this denial he interprets 351D–E ποιοῦντα ἡδονήν as an alternative to 'sharing in pleasure'; but, crucially, he does not say *how* it is an alternative. Cf. 325E for ποιεῖν meaning 'result in'.
285 Taylor takes this too lightly; see n. 211 above. Manuwald, 1975, cites *Rep.* 505B–C; but there the word 'define' (ὁριζόμενοι) makes all the difference.
286 Taylor has a full stop, Hubbard and Karnofsky a question mark at the end of this speech; among editors, Burnet has a question, the Adams a statement. In this interrogatory context (see Introduction pp. 6–7) the question mark is the more likely to represent Plato's intentions.
287 On this word see Saunders, 1968, and Vlastos, 1969, 83ff., on wanting and choosing. Taylor rightly contrasts ἑκών with compulsion, but his 'freely' is too narrow, and not quite to the point here. Cf. 358E for ἑκόντα picking up ἐθελήσει, and 358C for αἱρήσεται picking up ἑκών.
288 Taylor has here 'it seems to me', but 'to me' is not in the Greek.
289 Manuwald, 1975, 29–30 and 38, seeks to differentiate the passage with the 'many' from the transition back to the sophists.

He distinguishes between giving in to onself (358C2) and giving in to pleasure (357E2). The change is neither overt nor immediately useful, but, as Manuwald says, is helpful at 359D. But the change is minor and does nothing to show the serious discontinuity Manuwald wants between the two passages. It remains essential to see the hedonism passage (and indeed the dialogue as a whole) as a continuous discussion. Manuwald himself sees this (his 49), in several ways, especially in referring Socrates' new terminology ἔρχεσθαι ἐπί to Protagoras' ἴτας at 349E. But he has not seen that one must also refer back Socrates' use of 'knowledge' and 'opinion' to Protagoras' earlier usage: according to Manuwald, 360Aff., says nothing about opinion, only knowledge, and the advent of opinion is *ad hoc*. But at 360A ἀμαθία still bears its sense of 358A, until ἐπιστήμη replaces σοφία in the final paragraphs. Ἐπιστήμη there is fair both to Protagoras, who failed to distinguish the functions of knowledge and opinion in education and ethics, and to Socrates who has been trying to bring Protagoras to the proposition that goodness is knowledge or (equivalently) wisdom. Manuwald's anxiety to dissociate Socrates from what goes on in the dialogue with the 'many' is unnecessary, since Socrates only *questions* the 'many'.

290 Taylor, 205.
291 The phrase is Taylor's, 207–8.
292 Taylor, 208.
293 This version, after Taylor, avoids the logical 'demonstration'.
294 The Greek is ταύτῃ γε; LSJ offers (s.v. οὗτος C VIII 4) no support for 'therefore'; Ast, 1908, renders ταύτῃ with *idcirco*, citing *Rep.* 381B6, where it means rather 'in that case', and two irrelevant passages in the *Cratylus*. At 407A τοίνυν is added to ταύτῃ, suggesting that ταύτῃ is not so much 'therefore' in these passages as (perhaps) 'accordingly'. But none of Ast's passages has ταύτῃ γε.
295 1975, 40 and n. 41, controverting von Arnim, 1914, 19ff. Admittedly von Arnim spoke too readily of what *Plato* could or could not accept, without analysing the exact stance of Plato's *characters*. Von Arnim's distinction between the ostensible purpose of the many-passage and its true polemical purpose is hard to maintain. Manuwald is right that Protagoras and not Socrates is saddled with acceptance of the argument against the many, including the interchangeability of "good" and "pleasant". But that is equally true of all Protagoras' answers

to Socrates' questions, including the ones at 360A, whose connection with the many-passage Manuwald wishes to deny.
296 Zeyl, 1980, 259–60.
297 Cf. Aristotle's *Topics*, VIII, 1.
298 Manuwald, 1975, 40, well mentions the masses' view of war at 354B.
299 Santas, 1979, 174ff.
300 Taylor, 360B1 (A8 in Burnet's text). On Οὐκοῦν see above n. 269.
301 Taylor, 210, on 360B–5, points back to 350B and 351A–B, and sees that the mad and foolhardy are not there differentiated; but he then seeks to explain 360A from 'Plato's doctrine and terminology'; this implies Plato's commission of a basic *petitio principii* and fails to explain Protagoras' meekness.
302 The omission of shameful fears here may be due to MS error or to Socrates (and Protagoras) having in mind some version of the argument above for proposition D which makes the same cowardly act display simultaneously shameful fear and shameful daring.
303 See Sullivan, 1961; see further pp. 435, 438 below.
304 See pp. 274ff. above.
305 Cf. *Meno*, 98B.
306 Manuwald, 1975, 47, picks on this same proposition as the weak one; but he suggests merely that 'Sokrates also die Lehrbarkeit der Tugend niemals ernsthaft geleugnet hat'; he does not explain the passage where Socrates ostensibly adopts the unteachability of goodness.

Epilogue

1 See pp. 130 and 145 above.
2 See especially the careful and comprehensive analysis by Harvey, 1966, broadly accepted by Cartledge, 1978, and the more dashing utterances of Havelock, 1970 and 1982. Several of these references I owe in the first instance to Professor P. J. Rhodes. See also Burns, 1981, with brief bibliography at 371, n. 1. Burns' own treatment of the evidence strikes me as optimistic, e.g.: the quotations he offers from the dramatists are mostly *late* fifth-century – and the earlier, the less probative (I have no wish to be drawn into discussion of the date of *Prometheus Bound*, but observe that Aeschylus, *Eumenides*, 273, on Hades' δελτογράφῳ φρενί proves *nothing* about widespread

literacy); he assumes that the early prose writers were read by a wide cross-section of the population, which is open to doubt. See also n. 4, below.

3 Harvey's evidence (1966, 629–31) for schools teaching the skills of literacy as early as the 490s strikes me as extremely thin, and its gaps cannot be filled by *a priori* argument.

4 The most convincing piece of evidence is the scene from Euripides' *Theseus*, discussed by Harvey (1966, 603). I remain sceptical of the suggestion that the availability of Athenian public documents 'to him who wishes' implies (Harvey, 601, Burns, 1981, 383) 'at least a majority of literates' in view of the strong possibilities (a) that a relatively small proportion of literates read out to illiterates what the notices said, and (b) that the phrase σκοπειν τō βουλομενō on public inscriptions embodies a myth of democracy on similar lines to the notion that any Tom, Dick or Harry could come forward to address the Assembly. The equation of written laws and decrees with democratic government (Burns, 377) is subject to similar sceptical arguments. Strepsiades in Aristophanes, *Clouds* is indeed literate, but still needs to go to school rather than read books, and is in any case an uneasy mixture (from our present point of view) of a country bumpkin and the husband of a great lady. I believe Harvey may have misconstrued Aristophanes, *Wasps*, 959–60, where οὐδέ could mean 'not ... either' rather than 'not even'. But if we are convinced nevertheless by the *Theseus* scene we should observe that it does nothing (and Harvey indeed does not force it: see his 588 to the contrary) to prove that the reading of books was a widespread habit. Literature was doubtless still largely an oral matter. I should like to emphasize that this note is no substitute for, and does not do justice to, Harvey's excellent work.

5 'It remains true that Greek culture was much more a culture of the spoken word than of the written word' (Harvey 588, cf. e.g. Havelock, 1963, 38).

6 One does not have to take on board the whole of Ryle's views on Plato's life (see Ryle, 1966) in order to take seriously his suggestion that Plato composed the early and middle dialogues for performances.

7 Havelock, 1963, 57, n. 21.

8 Schofield, 1983, 31–58.

9 Sextus Empiricus discusses this argument at *Adv. Math.* IX, 133ff.: Schofield's interpretation, 1983, 38ff. makes it, I think, more explicit than we have any evidence that it was. In so

doing, it weakens the argument's force until it becomes a problem to draw 'any plausible conclusion nearly so strong as Zeno's from the two premisses'. But the argument looks like a cogent syllogism, with 'reasonably to be worshipped' as one of its terms. How is the atheist to escape without embarrassment?

10 This and Section III owe their existence to some pertinent and helpful questions from the anonymous reader of the Johns Hopkins University Press.
11 See C. H. Kahn, 1976, *passim*.
12 Note the work of K. Moors, 1981, on the *Republic*.

Bibliography

This Bibliography makes not the slightest attempt at completeness, but merely gives appropriate details of works referred to in text and notes.

In the notes I have cited normally only the author's surname and date. The following abbreviations should be noted:
Guthrie, HGP = W. K. C. Guthrie, *History of Greek Philosophy*
LSJ = H. C. Liddell, R Scott, and H. Stuart Jones, *Greek Lexicon*.
Note also that I have sometimes omitted the date in referring to editions and translations where the reference seemed to me quite clear without it.

J. Adam and A. M. Adam, 1905, *Platonis Protagoras*, with Introduction, Notes and Appendices ... (Cambridge 1893, 2nd edn, 1905).
A. W. H. Adkins, 1960, *Merit and Responsibility: a Study in Greek Values* (Oxford).
———, 1971, 'Homeric values and Homeric Society', *Journal of Hellenic Studies* 91, 1–14.
———, 1972, *Moral Values and Political Behaviour from Homer to the end of the Fifth Century* (London).
———, 1973, ''Ἀρετή, Τέχνη, Democracy and Sophists: Protagoras 316b–328d,' *Journal of Hellenic Studies* 93, 3–12.
———, 1978, 'Problems in Greek Popular Morality', *Classical Philology* 73, 143–58.
R. E. Allen, 1980, *Socrates and Legal Obligation* (Minneapolis).
A. Andrewes, *see* A. Gomme.
J. Annas, 1981, *Introduction to Plato's Republic* (Oxford).
J. Anton and G. Kustas, eds, 1971, *Essays in Greek Philosophy* (Albany NY).
M. T. W. Arnheim, 1977, *Aristocracy in Greek Society* (Aspects of Greek and Roman Life) (London).
H. von Arnim, 1914, *Platos Jugenddialoge und die Entstehungszeit des Phaidros* (Leipzig-Berlin).
F. Ast, 1908, *Lexicon Platonicum* ... condidit D. F. Astius (2nd edn, Berlin).
S. Baldwin, 1926, *On England and Other Addresses* (London).
R. Bambrough, ed., 1965, *New Essays on Plato and Aristotle* (London).

R. S. Bluck, 1955, *Plato's Phaedo*, trs. with introduction, notes and appendices (London).
———, 1961, *Plato's Meno*, ed. with introduction and commentary (Cambridge).
L. Bodin, 1975, *Lire le Protagoras: Introduction à la méthode dialectique de Protagoras*, ed. P. Demont (Paris).
L. Brandwood, 1976, *A Word-Index to Plato* (Leeds).
J. Brentlinger, 1970, *The Symposium of Plato*, trs. Suzy Groden, ed. J.B. (University of Massachusetts).
J. Burnet, *Platonis Opera*, vols. I–V (Oxford, my copies 1941–1952).
———, 1924, *Plato Euthyphro, Apology of Socrates and Crito* (Oxford).
A. Burns, 1981, 'Athenian Literacy in the fifth century B.C.', *Journal of the History of Ideas* 42, 371–87.
M. Burnyeat, 'Virtues in Action' in G. Vlastos, ed., 1971, *The Philosophy of Socrates*, 209–34.
R. G. Bury, ed., 1932, *The Symposium of Plato* (2nd edn, Cambridge).
P. A. Cartledge, 1978, 'Literacy in the Spartan oligarchy', *Journal of Hellenic Studies* 98, 25–37.
D. B. Claus, 1981, *Toward the Soul* (Yale).
D. Clay, 1975, 'The Tragic and Comic Poet of the Symposium', *Arion* NS 2/2, 238–61.
E. Coleridge, 1904, *The Plays of Euripides* (London)
———, 1905, *The Tragedies of Sophocles* (London).
C. Collard, 1975, *Euripides, Supplices*, ed. with introduction and commentary (Groningen).
F. M. Cornford, 1950, 'The Doctrine of Eros in Plato's *Symposium*', in *The Unwritten Philosophy*, ed. W. K. C. Guthrie (Cambridge).
M. Croiset and L. Bodin, 1923, *Platon, Protagoras* (Paris, Les Belles Lettres) (the 'Budé' *Protagoras*).
C. Cron, ed., 1891, *Platons Laches* (5te Auflage Leipzig).
J. Cronquist, 1980, 'The Point of the Hedonism in Plato's *Protagoras*', *Prudentia* 12, 63–81.
J. D. Denniston, 1954, *Greek Particles* (2nd edn, Oxford).
W. Detel, 1973, 'Zur Argumentationsstruktur im ersten Hauptteil von Platons Aretedialogen', *Archiv für Geschichte der Philosophie* 55, 1–29.
J. Deuschle, ed., Platons *Protagoras* in Platons *Ausgewählte Schriften* (Leipzig, various editions).
M. W. Dickie, 1978, 'The Argument and Form of Simonides 542 *PMG*', *Harvard Studies in Classical Philology* 82, 21–34.
R. Dieterle, 1966, *Platon, Laches und Charmides, Untersuchungen zur*

elenktisch-aporetischen Struktur der platonischen Frühdialoge (Dissertation, Freiburg im Br.).
E. R. Dodds, 1951, *The Greeks and the Irrational* (Berkeley).
———, 1959, *Plato, Gorgias,* A revised text with Introduction and Notes (Oxford).
K. J. Dover, 1965, 'The Date of Plato's *Symposium', Phronesis* 10, 2–20.
———, 1968, *Aristophanes' Clouds* (Oxford).
———, 1973, 'Classical Greek Attitudes to Sexual Behaviour', *Arethusa* 6, 75–90.
———, 1974, *Greek Popular Morality* (Oxford, Blackwell).
———, 1978, *Greek Homosexuality* (London).
———, 1980, *Plato Symposium* (Cambridge).
———, 1982, *The Greeks* (Oxford).
R. Duncan, 1978, 'Courage in Plato's *Protagoras', Phronesis* 23, 216–28.
P. E. Easterling, 1974, 'Alcman 58 and Simonides 37', *Proceedings of the Cambridge Philological Society* N.S. 20, 37–43.
M. T. Ferejohn, 1982, 'The Unity of Virtue and the Objects of Socratic Inquiry', *Journal of the History of Philosophy* 20, 1–21.
M. I. Finley, 1962, 'Athenian Demagogues', *Past and Present,* no. 21, 3–24.
W. H. Forbes, 1895, *Thucydides Book I* (Oxford).
J. W. Forrester, 1975, 'Some perils of Paulinity', *Phronesis* 20, 11–21.
Ed. Fraenkel, 1960, 'Eine Anfangsformel attischer Reden', *Glotta* 39, 1–5 (*Beiträge zur Klassischen Philologie* I (Rome 1964), 505–10).
Paul Friedländer, trs. H. Meyerhoff, 1965, 1969, *Plato: The Dialogues, First Period* (London, 1965) and *Second and Third Periods* (London 1969).
M. Gagarin, 1969, 'The purpose of Plato's Protagoras', *Tr. and Proceedings of the American Philological Association* 100, 133–64.
U. Galli, 1935, *Platone, Il Simposio, con Introduzione e Commento* (Turin).
D. Gallop, 1961, 'Justice and Holiness in the *Protagoras', Phronesis* 6, 86–93.
———, 1964, 'The Socratic Paradox in the *Protagoras,' Phronesis* 9, 117–129.
———, 1975, *Plato's Phaedo,* trs. with notes (Oxford).
V. Gardthausen, 1879, 1913, *Griechische Palaeographie* I (Leipzig 1879) and II^2 (Leipzig 1913).
V. Goldschmidt, 1947, *Les Dialogues de Platon* (Paris).

A. Gomme, A. Andrewes, and K. J. Dover, 1945–81, *A Historical Commentary on Thucydides*, vols. I–V (Oxford).
A. W. Gomme, 1962, *More Essays in Greek History and Literature* ed. D. A. Campbell (Oxford).
W. W. Goodwin, 1894, *Greek Grammar* (2nd edn) (London).
J. C. B. Gosling, 1975, *Plato, Philebus* (Oxford).
J. Gosling and C. C. W. Taylor, 1982, *The Greeks on Pleasure* (Oxford).
A. Graeser, 1975, 'Zur Logik der Argumentationsstruktur in Platons Dialogen "Laches" und "Charmides"', *Archiv für Geschichte der Philosophie* 57, 172–81.
G. T. Griffith, 1966, 'Isegoria in the Assembly at Athens', *Ancient Society and Institutions*, Studies presented to Victor Ehrenberg... ed. E. Badian (Oxford), 115–38.
G. Grote, 1888, *Plato and the Other Companions of Socrates* (4-vol. edn, London).
G. M. A. Grube, 1933, 'The Structural Unity of the *Protagoras*', *Classical Quarterly* 27, 203–7.
N. Gulley, 1971, 'Socrates' Thesis at *Protagoras* 358b–c', *Phoenix* 25, 118–23.
H. Gundert, 1977, *Platonstudien* (Amsterdam).
W. K. C. Guthrie, 1956, *Plato, Protagoras and Meno*, trs. with introduction, summaries, etc (Penguin Books).
———, 1962–81, *A History of Greek Philosophy*, vols. I–VI (Cambridge) (*HGP*).
W. Hamilton, 1951, *The Symposium by Plato*, trs. with introduction and notes (Penguin Books).
R. M. Hare, 1982, *Plato* (Oxford).
R. Harriott, 1969, *Poetry and Criticism before Plato* (London).
A. R. W. Harrison, 1968–71, *The Law of Athens*, vols. I–II (Oxford).
F. D. Harvey, 1966, 'Literacy in the Athenian Democracy', *Revue des Études grecques* 79, 585–635.
E. A. Havelock, 1957, *The Liberal Temper in Greek Politics* (London).
———, 1963, *A Preface to Plato* (Oxford).
———, 1970, *Prologue to Greek Literacy*, Semple Lectures 1966–70 (Cincinnati), 329–91.
———, 1978, *The Greek Concept of Justice* (Cambridge, Mass).
———, 1982, *The Literate Revolution in Greece and its Cultural Consequences* (Princeton).
R. S. W. Hawtrey, 1981, *A Commentary on Plato's Euthydemus* (Philadelphia, American Philosophical Society).

P. Huart, 1968, *Le Vocabulaire psychologique dans l'oeuvre de Thucydide* (Paris).
B. A. Hubbard and E. S. Karnofsky, 1982, *Plato's Protagoras: A Socratic Commentary* (London).
E. Irwin, 1974, *Colour Terms in Greek Poetry* (Toronto).
T. Irwin, 1977, *Plato's Moral Theory: The Early and Middle Dialogues* (Oxford).
———, 1979, *Plato, Gorgias* (Oxford).
B. Jowett, 1953, *Plato, The Dialogues* tr. into English with analyses and introductions by B. J. (4th edn revised, Oxford).
———, 1970, *Dialogues of Plato*, trs. by B. J., ed. R. M. Hare and D. A. Russell vols. I–V (London, Sphere Books).
———, 1956, *Plato's Protagoras*, trs. by B. J., revised by Martin Ostwald, edited, with introduction, by Gregory Vlastos (New York).
D. Kagan, 1965, *The Great Dialogue* (New York).
C. H. Kahn, 1976, 'Plato on the Unity of Virtues', *Facets of Plato's Philosophy*, ed. W. H. Werkmeister (*Phronesis* Supplementary vol. 2), 21–39.
———, 1979, *The Art and Thought of Heraclitus* (Cambridge).
———, 1983, 'Drama and Dialectic in Plato's Gorgias', *Oxford Studies in Ancient Philosophy*, 1, 75–101.
G. B. Kerferd, 1953, 'Protagoras' Doctrine of Justice and Virtue in the *Protagoras* of Plato', *Journal of Hellenic Studies* 73, 42–5.
———, 1981, *The Sophistic Movement* (Cambridge).
J. Klein, 1965, *Commentary on Plato's Meno* (Chapel Hill, NC).
G. Klosko, 1979, 'Toward a Consistent Interpretation of the *Protagoras*', *Archiv für Geschichte der Philosophie* 61, 125–42.
———, 1983, 'Criteria of Fallacy and Sophistry for use in the Analysis of Platonic Dialogues', *Classical Quarterly* 33, 363–74.
R. Kühner–B. Gerth, 1955, *Ausführliche Grammatik der griechischen Sprache*, IIe Teil, Satzlehre, vols. 1–2 (3rd edn. repr. Leverkusen).
J. Laborderie, 1978, *Le Dialogue platonicien de la Maturité* (Paris).
W. R. M. Lamb, 1967, *Plato, Laches, Protagoras, Meno, Euthydemus* (*Loeb* Plato vol. 2) with an English translation (London and Cambridge, Mass., my copy 1967).
M. Lefkowitz, 1981, *The Lives of the Greek Poets* (London).
D. Levy, 1979, 'The Definition of Love in Plato's Symposium', *Journal of the History of Ideas* 40, 285–91.
LSJ *A Greek-English Lexicon* ... by H. G. Liddell and R. Scott, 9th edn by H. S. Jones ... (Oxford, completed 1940).
G. E. R. Lloyd, 1979, *Magic, Reason and Experience* (Cambridge).
H. Lloyd-Jones, 1971, *The Justice of Zeus* (Berkeley).

J. Lyons, 1963, *Structural Semantics* (*Publications of the Philological Society* 20) (Oxford).

M. McDonald, 1978, *Terms for Happiness in Euripides*, *Hypomnemata*, Heft 54 (Göttingen).

D. M. MacDowell, 1978, *The Law in Classical Athens* (London).

M. M. Mackenzie, 1981, *Plato on Punishment* (Berkeley).

B. Manuwald, 1975, 'Lust und Tapferkeit: zum gedanklichen Verhältnis zweier Abschnitte in Platos *Protagoras*', *Phronesis* 20, 22–50.

E. Méron, 1979, *Les Idées Morales des Interlocuteurs de Socrate dans les Dialogues platoniciens de Jeunesse* (Paris).

J. Moline, 1969, 'Meno's Paradox', *Phronesis* 14 153–61.

K. Moors, 1981, *Glaucon and Adeimantus on Justice* (Washington, D.C.).

J. Moravcsik, 1971, 'Reason and Eros in the "ascent"–passage of the Symposium', in Anton and Kustas, eds, 285–302.

J. S. Morrison, 1941, 'The Place of Protagoras in Athenian Public Life', *Classical Quarterly* 35, 1–16.

―――, 1964, 'Four Notes on Plato's *Symposium*', *Classical Quarterly*, N.S. 14, 42–55.

C. Moulton, 1977, *Similes in the Homeric Poems*, *Hypomnemata*, Heft 49 (Göttingen).

A. Nehamas, 1975–6, 'Confusing universals and particulars in Plato's early dialogues,' *Review of Metaphysics* 29, 288–306.

H. North, 1966, *Sophrosyne* (Cornell Studies in Classical Philology) (Ithaca, NY).

M. J. O'Brien, 1961, 'The Fallacy in *Protagoras* 349d–350c', *Tr. and Proceedings of the American Philological Society* 92, 408–17.

―――, 1963, 'The Unity of the *Laches*', *Yale Classical Studies* 18, 133–47, and in Anton and Kustas, eds. 203–35.

―――, 1967, *Socratic Paradoxes and the Greek Mind* (Chapel Hill, N.C.).

L. Pearson, 1962, *Greek Popular Ethics* (Stanford).

T. Penner, 1973, 'The Unity of Virtue', *Philosophical Review* 82, 35–68.

R. Pfeiffer, 1968, *History of Classical Scholarship*, I (Oxford).

E. des Places, 1929, *Quelques particules de liaison chez Platon* (Paris, Les Belles Lettres).

―――, 1964, *Platon, Lexique* (Paris, Les Belles Lettres).

P. Plass, 1960, 'Socrates' method of hypothesis in the *Phaedo*', *Phronesis* 5, 103–15.

―――, 1978, 'Plato's pregnant lover', *Symbolae Osloenses* 53, 47–55.

Bibliography 501

M. Pohlenz, 1913, *Aus Platons Werdezeit* (Berlin).
A. W. Price, 1981, 'Loving Persons Platonically', *Phronesis* 26, 25–34.
H. Raeder, 1905, *Platons philosophische Entwicklung* (Leipzig).
G. F. Rettig, 1875, *Platonis Symposium* (Berne).
L. D. Reynolds and N. G. Wilson, 1974, *Scribes and Scholars* (2nd edn, Oxford).
J. Riddell, 1877, *Plato's Apology* (Oxford).
A. Riginos, 1976, *Platonica* (Leiden).
J. M. Rist, 1982, *Human Value* (Leiden).
L. Robin, 1951, *Platon, Le Banquet* (Paris, Les Belles Lettres, 5th edn) (The 'Budé' *Symposium*).
R. Robinson, 1953, *Plato's Earlier Dialectic* (2nd edn, Oxford).
C. Rodewald, 1974, *Democracy: Ideas and Realities* (London and Toronto).
J. de Romilly, 1980, 'Réflexions sur le courage chez Thucydide et chez Platon', *Revue des Études grecques* 93, 307–23.
G. Ryle, 1966, *Plato's Progress* (Cambridge).
D. Sachs, 1963, 'A Fallacy in Plato's Republic', *Philosophical Review* 72, 141–58, and in Vlastos, ed., 1970, *The Philosophy of Plato*, vol. 2, 35–51.
G. Santas, 1964, 'The Socratic Paradox', *Philosophical Review* 73, 147–64.
―――, 1969, 'Socrates at Work on Virtue and Knowledge in Plato's Laches'. *Review of Metaphysics* 22, 433–60, and in Vlastos, ed., 1971, *The Philosophy of Socrates*.
―――, 1979, *Socrates* (London and Boston).
T. J. Saunders, 1968, 'The Socratic Paradoxes in Plato's *Laws*', *Hermes* 96, 421–34.
―――, 1973, 'Plato on Killing in Anger', *Philosophical Quarterly* 23, 232–44.
D. Savan, 1964, 'Self-predication in *Protagoras*, 330–31', *Phronesis* 9, 130–35.
M. Schofield, 1980, *An Essay on Anaxagoras* (Cambridge).
―――, 1983, 'The Syllogisms of Zeno of Citium', *Phronesis* 28, 31–58.
W. C. Scott, 1974, *The Oral Nature of the Homeric Simile* (Leiden).
P. Shorey, 1933, *What Plato Said* (Chicago).
B. Snell, 1964, *Scenes from Greek Drama* (Berkeley).
F. Solmsen, 1975, *Intellectual Experiments of the Greek Enlightenment* (Princeton).

R. Kent Sprague, 1967, 'An Unfinished Argument in Plato's *Protagoras*', *Apeiron* I, no. 2, 1–4.
———, 1973, *Plato, Laches and Charmides*, trs. with introduction and notes (Indianapolis and New York).
———, 1976, *The Philosopher-King* (Columbia).
M. C. Stokes, 1971, *One and Many in Presocratic Philosophy* (Cambridge, Mass. and Washington DC).
J. P. Sullivan, 1961, 'The Hedonism in Plato's *Protagoras*', *Phronesis* 6, 10–28.
M. Tatham, 1888, *Plato, Laches* (London 1888, my copy 1938).
A. E. Taylor, 1937, *Plato, the Man and his Work* (4th edn, London).
C. C. W. Taylor, 1976, *Plato, Protagoras*, trs. with notes (Oxford).
———, 1980, 'Plato, Hare and Davidson on Akrasia', *Mind* 89, 499–518.
H. Telle, 1975, *Formen der Beweisführungen in der Platonischen Frühdialogen* (Bonn; dissertation Freiburg 1970).
E. Maunde Thompson, 1912, *Introduction to Greek and Latin Palaeography* (Oxford).
W. N. Thompson, 1979, 'The Symposium: a neglected source for Plato's ideas on Rhetoric', in K. V. Erickson, ed., *Plato: True and Sophistic Rhetoric* (Amsterdam).
E. Tigerstedt, 1977, *Interpreting Plato* (Stockholm).
E. G. Turner, 1971, *Greek Manuscripts of the Ancient World* (Oxford).
B. D. Turner, ed., 1891, *The Protagoras of Plato* (London).
L. Versenyi, 1963, *Socratic Humanism* (Yale).
P. Vicaire, 1963, *Platon, Laches et Lysis* (Paris).
B. Vickers, 1973, *Towards Greek Tragedy* (London).
G. Vlastos, 1969, 'Socrates on Acrasia', *Phoenix* 23, 71–88.
———, ed., 1970, *The Philosophy of Plato: a Collection of Critical Essays*, vols. 1–2 (Garden City, NY).
———, ed., 1971, *The Philosophy of Socrates: a Collection of Critical Essays* (Garden City, NY).
———, 1981, *Platonic Studies* (2nd edn, Princeton).
———, see Jowett.
———, see Bambrough.
R. Weingartner, 1973, *The Unity of the Platonic Dialogue* (Indianapolis).
U. von Wilamowitz-Moellendorff, 1920, *Platon*, vols. 1 and 2 (Berlin).
———, 1982, *History of Classical Scholarship*, trs. A. Harries, ed. with introduction and notes by H. Lloyd-Jones (London).
P. Woodruff, 1982, *Plato, Hippias Major*, trs. with commentary and essay (Oxford).

G. von Wright, 1963, *The Varieties of Goodness* (London).
D. Zeyl, 1980, 'Socrates and Hedonism: Protagoras 351b–358d', *Phronesis* 25, 250–59.

Index of passages referred to

The notes are indexed less fully than the text. This index title is to be taken strictly; where discussion of a passage *ends* is sometimes left for the reader to find. I find that I have sometimes used English and sometimes Latinized forms of titles, but hope this will not inconvenience the reader.

Using this index: Users should note that any numbers preceding a first comma refer to lines or sections of the latest previously mentioned work; a semi-colon is an instruction to construe the numbers between it and the first comma following as referring likewise to lines or sections of the latest previously mentioned work. All other numbers are those of pages of this book.

AESCHYLUS(?)   *Prometheus* 849–51, 471
AESCHYLUS   *Eumenides* 273, 492; *Septem* 610, 475
ARISTOPHANES   *Birds* 785, 485; 127ff., 486; *Plutus* 803ff., 486; 905, 473; *Wasps* 959–60, 493
ARISTOTLE   *Nicomachean Ethics* (*EN*) 1097b22–4, 155; 1115a4ff., 463; 1115b24–8, 459; 1129b7, 224; *Politics* 1317b3–4, 217; *Topics* VIII, 1(155b3ff.), 491; 157a1–3, 329, 483; 159b27–35, 462
BACCHYLIDES   15.67, 291
DEMOSTHENES   xviii. 217, 287; xxi. 67, 217; xxi. 183, 286; [xxv]. 84, 286; xxxix. 35, 286; [xlii]. 21, 286
EURIPIDES   *Alcestis* 164–9, 486; *Andromache* 420, 486; 439, 219–20; 683, 46; *Antiope* fr. 187 (Nauck), 486; fr. 196, 486; *Bacchae* 387, 291; *Cyclops* 476–82, 223; *Electra* 583–4, 219–20; 949ff., 46; 1050–4, 216; 1349–53, 220; 1357–9, 486; *Hecuba* 801ff., 220; 853, 220; 1235, 287; *Helen* 1031–2, 220; 1624–33, 217; 1647–9, 217; *Heraclidae* 2ff., 223; 415–9, 220; 901–9, 220; *Hippolytus* 382–3, 486; 426–7, 223; 942, 287; *Hypsipyle* fr. 60. 114–17, 223; *Ion* 439–43, 224; 658, 486; 1456–61, 486; 1574, 217; *Iph.Aul.* 161–3, 486; 399, 287; 1034–5, 220; 1368–1400, 223; 1430, 291; *Iph.Taur.* 601ff., 223; 1469, 220; *Medea* 276–7, 486; 1046–7, 486; 1090ff., 486; *Orestes* 416–7, 216–7; *Phoenissae* 154–5, 220; 214, 486; 1239, 223; *Supplices* 219–28, 220; 226–8, 475; 328–31, 220; 409–25, 190 and 472; 437, 226; 594–7, 220 and 223–4; 608ff., 220; *Fr.* 758 (Nauck), 222
HERODOTUS   III. 80, 485; IX. 71, 53
HOMER   *Iliad* IV. 184, 465; V. 398, 478; VIII. 39, 465
   Odyssey I. 1–10, 473; XV. 491, 486; XVII. 423, 486; XIX. 79, 486; XXIV. 457, 291
LYSIAS   xxv. 1–2, 191; xx. 5, 287
OLYMPIODORUS   *In Alcib.2* p.6 (Westerink), 35 and 457
PINDAR   *Pythian* II. 81–9, 472
PLATO   *Alcibiades I* 105C, 485; *Apology* 17A–18A, 472; 17D, 478; 21B–22E, 40; 21B–23B, 112; 21C–D, 187; 22B–C, 170; 29A–B, 468; 41C–D, 445; *Charmides* 159B, 77; 166E, 477; 167E, 155; *Crito* 45C–D, 474; 45C, 287; 48B–D, 287; 49C, 287; 51C–E, 287; 52B–C, 478; 52E, 287; 54B, 287; *Euthydemus* 292C, 473; *Gorgias* 453D, 23–4; 459C, 485; 460B–C, 481; 466–8, 155; 467–8, 397; 490C, 26; 491C–E, 74; 491C, 484; 494C–495A, 367; 495A, 487; 499B, 367; 502Dff., 473; 515C–D, 473; 521C, 228; *Hippias ma.* 284D, 4–6; 297B–C, 467; *Laches* 178A–E, 38; 178A, 38; 179B, 41, 63; 179C–D, 41; 179C, 38; 179E, 38; 180A, 100; 180B–C,

505

39; 180C, 58; 180E, 42; 181A–B, 39, 49, 85; 181A, 42, 51, 58; 181C, 58; 181D, 40; 181E–182A, 55; 182C, 55–6; 182D, 72; 183C, 38; 183D, 93; 184B–C, 44–8, 56; 184B, 72; 184C, 55, 58, 460; 184E–185A, 60–1; 184E, 40, 59; 185B, 40; 185C–E, 62–4; 185C, 40; 186B–C, 65; 187B–D, 65; 187D–E, 65; 188A–B, 55; 188A, 36; 188C–189B, 50; 188C–E, 227; 188C, 51; 188D, 51; 188E–189A, 85; 188E, 72; 189A, 51; 189B, 50–1, 65–6, 72; 189C, 65; 189D, 52; 189E, 66; 190B, 66; 190C–D, 67, 69; 190C, 67, 460; 190D, 44–5, 67, 70; 190E, 70–1; 191A, 72; 191C–D, 71; 191C, 44, 53, 72; 191E, 71; 192A, 76; 192B–D, 98; 192B–C, 75–6; 192B, 86; 192C–D, 79; 192C, 77, 81, 84–7; 192D, 77; 192E, 77, 81; 193E, 88; 194A, 88; 194B, 461; 194C, 91; 194D–E, 93; 194D, 84, 93, 99, 108; 194E–195A, 56, 91, 465; 195A, 93; 195C, 94, 104; 195D, 465; 195E–196A, 103; 195E, 95, 484; 196A–B, 95; 196C, 96–7; 197A–B, 98; 197A, 98; 197B, 56; 197C, 56; 197D–E, 99; 197D, 57; 197E, 461; 198A, 100, 464; 198B, 100, 104, 465; 198C, 103, 464; 198D–199A, 103; 198D–E, 102; 198D, 107, 464; 198E, 106; 199B, 103; 199C, 464; 199D, 462; 200A, 111; 200E, 112; 201B, 112; 201C–D, 112; *Laws* 643A, 485; 644C, 465; 646E, 465; 903C, 478; *Lysis* 219C–D, 5–7; 220A–B, 5–7; *Meno* 72A–C, 461; 73A–C, 15–16; 73A, 14–15, 21; 73E, 461; 74A, 461; 75A, 461; 75C, 20–1; 76C–D, 455; 77–8, 155; 77A, 461; 77B, 107; 77D–E, 461; 78D–79E, 460; 78D–79C, 460–1; 79A, 460; 80D, 21; 82A–86A, 11–24; 82B, 18; 82C, 12; 82D, 12; 82E–83B, 12; 82E, 18; 83B, 13, 21; 83C, 23; 83D, 21–2; 83E, 12; 84A–B, 468; 84A, 455; 84B–C, 18; 84E, 12; 85B, 12, 18; 85C, 23; 87B–C, 385; 87C, 267; 88A, 24; 98B, 492; *Phaedo* 100C, 271; 102D, 271; 103B, 269; 106D, 271; *Philebus* 11A, 353; 11B–C, 483–4; 20D, 155; 21A–B, 353; 33C, 485; 42E, 485; 51A, 468; 53A–B, 180; 64Eff., 467; *Politicus* 306Bff., 327; *Protagoras* 309A, 183–4; 309C, 183; 309D, 183, 203; 310Aff., 385; 310A, 184–5; 310B, 186; 310D, 204, 261; 310E–311A, 192; 310E, 185–6, 262, 386; 311B, 186; 311E–312B, 387; 312A–B, 387; 312Bff., 386; 312D–E, 188, 387; 313A–C, 387; 313C–314B, 387; 313C–D, 192; 313C, 472; 313D–E, 193; 313E–314C, 192; 314A–B, 387; 315B, 193; 315C, 193; 315D, 211; 316B–C, 193–4; 316B, 386; 316C, 209, 385, 388; 317A, 197, 207; 317B, 211; 317Eff., 198; 317E–318A, 386; 318A, 194, 198; 318B, 229; 318C, 474; 318D–319A, 232; 318D, 198–200, 386; 318E–319A, 309; 318E, 232, 308; 319A–320C, 375; 319A–B, 204, 385; 319A, 200, 203; 319Bff., 188; 319B–C, 204, 382; 319B, 227, 293, 354, 361, 385; 319C–D, 208; 319Dff., 206; 319D, 383; 319E–320B, 385; 319E, 204, 229; 320Dff., 349, 438; 320D, 249, 476; 321B, 292; 321C–D, 229–31; 321D, 282; 321E, 231, 475; 322A, 231, 237, 326, 375, 476; 322B–D, 277; 322B–C, 241; 322B, 232, 234, 239, 246, 253, 260, 282, 326; 322C–E, 382; 322C–D, 232, 256; 322C, 241, 256; 322D–323C, 209; 322D–E, 256; 322D, 244, 283, 375, 377; 322E–324A, 241; 322E–323A, 296, 308; 322E, 326; 323A–C, 233–4, 243; 323A, 233, 243, 283, 301, 376, 381; 323B–C, 335; 323B, 228, 243, 255, 297, 391, 476; 323Cff., 378; 323C–324B, 244–5; 323C–324A, 234; 323C–D, 379; 323C, 244–5, 283, 476; 323D–324A, 309; 323D–E, 301–2, 485; 323D, 391, 480; 323E–324A, 238, 303; 324A–D, 247; 324A, 381; 324B–C, 382; 324B, 284; 324C, 248, 488; 324D, 229, 234, 246, 256, 293, 476; 324E–325A, 245, 302; 325A–B, 209; 325A, 246–7, 284; 325Cff., 248; 325C–326E, 389; 325C, 256; 325D–326A, 249; 325D, 228, 249, 251, 285, 301, 389, 396; 325E, 326, 490; 326A–B, 249; 326A, 285, 299, 372; 326B–C, 251, 260, 285, 389–90; 326B, 228, 234, 251, 475, 476; 326C–E, 254, 389; 326C, 253, 326, 480, 488; 326D, 234; 326E–327C, 256; 326E, 303, 396; 327Aff., 255; 327A, 301; 327Bff., 254; 327 B–C, 209; 327B, 254–5, 303, 309; 327C–D, 234, 255; 327C, 232, 283, 474, 475; 327E–328B, 354; 327E–328A, 209, 213; 328A–B, 235, 256, 305, 335, 392; 328A, 232; 328B–D, 209; 328B, 323, 416; 328C–D, 234; 328C, 476; 328D–330B, 258–63; 328D–E, 245; 329B, 117; 329C–E, 306; 329C–D, 245, 305; 329C, 236, 238, 258; 329D, 259; 329E–332A, 343; 329E–330A, 261, 326; 329E, 231, 260, 267, 276, 483; 330–1,

480; 330Aff., 324; 330A–B, 264–5; 330A, 247, 262–3, 265, 267, 293, 300; 330B–C, 268; 330B, 266, 346, 485; 330C, 302; 330D–E, 271; 330E–331A, 272; 331A, 281, 467; 331B, 264, 274; 331C, 277; 331D–E, 270; 331D, 278; 331E, 279; 332A–333C, 289–305; 332A–C, 294; 332A–B, 296; 332A, 279, 290, 480; 332B, 300; 332C–D, 301, 436; 332C, 293, 301, 303; 332D–E, 294; 333B–334C, 305–311; 333B, 479–80; 333C, 305, 307; 333D, 306; 334C–338E, 312–3; 334C, 311; 334D, 307, 309; 335A–B, 311; 336C–D, 312; 337Cff., 312; 338C–E, 313; 338C, 312; 338Eff., 184; 338E–347B, 313–23; 338E–339A, 197; 339Aff., 195; 339A, 436; 339B, 313; 339D, 316; 340B, 317; 340C–D, 318; 340E, 318; 341B, 321; 341D, 270, 318; 342A, 319; 342B, 323, 484; 342E, 319; 343D, 485; 343E, 317; 344A–B, 314, 321; 344A, 485; 344D–E, 319; 345A–B, 320; 345D–E, 320; 346B, 320; 346C, 323; 346D, 320; 347A–B, 197, 314; 347A, 320–1; 347B–349B, 323–7; 347C–348A, 319; 349A, 324; 349B–351B, 327–49; 349C–D, 324; 349D, 279, 292, 328, 342, 372–3, 393, 421, 436; 349E, 328, 330–1, 333–4, 348, 367, 423, 430, 491; 350A–B, 343; 350A, 334, 336; 350B–C, 429; 350B, 328, 333, 337, 347, 429–31, 483, 492; 350Cff., 359; 350C, 329, 338–9, 344, 348; 350E–351B, 347; 351A–B, 372, 492; 351A, 349, 429; 351B–359A, 349–420; 351B–C, 415, 490; 351B, 192–3, 228–9, 351, 360, 365, 472; 351C–E, 394; 351C–D, 353–4; 351C, 360–1, 364, 395, 485; 351D–E, 490; 351D, 368; 351E, 361, 363–4, 368; 352A–B, 371; 352A, 370; 352B–D, 489; 352B, 346, 352; 352C–D, 353, 371, 437; 352C, 356; 352D, 395–6; 352E, 355; 353A–B, 355; 353B, 354; 353C–D, 393–4, 398; 353E–354E, 488; 353E, 398; 354A, 398; 354B–E, 438; 354B, 399, 405; 354C–E, 489; 354C, 400–2, 404; 354E, 402–3; 355A, 438; 355Bff., 403; 355B, 468; 355C, 20, 438; 355D–E, 438; 356A, 403; 356B, 405–6; 356C–357B, 418; 356C–D, 407; 356D, 409; 356E, 408–9; 357A–B, 409; 357B–358A, 200; 357B, 489; 357C–E, 408; 357D, 438; 357E, 408, 411, 434, 438, 490; 358A, 491; 410E, 327; 429B–C, 109; 434; 358B, 373, 384, 415–17, 435; 358C–E, 373; 358C–D, 418; 358C, 374, 435, 438, 490; 358D–E, 419; 358D, 109; 358E, 334, 422, 427, 490; 359A, 421; 359Cff., 423; 359C–D, 423; 359D–E, 430; 359D, 421–4, 490; 359E, 416, 424; 360, 436, 491; 360A–E, 428–9; 360A, 424–5, 427, 490, 491; 360B, 431, 434, 467, 492; 360D, 346, 436; 360E, 349, 437–8; 361A–C, 207, 336; 361A–B, 208, 267; 361A, 438; 361B, 438; 361C–D, 438; *Republic* 331E–332C, 456; 339E–400A, 459; 348C, 456; 353D–E, 351; 360B, 250; 381B, 491; 407A, 491; 410E, 327; 429B–C, 109; 442Eff., 250; 505B–C, 490; 586B–C, 180; *Symposium* 175E, 468; 194A–B, 116; 195A–B, 137; 195A, 116, 149; 195B–C, 128; 195B, 158; 195C–196A, 150; 195C, 147, 158; 195D, 116; 195E, 128, 140, 150, 175; 196A–D, 151; 196A, 118, 121, 128–9, 138, 149, 175; 196B–D, 171; 196B–C, 122; 196B, 128, 138, 149; 196C–D, 118, 135; 196C, 118, 120, 149, 173, 291; 196D–197B, 150, 161; 196D, 122, 143; 196E–197B, 175; 196E, 116, 125, 149, 157; 197A–B, 120, 151; 197A, 124; 197B, 118, 124–5, 133–6, 142, 144, 148, 153, 466; 197C–E, 152; 197C, 116; 197D–E, 116; 197D, 119, 121, 152; 197E, 116–7, 138; 198B, 117; 198C, 116; 199B, 117; 199C–D, 117, 130; 199C, 153; 200A–E, 123; 200A, 120–2; 200C, 128; 200D, 466; 200E–201B, 130; 201A–B, 135–6; 201A, 130, 136, 139, 145, 467; 201B, 145, 147, 466–7; 201C, 125, 145; 201D–E, 153; 201D, 117; 201E, 146, 152; 202A, 147; 202C, 148; 202D, 149; 203C, 143, 469; 203D, 150; 203E, 468; 204A, 151; 204B, 151–2, 166, 468; 204C, 153; 204D, 153, 161, 166; 204E, 153; 205A–D, 160; 205A–B, 156–7; 205A, 154, 157–8; 205D, 157; 205E, 155–6; 206A–B, 159; 206A, 158, 181; 206B, 160; 206C, 161–4, 166; 206D, 163; 206E–207A, 166–8; 206E, 164–5; 207A–208B, 167–8; 207A–C, 161; 207A–B, 168; 207A, 168; 207B–C, 168; 207C, 169; 208B, 167–8, 178; 208C–209A, 170; 208D, 181; 208E, 168; 209A–C, 172; 209A–B, 176; 209A, 171; 209B, 174; 209C–D, 172; 209C, 174; 209D–E, 173; 209E–210A, 173; 210A–E, 470; 210A, 173–4, 176; 210C, 174, 177; 210D, 175; 210E, 173–4, 178; 211A, 179, 269; 211C–D, 177; 211C, 181; 211D–

212A, 180; 212A, 178; 212B, 182; 212C, 182; *Theaetetus* 154A; 161E; 180D–E, all 478; 183B; 188A, both 485; *Theages* 126A, 194
PROCLUS   *in Timaeum* 128, 467
SEXTUS EMPIRICUS   *Adversus Mathematicos* IX. 133, 493
SOPHOCLES   *Ajax* 271–7, 486; 1342–4, 287; *Antigone* 1166–71, 486; *Electra* 983, 46; 1121, 478; *Oedipus Coloneus* 798ff., 486; *Oedipus Tyrannus* 425, 478; *Philoctetes* 1358–9, 469; *fr. incert.* 665, 486
THEOGNIS   147–8, 224
THUCYDIDES   I 73.2, 217; II 53.3, 485; II 87.3, 47; II 89.2, 46–7, 458; III 37, 472; III 40.4, 218; III 44, 218; III 47.3, 222; III 82–3, 459; V 85, 190, 472; V 89, 217, 222; V 104, 219; V 105.4, 224; VI 39.1, 191, 472; VI 83.2, 217
TIMOCREON of RHODES   Fr.1, 224
[XENOPHON]   *Ath.Pol.* i.13; vi, both 472
XENOPHON   *De Vectigalibus* i 1, 213

General index

The reader is asked to note (*a*) that I have not listed *all* proper names (some minor characters, mainly in non-Platonic writings, are omitted), and (*b*) that neither all nor only those pages are listed on which a given word actually occurs. This index is intended to be useful rather than totally complete. The notes are less fully indexed than the body of the text, particularly as concerns the names of scholars. For ancient authors see also the Index of passages referred to.

abstract(s): nouns 71–2, 227, 233; and collective(s) 133–5, 138, 176–7; and concrete 69–71, 132, 140
Achilles: 170, 291
actions: 242–3, 246–7, 250–5, 260, 269, 272–8, 292–300, 305–11, 325–7, 331, 333–5, 356, 377–84, 388–91, 396, 400–2, 409–10, 415, 418–20, 422–4, 434–5
Adam, J. and A. M.: 1
address, forms of: 69
ad hominem argument: 48, 52, 75, 151, 177, 286, 365, 374, 450. *See also under* Socrates, questions
Adkins, A. W. H.: 53, 210–27
advantage (of the agent): 306–9, 366, 371, 406, 435–6
advice, expert: 66, 256, 296, 375
Aelian: 172
Aeschines of Sphettus: 26
Aeschylus: 196
Agathon: 28, 114–46, 286, 291, 323, 441, 449–51; in the Diotima episode 146–61, 164–5, 167, 170–3, 175–82
age (old age): 137–40, 158–9
aidos: 227–8
akrasia: 298, 353–7, 382, 392–3, 402–3, 408–15, 422–5, 434–5, 438
Alcestis: 170
Alcibiades: 183, 198, 205, 312
'always': 128–9, 157–8
ambiguity: of a Greek expression 86–7, 92, 173, 223, 290–3; of

interlocutors in general 37, 183; of Laches 78; of Agathon 130, 133–6; of Protagoras 200, 202–3, 231, 235, 238, 242, 249–50, 257, 296–7, 300–1, 326, 337, 377, 416, 423; of Simonides 316–17; of Socrates 76, 107, 311, 339, 359–60, 409, 414; of Plato 358, 361–3, 412. *See also* 'always', 'and'
analogy: 60, 76, 163, 187, 213, 259, 263–89, 306, 325, 349–50, 411; as simile 371
Anaxagoras: 25
Anaximander: 25
'and' (meaning of): 50, 55, 120–1, 143, 173, 243, 252, 253–4, 265
andreia: meaning 36–7, 44–8, 50–2, 62, 74–5, 85–6, 92; and goodness 67–9, 75–6; and manliness 36; and knowledge 91–3. *See also* courage, manliness
Andrewes, A.: 219
animals: and courage 97–9; and love 126, 157, 163, 167; and punishment 381–2
antonym: *see* opposite(s)
Aphrodite: 118, 143, 166
aphrosyne: 290–5. *See also* folly
Apollo: 112, 120, 124–7, 143, 224
Ares: 122, 150
arete: 44–5; = courage 50–5. *See also* goodness
Aristides the Just: 38, 42, 195, 224–5

General index

Aristophanes: 196, 287, 290; in Plato's *Symposium* 116, 156, 181
Aristotle: 73, 80, 86, 155, 171, 217, 224, 329–30, 442
Arnim, H. von: 425
art(s): generally 124–7, 157, 200–1, 205, 213, 229–32, 334; political 206–7, 229–36, 239–40, 246, 345, 354–6, 385–6; of war, 70, 239–42, 245, 326, 336–7; and wisdom or knowledge 208, 319, 345–6, 350–2, 391, 395, 437; sophistic 186–7, 195–6, 207, 219, 229; and crafts 170, 375, 383, 386; of measurement 407–9, 418; and teaching 203–8. *See also* technical skills
assumptions: 115, 123, 130, 139, 144, 152, 169, 191, 271, 298, 335, 374, 400, 418, 431, 440, 447
Athena: 231
Athenagoras of Syracuse: 191
Athen(ian)s: education 195–6, 228, 251, 284–5, 355, 372, 389–90, 392–7; wisdom of 203–8, 212, 226–7, 248, 312, 314, 319, 356, 361–2, 385, 439; democracy 60, 191–2, 198, 203–9, 218, 256, 375–7, 382–5, 388–9; and rhetoric 189–90; on justice 221–5; statesmen 194, 204–6; in Thucydides' Melian Dialogue 219, 222–4; orators 215, 290

bad(ness): as opposite of 'good' (q.v.) 92, 124, 146, 186, 371–2; knowledge of good and bad 100, 103–8, 111; qualities 244–5, 248; bad for (harmful) 84, 95, 105, 155; bad at 284; inefficient 54; of a poem 195, 314; of pleasures or pains 367–8, 393–405; of actions 249, 372; of a life 359–60, 366; as object of fear 102, 110; and unjust 287
beautiful: meaning of 145, 151–2, 155, 465; things, as objects of love/desire 124–6, 131–6, 138–43, 153–5, 160–3, 174–6; possessed 153–4, 161, 165–7, and beauty 138–45, 178–80; the beautiful (itself) 143, 151–4, 161, 164–7, 176–81, 269; and fine 183, 465; and good 124–6, 142, 145–6, 149–57, 160–1, 165–7, 179–81, 467–8; and ugly 124–6, 135–6, 140–1, 145–7, 165–6, 174, 179–80; and wise 151, 166, 183–4, 269. *See also* fine
beauty: as object of Love 118, 124, 131–6, 139–44, 148–50, 153, 161, 165–6, 174–5, 469, 471; as property of Love 125–30, 133, 138, 142–5, 148–9, 165; as abstract 135, 138–144, 148, 154, 177–80, 269, 378; degrees of 144; of laws 173; of body and soul 174–7, 183; of individual 175
being (and becoming); 178, 316–17, 319
beloved: 6, 114, 121–2, 152, 157, 163–4
bold(ness): 45–6, 98, 328–35, 349, 428–33. *See also thrasys*, confidence
Brandwood, L.: 364
brave: 151, *and see* courage(ous)

Callias: 198, 211, 311
Callicles: 26, 74, 225, 228, 367
capability: 349–50
characters: *see* Socrates' interlocutors
Charmides: 77–8
Cimon: 194
citizen, the good: *see* good
city: historical 53; sphere of Protagoras' successful pupils 194, 200, 309, 387–8; in Socrates' approach to Protagoras 204; in Protagoras' Great Speech 232, 235, 239, 242, 245, 254, 285, 375–6, 383, 389–90, 396. *See also* political
clarification: obtained by Socrates,

General index 511

from Laches 87, from Nicias 93, 100, from Agathon 121, 135–6, from Diotima 161, from Protagoras 201, 207, 259, 263, 305, 349, 421, 423–4; given by Socrates 6, 71, 73, 76, 78, 93, 103, 119, 270, 367–9, 414
Cleon: 189, 218, 222
Clinias: 206
Codrus: 170
Coleridge, E.: 46
comic/comedy: 116, 287, 290, 314–15, 319, 322
common sense: 81, 92, 98, 258, 316, 371, 382, 399, 425–7, 431–3, 437, 452
common views: on people 184, 318, 323; on philosophical questions 16, 18, 68, 94, 220–1, 225–6, 274, 303, 353–5, 372–3, 378–80, 406. *See also* many, the, Greek usage, Athenians
comparatives (of adjectives): 336–7, 343–4, 347–8
concessional language: 68, 73, 151, 170–1, 184, 324, 327
confidence: 44–7, 55–7, 83, 328–41, 344–50, 356, 421–4, 428–34
confusions: 43, 48, 52, 69, 140, 202–3, 212, 270, 292, 296–7, 303, 310, 395, 449
consistency: of Socrates 32, 143, 314, 393; of interlocutors in general 32, 57, 438, 446; of particular interlocutors 83, 101, 103, 121, 134, 147, 178, 257, 259, 423, 426, 449; of Simonides 318, 321; of the Athenians 388. *See also* contradiction
contradiction: offered (or not) by Plato 6; by Socrates 23, 208; by interlocutors 28–35, 88; by Laches 52, 75, 84; by Agathon 126, 134, 147, 149; by Protagoras 201, 233–4, 247, 251, 257, 259–61, 266, 277, 297, 300, 306, 309, 324, 326, 339, 356–7, 382, 395, 424, 426, 431, 449

contradictory (and contrary) 239–41, 251, 270–3, 277, 281–9, 295, 299–301, 431
contrary: *see* contradictory and opposite(s)
Contrivance (mythical figure): 152
courage: meaning of, *see andreia*; definitions of 70–1, 78, 92–3; and goodness 44, 48–57, 66–9, 75–6, 95–111, 208, 214, 239–40, 253, 258–63, 276, 285, 324–7, 351–2, 393, 431, 448–51; and war 28, 44–57, 70–5, 82–3, 85, 91–4, 214, 239–40, 251–3, 257–60, 319, 323–6, 424; and endurance 71, 75–80, 83–91, 98, 106, 110, 451; and knowledge/wisdom 56, 79, 81–4, 92–111, 231, 267, 319, 323–4, 326–52, 356–7, 390, 393, 420–36, 449–51; parts of, 88, 103–4; mentioned 22, 295, 374. *See also* intellect, *andreia*, technical skills
cowardice: 45, 54, 252–3, 260, 285, 326, 373, 390–1, 421–33, 435–6
Critias: 312
Crito: 287

Damon: 111
definite article: 142, 177, 337–9, 348, 417, 427
definition(s): 69–71, 75, 77–8, 86–92, 99–104, 108–9, 199, 280–2, 399–400, 406, 419–20
deilos: 44–5, 56
Delium: 49–50, 58, 72, 85
democracy: 59–60, 188–91, 197–8, 203–13, 217–18, 235, 256, 382, 385–8
desire(s): 108, 118–35, 143–4, 149–50, 154–71, 175, 189–91, 319, 418, 452; Hippocrates' 194–5, 198; mentioned 74, 296
Detel, W.: 69, 78
dialectic: *passim*; see especially, in general 2, 114, 204, 210, 236–7, 411, 418–19, 422, 446; goals of 322, 343, 449–53; methods 10,

28, 32–5, 108–9, 115–16, 123, 135, 138, 152, 288, 293, 301–3, 322, 329, 346–9, 358, 382, 425–7, 440–3; distinct from proof 30–1, 83, 147–8, 178, 182, 451–2; especially skilful 170–2; as competition 312–14; criticized 399; in the Stoics 442–3

dialogue(s), dialogue-form: dramatic date 102; distinct from treatise 1–35, 148, 289; not historical 304, 447–8; and an audience 24, 441; purpose of 25–31, 52, 393, 440–2, 448–54; relevance of other dialogues 14, 29, 164, 307, 444–7; unity and construction 2, 11, 19–20, 36–7, 62, 75, 88–90, 110, 114, 169, 183, 188, 195, 200, 268, 304, 315, 322–3, 333, 352, 391, 411–2, 426, 433, 438, 453; to be read separately 187

Dieterle, R.: 36–7, 50, 59, 66, 87, 95, 99

Diogenes of Apollonia: 25

Diogenes Laertius: 25

Diotima: 114, 117, 143–4, 146–82; represents Socrates against Agathon 146–61, 165, 169–82

doctors: as examples 63, 80–3, 94, 96, 102–6, 398–9; as analogues 186, 319–20; mentioned 116, 124

Dodds, E. R.: 23, 226

Dover, Sir K. J.: 53–4, 114–18, 121, 127, 129, 137–8, 147, 149, 151, 156–8, 161–2, 165, 167

dramatic plausibility: 22, 36, 63, 65–6, 72, 74, 76, 190–1, 197, 307; drama and argument 3, 9, 26, 31, 312, 446

Duncan, R.: 237, 251–4, 262, 267, 326

education: general and Athenian 29, 38, 43, 189–90, 196, 204–6, 248–56, 299–301, 313–20, 354–5, 385, 387, 390, 395–6, 441, 454; sophistic 28, 196–9, 207, 313–18,

351–3, 390, 449; and Socrates 39–40, 61–2, 66, 112, 319; and Laches 72, 112; and Nicias 55, 57, 112; and the lover 174. *See also* teaching, parents

Electra: 46

elimination, argument by: 90, 125, 132, 141, 144

emotions: 75, 101, 109–11, 122, 165, 410–11, 414, 419–20, 426, 434–5

ends and means: 62–3

endurance: 71, 75–80, 83–91, 98, 106, 110, 170, 451. *See also* courage

Epimetheus: 249, 292–3. *See also* myth

episteme: 80. *See also* knowledge, technical skills, art(s), wisdom

equality: 209, 217–8

equivocation: 123, 133–5, 137–8, 153, 157–9, 289–93, 322–3, 346

eros: 116, 118, 125–8, 135, 140, 142–3, 149–52, 160, 162, 175. *See also* love

Eryximachus: 116

eupsuchia: 47, 64

Euripides: 190, 196, 215–28, 287, 291

expediency: 218–28. *See also* advantage

expert(ise)s: in education 59–64; and 'courage' 77, 81–2, 86, 92–6, 332–4, 340; and democracy 49, 188, 204–6, 209, 375–7, 383–5; and goodness 283–4, 319. *See also* art(s), knowledge, technical skills

fallacy: 33–4, 115–17, 315–16, 322, 329–32, 449. *See also* equivocation

fear(ful): 74, 90–6, 99–111, 220, 330, 333, 356, 373, 390–2, 421–32, 436; meaning/definition of 100–1, 104, 110–11, 419–20, 465

fictional (of Plato's characters): 89, 172, 211, 260–1, 270, 346, 357,

359, 362, 372, 391, 413, 445; meaning of 474
fine: meaning of 42, 155, 371; and courage 77–9, 83–8, 98; and beautiful 145, 183, 472; and good 64, 84–5, 155, 328, 332, 336, 366–7, 370, 394, 401–2, 415–17, 424–31, 435–6; and courage 77, 79, 83–8, 98; as 'opposite' 301
folly: 79–85, 92, 98, 220, 223, 261, 289–300, 325, 337, 463
Forms: 269, 445
Freud, S.: 175

Gallop, D.: 264, 267, 409
glory: 41, 169–70, 181, 194
Godley, A. D.: 53–4
gods: 95–7, 107–8, 124–7, 132–3, 142–3, 147–9, 169, 179, 219–23, 226, 237, 241, 249, 257, 277, 280–2, 317
good: meaning of, 51, 68, 198–9, 202–3, 325, 399–400; in itself 51, 402; at, 50, 74–5, 91–2, 194, 198–9, 387; for 94–5, 105–6, 154–5, 185–6, 192–3, 210, 223, 294, 296, 392, 397, 415–18; the good 154–7, 160, 166–7, 362, 369–70, 397, 400–2, 417–18; life 155, 350–5, 359–60, 365–7, 371, 406–8, 416–18; man 15–16, 41–3, 49–54, 199, 234, 245, 249, 256, 316, 319–20, 326, 437, 445; citizen 201–7, 228–30, 252, 283–5, 303, 306, 309, 356, 386, 437; possession of 149–67; doing well 308–9, 319, 407; and pleasant 357, 364–70, 373, 393–5, 398–405, 409–10, 413–20, 425, 428, 430, 438
goodness: political 206, 231–7, 242–6, 253, 256–8, 297, 300, 303, 334–5, 352, 375–80, 387, 437–9; teachable? 198, 205, 208–9, 245, 267, 284, 313, 320, 327, 335–6, 355, 375, 378, 382–7, 392, 395, 409–12, 434, 438–9; and 'art' 6, 229–35, 334; and knowledge/skill 66–7, 99–111, 199, 208, 385, 395, 412, 450–3; and particular virtues: justice 15–16, 64, 69–70, 223–6, 247–8, 254–6; courage 44–5, 48–58, 67–9, 75–6, 99, 231, 253, 260–1, 309–10, 328, 333–5, 393, 449; moderation 15–16; wisdom 91–111, 151, 170, 229–31, 234–5, 257, 260–2, 293, 320, 393, 412; unity and parts of 42–4, 51, 66–70, 73–4, 76, 88, 99–111, 170–85, 208–10, 213, 231, 233, 235–49, 251–311, 323–7, 332–6, 342–3, 346, 351, 373, 393, 430–1, 436–7, 445, 449–52; popular and philosophical 54, 326–7
Gorgias: 116
Gosling, J. C. B.: 7–9, 363–5
Graeser, A.: 69, 77–8
Greek usage: vocabulary 52–3, 77, 86, 90, 96, 98–9, 132, 156–7, 171, 187, 201, 227–8, 233, 244, 250, 253, 261–2, 279–80, 286–8, 290–5, 300, 317, 337, 354, 366, 399, 407; idiom 95, 118, 136, 163, 164, 180, 205, 230, 319, 369, 402, 406, 423, 432. *See also* particles
Grote, G.: 314–15
Grube, G. M. A.: 200, 230–1
Gulley, N.: 373
Gundert, H.: 318
gymnastics: 59–61, 186, 251–4, 387–90, 398

Hamilton, W.: 120, 128, 133, 135–6, 149, 155–6, 158–60, 162–3, 170, 174, 181
happiness: 126, 148–9, 153–5, 406
Havelock, E. A.: 201, 441
Hawtrey, R.: 25
hedonism: 7, 349, 357–8, 368, 407, 419, 425; psychological 396–7, 400–1, 406, 418; evaluative 397, 400, 406; weak/strong 414–18. *See also* pleasure
Helen: 46
Herodicus: 195

Herodotus: 53–4, 225, 290
Hesiod: 147, 173, 195, 319
Hippias: 2–5; in the *Protagoras*, 193, 196–7, 200, 232, 313–14, 319, 321, 420
Hippocrates (in the *Protagoras*): 184–8, 199, 202–5, 208–12, 229, 237, 261, 309–10, 355, 385–9, 434, 439
holiness: 236–8, 244–58, 263–4, 271–82, 285–8, 296, 324–5, 389, 395
Homer: 116, 173, 184, 195–6, 214, 227, 290–1, 366
homosexuality: 27–9, 114, 163–4, 172, 441, 449–51
Hubbard, B. A. F. and Karnofsky, E. S.: 3
humour (Plato's): 183–5, 193, 195
hybris: 291
Hyperbolus: 195

Iccus: 195
ignorance: Socrates' 7, 19, 21, 65, 112, 147; interlocutors' 11, 16, 67, 111–12, 150, 237, 385; other 98, 147, 151, 199, 219, 234, 283–4, 292, 328–9, 332–40, 344–5, 409–12, 421–2, 428–9, 434–6, 438
immoderation: 240–1, 244, 325, 421, 435
immortality: 19, 158, 162–70, 178–81
impiety: 237–8, 245–51, 272–3, 277, 287, 302, 327–8, 395, 421
induction: 60, 62, 301–3, 334, 343, 378, 403, 433
injustice: 24, 122, 185–6, 220, 224–6, 229–40, 245–55, 260–1, 269–73, 281–8, 290, 296, 302, 305–11, 322, 325, 328, 351, 381, 394–7, 421
intellect(ual): in general ethics 234, 262, 353–8, 371, 382, 387, 395, 414, 417, 420, 424–5, 436–7, 451–2; and courage 57, 77, 89–91, 106, 110–11, 253, 319, 334, 422,
426–7, 430, 435; and moderation 290–2, 297–301; and beauty 180
irony: Plato's 20, 65, 67, 69, 119, 207, 211, 323, 436; Socrates' 117, 182, 183–5, 193, 203–4, 312, 324, 354, 362, 384–5, 411, 437, 440; other 195
Irwin, T.: 5–7, 23, 88
Isocrates: 290

Jebb, Sir R. C.: 46
just(ice): meaning of 254; popular views of 213–27; as good quality 67–8, 100, 254–8, 262–89, 323–6, 376; and moderation 14–18, 108, 233–5, 238–51, 258, 305–13; and piety 236–7, 244–51, 258, 272–89; and wisdom, 171, 185, 259–61, 276; and courage 52, 57, 108, 253, 259–60; and violence 122; Laches on 50–2; in the *Protagoras* 209, 227, 232–64, 268–91, 300–1, 305–13, 323–6, 389, 394–6; in the *Republic* 351

Kerferd, G. B.: 2
Klosko, G.: 289, 315, 329–30
knowledge: and tenses 94–106; available to few 97; and the philosopher 151; that and how, 107–10; and wisdom/expertise/skill/art 55–6, 80–2, 93–7, 112, 185, 201, 208, 235, 262, 267, 319, 334, 339–40, 345–6, 350–3, 371, 395, 408–11, 417; and courage 55, 91–111, 328, 332–40, 347, 434–7; and justice 213; and good(ness) 56, 101, 106–11, 192, 322, 336, 351–2, 372–3, 385, 395, 408–11, 419, 434–8, 450–3; and opinion 109, 373–91, 416; and learning 207–8, 319, 332, 335, 345; beauty of 175; authority of 60–1, 262, 353–6, 370–2, 378–84, 389, 411–14, 417–18, 434–5, 452; attitudes to 111–13, 353–4, 370–2, 389, 411, 449–52; and pleasure 353–6, 371–4, 408–20,

438; and emotions 109–11;
of poetry 313; Socrates on 59, 85;
Socrates claims 437; Laches
claims 65; Stesilaus' 55. *See also*
art(s), *episteme*, technical skills

Laches: 36–58, 62–89, 92–103,
111–12, 227, 231, 449
law(s): 4–5, 173–4, 189, 216–17,
221–2, 254–6, 287, 291, 389–90,
396
Lexicon: 46, 252
like(ness): 263–6, 270–4, 277–80,
286, 324, 327–8; like-to-like 150
literacy: 186, 249, 320, 387, 441–2,
492–3
literary criticism: 318–9
Lloyd, G. E. R.: 31
logic(al): and dialectic, 13, 30, 32,
58, 80, 83, 125, 145–8, 162, 179,
357, 402, 422; of the argument
passim, esp. 36, 60, 69–71, 106,
117, 120–1, 130–9, 143, 270–1,
272–4, 281, 285–6, 414, 424–5,
431–2; Protagoras' 302–3, 329,
341, 349; Plato's knowledge of
293; of the *Crito* 287
love: 28–9, 114, 117–80, 448–52;
senses of 156–7; sexual 126–7,
137, 157, 161–5, 168, 174–6;
spiritual 160–4, 168; *of*
something, esp. 117–20, 131,
136, 139–43, 148, 153–4, 164–5.
See also eros
lover: 121–3, 140, 152, 157, 160,
163, 174–6
Lycurgus: 173
Lysias: 216, 221, 287
Lysimachus: 37–43, 51–2, 57–9, 65,
68–9, 73–4, 100, 112–13, 327

mad(ness): 228, 244, 283, 300–1,
329, 335, 347–50, 428–33
manliness: 36, 46–51, 54, 74, 76. *See
also andreia*, courage
Manuwald, B.: 373–4, 425
'many', the: in contrast to the brave
421–4; in discussion 203, 305–6,

328–33, 354–62, 367, 370, 373–5,
389–419, 422, 425, 434, 438, 452
Marathon: 219
mathematics (and its branches): 18,
22, 200, 232, 408–9, 418
Melesias: 37–9, 41–3, 57–63,
112–13. *See also* Lysimachus
Meno (as a character): 11, 15,
18–21, 24, 107
Méron, E.: 36–7, 44–6, 55, 83–4,
101, 110
metaphor(s): 75, 116, 119, 121,
137–9, 178–9
moderation: 14–18, 67, 77, 100,
107–108, 120, 149, 170, 213–4,
228, 232–63, 283–311, 324–5,
372, 389. *See also* just(ice),
wisdom, self-control, goodness
Morrison, J. S.: 162
Musaeus: 195
music: as a subject 55, 160, 186,
195, 198, 200, 299, 372, 387–9; as
illustration or metaphor 88,
283–5, 293–4, 297, 301
myth(s): Greek 124; of democracy
191–2, 226, 386–8; of Diotima
150–1, 165–6; of Protagoras
209–10, 213, 227–8, 231–2, 235,
246–9, 256–7, 280–4, 289,
292–3, 299, 349, 438

nature: 45, 380–1; and teaching 189,
194, 209, 234, 350–1, 378–9
necessity: 123, 128–9; as mythical
figure 147
Nehamas, A.: 69, 71
neutrals, between opposites (q.v.):
105–7, 124–5, 140–1, 146–7,
150–2, 165–6, 283–5, 320–2, 394.
See also contradictory
Nicias: 36–44, 52, 55–8, 61–2, 65–6,
87, 90–113, 449–52
North, H.: 291
nothing: 119

O'Brien, M. J.: 2, 323
Odysseus: 223, 291
Old Oligarch: 189

516   General index

oligarchy (and élitism): 189–90, 204, 212–13, 218–19, 235
opinion: *see* knowledge
opposite(s): 56, 124–6, 131–2, 140–1, 151, 166, 179, 239–41, 244, 246, 251, 269–73, 277–8, 281–95, 298–305, 309, 326–7, 332, 340, 378–80, 391, 429–36
ordinary language: esp. 41, 57, 68, 261–2, 369
Orestes: 216, 223
Orpheus: 195
Owen, G. E. L.: 1

Page, Sir D. L.: 317
pain: 74, 353–4, 357–60, 365–9, 390–410, 413–19
paradox: Meno's 19; 41, 104, 216, 290. *See also* Socrates
parents: of Desire 121; of Love 166–8; doctors as 81–2; as illustration 119; as punishers 382; as educators 38–43, 61–2, 205–6, 209, 228, 234, 248–51, 256–7, 285, 300–1, 327, 354–5, 385–6, 389, 394–6
Parmenides: 147, 317
particles, Greek: 59, 168, 173, 249, 269, 416, 424. *See also* 'and'
parts of face: 259, 263–9 274–6, 279, 289, 306
Pausanias, in the *Symposium*: 114, 172
Pericles: 194, 204, 206, 209–12, 218, 225, 229, 386
personification: 116–17, 148
Phaedrus, in the *Symposium*: 117, 143
Phormio: 46–7
phronesis: 77–82, 171, 356. *See also* wisdom
piety: *see* holiness
Pindar: 107, 190
Pittacus: 316–17, 320–1
des Places, E.: 54
Plataea, battle of: 72
Plato: *passim*: *Apology* 82, 203; *Gorgias* 1–2, 81, 205, 225, 353,

371, 444; *Hippias ma*. 1, 3, 6, 9; *Laches* 2, 27, 36–113, 208, 231, 239, 326–7, 451, 454; *Laws* 165; *Lysis* 9; *Meno* 11–24, 155, 205, 264; *Minos* 5; *Parmenides* 177, 180; *Phaedo* 446; *Philebus* 353, 364; *Protagoras*, 1–3, 7–9, 25–9, 183–439, 451, 454; *Republic* 6, 14–15, 109, 165, 196, 225, 350–1, 444, 446; *Sophist* 452; *Symposium* 26–9, 114–82, 258, 286, 323, 440, 445, 449–52; *Theaetetus* 201, 452; suspect of cheating (*see also* Socrates) 21, 63, 87, 180, 201, 211–12, 260–3, 270–1, 281–2, 288, 304, 372, 377, 384, 406, 415, 419, 445, 451; suspect of error 129, 134, 143, 158–9, 180, 211, 214, 271, 303–4, 311, 318, 329, 343; committed or not (*see also* Socrates) 2–3, 16–18, 183, 419, 425, 445; chronology or development 6, 26, 90, 184–5, 208, 264, 271, 445–8; methods 2–3, 34, 124, 135, 203, 338, 433, 448; motives 25–31, 211, 269, 304–5, 326, 336, 340, 345, 440, 449–53; distinguished from Socrates 7–10, 14–15, 20–1, 26–30, 34–7, 48, 54, 65, 75, 89, 130, 134–5, 139, 148, 172–3, 240–1, 260–1, 264, 269–75, 292–3, 296–7, 301, 303, 315, 320, 322, 343–5, 362, 368, 411, 417, 419, 440, 447–8; esoteric doctrine 29; aloof from readers 29; arrives often at same conclusion 28–30, 445. *See also* Socrates, dialogue
pleasure: 118–20, 164, 228–9, 313, 326, 349–50, 353–4, 357–74, 392–409, 425–30, 434, 438; immediate 403–6; pleasure and pleasures 368. *See also* hedonism
poets, poetry: 29, 114–17, 120–2, 126, 138, 143, 156–7, 160, 166, 170–4, 181, 184, 195–7, 233, 249,

256, 286–7, 290–1, 313–23, 389,
441, 449–50, 453
poiesis: 157
politics, political: art, skill, wisdom
202–10, 229–40, 246, 253,
257–60, 282, 345, 352–6, 383,
386; and justice 210–29; in general
60, 74, 191–5, 201–6, 209–10,
217–18, 222, 232, 234, 293,
300, 377, 385–8
Polus: 1
Polycleitus: 234
polysemy: 86
poverty: 150, 152
'powers': 76, 247, 251, 263–76,
279–81, 324, 343, 349, 373, 435,
437
predication: Pauline 268–9, 280,
330; 'sortal' 268–74, 278; 'plain'
269, 271, 280. *See also* self-
predication
premisses: interlocutors' 28, 30–1,
115, 165–7, 322, 325, 342, 360,
373, 378–81, 392, 436, 445;
Plato's/Socrates' 34, 146, 149,
153, 203, 209, 271, 289–305, 328,
332, 358, 383–6, 414, 417, 443–4
prevarication: 338–9
procreation: 127, 160–3, 166–7,
172, 178–81; of arguments 174
Prodicus: 57, 303; in the *Protagoras*
193, 312, 318–21
prologues (Plato's): 37–66 (esp. 40,
52), 99, 183–4, 318
Prometheus: 229, 249, 438
proof: 167, 244, 284, 295, 347, 400,
413. *See also* dialectic
prophecy/prophets: 95–6, 102–3,
124, 146, 157. *See also* Diotima
Protagoras: 183–439, *passim*;
historical 201, 211, 219, 237, 262,
326; character of 298, 300, 305–6,
313, 327, 340, 349, 353, 355, 363,
366–7, 372, 382, 394, 424, 435–7;
claims and pretensions 194–202,
213, 229–30, 235, 308, 310,
312–14, 324, 327, 329, 332,
335–6, 345, 354–5, 371–2,

General index 517

386–7, 392, 414, 417–18, 437,
449–51, 454; inexplicitly
conveys an impression
241, 244, 251, 331, 338, 340–1,
346, 348, 359; committed
or not 234, 248, 278, 289, 292–3,
359, 376–7, 390–1, 397, 418;
Great Speech 117, 209–15,
226–63, 271, 282–9, 292–305,
309, 325–7, 335, 354–5, 372,
374–83, 386, 389–97, 416, 421;
values, esp. 371
punctuation: 4–7, 12, 59, 412–3
punishment: 219–20, 244–8, 284,
302, 378–82, 389–90, 396–7

quantifiers: 141–2, 146
questions: *see* Socrates
questions, rhetorical: 8–9, 106

recollection: 18–19
reductio ad absurdum: 281, 430,
450
right(ly): esp. 291, 294–9, 313
Robin, L.: 154
Robinson, R.: 70
Ryle, G.: 24

Santas, G. X.: 1, 111, 155, 428, 433
Savan, D.: 263, 283–4
Schofield, M.: 25, 442–3
Scopas: 313, 441
Scythians: 72
self-control: 74–5, 120, 250. *See also*
moderation, *sophrosynê*
self-predication: 139–45, 148,
176–81, 268–74
Shorey, P.: 210, 316
similarity: *see* likeness
Simonides: 184, 195–6, 313–24,
348–9, 421, 429, 436, 441
Socrates: *passim*; historical 447–8;
his views 64, 91–2, 97, 109, 316,
322–4, 353–4, 357, 360, 385, 395,
422, 424, 430–1, 437; committed
or not 4–6, 13–17, 19, 59–60,
66–7, 88, 92, 100, 109, 207–8,
275, 358–91, 406–8, 413, 419,

425, 438–9, 444–5; questions or asserts 4–24, 29, 31, 58–61, 66, 73, 79, 85–96, 117, 172–3, 194, 207, 271, 275, 353–4, 358–61, 363–5, 412–14, 418–19; methods 21–9, 74–5, 300, 306, 342, 348, 359–60, 370, 384 (*see also* dialectic); suspect of cheating 36, 55, 182, 265, 279, 288, 295, 298, 372–91, 392, 399, 404, 406, 408, 415–8; conclusions of 4–5, 12–13, 28–30, 34, 67, 79–80, 82, 92, 98, 109, 132–4, 149, 304, 322, 336, 341–6, 360, 374, 413, 417, 431, 438, 445, 450–2; represents others, 65–8, 73–4, 92, 95–7, 100–1, 112–13, 146–184, 193–4, 198, 203–4, 235, 385–9, 439; questions fit interlocutor/context 28, 40–1, 62–3, 70–1, 80, 83, 88, 93, 96, 101, 106, 110, 116–22, 128, 130, 132, 134, 137, 139, 144, 146–8, 157, 172, 182, 190–1, 207, 210, 236, 239, 247, 251, 253–5, 258–63, 267–8, 272, 277, 289–94, 296–7, 299–304, 307–9, 340, 344, 346–8, 350–1, 355, 378, 387, 391, 404, 421–4, 429, 431, 435–6, 440; questions ordered 85, 329–30; argues inexplicitly 33, 296, 298, 440–3; paradoxes 41, 67, 73, 102, 106, 409–11, 418–19 (*see also* goodness, unity of); recapitulates inexactly 15, 135–6, 258, 329; memory 329; virtues of 39, 49–52, 55, 62. See also Plato
Socrates' interlocutors: *passim*: general 17–18, 31–3, 36–7, 55, 58, 60, 115, 143, 201, 444–53; their vocabulary 48, 54–5, 64, 68, 73, 149, 152, 294; their methods 28, 282–5, 314–22, 331, 348–9; views 41–58, 111–12, 313, 335, 366–7, 377, 422, 424, 435; characters 64, 89, 100, 102, 109, 172, 280, 311–13, 371, 388, 392, 446, 451; motives 37–41, 211

Socratic literature: 25–6, 457
Solon: 173
sophists: general 2, 29, 258, 310, 314, 351, 371, 434, 436; claims of 197, 203, 316, 327, 345, 355, 387, 409, 417–18; etymology of 'sophist' 229, 262, 312–13; as a group in the *Protagoras* 211, 319–22, 329, 354, 357, 362, 370, 374, 392–3, 400, 403, 411–19, 425, 427. See also teaching, Hippias, Prodicus, Protagoras
Sophocles: 217, 287
sophos: 187
Sophroniscus: 42, 49, 51, 69
sôphrosynê: 14–5; meaning of 171, 213–14, 227–8, 244, 290–2, 299, 305; mentioned 295, 304
soul: 64, 67, 73, 87, 102, 107, 174–6, 192–3, 252, 275–6, 350–1, 366, 387, 389, 452
Sparta(ns): 46–7, 53–4, 72, 224, 319, 323–4
speed: 76, 86, 294
Sprague, R. Kent: 50, 59, 62, 64, 71, 77, 80, 107
Stesilaus: 38, 44–5, 48–9, 52, 55–8, 63–4, 69–72, 83, 91–3, 112
Stoics: 73, 442
strength: 347–50
success: general 62, 195, 210, 213–14, 372, 454; and soul 192; and good(ness) 14, 42–3, 53, 57, 107, 198–9, 202, 205, 225–8, 366, 449; and courage 44, 46, 53, 57, 83–6, 91, 98, 448–9
Sullivan, J. P.: 358, 362
superlatives: 337, 339–45, 348, 436
suppliants: 217–20
syllogism(s): 139, 141–3, 146, 149–50, 442–3
synonyms: 93, 120–1, 303, 305, 331; for 'and' linking synonyms, see 'and', meaning of

Taylor, A. E.: 315
Taylor, C. C. W.: 1–2, 7–9, 25, 210,

233, 263–70, 274, 279–82, 292–8, 304, 307–8, 319, 325, 330, 332, 335, 339, 341, 346, 349, 356, 360, 363–71, 374, 379, 393, 399, 403–6, 410, 421–4, 430, 432
teaching: in general 66, 262, 284, 302, 379, 383–6; of professional teachers 249, 254, 285; of Socrates 18–23; of Love 124–6; of poets 196; of Pericles 205–6, 229; of Athenians or universal 209, 234–5, 254–7, 301; of the sophists 186–7, 191–210, 228–31, 235, 305–6, 309–10, 313, 316, 327, 332–6, 345, 351–5, 371–2, 388, 397, 409–12, 451, 454. *See also* Athenians, education, goodness, parents
technê: 300. *See also* arts and technical skills
technical skills: in war (and courage) 40–1, 45–56, 75–7, 79–82, 85, 87, 91–3, 103–5, 246–8, 251–3, 260, 332–3, 337, 340–1 (*see also* Stesilaus); and wisdom 79–82, 92–3, 126–7, 150–2, 157, 187, 293–4; and goodness 85, 95–6, 112, 199, 232–3, 249, 255, 283–4, 300–1, 334, 356, 377; and politics 188, 200, 213, 229–36, 246, 300, 334, 356, 377, 383–4; in education 186–7; and sophistry 185, 191–200, 231 (*see also* under 'and politics'). *See also* expertise, art(s) and wisdom
text, problems of: 295, 301, 337–9, 348, 416
Theages: 194
Themistocles: 194, 224–5
Theseus: 220, 224, 226, 241
Thrasymachus: 14, 225, 351
thrasys: 44–5, 56. *See also* bold, confidence
Thucydides (father of Melesias): 38, 42
Thucydides (historian): 46–7, 189, 215–16, 219, 222, 287, 290, 366

Tigerstedt, E. N.: 29
timeless truths: 94, 104–5, 111
Timocreon of Rhodes: 224–5
tolma (daring): 46
tragedy: 215–23. *See also* poets, Agathon
truth: and purity 179–80; and persuasion 189–90
Twin gods: 216, 220

ugliness: 124–6, 131–6, 139–41, 144–8, 165, 179–80, 269, 378–9. *See also* beautiful
unholiness: *see* impiety
unity: *see* goodness, dialogue
universal(s): *see* abstract(s)
univocity: 43, 86, 400
unjust: *see* injustice
unpleasant(ness): *see* pain
unwise: *see* folly
urbanity: Socrates' 89–90, 170–2, 312, 324, 440; Protagoras' 437

values: competitive and cooperative 210, 213–15, 218–19, 225–8, 298 (*see also* success); in the *Meno* 11, 14–16; of Laches 42, 44, 48–52, 85–7; of Nicias, 42, 44, 55–8, 94; of Lysimachus and Melesias 41–4, 66; of Socrates 58–66, 395; of parents 248, 251; of Hippocrates 202–3; of Protagoras 305, 394–5; of the 'many' 394–7, 400–6. *See also* good, goodness, hedonism
Vickers, B.: 217
virtues: *see* goodness
Vlastos, G.: 1–2, 102, 114, 263–4, 280, 373–4

weakness of will: *see akrasia*
wealth: 24, 229, 235, 399
Weingartner, R. H.: 2–3
wisdom: *sophos* 187; degrees of 129–30, 144; opposed to ignorance 147, 151; and art or technical skill 77–82, 91–2, 126, 171, 200, 229–30, 235, 261, 293,

300, 351–2, 355, 391; and knowledge 80–1, 190, 267–8, 339, 344–6, 351–2, 355, 371, 383, 417–20, 429, 436–7; and moderation 289–94, 299–300, 303–5, 372–3; and folly 289–94, 299–300; and Love, 126–7, 152, 157, 175; and Protagoras 183–7, 200, 203, 229, 257–8, 449 (not explicit in Great Speech 230–1); and sophists, *see* sophist, etymology, and 193, 197, 204, 312–3; of Hippias 312; of Pericles 205–6, 229; of the Spartans 319, 323–4

'wishingly': 122, 418, 423, 427–8
Woodruff, P.: 1–6
Wright, G. H. von: 366

Xenophon: 26, 213

Zeno (of Citium): 442–3
Zeus: 217, 220, 232, 235–6, 241, 244–6, 258, 299
Zeuxippus: 198
Zeyl, D. J.: 7–9, 12, 363, 425, 427